THE HIDDEN PLACES OF
IRELAND

By David Gerrard

Regional Hidden Places

Cambs & Lincolnshire
Chilterns
Cornwall
Derbyshire
Devon
Dorset, Hants & Isle of Wight
East Anglia
Gloucs, Wiltshire & Somerset
Hereford, Worcs & Shropshire
Kent
Lake District & Cumbria
Lancashire & Cheshire
Lincolnshire & Nottinghamshire
Northumberland & Durham
Sussex
Yorkshire

National Hidden Places

England
Ireland
Scotland
Wales

Hidden Inns

East Anglia
Heart of England
Lancashire & Cheshire
North of England
South
South East
Wales
Welsh Borders
West Country
Yorkshire

Country Living Rural Guides

East Anglia
Heart of England
Ireland
North East of England
North West of England
Scotland
South
South East
Wales
West Country

Published by: Travel Publishing Ltd, 7a Apollo House, Calleva Park, Aldermaston, Berks, RG7 8TN

ISBN 1-904-434-10-X

First published 1995, second edition 1997, third edition 2000, fourth edition 2002, fifth edition 2004

Printing by: Ashford Colour Press, Gosport

Maps by: © Maps in Minutes ™ (2004)
© Crown Copyright, Ordnance Survey 2004

Editor: David Gerrard

Cover Design: Lines & Words, Aldermaston

Cover Photograph: Nephin Mountain, Co Mayo © Failte Ireland

Text Photographs: © Failte Ireland and
© www.britainonview.com

Foreword

The Hidden Places series is a collection of easy to use travel guides taking you, in this instance, on a relaxed but informative tour of Ireland. Often called the "Emerald Isle", Ireland is indeed rich in greenery, but there is an abundance of every variety of landscape; rugged peaks and mountain ranges, scenic coasts and lush pastures. The country also offers the visitor plenty of fascinating historical sites, beautiful towns and villages and, above all, its people offer the most genuine of friendly welcomes.

The covers and pages of all *Hidden Places* titles have been comprehensively redesigned and the new format will ensure that readers can properly appreciate the beautiful scenery and the many wonderful places of interest in Ireland.

Our books contain a wealth of interesting information on the history, the countryside, the towns and villages and the more established places of interest. But they also promote the more secluded and little known visitor attractions and places to stay, eat and drink many of which are easy to miss unless you know exactly where you are going.

We include hotels, bed & breakfasts, restaurants, pubs, bars, teashops and cafes as well as historic houses, museums, gardens, and many other attractions throughout Ireland, all of which are comprehensively indexed. Most places are accompanied by an attractive photograph and are easily located by using the map at the beginning of each chapter. We do not award merit marks or rankings but concentrate on describing the more interesting, unusual or unique features of each place with the aim of making the reader's stay in the local area an enjoyable and stimulating experience.

Whether you are visiting Ireland for business or pleasure, or in fact are living here, we do hope that you enjoy reading and using this book. We are always interested in what readers think of places covered (or not covered) in our guides so please do not hesitate to use the reader reaction form provided to give us your considered comments. We also welcome any general comments which will help us improve the guides themselves. Finally if you are planning to visit any other corner of the British Isles we would like to refer you to the list of other *Hidden Places* titles to be found to the rear of the book and to the Travel Publishing website at www.travelpublishing.co.uk.

Travel Publishing

Note: International Calling

All telephone numbers throughout the book are shown with local dialling codes. Please note that for Northern Ireland numbers callers outside the United Kingdom should first dial the country code of 00 44 followed by the number shown with the leading zero dropped. For numbers in the Republic of Ireland the country code is 00 353 and again the leading zero should be dropped prior to dialling the number shown.

DONEGAL
LONDONDERRY
ANTRIM
TYRONE
FERMANAGH
ARMAGH
DOWN
SLIGO
MONAGHAN
MAYO
LEITRIM
CAVAN
LOUTH
ROSCOMMON
LONGFORD
MEATH
GALWAY
WESTMEATH
DUBLIN
OFFALY
KILDARE
LAOIS
WICKLOW
CLARE
CARLOW
LIMERICK
TIPPERARY
KILKENNY
WEXFORD
KERRY
WATERFORD
CORK

Contents

Republic of Ireland

Dunmanus Bay, Co Cork

"You arrive as a visitor and leave as a friend". The old tag may have originally applied to a pub or hotel but it's just as true of the country itself. The gentler pace of life away from the major cities, the Irish delight in music and dance, and the passion for *craic* (lively conversation) all beguile and entrance the visitor.

The cultural mix is just as fascinating. Some of the most astonishing prehistoric remains in Europe are found here; old Celtic myths and legends remain vivid in many parts of the country, while the legacy of St Patrick is evident in the great religious centres such as Clonmacnoise and the Rock of Cashel. English involvement with Ireland produced the Anglo-Norman castles, the estate villages of the 17th and 18th centuries, and the great Georgian houses built during the Protestant "Ascendancy".

Topographically, Ireland offers plenty of variety – rugged peaks and mountain ranges, 3500 miles of fretted coastlines, lush pastures, and hundreds and hundreds of lakes. The country's lakes and rivers make it an angler's paradise and one of the world's leading venues for angling holidays. Ireland also boasts some of the most beautiful and challenging golf courses in the world but it is horse racing that arouses the greatest enthusiasm amongst the Irish themselves. The Dublin Horse Show, held in July/August, is the principal sporting and social event in the country.

Mount Errigal, Co Donegal

Officially, the Republic's first language is Gaelic and some 40% of the population can speak it. In the Gaeltacht (Irish-speaking areas) that figure rises to around 75%. In these regions, mostly in the west and southwest, the signposts have English town names taking second place to the Irish form – if indeed they appear at all.

One final, rather surprising statistic. Ireland has a population of just under 4 million and more than half of them are under the age of 30.

Co Carlow

Shaped like an inverted triangle, County Carlow is the second smallest county in Ireland with an area of just 346 square miles and a population of less than 50,000. Most of the county is devoted to agriculture, especially the cultivation of sugar beet which is processed at a huge factory in Carlow Town. The most attractive areas are the Blackstairs Mountains in the south, and along the valley of the River Barrow which, for most of its length, forms the border with County Kilkenny. The river has long been of immense importance to Carlow as a means of communication and though no longer a commercial waterway, is still busy in season with pleasure craft, river cruisers and anglers.

The county has few grand houses or churches although it does boast the largest dolmen in Ireland at Browne's Hill near Carlow Town and a ruined Norman castle in the town itself. Generally however this is not a county for sightseeing but for enjoying the gentle landscape where traditional farming methods have preserved an unspoilt countryside with hedges and trees in abundance.

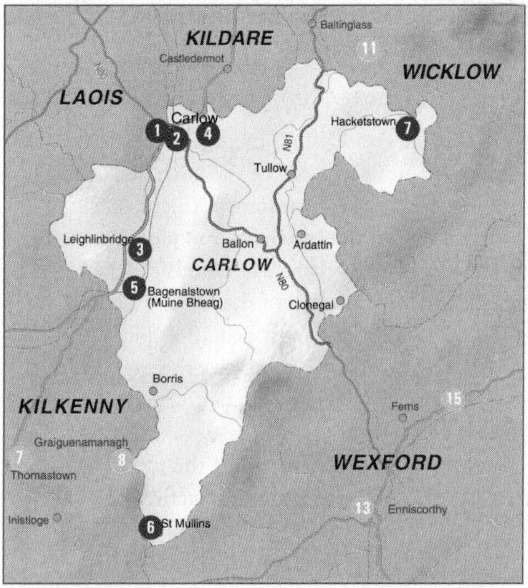

Carlow

Carlow was for centuries an important Anglo-Norman military base on the edge of a fiercely Gaelic area. Little is left to indicate its former status apart from the remains of **Carlow Castle**, a 13th century rectangular keep of which a wall and two flanking towers still stand near the bridge over the River Barrow. Its ruined state is only partly the result

PLACES TO STAY, EAT AND DRINK

The John Tyndall Bar & Restaurant, Carlow	1	Bar & Restaurant	p3
Carlow Guest House, Carlow	2	Guest House	p4
The Lord Bagenal Inn, Leighlinbridge	3	Pub, Restaurant & Accommodation	p4
Brownes Hill Dolmen, Carlow	4	Ancient Monument	p5
Knockrigg House, Bagenalstown	5	B&B	p6
Mulvarra House, St Mullins	6	B&B	p8
The Corner, Hacketstown	7	Pub with Food	p8

● Denotes entries in other counties

Carlow Castle

of the many battles that took place at this strategically sited town. Further damage was caused in 1841 by a certain Dr Philip Middleton. Attempting to reduce the thickness of the walls in readiness for converting the castle into a mental hospital, the good doctor rather over-estimated the amount of explosives required!

Perhaps the most impressive building in Carlow is the fine classical-style polygonal **Courthouse**, built in 1830 and with a Doric portico modelled on the Parthenon at Athens. It stands on a high plinth beneath which is a basement maze of cells and dungeons. This noble building was apparently intended for Cork but the plans were mixed up and it was erected in this small country town instead.

Another striking architectural feature of the town is the 151ft high lantern tower on the **Cathedral of the**

THE JOHN TYNDALL BAR & RESTAURANT

70 Tullow Street, Carlow, Co. Carlow
Tel: 059 914 1112
e-mail: dine@johntyndall.ie
website: www.johntyndall.ie

The John Tyndall Bar & Restaurant is named after the noted Irish physicist who was born at Leighlinbridge in Co. Carlow in 1820. Tyndall is best known for his work on heat but his enquiring mind also tackled topics such as the transmission of sound and the scattering of light by suspended particles – he was the first scientist to explain why the sky is blue. It's not known if he also enjoyed good food but if he did he would be pleased to know that the restaurant named after him has been designated 'Dining Pub' of the Year two years in succession.

Christy O'Mally's appetising menu specialises in seafood and steaks but there's also a wide choice of other dishes – "Old Reliables" such as traditional Irish Stew, for example, Joint of the Day, or Supreme of Chicken Vol au vent. Vegetarian options include Chinese Stirfry made with fresh market vegetables, or a fruit and vegetable curry. There's also a choice of salads, wraps, and sandwiches. Kiddies have their own menu – all the old favourites but accompanied with freshly made chips. Food is served from 10am to 10pm, Tuesday to Saturday; 10am to 9pm, Sunday and Monday, with a Sunday Lunch menu available from noon until 4pm.

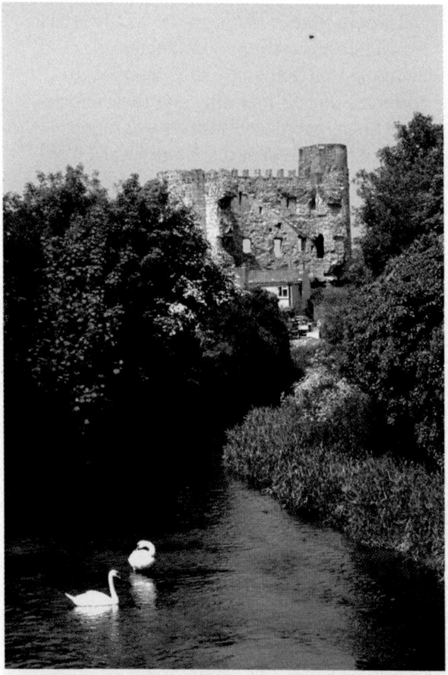

Carlow Guest House

Green Lane, Dublin Road, Carlow Town, Co. Carlow
Tel/Fax: 059 9136 0333
website: www.carlowguesthouse.com

Only a 5-minute walk from the town centre and standing in its own well-maintained grounds, **Carlow Guest House** was purpose-built in 2000 and designed to provide all modern amenities in comfortable surroundings. The 13 en-suite guest bedrooms have been meticulously designed to reflect the relaxed atmosphere that pertains throughout the house. Guests have a choice of places in which to wind down. There's a TV lounge where you can keep up to date with your favourite soap; a library offering a quiet retreat, and a new Coffee Dock where you can enjoy a cup of coffee and a glass of wine. There's also a large conservatory-style dining room where breakfast is served each morning from 7am to 10am with a menu that offers traditional, continental and vegetarian options.

Owners Gerard McCormack and Thomas Donagher are extremely dedicated to ensuring that you enjoy all your creature comforts during your stay and their efforts have been recognised with a 4-Diamond rating from the AA and a 3-star award from the Irish Tourist Board. There's plenty to see and do in the area, with a top championship golf course just 5 minutes away, and attractions such as Powerscourt, Glendalough, the Vale of Avoca and the Wicklow Hills all within easy reach. Log on to their web site and avail their 10% discount on multi night stays.

The Lord Bagenal Inn

Leighlinbridge, Co. Carlow
Tel: 0503 21668 Fax: 0503 22629
e-mail: info@lordbagenal.com
website: www.lordbagenal.com

In the heart of the picturesque and award-winning village of Leighlinbridge, **The Lord Bagenal Inn** has a reputation for fine food, excellent value for money, and a relaxing and friendly atmosphere. The Inn enjoys a lovely position beside the River Barrow and has its own private marina for up to 30 boats. The Inn itself is a rambling structure with lots of individual gathering spots as well as a very spacious lounge, restaurant, bars and function rooms. The Lord Bagenal's à la carte restaurant has won many national and international awards with a wide selection of fresh seafood in season its speciality. There is also the choice of daily Carvery.

The Inn has 12 guest bedrooms, all of them en suite, comfortably furnished and attractively decorated, and equipped with satellite colour television, hair dryers and hospitality trays. The 24-hour room service can be relied upon to furnish that little extra something should you require it. Children are welcome and the fully equipped playroom is open daily with supervision on site at weekends. Childminding services are also available. The beautifully maintained gardens provide a peaceful haven but if you are feeling active, there's plenty to do in the area. Anglers can hire boats for fishing on the River Barrow; hiking in the nearby Blackstairs Mountains is popular or you could choose to walk the Barrow Track to Graignamanagh or St Mullins.

Assumption, one of the first Roman Catholic churches to be built after the Emancipation Act of 1829. The driving force behind the building of the cathedral was James Doyle, Bishop of Kildare, who is commemorated inside the church by an acclaimed statue, the work of the celebrated sculptor James Hogan. Apparently Hogan forgot to include the bishop's ring and was so distressed by this professional lapse he committed suicide.

On the western bank of the River Barrow is a more sombre memorial which marks the **Croppies Grave**. This handsome monument rises above the site of an old sand pit where, following the failed Rebellion of 1798, the bodies of 640 slaughtered Carlow insurgents were thrown and covered with quick lime. The Croppies were so named because they cropped their hair to demonstrate their allegiance to the cause of Irish independence.

Back in the town centre, look out for the **Cigar Divan** in Dublin Street. There is another Cigar Divan in Mallow, Co. Cork, but this is the elder of the two. The name dates from the time when Turkish cigarettes were highly fashionable. The Victorian shop front has elaborate iron panels beneath the windows and several engraved glass advertisements.

County Carlow Military Museum is housed in a former 19th century church on Athy Road. The wide range of exhibits relate to the 10th Infantry battalion, Irish UN peacekeeping in the Congo, Lebanon and Somalia, Carlow in the Great War and a display dedicated to Captain Myles Keogh of the 7th Cavalry who was killed with General Custer at the Battle of Little Big Horn.

Lovers of fine ales will want to visit the **Carlow Brewing Company** where tours are available from May to September by appointment. This microbrewery won the highest accolade the brewing industry can bestow when its O'Hara's Stout won the Championship Trophy and a Gold Medal at the Brewing Industry International Awards in April 2000. The company also produces Curim Gold Celtic wheat beer and Molings, a traditional red ale. Visitors can enjoy these at the bar which overlooks the main brewing area and the brewing and fermenting vessels.

Brownes Hill Dolmen

Co. Carlow

About two miles to the east of Carlow Town stands the **Brownes Hill Dolmen**, arguably the most impressive sight in the county. A field monument of huge proportions, it has been dated to 2500 BC. Its colossal tilted capstone, supported by five granite blocks, weighs 100 tonnes and is believed to be the largest in Europe.

The location, setting and purpose of this Megalithic structure have been the subject of conjecture for centuries. The most likely explanation is that it marks the burial place of some prehistoric local king but the extraordinary monument has been invested with a rich overlay of myth and legend.

A good time to visit Carlow is mid-June when the town hosts its 10-day **Eigse,** a popular arts festival that showcases the work of Irish and international artists and performers. The festival includes extensive visual arts, theatre performances, film, music, crafts and a street entertainment programme when the streets come alive with the improbable combination of traditional Irish and samba beats.

About 2 miles to the east of Carlow Town stands the **Brownes Hill Dolmen** (see panel on page 5).

Leighlinbridge

8 miles S of Carlow on the N9/R705

Overlooking the River Barrow, the **Black Castle** (1547) stands on the site of an earlier fortress built in 1181, one of the first Norman strongholds to be erected in Ireland. The fine stone bridge nearby is reputedly one of the oldest functioning bridges in Europe. There are even more venerable structures in Old Leighlin, a couple of miles to the west. Here, the 7th century **Cross of St Lazerain** and his holy well are still venerated and attract many votive offerings. St Lazerain founded a monastery here which at one time accommodated some 1500 monks and was the location for an important church synod in AD 630 which was summoned to devise a formula for determining the date of Easter each year. The 13th century **Cathedral of St Lazerain** stands on the site of the monastery and has some interesting architectural features. Guided tours are available on request.

Also in Leighlinbridge is the **Millennium Garden,** built and designed by local people to commemorate the new millennium. The garden contains 7 small individual gardens, each with its own theme represented by trees, shrubs and stones to symbolize aspects

of life from birth to death. This attractive amenity no doubt helped the village to win a gold medal in the prestigious Entente Florale competition in 2001, the same year in which Leighlinbridge also carried off the award for being Carlow's Tidiest Village.

Bagenalstown (Muine Bheag)

13 miles S of Carlow on the R705/R724

This pretty little town on the River Barrow has some delightful riverside walks and is a popular fishing and hunting centre. In the 1780s when Walter Bagenal began building the town that bears his name, his plans were enormously ambitious - nothing less than a mirror image of Versailles with fine streetscapes and classical buildings. He made an impressive start with an imposing **Courthouse** which, like the one in Carlow Town, is modelled on the Parthenon at Athens. Then his grandiose scheme faltered. He failed to get the stage coach re-routed through his new town and serious financial problems finally put paid to his plans. All that remains are the Courthouse and his own home, **Dunleckney Manor,** just outside the town. This impressive 17th century house in the Tudor Gothic style has been fully restored and is now open for guided tours on weekdays during March, May and August.

Borris

16 miles S of Carlow on the R702

Set in a fertile valley of the River Barrow beneath the gentle curve of the Blackstairs Mountains, Borris is a handsome estate town created by the McMurrough Kavanaghs, lineal descendants of the Kings of Leinster. The family still live in the town at **Borris House**, a stately Tudor-style house which is open to group tours by arrangement. In the mid-1800s it was the home of Arthur McMurrough Kavanagh who amongst many other achievements was responsible for building the spectacular 16-arch railway viaduct at the lower end of the town. Arthur was born without arms or legs but nevertheless learned to ride, shoot and fish, and was an inveterate traveller. As a prominent landlord, he threw himself into improving the life of his tenants, largely rebuilding the villages of Borris and Ballyragget, establishing a sawmill and initiating a local lace industry. In 1866 he entered politics and was elected as Conservative Member of Parliament, first for County Wexford and later for County Carlow.

From Borris the circular **Mount Leinster Drive** strikes northeastwards through the Blackstairs Mountains, skirting the foot of Mount Leinster which at 795ft is the highest peak in the range. It's possible to

Mount Leinster

Mulvarra House

St Mullins, Co. Carlow
Tel: 051 424936
website: www.mulvarra.com

Situated in the picturesque and historic village of St Mullins, **Mulvarra House** occupies a superb position on the hillside overlooking the Barrow Valley. There are spectacular views from the 5 guest rooms, each of which has a balcony and en suite facilities. Built in 1991, Mulvarra House is the home of Harold and Noreen Ardill who have gone to great lengths to make the building as visitor friendly as possible with ramps to all the ground floor doors, double glazed windows and a comfortable residents' lounge well-equipped with books and board games as well as television and tea/coffee-making facilities.

Guests can also take advantage of the lovely garden with its wonderful views. The Ardills serve a generous breakfast, will provide packed lunches if required and evening meals by arrangement. There's a good local pub nearby, excellent fishing, and grand walking in the Blackstairs Mountains a few miles to the east. It's a great place to relax and if you want to unwind even more, Harold and Noreen offer a luxurious range of body treatments for both men and women. The treatments include Detoxing Body Wrap, Indian head massage, back, neck and shoulder massage, and also refreshing facials.

The Corner

Hacketstown, Co. Carlow
Tel: 059 64 71278

Surrounded by woods and farmland, Hacketstown is a small village set in the foothills of the Wicklow Hills that rise to their highest point a few miles to the northeast. **The Corner** is one of the oldest pubs in the village and has been dispensing hospitality since 1802. PJ and Liz Townsend took over here in September 2003, returning to their home village after some time in Dublin. Liz learnt the business from her father who has some 20 years experience in the licensed trade. "It's all about mixing the best ingredients together" says Liz, "quality food, great value for money – and a fantastic atmosphere!" You'll certainly find all that, along with a perfect pint of Guinness served in the comfortable lounge bar.

There's a good choice of appetising bar snacks, freshly prepared and attractively presented. Just to the south of Hacketstown is Eagle Hill, noted for its panoramic views that take in most of Co. Carlow – during the summer months the area is popular with parachutists. Horse riding is available just 5 minutes away; there's a golf course about 10 minutes distant, and a 20-minute drive will bring you to Carlow Town with its historic buildings and famous Brownes Hill Dolmen, the largest in Europe.

drive right up to the summit where the Nine Stones viewing point provides superb views over Carlow, Wexford, Kilkenny and Wicklow, and, on a fine day, across the Irish Sea to the Welsh coast. The Drive continues through the picturesque village of Bunclody in County Wexford and on to Clonegal in the Derry Valley, sometimes referred to as the "Switzerland of Ireland". The Drive then strikes westwards to Bagenalstown and back to Borris.

St Mullins

22 miles S of Carlow off the R729

The picturesque village of St Mullins, beautifully set beside the River Barrow, was once an important ecclesiastical centre, the burial place of the kings of Leinster. Little remains however of the monastery founded in AD 696 by St Moling. The early Christian and medieval ruins include the base of a round tower and a weathered granite cross. Down the slope from the churchyard is a medieval house with an unusual diamond window.

East of Carlow

Hacketstown

16 miles E of Carlow on the R727

Nestling in the foothills of the Wicklow Mountains, Hacketstown was the setting for a fierce clash during the rebellion of 1798. To the south of the town, Eagle Hill provides grand panoramic views across the whole of Co. Carlow.

Tullow

9 miles SE of Carlow on the R725/N81

The largest town in County Carlow, Tullow is a popular centre for anglers fishing the River Slaney for salmon and trout. There's a fine statue in the market square of Father John Murphy, the insurgent leader who was captured near Tullow and executed here on 2nd July, 1798. Otherwise, there is little to detain the visitor although you might care to travel a little further north to the delightful village of Rathvilly which has the distinction of having won the All Ireland Tidy Town competition three times over. Just south of the village, **Lisnavagh Gardens** were originally designed and laid out by Daniel Robertson in the 1850s. The Victorian Gothic mansion here (private), although much reduced in size, still provides an impressive focus for the ten acres of pleasure grounds, mixed borders and a magnificent array of rhododendrons, azaleas, camellias and many other unusual plants as well as some spectacular Irish yews. There's also a large walled garden with peacocks strutting their stuff amongst ancient fruit trees.

Ardattin

11 miles SE of Carlow off the N81

Anyone with an interest in unusual artefacts should pay a visit to **The Cottage Collection** in the little village of Ardattin. Inside the picturesque cottage is a fascinating collection that includes vintage radios from the early 1920s, wind-up gramophones, ancient sewing machines, toys and household implements. The Collection is open on Sunday afternoons from 2pm until 6pm; at other times by appointment.

Ballon

10 miles SE of Carlow on the N80

The charming village of Ballon lies just a few miles from the famous **Altamount Gardens**. These delightful formal and informal gardens lie in the grounds of Altamount House and are regarded by many as the "jewel in Ireland's gardening crown". Tended lawns sweep down to the large man-made lake whose perimeter walk provides a succession of ever-changing vistas of rare trees and shrubs. Within the grounds there's also a well-stocked garden centre, a large wild garden stocked with many rare shrubs, and a deep Ice Age glen leads to the Slaney River far below. The Gardens are open all year round, Monday to Friday.

Altamount Gardens

Clonegal

16 miles SE of Carlow off the N80

Clonegal is the southern starting point of the **Wicklow Way**, Ireland's first and oldest way-marked walking route. It runs for just over 80 miles through the glorious scenery of the Wicklow Mountains to the outskirts of Dublin. Clonegal itself is a peaceful village of winding streets, one of those places that seems happy to have stopped the clock somewhere around 1950. There are some restored 17th century thatched weavers' cottages now used for spinning demonstrations and evenings of story-telling, music, song and dance. In the centre of the village stands a fine building dating back to 1625 but extended and altered over the years, **Huntington Castle** (open by appointment only). Home to the Robertson family for many generations, the castle houses a museum of modern art and craft centre, a temple to the Goddess Isis (in the basement!) and, outside, a medieval herb garden and a magnificent yew walk. Visits to the house are by guided tour only.

Co Cavan

Blessed with some of Europe's most beautiful lake scenery, Co. Cavan has also benefitted from the restoration of the old Ballinamore-Ballyconnell canal which now links all four provinces of Ireland. The county has always been a watery place, until comparatively recently an impenetrable tract of lakeland and bog that frustrated potential invaders. But there's plenty of evidence of Neolithic peoples living here as long ago as 4000 BC. Their court cairn tombs are still visible but many of their *crannógs*, (artificial islands of branches and brush), have settled into the landscape and are now unrecognisable as man-made features. Apart from fishermen, for whom Cavan's 350 lakes, (one for each day of the year, almost), and sparkling rivers are an angler's dream, few tourists have yet discovered this wonderfully peaceful and unspoilt county.

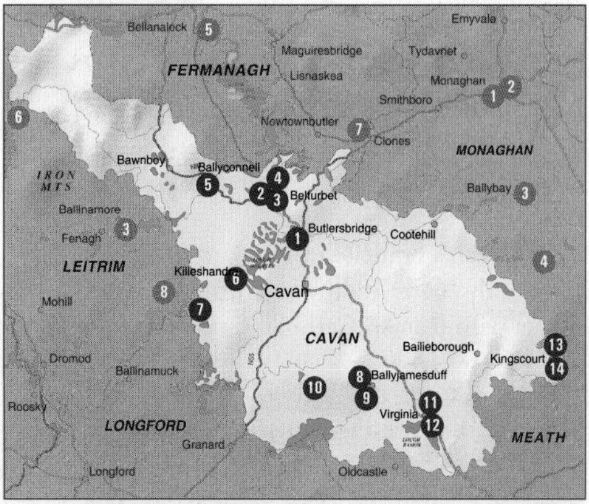

Cavan

The county town is a pleasant little place with a population of around 3500. It was at

PLACES TO STAY, EAT AND DRINK

Riverside Farm Guest House, Butlerstown	1	Guest House	p13
The Yukon Bar, Belturbet	2	Pub	p13
Church View Guest House, Belturbet	3	Guest House	p13
The Seven Horseshoes, Belturbet	4	Pub, Restaurant & Accommodation	p14
Pol O'D Restaurant, Ballyconnell	5	Restaurant	p14
Loughbawn Hotel, Killeshandra	6	Hotel	p15
Breffni Arms Hotel, Arvagh	7	Hotel	p16
Cavan County Museum, Ballyjamesduff	8	Museum	p17
The Bent Elbow & Restaurant, Ballyjamesduff	9	Pub with Restaurant	p18
The Pub, Kilnaleck	10	Pub with Food	p18
Corronagh Woods Log Cabin, Virginia	11	Self Catering	p19
Lakeside Manor Hotel, Virginia	12	Hotel	p19
Hilltown View, Kingscourt	13	B&B	p20
Wishing Well, Kingscourt	14	Pub with Food	p20

Denotes entries in other chapters

one time important as the stronghold of the O'Reillys who ruled the ancient kingdom of East Breffni. Their castle, **Clough Oughter,** stands on an island in Lough Oughter about 3 miles outside Cavan. It's a well-preserved example of a 13th century circular tower castle, rather surprisingly built on a crannóg. It looks very romantic when viewed from the lakeside but in the 1640s the castle served as a prison. Eoghan Roe O'Neill, the great leader of the rebels, was incarcerated and died here, poisoned it is said by his Cromwellian captors. The island can only be reached by hiring a boat.

Clough Oughter, Lough Oughter

Of Cavan's **Franciscan Friary,** founded in 1300, only the belfry tower still stands but the modern **Roman Catholic Cathedral,** consecrated in 1942, is well worth visiting for its fine sculptures. Other attractions in the town include **Cavan Crystal,** the second oldest lead crystal factory in Ireland, which offers guided tours during which visitors can observe glass blowing and crystal cutting in progress. A more recent visitor attraction is **Lifeforce Mill,** located in the heart of the town. Erected in 1846, the mill closed down in the 1950s but has now been fully restored and enjoys a new lease of life producing Lifeforce Stoneground Wholemeal Flour. On arrival, visitors are first invited to prepare a loaf of bread using the mill's own flour. This is popped into the oven and by the time the 35-minute tour is over the visitor's very own loaf is ready for collection. The mill also has a coffee shop housed in an old stone building which was transported some 50 miles here from the Boyne valley and re-erected stone by stone.

Cavan Cathedral

Around Cavan

Butlersbridge

5 miles N of Cavan on the N3

This attractive little village on the River Annalee is renowned for its coarse fishing and there are boats available for hire.

Riverside Farm Guest House

Deredis, Butlersbridge, Co. Cavan
Tel: 049 436 1371

Well hidden away in the Cavan countryside although only a mile and a half from the N3, **Riverside Farm Guest House** enjoys some lovely scenic views. It's the home of Jim Mullavey, a retired farmer, and his wife Margaret who have lived here for some 14 years. Because of the excellent fishing hereabouts many of their guests are anglers, including many Belgians and French. The house has 4 very spacious guest bedrooms, all en suite with an additional bathroom also available. Margaret serves a truly hearty Irish breakfast and is also happy to provide evening meals if required.

There's more good fishing in the numerous lakes extending to the south and west.

Belturbet

9 miles NW of Cavan on the N3

A market town, prettily set on the east bank of the River Erne, Belturbet is (surprise! surprise!) another major centre in Co. Cavan for coarse fishing. There are no conventional visitor attractions here but if you take one of the boat cruises along the Ulster Canal (available during the summer months) you glide through unspoilt countryside where even a single house

The Yukon Bar

Main Street, Belturbet, Co. Cavan
Tel: 049 95 22811

Don't be misled by the name – **The Yukon Bar** is as authentic an Irish country pub as you could hope to find, with lots of old beams and wooden floors. Sean and Margret Maguire have owned and run the bar for some 13 years and it's particularly popular with local fishermen and golfers – and with visitors who are lucky enough to know of it. Currently, The Yukon is currently a wet pub only (although soup and sandwiches may soon be available); there's a beer garden for fine days; pool and a large screen TV inside; traditional music on Friday evenings, and the bar also has its own off licence.

Church View Guesthouse

8 Church Street, Belturbet, Co. Cavan
Tel: 049 95 22358

Belturbet is located in the heart of Ireland's Lakeland fishing region but it's not just anglers who seek out Maura and Cahal Hughes **Church View Guesthouse**, a comfortable, modern 8-bedroom guesthouse in the centre of the town. Each of the spacious bedrooms is en suite and provided with a television and hairdryer. There's a guest living room with all the comforts of home and, for anglers, a walk-in coldroom for storing fishing bait. Golf, horse-riding and boating are all within easy reach and other attractions nearby include Florencecourt House, Cavan Crystal factory, Belleek China factory, Enniskillen Castle and the Marble Arch Caves

The Seven Horseshoes

Main Street, Belturbet, Co. Cavan
Tel: 049 95 22166
e-mail: info@sevenhorseshoes.com
website: www.sevenhorseshoes.com

Occupying a prime site on Belturbet's main street, **The Seven Horseshoes** has been owned and run by Francis and Dolores Cahill for more than 20 years. This delightful old inn is well-known for the excellent cuisine created by its award-winning chef – home-cooked Irish fare based on the freshest of local produce, meat and seafood. The restaurant is open for dinner every evening; bar food is available throughout the day, every day. The inn has 10 superbly appointed guest bedrooms in a newly refurbished extension and offers superior accommodation at value-for-money prices. The inn's Function Room is available for meetings, weddings and other functions.

appears as an intrusion.

A few minutes walk from the town centre, **Belturbet Railway Station** was one of the stops on the Cavan and Leitrim Railway (see Dromod, above). After the line closed in 1959 Belturbet Station stood abandoned for some 40 years but local volunteers have now restored the Victorian building and set up a small exhibition detailing the history of the railway.

Ballyconnell

14 miles NW of Cavan on the N87

A well-known centre for coarse fishing, Ballyconnell's popularity has increased even more since the completion of the Shannon-Erne waterway in the mid-1990s making it now possible to sail from the Shannon estuary to Belleek in Co. Fermanagh, a

Ballyconnell Arts and Crafts Centre

Pol O'D Restaurant

Main Street, Ballyconnell, Co. Cavan
Tel: 049 952 6228
e-mail: polod@oceanfree.net

The unusual name of **Pol O'D Restaurant** is derived from its owner Paul O'Dowd who arrived here in 2000 and with his wife has made this one of the county's most popular eating places. Paul is the chef and his appetising menu offers a wide choice that extends from Crispy Goats Cheese or Mixed Salad with Smoked Duck among its many starters to Cajun Salmon Fillet or Fillet Steak to name but a few main courses for dinner. Everything is home-cooked and prepared from the freshest ingredients. There is an unusually wide choice on the Dessert Menu and an excellent Wine List. A lighter menu is available at lunch-time.

Open for lunch 12.30pm-2.30pm (Tues-Fri) and for dinner 6.30pm-9.30pm (Wed-Sat).

distance of 239 miles. To the northwest of the village rises Sleive Russell from whose summit, 1331ft high, there are extensive views of the lake-studded countryside.

Brackley Lake, nr Bawnboy

Bawnboy

22 miles NW of Cavan on the N87

The tiny hamlet of Bawnboy is popular with walkers since it acts as a gateway to some scenic glens and mountains. You can follow the **Glen Gap Walk** and climb 1148ft (350m) to Glen Gap between the peaks of Cullcagh and Benbragh. A little further west, at Glangevlin, there are glorious panoramic views of the neighbouring counties.

Cootehill

14 miles NE of Cavan on the R168

This pleasant market town close to the border with Co. Monaghan and set amidst rolling drumlin hills was named after the Coote family who 'planted' the area when they were granted possession of confiscated O'Reilly lands in the 17th century. At the end of the long main street they built a church in the attractive Planters' Gothic style. A later member of the Coote family, Thomas, built Bellamont House in 1730. One of the finest Palladian structures in Ireland, the mansion is surrounded by the woodlands of Bellamont Forest. It was abandoned for many years, then lovingly restored by an Englishman. After the house had been completely refurbished, the owner received a claim from a member of the Coote family living in Australia. The house belonged to him, he insisted. The matter has still not been finally resolved.

Killeshandra

11 miles W of Cavan on the R199

Surrounded by a sparkling necklace of small lakes, Killeshandra is as unspoilt a place as you could hope to find in this most traditional of Irish counties. The town has

Breffni Arms Hotel

Main Street, Arvagh, Co. Cavan
Tel: 049 43 35117 Fax: 049 43 35799
e-mail: breffniarms@hotmail.com
website: www.breffniarms.com

Eamonn and Philomena Gray's newly refurbished **Breffni Arms Hotel** and leisure centre stands in an area famous for its fishing lakes, golf courses, horse-riding and leisure walks. Other activities available nearby include tennis courts, pitch and putt, snooker and a children's playground.

This outstanding hotel offers a wide range of amenities. The accommodation comprises 13 spacious en suite bedrooms, all luxuriously furnished and decorated and each provided with TV, telephone, computer point, hairdryer and hospitality tray.

A major attraction here is the quality of the food on offer. Guests can experience superb modern Irish cuisine in the newly decorated restaurant, or relax in the comfort of the hotel's main bar with its roaring open fire, where a wide choice of meals and drinks are available throughout the day. Here you can also enjoy live music on Friday and Saturday evenings, and dancing to live bands on Sunday evening.

Keep fit fans will be delighted with the newly appointed leisure centre which boasts a 15 metre indoor swimming pool, sauna, steam room, jacuzzi and a fully equipped fitness gymnasium to make your stay even more memorable – and healthy!

The Breffni Arms is a popular venue for wedding celebrations and offers a comprehensive value-for-money Wedding Package. The red carpet will be rolled out for your arrival, there's complimentary champagne for the bride and groom and there's complimentary fruit punch for the guests, along with tea or coffee. A free Banqueting Suite is provided for the reception and to commemorate your special day you will be presented with a specially commissioned souvenir. Bed and breakfast accommodation is provided free of charge for the bride and groom and the hotel offers specially reduced rates for guests staying overnight. Moreover, the bridge and groom will receive one year's membership of the Swimming Pool and Leisure Centre and will be invited back to the Breffni Arms for a complimentary dinner. Also included in the package are specially designed menu cards and place cards, a microphone for the speeches, changing facilities and, to top it all off, a 10% discount off your meal price for mid-week weddings, Monday to Thursday inclusive, excluding Bank Holidays.

Attentive personal service puts the seal on a stay in this friendly, relaxed hotel. Mastercard and Visa credit cards are accepted.

become a recognized centre of Irish music, song and dance which can be enjoyed regularly in the local pubs where you'll almost certainly see a performance of the renowned Cavan Set Dance.

Because of the superb angling all around, Killeshandra has hosted the King of Clubs Championship for the past several years. Bream, roach, pike, eel, tench and hybrids abound in the countless lakes and, moreover, the fishing is free. Bags as large as 200-250lbs are not unusual, and bait, tackle and boats are all readily available.

About 3 miles to the east, the 600 acres of **Killykeen Forest Park** offer woodland and lakeside trails, boating, horse-riding, excellent match fishing stretches and a splendid view of the 12th century Clough Oughter Castle, a stronghold of the O'Reilly family. Nearby Shantemon Hill is where their chiefs were inaugurated.

Lough Gowna

12 miles SW of Cavan off the N55

Lough Gowna enjoys the distinction of being the source of the River Erne which flows northwards from here through the centre of the county, spreading itself into fingers of water which in turn are dotted with islands. This watery landscape produces some fine views and the lake is also noted for the quality of its coarse fishing.

Ballyjamesduff

16 miles SE of Cavan on the R196

The Plantation town of Ballyjamesduff stands on the slope of a hill south of Lough Nadreegel. It has a slight claim to fame as the birthplace of William James who emigrated to America in 1789 and whose grandsons were the novelist Henry James and the philosopher William James.

Cavan County Museum

Virginia Road, Ballyjamesduff, Co. Cavan
Tel: 049 854 4070 Fax: 049 854 4332
e-mail: ccmuseum@eircom.net
website: www.cavanmuseum.ie

Originally built in the 19th century as the Poor Clare Convent, this impressive 3-storey structure now houses the **Cavan County Museum** which was established in 1996 with the aim of collecting, conserving, documenting and displaying all aspects of the culture, history and traditions of County Cavan and neighbouring counties. The core of the collection is the "Pighouse Collection", so named because of the buildings in which it was originally stored. Donated by Mrs Phyllis Faris of Cornafean, Co. Cavan, the collection consists of 18th, 19th and 20th century costume and folk life material. The folk life display takes visitors through the everyday life on a typical 19th century Cavan farm with exhibits including a thatched cottage, farmyard scene and folk craft items.

Amongst the items in the Archaeology Room are two well-preserved Sheela-na-Gigs – medieval stone carvings which with their explicit depiction of female genitalia are believed to be based on pagan fertility symbols. Other outstanding pieces in the Museum's collection include the 1,000-year-old Lough Errol Dug-Out boat, a 3-faced pre-Christian Corleck Head and, dating from 1724, the exquisite silver mace of the Borough of Cavan.

The Museum is open all year round, except at Christmas, from 10am to 5pm, Tuesday to Saturday, and on Sundays from June to September between 2pm and 6pm. There's parking for cars and coaches and the Museum has disabled access toilets.

The Bent Elbow & Restaurant

Dublin Road, Ballyjamesduff, Co. Cavan
Tel: 049 433 0055

Conveniently located on the N3 about 10 miles south of Cavan, **The Bent Elbow and Restaurant** combines a friendly traditional pub with a restaurant serving truly memorable food. Both pub rooms and the restaurant have recently been lavishly refurbished with an eye to customer comfort. In the 54-seater restaurant you'll find an impressive menu with Tian of Crab amongst the starters, Confit of Duck, Beef Fillet Gateau and Seafood Dish of the Day as some of the main courses, and some really appetising desserts. This gourmet's delight is open every lunchtime from 12.30pm to 3pm, and Wednesday to Sunday evenings from 6pm to 9.30pm.

The Pub

Main Street, Kilnaleck, Co. Cavan
Tel: 049 433 6666

There's no mistaking what function **The Pub** serves! Dating back to the early 1800s and recently upgraded, it has a striking yellow and black frontage and, inside, a full length marble bar and a spacious lounge. Slate and wooden floors add to the appeal.

Mine hosts Owen and Marie McCabe took over here in the summer of 2003 – their first venture in the hospitality business but it's clear that their enterprise is a decided success. The Pub serves soup and sandwiches from noon to 6pm, Monday to Friday, and if the weather is kind you can enjoy your refreshments in the charming beer garden at the rear.

Today the town is best known for the **Cavan County Museum** (see panel on page 17). Occupying a magnificent 19th century building, originally a Convent of the Poor Clares, the museum's collection consists of more than 3,000 items reflecting rural life from the 1700s to the present day, as well as a 1000-year-old Dug-Out boat, a couple of well-preserved "Sheela-na-Gigs" (ancient stone carvings of female figures believed to be based on pagan fertility symbols), and many other items connected with the county. The core of the collection is the "Pighouse Collection", so named because of the buildings in which it was originally stored before being donated to the museum by Mrs Phyllis Faris of Cornafean, Co. Cavan. The collection is devoted to 18th, 19th and 20th century costumes and folk life material.

About 5 miles east of Ballyjamesduff, the little village of **Killinkerne** also has a connection with the USA since it was the birthplace of General Phil Sheridan (1831-88) who later became Commander-in-Chief of the US Army.

Virginia

19 miles SE of Cavan on the N3

Beautifully situated on the edge of Lough Ramor, Virginia was founded during the reign of James I and named after his aunt, the virgin queen Elizabeth I. It's an orderly little town with rustic cottages lining the main street and a trim avenue of clipped yew trees leading to the Protestant church. The celebrated playwright Richard Brinsley Sheridan lived here for several years and was often visited by his equally famous friend Jonathan Swift. A sandy stretch on

Corronagh Woods Log Cabin

Lough Ramor, Virginia, Co. Cavan
Tel: 00353 (0)86 3724774

Surrounded by beautiful woodlands on the shore of Lough Ramor, **Corronagh Woods Log Cabin** offers top of the range self-catering accommodation in a wonderfully peaceful location. This Canadian-style log cabin has been tastefully designed to the highest standard and its many amenities include an open plan, spacious living area, kitchen, 3 bedrooms, a bathroom with shower, and a sauna with its own shower and dressing area. The lodge stands on its own site in around 0.75 acres.

Lough Ramor itself offers all kinds of water sports and boats are available to rent in Virginia. The lake is also an angler's paradise, providing great catches primarily of perch and pike. This unspoilt environment is also a safe haven for walking, cycling, horse riding and wild-life spotting. In Virginia – 5 minutes by boat or 5 miles by road and 1hr from Dublin Airport by car – you'll find a good range of bars, hotels, shops and its famous scenic 9-hole golf course which is open to visitors.

This Cabin is for rent by phoning the owner Frank on his mobile 00353 (0)86 3724774.

Lakeside Manor Hotel

Virginia, Co. Cavan
Tel: 049 854 8200 Fax: 049 854 8279
e-mail: info@lakesidemanor.ie
website: www.lakesidemanor.ie

Standing on the shore of Lough Remor, **Lakeside Manor Hotel** offers luxury accommodation, outstanding cuisine, lively entertainment and a range of water activities on the lough. Purpose-built to the highest standards in 1989, the hotel has 32 fully air-conditioned rooms, all with en suite facilities and panoramic views. In the stylish restaurant diners can choose from an extensive menu that includes superb fresh fish dishes. With its extensive facilities and on-site Nite Club, Lakeside Manor is a popular venue for conferences, banquets and weddings.

the lakeshore provides good bathing and rowing boats can be hired for fishing on Lough Ramor - quantities of pike, perch, rudd and bream are just there for the taking.

Kingscourt

22 miles SE of Cavan on the R165

This small town lies close to the borders with Counties Meath and Louth and is noted for the charming stained-glass windows in the Catholic church designed by the Dublin artist Evie Hone (1894-1955). A couple of miles north of the town is the entrance to the **Dun a Rí Forest Park** where visitors can picnic by the pretty Cabra River, follow the planned walks and nature trails, or maybe catch a glimpse of the wild deer among the trees. The park is part of the former Cabra demesne which

Hilltown View

Kells Road, Kingscourt, Co. Cavan
Tel: 042 966 8559 Mobile: 087 240 3327
e-mail: info@hilltownview.com
website: www.hilltownview.com

Within easy walking distance of Kingscourt town, **Hilltown View** stands at the end of a long tree-lined drive in a peaceful, secluded spot with lovely panoramic views. Guests arriving at this friendly B&B, the home of John and Annette O'Reilly, are greeted with welcoming refreshments. All the rooms in this beautifully decorated and maintained house are bright and spacious. All 5 bedrooms are en suite, including the four poster bed grand suite, have television and at breakfast time you'll find a good choice on the menu. If you prefer seif-catering the O'Reillys also have a superb chalet to rent which sleeps 5 guests in luxury.

Wishing Well

Main Street, Kingscourt, Co. Cavan
Tel: 042 966 7150

The oldest pub in Kingscourt, (and for many, the best), the **Wishing Well** stands in the heart of the town's main street, its brightly painted frontage looking very inviting. And you won't be disappointed by the interior, either. There's an olde worlde front bar with wooden flooring and a snug, friendly atmosphere, and a spacious lounge to the rear that extends a considerable distance. This is primarily a 'wet' pub but soup and sandwiches are available throughout the day. The Wishing Well is especially noted for its friendly, efficient staff led by manageress Berni, and another strong attraction here is the live music.

Dun a Rí Forest Park

belonged to the Lord of Cormey Castle. The medieval castle where both Oliver Cromwell and James II were entertained was bought in the early 1800s by a Colonel Joseph Pratt who rebuilt it in the Gothic style and renamed it Cabra Castle. It is now a luxury hotel.

Co Clare

The landscape of County Clare is defined by water and you are never far from it – nearly three-quarters of the county boundary is formed by either the Atlantic, the mighty River Shannon or the great expanse of Lough Derg. There is some outstanding coastal scenery in the southeast, around Loop Head, while further north the dramatic Cliffs of Moher tower almost 700ft above the Atlantic. Inland, Clare displays stark differences between the productive gentle pastures and fertile land by the Shannon and the lunar rockscape of the Burren, a wild wasteland irresistibly attractive to botanists, geologists and archaeologists exploring its many prehistoric sites.

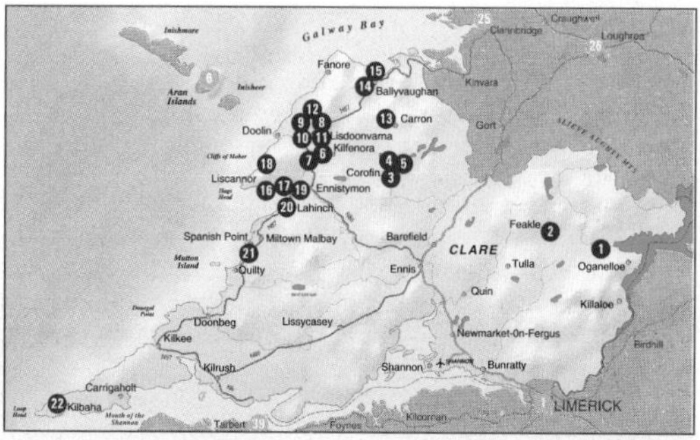

PLACES TO STAY, EAT AND DRINK

● Denotes entries in other chapters

The Burren

A busy and attractive town, the county capital grew up around a great bend of the River Fergus. Narrow, winding streets thread their way through the compact centre of Ennis with its quaint shops and shopfronts. A market is still held in the spacious market square every Saturday, just as it has every week since James I issued a grant in 1609.

Right in the heart of the town stand the substantial ruins of **Ennis Friary**. Founded around 1240, the friary is rich in sculptures and decorated tombs, most notably the 15th century MacMahon tomb with its striking alabaster carvings of the Passion.

Clare is known as both the "banner county" and the "singing county". The former epithet was earned by the fighting prowess of Clare's soldiers at the Battle of Ramillies, and later because of the courageous struggle of its people for Catholic emancipation. The "singing county" is self-explanatory – wherever you go you can be almost certain of finding a pub offering scheduled or impromptu sessions of traditional music.

Ennis

Ennis has an unusual distinction – more households here are linked to the Internet than anywhere else in the world. In 1997, Ennis was chosen by Eircom, the Irish telecommunications company, for an extraordinary social experiment. Every family was offered a new computer, with free Internet access and voice mail, and schools were provided with a computer for every nine students. Currently, more than 85% of households have computers and are linked to the Internet.

Dominating the main street is a much-maligned **Statue of Daniel O'Connell**, the great 19th century nationalist leader who was elected MP for Clare in 1828. As a Catholic he was legally barred from membership of the House of Commons but the Government, fearing violent civil unrest if O'Connell was not allowed to take his seat, was forced to pass the Catholic Emancipation Act the following year. Another statue, opposite the impressive neo-Classical Courthouse of 1850, commemorates Eamon de Valera who represented County Clare in the Dáil from 1917 until 1973; during many of those years he also served as President of the Republic.

A third statue, at the eastern end of the town, is known as **The Maid of Erin**. Erected in 1881, it commemorates three Irish nationalists executed in Manchester in 1867. A life size female figure atop the 23ft high column represents Erin who stands with her left hand placed on a Celtic cross. At her feet is an Irish wolfhound.

The town's museum, rather boastfully

Ennis Town

named **Riches of Clare**, tells the story of Clare from more than 6000 years ago to the present. It specialises in items associated with famous Clare people. Fans of Percy French, the Victorian painter and entertainer, for example, can see the old steam engine he immortalised in his song about the West Clare Railway (1887-1961), *"Are you right there, Michael, are you right?"* French's satirical song made fun of the WCR's propensity for its engines to stop anywhere other than stations and it led to him being sued for libel by the railway directors.

During the last weekend in May, Ennis plays host to the Fleadh Nua, a festival of authentic Irish music; there's an Ennis Arts Festival in October and, most popular of all, the Guinness Traditional Music Festival in mid-November which attracts all the leading musicians. If you would like to know more about Irish traditional music and dance, the town offers evening sessions every Wednesday during the season where you can learn some Irish dancing steps. Tea and brown bread is included in the small admission charge. And every Saturday night from May to October there are Oiche Céilí evenings featuring traditional Irish music where again guests are invited to participate.

Around Ennis

Barefield

3 miles N of Ennis on the N18

Just to the north of Barefield, **Dromore Wood** (free) is a 1000-acre nature reserve noted for the diversity and richness of its flora and fauna. The wood is open daily during daylight hours throughout the year; the visitor centre daily from mid-June to mid-September. Guided tours are available by arrangement at the centre, or you can buy a self-guiding booklet.

Tulla

11 miles E of Ennis on the R462

The pretty little village of Tulla is surrounded by a sprinkling of lakes and is a popular centre for coarse fishing. Torpey's bar is noted for its regular traditional music sessions and Tulla also hosts a 4-day music festival, known as the Humour of Tulla, over the first weekend in October.

Quin

7 miles SE of Ennis on the R469

Quin Abbey (free) is a well-preserved 15th century Franciscan friary set in beautiful surroundings. The Macnamaras who founded the Abbey cannibalised much of the fabric of Ennis's Anglo-Norman castle to build it. Although roofless, the remainder of the church is remarkably complete, with a high altar, cloisters and a graceful tower from the top of which there are excellent views.

Close by is **Craggaunowen Castle**, a fortified tower house built in 1550 and restored in 1975. Inside there's an impressive collection of 16th century European wood carvings but even more interesting are the reconstructions of

Crannog Lake Dwelling

ancient Irish homes and farmsteads in the surrounding grounds. The exhibits include a reconstructed *crannog*, (a Bronze Age lake dwelling), a 4th century ring fort and a *souterrain*, or underground chamber. These are all replicas but the *Brendan* is the real thing – the boat made of leather stretched over an ash wood frame in which the journalist and adventurer Tim Severin sailed from Ireland to Newfoundland in 1976 to prove that St Brendan the Navigator could have made the journey in the 6th century as old chronicles relate. Another genuine artefact is an actual Iron Age road, excavated from Corlea Bog in Co. Longford, and moved to this site. It's made of large oak planks placed over birch and alder branches, an ingenious and effective solution to the problem of crossing spongy bogland.

A couple of miles further south, **Knappogue Castle** is a massively impressive fortress, also built by the Macnamara family (in 1467), and held by them until 1800 with the exception of a brief period when they lost it to Cromwell. He used the castle as his headquarters, thereby saving it from the major damage he inflicted elsewhere. Fully restored, the castle has become a major tourist attraction and hosts medieval-style banquets.

Newmarket-on-Fergus

8 miles S of Ennis on the N18

Donal O'Brien, Lord Inchiquin, was passionate about horses so when he built Dromoland Castle here in the late 1700s he named the new settlement after the famous English race course at Newmarket and the local river. The O'Brien castle is now a luxury hotel.

In nearby Dromoland Forest, **Maughaun Fort** is one of the most extensive Iron Age hill-forts in Europe, covering more than 27 acres within three concentric walls. The inhabitants must have been very prosperous since an enormous hoard of gold ornaments was discovered close by in 1854 when a railway line was being constructed. Incredibly, many of the ornaments were melted down by dealers but a goodly number survived and are now preserved in the National Museum in Dublin.

Shannon

12 miles SE of Ennis on the N19

Shannon is effectively a dormitory town for the nearby international airport, the single most important employer in Co. Clare. The airport boasts several firsts. In 1947 it introduced duty free shopping for international travellers; it was the first to provide pre-flight US immigration clearance facilities; and it also claims to have invented Irish coffee to placate stranded transatlantic passengers in the days when smog-bound Heathrow was often closed and many planes were forced to land here. Shannon is also one of very few airports in the world to have an 18-hole golf course right next to it.

Bunratty

16 miles SE of Ennis on the N18

Bunratty village overlooks Ireland's greatest river, the Shannon, which at 240 miles is also the longest in the British Isles. A broad, slow-moving river, the Shannon drains almost one fifth of the area of the country and drops a mere 400ft in the course of the journey from its source in the hills of Co. Cavan. As the river approaches the estuary its waters are harnessed to provide a major source of hydroelectricity.

About 2 miles to the east of Shannon, **Bunratty Castle** stands on what was once an island. The Vikings were the first to fortify the site and the moat they constructed is still in place. The present impressive building, set beside a small stone bridge over the River Ratty, was erected by the Macnamaras around 1460 and fully restored 400 years later. The massive rectangular Keep houses an outstanding collection of furniture, tapestries, and paintings from the 14th to the 17th centuries. The imaginative restoration of the castle has created an authentic 15th century atmosphere, best experienced during one of the medieval-style banquets held here twice nightly at which guests are served and serenaded by winsome colleens in medieval costume.

In the grounds of the castle the **Bunratty Folk Park** contains a fascinating series of replicas of rural and urban Irish houses as they would have looked in the late 1800s. There's a grey limestone cottage from north Clare, a whitewashed mountain farmhouse from west Limerick, a smallholder's comfortable home from Tipperary's Golden Vale and nearby the kind of basic hovel his hired hands would have lived in. Additional attractions include a complete village street with shops and a pub, gift and tea rooms, and the well known tourist pub, Durty Nelly's. During the season, the park hosts **Traditional Irish Ceili Nights** featuring dances and songs which have been handed down through generations. Visitors can also savour the authentic flavour of a home cooked meal of Irish stew, apple pie and soda bread.

A recent addition to the Folk Park is **Hazelbrook House.** Built in 1898 it was the home of the Hughes brothers who later created HB ice cream which is still a household name in Ireland. Visitors can learn about the evolution of ice cream making from the domestic dairy to modern day production plant. The house also features the history of the Hughes brothers.

A couple of miles southeast of Bunratty, on the main N18 road, **Cratloe Woods House** is a unique example of a 17th century Irish Longhouse. It contains an exhibition of works of art, curios and horse-drawn farm machinery. The nearby woods from which the house takes its name are also notable since they contain some rare primeval oak forest.

Bunratty Castle

Killaloe

25 miles E of Ennis on the R463

Killaloe lies at the southern end of Lough Derg, where the Shannon narrows and passes beneath a lovely 13-arched stone bridge that links Counties Clare and Tipperary. Picturesquely set beside the lough, Killaloe is an excellent base for lough cruises or boat rentals and you can also hire wind-surfers, canoes, wet-suits and dinghies from the University of Limerick Activity Centre a couple of miles outside the town.

The centre of Killaloe is a network of narrow lanes running up the hillside and leading to **St Flannan's Cathedral**, an austere 13th century building with a squat tower and sturdy buttresses. Just inside the cathedral is a strikingly decorated Romanesque doorway from an even older church and next to it the massive Thorgrim Stone circa AD 1000 inscribed with unique ogham and runic inscriptions and believed to be the memorial to a Viking convert. In the churchyard stands **St Flannan's Oratory,** built in the 1100s and with its barrel-vaulted stone roof still intact. Even older is St Molua's Church in the grounds of the Catholic church. It was moved here from its original site on Friar's Island in 1929 when the island was flooded in the Shannon hydro-electric scheme.

Killaloe was the birthplace of Brian Boru (AD 940-1014) who subdued the Viking invaders and is generally regarded as the greatest High King of Ireland. The earthern fort known as Beal Boru, on the western shore of Lough Derg, may be the site of his palace, 'Kincora'. The **Killaloe Heritage Centre** tells the story of Brian Boru, explores the history of Celtic Ireland, the arrival of Christianity in the area, as well as the development of the Shannon River as a transport artery since the earliest times.

From Killaloe a scenic road (the R463) runs northwards alongside Lough Derg, passing en route the fort of Beal Boru, then through the fishing centre of Scarriff and the pretty lakeside village of Mountshannon before entering Co. Galway near Lough Alewnaghta.

Oganelloe

25 miles E of Ennis off the R463

This little village at the foot of Mount Caher lies on the 112-mile circular **East Clare Way,** a long distance footpath that passes through pastoral countryside, taking in rivers, lakes, woodlands and boglands, and crosses the southern flank of the Slieve Aughty Mountains where, at Cragnamurragh, it reaches its highest point, 1730 feet. En route, walkers can stop off for a boat trip on Lough Derg from Mountshannon, or visit the 10th century church in Tuamgraney which is the oldest Irish church still used for services. This ancient church is said to have been repaired in AD 1000 by King Brian Boru himself.

Feakle

20 miles NE of Ennis on the R468/R461

A secluded village on the slopes of the Slieve Aughty Mountains, Feakle is best known for its **International Traditional Music Festival** which is usually held over the second weekend in August. Throughout the rest of the year there are regular music sessions in the local pubs. Feakle also boasts two interesting literary connections. A teacher at a nearby school, the poet Brian Merriman (1749-1805), was one of the earliest pro-feminist writers. In his epic poem *The Midnight Court* he satirised the many small-minded customs prevalent in the region at the time, in particular the fact that most men avoided marriage until their

Peppers Bar

Feakle, Co. Clare
Tel: 061 924822 / 061 924980
e-mail: garypepper@eircom.net

Peppers Bar is known throughout the country for its traditional music sessions, held every Wednesday night of the year, and made famous by the late PJ Hayes and Francie Donnellan. This village pub has been host to the world's top class musicians, stars such as Martin Hayes, Liam O'Flynn, Matt Molloy, Sharon Shannon, Begley and Cooney and many more. In addition to the regular Wednesday sessions, during the summer months (May to September) there are also performances on Sunday evenings, when all musicians are welcome to come along and join in with the music and song, and monthly concerts are held in the intimate room adjoining the bar.

Peppers' music sessions have featured on both national and international networks such as Geantraí on TG4, and the Tulla Ceilí Band recorded their last CD here. As well as providing the best of traditional music, Peppers in recent years has expanded to offer a very extensive food menu available seven days a week and based on fresh local produce direct from the land. The excellence of the food recently earned Peppers the "Dining Pub of the Year Award" and the pub, with its traditional Liscannor flag floor, beamed ceiling and open hearth fire, has also received the "James Joyce Pub of the Year" and the "Traditional Pub of the Year" awards.

Corofin Country House

Station Road, Corofin, Co. Clare
Tel: 065 683 7791

Corofin Country House offers visitors to this scenic corner of the county the choice of either bed & breakfast or self-catering accommodation.

Just a 3-minute walk from the centre of the village, Corofin Country House is the home of Mary and James Shannon who have been in the hospitality business for some 25 years.

The house was purpose-built in 2001 as a guest house and has 4 attractive guest bedrooms, all of them with en suite facilities.

Self-catering guests have a choice of 3 cottages, all recently built in traditional style and all comprehensively equipped.

Connole's

Killeen, Corofin, Co. Clare
Tel: 065 683 7773
e-mail: connolesbandb@eircom.net
website: www.connolesbandb.com

Set beside Ballyculinan Lake, **Connole's** family-run bed & breakfast provides guests with Irish hospitality at its best. Your hosts, Michael and Anne Connole, offer luxury accommodation in their spacious purpose-built house with its open peat fires, sun lounge and peaceful garden. All the elegantly furnished and decorated guest bedrooms have en suite facilities and are equipped with television, power showers and tea-making facilities. All bedrooms are non-smoking. Guests have the use of a comfortable TV lounge and at breakfast time are presented with an extensive menu to choose from.

There's ample private parking and anglers will find good sport in the lake to the rear of the house. A mile or so down the road from Connole's is Corofin village, famous for its fishing and traditional music, and just a few miles further the bustling town of Ennis with its lively social life and shopping opportunities. This picturesque and historic market town with its narrow streets and character pubs resounding to traditional music is known as the Gateway to the Burren, a unique lunar landscape that provides a congenial habitat for some of the rarest of Irish wild flowers.

parents were dead and they had a "few punts (pounds) in their pockets". As late as 1946, the Republic's Censorship Board banned the publication of a translation of Merriman's Gaelic original because it contained these "immoral" lines:

A starved old gelding, blind and lamed
And a twenty-year-old with her parts untamed,
It wasn't her fault if things went wrong,
She closed her eyes and held her tongue;
She was no ignorant girl from school
To whine for her mother and play the fool
But a competent bedmate smooth and warm
Who cushioned him like a sheaf of corn.

A century after Brian Merriman's death, another local inhabitant, Biddy Early, became something of a celebrity when her vivid accounts of local folk-lore were collected and published by Lady Augusta Gregory in her book *Visions and Beliefs of the West of Ireland.*

Corofin

8 miles NW of Ennis on the R476

Set in pretty countryside near the shore of scenic Lough Inchiquin, Corofin is well worth seeking out in order to visit the **Clare Heritage Centre** (free), housed in the former St Catherine's Church which was built in 1718 by a cousin of Queen Anne. The centre has a museum which opens a fascinating window on the story of 19th century Ireland. It also houses a Genealogical Centre which was the first of its kind in the country. This brings together the most comprehensive research material

BOFEY QUINNS

Main Street, Corofin, Co. Clare
Tel: 065 683 7321 Fax: 065 683 7322
e-mail: trishcleary@eircom.net
website: www.corofin.eu.com

Eight miles northwest of Ennis on the R476, en route to the Burren or the Cliffs of Moher and situated in Corofin village is **Bofey Quinns**, one of Co. Clare's leading dining pubs and restaurant. Voted one of the top ten pub/restaurants in the country by the licensing world, and with several other awards from the Clare good food guide, plus Black & White awards, this family-run restaurant is well worth a visit. Diners are spoilt for choice as chef/proprietor Niall

Cleary caters for everyone with plenty of traditional Irish dishes such as Bacon & Cabbage, Irish Stew or, if you prefer, tender sirloin steak, fresh salmon or seabass – Niall has it all. Younger diners also have a wide choice from the pizza menu, pasta dishes or junior diners section.

Bofey Quinns also caters for those with a gluten free diet. The 48-seater dining room, which has wheel-chair access, is a must while visiting Ireland! Bofey Quinns also hosts a session of traditional Irish music in the bar every Wednesday night all year round and Corofin itself has its Traditional Music Festival over the first weekend in March. The restaurant and bar are open 7 days a week from 12 noon; most major credit cards and laser are accepted. While accommodation is not available in Bofey Quinns, Niall and Trish do rent out their traditional Irish cottage.

to help anyone with Co. Clare roots to trace their ancestry – parish and civil records, census returns, tombstone inscriptions and information from many other sources. Together, these materials provide the details of more than half a million former residents of Co. Clare. If you don't want to do the research yourself, you can pay a fee to the Centre's staff for either an initial or full-scale search.

A couple of miles south of Corofin, **Dysert O'Dea Castle** is an uncompromising rectangle of a building with blank walls pierced by a few narrow slits. This 15th century tower house was devastated by Cromwell's troops in 1651 but renovated in 1986 and is now home to a museum with hundreds of artefacts from the Stone Age to the War of Independence. A 20-minute audio-visual presentation introduces visitors to the 25 historic monuments to be found in the surrounding fields. The most notable are two Celtic forts, a ruined Round Tower, two Romanesque churches, a 12th century High Cross and a Holy Well.

Kilfenora

19 miles NW of Ennis on the R476

Nowadays, Kilfenora is best known for its lively year-round music pubs, especially Vaughan's Pub. But in medieval times the village's importance derived from **St Fachnan's Cathedral,** seat of the Bishops of Kilfenora from 1152 but now serving as a simple parish church. The bishopric never provided a rich living: when the worldly-wise Dr Richard Betts was offered the preferment by King Charles I he ungraciously declined, intimating that "he had no wish to become bishop of the poorest see in Ireland". Perhaps reflecting this poverty, the 12th century cathedral is tiny but it's worth going inside to see the exquisite sedilia (seats set into the wall) with their delicate stone traceries on the 3-arched design. An additional attraction at

The Boghill Centre

Boghill, Kilfenora, Co. Clare
Tel: 065 707 4644
e-mail: boghill@eircom.net
website: www.boghill.com

Situated in 50 acres of bogland just 2 miles from Lisdoonvarna and 3 miles from Kilfenora, the **Boghill Centre** is a perfect place to relax and unwind. During the summer, and at Christmas and New Year, it's also a great place to learn more about traditional Irish music in the regular weekly courses for all traditional instruments. The Centre also hosts a range of other workshops such as djembe and yoga. If you aren't interested in any of these but would like to stay here on holiday and visit the Burren and Co. Clare's many other attractions, the Centre offers a variety of accommodation options for up to 40 people.

There are 4 private en suite double rooms, 4 single rooms sharing 2 bathrooms, and value-for-money hostel accommodation in 2 large and 2 smaller dormitories which would be suitable for families. With its large workshop room and extensive grounds, the Centre is well-suited to many different activities and is available as a venue to hire. Past workshops have included Reiki, yoga, self-discovery, homoeopathy and computer training. Catering can be arranged. Visitors will find plenty to see and do in the area. The spa town Lisdoovarna, famed for its annual Matchmaker's Festival in September, is just a couple of miles away; the Burren and the Cliffs of Moher are both within easy reach.

Kilshanny House

Kilshanny, Co. Clare
Tel: 065 707 1660

Established in 1860, **Kilshanny House** is not just a splendid traditional pub but also offers quality bed and breakfast accommodation. The fine old stone house stands in a scenic rural location alongside the N67, about halfway between Lisdoonvarna and Ennistimon. Mine host Aidan Galvin, ensures that his customers enjoy "the best of drinks, great traditional music sessions, a warm welcome and great craic!" Open peat fires add to the atmosphere and overnight guests will find en suite rooms with orthopaedic beds and hospitality trays. Children are welcome and Aidan's traditional Irish breakfast provides a great way to start the day.

Kilfenora, in a field to the west of the church, is the array of medieval high crosses of which the most striking is the beautifully decorated 12th century Doorty Cross depicting Christ's entry into Jerusalem.

For an informative introduction to the Burren area and its history, a visit to the **Burren Display Centre** at Kilfenora is strongly recommended.

Lisdoonvarna

Ireland's premier spa town, Lisdoonvarna is also famous for hosting Europe's largest matchmaking festival. Its origins go back to

Ravine Hotel

Main Street, Lisdoonvarna, Co. Clare
Tel: 065 707 4043
website: www.ravinehotel.com

The **Ravine Hotel** occupies a prime position right in the centre of this popular spa town, beside the church and close to the town's tourist attractions. Owner Nellie O'Boyle has been in the hospitality business all her working life and used to own the well-known Lighthouse Bar & Lounge in the seaside town of Ardglass. She and her staff create a very warm and welcoming atmosphere and genuinely go out of their way to make guests feel at home. The hotel has 12 attractively furnished bedrooms, all with en suite facilities, direct dial phone, hospitality tray and complimentary toiletries. There's a separate restaurant and live entertainment every weekend.

Lisdoonvarna is the perfect base for exploring the other-worldly landscape of the Burren, an area of domed hills and limestone pavements which is a botanist's paradise – 1100 of Ireland's 1400 native plant species are found here. The area is also amazingly rich in prehistoric remains, most notably the Poulnabrone Dolmen which was built more than 6000 years ago. Lisdoonvarna itself is best known for its matchmaking festival, held each year in September when thousands of single people descend on the town in search of the perfect partner.

Rathbaun Hotel

Main Street, Lisdoonvarna, Co. Clare
Tel: 065 707 4009
e-mail: rathbaunhotel@eircom.net
website: www.rathbaunhotel.com

Rathbaun Hotel in the centre of Lisdoonvarna is a unique hotel for special guests. Quality accommodation, excellent food, genuinely personal service from John and Lynn Connolly, and brilliant value for money are the hallmarks of this hotel. It is also renowned for its live music. Throughout June, July and August there is traditional music from the resident group Ceolan, and during September there is dance music by Eclipse. The hotel has 12 guest bedrooms, all en suite, tastefully decorated and equipped with direct dial telephone, modem link and tea/coffee-making equipment.

Breakfast is served in the restaurant from 9am to 10.30am but if you decide to have a lie in it is also available in the bar/restaurant until noon. The bar also serves meals throughout the day from 10.30am until 10pm. A popular amenity here is the gift shop which is packed with value for money items. The hotel also operates a bureau de change – with no commission fees – and can provide information and brochures on tours and ferry times to the Aran Islands and the Cliffs of Moher. Maps of the Burren National Park are also available to the hotel's guests.

The Roadside Tavern

Lisdoonvarna, Co. Clare
Tel: 00353 65 707 4084
Fax: 00353 65 707 4303
e-mail: info@burrensmokehouse.ie
website: www.burrensmokehouse.ie

The Roadside Tavern is one of the best known pubs in north Clare, not least because it is one of the longest established, having been run as a hostelry by the Curtin family for over one hundred years. There is nothing fake or pretentious about "The Roadside", the music here isn't manufactured for the tourist market – it's real, and that's why The Roadside attracts a great fusion of local clients and visitors. The atmosphere here is relaxed and the emphasis is on fun and entertainment. Customers can enjoy traditional music 7 nights a week throughout the summer months and can listen to, or participate in, lively conversation at all hours of the day and night!

Peter Curtin's father and grandfather ran a bakery alongside the pub and while the smell of fresh bread no longer lingers, the tradition of fresh food is very much alive at 'The Roadside'. Meals are served from 12.30pm to 9pm daily throughout the summer months from May to the end of September, and from 12.30pm to 3pm for the remainder of the year. While delicious smoked fish, from the Burren Smokehouse feature strongly on the menu, so too do local high-quality produce, including a good selection of native cheeses.

the days when, having gathered their harvest in, local farmers came to the town in search of a wife. Today, the festival attracts visitors from all over the country for the month-long jamboree of singing, dancing, drinking – and wooing.

The matchmaking festival takes place in September but throughout the year the Victorian **Spa Complex & Health Centre** offers restorative baths, saunas, showers and massages using the spring waters which contain elements of magnesia, iodine and iron and are believed to cure a wide variety of ills. The waters are also mildly radioactive.

A very different process is on view at **The Burren Smokehouse** (see panel below) where huge slabs of salmon are deftly filleted and then smoked over an aromatic smouldering fire of wood chippings. A free video explains the procedure and the final product can be bought here or sampled in the next door tavern.

Lisdoonvarna is surrounded by the unique landscape of the **Burren**, an eerie moonscape of bare domed hills and limestone pavements called *clints*, perforated with vertical fissures called *grikes*. Water filters through these grikes into a vast underworld of caves, the most spectacular of which is Aillwee Cave near Ballyvaughan (*see below*). Although the treeless plateau of the Burren looks harsh and uninviting it is actually amazingly rich in plant life, with 1100 of Ireland's 1400 native species to be found here. And bleak though it is today, the area was widely settled by Stone Age people who left around 120 massive dolmens and wedge tombs. The most photographed of these is the **Poulnabrone Dolmen** about 4 miles south of Ballyvaughan off the R480. Dramatically sited on a limestone pavement, the dolmen with its massive

Burren Smokehouse

Lisdoonvarna, Co. Clare
Tel: 00353 65 707 4432
Fax: 00353 657074303
e-mail: info@burrensmokehouse.ie
website: www.burrensmokehouse.ie

Burren Smokehouse was started in 1989 as a small family-run smoking business, driven by the desire to achieve the highest possible standards. Since then, the quality of its produce has earned it an enviable international reputation. The smokehouse has won an array of top food awards including a Gold at the 2003 UK-based "Great Tastes Awards". Proprietors Birgitta and Peter Curtin welcome guests to the Burren Smokehouse Visitor Centre all year round. Visitors can stroll in to view an engaging video presentation on the art of fish smoking and to enjoy a tasting free of charge.

The Visitor Centre incorporates a gourmet store and craft shop featuring the highest quality locally produced food and gifts – from cheeses, jams and chocolates through to ideal gifts such as hand-made soap. You can purchase salmon, mackerel, trout or eel from the Burren Smokehouse during your visit, place a mail order to have some produce delivered to family or friends practically anywhere on the globe, or you can order at leisure on line. The Burren Smokehouse Visitor Centre welcomes over 30,000 visitors from all over the world every year. Opening hours are 9am to 5pm daily; 9am to 7pm in June and August; and weekends from January to March, 10am to 4pm.

O'Neill's Town Home

St Brendan's Road, Lisdoonvarna, Co. Clare
Tel: 065 707 4208 Fax: 065 707 4435
e-mail: isclo@indigo.ie
website: http://indigo.ie/~isclo

O'Neill's Town Home serves two functions: it offers quality accommodation and is also the home of The Burren Painting Centre which celebrated its 30th anniversary in 2003. The house itself is more than 100 years old with limestone walls some 3ft thick and was built by John O'Neill's great grandfather. Over the past 30 years, John and his wife Chris have carefully modernised the house while preserving its atmosphere and character. There's a comfortable residents' lounge with colour TV and a selection of books and magazines on art and the Burren.

An extensive collection of watercolours and oils decorate all rooms throughout the house. Arriving guests are greeted with complimentary tea or coffee; home-baked brown soda bread is made every day; and dinner is available if required two nights a week. There are 8 guest bedrooms, all with en suite facilities. Outside, there's a peaceful, lawned garden, private car park and the art studio which is the base for a series of courses, lasting from 2 to 6 days, available from May to October. The tutors are all well-established artists and the emphasis is on painting *en plein air*, taking full advantage of the unique Burren and north Clare landscapes and using a variety of media. The courses are available on either a residential or non-resident basis.

capstone was built more than 6000 years ago, probably as a ceremonial cemetery for tribal leaders.

A popular way to explore the 100 square miles of the Burren is to follow the circular drive from Lisdoonvarna along the coast to Black Head and Ballyvaughan, returning along the Corkscrew road to Lisdoonvarna.

Poulnabrone Dolmen, The Burren

Around Lisdoonvarna

Carron

10 miles E of Lisdoonvarna off the R480

The tiny hamlet of Carron stands in the heart of the Burren and is perhaps best known for **The Burren Perfumery** which, when it was established some 30 years ago, was the first of its kind in Ireland. It claims that its fragrances evoke "somewhere between Heaven and Earth, the mystery of Ireland and the purity of the Burren combined". Visitors can see natural essential oils being extracted and then blended using the traditional still. All the products are on display, available to sample and purchase in the showroom. The Perfumery also has a unique

Cassidy's Pub

Carron, Co. Clare
Tel: 065 708 9109 Fax: 065 708 9232
e-mail: info@cassidyspub.com
website: www.cassidyspub.com

Cassidy's Pub claims to be the only barracks in Ireland where you can buy a pint! Originally built by the British in the 1840s, it was destroyed by Irish volunteers in 1920 and lay in ruins until 1926 when it was rebuilt as a Garda barracks. The Cassidy family have deep roots in the area and were already operating a pub and grocery business in Carron by 1830. They moved to the present premises in 1956 and the original lock up cell door still stands as a reminder of the days when all you would be served here was bread and water! Today, you'll find an enticing choice in what must be the only Burren-themed bar food in the world.

The menu includes a selection of mionàin (kid meat) and Burren goat cheese dishes. These, with some of the wild herbs and plants native to the area, coupled with the distinct scenery will give a unique Burren feel to your dining experience. Everything served in the restaurant is home cooked and baked, and only natural ingredients are used in dishes such as The Bailiff's Bounty – "Burren smoked salmon from the poacher's bag served with cream cheese and hidden in greenery". An additional attraction at Cassidy's is the live entertainment each weekend at which musicians are always welcome and local singers are always ready to join in.

photographic exhibition and an excellent audio-visual presentation of the flora and history of the Burren. An interesting natural feature nearby is a "turlough" – in summer it's a meadow, in winter a lake.

Ballyvaughan

12 miles NE of Lisdoonvarna on the N67/ R480

In striking contrast to the bare, treeless wastes of the Burren, Ballyvaughan is an attractive little port set in a green, wooded valley and looks across the bay to the Galway hills. The village has several interesting craft shops and **Newtown Castle** nearby is unusual in being a circular fortified tower standing on a square base. Built in the 16th century, the castle has 4 storeys and contains some unique architectural features. Guided tours reveal its social, cultural, political and historical context, and the exhibits include a

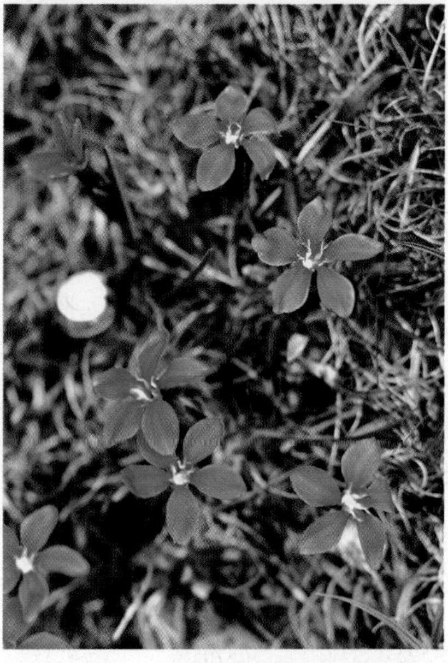

Burren Flora

AILLWEE CAVE

Ballyvaughan, Co. Clare
Tel: 065 70 77067 Fax: 065 70 77107
e-mail: fiona@aillweecave.ie
website: www.aillweecave.ie

Located just a couple of miles south of Ballyvaughan, **Aillwee Cave** is Ireland's premier show cave. There's a whole labyrinth of caves, pot-holes, underground lakes and streams beneath the surface of The Burren, but Aillwee is the only one that can be explored without the aid of special equipment. Discovered by a local herdsman in 1941, the cave has more than 3500 feet of passages. Visitors are guided on a 35-minute stroll through beautiful caverns, over bridged chasms, beneath weird rock formations, and alongside the thunderous waterfall that can sometimes gently spray the unsuspecting visitor. At one point there's a column from floor to ceiling formed by a stalactite and a stalagmite meeting.

Unique to Ireland are the Bear Pits – hollows scraped out by brown bears, one of the cave's original inhabitants. The entrance to the cave has been strikingly landscaped in stone with a design reminiscent of Ireland's prehistoric monuments. Inside, there's a tea room and potato bar, a farm shop, a dairy where you can watch cheese being made, and a craft shop with some unusual artefacts on sale. Outside, there's a terrace where you can enjoy both a glass of wine and stunning views stretching away to the Connemara

THE TEA JUNCTION

Main Street, Ballyvaughan, Co. Clare
Tel: 065 707 7289
e-mail: orchidhouse@oceanfree.net

Located in the centre of town and close to all the tourist attractions, **The Tea Junction** offers customers an enticing range of wholesome and appetising fare.

Gill Gregory's small and cosy tea room is noted for its wonderful home-made cakes but the menu also includes an all day breakfast and a good variety of vegetarian and vegan meals served by friendly staff.

The tea room has pine furniture and a truly traditional feel. Smoking is not permitted inside but in good weather you can sit outside at tables on the pavement and watch the world go by. The Tea Junction is open 7 days a week from March to November but closed on Tuesdays during the winter.

facsimile of the Book of Kells.

Just to the east of the village, at the Whitethorn Visitor Centre, the **Burren Exposure** provides an excellent introduction to the history, mythology and unique flora of the Burren with the help of giant screens.

Just a couple of miles south of Ballyvaughan is **Aillwee Cave** (see panel opposite), Ireland's premier show cave. There's a whole labyrinth of caves, pot-holes, underground lakes and streams beneath the surface of the Burren, but Aillwee is the only one that can be explored without the aid of special equipment. If you are feeling energetic, you could tackle the steep climb up the mountain behind the cave and reward yourself with an incomparable view over the sweep of Galway Bay.

A little way to the south of the cave are the **Gleninsheen Wedge Tombs,** a series of Bronze Age burial places constructed of slabs forming a box. Nearby, in the 1930s, a young lad found a gold neck collar, regarded as one of the most beautiful and undamaged in existence. It is now in Dublin's National Museum.

Fanore

8 miles N of Lisdoonvarna on the R477

Fanore stands on the spectacular stretch of coastline between Doolin and Black Head, and provides a good starting point for walks across the Burren. One of the best of these is the 9½ mile circular walk that takes in the Caherdoonfergus ring fort and the heights of Dobhach Bhrainin and Gleninagh.

Doolin

6 miles SW of Lisdoonvarna on the R478

Famous for the quality of its traditional music, this small village set around a sandy cove is also the embarkation point for ferries to the **Aran Islands** of Inisheer, Inishmaan and Inishmore which are actually part of County Galway *(see chapter 6)*. Life on these windswept islands provided the raw material for J.M.Synge's early play *Riders to the Sea* (1904) and little has changed since those days. The rugged beauty, the sweeping views and the astonishing wealth of prehistoric and early monastic ruins make a visit to the islands a memorable, even mystical, experience.

Liscannor

10 miles SW of Lisdoonvarna on the R478

This small fishing village was the birthplace of John P. Holland (1841-1914) who invented the submarine but Liscannor is much better known locally because of the **Holy Well of St Brigid** to the northwest of the village. A major place of pilgrimage, the well is approached by a narrow stone passage whose entrance is guarded by a remarkably lifelike full size plaster model of the 6th century saint. Testimony to the continuing power of St Brigid to heal the afflicted is displayed in the grotto with its collection of discarded crutches.

In the cemetery above St Brigid's Well rises the great column erected in memory of Cornelius O'Brien, MP for Clare from 1835 until his death in 1857. Cornelius took such a relaxed view of his Parliamentary obligations that Prime Minister Lord Palmerston remarked of him "He was the best Irish MP we ever had. He didn't open his mouth in 20 years". Cornelius was however a dutiful landlord, always concerned to improve the living conditions of his tenants. Unlike most other, often absentee, Irish landlords, he never evicted any of his tenants, even during the calamitous years of the Great Famine. There is a curious footnote, though, to the story of this much-loved man. After his death, the column mentioned above was erected. It bears an inscription recording that it was paid for by the donations of

The Rock Shop

Liscannor, Co. Clare
Tel: 0657081930 Fax: 0657081944
e-mail: therockshop@eircom.net
website: www.therockshop.ie

The area around Liscannor and the Cliffs of Moher is famous for its durable stone, known as "Liscannor Flag", which is widely used for paving, cladding, fireplaces and roofs. It's one of the many natural treasures on display and for sale at **The Rock Shop**'s innovative showroom where you'll also find crystals of quartz birth stones and healing crystals, stone vases and trays, superb Celtic carvings on stone and much more. Also on sale are jewels and jewellery to suit all tastes and fashions, and an extensive range of rock, fossil and mineral specimens from Ireland and around the world for collectors young and old. Qualified staff are on hand to help with your requirements, whether it be for a semi-precious stone or for flagstones, crazy paving or stone garden furniture. An audio-visual presentation illustrates quarrying methods through the ages and includes some spectacular shots of the Cliffs of Moher. There's also a fascinating collection of quarrying tools from the past, together with photographs of Liscannor in the 1800s.

The Rock Shop also has another "little gem" – its own excellent coffee shop serving refreshingly different salads, filled pitta breads and melt-in-the-mouth scones which come with Clare Jam and a mound of freshly whipped cream. Delicious!

Harvey Holiday Homes

Monanagh, Ennistymon, Co. Clare
Tel: 065 70 71145
website: www.lahinchholidays.com

With its mile-long sandy beach and multiple attractions, Lahinch is one of western Ireland's most popular resorts and an ideal base for touring the Burren, Cliffs of Moher, Lisdoonvarla and Doolin. From Doolin, a 20-minute boat trip will take you to the unique Aran Islands. **Harvey Holiday Homes** offers a choice of quality self-catering accommodation in Lahinch with 2 beautifully maintained properties, both attractively furnished and decorated, and comprehensively equipped to provide just about everything you could possibly need on holiday.

One of them, Craven Sea Lodge, is a recently built terraced town house situated beside the beach and close to Sea World and golf links. There are 3 upstairs bedrooms, 1 with a double bed, 1 with a double and single, and 1 with a single bed. The main bedroom enjoys a panoramic view of the Atlantic. All bed linen is supplied. The other one, 46 Summer Cove is 4 star, with a garden in a quiet cul-de-sac just 10 minutes walk from the beach It has a large lounge with fire place, large kitchen/dining area and 3 bedrooms (the master bedroom being en-suite). Heating is by electric storage. In addition to the area's scenic attractions, there is plenty on offer for the actively inclined – two golf courses (one of them a championship course), pitch and putt, walking, cycling, angling, riding, traditional music and set dancing.

The Cliffs of Moher

Liscannor, Co. Clare

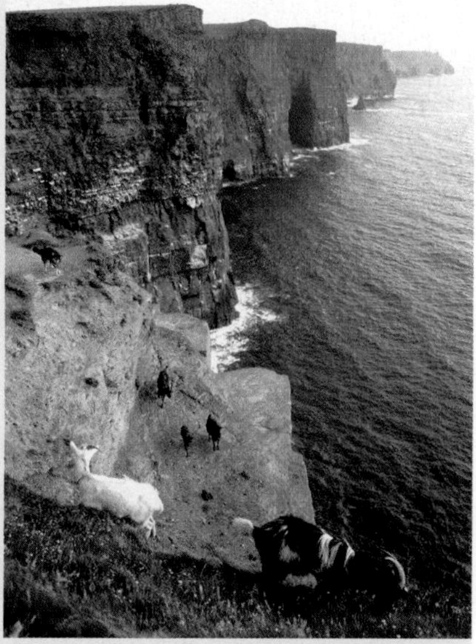

About three miles beyond Liscannor are the famous **Cliffs of Moher**, defiantly standing as giant natural ramparts against the might of the Atlantic. The cliffs stretch along the coast for some five miles and rise in places to 700ft. On the highest cliff stands **O'Brien's Tower**, built in the early 19th century as a viewing point for Victorian tourists. From its exceptional vantage position you can view the Clare coastline, the Aran Islands and mountains as far distant as Kerry and Connemara. There's a visitor centre here with a tourist information centre, crafts souvenir shop and tea room.

Found only in the area of the Cliffs of Moher, Liscannor Stone is a unique mineral that bears the fossil tracks of marine animals living in soil sediments more than 300 million years ago. It was used locally to floor farm dwellings and today provides beautiful natural stone for modern homes and buildings. The story of this unusual material is told in a 15-minute audio-visual presentation at the **Liscannor Stone Story & Rock Shop** near St Brigid's Well (see panel opposite). There's an exhibition of the working methods of cutting and dressing stone products and visitors can also browse in the Rock Shop which sells precious and semi-precious stones from Ireland and worldwide.

'grateful tenants'. It fails to mention the fact that an obligation to contribute to the memorial formed part of 'grateful tenants' tenancy agreements.

About 3 miles beyond Liscannor are the famous **Cliffs of Moher**, defiantly standing as giant natural ramparts against the might of the Atlantic (see panel above).

Ennistymon

7 miles S of Lisdoonvarna on the N85

This attractive market town and holiday centre, famed for its colourful shop fronts and traditional music, sits in a wooded valley beside the River Cullenagh where the waters hurl themselves over a series of rocky shelves. The river is noted for its excellent brown trout fishing, as is the Dealagh River just a couple of miles away. The town grew up around a castle built by Turlough O'Brien in 1588 but no traces remain of his fortress.

Up on the hillside stands a charming 19th century Gothic church. There are some grand views from here of the river winding its way out of the woods on its way to the sea at Liscannor.

Lahinch

9 miles S of Lisdoonvarna on the N67

Overlooking the broad sandy beach of Liscannor Bay, Lahinch has a permanent population of little over 500 but in summer that number is multiplied several times over since this is one of Co. Clare's most popular resorts. It boasts two 18-hole golf courses – one of them a championship course known as the "St Andrew's of Ireland". There's also an entertainment centre with a theatre, cinema, seawater swimming pool, aquarium,

The Sea Farer

Kettle Street, Lahinch, Co. Clare
Tel: 065 708 1050

Opened in the summer of 2003, **The Sea Farer** has quickly established itself as a restaurant for discerning diners to seek out. Chef Michael Allen, who owns and runs the restaurant with his wife Tracey, began in the kitchens of the Limerick Inn Hotel and subsequently worked in Europe and America. His cuisine is modern European with sea food dishes, based on locally caught fish, as his speciality. The décor at The Sea Farer is extremely stylish and elegant with dark wood chairs and black tables contrasting with light-coloured walls. Michael is happy to cater for parties of up to 30 and offers the choice of either an à la carte or set menu.

Dough Mór Lodge

Station Road, Lahinch, Co. Clare
Tel: 065 708 2063 Fax: 065 707 1384
e-mail: dough@gofree.indigo.ir
website: www.doughmorlodge.com

With its attractive front garden and striking limestone walls, **Dough Mór Lodge** looks very inviting as a place to stay. It was purpose built as a guesthouse in 1999 and conforms in all respects with the requirements of Bord Fáilte, the Irish Tourist Board, which has awarded the Lodge a 3-star rating.
The lodge is owned and run by Jim Foley who is an enthusiastic golfer and gardener – which explains the beautifully maintained garden with its interesting selection of shrubs. Jim is also an accomplished cook and produces memorable breakfasts. As well as a full Irish breakfast, there's a choice of omelettes and smoked salmon, along with cereals and fresh fruit, home-made bread and scones. Jim will also cater for vegetarian and other dietary requirements.

Guests have the use of a spacious and very comfortable lounge, complete with a welcoming open fire. Accommodation at the Lodge comprises 6 bedrooms (4 doubles, two twins), all en suite with power showers and direct dial telephone. All the rooms are light and airy, spacious and attractively furnished. Dough Mór Lodge is a mere 800 yards from the centre of Lahinch, a popular seaside resort which boasts a magnificent Blue Flag beach and one of Ireland's very best golf courses.

children's pool and play area. Lahinch is also a favourite destination for surfers challenging the rolling Atlantic breakers.

Southwest Co Clare

Miltown Malbay

20 miles W of Ennis on the N67/R474

Miltown Malbay is a Victorian seaside resort which somehow ended up being built inland. This quiet town comes alive in July for the Willie Clancy Summer School when it is thronged with traditional music enthusiasts. Willie Clancy (1921-73) is celebrated as Co. Clare's greatest performer on the *uileann* pipe, an instrument perfectly suited for his beautiful renderings of slow Irish airs.

East of the town, Slieve Callan, the highest point in west Clare, rises behind the main road to Ennis. If you follow this road you will pass Knocknalassa where there is an impressive wedge-shaped gallery grave. However, it is quite tricky to find, hidden from the road by a hummock

Spanish Point

23 miles W of Ennis off the N67

Spanish Point is so named because it was here in 1588 that several Armada ships were wrecked. A couple of miles offshore, at Mutton Island, one galleon was tossed on to the rocks and hundreds of sailors perished. Survivors from other ships managed to reach the shore only to be slaughtered by the locals on the orders of the Governor of Connacht. On the seafront stands a huge carved stone representing a galleon and an inscription in three languages commemorating a conciliatory visit by the King and Queen of Spain in the 1980s.

Spanish Point has its own wide golden beach, excellent for swimming, and there's another at Freach, just around the headland.

BAY VIEW GUEST HOUSE

Spanish Point, Miltown Malbay, Co. Clare
Tel: 065 708 4006
e-mail: bayviewguesthouse@eilcom.net

An attractive modern building, **Bay View Guest House** occupies a marvellous position enjoying uninterrupted views across the Atlantic Ocean to the Aran Islands. Ann Lahiff and her family have been welcoming bed & breakfast guests here for some 30 years.

All the guest bedrooms are individually designed with top quality decoration and furnishings, and all have en suite facilities and are equipped with TV, direct dial telephone, hair dryer and tea/coffee-making facilities.

There's a comfortable residents' lounge, private parking and the local golf course is just a 5-minute drive away. Bay View Guest House enjoys a 3-star rating from the Irish Tourist Board.

Quilty

24 miles W of Ennis off the N67

The unusual name of this little fishing village derives from the old Irish word, *coillte*, meaning 'woods', but today there are few trees on this flat part of the coast. Instead, the long lines of stone walls are draped with seaweed being dried for kelp making. The seaweed is either burnt to produce iodine-rich ash, or used to extract alignates which provide an unexpected constituent of Guinness, helping to create its rich, creamy head.

Quilty's church looks very Early Christian in style but in fact only dates back to 1907. Some shipwrecked French sailors who had been rescued by local people donated funds for its building.

Lissycasey

10 miles SW of Ennis on the N68

Lissycasey is the home of perhaps the best-known pub in Ireland, **Fanny O'Dea's**. It's Ireland's oldest family-run pub and with its long, low thatched roof and orange-washed walls, wonderfully picturesque. Inside, there's a clock which featured in the pub scene in the film *Ryan's Daughter*, and an open fire that has been burning continuously for 200 years.

The pub's history goes back to 1695 when Denis O'Dea settled in Lissycasey and set up a small inn which doubled as a Shibìn (unlicensed alehouse). When Denis retired the inn was bought by his niece Fanny who immediately displayed a remarkable flair for innkeeping – a great housekeeper and a charming host.

A particular attraction for her customers was the invigorating hot egg flip she had created to her own recipe, a recipe which contained a liberal lacing of Jameson whiskey. One winter's night in 1790, a High Court judge was caught in a blizzard and sought refuge at the inn. As he dried himself out by the fire, Fanny served him the speciality of the house, her famous egg flip. The judge sipped the concoction appreciatively and then remarked that he tasted spirits in the drink. Did she have a licence to sell spirits, he enquired. Fanny replied that she could not afford to pay for a licence and that she gave this drink to friends only. On hearing this, the judge opened his travel case and, taking out a form, filled it in, signed it Robert Vere O'Brien and handed it to Fanny, saying "There is your licence, now you may sell intoxicating drink". Fanny's descendants continue to serve the potent egg flip which provided the unlikely means by which their hostelry acquired its first licence.

Doonbeg

26 miles SW of Ennis on the N67

The tiny village of Doonbeg sits at the mouth of the Cooraclare River and boasts a fine white sandy beach. As at Spanish Point, an Armada ship ran aground here in 1588 and those sailors who managed to struggle to the shore suffered the same fate as their comrades further north.

Kilkee

30 miles SW of Ennis on the N67

A seaside resort since Victorian times, Kilkee is a bustling place during the season when its resident population of 2,000 increases to some 20,000. Sheltered from the Atlantic by the reef-like Duggerna Rocks, Kilkee is well-provided with all the essentials for a family holiday – a long golden beach, amusements, cafés and restaurants, golf, pitch and putt, and a major all-weather attraction, **Kilkee Waterworld**. Opened in 1998, Waterworld offers a Crystal Tower Flume ride more than 60 yards long, a Lazy River ride with some unexpected geysers and gushers, a

Bubble Pool, children's pool, and other fun features to keep all the family amused.

For fairweather days, there's a safe sandy beach which slopes very gently into the bay and boasts a Blue Flag rating. At the western end are 'pollock holes', so called because pollock and other varieties of marine life live in them. There are some marvellous clifftop walks stretching for miles in both directions, or you could follow the breathtaking 15-mile-long Loop Drive around the peninsula which takes in some of the highest cliffs in Ireland. Kilkee is a favourite with scuba divers and snorkellers, sea angling is easily arranged and inland the rivers Creegh and Cooraclare offer some excellent trout and salmon fishing.

"The fashionable bathing place" of Kilkee is mentioned in writings of the 18th century as a place to visit and immerse oneself in the healing waters of the Atlantic. The **Kilkee Thalassotherapy Centre** continues that tradition. Thalassotherapy, from the Greek *thalassa*, the sea, and *therapia*, to heal, is based on the healing virtues of sea water. The treatment was originally developed in France as a palliative for illnesses ranging from respiratory problems to heart conditions. Today it is a recommended therapy for men and women suffering from skin disorders, muscular and circulatory problems, backache and stress. The Kilkee Centre offers a whole range of treatments including Natural Seaweed baths, balneotherapy, algeotherapy/seaweed body wraps, cryotherapy and massage.

Kilrush

22 miles SW of Ennis on the N68

A lively maritime and market town overlooking the Shannon estuary, Kilrush has a Blue Flag beach, an adventure centre offering a wide range of activities for all ages, from archery to windsurfing, a golf club which claims to be the friendliest in Ireland, and the **Vandeleur Demesne**, a 420-acre woodland park with a restored Victorian walled garden.

The pubs in Kilrush enthusiastically live up to Clare's reputation as the "Singing County" but for an exceptional feast of traditional music the time to visit is mid-August when the 4-day **Éigse Mrs Crotty** takes place. Elizabeth Crotty was a famed concertina player in the early part of the 20th century and a pioneer of the movement to preserve Irish traditional music. The festival includes céilís, concerts, lectures, classes, traditional sessions in pubs throughout the town and a memorial mass.

Other events in Kilrush include the Kilrush Maritime Festival in the second week of July and a traditional horse fair and market in March, June, October and November.

The town once boasted a muddy tidal harbour but now has an excellent modern marina. From the marina there are daily cruises setting off in search of Ireland's only known resident population of bottlenose dolphins. More than 100 individual dolphins have been identified in the Shannon estuary and the cruise boat's hydrophone allows you to hear them communicating with each other. Another popular excursion is to **Scattery Island**, about 2 miles out in the estuary. The site of a 6th century monastery founded by St Senan, the island has the ruins of five medieval churches, a well-preserved Round Tower 120 feet high and about one thousand years old, and a gun battery from the time of the Napoleonic wars. The battery stands high on the southern tip of the island and from this viewpoint you have a good chance of seeing dolphins at play.

About 5 miles to the southeast of Kilrush is **Killimer Agricultural Zoo,** offering a close view of llamas, wallabies, pot-bellied pigs and many other farmed animals, and a little further east you can catch the regular vehicle ferry for the 20-minute trip across the Shannon to Tarbert in Co. Kerry.

Carrigaholt

8 miles SW of Kilkee on the R486

This Irish-speaking village on the Shannon has a tiny beach and a 15th century, 5-storey tower house overlooking the harbour. Between April and October, Carrigaholt is a popular departure point for dolphin-watching trips in the Shannon estuary. The school is one of only five known groups of bottle-nose dolphins in European waters. There are around 100 of them and it's rare for trippers to be disappointed, on occasions even spotting nursery schools of young dolphins. The village has an information centre and booking office which runs audio-visual displays about the dolphins.

Kilbaha

16 miles SW of Kilkee on the R487

In the little church at Moneen, near Kilbaha, is the 19th century curiosity known as **The Little Ark**. In penal times, Catholics were forbidden to celebrate mass on land. The ingenious residents of Moneen built a little hut on wheels which was kept on the beach and wheeled down below the high-water mark between tides, beyond the legal reach of the local Protestant landowner. The priest would say mass in the hut while the congregation knelt around it on the beach.

In June, Kilbaha, together with the nearby villages of Cross and Carrigaholt, hosts the annual West Clare Jazz School with classes in Kilbaha and free performances in the pubs of all three villages.

THE LIGHTHOUSE INN

Kilbaha, Kilrush, Co. Clare
Tel: 065 905 8358 Fax: 065 905 8944
e-mail: tomod26@eircom.net
website: www.kilbaha,com

The Lighthouse Inn occupies a lovely position near the tip of the Loop Head Peninsula overlooking the Atlantic Ocean and the Shannon estuary. The area including The Bridges of Ross is famous for its bird watching and fishing. Geologists travel from far and wide to study the unique rock formation that surrounds the peninsula. Fishing trips can be arranged and packages are available. The premises has been a public house with a rich and chequered history going back to 1850.

The current proprietors, Maureen Walsh and Tom O'Dwyer, have created one of *the* prime pub/ restaurants in County Clare serving the freshest food and fish menus. Their regular breakfast, lunch and evening menus are supplemented by tasty daily specials. In good weather, customers can enjoy their refreshments in the beer garden where there's also a barbecue. Maureen and Tom are happy to cater for parties of up to 150. If you are planning to stay in this area, famous for its wild and spectacular views, the Inn has 11 comfortable guest rooms, all of them with en suite facilities. If you are visiting Kilbaha in June you'll find the West Clare Jazz Festival in full swing, which offers classes and free performances in the village pubs.

Co Cork

The tourist board slogan "Ireland in Miniature" is actually a faithful description of this appealing county. In the north, the beautiful Blackwater Valley is framed by high mountains, while in the east a gentler landscape extends to the coast with its historic ports of Youghal and Cobh. To the west, a series of rocky peninsulas grope out into the Atlantic and scattered islands create some magical seascapes.

The southwest corner is where the Gulf Stream first hits land. Its moderating warmth creates a wonderfully mild climate that varies very little over the year. Glorious sub-tropical gardens like the one on Garinish Island flourish in these benign conditions and the accompanying rainfall has helped make Cork an important dairy county.

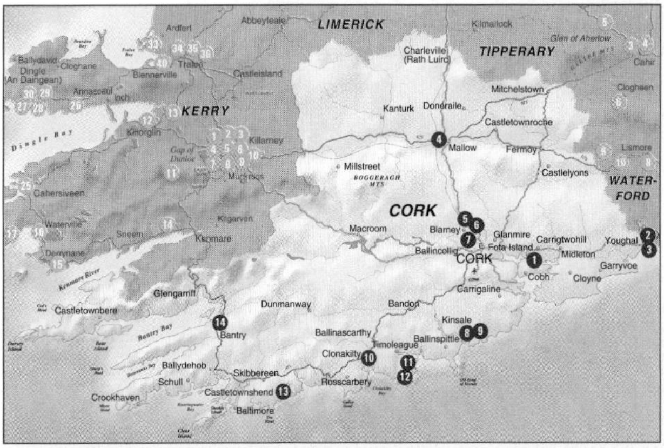

The county is also home to one of Ireland's premier attractions, the Blarney Stone at Blarney Castle where hundreds of visitors each day kiss the stone in the hope of

PLACES TO STAY, EAT AND DRINK

Fota House, Carrigtwohill	1	House & Gardens	p48
Aherne's Seafood Restaurant/Rooms, Youghal	2	Restaurant & Accommodation	p51
The Old Imperial Hotel, Youghal	3	Hotel	p52
Springfort Hall Hotel, Mallow	4	Hotel	p54
Blarney Castle Hotel, Blarney	5	Hotel	p55
Blarney Castle , Blarney	6	Historic Site	p56
Blairs Inn, Blarney	7	Pub with Food	p56
The Lord Kingsale, Kinsale	8	Pub, Food & Accommodation	p58
Charles and James Forts, Kinsale	9	Historic Site	p58
Emmet Hotel, Clonakilty	10	Hotel	p60
Sea Angling Centre, Courtmacsherry	11	Sea Angling	p61
Butlerstown House, Clonakilty	12	Self Catering	p62
The Castle, Castletownshend	13	B&B	p64
Vickery's Inn, Bantry	14	Pub, Restaurant & Accommodation	p68

● Denotes entries in other chapters

St Finbarr's Cathedral

acquiring the gift of eloquence. The castle itself is an outstandingly well-preserved 15th century building but the county has comparatively few grand buildings that pre-date the 19th century cathedral building boom. This saw the construction of ornate neo-Gothic structures such as St Finbarr's in Cork and St Colman's at Cobh. A notable exception is Bantry House, in the west, a gracious Georgian mansion packed full of fine furniture and works of art.

What it lacks in ancient buildings, Cork County makes up for with a wide range of holiday activities, most notably angling. If your interest is fine cuisine, the historic port of Kinsale is considered the gourmet capital of Ireland, and wherever you go in the county you'll never be far from a traditional pub resounding to the plangent strains of Irish music.

Cork

Ireland's second largest city and capital of the Republic's largest county, Cork is a captivating place with a character all of its own. It stands on an island in the River Lee so creating a compact city centre and a pleasing townscape of elegant bridges and old stone quaysides, all bathed in the soft reflected light of the water. This is a city to savour on foot, strolling the quaysides, browsing for bargains in **Coal Quay Market** (not too proud to describe itself as a "flea-market"), or wandering along French Church Street with its modish restaurants and pavement cafés.

The city's name comes from the Gaelic *Corcaigh*, meaning a marshy place, which is exactly what it was when St Finbarr established an Abbey and school here in the 7th century. The imposing triple-spired **St Finbarr's Cathedral**, an exuberant 19th century Gothic building designed by William Burges, stands on the site of St Finbarr's long-vanished Abbey. The opulent interior testifies to the prosperity of Cork in the late 1800s. Most of Cork's major buildings date from the same era as the cathedral and include some outstanding works by Pugin and Pain: together they give the city a satisfying architectural unity.

The city's lack of older buildings is the consequence of its unfortunate knack for invariably supporting the losing side in any conflict that might be under way – and getting ransacked as a result. The people of Cork rallied to Perkin Warbeck in his rebellion against Henry VII; they fought for Charles I against Cromwell; and threw in their lot with the hapless James II in 1690. It was this last misguided enterprise that led to the demolition of the city's medieval fortifications along with its Tudor and Stuart period houses.

Fortunately, some later buildings have survived, most notably the fine Georgian **Church of St Anne's** (1750). It's easy to find – just scan the skyline for a steeple topped by a huge weathervane in the form of an 11 foot long salmon. A climb to the top of the tower is rewarded by some grand views and the chance to ring out a tune on its famous bells. (Sheet music provided).

Close by is the **Cork Butter Exchange**, a complex of sturdy 19th century buildings with a façade in the Classical style which now houses an interesting colony of up-market craft shops. The old Butter Market itself is now home to the Firkin Crane Dance Theatre. Nearby, the **Butter Museum** illuminates the long and surprisingly interesting story of dairy production in the area, from churns of bog butter preserved in peat to the success story of Kerrygold butter which was created by local tycoon and sponsor of this museum Sir Antony O'Reilly.

At the castle-like **Cork City Gaol** an imaginative taped tour will guide you through the routine horrors of life in a Victorian penitentiary. The impact is heightened by amazingly lifelike figures and evocative sound effects. A separate exhibition within the gaol precincts is called the **Radio Museum Experience**. Back in 1927, the Governor's House was chosen as the unlikely base for radio station 6CK and this recently opened exhibition is housed in the original studio. It incorporates the Radio Telefis Éireann Museum Collection along with displays illuminating the early days of Irish and international radio broadcasting.

Irish art is well-represented at the **Crawford Art Gallery** (free), housed in the city's former Custom House. Ireland's most important art gallery outside Dublin, the Crawford has works by Jack B.Yeats, Sean Keating, Harry Clarke, William Gerard Barry and Edith Somerville, along with pieces by contemporary artists working in the city. British artists on display include Jacob Epstein, George Romney and Frank Bramley. The Gallery's stylish café is the "in" place for morning coffee and cakes.

Cork is the undisputed cultural capital of southern Ireland, hosting a major Film Festival in early October, a popular International Jazz Festival later that month, an International Choral Festival in early May, and a lively Folk Festival in September. Throughout the year, the Triskel Arts Centre, the Cork Opera House, the Kino art house cinema, and the Firkin Crane Dance Centre between them offer a huge variety of concerts, plays and ballet performances sufficient to sate the appetite of the most voracious culture vulture.

Cork City Hall

South & East of Cork

Glanmire

4 miles NE of Cork off the N8

A striking Georgian country house, **Dunkathel House** was built in 1790 for a wealthy Cork merchant and is notable for its magnificent bifurcated staircase of Bath stone. The house contains some Adam fireplaces, fine 18th century furniture and paintings but children (and many adults) are more impressed by the rare 1880s barrel organ which is still played for visitors. Open from May to October, the house also has antiques for sale and a pleasant tea room.

Carrigaline

6 miles SE of Cork on the R611

Near Carrigaline the road passes through delightful woodland and skirts the River Owenboy. A little further downstream the river broadens out into **Drake's Pool**, so named because it was here that Sir Francis Drake, pursued by the Spanish fleet, took refuge with his ships in 1587.

Once famous for its pottery, this picturesque village has a Perpendicular-style church noted for a remarkable effigy in lead of Lady Newenham who died in 1754. On a rocky cliff overlooking the village are the ruins of a castle built in 1177, and 2 miles to the northwest is Balla Castle (private), originally a McCarthy stronghold and now one of the oldest inhabited castles in the country.

Fota Island

10 miles E of Cork on the R264

A popular excursion by rail from Cork is to **Fota Wildlife Park** on Fota Island, one of several islands lying within Cork Harbour. Established with the intention of breeding endangered animals, Fota teems with wildlife – birds thronging the mudflats and apes, cheetahs, red pandas, ring-tailed lemurs and giraffes roaming the landscaped acres of the Fota House estate. In all, more than 90 different species of wildlife enjoy sanctuary here. **Fota House** (see panel below) itself, a striking early 19th century

Fota House

Fota, Carrigtwohill, Co. Cork
Tel: 021 4815543 Fax: 021 4815541
e-mail: info@fotahouse.com
website: www.fotahouse.com

Fota House formerly an 18th century hunting lodge, was the centrepiece of an estate which covered the whole of Fota Island, some 780 acres. Early in the 19th century it was enlarged for John Smith Barry by Richard Morrison and his son William Vitruvius, architects of some of Ireland's finest buildings, including Ballvfin, Lvons House and the court houses at Carlow and Tralee.

As well as providing a permanent home for the Smith Barry family, John embarked on a programme of work to turn the island into an estate of parkland, woods and pleasure grounds. He built the sea walls and enclosed the demesne with a stone wall punctuated by gates and lodges, and built a huntsman's house together with kennels, stables, stone barns, walled gardens, glass houses and numerous other outbuildings.

The arboretum, with its beautiful orangery, was begun by John's son, James Hugh Smith Barry, in the early 1840s; while, in turn, his son Arthur Hugh continued to develop the gardens and arboretum, as well as completing the house by adding the gallery and billiard room.

Fota House is open to the visiting public despite the fact that restoration work is still in progress. It is also available as a venue for a wide varietv of events including exhibitions, concerts and other performances, as well as for corporate and private functions.

mansion designed by Richard Morrison, is currently undergoing restoration and only the ground floor is open to the public. The most striking features here are the impressive entrance hall with its scagliola (mock marble) columns, the glorious gilded plasterwork of the dining room ceiling and the evocative servants' quarters. Other attractions in the park include a tour train, children's playground, self-service restaurant and the Serengeti Gift Shop. Visitors are also welcome at the estate's Arboretum (free) which was begun in the early 1840s and is stocked with many species of trees rarely seen elsewhere in Ireland.

Cobh Harbour

Cobh

12 miles E of Cork on the R624

Cobh (pronounced *Cove*) is a complete delight and should on no account be missed. Its huge neo-Gothic **St Colman's Cathedral,** designed by Pugin and built of blue-grey Dalkey granite, dominates the picturesque little town and its bustling harbour. Begun in the 1850s but not completed until 1915, the cathedral has a spire containing Ireland's biggest carillon – 47 bells covering four octaves with the deep bass bell weighing an incredible 7584 lbs.

Despite having one of the finest natural harbours in the world, the small fishing village of Cobh was virtually unknown up to the early 1800s, (although Sir Francis Drake did take temporary refuge here when his ships were outnumbered by those of the Spanish Armada). With the advent of the French Revolutionary and Napoleonic wars, between 1792 and 1815, the harbour became an important refuelling point for naval and commercial ships. Tall ships called to transport convicts to Australia and to carry Irish emigrants to North America. Later, the early transatlantic steamers and finally the great ocean liners continued the task of carrying the Irish to new lives in new lands. Between 1848 and 1950 more than 6 million adults and children emigrated from Ireland. Some 2½ million of them embarked at Cobh making it the single most important port of emigration.

The Queenstown Story

Today, Cobh's unique origins, its history and the legacy are dramatically recalled at **The Queenstown Story** – a multi-media exhibition housed in Cobh's Victorian railway station. (Cobh was renamed

Queenstown following a visit by Queen Victoria in 1849, a name it retained until the establishment of the Irish Republic in 1922). The exhibition also recalls two great ships associated with the town. The *Lusitania* was sunk by a German submarine off the coast here in 1915 and several hundred of the 1198 passengers who perished are buried in Cobh's old graveyard. Three years earlier, Cobh had been the last port of call for the ill-fated *Titanic*.

A more cheerful claim to fame is the town's historic **Yacht Club**, founded in 1720 and the oldest yacht club in the world. The Club hosts an annual Regatta in mid-August and in early September the town is the home port for the International Sea Angling Festival. The International Sailing Centre offers courses in sailing, canoeing and water-surfing; a more sedate exploration of the harbour can be enjoyed on cruisers leaving Atlantic Quay (summer months only).

Carrigtohill

9 miles E of Cork on the N25

Back on the mainland, near the village of Carrigtohill, stands **Barryscourt Castle** (Dúchas), the seat of the Barry family from the 12th to the 17th centuries. The present castle is a fine example of a 15th century tower house with 16th century additions and alterations. The original bawn (enclosure) wall with three corner towers is largely intact. Stage one of an ambitious restoration programme has been completed and successive areas of the castle will be opened to the public as the work proceeds. The ground floor houses an exhibition on the history of the Barrys and Barryscourt Castle and there's also a restaurant, tea shop and crafts shop.

Midleton

11 miles E of Cork on the N25

A bustling market town, Midleton was founded in the late 1600s by the Brodrick family, later Earls of Midleton. The Brodricks also established Midleton College as a free grammar school and later benefactors provided the town with an elegant 18th century Market House in the main street. The town is becoming known for its range of crafts workshops but Midleton's major attraction is undoubtedly **Jameson's Distillery** where visitors can join a guided tour, test their expertise at tasting, and marvel at the colossal copper pot still, the largest in the world, which boasts an incredible capacity of 32,000 gallons. The tour also takes in the old water wheel, which is still in operation, before concluding with a complimentary glass of *uisce beatha* – the "water of life".

Cloyne

14 miles E of Cork on the R629

About 4 miles south of Midleton, the somnolent village of Cloyne was an important religious centre for a thousand years and more. St Colman founded a monastery here in the 6th century on a site now occupied by the **Cathedral** bearing his name. This building dates back to 1250 but suffered badly at the hands of Victorian restorers. Nevertheless, it contains some striking monuments, amongst them the splendid alabaster tomb of the philosopher George Berkeley who was Bishop here from 1734 to 1753. Within the cathedral precincts stands the **Round Tower**, one of only two of these distinctive structures to be found in County Cork. Built in the 11th century, the Tower lost its conical roof in 1754 when it was struck by lightning. The 90 foot climb to the top of the Tower opens up some spectacular views.

Garryvoe

20 miles E of Cork on the R633

A popular holiday resort, Garryvoe has a long sandy beach fronting onto Ballycotton

Bay. The strand extends westwards to Shanagarry where the ruins still stand of a house once owned by the Penn family. It was a descendant of this family who founded the state of Pennsylvania. In Garryvoe itself there's a late medieval church and graveyard, and a 15th century tower house built by the Carew family.

Youghal

30 miles E of Cork on the N25

Unlike Cork, Youghal (pronounced *Yawl*) managed to be on the winning side during the various conflicts that troubled the land. Consequently its town walls, originally built on the orders of Edward I in 1275, are the best preserved in Ireland. The town is picturesquely set at the mouth of the River Blackwater with a Blue Flag beach nearby, popular with Irish families in the summer. For many centuries Youghal was a thriving port. The prosperity of those days is reflected in some striking buildings: **Tynte's Castle** in Main Street is a fine 15th century tower house, though in sore need of restoration; the **Red House** of 1710 is an attractive building in the then-popular Dutch style; and there are some lovely old almshouses founded by Richard Boyle, 1st Earl of Cork, in the early 1600s.

Of special historical interest is **Myrtle Grove** (private), an Elizabethan gabled

Youghal Town Walls

house which was for a while the residence of Sir Walter Raleigh who was Mayor of Youghal in the 1580s. Amongst the guests he entertained at Myrtle Grove was his fellow-colonist, the poet Edmund Spenser, author of *The Faerie Queene*. Inevitably, there are claims that it was at Myrtle Grove that Raleigh smoked the first pipe of tobacco in Ireland and also planted the first potatoes in the country.

AHERNE'S SEAFOOD RESTAURANT & ACCOMMODATION

North Main Street, Youghal, Co. Cork
Tel: 024 92424 Fax: 024 93633
e-mail: ahernes@eircom.net
website: www.ahernes.com

For over thirty years **Aherne's Seafood Restaurant & Accommodation** has been offering an impressive combination of top quality cuisine, superbly fitted-out bars, and stylish accommodation in the form of 13 superior en suite rooms. Owner John Fitzgibbon has resisted the temptation to develop this highly successful enterprise into

a hotel, preferring the more relaxed ambience of a restaurant with rooms. The outstanding locally-sourced seafood dishes served here have a modern Irish flavour. A bar menu is also available throughout the day.

The Old Imperial Hotel

27 North Main Street, Youghal, Co. Cork
Tel: 024 92435 Fax: 024 90268
e-mail: theoldimperialhotel@eircom.net
website: www.theoldimperialhotel.com

Occupying a prime position on Youghal's main thoroughfare, **The Old Imperial Hotel** was originally built in the 1700s as a stage coach stop for the Bianconi Line of superior conveyances that served much of the south of Ireland at that time. A disastrous fire in the mid-1800s destroyed that building but a new one was speedily erected. At one point this was occupied by the Loreto Convent but it was still a hotel in 1891 when the Youghal Gaelic Athletic Association held its inaugural meeting here.

A quarter of a century later, in 1919, McCarthy's Bar and General Grocery was established and its original timberwork, fittings and stained glass remain unaltered to this day. It's a wonderfully atmospheric place, complete with a glowing fire and friendly service, and genuinely popular with local people – always a reassuring sign.

In 1996, this splendid property was bought by James and Mary Browne who have spent lavishly on refurbishing the interior while taking great care to retain some of its original character. With customer care and comfort as their top priorities, the Brownes have created 18 luxurious en suite bedrooms, each with a sybaritic king size bed, television, trouser press, iron, hairdryer and hospitality tray; some rooms also have internet extension access. These spacious rooms, all stylishly furnished and decorated, provide a wonderfully peaceful retreat from the bustling town.

The Old Imperial is also a good place to eat. Tasty food is served daily in the Coachhouse Bar as well as in the intimate atmosphere of the upstairs restaurant. Everything on the menu is home-cooked with generous portions of fresh fish, beef or poultry amongst the house specialities. Food is available all day during the season and on Saturday and Sunday out of season; weekdays out of season from 12.30pm until 3.00pm and from 6pm to 9pm.

The hotel is well-placed for exploring this historic old town. Right next door is the famous Red House, built in 1710 in the then popular Dutch style, and close by is the Elizabethan Myrtle Grove, once occupied by Sir Walter Raleigh. Youghal also boasts the best preserved medieval town walls in Ireland and more modern attractions such as the miles of Blue Flag beaches, a top class golf club, pitch and putt, greyhound racing, 10-pin bowling and tennis. Excellent deep sea angling can be arranged and a popular excursion for visitors is a boat trip along the scenic River Blackwater.

Three other buildings in the town are also worth a look. There's an impressive **Clock Tower** built in 1777 to replace one of the medieval town gates. The tower originally served as a gaol – rumour had it that political prisoners were tortured within its walls and it's a fact that many of them were hanged from its windows. The 19th century **Lighthouse** stands on the site of St Anne's Tower, a 12th century lighthouse which was manned by nuns until the mid-1500s. And in William Street, the **Collegiate Church of St Mary's** is the largest medieval parish church in Ireland and also one of the oldest still in use. It dates back to the early 1200s and although much restored, contains some outstanding medieval tombs and monuments. The most notable of these is the flamboyant tomb of Richard Boyle which is generally regarded as one of the finest 17th century tombs in Ireland. He is depicted with his 2 wives on either side; his children below and, unusually, his mother-in-law is also present.

A rather unusual visitor attraction is **Fox's Lane Museum** which showcases an intriguing collection of offbeat domestic appliances. The vintage sausage-making machines are comprehensible but the cucumber straighteners and irons fuelled by petrol boggle the mind.

North and West of Cork

Fermoy

22 miles NE of Cork on the N8

Once a garrison town for the British Army, Fermoy developed along the banks of the River Blackwater whose waters are renowned for the quality of the salmon. Local people have a reputation for being incredibly expert on every aspect of catching the noble fish.

The town was once part of the vast estates of Lord Fermoy. Unfortunately, his lordship lost everything he possessed in a single night's gambling spree.

Castlelyons

20 miles NE of Cork off the N8

A peaceful and picturesque hamlet today, Castlelyons once enjoyed considerable importance. The ruins of a huge Norman castle, a stronghold of the Barry family, and the remains of a 14th century Carmelite friary bear witness to this former status.

Mitchelstown

29 miles N of Cork on the N8

The area around Mitchelstown is noted for the quality of its food products – mouth-watering farmhouse cheeses, butter, Galty bacon, sausages, hams and even venison. The town's name is most strongly associated with the Mitchelstown Caves but these are in fact a few miles over the county border in Co. Tipperary and are described in the Co. Tipperary chapter under the entry for Cahir.

Doneraile

23 miles N of Cork on the R581

About 6 miles north of the town, the **Doneraile Wildlife Park** is a remarkable example of an 18th century landscaped park designed in the style of 'Capability' Brown. There are many paths through the grounds with its mature groves of deciduous trees, several restored water features and roaming herds of deer. Within the grounds is the stately pile of Doneraile Court, the former residence of the St Leger family. This is currently being restored before being opened to the public.

It was at Doneraile Court that Elizabeth, wife of the 1st Viscount Doneraile, hid in a clock case so that she could watch a Masonic lodge meeting in progress. As the solemn ritual unfolded, Elizabeth found herself unable to suppress a fit of giggles

SPRINGFORT HALL HOTEL

Mallow, Co. Cork
Tel: 022 21278 Fax: 022 21557
e-mail: stay@springfort-hall.com
website: www.springfort-hall.com

Surrounded by tranquil woodlands, **Springfort Hall Hotel** is a handsome Georgian country manor house that evokes memories of a forgotten era of gentility and charm. Located about 4 miles north of Mallow, the estate dates back to the Norman invasion of Ireland in 1160 and over the succeeding generations has remained the property of landed gentry. It is now the home of the Walsh family who welcome visitors to this haven of peace and quiet – the perfect

seamlessly together to provide complete comfort and repose.

Over the years, the Walsh family has acquired a vast experience of co-ordinating wedding banquets and gala dinners, ensuring that all your requests are catered for with sensitivity and providing that all-important personal touch. The Hall also offers superb facilities for business meeting and functions. The conference and meeting rooms are bright and airy and a variety of seating layouts can be arranged to suit all requirements.

antidote to hectic modern living.

The Hall's gracious drawing room with its elegant proportions, blazing log fire and comfortable sofas and chairs is a perfect place to unwind and relax. The spacious dining room looks very inviting with its crisp white tablecloths and floral displays – here you'll find a dining experience with a difference whether enjoying a leisurely breakfast or a lingering evening meal. Four highly qualified chefs prepare fine Irish cuisine, offering menus created with imagination and flair, perfectly complemented by exquisite wines, unrivalled service and an intimate ambience.

The accommodation at Springfort Hall sustains the same high standards evident throughout the hotel. All of the 49 bedrooms command superb country views and are all en suite and provided with multi-channel television, direct dial telephone, tea and coffee-making facilities, hairdryer, garment press, iron and ironing board. Old world charm and contemporary conveniences blend

Guests at Springfort Hall will find plenty to see and do in the area. The 18-hole golf courses at Mallow, Fermoy, Kanturk, Douglas, Mitchelstown and the 9-hole course at Doneraile are all within easy reach. Also close by is the marvellous walking country of the Ballyhoura Mountains, the Blackwater Way, Avondhu Way (East) and the Duhallow Way (West), while Mallow itself boasts a wealth of equestrian attractions with the 200-acre racecourse as the highlight. For anglers, salmon fishing on the famous River Blackwater can be arranged for guests on both private and association beats.

and her hiding place was quickly discovered. Desperate to preserve the mystery of their arcane procedures, the masons decided they had no choice but to elect Elizabeth as a member and so she became the only woman mason in history.

Mallow

21 miles N of Cork on the N20

From Cork City the N20 strikes northwards through the rolling wooded foothills of the **Boggerach and Nagles** mountains to Mallow. Surrounded by good farming country, Mallow is a prosperous town which still bears signs of its fashionable past as a spa town with a Spa Well still in existence and a quaint half-timbered Clock House adding a distinctive touch to the main street.

Nowadays the town is best known for its excellent angling and for its racecourse.

Charleville

35 miles N of Cork on the N20

This important market town lies at the northernmost tip of Co. Cork, close to the border with Co. Limerick. All around is the rich farming land of the Golden Vale and Charleville boasts one of the largest milk and cheese processing plants in Ireland.

Castletownroche

29 miles N of Cork on the N72

Set beside the Awbey River and with the Nagles mountains rising to the south, Castletownroche is perhaps best known for the nearby **Anne's Grove Gardens**. Created in the mid-1800s in the 'natural' style pioneered by William Robertson, the gardens contain a wide variety of shrubs, magnolias and rare mallows. Walled gardens, hedged compartments and an impressive water feature all help to create a pleasant and relaxed atmosphere.

Blarney

6 miles NW of Cork on the R617

This small town, set around a spacious green, is home to one of the country's major tourist attractions – the **Blarney Stone** at **Blarney Castle** (see panel on page 56). Blarney Castle itself is one of Ireland's oldest and most historic castles. It was built in 1446, with walls 18 feet thick in places, by Dermot MacCarthy, King of South Munster, and was one of the strongest fortresses in Munster. The castle is open daily all year except over Christmas. Next door to the castle, **Blarney Castle House** is a late-Victorian turreted mansion that is still inhabited by descendants of the

BLARNEY CASTLE HOTEL

Blarney, Co. Cork
Tel: 021 438 5116 Fax: 021 438 5542
e-mail: info@blarneycastlehotel.com
website: www.blarneycastlehotel.com

Beautifully set overlooking the village green and just yards from the castle with its famous Blarney Stone, the **Blarney Castle Hotel** has been owned and run by the Forrest family since 1873. This charming old inn has a spacious traditional bar complete with open fire and an elegant restaurant offering a comprehensive menu that includes old favourites such as Irish Stew. There are 13 guest bedrooms, all individually designed, attractively furnished and decorated, and with en suite facilities. Open all year round, the hotel has a 3-star Recommended rating from the AA and RAC. Ample parking space; credit cards are accepted.

Blarney Castle

Blarney, Co Cork
Tel: 353 21 4385252
e-mail: info@blarneycastle.ie
website: www.blarneycastle.ie

The **Blarney Stone** is sometimes referred to as Ireland's equivalent of England's Crown Jewels and the queue waiting to perform the ritual of Kissing the Blarney usually equals that at the Tower of London. The stone itself is an unremarkable limestone slab, four feet by one foot, but it is embedded in the outer wall of Blarney Castle, 83 feet above the ground. Those in search of the gift of eloquence must lie on their back hanging over the parapet, legs held by two trusted friends, and then reach up to kiss the stone. If you have no head for heights (or lack two reliable friends) resign yourself to a life of being tongue-tied and inarticulate.

The custom of kissing the Blarney Stone became popular with tourists in late-Victorian times but the legend originates in a story from the reign of Elizabeth I. The Lord of Blarney at that time was a silver-tongued Irishman, Dermot MacCarthy, who "could talk himself out of a noose". While apparently enthusiastically co-operating with the Queen's colonising ambitions, he managed to do absolutely nothing to put them into effect. Receiving yet another of MacCarthy's procrastinating letters, Elizabeth fumed "This is Blarney, all Blarney".

Blairs Inn

Cloghroe, Blarney, Co. Cork
Tel: 021 381470
e-mail: blair@eircom.net

Anyone visiting for the first time will soon understand why **Blairs Inn** has been showered with awards and rave reviews, amongst them the Les Routiers Dining Pub of the Year (Ireland) Award 2002 and the Irish Pub Guide.com Dining Pub of the Year Award 2003. Occupying a lovely riverside setting in the heart of the country, this lively hostelry is an outstanding example of an authentic traditional family-run pub. John and Anne Blair are your hosts, a warm and friendly couple who extend a sincere welcome to regulars and newcomers alike.

Chef Raphael Delage's menus feature international dishes imbued with a nostalgic Irish flavour and include a large selection of seafood prepared from freshly-caught fish delivered daily from Kenmare and Dingle; poultry such as French-reared Poussin (baby chicken) and Irish-reared Duckling; lamb and steaks from prime Munster herds; and seasonal game that ranges from pheasant and partridge to quail and venison. If you have any special dietary requirements, just inform the helpful staff and they will do their best to accommodate you. You can enjoy your meal either in the Bar Lounge, Snug and Pantry or, in good weather, in the attractive garden beside the Owennageara, the Sheep River, where in summer trout can be seen to rise.

Blairs Inn is also a popular "local", a lively Irish pub with traditional music each Monday evening during the season and fireside guitar sessions on Sunday evenings throughout the year.

Jeffreys family who built it. The rooms open to the public are elegantly furnished and decorated in period style.

Before the Blarney Stone put the village on the tourist map, the main local industry was producing woollen goods, an industry which has been revived at the **Blarney Woollen Mills** whose factory shop offers some outstanding bargains along with a large selection of crystal, china and gifts.

Kanturk

26 miles NW of Cork on the R576/R579

A small market town, Kanturk stands at the junction of six major and minor roads and at the confluence of two tributaries of the River Blackwater, the Dulua and Allow. To the south of the town is **Old Court Castle,** a large fortified house built by the McCarthy family around 1609. Dermot MacOwen MacDonagh McCarthy had intended to construct an even larger building but the local English settlers became nervous and protested to the Privy Council that the house was "much too large for a subject". McCarthy was ordered to cut back on his expansive designs but even so the surviving castle has a quadrangle 120 feet by 80 feet with a large, square 4-storey tower at each corner.

Ballincollig

5 miles W of Cork

Set along the southern bank of the River Lee, the **Ballincollig Gunpowder Mills** are a rather unusual visitor attraction. The mills were established in 1794 and by the 1830s employed some 200 workers who produced about 16,000 barrels of gunpowder each year. Fifty years later the workforce had risen to 500 and included a wide range of craftsmen – coopers, millwrights, carpenters and others. The largest of their kind in Europe, the mills closed down in 1903 but re-opened as a visitor attraction some 90 years later. The buildings are scattered over a mile and a half and cover more than 130 acres. Guided tours are available and the Heritage Centre presents an interesting interpretation of events on the site, both the day-to-day work as well as the serious explosions that occurred.

Macroom

22 miles W of Cork on the N22

Macroom enjoys a beautiful setting beside the Sullane River, backed by the Boggerach Mountains within whose undramatic contours can be found a rich heritage of prehistoric remains – stone circles, wedge tombs, ring forts and standing stones. The town is dominated by its massive square castle which dates back to the 1400s. Cromwell granted the castle to Admiral Sir William Penn whose son later gave his name to the state of Pennsylvania. The younger Penn was a tireless missionary for Quakerism, but when his colonists demanded a more representative form of government he returned to England, harassed by financial problems and suffering from apoplexy.

About 10 miles southwest of Macroom the Pass of Keimaneigh leads to the **Gougane Barra Lake**, a broodingly romantic stretch of water that provides the source of the River Lee. In the centre of the lake rises a tiny half-acre island, reached by a causeway. This was once St Finbarr's hermitage, founded in the 7th century. A diminutive chapel and the remains of an 18th century building emphasise the loneliness of this secluded spot.

The Cork County Coast

Kinsale

18 miles S of Cork on the R600

Set around a broad sheltered harbour, Kinsale witnessed two of the most critical events in Irish history. The Battle of Kinsale

The Lord Kingsale

4 Main Street, Kinsale, Co. Cork
Tel: 021 477 2371 Fax: 021 477 4410
e-mail: info@lordkingsale,com
website: www.lordkingsale.com

Occupying a charming 200-year-old building on Kinsale's Main Street, **The Lord Kingsale** is one of the most appealing of the town's many hostelries. It's owned and run by Maureen and Michael Mortimer, who, in this gastronomic capital of Ireland, have established a reputation for serving outstanding home cooked food. Their accommodation is also of the highest quality, the 10 comfortable guest rooms all offer en suite facilities, Breakfasts are a speciality of The Lord Kingsale.

The Lord Kingsale also boasts a separate function room suite for small parties, weddings and conferences.

Charles and James Forts

Kinsale, Co.Cork

Kinsale has two forts: **James Fort** (1601) was built on the spit of land that curls around the harbour mouth. The fort is in ruins now, covered with creeper, but the location is a pleasant place to wander around.

A much more imposing building is **Charles Fort** (Dúchas) on the other side of the harbour at Summer Cove. Built in 1677, it's a classic example of a star-shaped fort and one of the largest military citadels in Ireland. The outer walls conceal a warren of barracks, ramparts and bastions, an impressive display of 17th century military ingenuity.

Charles Fort played its part in the other great event in Kinsale's history - the arrival of the deposed James II in 1690 who was proclaimed king in the Church of St Multose. His troops were billeted at Charles Fort before marching north to their decisive defeat at the Battle of the Boyne. The vanquished king returned to Kinsale where he set sail for France and an inglorious exile.

it's a classic example of a star-shaped fort and one of the largest military citadels in Ireland. The outer walls conceal a warren of barracks, ramparts and bastions, an impressive display of 17th century military ingenuity. Charles Fort played its part in the second great event in Kinsale's history – the arrival of the deposed James II in 1690 who was proclaimed king in the Church of St Multose. His troops were billeted at Charles Fort before marching north to their decisive defeat at the Battle of the Boyne. The vanquished king returned to Kinsale where he set sail for France and an inglorious exile.

There are more military echoes at **Desmond Castle** (Dúchas), a striking 16th century tower house in Cork Street which is also known as the "French Prison". At the height of the Napoleonic Wars, as many as 600 French prisoners were incarcerated here. Earlier, in 1754, a dreadful fire swept through the gaol and 54 prisoners, mostly French seamen, perished. Today, Desmond Castle houses the **International Museum of Wine** which documents the intriguing story of Ireland's wine links with Europe and the wider world from the early modern period to the present day.

Kinsale's own history is entertainingly brought to life in the **Kinsale Museum**, located above the old market with its Dutch-style façade. Within the same

Old Head of Kinsale

building is the former Courtroom, its 18th century interior left just as it was in 1915 when the inquest into the sinking of the *Lusitania* was held here. That appalling incident took place just off **Kinsale Old Head** with the Germans later maintaining that the ship was carrying munitions, a claim that the Americans hotly denied. Whatever the truth, the 128 American deaths among the 1198 victims helped sway public opinion in the US in favour of entering World War I.

Over recent years Kinsale has acquired a formidable reputation as the gourmet centre of southern Ireland. Many excellent (if sometimes expensive) restaurants are well-established here and the town hosts a 4-day International Gourmet Festival which begins on the first Thursday in October.

Ballinspittle

23 miles S of Cork on the R600

The fortunes of this little village high on a hillside above the river changed abruptly in the summer of 1985. Carved out of the hillside, 90 feet above the road, is a grotto containing a stone statue of the Virgin Mary. At dusk one evening in July a local girl, Clare Mahony, was passing and saw it rocking back and forth. Other villagers claimed to have observed the same phenomenon. Within days, hundreds and then thousands of people came to Ballinspittle each evening in the hope of seeing the **Rocking Madonna**. A team of psychologists from Cork University also came and were politely sceptical, pointing out that it was easy for one's eyes to be deceived when looking up at an illuminated statue 90 feet above the ground with dusk gathering in. However, most locals – and visitors – preferred the idea of supernatural intervention and the grotto has remained a popular place of pilgrimage.

Bandon

19 miles SW of Cork on the N71

The thriving town of Bandon stands at a major crossroads with good access to all areas of the county. So it's an appropriate location for the **Irish International Morris Minor Festival** in late July when many hundreds of devotees of these durable old cars gather in the town.

Bandon was once notorious for the Protestant zeal of its inhabitants – "Even the pigs are Protestant" according to one old saying. During the 1600s, someone painted a graffito on the town walls: "Jew, Turk or atheist may enter here, but not a Papist". Shortly afterwards a response appeared: "Whoever wrote this wrote it well, for the same is written in the gates of Hell".

In the Munster Arms Hotel hangs a photograph of the Irish patriot and Commander of the Free State Army,

Emmet Hotel

Emmet Square, Clonakilty, Co. Cork
Tel: 023 33394 Fax: 023 35058
e-mail: emmethotel@eircom.net
website: www.emmethotel.com

The **Emmet Hotel** takes its name from its location in the gracious Georgian square of the same name, an elegant area surrounding the Kennedy Gardens. The square was laid out between 1785 and 1810 to provide suitably impressive housing for the growing number of merchants prospering from the town's thriving port. It was originally named Shannon Square after the Earls of Shannon who were descendants of Richard Boyle, 1st Earl of Cork. The square's notable residents included the Sovereign (Mayor), several magistrates and the harbour master, but its most famous resident was Michael Collins who lived at no.7 with his sister while attending a local school.

Owner Robert O'Keeffe has recently completely refurbished the hotel to a very high standard, the tasteful décor adding to the relaxed atmosphere and charm, and popular with both locals and visitors alike.

What is striking from your very first contact with the hotel staff is the uncompromising level of service – personal, courteous and efficient, and something that Robert takes great care to maintain.

The Emmet is a very good place to eat – whether in the Bistro or bar which both offer a variety of enticing ideas, or in the award-winning O'Keeffe's Restaurant next door, housed in an exquisite Georgian house.

Offering innovative menus based on fresh local and organic produce, at very reasonable prices, O'Keeffe's has established itself as one of the leading restaurants in West Cork. The delightful and invigorating décor blends with the international menu to give you an evening to remember. All the food is cooked to order, so if you have any personal preferences or dietary requirements, just inform the helpful staff. Food is available in the hotel every day, with breakfast served from 8am to 10.30pm; lunch between 12.30pm and 2.30pm; and evening meals from 6pm to 9.30pm. The hotel also caters for private parties and outside catering.

Other amenities within the hotel include a conference room, function facilities, a garden patio, cocktail bar and a night club at weekends.

Accommodation at the Emmet maintains the same high standards evident throughout this outstanding hotel. There are 21 spacious guest bedrooms, all beautifully furnished and decorated and provided with en suite facilities, TV, direct dial telephone and hospitality tray.

Located close to the town centre with its lively music pubs, the hotel has its own car park; credit cards are accepted.

Sea Angling Centre

Courtmacsherry, West Cork
Tel: 023 46427
e-mail: csal@iol.ie
website: www.angling-erin.ie

The small fishing village of Courtmacsherry has established itself as one of Ireland's premier sea angling centres. At the **Sea Angling Centre** you'll find everything you need to make the most of your fishing holiday. The Centre has a fleet of 16ft self-drive boats and two 38ft purpose-built angling boats with a cruising speed of 18 knots to give you more fishing time. There's shark fishing and wreck fishing just 30 minutes away and the bay is prolifically stocked with ling, conger, pollack, coalfish, cod, bull-huss and many other species while further off-shore blue shark more than 2 metres long can be caught.

Michael Collins, who stopped at the hotel one day in August 1922 on his way to Cork. It was his final journey. Halfway there, his convoy was ambushed and Collins was shot dead by militant Republicans.

Timoleague

24 miles SW of Cork on the R600

This trim little village on the estuary of the Ardigeen river is dominated by the sprawling ruins of the 14th century **Timoleague Abbey**, most of it destroyed in 1649 by Cromwell's troops but the remains are still very impressive. Much less imposing are the minimal remains of Timoleague Castle.

However the big attraction here is the **Castle Garden** with its fragrant walled garden, a palette of dazzling colours during the season. Westwards from Timoleague stretches the **Seven Heads Peninsula,** its fretted coastline dotted with small fishing villages, a landscape that provides good walking as well as excellent bird watching.

Ballinascarthy

24 miles SW of Cork on the N71

This pleasant little village has a small claim to fame because it was the birthplace of William Ford. William emigrated to Detroit in the United States where his son, Henry Ford, was to become one of the titans of early 20th century industrial America.

Clonakilty

32 miles SW of Cork on the N71

Clonakilty stands at the head of one of the countless inlets along this stretch of coastline. A bustling little town, Clonakilty boasts one of southwest Ireland's best beaches on Inchadony Island, an "island" which is now permanently linked to the mainland by a causeway.

The Republican leader, Michael Collins, was born at Clonakilty in 1890 but the house where he was born, about 4 miles west of the town, was burnt down by the Black and Tans in 1921 and very little remains. The town's main claim to fame nowadays is its status as a major centre for traditional Irish music. There are plenty of lively pubs and the music making comes to a climax during the **Clonakilty Festival** in late June/early July.

Especially popular with children, the **West Cork Model Railway Village** depicts, in a miniature scale of 1:24, life and industry in West Cork as they existed 50 years ago. The theme is enhanced by the miniature working railway which re-creates the long-closed West Cork Railway. The already extensive layout will become even larger as other West Cork towns are added to the display.

Butlerstown House

Butlerstown, Clonakilty, West Cork,
Co. Cork
Tel/Fax: 023 40137
e-mail: mail@butlerstownhouse.com
website: www.butlerstownhouse.com

Why not be "Lord of the Manor" for a while? **Butlerstown House** provides a unique opportunity to enjoy a self-catering holiday in the impressive surroundings of an elegant Georgian mansion. The house was built in 1805 for Anglo-Irish ship owner, Jonas Travers, and designed by the architect Hutchins who drew his inspiration from the exploits of Nelson and his recent victory at the Battle of Trafalgar – most of the designs and internal features have a maritime theme.

This Georgian jewel of a house is now in the care of Roger and Lis Owen who have restored it to its original state of grace, preserving many of its early 19th century features but also installing the necessary modern amenities to make the house comfortable, warm and inviting all year round. It stands in its own grounds of some 10 acres which rise some 500ft above sea level, offering glorious uninterrupted views of rolling Irish countryside with the blue haze of mountains in the distance. Immediately surrounding the house is a mature, well-tended garden with a south lawn providing a peaceful seating area where guests can relax, enjoy the view or play a game of croquet. Also within the grounds are the original walled garden and woodlands.

In the house itself, the ground floor contains a hallway, study, drawing room, dining room, communications centre, games room and kitchen, while the first floor has 5 beautifully furnished and decorated bedrooms, 4 with en suite facilities, one with private shower room.

The house is available for self-catering rental for a minimum stay of 2 consecutive nights. Guests can arrive on any day that suits their flights and travel arrangements – the Owens don't insist on Saturday or any other day arrivals. As long as your stay is no less than 2 consecutive nights, you can stay for as long as you wish – whatever length fits in with your vacation arrangements.

Butlerstown House is centrally situated, enabling guests to explore the fabulous coastline of West Cork. As well as being within 40 minutes of Cork Airport, and less than an hour's drive from the City of Cork, all the well-known names of West Cork are easily less than 60 minutes away, including Clonakilty, Glandore, Baltimore, Bantry, Glengarriff, Blarney and Kinsale.

The most recent visitor attraction to open at Clonakilty is the **Lisnagun Christian Ring Fort** where children particularly will be fascinated by the inventive reconstruction, on the original site, of a 10th century village. The exhibit includes a thatched central house and replica weapons, clothes and tools of the period. The complex also contains a small wildlife park, home to a variety of animals ranging from rabbits to reindeer.

Drumbeg Stone Circlea

About a mile north of the town, the **Templebryan Stone Circle** has lost five of its original nine stones but not the mystical atmosphere that seems inseparable from these prehistoric monuments with which southwest Ireland is so liberally sprinkled.

Those keen to know more about Michael Collins should travel a couple of miles east to the **Arigideen Valley Heritage Park** where a distant relative of the great leader offers guided tours along a trail that features replicas of typical West Cork sights such as standing stones and exhibits that include a reconstruction of the site where Collins was ambushed. There's also a Michael Collins slide show and story-telling for children.

From Clonakilty the N71 runs mostly inland, just touching the coast at the small resorts of Rosscarbery and Glandore. About halfway between these two towns, a short detour will take you to the mightily impressive **Drumbeg Stone Circle**, splendidly sited in a field overlooking the sea. Dating from around 1500 BC, the 17 stones encircle a recumbent stone which is aligned to the position of the sun at the midwinter solstice. When the circle was excavated a cremated body was discovered in the centre of the ring. A little to the west of the stones stands a group of hut circles and a *fulacht fiadh* – an ancient cooking area. The stone troughs would have been filled with water heated by hot stones tossed into them from a fire. Then meat wrapped in straw was tossed into the water. This fascinating settlement has been dated to roughly AD 200.

Rosscarbery

9 miles SW of Clonakilty on the N71

Set around a broad bay, Rosscarbery is a pleasantly old-fashioned little town standing on an elevated position above the shore. The sea here offers good bathing and fishing, and the lagoons and sand flats are ideal for bird-watching – there are more than 60 resident species and half as many again are temporary visitors.

Five miles down the road, the village of **Leap** is renowned for Connolly's Bar, generally acknowledged to be the best live music venue in West Cork.

The Castle

Castletownshend, Co. Cork
Tel: 028 36100 Fax: 028 36166
e-mail: castle_townshend@hotmail.com
website: www.castle-townshend.com

The Castle at Castletownshend has been the seat of the Townshend family for many generations and is now the home of the Cochrane-Townshends who are direct descendants of the original Townshend family who took up residence here in 1649. The original castle was destroyed during the 17th and 18th centuries but its stones were used to build the two striking towers of the present building. It occupies a superb position, standing in spacious grounds overlooking the peaceful waterfront of Castletownshend harbour.

Inside, there's a gracious hall/ sitting room with fine old oak panelling and an elegant dining room which also looks out over the waterfront. Both of these rooms retain most of the original furniture and family portraits. Bed and breakfast accommodation comprises 7 attractively furnished and decorated rooms, each with en suite facilities and most enjoying lovely sea views. For those who prefer self-catering accommodation, The Castle offers a choice of two self-contained flats within the castle towers, both of which can sleep 2 guests; or three terraced cottages nearby – Mews Cottage which accommodates 2 people; Annie's Cottage which sleeps up to 4, and Church Hill Cottage which has accommodation for up to 5 people.

Castletownshend

17 miles SW of Clonakilty on the R596

The coastal village of Castletownshend is perched on a steep hill that dives down to a minuscule quay. A flourishing tree stands defiantly in the centre of the village's main road, an unexpected hazard that acts as an effective traffic calming feature. Castletownshend is something of a shrine for devotees of *The Irish RM* series of stories which recount the risible experiences of an English Resident Magistrate who is perpetually outwitted by the wily locals. The stories were written jointly by Edith Somerville and her cousin, Violet Ross, who assumed the nom-de-plume of Martin Ross. Edith spent her childhood at Skibbereen before settling down in Castletownshend where both she and her cousin are buried in the graveyard of St Barrahane's Church. The interior has many memorials to the Townshend and Somerville families, a mosaic floor designed by Edith Somerville and stained glass windows by Harry Clarke which Edith also commissioned.

Skibbereen

19 miles SW of Clonakilty on the N71

A lively market town, with a cattle market on Wednesdays and a country market on Fridays, Skibbereen stands at the gateway to the most southerly of the Cork and Kerry peninsulas. The town is home to the **West Cork Arts Centre** which puts on monthly exhibitions and occasional music and dance events.

During the Great Famine, Skibbereen was one of the worst affected areas in the whole of Ireland. At a mass grave in nearby Abbeystrewry almost 10,000 victims are buried. The horrors of those times are recalled at the **Skibbereen Heritage Centre** housed in an attractively converted former gasworks. A series of exhibits, dramatizations and interactive stations tell the gruesome story and the centre is also the starting point for a historical walking tour of old Skibbereen that visits sites with direct links to the famine.

For anyone with even a passing interest in gardens there are two of them close to the town that should not be missed. **The Liss Ard Experience** is a New Age garden where the emphasis is on conservation and natural growth – the landscaped garden here has been left unchanged since 1924. An extraordinary feature which is still in the process of being created is the Sky Garden, the work of an American artist, James Turell. The project when completed will include a pyramid, a crater, a mound, a sky walk and a grotto. At the time of writing, only the crater is finished, a vast grassy saucer with a single flat stone slab at its centre, an altar on which visitors lie down to view and to contemplate.

Creagh Gardens are somewhat more conventional, with woodland walks, grassy slopes leading down to the Illen estuary, and an early 19th century walled garden. But its late owner modelled this superb garden on the jungle paintings of Henri Rousseau – filling it with lush vegetation and sub-tropical plants. All that's missing is the occasional lion or tiger that Rousseau used to include in his tableaux.

Just to the south of the town, **Ceim Hill Museum** is a 500 year old farm house with an open hearth. The private collection housed here has artefacts from Neolithic times, Old and New Stone Age, Bronze and Iron Ages. The visitor can see old farm tools as well as lace, linen and West Cork cloaks while for history enthusiasts there is a "War of Independence" room.

About 4 miles southwest of Skibbereen, **Lough Hyne** is a lovely land-locked sea inlet surrounded by trees. There is a delightful walk through woods of oak and beech to a hilltop offering a sensational view of the West Cork coastline. An unusual feature of the lake is that it lies below sea level, cut off by a wall of rock. Only at high tide does the seawater flood over the barrier. Consequently, Lough Hyne is a saltwater lake but much warmer than the sea and so an unusual ecosystem has developed here with plants and animals more Mediterranean than northern European. Species such as the sea urchin and some sea slugs only exist in Lough Hyne and in the Mediterranean, and the lake is also home to rare species like the Red Mouth Goby.

Baltimore

9 miles SW of Skibbereen on the R595

Standing near the tip of the Skibbereen peninsula, Baltimore is the last mainland settlement on this, the most southerly part of Ireland. With only 200 permanent residents it's a charming fishing village clustering around a busy harbour and

The Beacon, Baltimore

overlooked by a 16th century castle. Back in the 1920s, Baltimore achieved a certain fame since it was here that the *Saoirse*, "Freedom", was built – the first Irish ship to sail round the world.

Almost 300 years earlier, in 1631, the town suffered a much more inglorious episode when a shipload of Algerians sailed in, massacred many of the inhabitants and carried off another 100 to a fate worse than death as white slaves.

Mizen Head Peninsula

Baltimore's harbour always provides a colourful and active scene with regular ferries during the season sailing to the nearby islands of Sherkin and Clear, and across the aptly-named Roaringwater Bay to Schull on the Mizen Head Peninsula. The harbour becomes especially busy during the last two weeks of July and the first weekend in August when the annual Regatta takes place.

Sherkin & Clear Islands

12 miles SW of Skibbereen

Not to be missed if you are staying in Baltimore is a trip on the ferry to the islands of Sherkin and Clear. **Sherkin Island** is the nearer of the two and it's extremely picturesque. The ruins of a 15th century Franciscan friary stand beside the harbour and fine sandy beaches stretch along the island's western coast. In June each year Sherkin Island, along with Baltimore and Clear Island, hosts the gathering of the O'Driscoll clan whose members vastly outnumber Sherkin's resident population of fewer than a hundred. Festivities centre on the lively Jolly Roger pub which is also very active throughout the rest of the year. Its traditional music evenings attract many aficionados from the mainland and if a band has been booked you'll usually find that a late night boat has been laid on to carry you and other revellers back to the mainland.

A little further south, **Clear Island** is the most southerly point in all Ireland. On your way there you may well see basking sharks, seals, and even occasional dolphins frolicking alongside the boat. About 3 miles long and barely a mile wide, Clear Island is a birdwatcher's dream come true, one of the most rewarding locations in Ireland for viewing seabirds. A bird observatory was established here in 1959: it welcomes visitors and has hostel-style accommodation available for the really dedicated twitcher.

On Clear Island, Irish is still a living language and there are regular summer schools for those wishing to master Gaelic's arcane vocabulary and beguiling rhythms. The island also hosts the County Cork Storytelling Festival in early September and a music and arts festival in late October.

The island's **Heritage Centre** is tiny but nevertheless succeeds in presenting a vivid record of local history, including the story of St Kieran who was born here in the mid-6th century. A holy well attributed to the saint stands close by the north harbour.

The most impressive building on the island is **Dún an Óir**, "Fort of Gold", an O'Driscoll fortress impaled on a great slab of vertical rock which becomes an island at high tide. It can be admired at a distance but, sadly, is not open to the public.

Across the water from the islands and sweeping out into the Atlantic, the **Mizen Head Peninsula** has a spectacular coastline of sea-beaten cliffs which are particularly dramatic along the northern shore. There are some fine sandy beaches, especially at **Barley Cove** on the western tip, a location that is also popular with surfers riding the great Atlantic rollers.

Ballydehob

9 miles W of Skibbereen on the N71

At the neck of the Mizen Head peninsula, the colourful little town of Ballydehob was once known as the hippy capital of the West because of the large numbers of disillusioned young Europeans who came here in the 1960s to "drop out". Most have returned to the rat race, leaving behind a legacy of health food, craft shops and resident artists to supplement the town's extraordinarily generous complement of lively pubs.

Fastnet Lighthouse

Schull

14 miles W of Skibbereen on the R592

One of the most appealing little towns on the Mizen Head Peninsula, Schull is a popular seaside resort and yachting centre which hosts sailing events during Calves Week at the beginning of August. The town enjoys a splendid setting around its large sheltered harbour, looking out to **Carbery's Hundred Islands** and with the great bulk of Mt Gabriel (1339 feet) rising to the east. During the season, there are regular ferries to Clear Island with its famous ornithology centre, Sherkin Island, the **Fastnet Lighthouse** and Baltimore. Should you happen to fancy some shark fishing, just call in at the Black Sheep Inn where they'll arrange everything you need!

Schull also boasts the only **Planetarium** in the Republic. It is attached to the Community College in Schull and gives regular 'Star Shows' during the season.

Crookhaven

24 miles SW of Skibbereen on the R591

About 12 miles from Schull, this remote village near the western tip of the peninsula has a sheltered anchorage that makes it a popular meeting place for yachtsmen.

Just beyond the village, the peninsula divides into three: Brow Head, Mizen Head and Three Castle Head. The most dramatic scenery is at **Mizen Head,** the most southwesterly point of mainland Ireland. The Signal Station here was built in 1910, manned until 1993 but is now automatic. A local community co-operative took over the de-manned building and established **Mizen Vision** with the aim of creating rural employment. The centre stands on

Cloghane Island, linked to the mainland by a narrow suspension bridge 150 feet above sea level a crossing which is an experience in itself. Visitors can explore the Keeper's House and Engine Room, and climb the 99 steps for the most spectacular views at the end of the peninsula. Standing on this exhilarating spot, it takes little imagination to see why such a great number of ships have foundered in Dunlough Bay to the north.

The spectacular walk around the bay, where the ragged cliffs have a notorious habit of ending abruptly, has recently been closed but you can still reach Three Castle Head by road. Here, a curtain wall and two turrets of an O'Mahoney stronghold still stand. They were once part of the chain of 12 castles built along the peninsula in the 15th century. From this point, the peninsula turns sharply east along a north coast that is all empty wild cliffs with breathtaking views.

Bantry

20 miles NW of Skibbereen on the N71

"Were such a bay lying upon English shore, it would be the world's wonder". That was the opinion of the popular Victorian novelist William Makepeace Thackeray when he visited Bantry Bay in the mid-1800s. Its northern shore dramatically framed by the Caha Mountains, the bay stretches for some 30 miles before it loses itself in the Atlantic Ocean. This appealing town has a refreshing sense of space – "It breathes" said one writer. At the town's heart is a large square which provides the setting for a traditional country market every first Friday of the month.

The waters of Bantry Bay have twice been violated by major French invasions. In 1689, French ships sailed up the Bay in a doomed attempt to restore James II to the British throne. Just over a century later, in

VICKERY'S INN GUESTHOUSE, BAR, RESTAURANT

New Street, Bantry, Co. Cork
Tel: 027 50006
e-mail: info@vickerys.ie
website: www.vickerys-ie

It was back in the 1850s that Thomas Vickery established what is now **Vickery's Inn**. At that time it was an important staging post for coaches carrying travellers on to Killarney and required a stud of between 75 and 100 horses to maintain its coaching service. In the present bar you can see a framed time-table of the services then available. Sadly, the interior was destroyed by fire in 1921 but was rebuilt, on the original walls, to its present design in 1926 by William Vickery, grandson of the founder. The Vickery family still own and run the business with the mother and son team of Hazel and Thomas now continuing the long tradition of hospitality.

Other traditional virtues also survive – courteous, attentive service, an old world atmosphere in the bar and restaurant, and value-for-money prices. The licensed restaurant serves a well-balanced range of dishes, anything from fresh fish or steaks to freshly made sandwiches. Starting with breakfast, food is served throughout the day. If you are planning to stay in this attractive old town, Vickery's has 13 well-appointed guest bedrooms, all with en suite facilities, TV and hospitality tray. Internet access is available; there's ample parking, and credit cards are accepted.

the winter of 1796, a formidable French Armada of 40 ships carrying 15,000 soldiers arrived with the intention of putting an end to British rule and establishing an independent Irish Republic. As with the Spanish Armada in Elizabethan times, it was dreadful weather that confounded the enterprise. For 6 days the French battled against storms but at times their ships were "close enough to toss a biscuit on shore". Finally, with 10 of their ships lying at the bottom of Bantry Bay, the remainder of the fleet turned for home.

The invasion had been urged on the French by the Irish nationalist Wolfe Tone who sailed with the fleet. His rôle in the luckless adventure is detailed at the **1796 Bantry French Armada Exhibition** which contains a life-size model of the famous patriot. Another model, a giant 1:6 scale replica of a frigate vividly illustrates life in the French Navy some 200 years ago. The Exhibition is housed in one of the courtyards of **Bantry House**, a gracious Georgian house occupying a superb position overlooking the bay. It was built in 1765 by Richard White, 1st Earl of Bantry, whose descendants still live here. The house and its contents provide a revealing insight into the lifestyle of the Anglo-Irish aristocracy during the Protestant Ascendancy. Gobelin tapestries, Aubusson carpets and fine furniture, Russian icons and mosaics from Pompeii, and a host of art treasures testify to the privileged way of life enjoyed by the English incomers. Bantry House provides a gracious venue for the prestigious **West Cork Chamber Music Festival,** a 10-day event that takes place in early July.

French Armada Exhibition

Another popular celebration is the **Mussel Festival,** held during the second weekend in May with lots of music, street entertainment and, of course, seafood.

There's more history on display at the **Bantry Museum** but here it's mostly of a domestic nature. The museum is run by Bantry's Local History Society and contains an eclectic collection of vintage household paraphernalia, old newspapers and other ephemera. The oldest artefact to be found in Bantry, however, stands in a field just south of the town. The **Kilnaruane Pillar** is a striking early-Christian carved stone depicting a cross, an apostle and four figures in a rowing boat.

To the southwest of Bantry, the **Sheep's Head Peninsula** extends for some 20 miles and forms the southern shore of Bantry Bay. A circular drive around the peninsula provides some attractive scenery which can be enjoyed even more if you walk the Sheep's Head Way. Starting from Bantry House, this 55-mile circuit is designed to be covered over 4 days although knowledgeable walkers avoid the less interesting last day's stage from Durrus back to Bantry.

Glengarriff

10 miles NW of Bantry on the N71

The huge mass of rock which gave the secluded deep Glengarriff valley and harbour their names is now covered by

Garinish Island Gardens

verdant growths of holly, arbutus, fuchsia, yew, pines and oaks. The natural shelter afforded by the surrounding mountains has endowed the valley and village with one of Ireland's most pleasant micro-climates and this is a lovely spot for boating, fishing and swimming. When Thackeray visited Glengarriff in 1842 he declared that tourists had no need to travel to Switzerland and the Rhine when such scenery existed closer to home.

During your visit you will almost certainly be accosted by a boatman offering a trip to **Garinish Island** and this is an offer you should not resist. Some 90 years ago, this 37-acre island was just barren rock. Then its owner, Annan Bryce, had tons of soil shipped over from the mainland and in collaboration with the architect and garden designer Harold Peto created a miniature botanical paradise. Garinish is known to horticulturists and lovers of trees and shrubs all around the world as an island garden of rare beauty. Garinish's sheltered position allows fragile species from every continent to flourish and provides a dazzling contrast to the bare mountains of the Beara Peninsula.

From Glengarriff, the R572 follows the northern shore of Bantry Bay with the Caha Mountains rising majestically to the right. This scenic route along the Beara Peninsula leads to Castletownbere which, confusingly, is also known as Castletown Bearhaven.

Castletownbere

32 miles W of Bantry on the R572

Castletownbere boasts the second largest natural harbour in Ireland and is still an active international fishing port where you are likely to hear Spanish and Portuguese being spoken in the bars, mingling with the soft Irish brogue of the locals. At the **Call of the Sea** visitor centre you can learn all about the town's maritime history with the help of videos, interactive displays and some interesting exhibits.

A mile or so outside the town there's an impressive stone circle and to the southwest stand the ruins of **Dunboy Castle**. Dunboy has been a mere shell ever since the day in 1602 when an English force of 4000 men surrounded the fortress, battered their way through its walls and killed the castle's defenders.

Close by is **Puxley's Castle**, another shell. This Victorian Gothic mansion was once the home of the Puxley family who made their fortunes from copper mining. Their story provided the inspiration for Daphne du Maurier's novel *Hungry Hill*. The house fell victim, not to the English, but to the IRA who set fire to it during the civil War of the 1920s. The story is depressing but the setting of Puxley's Castle is idyllic, a picturesque scene encompassing an inlet of Bantry Bay, leafy woodland and wild mountains.

West of Castletownbere, only a few small settlements have taken root and if you want to feel really remote, pay a visit to **Dursey Island**, a final fragment of Ireland flanked by 3 huge sea pillars named **The Bull, The Cow** and **The Calf.** There's no pub or shop and reaching the island involves a hair-rising trip in a Heath Robinson-designed cable car across the narrow and treacherous sound. The rewards are breathtaking views and the satisfying sense of having sought out one of the most isolated outposts of County Cork.

Co Donegal

Attached to the rest of the Republic by a mere sliver of land near Ballyshannon, County Donegal is geologically a continuation of the Scottish Highlands and boasts the highest cliffs in Europe at Slieve League. Few would disagree that the county also has the most spectacular scenery in Ireland – sweeping ranges of mountains, deep glens and shimmering lakes, and a frayed coastline that extends for more than 650 miles. The third largest county after Cork and Galway, Donegal has

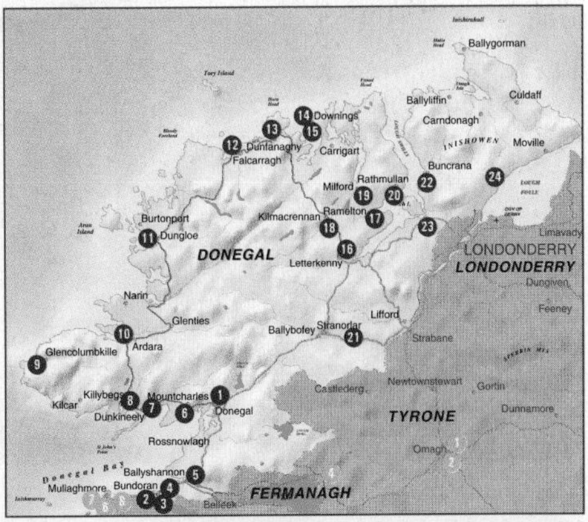

PLACES TO STAY, EAT AND DRINK

● Denotes entries in other chapters

Donegal Highlands

point, Bundoran, and travel northwards to Malin Head, the most northerly point in all Ireland.

Donegal

Despite its name, Donegal is not the county town – that honour is held by Letterkenny in the north, near the Ulster border. But Donegal has the atmosphere of a county capital, always busy with visitors especially around the central Diamond, or market square. A 25 foot high obelisk here commemorates the local Franciscan monks who compiled the **Annals of the Four Masters**, an encyclopaedic work which aimed to incorporate every known fact (and myth) about Ireland from 2958 BC (when Noah's granddaughter visited Ireland) up to the year when the book was completed, AD 1616.

Just off the Diamond, in Tyrconaill Street, is the well-restored **O'Donnell's Castle** which is actually a combination of a Norman-style tower house built in 1474, with a square tower and turrets added by the O'Donnells in 1505, and a Jacobean house built by Sir Basil Brooke, the English military commander of Donegal, in 1610. It's an attractive building both from the outside, with its mullioned windows, arches and gables, and inside where there are no fewer than 14 fireplaces, the most imposing of which bears the carved escutcheons of the Brooke family.

the largest Gaeltacht (Irish speaking community) in Ireland, partly because the English never troubled to colonise this remote corner of the country with its rich scenery but impoverished soil.

Another result of the absence of the English is the lack of any stately homes in the county but in compensation there's a rich variety of prehistoric and medieval remains, and a wealth of delightfully unspoilt villages and towns. We begin our tour of the county at its most southerly

Picnic at Lough Nacung, Mount Errigal

Also on Tirconaill Street is the **Donegal Railway Heritage Centre** where there's a model of the old County Donegal Railway which ran from Ballyshannon to Londonderry until its closure in 1959. The centre has some lovingly restored railcars, carriages and other steam age memorabilia and the enthusiasts who run the venture hope one day to re-open part of the old track.

Less than a mile outside Donegal Town on the Ballyshannon road, the **Forbairt Craft Village** has a number of craft workshops, attractively grouped around a central courtyard, where traditional crafts are expertly finished by skilled craftspeople. A good place to pick up a souvenir, be it hand-made pottery, batik, jewellery, an uilleann pipe or some handwoven Donegal tweed for which the town is famous. The complex includes a coffee shop and picnic area.

Autumn at Lough Eske

Atlantic Restaurant

Main Street, Donegal Town, Co. Donegal
Tel: 07 321080
e-mail: patriciamcgirr2000@yahoo.com

Standing on Donegal's main street, the **Atlantic Restaurant** has been owned and run by the Browne family for three generations – ever since 1958 in fact. It has a warm and relaxed atmosphere, enhanced by the soft music playing in the background. Patricia and Nicholas Browne's menu offers a good choice of wholesome and appetising food at value-for-money prices – an All Day Breakfast, light grills, lunch specials and evening meals with which you can enjoy a glass of wine Everything is freshly prepared at the time of ordering, (even the chips are made on the premises), and the service is fast and friendly. Children have their own choice of 'real' food and there's a smoking area at the rear of the restaurant.

The Atlantic has full wheelchair access and there's plenty of room between tables. An additional amenity in this busy part of town is the parking space at the back of the restaurant. And if you are planning to stay in Donegal, right next door to the Atlantic is a comfortable guest house run by another member of the Browne family.

The Maghery House Hotel

Brighton Terrace, Bundoran, Co. Donegal
Tel: 072 41234 Fax: 072 41929

Beautifully situated on the southern shore of Donegal and close to both the beach and the town centre, the **Maghery House Hotel** is a

friendly, family-run hotel, ideal for family holidays but also for anyone travelling on business. Owner Kathleen Moohan prides herself on the excellent cuisine, old-fashioned courtesy and personal attention which is given to all customers. The hotel dining room offers an extensive choice of cuisine with both table d'hôte and à la carte menus available. There's a Lounge Bar which is noted for its friendly atmosphere – a perfect place for a quiet drink or snack in comfortable surroundings. The bar also offers live music every week. The hotel has 16 guest bedrooms, all en suite and fully equipped with TV and direct dial telephone. There's a lot to see and do in the neighbourhood – golf, fishing, surfing, water sports, horse-riding, cycling, hill and coastal walks and miles of sandy Blue Flag beaches.

Kathleen also owns and runs a sister establishment in the heart of the village, **The Rougey Lodge**. Here you'll find the same high standards of cuisine and accommodation along with exceptionally friendly staff with a wealth of local knowledge they are happy to share. The Lodge is attractively furnished and decorated and has lots of character and charm. Bundoran itself is plentifully provided with all the attractions you would expect of a popular seaside resort, including Waterworld which offers a choice of heated pools, wave machine, water slides and seaweed baths. If you enjoy surfing, nearby Tullan Strand and Rossnowlagh beaches provide the opportunity of riding some mighty Atlantic billows – tuition is available here. Another natural attraction is the Puffing Hole through which the incoming swell forces spectacular spumes of water.

Lough Eske, a couple of miles north of Donegal, enjoys the reputation of being one of the most scenic places in the county. The name means "Lake of the Fish" and the main catch here is char, a small and tasty member of the salmon family. You might care to explore the Lough Eske Drive, a scenic route which circles the whole of the lake. A curiosity to look out for on the way is the colossal Famine Pot, almost 6 feet high and 6 feet round. During the potato famine, cauldrons like this were filled with maize provided by English landlords whose tenants would then fill their own household pots from it.

South of Donegal

Bundoran

19 miles SW of Donegal on the N15

One of Ireland's older seaside resorts, Bundoran is set on the south shore of Donegal Bay looking across to the Donegal hills. The town offers all the usual variety of seaside amusements as well as a golf course on the headland. Bundoran is known world-wide for possessing one of the most adrenaline-pumping surfing beaches, the 3-mile long Tullan Strand which in 2003 hosted the World Surfing Championships. The mighty Atlantic Sea creates another major visitor attraction, the Puffing Hole, where the incoming tide produces spectacular spumes of water. More exciting watersports are available at **Waterworld,** located on the seafront. Here you will find a choice of heated pools, along with a wave machine, water slides and seaweed baths. If you prefer outdoor activities, the town also has a riding school from which you can go pony trekking along the coastal sand hills, and there's also a cycle rental shop if you want to explore the country lanes round about.

Willards Bed & Breakfast

East End, Bundoran, Co. Donegal
Tel: 072 41888

Located a few hundred yards from Bundoran's famous Blue Flag beach, Willards Bed & Breakfast offers comfortable accommodation, good food and a warm greeting from the owner, Mary McMahon, who has been welcoming visitors here since 1997. Nothing seems to be too much trouble for Mary who also provides her guests with an excellent breakfast. There are 4 guest bedrooms, all attractively furnished and decorated, well-equipped and all with en suite facilities.

If you are looking for active pursuits you'll find plenty in the neighbourhood. Facilities for golf, fishing, surfing, water sports and horse-riding are all within easy reach; cycling, hill and coastal walks and miles of sandy beaches are all close by; it's just a 2-minute walk to the town's fun fair, 4-screen cinema and amusement arcades; and an easy drive to either Sligo or Donegal Town.

Slieve League Hotel

Main Street, Bundoran, Co. Donegal
Tel: 072 42099/29969 Fax: 072 29970
e-mail: slieveleague@eircom.net
website: www.pubsofdonegal.com/slieveleague

Centrally located on Bundoran's main street, the **Slieve League Hotel** offers quality accommodation, excellent cuisine and high quality service. This family-run hotel has been recently refurbished and now offers 21 luxury en suite bedrooms, all impeccably furnished to modern standards and equipped with remote control colour television, hairdryer, heated towel rail and tea/coffee-making facilities. Two of the bedrooms are designed for guests with restricted mobility and have full wheelchair access. A baby-sitting service is available if required. The hotel boasts an air-conditioned bar and restaurant. The bar is child-friendly and hosts live entertainment and traditional Irish music each week.

The restaurant also welcomes children and serves breakfast for residents – an all day breakfast is available – lunches daily, and from 5pm offers an à la carte menu. The restaurant is fully licensed and there's a good choice of fine wines to complement your meal. Guests at the Slieve League have exclusive use of the off-street parking at the rear of the hotel. Bundoran itself is a popular seaside resort with a wide range of attractions.

Inis Saimer House

Portnason, Bundoran Road, Ballyshannon, Co. Donegal
Tel: 071 985 1418
e-mail: inissaimerhouse@holidayhound.com
website: www.inissaimer.com

Inis Saimer House is an impressive Victorian property, built around 1860 and set in its own delightful grounds of woodland and orchard overlooking the estuary of the River Erne. Here, Sharon McGuinness offers a warm welcome to guests staying in her beautiful home with its antique furnishings, bedrooms with real fireplaces and there's even a Victorian bath and shower available. A specially attractive feature is the balcony overlooking the estuary.

Sharon is an accomplished cook and her full breakfast menu includes options such as smoked salmon but her specialities are the memorable omelettes. All breads, jams and jellies are home-made, the latter made with fruit from the nearby orchard. There are 4 guest bedrooms, three of them with en suite facilities, and all provided with TV and hospitality tray. Inis Saimer House is named after the island in the estuary where the earliest invaders of Ireland, the Parthalonians, made their first settlement. Ballyshannon itself, just a 10-minute stroll from Inis Saimer House, is a friendly place with plenty of activities available – there's a Leisure Centre with a 25-metre swimming pool, sauna and gym; a cinema; craft shop; and facilities for horse-riding, golf and water-sports.

Ballyshannon

14 miles S of Donegal on the N15

The people of this attractive small town, set on the steep banks of the River Erne, seem to like nothing better than a festival. They kick off in March, around St Patrick's Day, with an Amateur Drama Festival; on the first weekend of August the town is crowded for the Traditional Music Festival which has attracted performers such as Donegal's own Altan, Christy Moore, Dervish and Sean Keane; in September the long-established Harvest Fair celebrations take place; and towards the end of November, there's the Allingham Arts Festival for Writers. This festival is named after the poet William Allingham (1824-89) who was born at Ballyshannon and became a member of an artistic circle that included Tennyson and the Pre-Raphaelites. He is buried in the graveyard of St Anne's Church beneath a stone slab inscribed with just one word: "Poet".

A more recent celebrity born in the town is the blues-rock guitarist Rory Gallagher (1948-1995) whose best-known song is *Going to My Home Town*. Part of the song's lyrics are inscribed on a commemorative plaque opposite the library in East Port and the guitarist is celebrated by a weekend of music at the end of May. The town also has a connection with the British Prime Minister Tony Blair whose late mother came from Ballyshannon.

The town is also noted for a variety of china known as Parian ware because it resembles the clear white Greek marble quarried on the island of Paros. It is produced at the **Donegal Parian China Factory** on the Sligo road where visitors can join a free guided tour, browse in the Exhibition Room, purchase one of the delicate, hand-crafted products, or settle down for a cup of tea in the refreshment room.

On the outskirts of Ballyshannon are the minimal remains of Abbey Assaroe, founded by Cistercian monks in the late 12th century. In 1989, the Abbey Mill Restoration Trust acquired the derelict mills here, then restored the mill buildings and water wheels for use as an auditorium and coffee shop. It's a peaceful and picturesque spot and visitors to the interpretive centre, **The Water Wheels**, can view a video film on the heritage of the monastery and mill.

Ballyshannon is reckoned to be one of the oldest towns in Ireland. Legend has it that the first people to reach Ireland settled on Inish Saimer, an island in the Erne Estuary, just off the Mall Quay in the town. A similar claim is made for Lower Lough Erne, just a few miles to the east. Many of the small islands that dot the lake are actually *crannógs*, or artificial islands created by Celtic settlers in prehistoric times. During the summer season, there are regular cruises around Lough Erne, or you can hire a boat and explore it for yourself.

Rossnowlagh

5 miles NW of Ballyshannon off the R321

Best known for its magnificent beach, Rossnowlagh is also home to the modern **Franciscan Friary Centre of Peace and Reconciliation** where visitors are welcome to share in the peace of its lovely seaside setting. The centre is open daily from 10am until 9pm but if you wish to stay longer, the Friary has overnight accommodation available in rooms with splendid sea views.

A much more rigorous regime is in effect at **Station Island** in Lough Derg, about 15 miles inland. According to legend St Patrick spent 40 days and nights fasting in a cave on the island. The cave has been a place of pilgrimage for centuries, even during the years that Catholic observances were prohibited. During the period of the St Patrick's Purgatory Pilgrimage between June 1st and August 15th only genuine pilgrims

The Village Tavern

Main Street, Mountcharles, Co. Donegal
Tel: 07497 35622
e-mail: villagetavern@ireland.com
website: www.villagetavern@i.e

A typical traditional Irish pub, **The Village Tavern** is an attractive stone building on the main street of this neat little coastal village overlooking Donegal Bay. A major attraction here is the excellent choice of bar meals prepared by chef Graham Flannery who runs the hostelry together with Kim Kelly. An accomplished cook, Graham's training includes experience at the K-Club, Hibernian and Merrion Hotels. During the tourist season, the bar offers live music and the tavern also has comfortable accommodation available in 10 guest rooms, 7 of which have en suite facilities.

Castle Murray House Hotel

St John's Point, Dunkineely, Co. Donegal
Tel: 074 97 37022 Fax: 074 97 37330
e-mail: castlemurray@eircom.net
website: www.castlemurray.com

With its scenic location overlooking the sparkling waters of McSwynes Bay and with grand views of the Donegal Hills, **Castle Murray House Hotel** has been voted one of the top 50 most romantic places to stay in the world. And in the Black and White Awards of 2003 Castle Murray won the "Best Hotel Bar in Ulster" accolade. Originally built as a farmhouse, this friendly family-run hotel provides a luxurious base from which to explore the beautiful headland of St John's Point and the surrounding Donegal Hills. It stands just 2 minutes from the shore and a mere 2 miles or so from the beach.

Castle Murray's owner, Marguerite Howley, is a chef by profession so it's not surprising to find that the hotel's French restaurant is renowned for its cuisine. It offers the very best in fresh, locally caught sea foods, "of which there is none fresher" says Marguerite, "than a lobster chosen from the tank in the hotel itself!" To accompany your meal, there's an extensive wine list to choose from and a collection of more than 100 Irish and Scotch whiskeys to sample. The accommodation at Castle Murray maintains the same high standards seen throughout the hotel and comprises 10 individually themed bedrooms, all of them en suite.

are allowed on the island. During the 3-day penitential exercise they must go barefoot whilst making the Stations of the Cross and only one meal each day of dry bread and black tea is permitted. The first night is spent without sleep in a vigil in the basilica; on the two successive nights, pilgrims stay either in the modern hospices or in the "Penitential Beds" – remains of the stone cells of the early Christian monks.

North & West of Donegal Town

Mountcharles

4 miles W of Donegal on the N56

The birthplace of the celebrated Irish writer, Seamus McManus (1869-1960), the little town of Mountcharles clings to a steeply rising hill with splendid views over Donegal Bay. At the summit of the hill is a bright green water pump commemorating McManus, "*poet and seanachie*" (storyteller), who is buried in the churchyard at nearby Frosses village. Mountcharles and the neighbouring villages were once famous for hand embroidery work and it's still possible to find some embroidered linen on sale.

Dunkineely

10 miles W of Donegal on the N56

From Dunkineely, a scenic route offering some grand views goes south for 5 miles along a narrow peninsula to **St John's Point** where there's a secluded beach, a lighthouse and, nearby, the crumbly ruins of a castle. In Dunkineely itself, the exhibits in the **Killaghtee Heritage Centre** include a scale model of various local archaeological sites; the real places can be visited if you follow the designated Heritage Trail.

Killybegs

15 miles W of Donegal on the R263

If you ignore the large fish processing plant on the eastern side of the town, Killybegs is a picturesque place with sparkling whitewashed houses lining the narrow streets running up the sloping hillside from the harbour. It's also the busiest fishing port in Ireland with tons of freshly-caught fish off-loaded onto the quay every day. Killybegs hosts a huge **International Sea Angling Festival** in mid-July each year and throughout the year boats are available to hire for sea angling expeditions. If you have neither the time or inclination to catch the fish yourself, you can always wander down to the quay in the early evening when the fishing fleet hoves in, accompanied by flocks of raucous seagulls, and choose from that day's newly-arrived catch.

St Mary's Church, at the top of the hill,

Killybegs Fishing Harbour

Bay View Hotel & Leisure Centre

Killybegs, Co. Donegal
Tel: 074 9731950 Fax: 074 9731856
e-mail: bvhotel@iol.ie
website: www.bayviewhotel.ie

Occupying a splendid site overlooking the harbour, the elegant **Bay View Hotel & Leisure Centre** has a well-earned reputation for good food and a real Donegal welcome. The hotel was completely rebuilt in 1992, providing first class modern facilities. Taken over by Paul and Betty Sheeran in 2000 they have continued to upgrade the hotel and its amenities to the very high standard now in evidence. The main dining-room, The Captain's Table, overlooks the busy harbour and provides quality food presented with panache. Naturally, since this is Ireland's premier fishing port, many of the dishes feature fresh seafood prepared to spectacular recipes. For smaller appetites, snacks are available in the themed Wheelhouse Lounge off the main bar.

A popular area of the bar is the Writer's corner with its sketches of famous Irish authors. In addition to its top quality accommodation and outstanding cuisine, the hotel offers its guests free use of a fully supervised and comprehensively equipped leisure and fitness suite which includes a heated indoor pool, sauna, Jacuzzi, steam room and state-of-the-art gymnasium. If that isn't enough activity for you, Killybegs itself has facilities for golf, scuba diving, horse riding, hill walking and sea fishing. The comfortable cocktail bar adjoins the hotel's main function room where up to 300 people can be seated.

is worth visiting to see the 16th century tombstone of Niall Mór MacSweeney which is covered in Celtic carvings and preserved in a glass case.

Kilcar

25 miles W of Donegal on the R263

Northwards from Killybegs beckon the scenic splendours of west Donegal or you can strike due west along the coast road that tumbles and rolls over the cliff tops to Kilcar and Carrick. A pleasing village, Kilcar is a major centre for the Donegal tweed industry – at the Studio Donegal visitors can watch the craftsmen at work and purchase the finished products.

Kilcar is also well-known for its music pubs where you'll find traditional music every evening in summer and at weekends all year, and for its sea-angling festival at the beginning of August.

A few miles further west, a mile or so south of Carrick, the mighty cliffs of **Slieve League** rise almost 2000 feet from the shore, the loftiest sea cliffs in Europe. The view of the cliffs from the tiny Irish-speaking village of Teelin is awesome.

Glencolumbkille

30 miles NW of Donegal on the R263

Reached by a spectacularly scenic road from Killybegs, this peaceful and picturesque little resort takes its name from St Colmcille (c AD 521-597) who had a retreat house here. At midnight on the saint's day, June 9th, pilgrims begin a barefoot procession around the area, stopping to pray at the 15 Turas associated with St Colmcille, amongst them his chapel, holy well and the stone slab that served as his bed. The procession concludes at 3am with Mass in the village church.

The area surrounding Glencolumbkille is dotted with more than forty prehistoric monuments – portal dolmens, souterrains and cairns from the Bronze Age, some of them erected more than 5000 years ago.

This remote corner of Co. Donegal has always suffered from chronic poverty and unemployment. In 1951 a newly appointed parish priest, the energetic Father James MacDyer, began several initiatives to provide employment for local people and stem the constant drain of emigration. The most visible of Father MacDyer's projects is the **Folk Village and Museum** which features three reconstructed dwellings, replicas of those typical in the area during the 1720s, 1820s and 1920s. Each cottage is appropriately furnished with furniture, artefacts and utensils, and there's also a replica of a National School which has a display of interesting vintage photographs. There's a Shebeen where you can have a free taster of unfamiliar beverages such as fuchsia, honey or seaweed wine, and the site also includes a tearoom serving more traditional fare – home-made scones and soup. You're unlikely to want to sample the unappealing brew of maize porridge that is prepared daily for the "famine pot" standing in the yard outside.

A short walk from the Folk Village, the **Ulster Cultural Centre,** a thriving complex where local artists create distinctive tapestries and visitors can join courses that include Irish language, flute, whistle and bodhrán playing, dancing, painting and archaeology.

From the village there's an agreeable walk to the cliff top at Glen Head (769 feet) where there's a watch tower built in the early 1800s when a French invasion was expected. The site provides magnificent views of the jagged coastline. The path continues along the coast to the wonderfully remote **Valley of Glenlough** where the American landscape painter

Rockwell Kent (1882-1971) stayed in the 1940s and was inspired by the hauntingly beautiful terrain to create some of his finest paintings. A few years later the Welsh poet Dylan Thomas stayed in the same house but was not inspired. He departed abruptly and without paying his food and rent bills.

Ardara

23 miles NW of Donegal on the N56

From Glencolumbkille a staggeringly beautiful route passes through the spectacular Glengesh Pass to the sizeable Heritage Town of Ardara, attractively located at the head of a deep sea-lough. A centre for weaving, knitwear and homespun tweed for generations, Ardara is definitely the place to purchase your souvenir Aran sweater, either in the high street shops or in the half dozen factory shops where you can watch the manufacturing process in operation. The town's major product is celebrated in the town's Heritage Centre where you can watch a weaver at work, and also by the annual **Weavers' Fair** in midsummer, a popular local event when Ardara's many pubs are alive with traditional music and good craic.

Ardara's buildings are quietly pleasing rather than outstanding in any way but it's worth stepping inside the Church of the Holy Family to look at the striking stained glass window created by Evie Hone, one of the most important Irish artists of the 20th century.

Narin

6 miles N of Ardara on the R261

Beautifully located at the foot of low sheltering hills on the south shore of Gweebarra Bay, Narin is a popular little resort boasting a magnificent beach, 1½ miles long, and an 18-hole golf course. In late June, the village hosts a seafood

WOODHILL HOUSE

Ardara, Co. Donegal
Tel: 074 954 1112 Fax: 074 954 1516
e-mail: yates@iol.ie
website: www.woodhillhouse.com

Set in its own grounds with an old walled garden and looking out to the beautiful Donegal Highlands, **Woodhill House** is a historic manor house dating back in parts to the 1600s. It was formerly the home of the Nesbitts, local landlords and the last commercial whaling family in Ireland. The house is half a mile from the sea and just a quarter of a mile from the coastal town of Ardara. The house offers unusual and interesting accommodation, either in the main house or in the nearby Coach House. All the rooms, which enjoy a 3-star rating from Bord Failte, have en suite facilities and there's a choice of single, twin, double and triple rooms. There's a fully licensed lounge bar, which has occasional music sessions for tourists and locals alike, and a restaurant well known for its high quality and reasonable prices. The cuisine is French-based using fresh Irish produce, especially seafood from nearby Killybegs, Ireland's principal fishing port. Ardara itself is famous for its Donegal tweeds and woollen goods and the local factory shops offer outstanding bargains. There's excellent salmon and trout fishing in the Owenea River; breathtaking links golf courses at Murvagh, Donegal town and Portnoo/Narin; and the Blue Flag beaches nearby offer pony trekking along the strand, boating and surfing.

festival when all the bars lay on seafood specials and you can try your skills in an oyster opening contest.

Just offshore lies Iniskeel Island which has a ruined church and can be reached on foot at low tide. An even older construction stands on an island in nearby Doon Lough. More than 2000 years old, the circular stone fort covers most of the island and can easily be seen from the lake shore.

Glenties

18 miles NW of Donegal on the N56

The outstanding scenery around Glenties provides a popular location for film and TV producers. *The Hanging Game* was filmed here and most recently *Dancing Lunacy* in which Meryl Streep played the leading rôle. She also attended the première of the film in Glenties.

So it's perhaps not surprising to discover that the town has won the "Ireland's Tidiest Town" award five times, and the "Tidiest Small Town" title a further five times. Picturesquely situated where two glens converge, Glenties' wooded surroundings display a marked contrast with the ruggedness of much of the surrounding country.

This part of Donegal has always been noted for its strong tradition of Irish music and Glenties has a flourishing traditional music school which is constantly turning out a new generation of musicians. To experience this tradition at its best, visit the town on the first weekend of October when the **Fiddlers Weekend** attracts fiddlers from many parts of Ireland and around the world.

The most striking building in the town is the Roman Catholic **St Connell's Church**, a lovely modern church designed by the Derry architect Liam McCormack and consecrated in 1974. Imitating the nearby mountains, the church has a long sloping roof which sweeps down to within 6 feet of the ground. When it's raining, the water drips off the tiled roof and forms gleaming ornamental pools.

Glenties most famous son is Patrick MacGill (1890-1963) whose life got off to a poor start when his parents sold him at a hiring fair for servants. He escaped to Scotland where he worked as a farm labourer and navvy before his writing skills earned him a position with the *Daily Express*. His best-known book is *Children of the Dead End*, a semi-autobiographical account of the lives of itinerant navvies. In early August each year the town hosts the MacGill Summer School in honour of his work, a very Irish event celebrating his work with literary debates, lectures, workshops and exhibitions.

An exhibit at **St Conall's Museum and Heritage Centre** celebrates MacGill's life; others are devoted to the playwright Brian Friel (*Dancing at Lughnasa*) whose mother was born in Glenties; Donegal railways; the Great Famine, and local wildlife.

Dungloe (*An Clochán Liath*)

50 miles NW of Donegal on the N56

Dungloe lies in the heart of the Rosses, a name that means "place of many lakes" – in fact there are some 130 in all. This is one of Ireland's *gaeltacht* (Irish-speaking) areas so the name you will see on signs for the town is *An Clochán Liath*, referring to the stepping stones which were once the only way to cross the river. This lively and thriving little town with a population of fewer than a thousand is well known throughout Donegal for its **Mary from Dungloe Festival** which takes place over the August Bank Holiday each year. A relaxed local version of the Miss World beauty contest it provides a grand excuse for general celebration and extended licensing hours.

On Dungloe's main street stands the headquarters of the Templecrone Co-

Riverside Bistro

Lower Main Street, Dungloe, Co. Donegal
Tel: 075 21062 Fax: 075 22130
e-mail: riversidebistro@eircom

Opened in 1993, the family-owned **Riverside Bistro** offers its customers a cuisine that includes both traditional dishes such as steamed local mussels and less familiar ones like fillet of ostrich with a Madeira sauce. Chef/patron Eamon Diver's evening à la carte menu also includes crispy duck with redcurrant sauce, monkfish wrap in a cream sauce and, for vegetarians, Nut Wellington, stuffed pepper with risotto and cannelloni with ricotta, spinach and goat's cheese. At lunchtime the menu is simpler – amongst the dishes on offer are seafood chowder, Mexican chicken wraps, filled potato skins and club sandwiches.

A kids' menu is available and there's an extensive choice of wines. The bistro is open for lunch from 12.30pm to 3pm; for evening meals from 6pm to 10pm. From time to time, Eamon hosts theme nights and he is also happy to cater for private parties. All major credit cards are accepted. Dungloe itself is a thriving little town, best known for its annual "Mary from Dungloe" Festival held on the August Bank Holiday. It's a particularly Irish version of the Miss World beauty contests and provides great fun for everyone.

operative Agricultural Society, known locally as the "Cope". The Society was founded in 1906 by a local farmer, Paddy Gallagher, who took note of the fact that the price of manure was considerably less when purchased in quantity by societies. He extended this principle to buying more generally marketable commodities with the broad aim of helping local people shake off their dependence on the dreaded gombeen men, (moneylenders). By the time of his death in 1966 the "Cope" was a flourishing business with branches throughout the Rosses.

Burtonport *(Ailt an Chorráin)*

56 miles NW of Donegal on the R259

The unspoilt fishing village of Burtonport claims that more salmon is landed at the harbour here than at any other port in Ireland or Britain. There's a regular ferry from Burtonport to the island of Arranmore, a 20-minute trip, and boats can be hired for the even shorter journey to Rutland Island. It was on the latter island, during the 1798 rebellion, that James Napper Tandy landed with French troops. Unfortunately, before taking any belligerent action, James became intoxicated and had to be helped back on board his ship. More recently, the island has attracted some unorthodox residents. The Screamers were a group who believed in primal therapy and sexual liberation. The leaders of the commune eventually decamped to Colombia. The three Silver Sisters who arrived a few years later appeared a completely different kind of group. They dressed in Victorian clothes and seemed to lead a disciplined life. Exactly how disciplined emerged when their sado-masochistic practices were revealed. They too fled the island.

Bloody Foreland

32 miles NW of Letterkenny on the R257

About 7 miles offshore from Bloody Foreland is **Tory Island**, a barren windswept place reached by a ferry from Magheraroarty. The ferry is supposed to operate year round but the weather can be so bad that the crossing may be impossible for days on end. Indeed, in 1974 the islanders were cut off for 8 weeks by incessant storms so ferocious that even helicopters were prevented from landing. Following that experience two dozen families applied to Donegal County Council for housing on the mainland and it was subsequently revealed that the council had made plans for a total evacuation of the island. Then, as at Glencolmkille, a new priest arrived on the island. Father Diarmuid Ó Péicin encouraged the islanders to lobby every possible source of help, from the US Senator Tip O'Neill to Ian Paisley. Funds began to trickle in and conditions have gradually improved although life is still hard for the 150 or so permanent residents. The main occupation is fishing but the island also nourishes a school of primitive painters whose works are displayed at the **James Dixon Gallery** near the harbour.

Falcarragh

24 miles NW of Letterkenny on the N56

This peaceful little village is well-known locally for its lively music pub, The Gweedore Bar (*see below*), which has music sessions most summer evenings. The village has a 9-hole golf course and one of the loveliest beaches in the northwest, about 3 miles to the north. The view may be enchanting but don't be tempted into the water – a strong undercurrent makes the sea here dangerous for swimmers.

The Gweedore Bar & Restaurant

Main Street, Falcarragh, Letterkenny, Co. Donegal
Tel: 074 913 5293

Located in the heart of the Irish-speaking village of Falcarragh, the **Gweedore Bar and Restaurant** stands out with its striking terracotta and cream frontage. The bar and restaurant has been owned and run for nigh on a quarter of a century by Mary McGinley Friel and has become something of an institution in the area. In the traditional bar you'll find a good choice of snacks and, on most summer evenings, music of various styles. The first floor restaurant, serving an excellent selection of wholesome and appetising dishes, is ideal for special occasions. In the summer The Gweedore is open every day for meals from 12 noon to 10pm but during the winter this changes to 12.30pm -2.30pm each day and on Friday, Saturday and Sundays the Bar and restaurant serve food from 6pm untill 10pm.

The Oyster Bar

Main Street, Dunvanaghy, Co. Donegal
Tel: 074 36438 Fax: 074 36990
e-mail: evelyngamble@hotmail.com

Located on the main street of the picturesque estate village of Dunvanaghy, overlooking Sheephaven Bay, **McGilloway's Oyster Bar** is an award-winning pub with all the right credentials – open turf fires, regular traditional music sessions with live bands at weekends, and good craic throughout the year. Dessie and Connie McGilloway arrived here in 1997 and have made their pub a lively centre for both village people and tourists. Fully air-conditioned, the pub is open 7 days a week. If you are planning to stay in this wonderful corner of Donegal, Dessie has some attractive holiday cottages nearby, all with a 4-star rating from the Irish Tourist Board. In Dunvanaghy itself, a visit to the old Workhouse is highly recommended. Interactive exhibits relate the harrowing tale of how the Great Famine of 1845 affected the village and its inhabitants. And if you enjoy walking, there's a superb route from Dunvanaghy that leads to Horn Head, an imposing cliff some 600 feet high whose ledges swarm with countless guillemots and gulls, with a few puffins also resident.

Coastguard Holiday Cottages

Downings, Co Donegal
Contact: Noel McGinley, Pearse Road, Letterkenny, Co. Donegal
Tel: 074 912 5666 Fax: 074 912 4788
e-mail: coastguardcottages@eircom.net
website: http://homepage.eircom/-nmcginley

Downings is a picturesque fishing port, famous for the production of traditional Donegal tweed and an excellent base for exploring this lovely corner of Donegal. **Coastguard Holiday Cottages** are beautifully sited overlooking Sheephaven Bay, a great place, as owner Noel McGinley puts it, to "relax, reflect, restore your spirits and enjoy the charm and courtesy of a people renowned for their warm and gracious hospitality". Each 3-bedroom cottage has a spacious lounge off which is a comprehensively equipped modern kitchen designed to make light work of food preparation. A fully-tiled shower/toilet serves the double and twin bedroom, while the double master bedroom has a shower/toilet en suite.

The cottages are snug and cosy all year round with full oil-fired central heating as well as an electric heater in the lounge. There's plenty to see and do in the area. Downings village is on the Rosguill Peninsula, the starting point of the spectacular Atlantic Drive, and just a few minutes drive away from medieval Doe Castle, Ards Forest Park and Glenveagh National Park. Rosapenna's 18-hole championship golf links lies beside the cottages and nearby Carrigart boasts a magnificent links course and an equestrian centre.

Dunfanaghy

26 miles NW of Letterkenny on the N56

A plantation town built by English settlers, Dunfanaghy is often referred to as the Gateway to **Horn Head**, a mighty promontory with majestic cliffs rising sheer from the sea to a height of 600 feet. The views here are sublime: in one direction the vastness of the Atlantic Ocean broken only by numerous islands and headlands; and inland, mountain ranges crowned by the prominent peaks of Muckish and Errigal.

In Dunfanaghy itself the most striking building is the **Workhouse.** When it opened in 1845 there were just 5 inmates; two years later, as the Great Famine wrought its havoc, more than 600 people were crowded within its inhospitable walls. The terrible story is told here through the true-life story of one inmate, 'Wee' Hannah Herrity, who lived through the disaster and survived until 1926. The Workhouse is also used as a community centre, hosting music sessions and art exhibitions. There's also a pleasant coffee shop.

Carrigart

25 miles N of Letterkenny on the R245

An enticing village and peaceful holiday resort, Carrigart stands at the neck of the Rosguill Peninsula around which runs a beautiful circular route known as the **Atlantic Drive,** one of the finest scenic roads in Ireland. Carrigart has its own excellent beach, a superb golf course and several sandhill prehistoric buildings, or "kitchen middens", that have yielded numerous Bronze Age artefacts.

Downings

28 miles N of Letterkenny on the R248

A small resort popular with holiday-makers from Northern Ireland, Downings stands on the scenic Atlantic Drive. Fishermen are

BAILE AN TSLEIBHE

Downings, Co. Donegal
e-mail: moirascottage@hotmail.com
Tel: 074 9155661 Mob: 087 4146985
website: www.moirascottage.com

If you are looking for self-catering property 'away from it all', then **Baile an tSleibhe** is about as far away from it all as its possible to get. Set in the hills amidst some of the most beautiful scenery in Ireland, this lovely old property enjoys stunning views in all directions over sea and mountains. The

inside is romantic, charming, and full of character - just what you hoped an Irish country cottage would be like. There is an open hearth fire, antique furniture (including a 4-poster bed in one of the bedrooms), a cosy box bed by the fire, and an Aga in the kitchen. It sleeps 4-5 people. With its secluded location Baile an tSleibhe provides a perfect refuge from the stresses of modern living.

still active here and boats are available for trips to the islands of Tory and Inishbofin. There's a huge, unspoilt beach alongside the 18-hole golf course, a pier and, close by, a shop selling locally handwoven Donegal tweed.

In and around Letterkenny

Letterkenny

32 miles NE of Donegal on the N13

The commercial, administrative and ecclesiastical capital of Co. Donegal, Letterkenny is set beside the River Swilly where it flows into the lough of the same name. A thriving town, Letterkenny has attracted a healthy influx of new businesses on the outskirts but the centre still retains its country town appearance. It boasts one of the longest main streets in Ireland and also the only traffic lights anywhere in Co.

Donegal. An attractive feature of the town centre is a group of lifelike statues of naturally posed children. Even by Irish standards, Letterkenny is well-provided with lively pubs, many of them offering Irish music, and the younger generation has a choice of half a dozen nightclubs, a 6-screen cinema and a 10-pin bowling alley.

The town's most impressive building is the late-19th century **St Eunan's Cathedral,** designed in the Gothic style with flying buttresses and a strikingly lofty spire. The cathedral's walls of pearly Donegal sandstone gleam in sunlight and inside there are some interesting Celtic carvings and richly decorated ceilings.

The other main place to visit is the **Donegal County Museum** (free) on High Road which is housed in part of the former Workhouse and contains an interesting permanent collection of artefacts from early history and folk life as well as hosting travelling exhibitions.

CASTLE GROVE COUNTRY HOUSE

Letterkenny, Co. Donegal
Tel: 074 51118 Fax: 074 51384
e-mail: reservations@castlegrove.com
website: www.castlegrove.com

Approached by a mile-long avenue through a parkland of mature trees, **Castle Grove House** is a fine Georgian mansion built in the late 1700s and set amidst its own estate in one of the most beautiful parts of Ireland. The house enjoys a sheltered position, commanding a scenic view across Lough Swilly, and boasts a quality and gentle pace of life that is rare nowadays. The atmosphere at Castle Grove is that of an elegant country house – spacious rooms with gracious furnishings, congenial company and a comfortable informality. And outstanding food. The restaurant serves the very best of good fresh food – fish fresh from the sea, tender juicy roasts, and vegetables fresh from the hotel garden, all cooked with care and attractively presented.

To complement your meal, there's an excellent choice of wines from the hotel's cellar. The accommodation at Castle Grove maintains the same high standards. All 14 bedrooms are en suite and the emphasis is on retaining their individual character within the elegance and style that characterises the rest of the house. This is a great place to relax but there are also plenty of activities within easy reach – fishing, shooting and horse-riding, for example. A visit to Glenveagh National Park is a must and the Art Gallery at Churchill should also not be missed.

Letterkenny

Incidentally, if you are a devotee of Irish folk dance and music then the ideal time to visit Letterkenny is the middle of August when the Letterkenny Folk Festival is in full swing.

About 3 miles south of the town, **Newmills Corn and Flax Mills** (Dúchas) were once powered by one of the largest watermills in Ireland using the waters of the River Swilly; much of the vintage machinery is still in place.

A few miles west of Letterkenny is **Glenveagh National Park**. Within the National Park is Poison Glen which acquired its rather forbidding name from the legend of the cyclops, Balor of the Evil Eye. When he was slain by Lugh, Balor's eye rolled to the ground, tainting the whole area. In this Gaelic-speaking area, incidentally, the names on road signs also appear in their old Irish form. Bloody Foreland is Cnoc Fola, Gweedore appears as Gaoth Dobhair, and the county name is spelt Dhún na nGall.

Ramelton

9 miles NE of Letterkenny on the R245

Established as a plantation town by the Stewart family, Ramelton is a pleasing little town sitting on the eastern bank of the River Leannan, noted for its abundant salmon. The river was important during the 18th century as a major traffic route and the town became a thriving market centre. The elegant Georgian houses in The Mall and the sturdy stone warehouses beside the river testify to that period of prosperity and have earned Ramelton Heritage Town status, indeed it has more listed buildings than any other town in the Republic. A good time to visit the town is in July when the annual

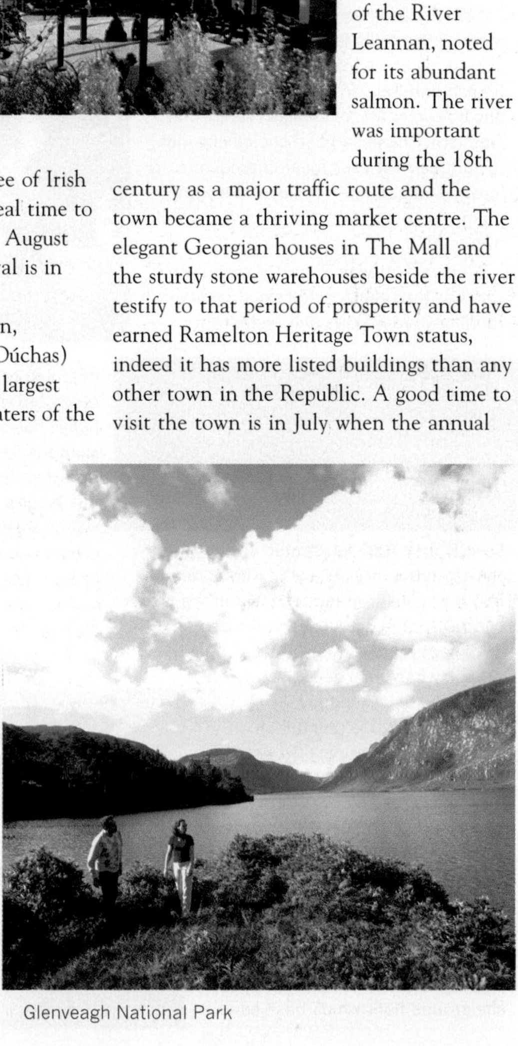

Glenveagh National Park

Donegal Shore

Aughnagaddy, Ramelton, Co. Donegal
Tel: 07491 52006
e-mail: huttomt@aol.com
website: www.donegalshore.com

Occupying an elevated site and enjoying spectacular views over Ramelton, Lough Swilly and Inishowen, **Donegal Shore** offers both outstanding food and quality accommodation. Joint owner Claire Hutton has a lifetime's experience in catering and hospitality and has created an enticing menu with a full à la carte choice with something of a continental flavour in the French and Belgian dishes. (Both Claire and co-owner Mervyn speak French and Flemish). There's a good choice of wines to complement your meal. Ingredients are locally sourced wherever possible with many of the vegetables coming from their own garden.

Mervyn Hutton is a master mariner who has also gained wide experience in running various pubs and restaurants. Both Claire and Mervyn have a wealth of local knowledge and maps of local walks are available. Donegal Shore has 4 comfortable guest bedrooms, all attractively furnished and decorated and all with en suite facilities. Nearby Ramelton is well worth exploring. It boasts the largest number of listed buildings of any Irish town, has one of the oldest pubs in the country (it featured in the film *The Hanging Gale*), and sits beside the River Lennan which is famous for its salmon fishing.

Fern House

Main Street, Kilmacrennan, Co. Donegal
Tel: 074 91 39218
e-mail: mailto@fern-house.com
website: www.fern-house.com

Fern House B&B is situated on the N56 in the attractive little village of Kilmacrennan, about 5 miles from Letterkenny in the most central spot in Co. Donegal. A traditional 19th century town house, the property has been sensitively renovated and tastefully modernised but is still full of character. For the past 30 years it has been the family home of Danny and Genevieve McElwee, a friendly and welcoming couple who make their guests feel very much at home.

Fern House has 5 guest bedrooms, all of them en suite and provided with TV and tea/coffee-making facilities. One of them is on the ground floor which has been modified to accommodate guests with restricted mobility or in a wheelchair – the house has a Wheelchair Accessible validation from the Irish Tourist Board. A full Irish breakfast is included in the tariff. For other meals, or a takeaway, a visit to the licensed Hilltop Restaurant is recommended. This is owned and run by Genevieve's sister Ann and offers a good choice of appetising food. The restaurant is open from midday, every day during the season; from 5pm at other times.

Ramelton Festival takes place with colourful floats passing through the town and pretty mavourneens competing for the title of "Queen of the Leannan".

Visitors in search of their Irish forebears will find copious resources available at **Donegal Ancestry**, housed in the former Steamboat Store on The Quay. For information about the town itself, a visit to the Ramelton Story is recommended: here you'll find an interesting audio-visual presentation of the town's history from medieval times up to the Georgian era. From Ramelton (which often appears on maps as 'Rathmelton') the journey along the R247 northwards around the Fanad Peninsula is one of Ireland's most scenic routes.

Kilmacrennan
7 miles N of Letterkenny on the N56

This pleasant little inland village has strong associations with St Columba who was fostered and educated here around AD 528. He later founded a monastery near the village but the ruins you see today are those of a 16th century Franciscan friary.

Milford
13 miles N of Letterkenny on the R245

Milford stands at the head of Mulroy Bay and is a good base for exploring the Fanad Peninsula which boasts some of the most impressive cliff scenery in Ireland. Follow the signposted **Fanad Peninsula Scenic Tour** which makes a 45-mile circuit that passes through some outstanding land and seascapes. En route you can take in the strange rock formation created by the incessant Atlantic waves and known as the Seven Arches, the dramatically-sited lighthouse and spectacular viewpoint at Fanad Head and, in summer, **Ballydaheen Gardens** with its 6 acres of flowers, herbs and vegetables.

MOYLEHILL HOLIDAY CENTRE

Moylehill, Milford, Co. Donegal
Tel: 074 9153866
e-mail: moylehill@oceanfree.net
website: www.moylehill.com

Standing within 70 acres of lovely open countryside and ideal for a large family or a party of friends, **Moylehill Holiday Centre** can accommodate up to 8 guests in 4 double bedrooms. These are all bright and airy – one has its own balcony, another is on the ground floor allowing easy access for the less mobile. The house boasts 3 bathrooms, 2 of them with showers; a walk-in hotpress; a large fully fitted kitchen with a balcony outside; and a spacious living area with a multi-fuel stove/open fire, TV and comfortable seating – perfect for a lazy evening indoors.

Other amenities include oil-fired central heating, logs for the open fire, fridge, freezer, microwave, washer/dryer, dishwasher, telephone, and barbecue area with balcony and garden furniture. Children are welcome – a cot and high chair are available on request; pets too are welcome. Owner Kenneth Bradley is always happy to answer any queries and to advise on the area's many activities: walking, cycling, shooting, golf, pony trekking, fishing, boating, scuba diving and wind-surfing, while there's good shopping in Letterkenny about 20 minutes away by car.

Rathmullan

16 miles NE of Letterkenny on the R247

Rathmullen

Rathmullan boasts a Blue Flag beach, which is classed amongst the cleanest in Europe, some striking multi-coloured houses, and the well-preserved ruins of a Carmelite friary that was built in 1508, converted to a fortified castle in 1618 and finally abandoned in 1814. Amongst the exhibits at the **Rathmullan Heritage Centre** is one telling the story of young Red Hugh O'Donnell, son of the Lord of Tyrconnel. In 1587 Hugh was lured by the promise of a "merry evening" into boarding a wine merchant's ship lying in the harbour. In reality, the vessel was an English naval ship. Hugh was arrested and spent 6 years in Dublin jail before managing to escape. It was also from Rathmullan harbour, in 1607, that the Earls of Tyrone and Tyrconnell fled with their retainers to France. Known as the 'Flight of the Earls', (many other nobles also decamped), this emigration of the elite effectively marked the end of centuries of Gaelic rule in Ireland.

From Rathmullan, the coastal road runs northwards past some of the most striking

An Bonnan Buí

Pier Road, Rathmullan, Co. Donegal
Tel: 074 9158453
e-mail: barrybcondron@eircom.net
website: www.info:anbonnanbui.ie

Gourmets and lovers of good wine will be in their element at **An Bonnan Buí**, an outstanding restaurant in a splendid position right on the pier with views across Lough Swilly to the Inishowen Peninsula. Iris Condron took over here in May 2003 and her menu, which changes each month, offers an appetising choice of lovingly prepared and beautifully presented dishes. Naturally, fresh fish dishes are prominent, along with others based on locally sourced ingredients according to season. The wine list is particularly satisfying with an excellent selection of wines from around the world.

The restaurant's décor is pleasing with attractive pine furniture, wooden floors and ethnic African original paintings on the walls. Children are welcome as well as larger groups by arrangement. Rathmullan itself is an attractive seaside town boasting a Blue Flag beach which has the distinction of being classed as amongst the cleanest in Europe. It's possible to hire boats at the pier and golfers will be delighted to find, just 2 miles outside the village, the Otway golf course which is reputed to be the oldest 9-hole golf course in the world.

cliff scenery in Ireland to the tiny seaside resort of Portsalon and on to Fanad Head where a dramatically sited lighthouse is accompanied by a solitary pub.

Stranorlar/Ballybofey

14 miles S of Letterkenny on the N15/N13

The Finn Valley has been described as "Donegal's best kept secret" – an area of spectacular mountain scenery which is also an angler's paradise. At its heart, standing on opposite banks of the River Finn, stand the Twin Towns of Stranorlar and Ballybofey. Finn Valley which, in addition to the superb fishing is Ireland's second-largest salmon and trout fishing river, offers a whole range of other activities and attractions. The golfer can enjoy a round on Ballybofey & Stranorlar's 18-hole course, with its tastefully appointed clubhouse and greens. The Finn Valley Athletic Centre is renowned throughout Europe and the centre manager was coach for the Irish team

at the Sydney Olympics. The Twin Towns are also home to the Premier Division League of Ireland soccer team, Finn Harps, and the county's gaelic pitch. Rally car events take place annually and walkers can enjoy trails in the Drumboe Woods and around Trusk Lough.

Ballybofey has a theatre and here you'll also find Donegal's largest department store, along with a wide variety of other shops. At Fintown, Donegal's only operational narrow gauge railway runs alongside the crystal waters of Loch Finn where the scenery was described by the actress Meryl Streep as "the most beautiful view she had seen". Near Raphoe stands the fascinating **Beltony Stone Circle,** the "Stonehenge of Donegal" which, in fact, has been dated as being 200 years older than Stonehenge. So it's clearly worthwhile discovering "Donegal's best kept secret" for yourself. Agatha Christie did so in the early 1900s and became a regular visitor to the area.

THE CROSS BAR

Crosswinds, Killygordon, Co. Donegal
Tel: 074 49218

Located about one mile off the N15 at Killygordon, **The Cross Bar** is well worth seeking out, especially if you are a football fan. There's lots of football memorabilia and a large screen TV for all those important matches. The atmosphere here is just what

you'd hope to find in an Irish bar, relaxed, convivial and with lots of good craic.

Owner Ben Browne has been in the hospitality business for some 56 years and possesses a wealth of local knowledge. The Cross Bar was established in 1938 and extensively refurbished in 1997 to a very high standard.

O'Flaherty's Bar

Main Street, Buncrana, Co. Donegal
Tel: 077 61305
website: www.oflahertysbar.net

Located in the centre of Buncrana, **O'Flaherty's Bar** stands out with its smart and distinctive black and gold frontage. Inside you'll find a friendly and welcoming atmosphere that will make you feel instantly

at home. "It's a place where everyone can come and enjoy a great pint and the best of craic in the true Irish tradition" says owner Jean Flaherty. Leather upholstered seating, an open fire, some striking paintings and even a sizeable library all add to the charm.

Jean is the second generation of her family to own and run the bar which was established in 1939 and was formerly known as the Dunree Bar. Once a family run general store and pub supplying goods to Dunree Fort, it is now renowned for its extensive selection of beers, wines and spirits and for its excellent food which is served from noon to 3pm, Monday to Friday.

O'Flaherty's is also famous for its live music, especially the Irish traditional sessions which take place every Wednesday night with local act Shandrum and friends taking to the stage. One of the country's greatest fiddle players, Dinny McLaughlin, heads this group of talented musicians who, as well as playing the best Irish music and songs, also tell an odd joke here and there. Other musicians, incidentally, are welcome to join in.

The other big music night here is Friday when local bands play a variety of music ranging from blues to rock'n'roll. These sessions are now establishing themselves as very popular amongst tourists and locals alike. "And with a different band playing every Friday night" adds Jean, "you're sure never to get bored with the line-up of acts playing!"

There's even more music on offer during Buncrana's annual music festival held in the last week of July and the town's other attractions include a superb 3-mile long beach, a Vintage Car Museum and the 15th century O'Doherty's Keep standing guard by the bridge over the river Crana.

Lifford

15 miles SE of Letterkenny on the N14

Lifford sits beside the River Finn which separates it from the much larger town of Strabane in Co. Tyrone. The Finn is valued as a good salmon river for spring fish and this tiny town with a population of around 1500 also boasts the only greyhound racing track in Co. Donegal. A more spiritual claim to fame is the fact that Cecil Frances Alexander, the writer of such enduring hymns as *All Things Bright and Beautiful* and *Once in Royal David's City*, was born here in 1818.

The main visitor attraction in Lifford is the **Seat of Power Visitor Centre** housed in the superbly restored Courthouse of 1746. With the aid of state-of-the-art audio-visual and talking heads techniques visitors can witness the re-enactment of famous trials in the courtroom and relive the harrowing experiences of prisoners in the cells below.

About 2 miles northwest of Lifford, **Cavanacor House** is a gracious 17th century mansion which welcomed amongst its earliest visitors James II who dined here in 1689. It later became the ancestral home of the Polk family whose most distinguished son was James Knox Polk, 11th President of the USA from 1845-49. The house has a small museum and an art gallery displaying changing exhibitions of work by contemporary artists.

The Inishowen Peninsula

One tends to be somewhat sceptical about tourist board literature promoting its own particular area as "undiscovered country" but in the case of the Inishowen peninsula, a great hammerhead of land jutting out into the Atlantic to the northeast of Letterkenny, the claim is entirely credible. Despite being part of the Republic, ("Southern Ireland"), the northern tip of Inishowen, **Malin Head**, is also the most northerly point of all Ireland.

The best way to explore this unique part of the country is to follow the 100-mile circular tour that starts at Buncrana in the southwestern corner of the peninsula.

The Inishowen Peninsula has one of the most impressive prehistoric relics in the

Grianan of Aileach

Letterkenny, Co. Donegal

The Inishowen Peninsula has one of the most impressive prehistoric relics in the country, the **Griánan of Aileach**, about 14 miles northeast of Letterkenny. This massive circular stone fort occupies a spectacular and impregnable location on the summit of Greenan Mountain (803ft) and commands grand views over Loughs Swilly and Foyle. The Griánan is marked on Ptolemy's 2nd century map of the world and was for several centuries the stronghold of the O'Neill kings. Built around 1700BC the fort has walls 17ft high and 13ft thick at the base, and near the entrance there are passages running inside the walls. The enclosure is 77ft across and three circular embankments form the outer defences. The inside of the walls is terraced which has led to speculation that it was designed for sun-worshipping rituals - *griánan* means a "sun palace". The fort's remarkable state of preservation is due to restoration in the 1870s. At the foot of the mountain is another place of interest: Burt Church, designed in the mid-1960s by Liam McCormack to harmonise with the fort and regarded by many as the most beautiful modern church in all Ireland.

country, the **Griánan of Aileach**, about 14 miles northeast of Letterkenny (see panel on page 95).

Buncrana

12 miles NW of Londonderry on the R238

The largest town in Inishowen, Buncrana is a favoured resort for holidaymakers from Londonderry and is well-supplied with amusement arcades, shops, bars and a Vintage Car Museum. The town is sheltered on three sides by hills and to the south there's a three-mile-long beach. The 15th century O'Doherty's Keep stands by Castle Bridge and on the other side of the river are the remains of Buncrana Castle, a once handsome building from the early 1600s. Around the town are a number of megalithic monuments, most notably a Bronze Age burial cairn at Crockcashel, a mile to the north.

Ballyliffin

23 miles N of Londonderry on the R238

A busy little resort, Ballyliffin's major out of season attraction is its **Folksong & Ballad Festival** held on the last weekend in March. Just to the north of the town, **Carrickabraghy Castle** is a weather-beaten 16th century fortress of the O'Dohertys overlooking beautiful Pollan Strand where huge Atlantic breakers roll in making it dangerous to swim here.

Doagh Isle

25 miles N of Londonderry off the R238

A popular attraction in the area is **Doagh Farm and Heritage Centre** on Doagh Island. Here, a mid-19th century Inishowen village has been re-created, providing visitors with a fascinating insight into the hardships experienced by local people during the period of the potato famine. The horrifying story is vividly presented in a series of traditional dwellings although a lighter note is struck in the Fairy House, home to Fergus McArt, one of Inishowen's best-known fairies "who is known to pop up from time to time!" Children will also love the play area, beach, farm zoo and boating pool while parents can indulge themselves in the thatched Tea Room or browse around the Craft Shop. (Doagh Island, incidentally, is not an island any more; the channel which once divided it from the mainland has silted up over the centuries).

Carndonagh

21 miles N of Londonderry on the R238/ R240

This thriving little town stands at Inishowen's main crossroads and home to one of the most far-famed Christian relics in Ireland, the **Donagh Cross**. Also known as St Patrick's Cross, it's said to be the oldest standing cross in the country, dating from around AD 650. Richly decorated and well-preserved, the cross stands in the Church of Ireland graveyard where the other interesting monuments include the Marigold Stone, so called because of the colouring of the stone.

There are more prehistoric remains scattered across the countryside to the east of Carndonagh: the Carrowmore high crosses; the Cloncha cross; the Temple of Deen (the central chamber of a huge cairn); and the Bocan stone circle, erected some 3000 years ago but now with only 7 of its many stones still standing.

Ballygorman

12 miles NW of Carndonagh off the R242

From Carndonagh, the road runs northwards to the pretty village of Malin (another winner of the Tidy Towns competition) and on towards **Malin Head,** the most northerly point in Ireland. About 5 miles before reaching Malin Head, a road off to the right leads to Ballygorman, the most northerly settlement in the country. There are some good coastal walks from here, one of which leads to Hells Hole, a 250 foot-deep chasm in the cliffs where the inrushing sea pounds and roars. Another will bring you to the Wee House of Malin, a hermit's cliff-side cell once the austere dwelling place of St Muirdealach.

Culdaff

7 miles NE of Carndonagh on the R238

Returning southwards, about 6 miles east of Malin is the secluded little village of Culdaff, set around a picturesque old bridge. The village boasts a very good beach and there is impressive coastal scenery all around; it hosts a major sea angling festival at the end of June and in early October a cultural weekend commemorating the 18th century actor Charles Macklin. But what this remote community is perhaps best known for is the world-quality live music entertainment regularly offered at McGrory's bar.

Moville

21 miles NE of Londonderry on the R238

Many emigrants to the New World embarked on their journey at the little port of Moville, set on the shore of Lough Foyle. Today, it's a peaceful leisure resort with a well-tended village green and great variety of scenery all around. To the northwest of the village, at **Cooley,** are some extensive archaeological remains. These include an ancient ruined church and, just outside the entrance, an unusual slender stone cross that stands some 10 feet high. There's also a small building known as the **Skull House**, a beehive-shaped building in which the bones of early monks were preserved. The bones have long since disappeared.

About 4 miles northeast of Moville, from the pretty little resort of Greencastle, there's a ferry every weekday that makes the 70-minute trip across the mouth of Lough Foyle to Co. Londonderry in Northern Ireland.

THE POINT LODGE

Quigley's Point, Inishowen, Co. Donegal
Tel: 074 9383428 Fax: 074 9383456
e-mail: thepointlodge@eircom.net
website: www.thepointlodge.net

Located in the peaceful village of Quigley's Point, just 8 miles from Derry City, **The Point Lodge** offers quality food and accommodation in a new style mini-hotel complex. It occupies the site of a former cabaret venue dating back to the 1950s which was badly damaged by a fire in 1999. It has been totally rebuilt and redesigned to host 16 en suite rooms with all modern facilities, a function room, a sizeable restaurant and a new style bar. The relatively small number of rooms and the fact that the hotel is family run assures visitors of a warm and friendly welcome and individual attention at all times. The O'Neill family also own and run the Foyleside Caravan and Camping

Park which overlooks beautiful Lough Foyle. The site offers 40 static pitches and 20 touring sites and provides all the facilities necessary for a very enjoyable and peaceful camping holiday. Permanent sites are also available. Golf and other leisure activities are just 5 minutes away and Quigley's Point is an ideal base for touring this lovely part of Donegal, the most northerly peninsula in Ireland. It is also a good starting point for the Inishowen 100 – a 100-mile circular scenic tour around the peninsula.

Co Dublin

Dublin

The old ballad sings of *Dublin's Fair City*, the Irish poet Oliver St John Gogarty lauded it as *No Mean City*, while James Joyce – along with most of his contemporaries – always referred to "*dear, dirty Dublin*". Anyone who spends any time in Dublin will almost certainly share Joyce's affection for the city, but it is "dirty" no longer. For one thing, the legendary Irish charm has beguiled the European Commission into lavishing more euros per capita on the Republic than on any other of its member nations. The money hasn't always been wisely spent as some of the truly dreadful modern buildings spatchcocked into the elegant Georgian squares bear witness. But the new "Celtic Tiger" economy has brought a real buzz to the city and stemmed the flow of young emigrants to other countries that drained the Republic for so long. Today, more than half of Greater Dublin's population of around 3.7 million is under 25.

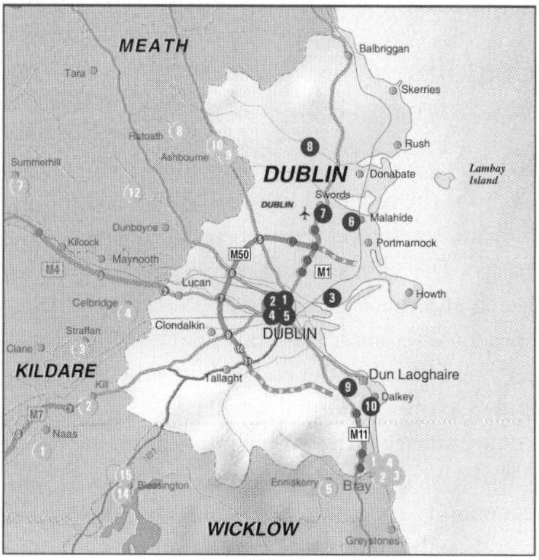

The first record of this attractive and vibrant city appears on Ptolemy's famous map of AD 140. It shows a settlement on the River Liffey which he named Eblana but which was known to its Celtic inhabitants as *Dubh Linn*, the "Dark Pool". The Vikings arrived in AD 860, ejected the Celts and set up a trading post on the south bank of

PLACES TO STAY, EAT AND DRINK

Washerwomans Hill Restaurant, Dublin	1	Restaurant	p99
Trinity College, Dublin	2	Historic Building	p100
Twin Eagles, Dublin	3	B&B	p107
National Botanic Gardens, Dublin	4	Gardens	p108
Dun Aoibhinn, Dublin	5	B&B	p108
Malahide Castle, Malahide	6	Historic Building	p111
Cedar House, Swords	7	B&B	p112
Hollywood B&B, Ballyboghil	8	B&B	p112
Marino House, Monkstown	9	B&B	p115
Nosh Restaurant, Dalkey	10	Restaurant	p116

● Denotes entries in other chapters

Grand Canal, Dublin

the Liffey. A century and a half of intermittent warfare followed until the Celts finally defeated the Vikings at the Battle of Clontarf in 1014. For another century and a half the Celts were left in peace. Then, in 1169, the Anglo-Normans arrived, the first chapter in a long and tragic saga of conflict between Ireland and England that would only end, (in the south, at least), with the establishment of the Irish Free State in 1921.

There was one short and glorious period however when hope of a peaceful resolution of Anglo-Irish hostilities seemed possible and even likely. During the last quarter of the 18th century, Ireland had its own parliament and although only Protestants could be elected, amongst their number were many liberal landowners who favoured Catholic emancipation. During this period, known as the "Anglo-Irish Ascendency", a building boom endowed the city with the dignified Georgian houses, squares and public

Washerwoman's Hill Restaurant

60 Glasnevin Hill, Glasnevin, Dublin 9
Tel: 01 837 9199 Fax: 01 837 9492
website: www.leadingrestaurant.com

One of the oldest buildings in Glasnevin, **Washerwoman's Hill Restaurant** takes its name from the old washhouse which once stood on the hill. Erected in the 1700s by Hugo Bath, this fine old building has a bright and open interior with highly polished wooden floors, robust country furnishings and original paintings by George MacAra Dawson.

Executive chef Matthew Hinde has created an impressive menu with Spiced Potato Rosti, Topped with Smoked Cod, lemon & coriander salad amongst the starters, main courses that include; Grilled Chicken Supreme Florentine with wilted spinach, paprika baby potatoes, cheddar veloute & wholegrain mustard; Crisp Roast Duck with Asian Flavours, marinated starfruit, cucumber, coriander & pickled ginger; and Sesame & Lime Crusted Salmon Steak, Thai rice, lemongrass and lime butter. Matthew and his team of chefs follow the principles of the HACCP in sourcing and preparing all their dishes. All meats are cooked to order, thus preserving the freshness and vibrancy of their flavours, and if you fancy something that isn't on the menu, they will do their very best to provide it.

This outstanding restaurant is open for lunch Monday to Friday from 12.30pm to 3.30pm, for Sunday lunch between 1.30pm and 4.30pm, and every evening for à la carte or table d'hôte meals from 6pm, with a pre-theatre menu served at 6pm (booking is essential).

buildings which still give Dublin such a distinctive architectural character. Then came the French Revolution and, in 1798, a countrywide rising by the United Irishmen. The rebellion failed but a panicky British government resumed direct control of Ireland in 1800, provoking yet another century of intermittent and violent resistance.

The ghosts of Henry II, the Earl of Essex, Cromwell, William of Orange and the Black & Tans still haunt Irish history but visitors to this friendly city will find only warmth, openness and a voracious appetite for "craic" – the delight in conversation and good fellowship. On Irish tongues, the English language sings and dances; a way with words also evidenced in the pantheon of Irish writers that ranges from Dean Swift, Sheridan and Oliver Goldsmith in the 18th century to Oscar Wilde, W.B. Yeats, James Joyce, George Bernard Shaw, Samuel Beckett and Seamus Heaney in more recent times.

Our tour of the city begins at the O'Connell Bridge, a central point which provides a stirring view of the river and some of Dublin's most famous buildings. Facing College Green, the monumental **Bank of Ireland** was designed in 1729 but not completed until 1789. Regarded as one of the finest specimens of the 18th century neo-classical style, the grandiose building provided an imposing setting for the short-lived Irish Parliament that gathered here between 1783 and 1801. Two years later, the Bank of Ireland acquired the building for a colossal £40,000 and it's still in business here today. Guided tours, available during normal banking hours, lead visitors through the former House of Lords, where there's a magnificent coffered ceiling and a splendid Waterford chandelier dating from 1765, and to the old House of Commons which has two fine 18th century tapestries depicting two famous Protestant victories, the Battle of the Boyne and the Siege of

Trinity College

College Green, Dublin 2

Across the busy main road from the Bank of Ireland is the entrance to **Trinity College** whose famous alumni have included Oliver Goldsmith and Edmund Burke (both commemorated by statues), Dean Swift, J.M. Synge the playwright, Samuel Beckett and the author of *Dracula*, Bram Stoker.

The college was founded in 1591 by Elizabeth I but the oldest surviving portion dates back to 1722. Trinity's design emulates the colleges of Oxford and Cambridge, with buildings of cream-coloured stone set around cobbled quadrangles. There's a finely-proportioned Chapel and Examination Hall (both 1787), and a Museum of 1857 whose walls contain some exuberant stone carvings by the famous O'Shea brothers.

But the highlight here is the **Trinity College Library**, a gracious building completed in 1732. It contains well over half a million printed books, as well as more than 140 Irish manuscripts, some from the 6th century, Greek and Latin manuscripts, and Egyptian papyri. The Library's greatest treasure though is the priceless Book of Kells, a beautifully illuminated manuscript of the gospels created sometime in the 8th century. There are 680 pages in all, now bound in four separate volumes, and each day a page is turned to reveal yet more fantastic and intricate designs, so finely drawn that even when magnified they reveal no flaws. Of equal interest is the **Book of Durrow**, dating from between AD 650 and 680 - the earliest surviving example of the great Irish illuminated manuscripts.

Derry. Also on display is the Parliament's Golden Mace. What visitors don't get to see is the bank's safe depository which still contains unopened trunks left there by victims of the *Titanic*.

Across the busy main road from the Bank of Ireland is the entrance to **Trinity College** (see panel opposite). Within the peaceful Trinity College campus are the redbrick **Rubrics**, dating from around 1700 and once occupied by Oliver Goldsmith as a student; the **Douglas Hyde Museum of Modern Art** which stages frequent exhibitions of major Irish artists; and the **Provosts' House**, a handsome mansion of 1760.

South of Trinity College, a stroll along pedestrianized Grafton Street takes you through the heart of the city's smart shopping area, well supplied with cafés, bars and restaurants, where the entertainment includes lively street theatre and buskers. At the southern end of the street is **St Stephen's Green**, laid out as a public park in 1890 by Sir Arthur Edward Guinness of the drinks dynasty. Tree-lined walks, shrubberies, colourful flower beds, an ornamental lake and lunchtime concerts during the summer make this a pleasant place to wile away a quiet hour. In Georgian times, the houses surrounding the Green provided the smartest addresses in town. Sadly, most of these elegant buildings fell victim to ruthless "development" in the 1960s. (Nearby Ely Place and Harcourt Street were more fortunate and contain some of the best-preserved domestic Georgian architecture in Dublin).

St Stephen's Green

On the south side of St Stephen's Green, however, there is one outstanding Georgian survivor, **Newman House**. It is actually two houses, both built around 1738 and famous for their spectacular plaster decoration and magnificent 18th century interiors. The house is named after Cardinal Newman who in 1853 became first Rector of the newly-established Catholic University of Ireland which is still based here. The Jesuit priest and poet, Gerard Manley Hopkins, was Professor of Classics here from 1884 to 1889, and the attic room in which he lived has been restored in his honour. The University's most famous alumnus was James Joyce, a BA student here from 1899 to 1902; a classroom, decorated as it would have been in his time, survives and is included in the guided tour.

Leading northwards from St Stephen's Green, Kildare Street contains the mightily impressive building frontage of **Leinster House**, built in 1745 as a town house for the Duke of Leinster. It is now home to not only the two houses of the Irish Parliament, the *Dáil Éireann*, but also the **National Library** and the **National Museum** (free), each with a huge rotunda over its entrance. The National Museum houses the treasures

Halfpenny Bridge

of ancient Ireland – beautifully crafted Celtic jewellery ranging from the 8th to the 1st centuries BC, along with spectacular medieval pieces such as the exquisite Tara Brooch, generally regarded as the finest piece of Irish metalwork to have survived.

Incorporated in the National Museum is the **Natural History Museum** (free) which contains collections illustrating the wildlife of Ireland, along with an extensive African and Asian exhibition. Children especially will be impressed by the two huge skeletons suspended from the ceiling of whales which had been stranded on the Irish coast.

Backing on to Leinster House is the **National Gallery** (free) which boasts a collection of more than 2,500 works, representing every major European school of painting. Amongst them are works by Jack Yeats, (brother of the poet WB Yeats), Hogarth, Reynolds, Gainsborough and Turner, along with an extensive array of fine European painting from the Renaissance onwards. Highlights include a recently rediscovered Caravaggio, *The Taking of Christ* (1602), and Degas' *Ballet Girls*. A riveting collection of Irish portraits lines the grand staircase at the top of which is one of Countess Markiewicz, the fervent Nationalist who was incensed when she was pardoned for her rôle in the Easter Rising.

To sample contemporary Irish arts and culture, the place to make for is **Temple Bar**, just to the west of Trinity College. Clustered around Meeting House Square, a spectacular open air performance area, are the Gallery of Photography, the Irish Film Centre, the Temple Bar Music Centre, "Arthouse" – a multi-media centre for the arts, "The Ark" – a cultural centre for children and, every Saturday, The Book Market provides a gathering place for independent booksellers and readers of all tastes and genres. Temple Bar mounts a free programme of events throughout the day and into the evening and an additional attraction is the unique Food Market (Saturdays only) where small producers and growers offer a huge range of home produced goods – farmhouse cheeses, venison, smoked fish, organic vegetables, chocolate and fudge.

Across the road from Temple Bar is one of Dublin's most famous bridges, the pedestrian-only **Halfpenny Bridge**. Erected in 1821, it was one of the earliest cast iron structures of its kind in Ireland. Until the early 1900s, a toll was charged to cross it – hence the name.

A few steps from Temple Bar, **Dublin's Viking Adventure** takes visitors on a fascinating journey back through time to the Viking town of "Dyflin", imaginatively and accurately re-created and brought to life. You can walk the narrow streets, chat to the "locals", observe their daily work and experience the sounds and smells of the

Dublin Castle

city. Within the complex, the Viking Museum features a collection of the artefacts discovered during the excavation of Viking Dublin, the most important collection outside Scandinavia.

Another short walk brings you to **Dublin Castle**, originally built for King John's visit in 1207. Of that early fortress, only the massive stone Record Tower still stands, and the Great Courtyard is surrounded by an architectural medley that includes a graceful 18th century mansion, a rather fussy neo-gothic church of 1803, and an Inland Revenue office building as alluring as its function. But the superb State Apartments are well worth visiting. Built as residential quarters for the English Viceroy, they are now the venue for Ireland's Presidencies of the European Community, Presidential Inaugurations and other state functions.

Located within the castle, the **Chester Beatty Library** (free) was bequeathed to the city by the New York-born Chester Beatty but only a small part of his collection, which weighed some 35 tons, is on display at any one time. Beatty was fascinated by the Orient and the priceless collection includes Chinese jade books, Turkish miniatures, rare Japanese and Thai texts, samurai armour, Buddhas and more than 250 copies of the Koran. The most sumptuous of these is a 10th century fragment written in gold on blue-dyed vellum.

Of Dublin's many churches, the grandest is **St Patrick's Cathedral** which stands on the site where, it is said, St Patrick baptised converts in a well beside the building. A church has stood here since AD 450 but the present building dates from 1191 and was much restored in Victorian times. The national cathedral of the Protestant Church of Ireland, St Patrick's is the largest church in Ireland. Its interior is notable for some imposing tombs and memorials, the most striking of which is the flamboyant 17th century monument to the Boyle family, Earls of Cork. In the Choir are the Banners and the Stalls of the Knights of St Patrick (1783) and in the transepts hang the old Irish regimental banners.

The cathedral contains several mementoes of Jonathan Swift, author of *Gulliver's Travels*, who was Dean of St Patrick's from 1713 to 1745. His pulpit, table and chair are here, and he himself is buried in the cathedral alongside his wife Stella. A plain black slab is engraved with the epitaph he wrote himself, but there's an even more telling inscription on a tablet at the east end of the church. In just two lines, William Taylour sums up the human condition:

As You are, so were Wee
And as Wee are, so shall You be.

At the west end of the cathedral, the medieval door to the Chapter House has a roughly hewn hole in it which is believed to have given rise to the phrase "chancing your arm". In 1492, the Earl of Ormonde and his supporters were barricaded within the cathedral, resisting an attack by their enemies, the Earl of Kildare and his followers. Eventually, Kildare decided to make peace, hacked a hole through the door and put his arm through it, urging Ormonde to shake hands. Kildare's gamble paid off, Ormonde shook hands and peace was restored.

Dublin's other Church of Ireland cathedral is **Christ Church**, some 30 years older than St Patrick's and with much more of its original fabric still intact. The crypt, dating from 1172, is unique in Ireland for its scale and size, being almost as large as the entire upper church. It contains some interesting relics, amongst them the punishment stocks from the old 'liberty' of Christ Church, the 1689 candlesticks and tabernacle of James II, and a mummified cat and mouse discovered in the old organ pipes.

Located beside Christ Church, **Dvblinia** tells the story of the development of Dublin from the arrival of Strongbow and his Anglo-Norman knights in the 12th century to the era of Henry VIII. Life-size reconstructions bring history to life, while medieval artefacts from the Wood Quay excavations are on display in the museum area. Visitors can take part in a 'Medieval Fayre' and climb the 17th century St Michael's tower for a unique, panoramic view of the city.

Just outside the main entrance to Christ Church, **Marsh's Library** is the oldest public library in Ireland. Built in 1701 by Archbishop Narcissus Marsh, it contains some 25,000 volumes, most of them dating from the 16th to the 18th centuries, along with 250 volumes of manuscripts. The beautiful dark oak bookcases and the tiny reading cubicles are still here, so too are the three original wired 'cages' where readers consulting rare books used to be locked in.

To the west of Marsh's Library is one of Ireland's most popular visitor attractions, the **Guinness Storehouse** in St James' Gate. Back in 1759, Arthur Guinness purchased a run-down old brewery near here and began brewing the famous black stout with its distinctive creamy head. The handsome 4-storey building houses the "World of Guinness Exhibition"; an Advertising Gallery displaying the inspired posters used over the years; an audio-visual show on the history of Guinness in Ireland; a model Cooperage and Transport Museum; and an Art Gallery devoted to the work of John Gilroy. There's also a coffee shop and a lively bar where you can sample what must surely be the best pint of Guinness in the city.

Before crossing the Liffey to north Dublin, two more buildings on the southwest edge of the city are well worth a visit. The **Irish Museum of Modern Art** (free) is housed in a glorious classical building of 1680, formerly the Royal Hospital Kilmainham for wounded army pensioners. The Museum, opened in 1991, owns only a small number of paintings itself but puts on a regularly changing collection of works borrowed from other galleries.

From the Museum, a long tree-lined avenue leads to the forbidding bulk of **Kilmainham Gaol**, now the largest unoccupied gaol in Ireland and used as a location in the film *In the Name of the Father*. It was opened in 1796, just in time to receive the leaders of the rebellion of 1798. A roll-call of Irish nationalists – Robert Emmet, Charles Stewart Parnell, De Valera – were to follow them through its forbidding portals. The admission price to the gaol includes an audio-visual presentation, an exhibition and a guided tour which gives a realistic insight into 19th century notions of punishment and correction. Perhaps the most poignant moment of the tour is a visit to the chapel where, on 4 May 1916, Joseph Plunkett – one of the leaders of the 1916 Easter Rising – was married by candlelight to Grace Gifford. The ceremony concluded at 1.30am: at 3.30am Plunkett was executed by firing squad. He had spent a total of ten minutes alone with his wife.

North of the Liffey

Extending northwards from the O'Connell Bridge is the widest city thoroughfare in Europe, **O'Connell Street**, a grand sight with its central strip dotted with statues. The most striking building here is the **General Post Office** (GPO), opened in 1818 and almost a century later the scene of one of the most significant moments in the struggle for Irish independence. On Easter Monday 1916, a group of rebels led by Pádraig Pearse seized the building and proclaimed the Irish Republic from its steps. British troops surrounded the building and shelled it from a gunboat anchored in the Liffey, wrecking the building and much of O'Connell Street as well. The rebels held out for 5 days before being overwhelmed. Sixteen of the rebel leaders were summarily shot; 2000 others imprisoned. Inside the GPO, a superb sculpture by Oliver Sheppard of the mythical Celtic warrior Cúchullain honours the heroes of the Easter Rising.

The most recent sculpture to be erected in O'Connell Street was unveiled to celebrate Dublin's millennium in 1988. The **Anna Livia Fountain** shows a recumbent woman bathed by the waters of the fountain. It represents Anna Livia Plurabella, a character in James Joyce's novel *Finnegan's Wake* who personifies the River Liffey. Striking though it is, the sculpture is usually referred to irreverently as the "Floozie in the Jacuzzi".

The final statue at the northern end of O'Connell Street commemorates Charles Stewart Parnell (1846-1891), the Nationalist leader whose distinguished political career was destroyed because of his involvement in a divorce case. The square behind his statue also bears his name and contains some of Dublin's earliest Georgian buildings. One of the most impressive is Charlemont House, built for the Earl of Charlemont in 1762 and now home to the **Hugh Lane Municipal Gallery of Modern Art**. The Gallery houses an extensive collection of 20th century Irish art as well as half the French Impressionist collection amassed by Sir Hugh Lane. Sir Hugh was a passenger on the *Lusitania* when it was torpedoed by a German submarine in 1915. In his will he had bequeathed his collection to "the Irish nation", a bequest which caused problems when the Republic was established. The outcome was that half the paintings are now permanently held in Belfast. Since Sir Hugh's death, the most significant donation to the Gallery has been

Millenium Bridge

the gift of the Francis Bacon Studio and the artist's unfinished *Self-Portrait*. (Bacon was born in Dublin in 1906 and lived in Ireland until 1925).

Also in Parnell Square is the **Dublin Writers Museum** which celebrates Ireland's illustrious literary tradition. Housed in a magnificent 18th century mansion, the collection features the lives and works of the city's literary celebrities over the past 300 years. Swift and Sheridan, Shaw and Wilde, Yeats, Joyce and Beckett are among those presented through their books, letters, portraits and personal items. The museum holds exhibitions and readings and has a special room devoted to children's literature.

The Four Courts

A short walk from Parnell Square, in North Great George's Street, a titan of Irish literature has his own personal museum – **The James Joyce Centre**. Located in a beautifully restored Georgian townhouse, the Centre is dedicated to promoting interest in the life and works of the author of *Ulysses*. The Centre's amenities include audio-visual material relating to Dublin's most local and yet international writer; an excellent bookshop; lectures, and walking tours through the heartland of Joyce's north inner city. There's also a coffee shop, the "Ulysses Experience", which features a mural based on the people and events recorded in Joyce's most famous novel.

Yet another Dublin literary shrine is the **Shaw Birthplace**, at 33 Synge Street on the southern edge of the city centre. It was here that George Bernard Shaw was born in 1856 and spent his early years. The interior of the neat little terrace house has been restored to its Victorian appearance and looks as if the family has just gone out for the afternoon. The displays provide a fascinating insight into domestic life in Victorian Dublin as well as celebrating the early years of one of Dublin's Nobel prize winners for literature, a prize incidentally that Shaw declined to accept.

Returning to the north bank of the River Liffey, a short walk eastwards from the O'Connell Bridge brings you to the famed **Abbey Theatre**, Ireland's national theatre. Founded in 1904 by W.B.Yeats, J.M.Synge and Lady Gregory, the Abbey has premiered the work of every leading Irish playwright, at times sparking off riots such as those that followed the première of Sean O'Casey's *The Plough and the Stars*, a revisionist view of the heroes of the Easter Rising. A fire in 1951 destroyed the original theatre and the brutalist building that rose in its place now contains two theatres: the Abbey which is devoted to the Irish classics, and the smaller Peacock which specialises in experimental drama.

A little further east from the Abbey Theatre stands one of Dublin's finest heritage buildings, the **Custom House,** completed in 1791. Designed by the celebrated architect James Gandon (1743-1823), this noble building with its elegant portico and great dome stands on the quayside overlooking the River Liffey. During the War of Independence in 1921 the Custom House, as a symbol of English government, was set alight by Republicans and burned fiercely throughout five days and nights. It has twice been refurbished since then and once again houses government offices. The Visitor Centre has an exhibit recording the history of the Custom House, including the 1921 fire; displays on the many government characters who have worked in the building; and a Gandon Museum detailing the great architect's life and work.

Another of Gandon's magnificent buildings also stands on the north bank of the Liffey, about half a mile west of O'Connell Bridge. **The Four Courts** were completed in 1786 as the seat of the High Court of Justice of Ireland and although they, like the Custom House, suffered massive damage during the 1921 civil war, they have been thoroughly restored. A graceful Corinthian portico supports a statue of Moses, and the figures of Justice and Mercy, while above the circular entrance hall rises a colossal pillared dome.

If you have a taste for the macabre, a visit to **St Michan's Church,** the oldest building in north Dublin, should prove very satisfying. An unusual combination of dry air, constant temperature, and methane gas from rotting vegetation beneath the 11th century crypt, has kept the bodies stored here in a state of mummification. The best preserved are on display, some of them more than three centuries old. The church also has an early 18th century organ. Handel played this organ when he was in Dublin for the very first performance of *The Messiah* in 1742.

A mile or so to the west of the Four

TWIN EAGLES

196 Kincora Road, Clontarf, Dublin 3
Tel/Fax: 01 8333 270

Twin Eagles offers comfortable and beautifully appointed accommodation in a stylish house decorated to modern day standards, with fire alarm system, security lights and private parking. Situated in Clontarf it enjoys a quiet location but is only a short walk from the waterefront and close to bus, shops, pubs and restaurants. Also

close by is the Royal Dublin Golf Course, Dollymount Beach and Bird Sanctuary and St Annes Park and Rose Garden, with Golf Course.

There are 4 attractively furnished ensuite bedrooms, all with TV, refrigerator, hair dryer and tea/coffee-making facilities.

Approved by Bord Failte, Twin Eagles is situated just 2.5 miles from Dublin City Centre, 15-20 minute drive from the Airport, 15 minutes drive to Dublin Ferry Port and 10 minutes from Point Theatre.

National Botanic Gardens

Glasnevin, Dublin
Tel: (01) 374388

One of Dublin's "must see" attractions lies about a mile to the northeast of Phoenix Park. The **National Botanic Gardens** (free) were founded by the Royal Dublin Society in 1795 and the 48-acre site contains some 20,000 species of plants and trees. There's an arboretum, rock garden and burren areas, extensive herbaceous borders, a student garden and an annual display of decorative plants, including a rare example of Victorian carpet bedding. Amongst the notable specimens thriving here are a fine, weeping Atlantic cedar, venerable Chusan palms, and the "Last Rose of Summer" of the famous ballad.

The botanical treasures are enhanced by a superb range of curvilinear glasshouses more than 400 feet in length, designed and built by the Dublin ironmaster Richard Turner between 1843 and 1869.

Adjacent to the gardens is Prospect Cemetery, the final resting place of many famous Dubliners, including Michael Collins, Daniel O'Connell and Charles Stewart Parnell.

Dûn Aoibhinn

30 Sutton Park, Dublin 13
Tel: 01 832 5456 Fax: 01 832 5213
e-mail: mary_mcdonnell@ireland.com
website: www.dunaoibhinn.com

Located in the quiet residential area of Sutton, **Dûn Aoibhinn** is a luxurious detached house where Mary McDonnell offers quality bed & breakfast accommodation. Mary is an assiduous host, determined to make your stay as relaxing and comfortable as possible. Her home stands on a large corner site in a peaceful quarter of this favoured and much sought-after Dublin suburb. The coast road runs close by, the DART train with its fast link to Dublin city centre is just a 5-minute walk away, as are some half a dozen bus routes. Dûn Aoibhinn was purpose built as a guest house so it is well equipped with all up-to-date amenities.

You'll find a spacious, well-furnished guest lounge instantly heated by a natural gas fire and complete with TV and video along with tea/coffee facilities available 24 hours a day. There are 3 guest bedrooms, all of them en suite, and all attractively furnished and decorated. Mary serves a copious breakfast offering a good choice of menu – more than enough to set you up for the day! Dûn Aoibhinn is open all year except over the Christmas period and provides a perfect base for exploring Ireland's capital city and the surrounding countryside.

Courts is Dublin's playground, **Phoenix Park**, a huge lung covering 1,760 acres and with a circumference of 7 miles – about five times the size of London's Hyde Park. Originally priory lands, the area was seized in the 1640s and made into a royal deer park. A Viceroy's Lodge was built here which is now the *Aras an Uachtaráin*, the Irish President's official residence. Visible from most corners of the Park is the towering, 205 feet high **Wellington Monument**, erected in honour of the victor of Waterloo who was born in Dublin in 1769. The Iron Duke didn't seem particularly proud of his Irish origins. When someone remarked on Dublin being his birthplace, Wellington retorted, "Being born in a stable doesn't make one a horse".

Thirty acres of Phoenix Park are occupied by the landscaped grounds of **Dublin Zoo**, opened in 1830 and now home to some 700 animals and tropical birds from around the world. "Fringes of the Arctic" features polar bears, snowy owls and arctic foxes; "World of Cats" includes jaguars, lions and snow leopards; and an innovative "Meet the Keeper" programme allows visitors to learn about the many rare and endangered species which have found a sanctuary here. Other attractions include a train ride around the zoo, children's play areas, a pet care area, discovery centre, restaurants and gift shop.

One of Dublin's "must see" attractions lies about a mile to the northeast of Phoenix Park. The **National Botanic Gardens** (free - see panel opposite)

County Dublin

Though the county of Dublin only includes the city and a coastal strip to the northeast, it contains many places of interest, most notably Malahide Castle and Newbridge House. Much of the county is easily accessible thanks to DART – the Dublin Area Rapid Transit railway, which runs fast and frequent electric trains from Howth right around Dublin Bay to Bray just across the border in Co. Wicklow. The route offers some great views, especially between Dalkey and Killiney, so it's worth taking a trip even if you have your own transport. We begin by travelling northwards from the city centre.

Marino

3 miles N of Dublin city centre off the R105

Marino is an unassuming suburb but it does have one attraction well worth taking the trouble to find: the 18th century **Marino Casino**. It's not a gambling den but an extraordinary folly built as a summer residence for the Earl of Charlemont in the 1750s as a Neo-classical foil to his villa here. The villa has long since gone but the Casino with its massive columns and elaborate urns concealing chimney stacks, and its 16 finely decorated rooms, was fully restored in 1984. Lord Charlemont's villa was designed to command a panoramic sea vista but a local painter named Ffolliot spitefully erected a row of town houses deliberately intended to block the view. To compound the insult, Ffolliot made the backs of the houses in Marino Crescent as unsightly as possible with ill-proportioned windows and ramshackle sheds.

Howth

9 miles NE of Dublin on the R105

Howth (pronounced to rhyme with 'both') stands on a peninsula which forms the northern horn of the Dublin Bay crescent. Once the main port for the steam packets from Britain, today it's a popular seaside resort for Dubliners and also a busy fishing centre. From Howth Head there are wonderful views across the bay to the Wicklow Mountains and even, on a clear day, to the mountains of Wales. From the harbour there are boat trips available, one of which will take you to **Ireland's Eye**, a

Howth Harbour

small island bird sanctuary about a mile off shore, a popular place for walkers and picnickers. On the west side of the town, **Howth Castle** is a long battlemented building dating from 1564 and enjoys the status of being the oldest inhabited house in Ireland. The castle itself isn't open to the public but you can wander through the extensive grounds (free) which are a brilliant sight in early summer when the azaleas and rhododendrons are in flower. The grounds also contain the ruined square tower of Corr Castle and a huge dolmen made of ten enormous masses of quartzite, with a capstone said to weigh 70 tons. Known as **Aideen's Grave**, it is reputed to cover the grave of Aideen, wife of Oscar, who was slain near Tara at the end of the 3rd century. Also within the Howth Castle Demesne is the **National Transport Museum** which has specimens of just about every vehicle to have travelled an Irish road, from Victorian carriages to early trams and fire engines. Walkers will enjoy Howth's famous **Cliff Walk** which extends for about 5 miles and opens up some fine views of the Wicklow Mountains to the south.

Portmarnock

8 miles NE of Dublin on the R106

This popular little seaside resort has a beach 3 miles long with sand so soft it has been named the 'Velvet Strand'. Portmarnock is also well known to golfers for its championship course. A couple of miles west

Portmarnock

of the town, **St Doulagh's Church** is an interesting building that stands on the site of the anchorite cell of the 7th century St Doulagh. The present structure, its oldest parts dating from around 1200, includes the last anchorite cell built on this site, a 14th century tower and a Victorian rebuilding of the parish church which is still in use.

Malahide

9 miles NE of Dublin on the R107

With its fine sandy beaches, Malahide is another popular seaside resort for Dubliners, but its greatest glory is the splendid **Malahide Castle** (see panel below). The castle is surrounded by 250 acres of beautiful gardens and parkland, and model railway buffs will be delighted to find within the castle grounds the **Fry Model Railway Museum**, a unique working collection of handmade models of Irish trains from the beginning of rail travel to modern times. The beautifully engineered models were created in the 1920s and 1930s by Cyril Fry, a railway engineer and draughtsman. The huge O-gauge layout

Malahide Castle

Malahide, Co Dublin
Tel 353 1 846 2184 Fax 353 1 846 2537
e-mail: malahidecastle@dublintourism.ie
website: www.visitdublin.com

Set on 250 acres of parkland in the pretty seaside town of Malahide, the Castle was both a fortress and a private home for nearly eight hundred years, and is an interesting mix of architectural styles. The Talbot family lived here from 1185 to 1973, when the last Lord Talbot died.

Many original 18th century furnishings are still in place together with an extensive collection of Irish portrait paintings, most of them from the National Gallery. Also on display are the Boswell Papers, travel journals written by Dr Johnson's biographer, James Boswell, who was related to the Talbots. These fascinating accounts of 18th century travel didn't come to light until a few years ago when they were discovered in a croquet box at the castle.

The history of the Talbot family is recorded in the Great Hall, with portraits of generations of the family telling their own story of Ireland's stormy history. One of the more poignant legends concerns the morning of the Battle of the Boyne in 1690, when fourteen members of the family breakfasted together in this room, never to return, as all were dead by the end of the battle.

A major feature of Malahide Castle Demesne is the beautiful Talbot Botanic Gardens. The gardens, as they exist today, were largely created by Lord Milo Talbot between 1948 and 1973.

Cedar House

Jugback Lane, off Watery Lane, Swords,
Co. Dublin
Tel: 01 840 2757 Mobile: 087 2474441
Fax: 01 840 2041

Located just 5 minutes from Dublin Airport, **Cedar House** offers first class bed and breakfast accommodation in peaceful and relaxed surroundings. This spacious and elegant modern house is the home of Kathleen Keneghan, an extremely friendly lady who makes her guests feel really welcome. There are 5 guest bedrooms, (including a family room), all beautifully appointed with en suite facilities, multi-channel television and hospitality tray. Kathleen provides a hearty breakfast, complete with home-baked bread and home-made preserves and if you have an early start to catch a plane or ferry, she is happy to arrange an early breakfast.

Cedar House is perfectly situated for exploring the city of Dublin – buses 41 and 33 pass close by and will get you right into the heart of the historic city in a matter of minutes. There's also a train service into the city from nearby Malahide, a popular seaside resort with fine sandy beaches and a splendid castle set in 250 acres of gardens and parkland. Cedar House has its own private car parking and, best of all, a wonderful home-from-home atmosphere.

Hollywood B&B

Hollywood, Ballyboghil, Co. Dublin
Tel/Fax: 01 843 3359
e-mail: hwood@indigo.ie
website: www.hollywoodbb.com

Only 15 minutes from Dublin airport and 25 minutes from the city centre, **Hollywood B&B** is a delightful country house set in open countryside and enjoying grand rural views. Its location makes it ideal as a stopover when arriving or leaving Ireland, or as a place to stay when visiting Dublin. Hollywood is the home of Margaret and Donal Farrell, a friendly and welcoming couple who do all they possibly can to make your stay as enjoyable and relaxing as possible. All the bedrooms here are non-smoking and are provided with en suite facilities, television, hairdryer and hospitality tray.

At breakfast time you'll find plenty of choices, including a full Irish breakfast, all served in the country-style dining room overlooking the garden. Guests are welcome to relax in this beautifully maintained garden and there's also ample space for parking. Room rates represent very good value for money; Visa, Access and Mastercard are accepted, as are Travel Agent vouchers, Town & Country Vouchers, TC Home & Farmhouse vouchers. Hollywood is close to Swords village with its castle and choice of restaurants, pubs and shops; other visitor attractions within easy reach include Malahide Castle, Newgrange, Newbridge Demesne and Skerrries Mills.

includes immaculately crafted stations, bridges, trams, buses, barges and even the River Liffey. The museum also contains a book shop and model shop.

Another attraction at Malahide Castle is **Tara's Palace,** undoubtedly one of the world's most magnificent Doll's Houses. Meticulously constructed by some of Ireland's finest craftsmen, it took over ten years to complete and additions are still being made. Designed and built to one-twelfth scale, it re-creates the grandeur and elegance of three of Ireland's greatest 18th century mansions: Castletown House, Leinster House and Carlton.

Also within the castle grounds, the 20-acre **Talbot Botanic Gardens** offer a walled garden, conservatory and some 5000 species of plants from Chile, Australia and New Zealand.

Malahide Castle was the seat of the Talbot family from 1185 until 1976(see panel on page 111). Malahide Castle's medieval Great Hall is particularly striking, the only one in Ireland to be preserved in its original form. It was in this room on the 1st July 1690 that fourteen members of the Talbot family sat down to breakfast. By nightfall they were all dead, killed in the Battle of the Boyne, William III's decisive victory over James II.

Swords

9 miles NE of Dublin on the N1

It was in AD 563 that St Columba founded a monastery beside the estuary of the River Ward where the town of Swords now stands. Over the centuries, the foundation flourished so much that it became known as the "Golden Prebend" and the monks built a round tower, 74 feet high, in which to protect their precious manuscripts and bejewelled crosiers.

The ruins of the round tower still stand but no trace remains of the monastery. At the northern end of the town, Swords Castle is an unusual 5-sided construction, built around 1200.

Donabate

12 miles N of Dublin on the N1

A good investment is to buy the joint ticket that gives you entry to both Malahide Castle and **Newbridge House**, just outside the trim little town of Donabate. Set in 350 acres of parkland, Newbridge House is a delightful 18th century manor built in 1737 for Charles Cobbe, later Archbishop of Dublin. His descendants still live here although the estate is now owned by Dublin County Council. The house is reckoned by most experts to have one of the finest Georgian interiors in Ireland. Each room open to the public has its own style of antique and original furniture, and the period atmosphere is enhanced by a fully restored courtyard, surrounded by a dairy, estate worker's house, carpenter's shop and a blacksmith's forge, all displaying 19th century tools and implements. The grounds also contain a 29-acre traditional farm, complete with farmyard animals, a deer park, walled garden and arboretum. Collectors of curiosities will be pleased to find that the Cobbe family displayed the same propensity. A charming small museum contains oddities from around the world, amongst them exotic weapons, an African chief's umbrella and the mummified ear of an Egyptian bull. And cinema buffs with a good memory may recognise Newbridge House as a major location for the 1965 film *The Spy Who Came in from the Cold*, starring Richard Burton and Claire Bloom. The Cobbe family used part of the location fee to have electricity installed for the first time.

Skerries

18 miles N of Dublin on the R127

One of the largest resorts on the northeast coast, Skerries takes it name from the islands just offshore: in Gaelic, *skerries* means 'sea rocks'. From the pretty harbour here there are boat trips to St Patrick's Island, notable for a ruined church in which a national synod was held in 1148, and to Red Island where some strange indentations in the rocks are said to be St Patrick's footprints.

Skerries Mills

Also worth visiting in the town itself are **Skerries Mills,** a complex containing a watermill, a 4- and 5-sail windmill with associated mill races, mill pond and wetlands. The history of the mills can be traced back to the early 1500s and all three have been restored to working order. The complex also includes a bakery selling bread made from the wholegrain flour ground in the mills, a tea room and craft shop.

South of Dublin

Dun Laoghaire

5 miles SE of Dublin on the N31

"Dun Leary" for English tongues; "Dun Lay-ray" for the Irish, Dun Laoghaire still retains something of its character as a Victorian resort – brightly painted houses, broad promenades and tree-lined avenues, and two piers each of which is more than a mile long. As well as being the major port of entry to the Republic, Dun Laoghaire is also Ireland's chief yachting centre with races held regularly during the summer months. For almost exactly one hundred years, it was known as Kingstown in commemoration of a visit by George IV in 1821. With the establishment of the Irish Free State the town reverted to its earlier name which refers to the 5th century High King of Tara, Laoghaire, who permitted St Patrick to begin his mission in Ireland.

The town's seafaring history is detailed in the **National Maritime Museum**, housed in the former Mariners' Church on Haigh Street. Amongst the prize exhibits are a French longboat, sent to aid the nationalist rebels but captured at Bantry Bay in 1796, and the massive old optic from the Baily Lighthouse on Howth Head.

About a mile south of Dun Laoghaire, at Sandycove, the **James Joyce Martello Tower** is an essential stop for anyone following the James Joyce trail. The tower features in the first chapter of *Ulysses* with "stately, plump Buck Mulligan" performing his morning ablutions on the open top of the tower. Mulligan is based on the Irish poet and wit, Oliver St John Gogarty, with whom Joyce spent a few days here in August

1904. His stay had been intended to be much longer but one night another guest had a nightmare and fired several shots into the fireplace of the room where they were sleeping. Gogarty then shot at a row of saucepans above Joyce's head, shouting "Leave him to me!" Joyce departed early the next morning. The tower has a small museum set up by Joyce's publisher, Sylvia Beach, which contains memorabilia of the author, amongst them his death mask and a tie given by Joyce to Samuel Beckett. On the seaward side of the tower is the Forty Foot Pool where, in *Ulysses*, Mulligan has a morning dip in the nude. The pool was for many years a men-only swimming place where nudity was the rule. Today, women can also swim here but a curt sign advises "Togs required - By Order".

A fairly recent addition to Dun Laoghaire's attractions is the **Dublin Bay Sea Thrill** which operates from the East Pier. Instead of a leisurely cruise around the bay, participants get a sea version of white water rafting on marine rescue boats. Kitted out in weatherproof sailing suits, passengers are perched on the buoyancy tubes of the boat to ensure maximum thrills. The trip lasts 40 minutes and there are departures from sunrise to sunset, 7 days a week.

Dalkey
6 miles SE of Dublin on the R119

Pronounced "Dawkey", this delightful little seaside town was the birthplace of the Elizabethan composer John Dowland who is commemorated by a statue in the park. The town also provided the material for Flann O'Brien's satirical novel *The Dalkey Archive*. Another of Ireland's great writers, George Bernard Shaw, lived at Torca Cottage on Dalkey Hill between 1866 and 1874.

MARINO HOUSE

83 Monkstown Road, Monkstown, Co. Dublin
Tel: 01 280 7520

Passengers arriving or leaving by ferry at Dun Laoghaire will find **Marino House** a particularly convenient place to stay for bed & breakfast. Anne and Richard Donnelly's home is also close to a DART railway station providing fast access to the centre of Dublin and is near a stop for the No. 7 bus to the airport.

The Donnellys are friendly and welcoming hosts who go out of their way to ensure that guests feel at home. An excellent breakfast is included in the tariff and offers extras such as freshly squeezed orange juice, home-baked bread and home-made preserves.

Nosh Restaurant

111 Coliemore Road, Dalkey, Co. Dublin
Tel: 01 284 0666 Fax: 01 281 4489
e-mail: commentsatnosh
website: www.nosh.ie

Sacha and Samantha Farrell opened their **Nosh Restaurant** in 2000 and within months had received a raft of favourable reviews and awards. All the Irish national newspapers carried very positive reviews and the restaurant was included in the Bridgestone Guide's selection of the Best 100 Restaurants in Ireland in both 2003 and 2004. The menus at Nosh are changed every 3 months but some sample dishes give an idea of the treats on offer.

At Brunch, for example, the Buttermilk Pancakes with grilled bananas and maple syrup or the Nosh Cheese Steak Sambo with Nosh chips and caramelised onions are "signature" dishes of the house. The Nosh chips, incidentally, are made with home-made fat and have become well-known for their delicious flavour.

Other notable dishes include Prawn Pil-Pils or sugar-cured Beef Bruschetta amongst the starters; and Deep fried Fish & Chips with tartare sauce or Rack of Lamb stuffed with coriander hummus, crisped potatoes with feta and black olives, and lemon salsa verde as main courses. To accompany this fine fare, there's an interesting wine list of mostly European wines with several of them also available in half bottles.

The town once had seven castles. Archibold's Castle is now the town hall and has a Visitor Centre with many exhibits relating to Dalkey's history. The most striking of these old fortresses is **Dalkey Castle,** an imposing 15th century restored castle which dominates the main street and whose battlements command magnificent views of the Wicklow Mountains. The castle houses a Gulbenkian Award-winning museum and Heritage Centre with exhibits detailing the development of the town from medieval times. The museum also hosts art, sculpture, photographic and craft exhibitions throughout the year, and entrance to the centre includes a tour around the wonderfully atmospheric 11th century church of St Begnets.

From the harbour there are boat trips to **Dalkey Island**, a treeless, low-lying island crowned by another of the Martello Towers erected to defend the realm from attack during the Napoleonic wars. There's a bird sanctuary here and the fragmentary ruins of the early Irish St Begnet's Oratory.

Just south of Dalkey is Killiney (*"kill-eye-*

Killiney Harbour

nee") where there's a public park atop **Killiney Hill** offering breathtaking views of Dublin Bay and the Wicklow Hills. You can also enjoy this stunning view by taking the DART train for the short trip from Dalkey to Bray, just over the county boundary in Co. Wicklow.

Co Galway

The second-largest county in Ireland, Galway has an unusual shape – split into two distinct parts with the great expanse of Lough Corrib almost separating them completely. Only a narrow strip of land around Galway City links the Connemara area in the west to the more extensive inland districts. For many, Connemara is archetypical Ireland, a region of magnificent scenic grandeur typified by the rocky mountain range known as the Twelve Bens. Most of the inhabitants are Irish speakers and the ancient Gaelic culture is enthusiastically preserved. To the east stretch fertile fields corralled by dry stone walls, meandering rivers and streams and the houses and castles of a bygone age.

The unofficial "capital of west Ireland", Galway City has a population of around 60,000 – almost one third of the county's inhabitants but despite the city's enormous growth over the last 20 years it has retained its intimate and friendly atmosphere. Dating back to medieval times, this fishing port, and thriving commercial and

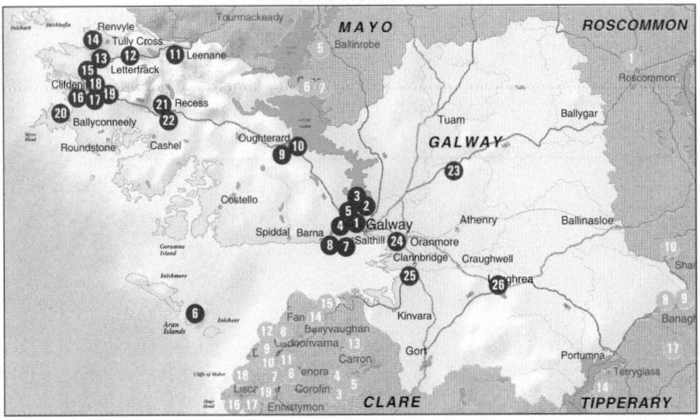

PLACES TO STAY, EAT AND DRINK

Nimmo's Restaurant & Wine Bar, Galway City	1	Bar & Restaurant	p120
Harbour Hotel, Galway City	2	Hotel	p120
Corrib Haven, Galway City	3	B&B	p121
The Malt House, Galway City	4	Restaurant	p122
The Galway Plate Restaurant, Galway City	5	Restaurant	p122
Aran Islands, Galway Bay	6	Islands	p124
Rockbarton Park Hotel, Salthill	7	Hotel	p125
Cashelmara Lodge, Salthill	8	B&B	p126
Western Star House, Oughterard	9	B&B	p127
Aughnanure Castle, Oughterard	10	Historic Building	p128
Killary Lodge, Leenane	11	Guest House	p129
Kylemore Abbey Estate, Connemara	12	Visitor Attraction	p130
Panguir Ban Restaurant, Connemara	13	Restaurant	p130

● Denotes entries in other chapters

Lough Corrib, Co Galway

cultural centre is a vibrant, cosmopolitan place where there always seems to be an event of some kind in progress.

Galway City

Despite being the third largest city in Ireland, (and blemished by some dispiriting modern development), Galway retains a village-like atmosphere, a place where everyone seems to known everyone else. As home to the National University of Ireland, a vibrant youth culture flourishes here and although Galway is not over-endowed in the way of top-flight historical sites or conventional visitor attractions, the city makes up for it by its vivacity and sense of fun. There are lively pubs, frequent concerts featuring top-calibre Irish folk groups, lots of street entertainment and a succession of popular festivals and events. The most popular of these are the 6-day Race Week at the end of July, the Galway International Oyster Festival in late September, and the Galway Arts Festival in mid-July, a two-week-long celebration of the performing and visual arts which is widely regarded as Ireland's most popular arts extravaganza. Irish literature is celebrated at the Cúirt Festival in late April; movie enthusiasts flock to the city in mid-July for the week-long Film Fleadh.

A good way to explore the city is to start by parking your car at the Eyre Square

PLACES TO STAY, EAT AND DRINK

The Olde Castle House, Connemara	14	B&B	p131
Clifden Glen Holiday Village, Connemara	15	Self Catering	p132
Mitchell's Restaurant, Connemara	16	Restaurant	p132
Connemara Country Lodge, Connemara	17	B&B	p133
Dolphin Beach Country House, Connemara	18	Guest House	p134
Lighthouse View, Connemara	19	B&B	p134
Erriseask House Hotel, Connemara	20	Hotel	p135
Lough Inagh Lodge Hotel, Connemara	21	Hotel	p137
Connemara Country Cottages, Connemara	22	Self Catering	p138
Crumlin Lodge, Tuam	23	Self Catering	p138
The Bistro, Oranmore	24	Bistro	p139
Paddy Burkes, Clarinbridge	25	Bar & Restaurant	p140
Cartron House Farm, Loughrea	26	B&B and Self Catering	p142

● Denotes entries in other chapters

Nimmo's Restaurant & Wine Bar

Long Walk, Spanish Arch, Galway City
Tel: 091 561114

Situated next to the historic city wall and the Spanish Arch, **Nimmo's Restaurant and Wine Bar** is a striking old stone building set beside the River Corrib. The views are mesmerising but the reason customers flock here is the spontaneous, creative cuisine that is hard to find these days. Owner Harriet Leander describes the style as Irish-European with the European elements inspired by Italy and Spain. Fresh fish is a speciality of the house – mussels, clams, sole, dory, wild salmon – but you'll also find game in season and chicken and red meat throughout the year. And there are always vegetarian dishes. Amongst the starters you'll find some intriguing items – curried courgette soup, warm salad with port dressing, or duck and prune pâté, for example. The restaurant is on the first floor; the ground floor is occupied by the informal wine bar with its soft blue and green floor tiles, pale lemon walls and signs from fun fairs of days long since gone. One visitor warmed to the décor with its "kitchen supplies stacked in the corners, mismatched chairs and crockery" and decided that it was "stylish-eccentric rather than ugly-eccentric (no dirt, attitude or chrome)". The wine bar is popular with local people so the atmosphere is always"raucous, fun and loveable".

Harbour Hotel

New Dock Road, Galway, Co. Galway
Tel: 091 569466 Fax: 091 569455
e-mail: bridiejoyce@harbour.ie
website: www.harbour.ie

Opened in 2001, the **Harbour Hotel** is Galway City's most contemporary and chic hotel and is located right in the heart of the City's cultural and shopping districts, adjacent to the waterfront area. With only a few minutes walk from Galway City's Train and Bus Station, the hotel provides an ideal base for shopping trips, sightseeing in Connemara or simply to get away from it all in the City of the Tribes. This stylish hotel offers 96 spacious en suite rooms, elegantly designed with crisp, warm tone furnishings and offers a sophisticated, welcoming and relaxing atmosphere with emphasis on personal service. A choice of smoking and non-smoking guestrooms are available and are all provided with ensuite facilities, direct dial telephone, fax/modem port, satellite television, trouser press, hair dryer and hospitality tray. In "Krusoes" bar and restaurant our guests can enjoy modern Irish cuisine with an Italian twist in a comfortable and lively setting. Our restaurant is fully air-conditioned.

A popular amenity at the hotel is the new exclusive Spa and Leisure Suite, which includes a state of the art gymnasium, beauty and treatment rooms, relaxing lounge area, contemporary style breakfast terrace and an elegant guest dining area. Private meetings and functions are catered for by the Harbour Hotel's boardroom and state of the art meeting rooms, which facilitate up to 80 people.

Galway City

Centre, a modern shopping centre with more than 200 different shops which, amazingly, manages to blend up-to-date shopping facilities with a respect for the past. Incorporated within the Centre is a large section of the medieval town wall, built by the Anglo-Normans who settled here on the banks of the River Corrib in the 13th century. A short walk from the Centre brings you to the **John F. Kennedy Memorial Park** where the American President addressed the people of Galway when he received the freedom of the city in 1963. Within the park are some strong iron cannons which were used in the Crimean War of 1853-6; a statue of Pádraic

O'Conaire (1882-1928) who was a pioneer of the Irish Literary Revival; and, a real oddity, the freestanding Browne Doorway. This 2-storey portal was removed here in the 1920s from an old town house and bears the arms of the Browne and Lynch families, dated 1627.

The Lynch, or Lynche, family was one of the "14 Tribes of Galway" – leading Anglo-Norman families who dominated the county in the Middle Ages and whose surnames still take up many pages of the telephone directory. The Lynch family is also recalled by **Lynch's Castle** (free) in the city centre, an imposing building with an elaborately decorated frontage which dates back to 1320 and is regarded as one of the finest medieval town houses in Ireland. It is now a branch of the Allied Irish Bank but in 1493 was the home of James Lynch Fitzstephen, Mayor of Galway. In that year the Mayor's son, Walter, was found guilty of murdering a Spanish visitor who had "made eyes" at Walter's girl friend, Agnes. As Chief Magistrate, James was forced to condemn

CORRIB HAVEN

107 Upper Newcastle, Galway City,
Co. Galway
Tel; 091 524171 Fax; 091 582414
e-mail: corribhaven@eircom.net
website: www.corribhaven.com

An attractive creeper-clad house standing in mature gardens, **Corrib Haven** offers quality bed & breakfast accommodation in a home-from-home atmosphere. Your hosts are Angela and Tom Hillary. Corrib Haven has 9 guest bedrooms, all non-smoking and with en suite facilities, TV and direct dial telephone. There are 3 double rooms on the ground floor as well as a comfortable residents' lounge where tea and coffee is available. Visa and Mastercard accepted; closed for two weeks at Christmas. Corrib Haven is situated on the N59 road to Clifden.

The Malt House

High Street, Galway City, Co. Galway
Tel: 091 567866 Fax: 091 563993
e-mail: info@malt-house.com
website: www.malt-house.com

Located right in the heart of the city, **The Malt House** is a restaurant of distinction offering top quality cuisine every lunchtime,12.30pm to 2.30pm, Monday to Saturday, and every evening from 6.30pm to 10.30pm during the high season. Owners Barry and Thérese Cunningham have won awards each year since 1999 for the outstanding food on offer, with fresh seafood, shellfish, Rack of Lamb, Duckling and vegetarian dishes always available. Not surprisingly, with such appetising fare being served, reservations are advisable at all times.

The elegant restaurant, its tables set with crisp white linen cloths and candles, is fully licensed to sell draught beer, wine and spirits. If you prefer dining earlier in the evening, The Malt House offers a special Early Bird menu which is served between 6.30pm and 7.30pm. The restaurant is just yards away from two of the city's most famous buildings: Lynch's Castle is a wonderfully preserved building with a frontage dating back to 1320 – it's generally regarded as one of the finest medieval town houses in Ireland. Nearby is St Nicholas' Church, the largest medieval church in Ireland where, it's said, Christopher Columbus prayed before starting his fateful transatlantic voyage.

The Galway Plate Restaurant

Tuam Road, Galway City, Co. Galway
Tel: 091 770589 Fax: 091 773549

Kieran Nolan's love affair with food began when he started working in the kitchen of the GBC where his father was Head Chef and his mother manageress. That experience, and a period working in Australian restaurants, provided good training for when he opened **The Galway Plate Restaurant** which has quickly established itself as one of the city's most satisfying eating places. Kieran's comprehensive menu changes regularly but always has something for everyone – traditional dishes such as Roast Rib of Beef, Roast Chicken with all the trimmings, steaks and seafood, as well as vegetarian options like Spaghetti Ragu.

Amongst the starters you may well find Crispy Potato Skins with Mozzarella cheese & bacon topping, or a Spicy Chicken Salad with sweet chilli dressing. Save some room for one of the memorable home-made desserts – tiramisu perhaps, Warm Apple Crumble & Ice Cream or Carrot & Walnut Cake with a mango coulis. To accompany your meal there's an extensive choice of wines, beers or coffee. Kieran also offers an All Day Breakfast, a sandwich bar and snackfood, and a Carvery every day from noon until 3pm. Wheelchair-friendly, the restaurant is open from 8.30am to 9.30 or 10pm, every day.

Walter to death and when no-one could be found to carry out the sentence, the Mayor hanged his own son himself. A broken man, he retired into seclusion and died soon afterwards. Some historians dispute that this tragic event ever took place but the story is now firmly embedded in Galway's folk lore.

Mayor Lynch's tomb can be seen in **St Nicholas' Church**, a couple of hundred yards from Lynch's Castle. It's the largest medieval parish church in Ireland and an enduring tradition asserts that Christopher Columbus prayed here before crossing the Atlantic. The church is dedicated to St Nicholas of Myra, better known now as Santa Claus, but in those days much more important as the patron saint of sailors. Whether Columbus prayed here or not, it is a fact that a Galway man named Rice de Culvy did accompany the great explorer on his pioneering voyage. Above the entrance porch of the church there's a tiny room which was formerly used as the living quarters for the sexton – the last sexton to live here shared the cramped accommodation with his wife and eight children.

Spanish Arch

Just around the corner from St Nicholas' Church, number 8, Bowling Green Lane was the **Home of Nora Barnacle**, the fiery-tempered, auburn haired woman who married the novelist James Joyce in 1931. Joyce regularly visited the tiny house where she grew up and the small museum here contains, amongst other Joycean memorabilia, copies of the letters they wrote to each other.

A short walk from Nora Barnacle's house leads to the riverside and one of the city's most historic landmarks, the **Spanish Arch**. This rather plain but functional building dates back to the 1500s when it was used to store barrels of wine and rum being offloaded from Spanish galleons. The Arch leads to the famous Long Walk where in times past Galway gentryfolk strolled along the river bank.

If you follow this riverside walk and cross the Salmon Weir Bridge you will come to the **Cathedral of Our Lady Assumed into Heaven and St Nicholas,** a bleak 1960s construction whose limestone walls are streaked with green copper stains drifting down from its dome. The interior, with its overly lavish use of Connemara marble, has been described as having the spiritual impact of a hypermarket. Nearby are two buildings that are much easier on the eye – the Neoclassical courthouse and the municipal theatre.

Another popular attraction is the **Galway Irish Crystal Heritage Centre** on Dublin Road where visitors can watch mastercutters creating intricate designs. Housed in an imposing Georgian mansion, the Centre has a showroom displaying a dazzling range of Galway Irish Crystal, Belleek Pottery and Aynsley China, and offers an audio-visual presentation, City of the Tribes. Guided Heritage Tours are available and there's also a spacious restaurant. Amongst the centre's exhibits depicting old Galway, one of the most interesting tells the story of Claddagh

ARAN ISLANDS

Galway Bay, Co. Galway

The **Aran Islands** lie about 30 miles out in Galway Bay. The three islands, Inishmore, Inishmaan and Inisheer, are unique in their archaeology, in their Celtic and early Christian heritage and in their landscape, which is akin to the stark limestone moonscapes of the Burren in County Clare. The other-worldly nature of the

sea. The fort's three concentric ramparts are 18ft high and 13ft deep; their precise age and purpose still a mystery. **Dún Chonchúir** on Inishmaan is dramatically sited on the highest point on the island and has been vaguely dated to somewhere between AD 100 and AD 700. The great oval wall is 18ft high and 16ft deep and remarkably well-preserved.

In addition to the Galway ferry, the islands can be reached by ferries from Doolin in County Clare and by air from the airstrip near Inveran on the Galway coast. All forms of transport are dependent on the west coast's unpredictable weather.

islands is enhanced by the fact that most of the 1,500 islanders speak Gaelic as their native tongue. They still use the traditional canvas-covered boats, *curraghs*, for fishing and for access to the smaller islands where the ferry cannot dock.

At the **Aran Heritage Centre** (Ionad Arann) in Kilronan, visitors can watch the ground-breaking documentary film *Man of Aran,* produced in 1934 by Robert Flaherty. This historic film amazed cinemagoers of the period with its stark portrait of the primitive way of life endured by the remote islanders.

The island's prehistoric sites are too numerous to detail here but there are at least two that should not be missed. **Dún Aengus** on Inishmore is a spectacular ring fort covering about 11 acres and perched on the edge of cliffs that plummet 300ft into the

Village which was here long before the present town grew up alongside it. **Claddagh** lies to the south of the city and at one time had its own laws, ruler, customs, dress and a thriving economy based on fishing using the Galway Hookers. These distinctive vessels are still built here but are now mostly used for pleasure boating rather than fishing. The village is known to Irish people around the world as the originator of the traditional Claddagh Ring which shows two hands – the symbol of friendship – holding a heart, the symbol of love. Some seventy years ago, Claddagh Village was a picturesque huddle of thatched cottages but in 1937 these were demolished to provide modern housing. Fortunately, some lively bars and value-for-money eating places have survived.

To the east of the Spanish Arch is the harbour where you can catch one of the regular ferries to the famous Aran Islands (see panel opposite).

Around Galway City

Salthill

1 mile S of Galway City on the R338

Salthill is Galway City's seaside suburb, one of Ireland's leading resorts. It offers a promenade 2½ miles long, good bathing, sailing, band concerts, amusements and a huge entertainment complex, **Leisureland,** providing a wide range of all-weather activities including a 65 metre waterslide. At the **Galway Atlantaquaria**, the National Aquarium of Ireland, visitors can follow the trail of the famed Galway Salmon, the bradán, on its journey from the Corrib River to Galway Bay and beyond. The many exhibits here display native Irish aquatic life in a manner that reflects their natural habitat. The complex includes the Lighthouse Café, which looks onto Galway Bay, and the Mermaid's Gift Shop. Multiple same day entry is permitted

Rockbarton Park Hotel

Rockbarton Park, Salthill, Co. Galway
Tel: 091 522018 / 091 522286
Fax: 091 527692
e-mail: tysonshotel@eircom.net
website: www.travel-ireland.com/irl/rckbrton.htm

Although only two minutes walk from the shore of Galway Bay and a short stroll from the Leisureland entertainment complex, **Rockbarton Park Hotel** enjoys a secluded quiet residential location. This friendly, welcoming hotel is owned and run by Terry and Patricia Tyson who have been dispensing hospitality to locals and visitors in Galway for more than 30 years. During that time they have established the hotel restaurant as one of the finest in Galway, noted for its fine cuisine and fish specialities. The fully licensed restaurant also caters for intimate family weddings or private parties of around 50 people.

Accommodation at Rockbarton Park comprises 11 rooms, all of which have private bath or shower and toilet; telephone and television. Registered with the Irish Tourist Board and AA Approved, the hotel has its own private car park and is within easy reach of a wide range of attractions. Lough Corrib, one of Europe's finest fishing lakes, is about 3 miles away; there's a championship golf course a few minutes walk from the hotel; good stables close by with trekking available; and a day's shooting can be arranged for small parties. The hotel is also an ideal base for those attending conferences and exhibitions at the nearby Galway Conference Centre.

Cashelmara Lodge

3 Cashelmara, Knocknacarra Cross, Salthill, Galway City
Tel: 091 520020
e-mail: cashelmara@eircom.net
website: www.galway.net/pages/cashelmara

Situated on the scenic Coast Road 5 minutes from Galway City and at the gateway to Connemara, **Cashelmara Lodge** is one of the most opulently appointed houses in the county. It occupies a superb position overlooking beautiful Galway Bay with long sandy beaches, swimming pool and watersports nearby. A particularly popular feature of the Lodge is the large balcony where guests can relax and unwind on those long summer evenings and listen to the natural stone waterfall in the front garden. The interior is quite breathtaking with its elegant furnishings and decorations, lavishly laid out and comfortable throughout.

Each of the luxurious en suite bedrooms features top quality fabrics, multi-channel television, hairdryer, tea/coffee-making facilities and direct dial phones. There's a stylish dining room where breakfast is served and your charming hostess, Christina Fahey, will do her utmost to ensure your stay is both a relaxed and enjoyable one. As well as being an ideal base for touring Connemara, the Aran Islands and Galway City, the Lodge is close to a huge range of amenities – there are riding stables nearby; a golf driving range just a 2-minute walk away while a 10-minute walk will bring you to Galway Golf Club. Galway Aquarium is also in easy walking distance and there's a tennis club only a 5-minute drive away.

and a Family Fun Day ticket which also gives admittance to nearby Leisureland. Salthill's spacious sandy beaches are rarely crowded and they enjoy splendid views across the sparkling bay to the Burren hills of County Clare. Perhaps the most appealing of the beaches are Silver Strand to the west, and Ballyloughrun to the east.

Barna Village (Bearna)

5 miles W of Galway on the R336

An excellent way of exploring Connemara is to follow the Great Figure Eight Tour, a 150 mile drive that describes a figure-of-eight through one of the most beautiful regions of Ireland and also one of the most barren. Much of it lies in the Gaeltacht area where Irish is still spoken so be prepared for road and town signs in Gaelic and for the fact that the spelling of Gaelic words is highly variable. Beginning the tour at Salthill and travelling westward, the first place of note is the picturesque little fishing village and resort of Barna – or *Bearna* since this village is part of the Gaeltacht.

Spiddal (An Spidéal)

10 miles W of Galway on the R336

The small coastal town of Spiddal is a charming little holiday resort with a fine sandy Blue Flag beach. It lies in the heart of the Gaeltacht and has some lively pubs and a **Craft Centre** where craftspeople from 8 workshops produce some top quality sculpture, ceramics, candles, fabrics and jewellery.

From Spiddal the Figure Eight Tour continues along the coast as far as the little airport at Inveran (which has regular flights to the Aran Islands) and then turns inland to the village of Casla (*Costello* in Gaelic), home to the Gaelic radio station *Raidió na Gaeltachta* and the recently opened Tropical Butterfly Centre. North of Casla the route passes through wild and scenic countryside to Maam Cross, the crossover point of the figure-of-eight which has been dubbed the "Piccadilly Circus of Connemara". The drive continues northwards through the beautiful Maam Valley to the area known as Joyce Country – nothing to do with the great novelist but named after the Joyce family who settled here in the 13th century and whose name is still common in the district.

excellent salmon fishing river. From Rossaveel, just down the road, there are regular passenger ferries to the Aran Islands and, in the hamlet of Rosmuc near Carraroe, **Pádraig Pearse's Cottage**. The poet, dramatist and patriot built the cottage himself in the traditional style as testimony to his belief in Irish language and culture. During the Easter Rising of 1916 he was Commander in Chief of the Irish Republican forces but after a week of fighting he and his troops surrendered. Pearse was court-martialled and executed.

The coastline near Costello is deeply indented and scores of small, low-lying islands speckle the bays. The area is very sparsely inhabited with just a scattering of isolated houses and farmsteads, ideal if you are looking for peace and solitude.

Costello (Casla)

22 miles W of Galway on the R336

Costello boasts a lovely coral beach and an

Oughterard

14 miles NW of Galway on the N59

Lying a mile or so inland from Lough

WESTERN STAR HOUSE

Rosscahill, Oughterard, Co. Galway
Tel: 091 550162
e-mail: westernstar@eircom.net

Ideally located on the N59, about 12 miles west of Galway City, **Western Star House** provides a perfect base for exploring the scenic glories of Connemara. This award-winning country house, surrounded by beautifully maintained landscaped gardens, has recently been refurbished and upgraded to provide maximum comfort and a warm and homely atmosphere. There's a spacious guest television lounge with quality furnishings and decorations, and an elegant dining room overlooking the delightful gardens. Owner Teresa Hession has added an unusual amenity in the form of a purpose built art and craft studio where guests can paint.

For more information on the many courses available please contact Teresa on the above telephone number. Western Star House has 8 beautifully

appointed guest bedrooms, all of them with en suite facilities, and the excellent breakfast included in the tariff offers a wide choice to suit all tastes. Guests will also find an extensive range of activities available nearby. There are many quality golf courses to choose from; fishing for salmon and trout on Lough Corrib; hill and forest walks; horse riding; cruises on Lough Corrib; day trips to Connemara National Park, Kylemore Abbey or Aughnanure Castle, and much, much more.

Carrib, Oughterard is a major centre for anglers. There are plenty of boats available to rent either for fishing or to visit the uninhabited islet of **Inchagoill** in the centre of the lough. It has two ruined churches – St Patrick's, believed to date back to the 5th century, and the 12th century *Teampall na Naomh* (Church of the Saints) which has an impressive Romanesque doorway and some interesting carvings. Outside, the 3 foot high Lia Luguaedon Mac Menueh (Stone of Luguaedon, son of Menueh) is believed to bear the oldest Latin inscription of Christian origin in Europe. The atmosphere on the island is quite magical.

Aughnanure Castle

Oughterard, Connemara, Co. Galway

A couple of miles east of Oughterard, **Aughnanure Castle** is a 6-storey tower house occupying a daunting position on a rocky island surrounded by a fast flowing stream. In the 1500s it was the main stronghold of the O'Flahertys and said to be one of the strongest fortresses at the time Cromwell was blockading Galway. Visitors to the castle are shown an interesting device constructed by the O'Flahertys to deal with unwelcome visitors. In the main hall, one of the flagstones was hinged downward so that any offending characters could be tipped into the stream below. The hall has followed the same route, collapsing over the years into the rushing water, but the rest of the castle has been restored and is open daily throughout the season. At other times, the key can be collected from the caretaker.

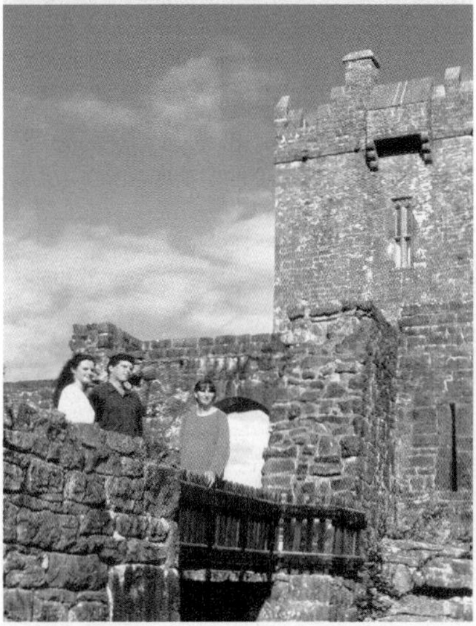

Back on the mainland, **Glengowla Silver & Lead Mine** is Ireland's only show mine. Opened in the 19th century, the mine was one of the richest and most productive of its time. Visitors are taken to a depth of 65 feet underground and guided through the large marble chambers and caverns where the walls glitter with quartz, silver, lead, calcite and other mineral formations. On the surface, the Visitor Centre contains many specimens of minerals from the mine, a restored Agent's Cottage, a Gunpowder House and a Winding Stow.

A couple of miles east of Oughterard, **Aughnanure Castle** is a 6-storey tower house occupying a daunting position on a rocky island surrounded by a fast flowing stream (see panel opposite).

Leenane

41 miles NW of Galway on the N59/R336

The attractive village of Leenane is an angling resort, a centre for climbers tackling the nearby Maamturk Mountains, and perhaps best known as the main location for the 1990 film *The Field*, starring Richard Harris and John Hurt. The **Leenane Cultural Centre,** overlooking the harbour at Killary, interprets the local sheep and wool industry by means of demonstrations of carding, spinning, weaving and the use of natural dyes. A continuous audio-visual display introduces visitors to such topics as the 20 different breeds of sheep that graze on the lands around the centre. Other amenities include a wool craft shop and a restaurant. Nearby, you can take a 90-minute cruise around Killary Harbour,

Killary Lodge

Leenane, Co. Galway
Tel: 095 42276 Fax: 095 42314
e-mail: lodge@killary.com
website: www.killary.com

Originally built in 1852 as a hunting and fishing lodge for the Lambert family, **Killary Lodge** was fully renovated in 1989 and now provides a base from which discerning travellers can experience the glorious scenery of Connemara and the splendour of Ireland's only fjord, the Killary. The Lodge stands overlooking the harbour with views across the water to Mweelrea mountain, Connemara's highest peak. This area has been aptly described as combining "two extremes of scenery; grand, solitary savageness and minute, verdant beauty". Owner Kathy Evans describes the Lodge as a place that combines "simple, old-fashioned hospitality with an atmosphere of unhurried calm".

Guests can choose to relax and unwind by the water's edge or explore the surroundings with a choice of activities to suit all tastes. The friendly and courteous staff at the Lodge come from a variety of backgrounds and cultures and are always ready to assist guests when required whether they wish to explore the region by foot, mountain bike, catamaran or even helicopter! They can provide access to all the necessary equipment and expertise to whatever level required. The Lodge's unique combination of location and old-fashioned hospitality has ensured that many guests come back to stay here again which, as Kathy says, "is the ultimate compliment!"

which is actually an 8-mile long waterway flanked by bare mountains and is Ireland's only fjord.

Killary Harbour, nr Leenane

Connemara

Letterfrack

52 miles NW of Galway on the N59

West of Leenane the route passes **Kylemore Abbey** (see panel on page 130), a 19th century mock-Tudor extravaganza of towers and turrets erected by an English shipping magnate and enjoying a spectacular lakeside location.

About 4 miles further west at the quiet village of Letterfrack is the entrance to the **Connemara National Park,** a wild expanse of bog, heath and granite mountains which includes part of the famous Twelve Bens range of mountains. The Park's Visitor Centre has copious information about the fauna, flora and geology of the area, and the helpful staff can guide you to safe hiking trails in this potentially dangerous terrain. Free guided nature walks lasting 2 to 3 hours are available on Monday and Friday mornings in July and August.

Kylemore Abbey Estate

Connemara, Co. Galway
Tel: 095 41146 Fax: 095 41145
e-mail: info@kylemoreabbey.ie

Kylemore Abbey Estate, set in the heart of the Connemara Mountains, is the home of the Irish Benedictine Nuns since 1920. Famous as an international boarding school it is equally famous as a premier tourist attraction thanks to the beautiful surroundings, the splendid neo- gothic church, one of the finest craft shops, an excellent restaurant and last but not least, the Victorian Walled Garden. The castle was built in 1868 and is one of the great Baronial castles of this period remaining in Ireland today. An exhibition of the history is on view in the restored reception rooms at the Abbey which have been opened to the public. One of the major attractions at Kylemore is the restored neo-gothic church (circa 1870). Described as a 'cathedral in miniature' the church has impressive stained glass windows, columns of colourful marble and intricate stone carvings throughout.

The Victorian Walled Garden is an impressive six acre walled garden. Most of its features and buildings have been restored like the formal flower and kitchen garden, borders and walks, head gardeners house, bothy and toolshed. Two of the original range of seventeen glasshouses, have been restored (one open to the public). A visit to Kylemore Abbey will not be complete without visiting the craft shop and the restaurant where quality Irish products and home-made food are on sale. Many products are unique to Kylemore, like the home-made jams and jellies and the Kylemore Abbey pottery. A visit to Connemara is not complete without visiting Kylemore Abbey and Garden.

Pangur Bán Restaurant

Letterfrack, Connemara, Co. Galway
Tel: 095 41243
e-mail: pban@indigo.ie
website: www.pangurban.com

Extremely popular with both locals and visitors alike, the **Pangur Bán Restaurant** occupies a delightful picture-postcard thatched cottage in the Connemara village of Letterfrack. The 300-year-old stone cottage has been beautifully restored and furnished in traditional style, and an open fire adds to the cosy cottage feeling.

If the building is distinctive so is the cuisine on offer. Owners John Walsh and Mairead Tucker-Mamalis believe that "an adventurous use of the world's more exotic flavours and an abundance of fresh, local produce combine well to set us apart". They are confident that once tempted inside, you'll find it difficult not to fall under the spell of the innovative cooking and friendly, informal ambience. Their menu changes regularly but fresh seafood dishes are perennially popular, as are the succulent, locally-sourced steaks. The choice of dishes is extensive, with something to gratify every palate. Pangur Bán is open for dinner, opening times vary so please contact them, to find it, just follow the distinctive blue signs from Clifden or Kylemore. After sampling the outstanding fare on offer here, you may well be interested in enrolling in the Pangur Bán's Cookery School – the first such school to be established in Connemara.

In Letterfrack itself, scenic and wildlife cruises, and short sea angling trips can be arranged through the **Ocean's Alive Sealife Centre**. Their cruiser has an upper deck seated area with telescopic stands, ideal for viewing the surrounding mountains, amongst them the famous Twelve Bens. The centre also contains an aquarium and maritime museum.

Tully Cross

6 miles N of Letterfrack on minor road off the N59

Tully Cross stands on the Renvyle Peninsula, a remote promontory which has been described as "the loveliest landscape on earth". Bounded by the Twelve Bens mountains, Killary fjord and the Atlantic, its isolation has spared Renvyle from the worst excesses of modernisation. Signs of prehistoric occupation, on the other hand, are commonplace – ancient forts, tombs, standing stones and shell middens. Also evident is the legacy of 19th century poverty and emigration – famine burial grounds and the ruins of deserted villages.

On a more positive note, a strong tradition of music, song and dance still flourishes here, both in the local pubs and also in the community-owned Teach Ceoil, the 'House of Music'.

Renvyle

10 miles NW of Letterfrack off the N59

The distinguished writer and surgeon Oliver St John Gogarty (1878-1957) described this area as the *"faery land of Connemara at the extreme end of Europe where the incongruous flowed together at last and the sweet and bitter blended"*. Gogarty lived at Renvyle House where he entertained other literary luminaries of the day such as Yeats, Shaw and AE (George Russell). Renvyle House is now a hotel.

The Olde Castle House

Curragh, Renvyle, Connemara, Co. Galway
Tel: 045 43460
e-mail: oldecastle@hotmail.com

"The only problem about visiting Connemara is that you'll probably want to stay for ever". That's especially true if you are staying at the Davin family bed & breakfast establishment, **The Olde Castle House**, located at the tip of the picturesque Renvyle Peninsula. The gleaming white-washed building stands beside a 15th century castle looking out across the Atlantic Ocean, a superb setting that attracted the director of the famous French film *The Purple Taxi* which features the house and surrounding area. Guests at The Olde Castle can relax in the cosy lounge with its turf fire, TV and a selection of old books and information about local places of interest.

At breakfast time you can enjoy your full Irish breakfast while enjoying grand views through the large picture windows of the breathtaking scenery of the Mountains of Mweelrea and Croagh Patrick. Evening meals are available on request – just inform the family before noon so that fresh ingredients can be bought in. The Olde Castle can accommodate up to 12 guests in the 6 charming bedrooms, 5 of which have en suite facilities, the other has a private bathroom. The Olde Castle is open from early March until the end of October.

Clifden Glen Holiday Village

Clifden Glen, Clifden, Co. Galway
Tel: 095 21401 Fax: 095 21818
e-mail: clifglen@eircom.net
website: www.clifdenglen.com

John Baragwanath and Balithin de Sachy run the unique **Clifden Glen Holiday Village** set on a 210-acre private estate in the heart of Connemara just one mile outside the town of Clifden. Guests have a choice of accommodation: 4-star self-catering lodges with all the conveniences of home, or luxury ApartHotel cottage suites providing accommodation on a B&B, full or half board basis. Each of the lodges has an en suite double bedroom; two more bedrooms sharing a bathroom; and a large, comprehensively equipped living/dining area. There are 44 ApartHotels – semi-detached cottage suites standing on the banks of the Owenglen river. Each comprises an en suite bedroom and an open plan living area with TV, phone, fridge and many other accessories.

Also on the estate are a traditional Irish pub with evening entertainment, a restaurant serving top quality cuisine, three tennis courts, crazy golf, croquet, boules, football pitch and a children's play area. There are some lovely walks in the area – to the Owenglen salmon spate river, for example – and facilities for cycle hire, horse riding, golf, sea fishing and scuba diving are all available locally. A special weekly rate for holiday village residents is available at the luxury all-weather leisure centre at Station House Hotel in Clifden.

Mitchell's Restaurant

Market Street, Clifden, Connemara,
Co. Galway
Tel: 095 21867
Fax: 095 21770

Located right in the heart of this attractive little town, **Mitchell's Restaurant** is one of the most popular in Clifden, patronised by locals and visitors alike. Elegant and stylish, the 75-seater restaurant is owned and run by JJ Mitchell who offers his customers an extensive menu of uncomplicated and appetising dishes which is available throughout the day.

Seafood is the speciality of the house with specials of the day based on the latest fresh catch. Mitchell's is fully licensed and has an especially interesting wine list with well-chosen varieties from all around the world.

Clifden

10 miles S of Letterfrack on the N59

Clifden

The main town of Connemara, (although with a population of little more than 1000), Clifden is beautifully set on the edge of the Atlantic with the elegant spires of its two churches rising against a magnificent backdrop of the Twelve Bens mountains. The well-planned town was founded in 1812 and today it's the centre of Connemara pony breeding. The annual **Connemara Pony Show,** on the third Thursday of August, is the main event in the Clifden calendar, although the lively arts festival in the last week of September is increasingly popular.

It was near Clifden that the pioneer aviators Alcock and Brown landed after completing the first ever non-stop transatlantic flight in June 1919. Flying a converted Vickers Vimy bomber, they were in the air for 16 hours 27 minutes. The **Alcock & Brown Memorial,** 4 miles south of the town, takes the form of a huge aeroplane wing carved in limestone and emerging from the bog.

About 3 miles east of Clifden, at **Lettershea, Dan O'Hara's Homestead** is the restored cottage of Dan O'Hara, a man made famous in song and story. A tenant farmer, he was evicted from his home in

Connemara Country Lodge

Westport Road, Clifden, Connemara,
Co. Galway
Tel/Fax: 095 21122
e-mail: connemara@unison.ie
website: www.bedandbreakfastgalway.com

Bed & breakfast with music is the unusual combination on offer at the **Connemara Country Lodge.** This spacious house, set in 2 acres of extremely peaceful grounds, is the home of Mary Corbett, an accomplished violinist and singer who will not only sing for your breakfast but also arranges Irish song and dance evenings for her guests. The multi-talented Mary, who also speaks no fewer than 4 languages, bakes all her own various breads and scones which are served to her guests each morning. A friendly and welcoming host, Mary makes every effort to ensure that a stay here will be a memorable one. Open all year with private car park.

Mary also owns and runs the Connemara Woollen Mills Craft Shop, right next door. Housed in a delightful two-storey thatched cottage, this is every shopper's dream – packed full of all kind of beautiful sweaters including Aran and machine knits. The selection is unbelievable: there are sweaters hand-knitted in local homes together with matching scarves and caps, and Aran sweaters in every colour imaginable. Other choices include sweaters in merino wool and lambswool, all at extremely good prices. The shop is open daily from 9.30am to 7pm (8pm in July and August); mail order available.

Dolphin Beach Country House

Lower Sky Road, Clifden, Connemara,
Co. Galway
Tel: 095 21204 Fax: 095 22935
e-mail: dolphinbeach@iolfree.ie
website: www.connemara.net/dolphinbeachhouse

Originally a Connemara homestead/farmhouse dating back to the early 1800s, **Dolphin Beach Country House** belongs to a family whose hotel pedigree is almost without equal in Ireland. The house enjoys a superb position, surrounded by 14 acres of wilderness and with a beach providing very safe swimming just a short walk through the gardens. Few country houses can boast of having the Atlantic Ocean at the foot of their garden – the atmosphere here is idyllic with no music or noise other than the rhythmic soughing of the sea.

The house itself has been extensively refurbished and now comprises of the original house with newly built bedrooms. All of these have been finished to a very high standard with high ceilings, wooden floors, modern bathrooms and underfloor heating. The dining room has large picture windows looking out to sea and an attractive décor of warm-coloured pine set off by the crisp blue and white linen tablecloths. The cuisine here concentrates on simply prepared dishes based on local ingredients. All vegetables served are organically grown and there's a plentiful supply of free-range eggs from their ducks and chickens.

Lighthouse View

Sky Road, Clifden, Connemara, Co. Galway
Tel/Fax: 095 22113
e-mail: lighthouseview@eircom.net
website: www.lighthouseview.com

The Sky Road, running north-westwards from Clifden, is famous for its spectacular views and it's about a mile along this road that you'll find **Lighthouse View,** Jane Andrews friendly family-run bed and breakfast establishment. Enjoying glorious views, the house stands across the road from Clifden Castle and in addition to welcoming human guests also has 3 dog runs so you can bring your pet with you if you wish. Jane also breeds the famous Connemara ponies whose annual Pony show takes place in Clifden on the third Thursday in August.

Jane is an enthusiastic cook so breakfast here is definitely rather special – to accompany the good choice of breakfast fare, for example, you'll find delicious freshly-baked soda bread. Registered with Bord Fáilte, Lighthouse View has 4 guest bedrooms – 2 doubles, 1 twin and 1 family room that can sleep up to 4 people. All the rooms are attractively furnished and decorated, non-smoking, and provided with en suite facilities, hairdryer and hospitality tray, the family room also has a TV. The house has a private car park and credit cards and vouchers are accepted.

1845 and forced to emigrate. During the voyage to America he lost his wife and three of his children; arriving penniless in New York he was reduced to selling matches on the street. His 8-acre holding is farmed as it would have been in pre-famine times. An old style pony and trap takes visitors on a guided tour and in addition to Dan's humble cottage the site includes a visitor centre with an audio-visual presentation; reconstructions of a *crannóg*, (a prehistoric lake dwelling), a ring fort and a *clachaun* (an early Christian oratory); a large craft shop and a tea room. Also on site is an art gallery displaying many interesting works by up-and-coming Irish artists.

About 6 miles northwest of Clifden, the pleasant seaside village of **Cleggan** is the departure point for the 30-minute trip to **Inishbofin Island,** a journey during which your boat is likely to be accompanied by colonies of local seals or dolphins. A full commentary is provided during the trip and

guided walks exploring the fertile island and its sheltered sandy beaches are also available. The island, 4 miles long and less than 2 miles wide, has a resident population of about 200 and a wealth of historical sites, most notably the ruins of the 13th century St Colman's Abbey and the remains of a star-shaped Cromwellian Barracks. A horrible story from Cromwell's time is attached to **Bishop's Rock** which is only visible in the harbour at low tide. Cromwell used Inishbofin Island to sequester priests and other 'rebels'. He had one of them chained to the rock and watched with his troops as the incoming tide drowned the poor man.

Ballyconneely

6 miles S of Clifden on the R341

Ballyconneely lies on the coastal road around the southwest corner of Connemara, a route known locally as the "brandy and soda road" because the sea breezes here are

ERRISEASK HOUSE HOTEL & RESTAURANT

Ballyconneely, Connemara, Co. Galway
Tel: 095 23553 Fax: 095 23639
e-mail: info@erriseask.com
website: www.erriseask.com

Located on the remote and beautiful western edge of Connemara, **Erriseask House Hotel & Restaurant** is probably one of the nicest family run hotels in the west of Ireland. It enjoys a superb position on the edge of the wild Atlantic Ocean with its own private beach and mature gardens. Some of the guest rooms have their own private sitting room and balcony commanding splendid views of Mannin Bay and the Twelve Bens Mountains. There are 12 guest rooms in all, including 5 superior demi-suites with en suite facilities (including power showers) and separate sitting areas in split-level rooms overlooking the bay.

Each tastefully decorated room is provided with multi-channel TV, direct dial telephone and hospitality tray. Seven standard bedrooms are also available. The hotel's restaurant is noted for its fresh seafood, poultry and dairy dishes, all based on local produce – Connemara Oysters on Crushed Ice, for example, or Barbary Duck in Five Spices. The restaurant is open between 6.30pm and 9.30pm for both residents and non-residents, and in addition to the à la carte menu, a Bar Menu is also available. The restaurant also serves Sunday lunch all year round and is especially experienced in catering for family functions such as birthdays or christenings and other small private functions.

Roundstone Harbour

so inspiriting. The village stands close to Mannin Bay, a broad, square inlet noted for its Coral Strand. It's not actually coral at all but the debris of a seaweed that dries and disintegrates into a substance that looks just like white sand.

Roundstone

15 miles SE of Clifden on the R341

A delightful little fishing village with a picturesque harbour and a clutch of art and craft workshops, Roundstone sits at the foot of Errisberg mountain. A couple of hours undemanding walking will take you to the top and to some wonderful views. To the south stretches the fretted coastline; to the west lie a string of brilliantly white sandy beaches; northwards the bleak wastes of **Roundstone Bog** extend towards the Connemara mountains.

The low-lying blanket bog, dimpled by a hundred little lakes, is crossed by a single road, more of a track really. Some local people refuse to pass along it, especially at night. Many years ago, it seems, two old ladies lived in the only house along this road. A benighted traveller took refuge there, only to be robbed and murdered. His ghost is said to haunt the lonely road.

Best to avoid that road then and make for Roundstone's local beaches, Gurteen and Dog's Bay, which are both totally unspoilt and rank amongst the most beautiful beaches in Europe.

An unusual attraction in the village itself is the workshop of **Malachy Kearns,** a master craftsman who makes bodhráns, the distinctive Irish drum made with a birch frame and goatskin. Visitors can exercise their own percussion skills in the testing room and the centre, housed in a former Franciscan monastery, also has a crafts shop, record store and coffee shop.

Cashel

18 miles SE of Clifden on the R342

Not to be confused with the great religious centre in Co. Tipperary, Galway's Cashel is a popular angling centre located at the head of Bertraghboy Bay. Here, traditional fishing boats, *curraghs*, are used not just for fishing but also for towing *climains* –great tangled fronds of seaweed on their way to the processing factory at Kilkerrin.

Bertraghboy Bay is a breeding ground for common seals which can often be seen sunning themselves on the rocky shoreline. Further out, there are regular sightings of dolphins and porpoises disporting themselves in the waves.

Small though it is, Cashel boasts two hotels of interest. The Zetland Hotel, originally the Viceroy's Rest, was renamed in honour of the Earl of Zetland, Lord Lieutenant of Ireland, who often stayed here between 1880 and 1890. An even more famous guest was Gugliemo Marconi who experimented with a radio mast on nearby Leithenach Mor Hill before settling on a site near Clifden for his transatlantic radio station.

Cashel House Hotel was built in 1847 and became a hotel in 1967. The star name in its Visitors' Book is that of General Charles de Gaulle who stayed here on holiday in 1969.

Traditional Sailing Boats, Bertraghboy Bay

Recess

18 miles E of Clifden on the N59

Recess is one of Connemara's most famous beauty spots, set amidst wonderful lake and mountain scenery with Glendalough Lake on one side, Derryclare Lough on the other. East of Recess, the Great Figure Eight Tour passes through some of the best scenery in Connemara. The road skirts the shores of

Lough Inagh Lodge Hotel

Inagh Valley, Recess, Connemara, Co. Galway
Tel: 095 34706 Fax: 095 34708
e-mail: inagh@iol.ie
website: www.loughinaghlodgehotel.ie

Built in the 1880s as a fishing lodge, **Lough Inagh Lodge Hotel** occupies a spectacular position on the shore of one of Connemara's most beautiful lakes, framed by a backdrop of magnificent mountains. Open log fires in the library and an oak-panelled bar intensify the country house atmosphere; guests can also relax in a charming sitting room with morning coffee or afternoon tea. In the elegant restaurant, specialities of the house such as seafood and wild game dishes are complemented by an outstanding wine list. The accommodation at the Lodge maintains the same high standards.

All of the 12 beautifully furnished en suite bedrooms (5 deluxe and 7 superior) enjoy marvellous views over Lough Inagh to the Twelve Bens Mountains. Each room is provided with a television set, a comfortable seating area and a separate dressing room. Pets are welcome – there are some lovely walks in the area that even their owners might enjoy! The Lodge is a perfect base from which to explore magical Connemara with the Twelve Bens Mountains, the Connemara National Park and Kylemore Abbey all within easy reach. And if you enjoy being active on holiday, facilities for fishing, shooting, golf, hill-walking and pony trekking are all close by.

Connemara Country Cottages

Leam East, Recess, Connemara, Co. Galway
Tel: 091 552514 Fax: 091 552976

Set deep in the glorious Connemara countryside with its miles of rolling hills and mysterious peat bogs, **Connemara Country Cottages** provide the perfect place for a peaceful and relaxing holiday. Holiday-makers have the choice of either renting a cottage or purchasing one or more weeks stay through a Timeshare arrangement. The 6 attractive thatched buildings stand on a hillside enjoying wonderful panoramic views of one of the few remaining unspoilt corners of Europe.

The 2- or 3-bedroomed cottages have been built to international timeshare standards and all are centrally heated, fully carpeted, and include a modern fitted kitchen, 2 bathrooms with shower and a lounge/dining room with furniture made from natural wood, a TV/video and many other amenities. The cottages even have their own sauna. The spacious lounge has a high panelled ceiling, an open fire crowned with a copper canopy and flanked by baskets for peat and kindling. In the kitchen you'll find a dishwasher, mixer, fridge/freezer, robot chef and just about every utensil you are ever likely to use. There's also an outhouse with washing machine and dryer. Those who choose the Timeshare option can exchange their Connemara week(s) for holidays elsewhere through Resort Condominium International which links Timeshare owners worldwide.

Crumlin Lodge

Crumlin Bridge, Ballyglunin, Tuam,
Co. Galway
Tel: 093 43703
e-mail: info@crumlinlodge.com
website: www.crumlinlodge.com

Located in "Quiet Man" country in the heart of East Galway, **Crumlin Lodge** offers quality self-catering accommodation in a wonderfully peaceful rural setting. Originally a schoolhouse, part was built in 1885; the rest in 1901. Both parts have been expertly modernised while keeping some of the original features and they now provide comfortable accommodation for 4 people in each of the two apartments. The attractively furnished and decorated rooms have wooden floors and open fires, and both apartments have a 4-star rating from Bord Fáilte.

Visitors will find plenty to see and do in the area. Walkers will enjoy the route along the old railway track that runs directly in front of the Lodge with a beautiful stone bridge just outside the front door. The track leads to Ballyglunin Station which featured in the film *The Quiet Man.* Golfers are well-provided for with some of the best courses at Athenry, Tuam, Oranmore and the Galway Bay Country Club. There's excellent fishing in Lough Corrib and Lough Mask, and horse racing at Galway Racecourse just 10 minutes away. Also a 10-minute drive is the historic town of Athenry and even closer is the lovely Lackagh museum, which hosts a collection of old farm machinery and household items used many years ago by the Irish people.

Lough Shindilla and Lough Oorid with the Maamturk peaks rising to the left.

East of Galway City

Tuam

25 miles NE of Galway on the N17

The main town in northeast Galway, Tuam (pronounced *Choom*) was an important political and ecclesiastical centre in medieval times. The powerful O'Connor Kings of Connacht made it their base and the town was also the seat of an Archbishop. Little remains as witness of Tuam's former eminence. Two exceptions are the magnificent Norman arch which has been incorporated into the 19th century **St Mary's Cathedral**, and the Cross of Tuam in the Market Square. The Cross dates back to the 1300s and its base carries inscriptions in memory of Abbot O'Hoisin of Tuam and of Turlough O'Connor, King of Connacht.

Oranmore

5 miles E of Galway on the N6

The picturesque village of Oranmore lies on the shore of Galway Bay to the south of the city in the area known as "Oyster Country", the focus of the celebrated **Galway International Oyster Festival** in late September. This popular event attracts visitors from all over the world to sample the succulent delicacy, usually washed down with a pint of rich, creamy Guinness, and to enjoy the street theatre, free concerts and parades that take place in Galway City.

Another attraction at Oranmore is **Rinville Park**, an attractive amenity created around an ancient castle, a stately home, and a fine estate demesne dating from the 16th century. Open all year round, the park has an extensive network of walks through woodlands, open farmland and by the sea. There are some fine views of Galway Bay, Galway City and the Burren of

THE BISTRO

Oranmore, Co. Galway
Tel: 091 792600
e-mail: dymphnabrady@eircom.net

During her ten years in the restaurant business, Dympna Brady has worked as a chef for several years in America, including a stint at the World Trade Centre, as well as major restaurants in Australia and Galway before opening her own place, **The Bistro** in Oranmore. This is an elegant eating place with a smart cream and black exterior and a stylish black and white décor inside. It's extremely popular with local people which is always a good sign.

They flock here for the house specialities of fresh seafood and steaks but Dympna's menu also offers a wide range of other dishes. Amongst the starters for example you'll find a Bouchee of Smoked Chicken; Deep Fried Brie on a sweet pear puree and minted crème

fraiche; or a tasty home-made Soup de Jour. For your main course, as well as fresh fish and steak dishes, the choice includes Roast Barbary Duck Breast with toasted almonds in a mandarin and Cointreau sauce; Roast Rack of Lamb in Dijon mustard & rosemary crust served on a garlic and honey sauce; and a delicious Supreme of Chicken with a centre of apricot and red pepper on a garlic and thyme reduction. To round off your meal there's a selection of divine desserts. An extensive wine list offers an excellent choice of vintages from around the world.

Co. Clare, and ravens, grey herons and otters are among the fascinating fauna to be seen here. The park has picnic areas, a children's playground, a coffee shop (summer season only) and – an additional attraction, admission is free.

Clarinbridge

10 miles SE of Galway City on the N18

At Clarinbridge you can ignore the old rule about only eating oysters if there's an 'r' in the month. The ones raised in the calm tidal waters around the village are farmed ones from Portuguese stock and it's perfectly safe to eat them at any time of the year. Under the banner "The World is your Oyster....Clarinbridge is its home", the village hosts its very own **Oyster Festival** a couple of weeks before Galway City's more extensive celebrations.

Kinvara

18 miles SW of Galway on the N67

Set on an inlet of Galway Bay, Kinvara is a delightful quayside village, a popular destination for day visitors from Galway City. Overlooking the village with its thatched inn and harbourside cafés is **Dunguaire Castle,** an outstanding example of an early 16th century tower house. It stands proudly on the site of the 7th century stronghold of the Kings of Connacht. In the 1920s, the castle became the retreat of Oliver St John Gogarty, contemporary and friend of WB Yeats and Lady Gregory. Now it has been restored by Shannon Heritage and the displays give an insight into the lifestyle of the people who lived there from 1520 to modern times. Reflecting the great entertainments that took place here during the Middle Ages,

PADDY BURKES

Clarinbridge, Co. Galway
Tel: 091 796226 Fax: 091 796016
e-mail: info@paddyburkesgalway.com
website: www.paddyburkesgalway.com

"If you're not in the mood to get right down to work Have a dozen deep shells from our friend Paddy Burke".

This entry in the Visitors Book at **Paddy Burkes** famous Oyster Inn was penned by a Mr Vickerman in 1959, just 5 years after Clarinbridge village held the first of its now famous Oyster Festivals. From that first celebration held at Paddy Burkes and attended by a total of 34 diners the festival has burgeoned into a world-renowned event attracting some 10,000 visitors from both Ireland and abroad. The celebration is held over the second weekend in September but lovers of good food can indulge themselves throughout the year at Paddy Burkes, either in the traditional bar with its beamed ceiling or in the elegant à la carte restaurant.

Naturally, seafood takes pride of place with dishes such as Galway Bay Chowder amongst the starters, and Fresh Atlantic Crab Salad and Cod & Salmon Bake amongst the wide choice of main dishes. But you'll also find a good selection of meat , poultry and vegetarian options – Roast Rack of Connemara Lamb, for example, Stir Fry Chicken & Vegetables, or a Pasta Bake with a garlic, cheese & tomato sauce. Or, of course, you could just stay with those succulent oysters!

Dunguaire Castle

the Castle plays host during the season to twice-nightly Medieval Banquets "*with food to please the palate and entertainment to lift the soul*". A harpist plays softly as you enjoy your meal and Dunguaire's artists present humorous and inspirational excerpts from the work of Synge, Shaw and O'Casey. All in all, a memorable evening.

Gort

22 miles SE of Galway on the N18

Just north of this small town is **Coole Park**, the former demesne of the house of Lady Gregory, much visited by WB Yeats and the subject of some of his most famous work. Little remains of the house but the grounds and lake are now a particularly beautiful forest park. The 'autograph tree' which bears the graffiti of George Bernard Shaw, Sean O'Casey and Augustus John amongst others now stands behind railings to deter anyone else with a literary bent adding their thoughts. In late September the park is the setting for a 3-day annual Autumn Gathering which features a programme of plays, lectures and visits to places in the locality associated with Yeats and Lady Gregory.

One such place is **Thoor Ballylee** nearby. Yeats bought this ancient Norman tower and the adjoining cottages in 1916 for £35. It was to become his inspiration and his retreat. His collection of poems, *The Tower*, contains several pieces written at or about Thoor Ballylee. The ivy-clad tower has been lovingly restored and now looks much as it did in the 1920s when Yeats and his family lived here. An audio-visual presentation evokes Yeats' life and times, there's a bookshop specialising in Anglo-Irish literature, an excellent tearoom, picnic area and a beautiful riverside walk leading to an ancient mill.

Portumna

38 miles SE of Galway on the N65

The traditional market town of Portumna stands on the northern shore of Lough Derg. It's well known as an angling centre and now has a busy marina serving the lough and the Shannon. Hour-long cruises along the lough or over to Terryglass in Co. Tipperary are available during the summer months.

On the south side of the town are the easily accessible ruins of a **Dominican Priory**, built in 1426, and **Portumna Castle**, a Jacobean mansion of 1618 currently undergoing restoration but the ground floor is open to the public. The castle's estate is a wildlife sanctuary with a resident herd of fallow deer. Nearby, the 1000-acre **Portumna Forest Park,** bordering Lough Derg, is also a wildlife sanctuary with a well laid out nature trail and many pleasant woodland walks.

About 4 miles north of Portumna, tiny **Clonfert Cathedral** stands on the site of a Benedictine monastery founded around AD

560 by St Brendan. The present cathedral was built in the late 1100s and has an outstanding Romanesque doorway made up of six perfect semi-circular arches radiating outwards from the portal, each decorated with carvings of heads, plants and animal figures. There are more bizarre animal heads adorning the tops of the pillars and the chancel arch is decorated with angels, rosettes and a mermaid admiring herself in a mirror. The Bishop's Palace in the cathedral precincts was the home of the English fascist leader, Sir Oswald Mosley, following his release from prison but the building was later badly damaged by fire and is now derelict.

Loughrea

20 miles SE of Galway on the N6

This little market town sits on the north bank of the lough from which it takes its name and at its centre survive the well-preserved remains of a **Carmelite priory** built by the de Burgh family in the 1300s. Little remains of the medieval town walls apart from the southeastern gate tower which is now the **Clonfert Museum** (by appointment only) containing some interesting exhibits – notably some exquisite 16th century gold and silver chalices. Alongside the tower stands **St Brendan's Cathedral,** completed in 1903, which features some stained glass created by the modern Dublin School of Stained Glass.

About 4 miles north of Loughrea, signposted from the hamlet of Bullaun, stands the **Turoe Stone**, the finest stone of its kind in Ireland. It's a rounded pillar, just over 3 feet high, richly decorated with an eddying mass of spirals, a form of decoration known as the Celtic La Tene style and much more commonly found in Brittany. Dating from the 1st century AD at the latest, the stone is believed to be a fertility

Cartron House Farm

Ballinakill, Kylebrack, Loughrea, Co. Galway
Tel: 090 97 45211 Mobile: 086 1089329
Fax: 090 97 45987
e-mail: cartronhouse@hotmailcom
website: www.cartronhouse.com

Set in the lush Galway countryside and surrounded by spacious lawns and fields, **Cartron House Farm** dates back to 1770 and still retains much of its original character and style. Owners Ann and Tim offer their visitors the choice of either bed & breakfast or self-catering accommodation. Bed & breakfast guests stay in a wing of the house which on its ground floor has a large comfortable sitting room with television, a large dining room and a small kitchen where guests can make tea or coffee at all times. Also on the ground floor, with separate access to the courtyard, are 2 en suite rooms, one of which is specially designed for disabled guests.

The 7 guest bedrooms, all with en suite facilities, are traditionally furnished with an emphasis on comfort. Mealtimes are flexible and Ann prides herself on her ability to cater for special diets. The cuisine specialises in delicious traditional Irish food served with home-baked bread and locally produced, organically grown salads and vegetables wherever possible. For those who prefer self-catering, Ostlers Cottage next to the main house is cosy and self-contained. It is fully equipped for a self-catering holiday for 2, with a ground floor kitchen/living room with open fire, and a double bedroom with shower and w.c. on the first floor.

symbol used in pagan rituals.

Four miles east of Loughrea, visitors to the **Dartfield Horse Museum** can watch audio-visual displays with an equestrian theme, try out a riding machine and examine some fine horse-flesh in the stables. Also available are pony and carriage rides, trekking and horse-riding lessons.

Craughwell

14 miles E of Galway on the N6

This pleasant little village set beside the River Raford was for some years the home of the celebrated film director John Huston who lived at the house named St Clerans. A gregarious man, he made the most of the village's three pubs which are famed for their music and dance sessions. Less well-known outside Galway, the poet Ó'Reachtaire is buried in the churchyard here.

Athenry

14 miles E of Galway on the R348/R347

In a way, the people of Athenry should be grateful to Red Hugh O'Donnell who in 1597 attacked the town with such savagery that it didn't recover for centuries. The town became fossilised with the result that Athenry today is the classic Irish medieval town with an unmatched wealth of remains from the Middle Ages.

Visitors to **Athenry Heritage Centre** will find a focal point for the many medieval monuments scattered across the town. Amongst them are Athenry Castle (1235), the Dominican Priory (1241), Market Cross, North Gate, and the longest medieval walls in Ireland. They will also find receptionists dressed in resplendent medieval garb and guided tours are available during the season. A variety of leather goods and handmade dolls are among the local crafts on offer in the Centre's shop. The Centre is open daily from Easter to the end of September.

The walled garden located to the rear of the Heritage Centre provides the opportunity for visitors to try their skill in archery and the town's Medieval Festival in mid-August transports spectators back to the colour and spectacle of the Middle Ages.

Athenry was the birthplace of the poet Padraic Fallon who includes several references to the town in his poem, *The Fields of Athenry*, a moving reflection on the horrors of the famine years. Set to music, it is now heard around the world and has been adopted by thousands of Glasgow Celtic supporters as their theme song. Fallon's son, Connor, is an accomplished sculptor and an example of his work, created in honour of his father, holds pride of place in the town.

Ballygar

42 miles NE of Galway on the N63

This little village lies close to the River Suck which here provides the boundary between Galway and Co. Roscommon. It's a good point at which to join the **Suck Valley Way,** a 56-mile fully marked walk that passes over woodland, bogs and wetlands. Full details of the walk and other local attractions can be found at the **Angling/ Visitor Centre** which is housed in a former Church of Ireland building at Athleague.

Co Kerry

The most-visited county in Ireland, Kerry offers some of the most beautiful scenery in the country, and some of the friendliest people. Ireland's most impressive mountain range, Macgillycuddy's Reeks, is crowned by Ireland's tallest peak, Carrauntoohil (3411feet). The Reeks rise majestically above the lakes surrounding Killarney, the county's largest town. Killarney is a good starting point for the Ring of Kerry, the famous 110-mile

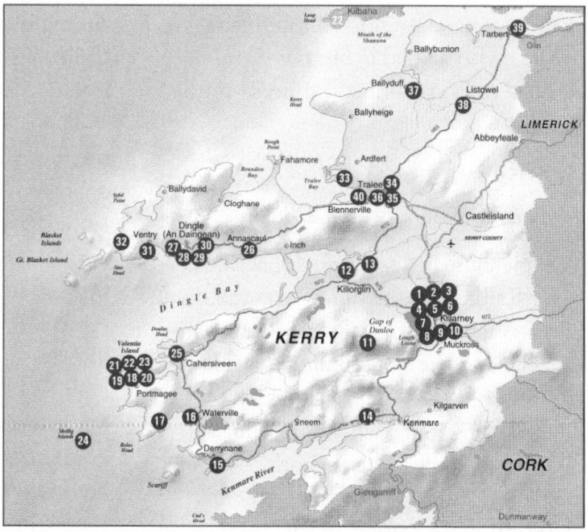

PLACES TO STAY, EAT AND DRINK

Arbutus Hotel, Killarney	1	Hotel	p146
Lord Kenmare's Restaurant & Rooms, Killarney	2	Restaurant & Accommodation	p146
Failte Hotel, Killarney	3	Hotel	p147
Foley's Town House & Restaurant, Killarney	4	Hotel	p148
Gabys Seafood Restaurant, Killarney	5	Restaurant	p148
The Old Presbytery Restaurant, Killarney	6	Restaurant	p149
The Laurels Pub, Killarney	7	Pub with Food	p150
Nashville, Killarney	8	B&B	p150
Ross Castle Lodge, Killarney	9	B&B	p151
Darby O'Gill's, Killarney	10	Hotel	p151
The Climbers Inn, Killarney	11	Pub, Food & Accommodation	p152
O'Grady's Canberra House, Killorglin	12	Bar & Accommodation	p154
Larkin's Pub, Restaurant and B&B, Killarney	13	Pub, Restaurant & Accommodation	p154
The Vestry Restaurant, Kenmare	14	Restaurant	p155
The Blind Piper, Caherdaniel	15	Pub with Food	p157
The Huntsman Restaurant & lodge, Waterville	16	Restaurant & Accommodation	p158
Beach Cove B&B, Ballinskelligs	17	B&B	p158
The Waterfront, Portmagee	18	B&B	p159
The Fisherman's Bar & Restaurant, Portmagee	19	Bar & Restaurant	p159
Portmagee Seaside Cottages, Portmagee	20	Self Catering	p160

● Denotes entries in other chapters

scenic drive around the Iveragh peninsula. Perhaps the most enchanting corner of this captivating county is the Dingle Peninsula, running westwards from Tralee. Irish is still a living language here and the wealth of prehistoric and early Christian remains all contribute to the indefinable, mystical quality of the area. Within the county boundaries lie the now-uninhabited Blasket Islands, and the Skellig Islands where St Patrick is credited with exterminating the last of Ireland's venomous snakes.

Curragh Boatmen, Co Kerry

PLACES TO STAY, EAT AND DRINK

Denotes entries in other chapters

Arbutus Hotel

College Street, Killarney, Co. Kerry
Tel: 064 31037 Fax: 064 34033
e-mail: stay@arbutuskillarney.com
website: www.arbutuskillarney.com

This historic townhouse hotel has been owned and managed by the Buckley family since 1926 and although it is located in the heart of a vibrant Killarney, has the relaxed atmosphere of a quiet country manor. Guests and non-residents alike can enjoy a fine pint and the Kerry *craic* in the award-winning bar, or sample the outstanding food on offer in the restaurant. This is presided over by Norrie Buckley ("Mom" to her family and many of her customers!) Norrie oversees the restaurant with pride and passion – here you will find the inspired blending of traditional Irish and international recipes, all prepared from the very best local ingredients. You won't be surprised to learn that Norrie and her team have received an AA rosette each year for the last 8 years.

Breakfast at the Arbutus is also something of a feast – "as refreshing and fulfilling as a walk on nearby Rossbeigh beach!" says Norrie. The menu offers a huge choice that includes all the usual favourites along with omelettes, fish of the day, French toast, a cold meats and cheeses selection, and much more. The excellent accommodation here comprises 35 rooms, all of which have been carefully renovated and enhanced over the last few years. The Arbutus Hotel is one of Killarneys best kept secrets.

Lord Kenmare's Restaurant & Murphy's Accommodation

College Street, Killarney, Co. Kerry
Tel/Fax: 064 31294
e-mail: info@murphysofkillarney.com
website: www.murphysofkillarney.com

With its excellent restaurant, two inviting bars and top quality accommodation, **Lord Kenmare's Restaurant & Murphy's Accommodation** provides everything you need for a memorable evening – and night – out on the town. The oldest part of the complex is Murphy's Bar, a traditional Irish public house of world renown which was established in 1955. Its stone-built walls, wooden beams and local historic décor create an atmosphere that attracts locals and visitors alike. The lively traditional music and natural, homely character is complemented by a superb bar menu served all day and, of course, the finest pints of Guinness in Kerry! In the other bar, Squires, a modern yet cosy ambience has been created, a perfect setting in which to sample the range of foreign beers and the selection of fine food. Lord Kenmare's Restaurant, named after the Earls of Kenmare, Killarney's great landowners, offers an enticing menu that combines the rich culture of the Mediterranean with the flavour of modern Irish cuisine.

The extensive range of dishes is complemented by a truly comprehensive wine list from the finest wine producers around the globe. And if you are planning to stay in this popular little town, Murphy's accommodation is newly refurbished to the highest standards, its 20 spacious rooms all en suite, with elevator access, and provided with television, telephone and hospitality tray.

Killarney

Killarney's tourism history goes back to the 1750s when the local landowner, Lord Kenmare, capitalised on the newly-discovered appreciation of "Romantic" scenery by creating a purpose-built resort around the village of Cill Áirne (Church of the Sloes) for the well-heeled travellers of the time. Killarney's surroundings are indeed glorious – magnificent vistas of loughs and mountains open up in every direction, with much of this superb scenery lying within the boundaries of the **Killarney National Park**. A popular excursion from the town is a day trip through the park in a "jarvey" or "jaunting car" (pony-trap) driven by a silver-tongued guide who will regale you with some highly inventive history along with fanciful tales of leprechauns and legends. Their charges can also be somewhat fantastic so do negotiate a price before you set off.

Another satisfying excursion is a boat trip around the three lakes, Lough Leane, Muckross Lake and the Upper Lake – all of them framed by the highest mountains in Ireland, **Macgillycuddy's Reeks** which rise to 3410 feet. Killarney is also a natural starting-point for the **Ring of Kerry**, a 110-mile circular drive around the Iveragh Peninsula which takes in some of the finest scenery in Ireland. The **Kerry Way** is the walker's alternative – a 133-mile hiking trail around the neck of the peninsula which takes in some especially dramatic scenery near Torc Mountain and Windy Gap.

Killarney itself, despite its long history as a tourist resort, is surprisingly lacking in architectural interest. Its one building of any consequence is the Catholic **Cathedral of St Mary**, a flamboyant exercise in neo-Gothic style designed by Augustus Pugin and consecrated in 1855. Its construction

FÁILTE HOTEL

College Street, Killarney, Co. Kerry
Tel: 064 33404 Fax: 064 36599
e-mail: failtehotel@eircom.net
website: www.kerry-insight.com

Located in the town centre, the **Fáilte Hotel** is one of Kerry's most popular bars and has won a clutch of awards for its old style décor and unique atmosphere. It's owned and managed by Dermot and Eileen O'Callaghan together with their son Paudie, a friendly and welcoming trio who are

dedicated to providing top quality food, drink and accommodation. In the cosy bar you'll find "good pints and good company" along with appetising bar food served throughout the day – home-made soup, freshly made sandwiches, hot baguettes, seafood specials and a good selection of main dishes. The bar is also the venue for regular live music sessions.

The first floor award-winning restaurant is undoubtedly one of Killarney's finest – a favourite with locals and visitors alike. The menu changes regularly to include all the specialities of the house and among the varied tasty dishes you'll find baked oysters, game terrine, hot buttered lobster, roast quail, pheasant, guinea fowl and seafood selections. The accommodation here maintains the same high standards seen throughout the hotel – all the bedrooms have recently been refurbished and each now has en suite facilities, colour television and direct dial telephone. Some rooms also have air conditioning.

Foley's Town House & Restaurant

23 High Street, Killarney, Co. Kerry
Tel: 064 31217 Fax: 064 34683
e-mail: info@foleystownhouse.com
website: www.foleystownhouse.com

Located in the charming town centre of Killarney, **Foley's Town House & Restaurant** was originally built in 1795 as a coaching inn and has hosted generations of travellers. In the late 1800s part of the building was occupied by the Royal Irish Constabulary and local Fenian rebels were jailed here during the 1867 rebellion. Today, newly refurbished and extended by its owners Denis and Carol Hartnett, Foley's now boasts 4-star and 5-diamond ratings. The hotel is especially noted for its award-winning restaurant where Carol provides superb meals based on the very best of fresh local produce.

An extensive range of fresh fish and prime meats are used and local farmhouse cheeses complement the home-baked bread and pastries. To accompany your meal, there are more than 300 wines to choose from. The accommodation here is quite outstanding – each of the luxurious bedrooms has been individually designed for comfort and elegance and is provided with every modern amenity. All 28 rooms are en suite – 16 of them with Jacuzzi baths – and each has its own television, trouser press and hospitality tray. The service at Foley's is both friendly and efficient and another important advantage in busy Killarney is that the hotel has its own secure parking.

Gaby's Seafood Restaurant

27 High Street, Killarney, Co. Kerry
Tel: 064 32519 Fax: 064 32747

No visit to Killarney would be complete without sampling a meal at **Gaby's Seafood Restaurant,** one of Ireland's longest established and most famous seafood restaurants. Gert Maes, who owns and runs the restaurant together with his wife Marie, is an inspired chef who has won countless awards for his cuisine. As one visitor put it "Gert Maes must understand the secret of eternal youth for his long tenure in Killarney hasn't dimmed his energy and determination to be his best!"

Gastronomes from around the world make their way here to wax lyrical about dishes such as Atlantic salmon with chive & lemon cream; a tempura of prawns and scallops served with champ; sea bass with savoy cabbage, or Gert's speciality – lobster cooked to his own secret recipe. To complement this heavenly fare, there's a fine selection of wines from Gaby's cellar. Before or after your meal, enjoy a drink in the cosy bar with its open fire and pleasantly informal

was halted by the Great Famine of 1845-51. During those dreadful years, the only completed part was used as a hospital for the victims of starvation and disease.

Just across the road from the Cathedral is the entrance to the Knockreer Estate where the main path leads to the impressive ruins of 15th century **Ross Castle,** the last fortress in southwest Ireland to succumb to Cromwell's forces in 1652. Recently restored, the castle contains a fine collection of 16th and 17th century oak furniture. (Entrance by guided tour only). The castle stands beside Lough Leane; boat trips around the lake are available from the nearby quay.

From Lough Leane there are grand views of Macgillycuddy's Reeks and Innisfallen Island, the largest of the 30-odd islands scattered across the lough. It's well worth hiring a boat for the short trip to the island to see the picturesque ruins of **Innisfallen**

Ross Castle

THE OLD PRESBYTERY RESTAURANT

Cathedral Place, Killarney, Co. Kerry
Tel: 064 30555 Fax: 064 30557
e-mail: oldpresbytery@eircom.net
website: www.oldpresbytery.com

Located opposite St Mary's Cathedral, with its own private car park, **The Old Presbytery Restaurant** echoes the superb architecture of the cathedral, designed by Pugin in 1842. A gracious 3-storey Georgian building with a unique copper roof, the restaurant has many elegant features and has been restored with integrity and with the warmth and comfort of the diner in mind. But the major attraction of course is the superb food with creative dishes designed to satisfy the most demanding of "foodies" – Honey Roast Chicken Spring Rolls, Wok Fried Vegetables, Sweet Sour and Soy Sauce, Mixed House Salad

with Toasted Pine Nuts, Sun-dried Tomatoes and Bacon, Roast Kerry Rack of Lamb with Espelette Chilli Crust and Red Pepper coulis, followed by warm and melting Chocolate Cake, Mango Sauce, Vanilla Ice Cream are Signature Dishes and head an extensive Menu. The generous portions are satisfying, but allow room for light desserts such as Hazelnut Creme Brulee or you could linger with the selection of French and Irish Cheeses.

To accompany your meal there's a vast range of carefully selected wines from around the world – more than 120 varieties, including many classics. The restaurant has received many awards including "Les Routiers Restaurant of the Year 2003". Reservations are advisable.

The Laurels Pub

Main Street, Killarney, Co. Kerry
Tel: 064 31149 Fax: 064 34389
e-mail: info@thelaurelspub.com
website: www.thelaurelspub.com

This busy tourist town is well-supplied with good hostelries but one that stands out is **The Laurels**, a wonderfully traditional Irish inn run by the father and daughter team of Con O'Leary and Kate Lee. Con's family has run the pub for almost a century and little has changed during that time. Tiled floors and beamed ceilings, lots of alcoves and dimly lit corners, friendly and attentive staff, all contribute to the charm of this most characteristic of Irish pubs.

Appetising food is served all year round. Expect to find the best traditional fare around, prepared not with just a little flair, entirely from local ingredients. Bantry Bay mussels come in a tureen of white wine, garlic and fresh cream with home-made soda bread; Irish stew with crusty home-baked rolls; and traditional potato-cakes filled with chicken and smoked bacon on a mushroom sauce. These are found happily rubbing shoulders with dishes of decidedly more cosmopolitan persuasion such as bruschetta topped with roasted vegetables and mozzarella. Also promised is 'the best pizza in town!' And then there's the music. Irish 'airs' first lifted the rafters of The Laurels in 1966 and immediately established its reputation for great entertainment. Dick Willis, Tim Brosnan, Mike Sexton and David Stone, accompanied by 'The Laurels Lassies' Irish Dancers, combine to ensure a great night's craic.

Nashville

Airport/Tralee Road, Killarney, Co. Kerry
Tel/Fax: 064 32924
e-mail: nashville@eircom.net

Nashville is a spacious modern house standing in its own extensive and beautifully maintained grounds. The house was built by David Nash who lives here with his family and has been welcoming bed and breakfast guests since 1984.

There are 6 guest bedrooms (2 doubles; 2 twins; 2 family rooms), all of them spacious and provided with en suite facilities, TV, hairdryer and tea/coffee-making facilities. All are attractively furnished and decorated and three of them have lovely views across to the Macgillycuddy Reeks.

A full Irish breakfast is served in the airy dining room and David is happy to cater for any special dietary requirements. Evening meals are available on request.

Ross Castle Lodge

Ross Road, Killarney, Co. Kerry
Tel/Fax: 064 36942
e-mail: rosscastlelodge@eircom.net
website: http://killarneyb-and-b.com

On the edge of Killarney town, in woodland alongside magical Lough Leane, **Ross Castle Lodge** offers luxurious bed & breakfast accommodation in relaxed and comfortable surroundings. This non-smoking establishment is run by Denis and Rosaleen O' Leary who will give you a warm welcome and outstanding hospitality. The elegant twin, double and triple en-suite bedrooms all have colour TV, hairdryer, orthopaedic beds, clock/radio, trouser press & tea/coffee facilities, and guests have the use of a residents' lounge and large, mature gardens. A popular feature here is the Wishing Well where people from all over the world have made their secret wishes.

Abbey, an important ecclesiastical centre for more than a thousand years. The 11th century High King, Brian Boru, is believed to have been educated here and it was monks at the Abbey who compiled the *Annals of Innisfallen*, a fascinating chronicle of world and Irish history recording events between AD 950 and 1350.

History of a different nature is on display at the **Irish National Transport Museum** in Scotts Gardens. A unique Silver Stream of 1907 is the star of a show that includes veteran, vintage and classic motor cars, fire engines and Irish historical memorabilia all preserved in their original condition. Period signs, thousands of motoring accessories and

Darby O'Gill's

Lissivigeen, Mallow Road, Killarney, Co. Kerry
Tel: 064 34168 Fax: 064 36794
e-mail: darbyogill@eircom.net
website: www.darbyogillskillarney.com

Situated just outside Killarney in the heart of the Kingdom of Kerry, **Darby O'Gill's** is an ideal spot to stop and enjoy the authentic atmosphere of an Irish country house. The hotel takes its name from the lovable hero of the Walt Disney film *Darby O'Gill and the Little People* which depicted Ireland in its most appealing aspects – a heady brew of enchanting stories, ancient legends and beautiful traditional music. Owner Pat O'Gill and his wife Joan have a long experience in the catering industry and have transformed the small country pub they bought in the mid-1990s into an inviting country house hotel with a 3-star rating.

The 25 guest bedrooms here are some of the most charming in the Kingdom – all en suite and finished to a very high standard. All are furnished in country pine to give a very homely atmosphere. There's a spacious Lounge Bar where plate lunches are served daily and entertainment is provided nightly during the summer, and also a cosy Bar which is just as an Irish pub should be – the art of conversation still thrives here and darts, rings and cards are actively played. Darby's Restaurant serves only the best of Irish cuisine with à la carte and table d'hôte menus both available; there are half portions for children, and an excellent selection of wines.

rare memorabilia are also displayed, while the Cycle Road demonstrates the evolution of the bicycle from a Hobby Horse of 1825 to the modern safety bike.

The transport theme is continued at the **Killarney Model Railway,** located beside the Tourist Office on Beech Road. This is one of the world's most extensive model railways with trains rattling along more than a mile of track and transporting its miniature passengers through the landmark cities of Europe.

Around Killarney

Muckross

3 miles S of Killarney off the N71

Located about 3 miles south of Killarney, the 11,000 acre **Muckross Estate** was a gift to the nation by an American, Bowers

Muckross House

Bourne, and his son-in-law Senator Arthur Vincent. Now part of a 25,000 acre National Park (where cars are banned) the estate covers most of the lake district and contains the beautifully situated ruins of **Muckross Abbey** (free), founded in 1448 and one of the best preserved abbeys in the country despite being despoiled by Cromwell's troops in 1652. The Abbey's lovely setting is enhanced by superb

THE CLIMBERS INN

Glencar, Killarney, Co. Kerry
Tel: 066 976 0101
e-mail: stevebessant@f2s.com
website: www.climbersinn.com

Glencar lies at the heart of Ireland's highest mountain range and right in the centre of this spectacular glen is **The Climbers Inn,** ideally located for those prepared to tackle the challenge of Macgillycuddy's Reeks. Dating back to the 1870s, the inn is recognised as the oldest walking and climbing establishment in Ireland – many world-famous mountaineers have limped through its doors after a day on the Reeks. Walkers here are rewarded with some of the finest

scenic routes in Ireland, including the famous Kerry Way which actually passes the inn's front door.

The inn has a drying room for wet clothes and kit, and the excellent en suite rooms are provided with jet showers to rejuvenate tired bodies. Owner Sheila O'Sullivan prides herself on the inn's home cooking, all of it based on prime local produce – dishes such as wild salmon, sea trout, fish game soup, venison, highland lamb or vegetarian choices. The inn also hosts nights of live Irish music when locals and guests join together in a genuinely relaxed atmosphere. As well as climbing and walking, the area offers an abundance of other activities – golf, mountain biking, horse trail riding, game and sea fishing, archaeology tours, wildlife and wilderness tours, and more.

gardens, dominated by a gigantic yew tree. Also within the Park is **Muckross House**, a magnificent early-Victorian mansion built in the Tudor style. The main rooms are furnished in opulent fashion and the rest of the house has been transformed into a museum of Kerry folk life where live blacksmiths, weavers and potters demonstrate their time-honoured skills. Within the extensive grounds there's a traditional working farm, an excellent tea room and superb gardens noted for their dazzling rhododendrons and azaleas during early summer. A short walk from the grounds brings you to two of Killarney's most famous beauty spots, the lovely Meeting of the Waters, and the spectacular **Torc Waterfall** which tumbles 60 feet down the flank of Torc Mountain.

About 2 miles further south, the park's boundary is formed by the shore of the Upper Lake. The lakeside road leads to Ladies' View which provides a stunning vista of the Gap of Dunloe and the remote and cheerless Black Valley beyond the lake.

Torc Waterfall

Gap of Dunloe

8 miles SW of Killarney on minor road off the N72

Running south from Beaufort, the Gap of Dunloe is one of Kerry's premier attractions and was already a tourist attraction in the early 1800s when Charlotte Brontë paid a visit while on her honeymoon. During the season, part of this beautiful glacial valley, 8 miles long, that lies between Macgillycuddy's Reeks and the Purple Mountains can become congested with cars and jarveys. But a tour of County Kerry would be seriously incomplete if you missed out on its magnificent views of mountains, loughs and tarns.

A popular starting point for a scenic pony trek through the Gap of Dunloe is **Kate Kearney's Cottage**, a famous hostelry which has been owned and run by the same family for more than 150 years. Kate Kearney was a well-known beauty in Ireland during the years before the Great Famine of 1845-49 and her legend has captured the imagination of people from far and wide over the years.

Killorglin

12 miles W of Killarney on the N72

This pleasant little town stands on a hill above the River Laune with Macgillycuddy's Reeks dominating the landscape to the south. The ruins of 13th century Conway Castle are a rather minor attraction and the town is best known for its **Puck Fair**, held in mid-August every year. Originating in pagan times, the fair is believed to have been a celebration of the approach of harvest time. Another tradition claims that it commemorates an occasion when the stampeding of goats (pucks) alerted the townspeople to the approach of English

O'Grady's Canberra House

Upper Bridge Street, Killorglin, Co. Kerry
Tel: 066 976 2012
e-mail: ogradystephen@eircom.net
Proprietors: Stephen & Catherine O'Grady

Nestled between the McGillacuddy Reeks and Sliabh Mish the town of Killorglin is the setting for this cosy bar which is enjoyed by the local and visitor alike. Learn about local history while sitting in front of an open fire with members of the business and farming community who frequent this popular hostelry. Home of the Puck Fair, which takes place annually on August 10th, 11th and 12th, Killorglin on the Ring of Kerry is only 13 miles from Killarney and 15 miles from Farranfore airport. Accommodation is provided in newly refurbished en suite bedrooms with t.v. and tea/coffee making facilities.

Larkin's Pub, Restaurant & B&B

Main Street, Milltown, Killarney, Co. Kerry
Tel: 066 976 7217 Fax: 066 976 7515
e-mail: larkinsbar@hotmail.com
website: www.hotmail.com

Close to both Killarney town and the scenic Dingle Peninsula, **Larkin's Pub, Restaurant & B&B** has all the character and atmosphere you could hope to find in an authentic Irish pub. This spacious mid-19th century hostelry is owned and run by Mike and Breda McCarthy who have made it the kind of place where you "arrive as a stranger and leave as a friend". As well as serving one of the best pints of Guinness you'll find in County Kerry, Larkin's also offers great value-for-money pub cuisine which is served 7 days a week and ranges from breakfasts, through bar snacks to hearty evening meals.

forces. The festivities begin when a wild goat is captured in the mountains, brought to Killorglin and, its horns beribboned, is enthroned in a cage in the centre of the town. The "coronation" signals the beginning of 3 days of cattle and horse sales, and "unrestricted merry-making".

Kenmare

If you travel the scenic Ring of Kerry route in a clockwise direction from Killarney, (both directions are equally satisfying, incidentally), the first town of any size you come to is Kenmare. Picturesquely set on the estuary of the River Kenmare, this

Sheen Falls, Kenmare

and cafés, and its position at the meeting point of both the Iveragh and Beara peninsulas makes Kenmare a popular base for tourists. From the pier, there are boat trips around Kenmare Bay with almost guaranteed sightings of sea otters and grey seals with the occasional minke or killer whale as a bonus.

There's evidence of early occupation of this pleasant site in the **Druid's Circle**, standing just outside the town on the banks of the River Kinnihy. The 15 small stones form a circle about 50 feet across around a dolmen supporting a large capstone. Another relic from the past is **St Finan's Holy Well,** southeast of the town, whose waters are credited with healing powers and which still attracts many pilgrims seeking a

prosperous little town is well supplied with craft and speciality shops, bars, restaurants

THE VESTRY RESTAURANT

Templenoe, Kenmare, Co. Kerry
Tel/Fax: 064 41958
e-mail:carolbaines@oceanfree.net
website: www.neidin.net/vestry

Ideally situated between Kenmare and Sneem in the beautiful village of Templemoe, **The Vestry Restaurant** enjoys a superb location overlooking Kenmare Bay. This unique eating place occupies a former Church of Ireland building, constructed between 1790 and 1816 by the Mahony family and used for services until it was deconsecrated in 1987. It was then converted into a restaurant, retaining many of the original features, including the wonderful 5-paned 19th century stained glass window.

The present owners, David and Carol Hillier, tastefully re-furbished the interior in 2002-2003 and have created a delightful setting, full of charm and character in which to relax and enjoy their outstanding cuisine. A full à la carte menu is available supplemented by daily specials such as

ostrich, wild venison and sea trout dishes, as well as vegetarian options; fresh lobster and oysters are also available with 24 hours notice. The restaurant can seat up to 60 diners, including seating upstairs in the Minstrels' Gallery, and in good weather customers can eat outside in the scenic Vestry Garden overlooking the bay. (Look out here for the life-size model of Jenny the donkey and her cart!). The Hilliers are happy to accept bookings for weddings, tours and groups of 10 or more – live music can also be organised on request.

cure. Nearby are the ruins of a church traditionally associated with the saint.

But modern Kenmare's history really began in the mid-1600s, thanks to William Petty, Cromwell's Surveyor-General. William amassed a colossal fortune wheeling and dealing in Irish real estate following the English Civil War. The cash-strapped Commonwealth government had rewarded its supporters with confiscated lands in Ireland but many of these beneficiaries baulked at the idea of actually removing themselves to what was seen as virtual exile. William came to the rescue, providing ready cash in return for the freeholds. His acquisitions provided the basis for the vast Lansdowne estate that once surrounded Kenmare where he established mines and ironworks and helped develop a fishing industry. In addition to being a canny businessman, William was gifted in other ways – he became a professor of music at Oxford at the age of 27, was a founder member of the Royal Society in London, and so politically adroit that when Charles II was restored to the throne William managed to acquire yet more land – and a knighthood. It was his descendant, the 1st Marquess of Lansdowne, who in 1775 laid out the town on a pleasing X-plan. The story of the town's development is recounted in the **Heritage Centre** in the main square, where you can pick up a leaflet detailing the Kenmare Heritage Trail and also visit the **Kenmare Lace & Design Centre** to see lace being made in the traditional style.

From Kenmare, the R571 crosses the River Ken to the Beara Peninsula which County Kerry shares with County Cork. The peninsula here is a rocky, wild and barren place but the R571 clings to the shoreline, opening up marvellous views of mountains, loughs and the estuary of the River Ken.

Around Kenmare

Kilgarvan

7 miles E of Kenmare on the R569

A short diversion from the Ring of Kerry brings you to this busy little town set beside the River Kenmare and backed by the foothills of the Derrynasaggart Mountains. Anyone with an interest in motoring history will want to pay a visit to the **Kilgarvan Motor Museum** which displays a large collection of vintage and classic cars and is open all year.

Sneem

12 miles W of Kenmare on the N70

Westwards from Kenmare, the Ring of Kerry skirts the Kenmare Estuary, passing some wonderful river and mountain scenery, leading to the well-known beauty spot of Parknasilla where palms and tender shrubs thrive in the mild Gulf Stream climate. At Parknasilla, the road turns inland for a mile or so and brings you to the picture-postcard village of Sneem, its colour-washed cottages set beside the River Ardsheelaun and with lofty Knockmoyle (2245feet) as a backdrop. Locals will assure you that the different hues have a very practical purpose – the varying colours make it easier to distinguish your own residence after a long evening of merry-making! There's good fishing hereabouts, a fact celebrated by the salmon-shaped weathercock that crowns the tower of the Protestant church that dates back to Elizabethan times. The village's Catholic church was built much later, in 1865, and contains the grave of Father Michael Walsh, Sneem's parish priest in the mid-1800s and immortalized in the popular song, *Father O'Flynn*. An even more famous figure is commemorated by a monument on the village green to General de Gaulle who once spent two weeks here: local people refer to it

The Blind Piper

Caherdaniel, Co. Kerry
Tel: 066 94 75126

In the heart of this little village on the Ring of Kerry, **The Blind Piper** is named after Mici Cumba O'Sullivan who was born nearby in 1835 and became one of Ireland's most famous pipers. You can read about him in the bar of this friendly hostelry which is also noted for its excellent food. Sandra O'Farrell's extensive menu offers a wide choice of wholesome and appetising dishes, as well as hearty sandwiches, salads, vegetarian options, a Kids' Menu and daily specials. In good weather you can enjoy your refreshments at the picnic tables outside.

affectionately as "Da Gallstone". They also have their own term, "The Pyramids", for the **Sneem Sculpture Park** where, along with unusual sculptures from Asia and elsewhere, are some exhibits inspired by the beehive huts of prehistoric Staigue Stone Fort.

Continuing clockwise around the Ring of Kerry, the road passes through an area rich in ancient forts and standing stones, one of the best of which is **Staigue Stone Fort**, signposted off the main road between Nedanone and Caherdaniel. This extremely well preserved ring fort, some 3000 years old, is believed to have been a fortress of the Kings of Munster. The walls, 13 feet wide at the base and around 18 feet high, enclose a space of about 90 feet across. The only entrance is through a small doorway with sloping sides. From the bank on which the fort stands there are superb panoramic views. (Don't forget to respond to the notice on the honesty box which requests a small sum – currently • 1 – to compensate the farmer for "trespass").

Derrynane

28 miles SW of Kenmare on the N70

This pleasant little village with its expanses of sandy beaches and dunes, was the home of one of Ireland's most significant and attractive statesmen, Daniel O'Connell (1775-1847), the nationalist leader and social reformer. A powerful orator and skilled organizer, O'Connell's election as MP to the Westminster Parliament in 1829 forced the British government to repeal legislation which banned Roman Catholics from sitting in the House of Commons. **Derrynane House**, remodelled by "the Great Liberator" himself, is a rather austere building but it enjoys a lovely setting overlooking the sea and is surrounded by a 300-acre park. The house contains a wealth of family memorabilia (including Daniel's duelling pistols) and it's worth watching the video which commemorates the life and times of a man who ringingly declared that "no political change whatsoever is worth the shedding of a single drop of human blood".

Waterville

35 miles SW of Kenmare on the N70

From Derrynane, the Ring of Kerry twists its way through the spectacular Coomakista Pass to the resort town of Waterville with its sandy beach, thriving palm trees and wild Atlantic views. According to legend, Waterville was founded by Noah's granddaughter, Cessair. Having filled his Ark with animals, the patriarch discovered he had no room left for Cessair so she set sail with a retinue of 49 women and 3 men for an island which, she was assured, was "free of monsters, reptiles and sin, and would therefore escape the flood". Two of the men died after arriving at Waterville; the sole surviving male flinched from facing his awesome responsibilities and ran away. These stirring events took place, apparently, in the year 2958 BC.

Waterville stands on a narrow neck of land that separates Ballinskelligs Bay and Lough Currane, one of the most beautiful lakes in Ireland and noted for its salmon fishing. The town developed in Victorian and Edwardian times and still retains a dignified air despite the advent of more recent and less appealing "amenities".

The Huntsman Restaurant & Lodge

Waterville, Co. Kerry
Tel: 066 947 4124 Fax: 066 947 4560
e-mail: huntsmanclub@eircom.net

The Huntsman Restaurant & Lodge occupies a striking modern building set right at the ocean's edge and enjoying grand views across Ballinskelligs Bay. This award-winning restaurant, lodge and oyster bar offers just about everything you could want for a wonderfully peaceful "away-from-it-all" holiday break. Settle down in the bar with its red-wine leather couches, warm walnut tables and open peat fire, and admire the fishing memorabilia displayed around the walls – witness to the ones that "didn't get away". A well-stocked bar helps along the anglers' stories of heroic fights with Mother Nature and her "scaly bounty".

The relaxing atmosphere is enhanced by the resident professional pianist, David Appleby, who helps the day wind down with soft classical music. The Huntsman is owned and run by Raymond and Deirdre Hunt – Raymond is the master chef and his award-winning restaurant offers an enticing gourmet menu with seafood as the speciality of the house, supplemented by some appetising meat and poultry dishes. And if you are planning to stay in this magical corner of Co. Kerry, The Huntsman offers a choice of either bed & breakfast or luxury time-share accommodation.

Beach Cove B&B

St Finian's Bay, Ballinskelligs, Co. Kerry
Tel: 066 947 9301
e-mail: beachcove@eircom.net
website: www.stayatbeachcove.com

Beautifully located on the beach at St Finian's Bay, overlooking Skelligs Rock, **Beach Cove B&B** offers first class bed & breakfast accommodation in wonderfully peaceful surroundings. Your host, Bridie O'Connor, has been welcoming guests here since 1997, amongst them walkers, cyclists, anglers, golfers and anyone who appreciates seclusion and tranquillity. All the beautifully furnished and decorated guest bedrooms have en suite facilities and Bridie's hearty breakfasts include home-made bread and preserves. As well as being surrounded by glorious scenery, Beach Cove is also close to the Skellig Heritage Centre and the Ring of Skellig, a scenic route around the peninsula.

Portmagee

43 miles SW of Kenmare on the R565

This small village on the Iveragh peninsula, just off the Ring of Kerry, is known as "An Caladh", or "the Ferry", in Irish because of the once constant traffic back and forth between the village and nearby Valentia Island. Today, the two are linked by a road bridge. Portmagee is also the holder of an unusual custom called the "Old Year", a parade that is held on New Year's Eve.

Valentia

45 miles W of Kenmare on the R565

Linked to the mainland by a bridge at Portmagee, Valentia is an intensively

The Waterfront

Scenic Skellig Ring, Portmagee, Co. Kerry
Tel: 066 947 7208
e-mail: thewaterfront@eircom.net

As it name suggests, **The Waterfront** stands right beside the sea on the outskirts of this peaceful little harbourside village. It's the home of Christina Murphy, a friendly lady who welcomes bed & breakfast guests to this charming property which is much more spacious than it first appears. In fact, there are 5 guest bedrooms in all, each with en suite facilities and beautifully furnished and decorated. Guests have the use of a comfortable TV lounge with a wood-burning stove and there are facilities for fishing, horse-riding and golf nearby with restaurants, bars, music sessions and dancing just a 3-minute walk away.

The Fisherman's Bar & Skellig Restaurant

Portmagee village, Co. Kerry
Tel: 066 947 7103

The tiny but thriving fishing village of Portmagee is one of Co. Kerry's best-kept secrets. Overlooking the little harbour is **The Fisherman's Bar & Skellig Restaurant**, a delightful place full of charm and character with its Valentia slate floor and subdued lighting. Naturally, there's a lot of fishing memorabilia scattered around the walls of the bar and fish takes pride of place on the appetising menu. All the fish dishes served here are based on catches by local fishermen landed at Portmagee harbour. If fish is not your preference, the menu also offers a good choice of meat and other dishes with lunch menu specials served all day. There's also a selection of freshly made sandwiches for lighter appetites and a full Irish breakfast served daily from 8am until noon.

The Skellig Restaurant, which occupies a former bank building, also serves a renowned Sunday lunch from 12.30pm. To accompany your meal, there's an extensive range of beverages, including a fascinating collection of special whiskeys from around the world. No visitor to Portmagee should leave without taking the boat trip to the great sandstone pyramid of Skelligs Rock – bookings for this, and for angling trips, can be made in The Fisherman's Bar.

Portmagee Seaside Cottages

Kilkeaveragh, Portmagee, Co. Kerry
Tel: 066 94 77151
e-mail: jlynch@indigo.ie
website:
www.portmageeseasidecottages.com

Located just 2 miles from the fishing village of Portmagee in a beautiful rural area, **Portmagee Seaside Cottages** enjoy a wonderful position on the water's edge. There are 6 properties in all – Puffin, Gannet, Crab, Periwinkle, Skellig and Blasket – and all boast a 4-star rating from the Irish Tourist Board. A stone fireplace, wooden floors throughout, an oak kitchen, beamed and wooden ceilings all add to the charm. On the ground floor there's a sitting/dining room with open fire (turf supplied free), a patio, a well-equipped kitchen, a bathroom with Jacuzzi, WC and hand basin, a twin bedroom and a double bedroom.

The first floor has another twin and double bedroom, each with en suite bathroom with shower, WC and handbasin.

Each cottage can sleep up to 8 guests, plus a cot. Other amenities include oil-fired central heating, a fridge/freezer, washing machine/dryer, microwave, dishwasher, colour TV and barbecue. Linen and towels are supplied free; electricity and oil are charged as used. Each cottage, with boat moorings, has direct access to the shore for some wonderful coastal walks; Portmagee with its shops, pubs, restaurants and boat trips, is close by as are numerous sandy beaches, facilities for golf, fishing, scuba-diving and horse riding, and historic Derrynane House.

Glanleam House & Gardens

Glanleam Estate, Valentia Island, Co. Kerry
Tel: 066 947 6176 Fax: 066 947 6108
e-mail: info@glanleam.com
website: www.glanleam.com

Surrounded by the most westerly garden in Ireland and Europe, **Glanleam House & Gardens** offers a unique bed and breakfast experience. The house was originally built in 1775 as a linen factory by the Knights of Kerry. In the 1830s, the 19th Knight couldn't resist turning the building into an elegant manor. Taking advantage of the virtually frost-free conditions, he also laid out 40 acres of gardens in a wild Robinsonian style – interplanting natural habitat plants with exotics which are found nowhere else in Europe.

The gardens also boast the tallest tree ferns in Europe, giant groves of bamboo, lily-of-the-valley trees that perfume the whole garden, and a walled garden with a picnic area. The gardens also command magnificent views across the bay to the distant Kerry mountains. Today these private gardens are open to the public and the manor house is now an elegant guest house where beautiful antiques mingle with contemporary styles to provide every possible comfort. If you prefer self-catering, Glanleam also has 3 beautifully restored holiday homes to let: the Boathouse, directly on the beach, the old Gardener's Cottage within the Walled Garden, and the original Estate Manager's house.

cultivated island, 7 miles long and 2 miles broad, boasting the most westerly harbour in Europe, Knightstown. It was from here that the first transatlantic cable was laid in 1857, and for decades Valentia enjoyed far superior communications with New York than with Dublin.

Valentia's **Heritage Centre**, housed in the former National School, has interesting information on the cable station and also features local craft industries. One exhibit is devoted to the local slate quarries. These are now defunct but throughout Victorian times Valentia slate was highly prized for its

Valentia Island

Shealane Country House

Corhamor, Valentia Island, Co. Kerry
Tel: 066 9476354
e-mail: marylane@eircom.net
website: www.shealane.com

On the road bridge adjacent to the Skellig Experience Centre and less than a mile from Portmagee Village on the mainland, **Shealane Country House** offers Irish hospitality at its best. Mary and James Lane guarantee their guests personal attention – including an extensive breakfast menu that offers many choices (including grilled Atlantic kippers) and caters for all tastes including vegetarians. The spacious en-suite bedrooms - all with sea views – are individually decorated and the facilities include electric blankets, cd/clock radio, and hospitality tray. Local maps and brochures are provided and boat trips to the famous Skellig Rocks can be arranged.

Glenreen Heights

Knightstown Road, Valentia Island, Co. Kerry
Tel/Fax: 066 94 76241
e-mail: glenreen@eircom.net
website: www.glenreenheights.com

With its mild, balmy climate Valentia Island is understandably popular with holiday-makers looking for an unspoilt, peaceful retreat. If you are also looking for quality bed & breakfast accommodation, **Glenreen Heights** is strongly recommended. This stylish modern house is the home of Julie O'Sullivan, an accomplished cook whose generous breakfasts, complete with home-baked bread, are a real treat. There are 4 guest bedrooms, all with en suite facilities and attractively furnished and decorated. Guests also have the use of a comfortable lounge with a welcoming open fire. Golf, fishing, horse-riding and some grand walks are all available nearby.

Skellig Islands

Co.Kerry

The **Skellig Islands** rise abruptly and forbiddingly from the sea. Little Skellig is a sanctuary for some 40,000 gannets and landing is not permitted but, if you are able and willing to negotiate a ladder set into its harbour wall, you *can* visit Great Skellig, or Skellig Michael as it's also known. Another steep climb, on steps carved out of the solid rock, leads to a remarkable cluster of ecclesiastical ruins, the arched stone remains of St Fionan's Abbey (AD 560), a somewhat larger church dating back to the 10th century, several burial enclosures, some rough-hewn crosses and two wells. The most evocative remains, though, are the six distinctive beehive cells in which monks of the Dark Ages passed an appropriately murky existence.

It's difficult to credit that these neat and intricate drystone constructions have survived almost a millennium and a half of onslaughts from Atlantic gales. The cliffs of Great Skellig rise some 700 feet and it was from their awful summit that St Patrick drove the last venomous snakes of Ireland into the sea. Several local companies offer boat trips to the Skelligs but if you book with **The Skellig Experience,** at Portmagee on the mainland, the package includes entry to the visitor centre which provides informative audio-visual displays on all aspects of the island's history.

"cleavage" – the ease with which tiles could be split from the block. Valentia tiles protected many notable buildings, ranging from London's Houses of Parliament to the San Salvador railway station in South America.

If you were to travel due west from Valentia, the first landfall would be Newfoundland, 1900 miles distant, but a much shorter boat trip, about 9 miles to the southwest, will bring you to the fascinating **Skellig Islands** (see panel above).

Cahersiveen

42 miles NW of Kenmare on the N70

From Valentia, the Ring of Kerry runs northwards to the resort town of Cahersiveen, birthplace of Daniel O'Connell, "The Liberator", in 1775. His story, and an introduction to the area, are on display in the impressive **Heritage Centre,** housed in a restored former police barracks. The great statesman is also commemorated by the Daniel O'Connell

O'Shea's B&B

Church Street, Cahersiveen, Co. Kerry
Tel: 066 947 2402
e-mail: osheasbnb@eircom.net
website: www.osheasbnb.com

Conveniently located in the centre of this popular little resort but enjoying some grand sea and mountain views, **O'Shea's B&B** is a family run business offering first class accommodation and food. All 4 guest bedrooms have en suite facilities and TV, and the generous breakfast includes some tasty home baking. Your hosts, Eileen and Patrick O'Shea are a friendly couple who have been welcoming guests since 1994. They have a wealth of local knowledge and can guide you to the many local amenities – golf, fishing, scenic walks, swimming, scuba diving, cycling, archaeological trips and boat trips to Skellig Rock.

Slea Head, Dingle Peninsula

Park, set beside the River Fertha and, even more remarkably, by the Daniel O'Connell Memorial Church, a rare instance of a church being dedicated to a politician rather than a saint.

About 10 miles north of Cahersiveen, the Ring of Kerry joins the southern coastline of Dingle Bay. From this point, there are grand views across the bay almost all the way to Killorglin. A worthwhile stop en route is at Glenbeigh where the **Kerry Bog Village Museum** is a unique development which includes theme cottages, an old forge equipped with all its utensils, a stone hen house, vegetable garden and a bog. The dwellings are exact replicas of those built in Ireland in the early 1800s.

The Dingle Peninsula

The most northerly of County Kerry's promontories, the Dingle Peninsula stretches westwards for 30 miles with the Blasket Islands scattered off its southwestern tip. The dramatic scenery of its mountain backbone, a spectacular coastal road, a wealth of ancient remains and traditional customs, crafts and lore have made the peninsula one of the most popular tourist destinations in the west. There's a lively music scene in this Irish-speaking enclave and a visit is made even more enjoyable by the excellent seafood available, especially in and around the delightful fishing port of Dingle. We begin this survey in the southeastern corner, at Inch, and travel clockwise around the peninsula to Tralee, the capital town of County Kerry.

Inch (*Inse*)

14 miles E of Dingle on the R561

At Inch a long narrow sandbar stretches across the mouth of Castlemaine Harbour providing shelter for the bird sanctuary on its eastern side. In the 18th century Kerry wreckers had the brilliant wheeze of tying a lantern to a horse's head and leaving it to graze on the dunes on stormy nights. Sailors would mistake the moving light for another boat, steer towards it and find themselves aground on the strand.

Four miles long and with a backdrop of the Slieve Mish mountains, the beach at Inch is probably the finest in Ireland. At low tide, you can walk a mile out to sea and

Inch Strand

the water will still be only an inch deep. The beach featured in the film *Ryan's Daughter* and you could easily imagine Robert Mitchum striding across the sands towards you.

Annascaul *(Abhainn an Scáil)*

9 miles E of Dingle on the N86

In this tiny village, a mile or so inland, you can get a drink at the South Pole or more precisely, at the South Pole Inn *(see separate entry)*, so named because it was once owned by Thomas Crean, a member of both Scott's and Shackleton's expeditions to the Antarctic. Another pub in the village, Dan Foley's Pub used to be run by the popular magician of that name and is much photographed because of its shocking-pink frontage. About 3 miles outside the village is **Minard Castle.** The largest fortress on the peninsula, it was a stronghold of the Knights of Kerry but was virtually destroyed by Cromwell's troops in 1650.

Dingle (*An Daingean*)

40 miles NW of Killarney on the N86

Dingle, which bills itself as "the westernmost town in Europe", is a busy fishing port with brightly-coloured houses clustered around a huge natural harbour. Fishing is still carried on in the traditional way with small boats and low-tech methods, but the catches are copious and excellent fresh seafood features on most menus in the town's many restaurants and cafés. The town also boasts a first-class bookshop/café, "An Café Liteartha", several good craft shops, an internet café, The Dingle Web, and plenty of good old-fashioned pubs where you'll find music most evenings.

In medieval times Dingle was a major port, trading mostly with Spain. When that commerce petered out, the town took advantage of its remote position to become an active centre for smuggling. The proceeds from this illicit traffic were so

South Pole Inn

Main Street, Annascaul, Co. Kerry
Tel: 066 91 57388
e-mail: info@southpoleinn.ie
website: www.southpoleinn.ie

Named in honour of Annascaul's most famous son, the Antarctic explorer Tom Crean who ran the pub between 1920 and 1938, the **South Pole Inn** provides a welcome contrast to the rigours of the frozen south with its open fire, warm timber floors and wonderful atmosphere. This hundred-year-old pub is a family-run business with Eileen and Trevor Percival, son Gary, daughter-in-law Jane, Eileen's brother Tim O'Shea and his partner Pauline Smith all helping to make it as popular as it is. One of the big attractions here is the wholesome and appetising food which is served every day of the week from noon until 8pm and includes a Kid's Menu.

Live music sessions are held every weekend and the inn also has a first floor function room for parties and also for occasional lectures connected with Tom Crean's Antarctic adventures. The pub walls are hung with many pictures of Tom who was born near Annascaul in 1877, enlisted in the British Navy in 1893 as a "Boy, 2nd Class" and was to be a valued member of Scott's two Antarctic expeditions, and also took part in Shackleton's doomed attempt to cross the Antarctic. On December 12th, 2001, the centenary of Tom's first departure, Eileen and Gary founded the Tom Crean Society which has been addressed by Sir Edmund Hillary and relatives of both Scott and Shackleton.

Dingle Town

abundant that for a while the town minted its own coinage. Today, Dingle's prime industry is tourism, with visitors drawn here by the town's scenic location, surrounded on three sides by hills, its good angling and attractions such as **Oceanworld** which reveals the fascinating species that inhabit the nearby waters and offers a journey through the Peninsula's ancient sea culture from pre-Christian times to the present. Interactive screens allow visitors to follow in the footsteps of St Brendan the Navigator and to examine some artefacts salvaged from wrecked ships of the Spanish Armada. The highlight of a visit is an underwater walk through the Tunnel Tank with long-snouted sharks gliding eerily above you.

But Dingle's most popular attraction has to be **Funghie,** the 660 lbs bottlenose dolphin who arrived in the harbour in 1983 and has been delighting visitors ever since with his frolicsome ways.

JOHN BENNY MORIARTY

The Pier, Dingle, Co. Kerry
Tel: 066 915 1215
e-mail: jbenny@eircom.net
website: www.johnbennyspub.com

With its brightly painted frontage **John Benny Moriarty's** pub is easy to find and is well worth seeking out for its great food, wonderful atmosphere and regular traditional music sessions. Mine host, John Benny Moriarty, is a larger than life character who dispenses hospitality and keeps the craic going with equal aplomb. John's wife, Eills ni Chinneide, is a professional singer which possibly explains why the pub has such an outstanding reputation for good music. There are live traditional music sessions every Monday, Wednesday, Friday and Saturday nights throughout the year, with Monday evenings dedicated to set dancing.

Another major attraction here is the excellent food on offer. The style is traditional Irish cuisine, all of it home cooked and with the emphasis on fresh local seafood – look out particularly for the wonderful scallops dish. Food is served from 12.30pm to 9.30pm, every day; credit cards are accepted. If you are planning to stay in this popular little town, Moriarty's has 3 luxury self-catering apartments available. Set in a secluded garden setting, these delightful apartments can sleep up to 5 guests and are fully equipped with all modern conveniences.

Paul's

Geany's Bar & Steakhouse, Main Street,
Dingle, Co. Kerry
Tel: 066 91 51238
e-mail: paulgeanysbar@eircom.net

Those in search of a traditional Irish pub with plenty of atmosphere but one which also serves superior bar food should make their way to **Paul's**, a smart-looking establishment on Dingle's Main

Street. Mine host, Paul Geany, is a young man with a real relish – and flair – for his job, qualities which explain why his hostelry is so popular. Well-maintained ales complement the excellent food which, during the season, is served from noon until 4pm, and from 5.30pm to 9.30pm.

Greenmount House

Upper John Street, Dingle, Co. Kerry
Tel: 066 915 1414 Fax: 066 915 1974
e-mail: greenmounthouse@eircom.net
website: www.greenmount-house.com

Beautifully located overlooking Dingle town and harbour, **Greenmount House** is a 4-star luxury guesthouse where the Curran family promise guests "a warm welcome from a real Dingle family". Their family home has been extended over the years to incorporate 6 top-class en suite rooms and 6 newly-developed superior rooms each enjoying those wonderful sea views. Each room has a full bathroom and large sitting area and is equipped with television, direct dial phones, tea/coffee-making facilities and many other extras.

The house has been decorated to the highest standards throughout and the guest lounges, with their warm fires, are wonderfully comfortable and ideal places to relax in after a long day exploring the scenic Dingle peninsula. A particular attraction at Greenmount House is the magnificent breakfast – a feast for which the Currans are renowned, having twice been regional winners of the Galtee Breakfast Award and the Jameson Guide Breakfast Award Winner in 2001. The house is ideally located for those who want to experience this gloriously unspoilt corner of Ireland – Dingle town is just a short stroll away and the many attractions of the peninsula are never more than a few minutes drive away.

THE LANTERN TOWNHOUSE

Main Street, Dingle, Co. Kerry
Tel: 066 915 1088
e-mail: thelantern@ireland.com
website: www.dinglebedandbreakfast.com

In the heart of this popular resort, **The Lantern Townhouse** offers quality bed and breakfast accommodation in relaxed and informal surroundings. The house is furnished to a very high standard and each of its en suite guest bedrooms is tastefully designed and equipped with direct dial telephone and TV. Guests also have the use of a comfortable lounge, well-stocked with books, and owner Linda Clifford is happy to arrange any outdoor pursuits such as golf, fishing, sailing, surfing, cycling, horse trekking, mountaineering and ornithology. The house is close to restaurants and pubs with traditional Irish music.

An early morning boat takes out those who want to swim with Funghie and, weather permitting, boats leave at 8am and 10am to join him. In the unlikely event of Funghie not appearing, you get your money back. Other waterborne journeys available are eco-tours up the coast, trips across the bay to Valentia Island, and ferries to Great Blasket Island.

Ventry *(Paróiste Fionn Trá)*
5 miles W of Dingle on the R559

Like Dingle, Ventry boasts a fine natural harbour but the wide curve of sandy beach, dotted with a sprinkling of houses, shops and a pub, gives little indication that this was once the main port on the peninsula. Westwards from Ventry the road is carved

BALLYMORE HOUSE

Ballymore, Ventry, Dingle, Co. Kerry
Tel: 066 915 9050
e-mail: info@ballymorehouse.com
website: www.ballymorehouse.com

Located 3Km west of Dingle on the R559 Main Slea Head Drive, **Ballymore House** is a spacious country home with sea view offering high quality bed and breakfast accommodation in peaceful rural surroundings. This traditional house is the home of Maurice and Therese O'Shea, a warm, friendly and welcoming couple who greet arriving guests with complimentary tea/coffee and home baking beside the open coal fire. Therese and Maurice take great pride in their home cooking and home cooked dinner at Ballymore House is a must. Dinner may be prebooked by visa/mastercard. Seafood is our speciality along with Dingle Organic Mountain Lamb.

Breakfast is equally appetising with an extensive choice of cereals and juices, smoked salmon, smoked mackeral, vegetarian dishes, Irish breakfast, fruit and yogurt and boiled eggs. Any special requirement will be looked after on request. Guests at Ballymore House can enjoy TV lounge with open fire or reading lounge for those that want to relax. Accommodation comprises of 6 bedrooms all with private facilities, 5 with seaview, with a choice of doubles, twins or triples. Numerous recommendations, Bord Failte 'Irish Welcome Award' 2002 and 2003. Open all year including Christmas. Ballymore House is a must for any person traveling to Dingle Penninsula. Private car park.

into the precipitous flank of Mount Eagle (1696 feet) and passes through an area renowned for its abundant archaeological remains. The most dramatic site is **Dún Beag**, a 1200-year-old cliff-top fort about 4 miles west of Ventry. A great wall, 22 feet thick, is girdled by four rings of earthworks, beehive huts stand nearby, and an elaborately constructed souterrain, or underground escape passage, testifies to the engineering sophistication of the medieval occupants of this lonely outpost. Dún Beag is part of the astonishing **Fahan Group** which includes no fewer than 414 clochans, (unmortared beehive huts), 19 souterrains, 18 standing inscribed stones, 7 earthen ring forts and 2 sculptured crosses. Not to be missed.

Continue westwards along the R559 to Slea Head where there's a magnificent panoramic view of the **Blasket Islands**, a group of seven islands and many rocks. These bare, inhospitable islands, uninhabited since 1953 except for summer stayovers, nevertheless proved to be a fertile source of memorable literature. Books such as Maurice O'Sullivan's *Twenty Years A-Growing* and Thomas O'Crohan's *The Islander* give a vivid impression of life on these sequestered isles where few could read or write but all contributed to a rich tradition of oral folk lore and legend. During the summer, there are boat trips to Great Blasket island where you can land and wander the many paths or find a secluded beach. Boats leave from Dunquin, a small village on the mainland where you'll also find the **Blasket Island Centre**, *Ionad am Bhlascaoid Mhóir*, which provides an introduction to the islands and contains a comprehensive archive of books, tapes, films and photographs relating to the Blaskets.

Blasket Islands

From Dunquin, the R559 continues around the western tip of the peninsula to Ballyferriter and the broad inlet of Smerwick Harbour, overlooked by **Dún an Óir**, "the Golden Fort". In September 1580 the beach here, wonderfully peaceful now, became an abattoir. Spanish, Italian, English and Irish supporters of the Catholic rebellion against Protestant England were defeated at Smerwick by English forces led by Lord Grey. Despite having surrendered, some 600 men, women and children were slaughtered on the sands. A monument erected in 1980 records this dismal event.

A mile or so inland from Smerwick Harbour stands one of the best preserved early Christian church buildings in Ireland. **Gallarus Oratory** (free) dates from somewhere between AD 800 and 1200 and at that time its design, (shaped rather like an inverted boat), was a major architectural advance on the earlier beehive constructions. A doorway that narrows towards the top leads into a space only 15 feet by 10 feet, with just a single loophole window at the eastern end providing a "dim, religious light". Despite the fact that the Oratory was built so many centuries ago, with unmortared stone, it remains completely watertight. Only a slight sagging in its roofline admits to the weight of years.

Ballydavid *(Baile na nGall)*

7 miles NW of Dingle on minor road off the R559

Sometime in the 5th century AD, St Brendan set sail from Ballydavid Head in search of the "Islands of Paradise" which had been revealed to him in a vision. His course lay due west, giving rise to the enduring legend that he was the first European to discover the Americas. He sailed in a currach, a boat whose construction is peculiar to the west of Ireland. The currach's wooden framework is covered by a tarred canvas and its high prow is well-designed to slice through oncoming waves. Ballydavid is one of the very few places in Ireland where these sturdy craft are still built. It's not known whether St Brendan's currach did indeed convey him to America some 900 years before Columbus arrived there, but whether he did or not, Brendan has been adopted as the patron saint of County Kerry and the mighty hill that rises to the east of Ballydavid has been named Mount Brandon in his honour.

Cloghane *(An Clochán)*

7 miles NE of Dingle on minor road off the N86

As the crow flies, Cloghane is less than 8 miles from Ballydavid but with the bulk of Mount Brandon intervening it's necessary to return to Dingle and then take the dramatically scenic route northwards through the Conor Pass. The road rises to 1500 feet and provides some magical views over Dingle Bay and Tralee Bay. The little village of Cloghane boasts some lovely beaches and makes a good starting point for exploring the superb coastal scenery between Brandon Point and Brandon Head. A gruelling pathway up the mountainside leads to a shrine at the summit, marking the place where St Brendan received his vision of the "Islands of Paradise".

Fahamore

32 miles NW of Killarney off the R560

Hidden away on the northern tip of the Dingle Peninsula, the seaside village of Fahamore has some fine sandy beaches and is the departure point for boats ferrying passengers to the Maharees Islands, the "Seven Hogs", a mile or so offshore. The most interesting of the islands is **Illauntannig** where there are the remains of an early Christian monastery attributed to St Seanach. A protective wall encloses the ruins of two oratories, three beehive cells and a small cross.

THE TANKARD

Kilfenora, Tralee, Co. Kerry
Tel: 066 713 6164 Fax: 066 713 6516
e-mail: tankard@eircom.net
website: www.traleegoodfoodcircle.com

Owned and run by the O'Sullivan family for more than 28 years, **The Tankard** is well-established as one of Tralee's most popular hostelries. Known to its many local patrons as "The Tank", it occupies a splendid position overlooking the broad sweep of Tralee Bay, backed by the distant summits of the Slieve Mish Mountains.

Originally built in 1874, the pub has been extended many times over the years and now boasts a 130-seater restaurant looking out over the bay, a conservatory style lounge, a huge public bar complete with piano, a snug and a games room. The yellow exterior reflects the warm and welcoming atmosphere that the Tankard has to offer and nowhere is this more evident than in the bar.

Producing outstanding food is the priority here and The Tankard's excellent cuisine has won plaudits from just about every major food writer and good food guide. All the food is freshly prepared and the chef prides himself on the superb quality of the beef and seafood on offer. Fresh fish and lobster landed daily from Fenit pier, and Tralee Bay oysters and mussels from Cromane make dining at the Tankard a memorable experience. A huge wine list is also available here with more than 100 wines to choose from. There's a choice of two menus – wholesome and appetising bar food or the enticing à la carte options. Bar food is served from 1pm to 10pm, seven days a week; the restaurant is open from 6pm until 10pm – credit cards are accepted. In addition to the wonderful food, you'll find that landlord Jerry O'Sullivan pulls a "divine" pint of Guinness. Currently, The Tankard has no accommodation but plans are under way to provide guest bedrooms in the near future.

Kilfenora itself is well known for its annual festival of traditional music that takes place over the October Bank Holiday weekend. Other attractions in the village include the Burren Display Centre devoted to the history and geology of the Burren, and Kilfenora Cathedral which is noted for its fine 12th century high crosses.

Tralee

If you are female and can claim some Irish ancestry, you too could be the "Rose of Tralee". As part of the **Kerry Festival,** held in the last week of August, any lady of Irish descent can compete in a decorous beauty, or rather personality, contest to win the title of "Rose Queen". The sentimental Victorian song, *The Rose of Tralee*, was written by a local man, William Mulchinock, who lived near the town at Cloghers House, Ballymullen.

Tralee enjoys festivals. There's another one that takes place over the Easter weekend, the **International Pan Celtic Festival**, founded in 1971. The festival is designed to strengthen the bonds of friendship between the six Celtic nations – Ireland, Scotland, Wales, Brittany, Cornwall and the Isle of Man, and to promote their traditional music, song and dance. The week-long festivities culminate on the Sunday with an inter-denominational Mass which features musical contributions from all six nations.

The town calls itself "the Happy Holiday Centre" and there is plenty here to keep visitors entertained – historic buildings, spacious parks, quality food and shopping, a bowling centre, horse and greyhound racing, golf, arts and crafts, a vibrant night life and a range of all-weather visitor attractions unmatched anywhere else in

Irish National Folk Theatre, Tralee

Ireland. One of the most popular is the **Aqua Dome**, Ireland's largest waterworld, where visitors can battle raging rapids, splash out in the wave pool or plummet down the water flume. Children have their own pool and slides, while adults can relax in the extensive Sauna Dome. Other amenities include an 18-hole miniature golf course, a restaurant and ice cream parlour, and a shop selling a variety of water-related

David Norris Restaurant

Ivy Terrace, Tralee, Co. Kerry
Tel: 066 718 5654
e-mail: restaurantdavidnorris@eircom

Outstanding Irish cuisine with an international flavour is the order of the day at the **David Norris Restaurant**, an elegant small eating place located close to the town centre. David opened his own business here in 2001 after many years working as a chef in some of Munster's top-class restaurants. His menu changes regularly in response to the best available produce but always includes a Fresh Fish Dish of the Evening and vegetarian choices. Crisp white linen, stylish cutlery, sparkling glassware, intimate lighting and well-spaced tables all combine to make dining here a real pleasure. The restaurant is fully licensed and open from 5pm to 10pm, Tuesday to Saturday.

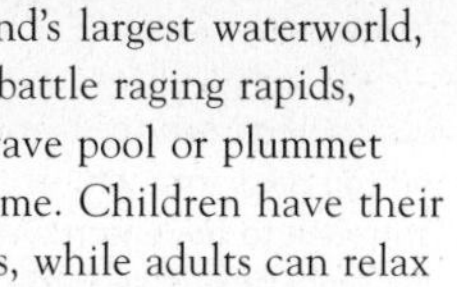

St Joseph's

2 Staughtons Row, Tralee, Co. Kerry
Tel: 066 712 1174 Fax: 066 712 1254

Close to the town centre and dating back to 1818, **St Joseph's** is an elegant late-Georgian building which still has its original front door, ceiling cornices and fireplace. Quality furniture and decoration, along with some fine Irish antiques all add to the appeal. For the last 40 years or so, St Joseph's has been the home of Hannah Foley who welcomes bed and breakfast guests all year round. Her 6 guest rooms are beautifully furnished, all have en suite facilities and all are provided with TV.

Registered with Bord Failte, this town centre establishment offers exceptional value for money.

items such as buoyancy aids and water toys.

On a more cultural level, the outstanding **Kerry the Kingdom** contains three separate attractions. "Kerry in Colour" provides a panoramic, multi-image audio-visual tour of County Kerry celebrating its scenery, historic sites, people and traditions. In the "Geraldine Tralee" exhibit, visitors are seated in time cars and transported 600 years back in history to the reconstructed streets, houses, Abbey and Castle of medieval Tralee, complete with sounds and smells. The Museum itself uses interactive media and life-size models, along with priceless treasures dating from the Stone and Bronze Age, to recount the story of Kerry and Ireland over 8000 years.

Just along the road from Kerry the

Harty's

Lower Castle Street, Tralee, Co. Kerry
Tel: 066 712 5385

As you pass through the brightly coloured entrance to the enormously long bar, you instantly recognise **Harty's** as a truly authentic traditional Irish pub. One of Tralee's best-known landmarks, Tom and Rony Harty's popular hostelry has been owned and run by their family for more than 60 years – their parents opened the pub way back in 1940.

It's noted for its excellent, value-for-money food, (just try their Irish Stew or one of the mighty steaks), for serving the best Guinness in town, for friendly and efficient staff – and for generating the best craic in the county!

Food is served from 10am to 9pm, Monday to Saturday, and at lunchtime on Sundays. Friday nights are especially popular since that is when the pub resounds to the strains of traditional Irish music.

Harty's also has another claim to fame. It was here that the seeds of the famous "Rose of Tralee" contest were sown. Any lady with Irish ancestry can take part in this good-natured personality competition to win the title based on the Victorian song written by a local man, William Mulchinock. The contest is Ireland's largest pageant and now forms part of the Kerry Festival which takes place during the last week of August each year.

Kingdom, the **Siamsa Tíre Theatre** is the home of the acclaimed National Folk Theatre of Ireland whose aim is to present on stage a dance/theatre entertainment based on the wealth of Irish music, folklore and dance. The performances do not use dialogue and so are immediately accessible to visitors from every land.

A disastrous fire in 1580 consumed Tralee's ancient buildings and the heart of the town is mostly Victorian with a sprinkling of Georgian houses. Two churches are well worth visiting – the neo-Gothic Dominican **Church of the Holy Cross**, designed by Pugin and with some fine stained glass by Michael Healy, and the prominent landmark of **St John's Church**, a masterpiece of the Gothic Revival style in Ireland which also has some dazzling Victorian stained glass and a sculpture of St Brendan by Gabrielle Hayes.

Devotees of steam railways will be delighted with the narrow-gauge **Tralee & Dingle Steam Railway** whose station is located on the southern outskirts of the town, close to the River Lee. This is Europe's most westerly line and was part of the famous Tralee & Dingle Light Railway which functioned from 1891 to 1953. During the season, steam trains depart on the hour, every hour, from 11am to 5pm, for the 2-mile jaunt to Blennerville.

Around Tralee

North of Tralee, the Stacks Mountains stride eastwards into County Limerick while the rest of this area is undulating farmland bounded by the Atlantic to the west and the River Shannon to the north. There are fine beaches at Banna and Ballyheige, and Ballybunnion, near the mouth of the Shannon, is a delightful resort, famous for its seaweed baths. There are few ancient buildings although Ardfert boasts a fine Norman cathedral and Carrigafoyle Castle occupies a striking location overlooking the Shannon. Listowel is well known for its annual Writers' Week while at Tarbert the Bridewell Jail is worth a visit. From Tarbert you can also take a ferry across the Shannon to County Clare.

Ardfert

5 miles NW of Tralee on the R551

The town's principal attraction is **Ardfert Cathedral**, a noble Norman building dating back to the 13th century. It stands on the site of a monastery founded by St Brendan in the 7th century and in medieval times the cathedral was County Kerry's ecclesiastical centre. A striking effigy of a bishop of those days was discovered here in 1830 and now stands in a niche in the building. The cathedral's most impressive features are its superb Romanesque west door and an elegant triple-lancet window in the Gothic style. Just down the road and also worth visiting is a rather austere 15th century Franciscan friary and church.

About a mile west of Ardfert, **Banna Strand** commands splendid views over Tralee Bay. In April 1916, on the eve of the Easter Rising, the Irish patriot Sir Roger Casement, who had been trying to get Germany to commit troops to an invasion of Ireland, was brought here by a German submarine. Casement was promptly arrested by the British, tried and executed as a traitor a few months later. His plea to be buried in Ireland was rejected at the time but his body was finally returned to his homeland in 1965 and was buried at Glasnevin Cemetery in Dublin following a state funeral.

Ballyheigue

12 miles NW of Tralee on the R551

Set in a corner of Ballyheigue Bay, this is a pleasantly peaceful little resort with an excellent sandy beach overlooked by the striking ruins of Ballyheigue Castle, actually a 19th century mansion. There is some fine coastal scenery here, especially around

SHANNON VIEW

Ferry Road, Ballyduff, Co.Kerry
Tel: 066 713 1324

Immaculately maintained modern bungalow standing in mature well-tended gardens, **Shannon View** is the home of Nuala and David Sowden who have been welcoming bed & breakfast guests since 1992. A major attraction here is David's cooking, a professional chef he offers a superb evening meal based on fresh local seafood, beef and lamb, complemented by fresh local vegetables. There are 4 guest bedrooms, two en suite and two with adjoining bathroom.

Seven minutes drive to Ballybunion Golf Course and sandy beaches, twenty minutes to Ballyheigue, forty minutes from Tarbert Car Ferry. En-route to Cliffs of Maher Dingele and Ring of Kerry.

Kerry Head which shelters the bay from the north.

The cliffs and rocks of Kerry Head contain large numbers of amethysts and the so-called "Kerry diamonds" – almost perfectly formed quartz crystals either purple in colour or clear.

Ballyduff

13 miles N of Tralee on the R551

The little village of Ballyduff is home to the **Rattoo Heritage Complex**, established in 1990 as a voluntary non-profit making body pledged to protect, promote and preserve the historic, cultural and environmental aspects of the Kingdom of Kerry. Its museum contains more than 1000 exhibits dating from antiquity to present times and the Ratto Society has produced three major historic films on the villages of Ballyduff, Causeway and Ballybunion.

A lane at the southern end of the village leads to Rattoo Church, built in the 15th century using materials from a much older church and, nearby, the 92 feet high Rattoo Round Tower.

Ballybunion

20 miles N of Tralee on the R553

A decorous resort at the mouth of the Shannon, Ballybunion has some good sandy beaches, and with its caves, coves and

rugged cliffs is popular with families. The town boasts a magnificent cliff-top 18-hole golf course, boats are available for angling or pleasure trips, and during the season there's a variety of stage performances and dances. Ballybunion's most unusual attraction however is its **Seaweed Baths** which occupy two 1920s bathing houses on the North Beach. Bathers settle down in their own private bathroom, supplied with an inexhaustible stream of hot sea water and a generous quantity of seaweed gathered earlier in the day from the Black Rocks. A good soak relieves any aches and pains you may have and afterwards you can take a tray of tea and apple tart onto the beach.

Listowel

17 miles NE of Tralee on the N69

Set beside the River Feale, Listowel has a ruined 15th century castle in the town square which belonged to the Lords of Kerry and was the last to resist the Elizabethan forces during the Desmond revolt. When the castle finally fell to English troops in 1600 the whole garrison was put to the sword.

This quiet little town bursts into life in the third week of September when the annual **Listowel Races** attract farming people, their harvests gathered in, from all over Ireland. A more sedate event takes place in June when the town hosts a week-

North County House

67 Church Street, Listowel, Co. Kerry
Tel: 068 21238 Fax: 068 22831
e-mail: bryanmonica1@eircom.net

Conveniently located on Listowel's main road, **North County House** is a luxurious family-run guest house which at the time of writing is being extensively remodelled and refurbished to create a stylish "town house" environment. Owner Monica Quille is a friendly and welcoming lady who is renowned for her wonderful full Irish breakfast, a hearty feast that will set you up for the day. This non-smoking house has 8 spacious guest bedrooms, all attractively furnished and decorated and with en suite facilities. Guests also have the use of a comfortable residents TV lounge; golfers can enjoy a fee reduction at the 18-hole Ballybunion Golf Club a few miles down the road.

long festival of writers' workshops and meetings. Several notable writers live and work in Listowel although the town's most famous author is probably John B. Keane whose *Man of the Triple Name* is a lively account of matchmaking shenanigans in North Kerry in the 1930s and 1940s. John runs John B. Keane's Pub, as authentic an Irish pub as you could hope to find anywhere in the country.

Located in the main square and occupying a former church, the **St John's Theatre & Arts Centre** offers a wide variety of drama, dance and music performances, as well as art exhibitions. In July and August, guided walks around the town start from the theatre. During these months also, three of the town's pubs host free theatre performances.

A recent addition to the town's amenities is **Seanchaí**, the Kerry Literary and Cultural Centre where you'll find a room devoted to John B. Keane along with others featuring local writers such as George Fitzmaurice, Brendan Kennelly, Brian McMahon and Maurice Walsh. Recorded extracts from their works are played and there are videos of Eamon Kelly, Ireland's most famous seanchaí (story-teller), and writers talking about their work.

Tarbert

28 miles NE of Tralee on the N69

The small village of Tarbert stands on a

Dillane's Farmhouse

Doonard, Listowel Road, Tarbert, Co. Kerry
Tel: 068 36242
e-mail: dillanesfarmhouse@eircom.net
website: www.dillanes.com

Set well back from the main Tarbet to Listowel Road, **Dillane's Farmhouse** occupies a wonderfully peaceful location just a short stroll from the village and a 5-minute drive from the car ferry across the Shannon. Your host is Tom Dillane whose family has lived in these parts for more than 200 years – he's also a well-known musician, renowned for his renditions of traditional Irish music. The farmhouse has 4 good sized guest bedrooms, all en suite and equipped with TV and hospitality tray. An ideal base for touring Kerry, Limerick and Clare, the farmhouse is also within easy reach of some good restaurants and pubs.

The Courtyard

Blennerville, nr Tralee, Co. Kerry
Tel: 066 712 4494 Fax: 066 712 7751
e-mail: myra@countykerryholidays.com
website: www.countykerryholidays.com

National Winners of the Self-Catering Award 2001 and with a 4-star rating from Bord Failte, **The Courtyard** are a group of charming cottages set in a courtyard setting dating back to 1832. Originally a stable yard these cottages have been tastefully decorated by Derry and Myra Daly to provide six stone cottages each refurbished to the highest standard with wooden floors and antique furniture. Myra, a knitwear designer, has personally designed each cottage.

On arrival there is a complimentary wine and hand-made chocolates and the Dalys will personally ensure that you receive a warm Irish welcome. All the cottages have open fires where guests can relax before retiring to handmade beds with crisp white bedlinen.

On site there is a secluded garden, barbecue, area playground and tennis court.

The courtyard is an ideal location for touring Kerry. It is close to equestrian centres, championship golf courses at Tralee, Ballybunion and Kilarney. Sea fishing, angling, windsurfing, hillwalking and a number of renowned walks start at their doorstep.

Tralee town is only 2km with its many attractions – amongst them the Siamsa Tire National Folk Theatre of Ireland and the Aquadrome (Ireland's largest water theme park). The Courtyard is only 5 minutes drive to the sandy Atlantic Ocean beaches.

steep slope overlooking one of the most attractive stretches of the River Shannon. A year-round vehicle ferry operates from here making the short crossing to County Clare in a matter of minutes. While waiting for the ferry, you might care to spend a while in the **Bridewell Courthouse & Jail** (1831) which has been restored with tableaux and exhibits to show how the judicial system worked in those days. Open from April to October, the Bridewell also serves an excellent afternoon tea

Castleisland

12 miles E of Tralee on the N21

Standing at the eastern end of the Vale of Tralee, Castleisland is a thriving market town that takes its name from a castle built here in 1226 by Geoffrey de Marisco. The ruins can still be seen.

The town is noted for its red marble, a colouring that results from iron oxide in the local rock. To the north of Castleisland is Knight's Mountain (1080 feet) and, nearby, Desmond's Grave – resting place of the 15th and last Earl of Desmond who was executed here in 1583.

Just outside the town to the east, **Crag Cave** is a remarkable cave system stretching for some 2 miles underground. Grotesquely shaped stalagmites and stalactites a million years old line the caves which were only discovered by accident in 1983. Guided tours are available and there's also a restaurant and craft shop.

Blennerville

2 miles SW of Tralee on the N86

Blennerville was the main port of emigration from County Kerry during the Great Famine and that story is told in an exhibition and audio-visual presentation at the **Blennerville Windmill Visitor & Craft Centre.** The windmill itself is the largest working mill in the British Isles and is beautifully set beside the bridge with the Slieve Mish Mountains as a backdrop. A miller is always on hand to explain the flour making process and the complex also includes craft workshops, gift shop and restaurant.

Co Kildare

County Kildare is traversed by several of the arterial roads leading away from Dublin and these convey visitors along without taking them near the best that Kildare has to offer. One of the most satisfying ways to discover the county is by following the Grand Canal, either by hiring a cruiser or just walking along the towpath. The landscape is relatively flat, offering panoramic views of rolling farmland and the stone walls surrounding the old estates.

The Irish love of horses is legendary and Kildare is famous for its racecourses at Punchestown, Naas and, most famous of all, The Curragh at Kildare Town where the Irish National Stud is also located. Amongst the county's most notable buildings are the magnificent Classical pile of Castletown House at Celbridge, and Kilkea Castle at Castledermot, a largely 19th century restoration but none the less impressive for it.

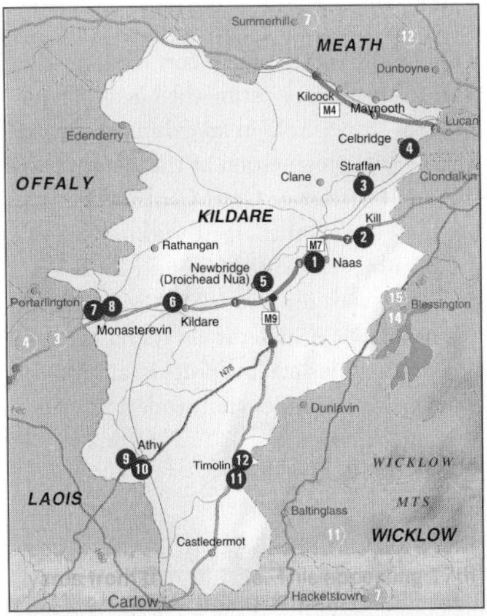

Naas

Barely 20 miles from the centre of Dublin, the county town of Naas (pronounced *Nace*) is fast becoming a commuter suburb of the capital. Although it was once one of the seats of the Kings of Leinster, all that remains of that regal past is a large *motte*, or man-made hill, in the centre of the town. The principal attraction for visitors is

PLACES TO STAY, EAT AND DRINK

Harbour Hotel & Restaurant, Naas	1	Hotel	p179
Olthove House, Kill	2	Guest House	p180
Morell Farm, Straffan	3	Visitor Attraction	p181
Setanta House Hotel, Celbridge	4	Hotel	p182
Red House Country Hotel, Newbridge	5	Hotel	p184
Silken Thomas, Kildare	6	Pub, Restaurant & Accommodation	p186
Cloncarlin House, Monasterevin	7	B&B	p187
The Hazel Hotel, Monasterevin	8	Hotel	p188
Tonlegee House & Restaurant, Athy	9	Restaurant & Accommodation	p189
Aurora B&B, Athy	10	B&B	p190
Woodcourte House B&B, Athy	11	B&B	p191
Sportsman's Bar & Restaurant, Moone	12	Bar & Restaurant	p191

● Denotes entries in other chapters

Collcarrigan Gardens, Naas

nearby **Punchestown Racecourse** whose main meeting of the year is the 3-day steeple-chasing festival in late April.

Motor-racing enthusiasts will find racing events most weekends at the **Mondello Park** circuit where, for a fairly substantial fee, they can experience the thrill of driving a single-seater racing car around the track.

Around Naas

Kill

5 miles NE of Naas on the N7

In the past this small village was notorious for its sheebeens – one of its pubs dates from 1794. Kill (meaning 'church') is better known today for **Goffs Bloodstock Sales Ring** which is famous throughout the world and also plays host to the Irish Masters Snooker Championships each year. The village

Olthove House

Newtown, Kill, Co. Kildare
Tel: 045 877022 e-mail: olthove@eircom.net
website: www.olthovehouse.com

Located in the picturesque village of Kill, **Olthove House** enjoys a charming setting, standing within 3 acres of mature gardens (including a full size croquet lawn) with a river running past. Tom and Olivia Meagher and their family relish the fact that the house is far enough out of the city to enjoy all the advantages of a countryside location whilst being a mere half an hour from the centre of Dublin. The 5 guest bedrooms here are all en suite with colour TV and guests have the use of a spacious living room and a dining room where breakfast is served from 6.30am.

boasts a number of equestrian riding centres and also sports a number of well-known golf clubs including the **K-Club**

Clane

5 miles N of Naas off the R403

Just a small village nowadays, Clane was an important ecclesiastical centre in medieval times. Sir Gerald Fitzmaurice founded a Franciscan abbey here in 1258 and its ruins still stand. Nearby Bodenstown churchyard is the final resting place of the Irish nationalist Wolfe Tone (1763-98). He was captured by the British during the rebellion of 1798 and committed suicide while under sentence of death.

Straffan

7 miles NE of Naas off the R403

Occupying a former Victorian church which has been transplanted here stone by stone from Dublin, the **Straffan Steam Museum** contains some surprisingly smooth-running steam engines, a display of miniature models of steam engines and exhibits detailing the impact of the "Iron Horse" on Ireland's history. In early August each year, the village resounds to the chuntering of steam engines gathering here for the annual Steam Rally.

At the nearby **Straffan Butterfly Farm** huge colourful butterflies flitter around freely while various creepy-crawlies, reptiles and tarantulas are considerately displayed behind glass. Gardeners will be attracted to **Lodge Park Walled Garden**, an 18th century creation that has a long walk bordered by gardens and leading to a delightful rose bower. The recently restored walled garden contains an orchard, topiary,

Lodge Park Walled Garden

Morell Farm

Turnings, Straffan, Co. Kildare
Tel: 01 628 8636

A grand day out for the family is assured at **Morell Farm,** a unique open farm with a personal, welcoming difference. The owner, Audrey Wilson, aims to provide visitors with an awareness of the farming countryside so they are encouraged to listen and touch at every opportunity, to have their questions answered and their understanding of what they are seeing enhanced. Children (and adults) can say "Hello!" to Daisy, the Jersey cow, and Sadie, the saddleback pig; hold and feed the many guinea pigs; meet the red deer and the arctic foxes; feed the kid goats and see the new born lambs with their mothers. They can also discover a huge variety of pheasants, ducks, geese and birds - the farm has the largest collection of rare poultry in Ireland and the greatest number of foreign birds and parakeets from Australia and India to the USA. There's also a collection of rabbits from all over the world, including Angora rabbits, peacocks from India, Anglo-Nubian goats, rare Egyptian geese, the chipmunks "Chip" 'n' "Dale" from America, and Minnie and Micky Marmoset and family. (Audrey recommends incidentally that children should be appropriately dressed in Wellingtons and bring a change of clothing).

Scattered around the farm is a large selection of antique farm machinery and there's also a picnic area beside a stream where visitors can enjoy lunch surrounded by peaceful countryside, or you can sample real home-made country baking in the coffee shop.

salad parterre and a greenhouse with an interesting collection of plants from around the world. At **Morell Farm** (see panel above) visitors will find rare and endangered breeds of farm livestock and poultry; a horse museum; antique farm museum and a nature walk.

Celbridge

11 miles NE of Naas on the R403

The little village of Celbridge on the River Liffey boasts two major visitor attractions. **Castletown House** is Ireland's largest and finest Palladian country house, built around 1722 for the Speaker of the Irish House of Commons, William Conolly. Conolly began life as the son of a publican in Donegal and became the richest man in Ireland by trading in forfeited estates following the Battle of the Boyne. The house was conceived on a massive scale. Conolly engaged the "best architect in Europe", the Italian Alessandro Galilei, to design the palatial mansion and while the exterior is restrained and formal with its regular rows of pedimented windows, the interior is much more flamboyant. The person mainly responsible for the striking decoration was Conolly's daughter-in-law, Lady Louisa Lennox, (one of the wayward Lennox sisters featured in the 1999 TV series *The Aristocrats*). It was she who commissioned the Lanfranchini brothers to produce the great hall's dazzling plasterwork; created the charming Print Room; and ordered the incongruous Murano glass chandeliers for the delightful Long Gallery, decorated in the Pompeian style. The Conolly family sold the house in 1965 and the majestic mansion was threatened with demolition so that a property developer could build "executive homes" on the site. Fortunately, the developer went bankrupt before demolition could begin and, even more happily, Desmond Guinness bought the house and presented it to the Irish Georgian

Setanta House Hotel

Clane Road, Celbridge, Co. Kildare
Tel: 01 627 1111/1112/1113
Fax: 01 627 3387 Mobile: 086 251 0188
website:
www.setantahousehotel@eircom.net

Back in 1729 William Connolly, Speaker of the Irish House of Commons, left a substantial sum in his will for the building of a school near Celbridge. The building was designed by the celebrated architect Thomas de Burgh who excelled himself by creating a magnificent mansion in soft grey local stone. Today, the elegance and atmosphere of the original building has been fully restored, creating a dynamic new ambience as the **Setanta House Hotel**. This family-owned and run hotel offers 66 newly refurbished guest bedrooms, luxuriously appointed with full en suite facilities and a wide variety of rooms and bed sizes, including some grand 4-poster beds and a number of DeLuxe rooms . All of the rooms are designed to reflect the historic character of the hotel in an elegant yet refreshingly cosy manner. Each is provided with colour TV, direct dial telephone, tea and coffee-making facilities and hairdryer as standard. The hotel offers an indulgent variety of services including personalised wake-up call and for an added tier of comfort and convenience Deluxe Rooms are available.

During their stay, guests can relax in the lovely secluded and landscaped gardens, enjoy the friendly ambience of the lounge areas and bars, and take advantage of the myriad of local amenities that includes golf, horse-riding, botanical gardens and more. One attraction that should not be missed is Castletown House, one of the grandest mansions in all Ireland which, like the hotel, was built for William Connolly.

Setanta House Hotel is an ideal venue for

business meetings of every kind with its attentive staff committed to making the event run smoothly and efficiently. It offers a full line of executive services, including fully equipped training rooms and conferencing facilities, Internet access, secretarial services and assistance with travel arrangements. The hotel can also provide companies with "off-site" days, summer barbecues and Christmas parties. The staff take pride in their attention to detail, another example of the hotel's continuing effort to provide a productive environment that fully complements and supports the customer's business activities.

The Setanta House Hotel's superb architecture and lovely grounds make it an ideal venue for weddings so a comprehensive wedding package is available for that very special day. It includes a red carpet and champagne on arrival for the bride and groom; complimentary reception of tea/coffee and biscuits on arrival for the guests; floral decorations on all tables; complimentary accommodation for the bride and groom in the Bridal Suite and special rates for wedding guests wishing to stay overnight.

Society. Castletown House was transferred to State care in 1994 and after extensive restoration and refurbishment in 1998/9, the house is once again home to a fine collection of 18th century Irish furniture and painting.

The grounds of Castletown House are as satisfying as the house, the extensive views enhanced by the follies erected by Conolly's widow. One has been described as *"140 feet of what appears to be a monument to chimney-sweeping"* while another, an Obelisk, enraged Lady Conolly's sister because of its cost – *"Three or four hundred pounds at least"*. Yet another, the "Wonderful Barn" (private), is a curious conical structure five storeys high which Lady Conolly nonchalantly erected on somebody else's property. Like so many follies of the time, they were erected to provide relief work in time of famine or unemployment.

Celbridge Abbey Grounds, situated on the River Liffey and its Millrace, are being developed by the St John of God Order as a historical, cultural and environmental amenity for the public. The magnificent grounds were planted by Vanessa Homrigh for her friend and admirer Jonathan Swift who was a frequent visitor. "Vanessa's Bower" is a delightful, secluded spot with a view of the weir where they spent many hours together. The nearby Rockbridge is believed to be the oldest remaining stone bridge over the Liffey. Celbridge Abbey itself, built in 1697 for Vanessa's father, Bartholomew Van Homrigh, Lord Mayor of Dublin, is a private residence and not open to the public but its handsome crenellated exterior provides an attractive focus to the grounds. A popular venue for family outings, the Abbey Grounds contain a well-stocked Garden Centre, a model railway reproducing a typical Irish railway in the 1950s, a crafts centre, children's playground, picnic areas, a restaurant, and there are also themed walks and an ecology trail.

Maynooth

14 miles N of Naas on the R408/R148

Maynooth is best known for St Patrick's College, Ireland's centre for training Catholic clergy. The seminary was established in 1795 on the site of an earlier college and its library contains some rare manuscripts and old printed books. The present building, started in 1847, was designed by Augustus Pugin in the Victorian Gothic style but does not represent his finest hour.

The **Maynooth College Visitor Centre & Museum** offers a variety of attractions, including an ecclesiastical museum with exhibits illustrating the history of the church in Ireland, a chapel and gardens. Guided tours are available during the summer months. Standing just outside the college grounds, the substantial ruins of **Maynooth Castle** date back to the 1200s and boasts one of the largest keeps of its type in Britain. Re-opened in 2002 after restoration work, the castle was a stronghold of the Anglo-Norman Fitzgerald family who effectively controlled much of Ireland from the 1200s until Tudor times.

A rather unusual attraction in Maynooth, only open during the summer months, is the **Maze in the Maize** where visitors can test their sense of direction in a maze created in a field of maize.

About 3 miles east of Maynooth, the 12th century **Leixlip Castle** stands overlooking the Liffey and with its front gates on the village main street. It is privately owned by Desmond Guinness who has written two books on county houses and castles in Ireland. He will provide a slide talk on Irish architecture by arrangement. The castle has a Georgian interior and contains some interesting Irish furniture and pictures but is only open on weekday mornings in February, May and September.

Kilcock

14 miles N of Naas on the R407

Way back in 1830 the Ordnance Survey described what is now **Larchill Arcadian Garden** as *"The most fashionable garden in all of Ireland"*. It's also one of the most fascinating, a rediscovered rococo fantasy in an Irish pastoral setting. The 63 acres of landscaped gardens enjoy breathtaking views of the Dublin mountains and contain Europe's only remaining *ferme ornée* – an "embellished farm". A circular walk links 10 Gothic and castellated follies, amongst them a romantic island fortress and temple on an 8-acre lake, an exquisite shell-lined tower in a formal walled garden, and the notorious "Fox's Earth" – a refuge prepared for a Mr. Watson, an 18th century enthusiastic fox hunter who was convinced that he would be re-incarnated as a fox. The gardens are also home to a large collection of rare breeds of cattle, ponies and four horned sheep, and other attractions include a walled garden, pets' corner for children and a pleasant tea room.

Newbridge (Droichead Nua)

7 miles SW of Naas on the R445

Set on the banks of the River Liffey, Newbridge developed as a garrison town and is now a busy industrial town. To the southwest of the town the emerald green grass of **The Curragh** extends for miles. Numerous race meetings are held here between March and November of which the most famous are the Irish Sweep Derby in midsummer, the Irish 2000 guineas, the Irish Oaks and the Irish St Leger.

Kildare

The pleasant little town of Kildare owes its foundation to Ireland's most revered female saint, Brigid, who came here sometime in the 6th century and spread her

Red House Country Hotel & Restaurant

Newbridge, Co. Kildare
Tel: 045 431516
website: www.redhouse.ie

Established in 1965, the **Red House Country Hotel & Restaurant** is one of the longest running family restaurants in Ireland and the number one venue in Co. Kildare. Formerly one of the Bianconi staging inns, the Red House has dispensed hospitality to many a hungry, thirsty and weary traveller throughout the past 300 years. During its ownership by the Fallon family, the restaurant here has built up a great reputation because of its dedication to serving only the best of fresh produce and its successful combination of modern influences with traditional fare. As Brian Fallon says "We have been 30 years perfecting a product we feel our customers will be very happy with".

With the addition of bedrooms in 1995, the Fallons successfully transformed the premises into a boutique hotel attracting a varied clientele of both leisure and business travellers. Twelve individually designed bedrooms, 6 of which are set in the mature gardens at the rear of the building, provide all the comforts one a country home along with the services of a large hotel. Each room is provided with TV/DVD, direct dial telephone, internet access, ISDN, fax facility, hairdryer and hospitality tray, while the family rooms are also fitted with a Playstation 2.

handkerchief on the ground. The area it covered was granted to her in perpetuity by the local king and here she built a convent. **St Brigid's Cathedral** stands beside the market square but little of its 13th century fabric remains. It was pillaged and burnt many times and between 1641 and 1875 lay in ruins. The present building is notable for some fine monuments and a three light stained glass window depicting Ireland's greatest saints – Brigid, Patrick and Columba. Nearby stands a 10th century Round Tower, the second highest in Ireland, which is open to visitors during the summer months; from its summit there are grand views of the rolling horse country all around.

In the market square is the oddly named **Silken Thomas** pub (see panel on page 186). The inn takes its unusual name from a member of the Fitzgerald family, Lords of Kildare, who was dubbed Silken Thomas because of the richness of his clothes and the silken banners carried by his standard bearers. In 1536, duped into believing that his father had been executed in the Tower of London, he led an uprising against Henry VIII. The rebellion was ruthlessly suppressed and Silken Thomas was beheaded at Tyburn.

With its brightly painted shop-fronts, busy pubs and, of course, well-patronised betting shops, Kildare is a lively place but its three major visitor attractions are located just outside the town. **The Irish National Stud** was the brainchild of a Scotsman, Colonel William Hall-Walker, who in 1900 decided to breed thoroughbred horses at Tully Farm. The Colonel was convinced that the moon and stars dictated the destiny of all living creatures so he insisted on skylights being incorporated into the roofs of the stables. His theories seem to have been vindicated since one of his horses was the Derby winner, Minoru. In 1915 the Colonel presented the estate and horses to the Crown and it was handed over to the Irish state in 1943. Visitors can tour the neat buildings, watch the horses being exercised and groomed, or just roaming free in the paddocks. Also within the grounds are the Irish National Stud Museum where, amongst many other exhibits devoted to horses and racing, stands the skeleton of the legendary 1960s steeplechaser, Arkle.

Next door to the Stud and in complete contrast are the **Japanese Gardens**. These were also the inspiration of Colonel Hill-Walker. He commissioned the Japanese landscape gardener Tassa Eida and his son Minoru to create what are now acclaimed as the finest Japanese Gardens in Europe. They symbolise the journey of a soul from Oblivion to Eternity, the 20 different stages including a Marriage Bridge, a Hill of Ambition and a Tunnel of Ignorance.

Close by is the peaceful **St Fiachra's Garden**, created in memory of the 7th century monk who travelled through Ireland and Scotland bringing the message of the Gospel before settling in France and founding a monastery at St Breuil. His followers were exhorted to cultivate gardens to grow food for the poor. He later became the French patron saint of gardeners.

A couple of miles east of Kildare is the **Curragh Racecourse**, the centre of the

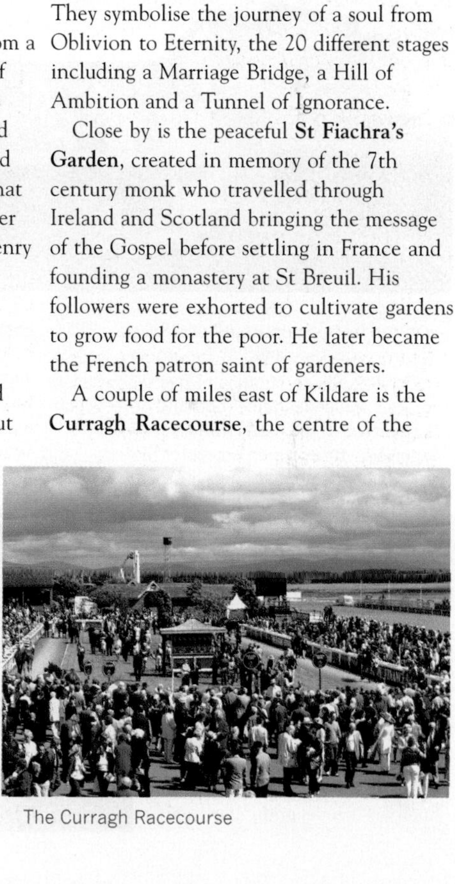

The Curragh Racecourse

Silken Thomas

The Square, Kildare Town, Co. Kildare
Tel: 045 522232 / 521264
Fax: 045 520471
e-mail: silkenthomas@eircom.net

One of Co. Kildare's most famous hostelries is the oddly named **Silken Thomas** pub in the main square of Kildare Town. The inn takes its unusual name from a member of the Fitzgerald family, Lords of Kildare, who was dubbed Silken Thomas because of the richness of his apparel and the silken banners carried by his standard bearers. In 1536 he was duped into believing that his father had been executed in the Tower of London. Vowing revenge, Thomas led an uprising against Henry VIII but the rebellion

was ruthlessly suppressed and Silken Thomas was beheaded at Tyburn.

Today's Silken Thomas pub is renowned for its excellence in fine food and drink which is reflected in the many awards it has received – three times winner of the prestigious "County Kildare Pub of the Year", and also voted one of "Ireland's Best 100 Pubs". More of an entertainment complex than a pub, Silken Thomas offers 3 lively bars, a restaurant and a recently opened state-of-the-art disco. The main lounge bar with its opulent Victorian décor serves excellent food from 11am to 9pm daily; the Squires Gannon bar is crammed with sporting memorabilia; while Lil Flanagan's (named after the owner's late mother) is a delightful thatched cottage traditional style pub where you step back in time to a world of wooden floors, brick walls, oak beams and open fires. Then there's the popular restaurant where you'll find exceptional cuisine, including vegetarian choices, at remarkable value for money prices. A Carvery meal is served daily from 12.30pm until 3pm, and again from 5pm until late.

At the rear of the pub, the "Lord Edward" provides quality accommodation in 18 en suite rooms furnished, decorated and equipped to 4-star standard, complete with TV and tea/coffee-making facilities.

Kildare Town and the neighbourhood offers a variety of attractions. Across the square from Silken Thomas stands St Brigid's Cathedral and a 10th century Round Tower, while to the rear of the pub is a Fitzgerald castle dating back to the 13th century. Just a mile from the town centre are the famous Japanese Gardens and the Irish National Stud and Horse Museum. And if you fancy a day at the races, the Curragh Racecourse, venue for all the classic Irish races, is a mere 2 miles away.

Irish racing world and host to all the classic Irish races. The racecourse is surrounded by some 6000 acres of grassland where in the early morning you can see strings of magnificent thoroughbred racehorses exercising. The word Curragh actually means "racecourse" and there has been organized racing here since at least the 1700s

Around Kildare

Rathangan

6 miles NW of Kildare on the R401

For centuries, peat has been a vital part of rural life in Ireland. A cheap and efficient fuel in bad times and good, the peat fire provided a focal point in the hearths of cottages and farmhouses. At **Peatland World,** in the heart of the Bog of Allen, visitors can discover some more versatile aspects of this ancient fuel which in recent years has been used in cosmetics, clothing, insulation, and even postcards. The past is represented by prehistoric artefacts preserved in bogland, a reconstruction of a typical Irish cottage kitchen from the early 1900s with a turf fire and traditional hearth, and examples of turf-cutting implements and equipment.

Another take on the area's pre-history can be experienced at nearby **Lullymore Heritage & Discovery Park** which has reconstructions of a Mesolithic settlement, a Neolithic farm, exhibits on early Christian history, and others on social history from the 1700s to the present day.

Monasterevin

7 miles W of Kildare on the N7

Named after the 6th century St Evin who founded a monastery here, Monasterevin likes to be known as the "Venice of Ireland" since from one point twelve bridges can be

Cloncarlin House

Nurney Road, Monasterevin, Co. Kildare
Tel: 045 525722
e-mail: marie@cloncarlinhouse.com
website: www.cloncarlinhouse.com

Located in pleasant and peaceful surroundings close to the Co. Laois border, **Cloncarlin House** is a spacious 18th century period farmhouse based on a 180-acre beef farm. It stands on an elevated site with superb views of the surrounding countryside with the nearby Barrow River and Grand Canal adding to the tranquillity and beauty of the area. This charming old house with its feature conservatory is the home of the McGuinness family who have lived here since 1990 and make their guests feel truly at home.

There are 6 luxuriously furnished and decorated guest bedrooms, 5 of which are en suite while the other has its own private bathroom. Both family rooms and twin rooms are available and all are provided with TV and hospitality tray. A copious Irish breakfast is included in the tariff. The house stands in mature gardens where in good weather guests can take the air at the garden tables and chairs provided. Monasterevin itself is a pleasant little market town through which pass both the River Barrow and the Grand Canal – an angler's paradise! The Curragh, Ireland's horse-racing capital, is just 6 miles away and provides guests with the opportunity of watching thoroughbreds in training and enjoying the electric atmosphere of a race day. It is only a 15 minute drive to the National Stud or Japanese Gardens.

The Hazel Hotel

Dublin Road, Monasterevin, Co. Kildare
Tel: 045 525373 Fax: 045 525810
e-mail: sales@hazelhotel.com
website: www.hazelhotel.com

At **The Hazel Hotel** in Monasterevin you'll find a wonderful venue for dinner, a wedding, entertainment and music, a banquet or a business conference. Owner John Kelly, his family, management and staff have a mission to provide their guests with excellent service to ensure their needs are met, and that the high quality standards are always maintained. Naturally, great care is taken to provide the very best cuisine. Head Chef John Muldowney oversees an excellent range of menus with dishes based on meat supplied by the local butcher in Portlaoise and the hotel's greengrocer in Kildare. All beef served is sourced locally, is Irish quality assured and of the highest standard. The menu ranges from the traditional to the Oriental – from Sirloin steak to spicy Szechuan chicken – along with many other appetising dishes. A candlelit dinner is served from 6pm and, to complement your meal, the hotel's cellars contain an outstanding selection of wines from around the world. If you are pressed for time, then the Bistro or the Servery off the Bar offers excellent fare for both lunch and dinner, and can usually make sure that your meal is competed within 30-40 minutes. The self-service Carvery offers a wide selection that includes roast joints and fresh country vegetables and is open from 10am to 10pm for light snacks.

As you would expect from a hotel of this standard, the accommodation is everything you could wish. All the 24 luxurious bedrooms have en suite facilities, multi-channel TV, direct dial telephones, hair dryers and hospitality tray. Other amenities at The Hazel Hotel include a lounge and bar where guests can relax, meet friends or have a light meal and drink throughout the day. Also very popular are the live music and dancing sessions held every Sunday and Monday evening.

There's plenty to see and do in the area with local attractions including the towns of Monasterevin and Leixlip, the Grand Canal, horse racing at the Curragh, motor racing at Naas, many golf courses and places associated with the poet Gerard Manley Hopkins.

Over the years, the hotel has established a fine reputation for hosting wedding receptions. You can choose either the elegant Garden Room or the spacious hotel Ballroom which can cater respectively for up to 120 or 300 guests. The hotel provides free of charge your very own personal wedding co-ordinator who will ensure that the celebration runs smoothly. There are many beautiful locations close to the hotel, such as the Japanese Garden, which are ideal for wedding photographs.

seen. It lies on the scenic River Barrow and the Barrow Line Canal which, when it was built in the late 1700s, gave the little market town a considerable economic boost. Prosperous merchants built the attractive Georgian houses that still

Kilkea Castle

distinguish the town while the canal engineers left the even more impressive aqueduct that carries the canal across the river. There's an enjoyable canalside walk from Monasterevin to Rathangan and the town hosts the popular **Monasterevin Canal Festival.**

The town follows the familiar layout of a Pale town with its houses grouped around the 'big house' – in this case Moore Abbey (private). Built on the site of an ancient Cistercian foundation, it was for a while the home of the famous Irish tenor Count John McCormack.

Athy

14 miles S of Kildare on the N78 and R415

Located on the border with County Laois, near the point where the Grand Canal meets the River Barrow, Athy (pronounced *a-thigh*) is

TONLEGEE HOUSE & RESTAURANT

Athy, Co. Kildare
Tel: 059 863 1473 Fax: 050 731473 e-mail: Marjorie@tonlegeehouse.com
website: www.tonlegeehouse.com

A warm welcome awaits visitors at **Tonlegee House & Restaurant** where Marjorie Molloy ensures that every guest, whether to dine or stay overnight, enjoys a memorable occasion. The house is an elegant Georgian building dating back to 1790 which has been restored to its former state of grace, a place of warmth and character complete with antique furnishings and open fires.

Tonlegee House has become well known for its intimate and cosy restaurant where you'll find country house cooking at its best. Everything is cooked to order so you can relax in the gracious drawing room with a drink while your meal is being prepared. A special favourite with regular customers is the roast quail in pastry with wild mushroom sauce but the fresh fish and game in

season are other specialities which alone make a visit worthwhile. Organic vegetables and salads come from the house's own walled garden. If you are planning to stay in this attractive part of the county, Tonlegee House has 12 guest bedrooms, all with en suite facilities. There's also a meeting room available which will accommodate up to 20 people for interviews, meetings, presentations and conferences – a relaxing room where you can conduct your business in peace and quiet.

Aurora B&B

Prusselstown, Kildare Road, Athy, Co. Kildare
Tel: 059 863 3103 Mobile: 085 723 0423 e-mail: aurorahouse@eircom.net
website: www.aurorahouse.net

Your hosts at **Aurora B&B**, Chris Bradshaw and Teresa Fitzpatrick, are both internationally acclaimed chefs who have gathered many awards and trophies, including Jersey's Junior Chef 1989, and Chef of the Year 1990. So breakfast here is definitely rather special with an extensive menu that includes, in addition to a full Irish breakfast, heart-warming porridge, poached eggs on home-made toasted brown soda bread, scrambled eggs draped with smoked salmon, and warmed pancakes drizzled with maple syrup. Evening meals are also available and Chris and Teresa will cater for any special dietary requirements. "It's always been our dream to own a bed and breakfast" they say, "and finally after a hard 6 years we completed our dream, building our own bed and breakfast in the beautiful town of Athy".

The stylish modern house, set in a spacious garden, has 3 beautifully furnished guest bedrooms, each with en suite facilities, central heating, television, and hair dryer. Children are very welcome – there's a play area for them, children's meals, a babysitting service, cot and high chair are all available as required. Pets too are welcome outside. The house is just a 10-minute walk from the Heritage Town of Athy with its open air Sunday market, fishing, golf and peaceful towpath or woodland walks.

the largest town in County Kildare. Overlooking the bridge over the River Barrow is White's Castle, built in the 16th century by the Earl of Kildare to protect this strategic crossing. There are some fine Georgian houses, an elegant market square, and a curious, pentagon-shaped modern church built of massed concrete about whose architectural merits opinions vary from dubious approval to outright hostility.

The Antarctic explorer Sir Ernest Shackleton was born in nearby Kilkea and his exploits are recalled in the **Athy Heritage Centre**, housed in the 18th century Town Hall, along with displays recalling major events in the town's history. In Kilkea itself, **Kilkea Castle** was another Fitzgerald stronghold, built in 1180. It was remodeled in the 1600s but most of the present building is a 19th century restoration and very imposing it is. Comprehensively renovated again in the 1980s, the castle is now a luxury hotel.

Timolin

12 miles SE of Kildare on the N9

At the **Irish Pewter Mill & Craft Centre** in Timolin visitors can watch pewter being cast (times vary) and browse amongst the displays which are mostly of jewellery and tableware.

A couple of miles north of Timolin, the village of Ballitore is an old Quaker settlement which has a small claim to fame as the place where the philosopher Edmund Burke (1729-97) was educated before moving on to Trinity College, Dublin. The village's Quaker heritage is explored in the

Woodcourte House B&B

Timolin, Moone, Athy, Co. Kildare
Tel: 0598 624167
e-mail: woodcourtehouse@hotmail.com
website: www.woodcourtehouse.com

Former farmer Tony Donoghue and his family have been welcoming bed & breakfast guests at **Woodcourte House** for some 16 years now. This stylish modern building has a delightful dining room looking out over lush pastures with grazing cows and 4 beautifully furnished and decorated non-smoking guest bedrooms, all of them with en suite facilities. A full Irish breakfast is served from 7-10am and tea/coffee-making facilities are always available. All the rooms are Bord Fáilte approved and Fire Department inspected, and they include family rooms. Guests are welcome to stay on either a bed & breakfast or full board basis.

Sportsman's Bar & Restaurant

Timolin, Moone, Co. Kildare
Tel: 0598 624228

Located in the centre of the quiet village of Timolin, the **Sportsman's Bar & Restaurant** is a fine old traditional Irish pub which has been owned and run by the Kelly family for almost a quarter of a century. There's pool, darts and regular traditional Irish music sessions and a choice of wholesome food – snacks and light meals in the bar or full à la carte meals in the restaurant with its open fire where breakfast is also served from 9.30am. Wheelchair-friendly, the Sportsman's Bar is open 7 days a week and has ample parking for both cars and coaches.

Ballitore Quaker Museum (free) which is housed in the former Friends Meeting House.

Castledermot

17 miles SE of Kildare on the R408/N9

This little town in the southeast corner of the country is notable for its rich cluster of ecclesiastical remains. The group includes the substantial ruins of a 13th century Franciscan friary, two finely carved 10th century High Crosses and a truncated Round Tower. Castledermot was once a place of some importance – a walled town in which Hugh de Lacy built an Anglo-Norman fortress. The castle was sacked by Cromwell's troops in 1649 and only one of the town gates still stands, but Castledermot seems at peace with its much quieter modern rôle.

Co Kilkenny

With Ireland's medieval capital at its heart, County Kilkenny is rich in heritage and its lush, well-cultivated landscapes offer some of the most appealing scenery in the southeast. The county's military importance in medieval times is reflected in the string of dramatic castles set along the river valleys of the Nore and the Barrow; the splendid ruins of Kells Priory and Jerpoint Abbey; and most notably in Kilkenny Town itself with its magnificent castle and the largest concentration of medieval churches in the country. Outstanding natural features include the extraordinary underground chambers of Dunmore Cave. As the self-styled "Creative Heart of Ireland" and home to the Irish National Design Centre the county prides itself on having fostered the survival of traditional skills, producing an impressive range of original works and giftware in glass, clay, precious metals, leather and textiles.

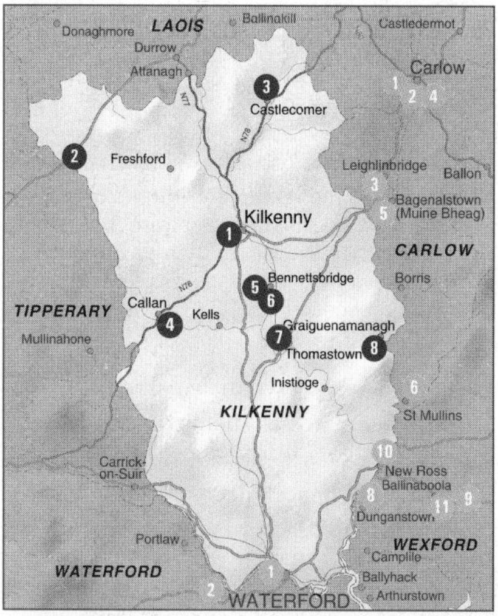

Kilkenny

Despite having a population of less than 9000, Kilkenny insists on being called a city, and with some justification. Before the Normans arrived, it was the capital of the Kingdom of Ossary, and the Confederate Parliament sat here between 1642 and 1648. Kilkenny suffered grievously from the vandalism of Cromwell and his troops when they were quartered here in 1650, but the city retains an astonishing wealth of medieval buildings.

Kilkenny has been described as a mini-Edinburgh because, like the Scottish capital, it has a main thoroughfare lined with fascinating buildings and bracketed at one end by a cathedral, at the other by a **Castle** (see panel opposite).

PLACES TO STAY, EAT AND DRINK

Kilkenny Castle, Kilkenny	1	Historic Building	p193
Butlers Inn, Urlingford	2	Pub with Food	p195
The Avalon Inn, Castlecomer	3	Pub, Restaurant & Accommodation	p195
Adelphi House, Callan	4	Pub, Food & Accommodation	p196
Nore Valley Park, Kilkenny	5	Visitor Attraction	p197
Aard Oakleigh, Bennettsbridge	6	B&B	p197
Kilfane Glen & Waterville, Thomastown	7	Scenic Attraction	p198
Brandon View B&B, Graiguenamanagh	8	B&B	p199

● Denotes entries in other chapters

From the castle, The Parade runs parallel to the River Nore and just off to the right, in Rose Inn Street, is the **Shee Alms House**, built in the late 1500s by local landowner Sir Richard Shee. This lovely old building is one of the very rare Tudor almshouses to be found in Ireland. It now houses the tourist information office where visitors can watch a video presentation of Kilkenny's history or join one of the regular walking tours around the city, an excellent way of discovering its many treasures.

A little further north along The Parade is the arcaded **Tholsel**, built in 1761 of black Kilkenny marble as a toll-house or exchange, and now serving as the Town Hall. Beyond The Tholsel the road becomes Parliament Street, running through the heart of medieval Kilkenny with its narrow "slips", or alleys, darting off in all directions. **Rothe House** is a striking Tudor building of 1594, the only surviving example in Ireland of a wealthy merchant's town dwelling. It contains three distinct houses, connected by courtyards – spacious lodgings necessary to house John Rothe's family of 12 children. The house is now home to Kilkenny's Archaeological Society Museum and a Costume Museum with a fine collection of waistcoats, bonnets and gowns from the 18th century onwards. Just

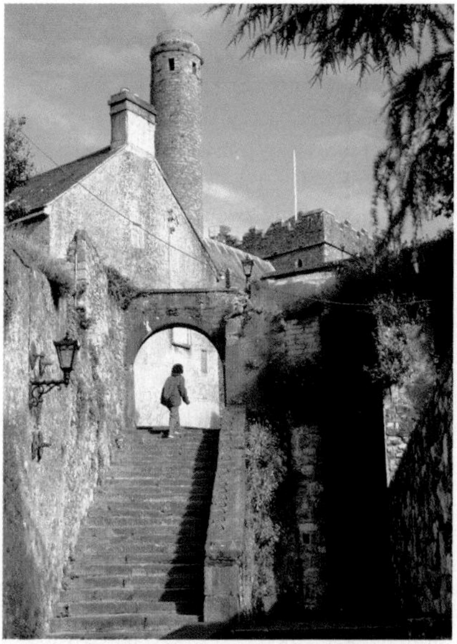

Kilkenny Medieval City

Kilkenny Castle

Kilkenny, Co Kilkenny
Tel: 056 21450 Fax: 056 63488

Kilkenny Castle stands on high ground overlooking the River Nore and dates back to the late 1100s when it was erected by Theobald Fitzwalter, Chief Butler of Ireland. His family took the name Butler and as Earls, Marquesses and Dukes of Ormonde lived in the castle until 1935. Extensive additions took place in the 18th and 19th centuries but the castle's medieval origins are plain to see in the grand scale of the rooms, the deeply recessed windows and mighty fireplaces. The Butler family's long tenure of the castle is reflected in the serried lines of family portraits dating back to the 13th century which are displayed in the spectacular Long Gallery. The castle is set in extensive grounds which also contain the Butler Gallery, dedicated to exhibitions of modern art, and the Irish National Design Centre, housed in the 18th century stables, which offers a wide range of high quality Irish

across the road from Rothe House rises the stately Court House built in 1794 and, a little further north, St Francis's Brewery which occupies part of the site of a 13th century Franciscan friary whose remnants stand nearby. The Brewery is open to visitors during July and August, offering a video of the production process and a tasting in the cellar bar. Tickets are free and can be obtained at the Tourist Information Centre.

At the northern end of the main street, **St Canice's Cathedral** is a magnificent 13th century building which boasts the second longest nave in Ireland after St Patrick's Cathedral in Dublin. It has an important Library with more than 3000 early and rare volumes, a wealth of carvings and a remarkable collection of tombs and monuments. The oldest one is dated 1285 and many of them commemorate members of the Butler family of Kilkenny Castle. In the Cathedral precinct, a Round Tower is all that remains of the monastic settlement founded here in the 6th century by St Canice. It's possible to climb the tower and there are some superb views from the top.

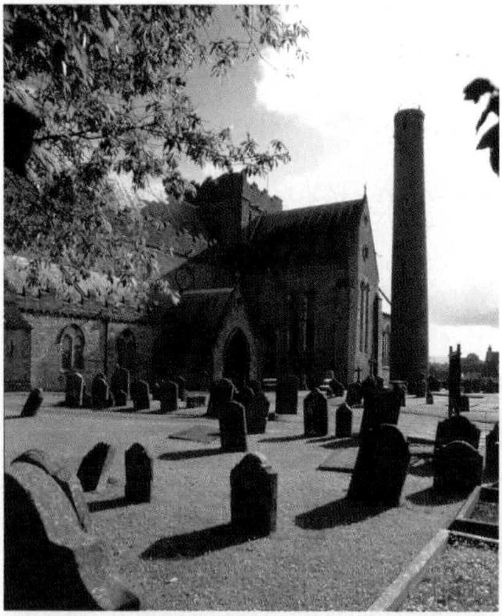

St Canice's Cathedral

Scattered across the city are many other medieval remains. The most notable are the **Black Abbey**, founded in 1225 and carefully restored, which has some fine stained glass along with interesting carvings and sepulchral slabs, and St John's Priory with a roofless chancel and an impressive seven-light window dating from 1250.

A secular building of interest is **Kyteler's Inn**, the oldest dwelling in Kilkenny. It has changed little since 1324 when it was owned by Dame Alice Kyteler. Alice outlived four wealthy husbands but her good fortune wavered when she was charged with witchcraft by the local bishop. Alice made a speedy departure for France and it was her maidservant Petronella who was burned at the stake in her place.

One of County Kilkenny's major visitor attractions is **Dunmore Cave**, about 7 miles northeast of Kilkenny Town off the N78. The series of chambers here were formed over millions of years and contain some of the finest formations of stalactites and stalagmites to be seen in Ireland. You may well share the response of one visitor who described Dunmore Cave as having "a dreadful romantic appearance, as if one stood in the mouth of a huge wild beast". The cave is first mentioned in the 9th century Irish Triads and the Annals tell of a Viking massacre here in AD 928. In 1967, the skeletons of 46 women and children were found in the cave along with coins dating from between AD 897 to 926. The well-presented caverns are open daily during the season; at weekends and Bank Holidays only in the winter. Access is by guided tour only.

Around Kilkenny

Freshford

9 miles NW of Kilkenny on the R693

Nestling in a gap in the Slieveardagh Hills, Freshford has some handsome Georgian

Butlers Inn

Main Street, Urlingford, Co. Kilkenny
Tel: 056 883 1366

Jim Butler has been in the hospitality business for more than a quarter of a century, for the past 6 years as mine host of **Butlers Inn** in Urlingford. This friendly old hostelry is well-known for its good food with a menu that includes an all day Irish breakfast, daily specials at lunchtime, and an à la carte choice in the evening. Urlingford itself is conveniently located on the N8, almost exactly halfway between Dublin and Cork, and is surrounded by the glorious scenery of the Slieve Ardagh Hills. There's an 18-hole golf course a few miles up the road and horse-riding and go-karting are both available locally.

houses, a pleasant green and an interesting church. St Lactin created a religious foundation here in the 7th century, though his church was replaced in the 1100s and again in the 18th century. This most recent one incorporates the west gable and Romanesque porch of the 12th century structure and has an Irish inscription invoking a prayer for the builders.

Castlecomer

12 miles N of Kilkenny on the N78

A pleasant little town in the hilly northern part of the county, Castlecomer was laid out in the style of an Italian village by Sir Christopher Wandersforde in 1635. Of the Anglo-Norman castle that gave the town its name, only a mound remains. Anthracite

The Avalon Inn

The Square, Castlecomer, Co. Kilkenny
Tel: 056 444 1302
website: www.avaloninn.com

A handsome Georgian mansion with creeper-clad walls, **The Avalon Inn** is a bar and restaurant also offering quality bed & breakfast accommodation. It has great charm and elegance and is owned by the O'Hanlon Family. Margaret Fitzgerald (nee O'Hanlon) who manages the Inn clearly has an eye for interior decoration.

There are 3 bars in all, one with a large screen TV for sporting events, and a dining room serving a full breakfast menu from 8am, lunches and evening meals. Margaret is also happy to cater for wedding parties and other private functions.

If you are staying in Castlecomer, the inn has 10 comfortable guest bedrooms, all en suite and attractively furnished and decorated.

was discovered here in the 1600s and Castlecomer became the centre of the country's largest coalfield which attracted skilled Welshmen to work in the mines. These finally closed in the 1970s and today the town and the surrounding area have a scenic appeal not usually associated with mining areas.

Callan

9 miles SW of Kilkenny on the N76

Standing in the centre of a fertile plain, Callan is an ancient market town which received its first charter in 1271. A major battle was fought here in 1408 when the Prince of Ossory and 800 of his men were slain by the English. Callan suffered again in 1650 when Cromwell's troops bombarded the town and destroyed most of its Norman castle. Only a few traces remain. In the main street stands a fine memorial in Kilkenny limestone to Edmund Ignatius Rice (1762-1844) who founded the influential teaching order, the Christian Brothers. A plaque on a thatched cottage at Westcourt, just outside Callan, marks the place where he was born.

Callan has two other notable sons: Robert Fulton, who designed the world's first steam engine in the early 1800s, and James Hoban (1762-1831), the architect of the White House in Washington.

Kells

7 miles S of Kilkenny on the R697

Not to be confused with Kells, Co. Meath, where the famous *Book of Kells* originated, this Kells is a delightful riverside village with a huge bridge and an ancient stone water mill standing beside the river. Nearby, set within emerald green fields, are the ruins of **Kells Priory** (free), a walled monastery with the appearance of a medieval town. The remains of the 12th century foundation are immensely impressive, with a complete curtain wall fortified with square towers and a sturdy gatehouse. Extending over 5 acres, Kells is one of the largest and most satisfying ecclesiastical sites in Ireland – definitely not to be missed.

About two miles south of this beguiling little village are the 95 feet high Kilkree Round Tower, one of many such structures in this area, a ruined church and a High Cross with some badly-weathered biblical carvings.

Bennettsbridge

6 miles SE of Kilkenny on the R700

A popular family attraction near the town of Bennettsbridge is the **Nore Valley Park Open Farm** (see panel opposite). There's a

ADELPHI HOUSE

Bridge Street, Callan, Co. Kilkenny
Tel: 0567 725210

Good food and drink, a great atmosphere and comfortable accommodation are all on offer at **Adelphi House,** a friendly family-run hostelry with Benny and Mary Grogan as the genial hosts. They pride themselves on giving personal attention and will do everything they can to make your visit a happy one, whether it's just for a drink in the bar, a tasty meal or an overnight stay. There are 5 guest bedrooms, all with TV and en suite facilities – children are welcome and a cot is available if required. A full Irish breakfast is included in the tariff. Historic Kilkenny City is just 10

miles away and there's an 18-hole golf course just over a mile down the road.

Nore Valley Park

Annamult, Bennettsbridge, Kilkenny,
Co. Kilkenny
Tel: 056 27229 Fax: 056 27748
e-mail: norevalleypark@eircom.net
website: norevalleypark.tripod.com

An excellent option for a satisfying family day out is a visit to **Nore Valley Park,** an open farm located a couple of miles south of Bennettsbridge on the R700. This open farm offers many attractions for children of all ages. A wide variety of animals can be seen in a specially designed area with an American style fort in the centre providing a viewing point. Children can feed the animals - lambs, chicks, rabbits, ducks and even deer. There's a children's playground, complete with sandpit and a straw bouncing area for energetic youngsters, while older visitors can enjoy a picturesque river walk.

Other attractions include crazy golf, pedal go-karts and trailer rides. Visitors can relax in the picnic area and if you haven't brought your own provisions, hot and cold drinks are available along with a selection of tasty cakes and scones. Families can look around at their own pace with no time restrictions but pre-booked tours are also available for larger parties. If you intend to make the stay a little longer, why not take advantage of the Caravan and Camping Park alongside the farm. The family-run site is located in a quiet peaceful valley and is personally supervised at all times. A high standard of cleanliness is a priority throughout the site and its amenities. There are warm showers, toilets, electric points, pot wash and laundry, and TV room with pool table. Patrons of the site enjoy free entry to the Park.

wide variety of animals to see in a specially designed area with an American style fort in the centre as a viewing point. Children can help feed lambs or kids in season and handle chicks and rabbits. Other attractions included in the admission charge are a children's playground, sandpit and straw bounce, picnic area and a 2-mile river walk. An additional charge is made for the crazy golf, pedal go-karts and trailer rides. Also on site is a tea room serving home-baked cakes and scones. The farm is open 9am to 8pm, daily except Sunday, from April to September.

Thomastown

11 miles SE of Kilkenny on the R700/N9

South of Kilkenny Town, the valley of the River Nore is renowned for its beauty. The river flows through fertile pastures, past

Aard Oakleigh

Ballyreddin West, Bennettsbridge,
Co. Kilkenny
Tel. 056 772 7388 e-mail: greer@iol.ie

Located on the R700 just outside the craft village of Bennettsbridge, **Aard Oakleigh** offers quality bed & breakfast accommodation in peaceful surroundings. This stylish modern house is the home of June Greer who extends a real Irish welcome to her guests. There are 4 non-smoking guest bedrooms, all with en suite facilities, TV, hair dryer – and a nice view. Smokers can take advantage of the smoking balcony and all guests have the use of a cosy lounge with TV, writing table and tea/coffee-making facilities. June serves a hearty breakfast with lots of choices, including French toast with maple syrup, home produce and home-made jams and marmalade.

Jerpoint Abbey

peaceful villages and ancient ruins. The most striking of the ruins are the substantial remains of **Jerpoint Abbey**, near Thomastown. This outstanding Cistercian abbey, founded in the late 1100s and built in oat-coloured stone, is noted for the unique carvings of medieval lords and ladies in the cloister, some fine 13th century tombs and the serene peacefulness of its setting. The small Visitor Centre houses an informative exhibition and there's good access for visitors with disabilities.

Two miles north of Thomastown, **Kilfane Glen and Waterfall** (see panel below) is one of County Kilkenny's prime beauty spots. Its Romantic-era garden, laid out in 1790, was only rediscovered a few years ago and has been beautifully restored. This magical garden, complete with waterfall, hermit's grotto and a cottage ornée, is reached by winding paths which open up some lovely views.

Inistioge

11 miles SE of Kilkenny on the R700

Pronounced *Inisteeg*, this delightful village

Kilfane Glen & Waterfall

Thomastown, Co. Kilkenny
Tel: 056 24558
website: www.nicholasmosse.com

Kilfane Glen and Waterfall is a pristine example of a romantic era garden dating from the 1790s. Untouched for 200 years, it is a picturesque paradise with a dramatic waterfall tumbling its way to a rushing stream, and woodland paths leading to a cottage orné. Tiny bridges sit among ancient trees surrounded by wild foxgloves, ferns and other historically correct 18th century planting. Nicholas and Susan Mosse, the owners of Kilfane Glen and Waterfall, have carefully overseen its restoration during the last few years. While restoration of the cottage and glen was taking place, a different project emerged in the upper garden.

The Kilfane Trust was established to help introduce new art and artists to Ireland. Artists are invited to propose work and then the accepted proposals are created in situ. Currently, there are half a dozen of these fascinating pieces, created by Irish, British and American artists. The open areas and woods, covering about 15 acres of natural landscape with inter-connecting paths, provide excellent spaces in which to work. The garden is listed as an Irish Heritage garden and was awarded assistance in 1993 by the European Union Cultural Commission. Kilfane Glen is open to the public daily in July and August, group booking and facilities are also available.

lies in a scenic part of the Nore valley where the river winds between wooded banks. It passes beneath the fine 10-arched stone bridge at Inistioge, close to the tree-lined square. Rows of small 18th and 19th century cottages line the twisting lane that climbs the hill. Some striking remains of an Augustinian priory, founded in 1210, still survive, amongst them a tower which contains monuments of the Tighe family. One of these is an effigy by Flaxman of Mary Tighe (died 1810) the author of *Psyche*.

The former home of the Tighes, Woodstock House, once stood in woodlands south of the village. The house was burnt down in 1922 after it had been requisitioned by the British Black and Tans but the impressive formal gardens are open to the public. As an alternative, there's a pleasant riverside walk starting from the centre of the village.

Graiguenamanagh

22 miles SE of Kilkenny on the R703/R705

Picturesquely sited on a mountain ravine, Graiguenamanagh is a prosperous market town popular with anglers who come to fish for salmon and trout in the River Barrow. Graiguenamanagh ("the granary of the monks") was once an important ecclesiastical centre, based on **Duiske Abbey** which dominates the town. Founded in 1204, the Abbey was the largest Cistercian abbey in Ireland, its precincts including much of the area of the present town. The Abbey's interior has been lovingly restored and amongst many interesting features are a superb effigy of a knight in chainmail and a richly decorated, marvellously preserved Romanesque processional door. Outside in the churchyard are two 9th century stone crosses and a 6th century font.

BRANDON VIEW B&B

Ballyling Lower, Graiguenamanagh,
Co. Kilkenny
Tel: 059 972 4625
e-mail: hdoylebrandonview@eircom.net
website: www.brandonviewbandb.com

Beautifully set in scenic countryside on the R729, **Brandon View B&B** is a stylish modern house with an elegant conservatory, surrounded by attractive gardens. Proprietor Helen Doyle greets arriving guests with a warm welcome – and refreshments. Helen has been welcoming visitors to her charming home for some 10 years and makes sure that all of them receive her personal attention. Guests have the use of a spacious and comfortable residents' lounge with TV, games, tea/coffee-making facilities, and a library of local places of

interest and of activities nearby. These include fishing less than a mile away; golf just over a mile; quad-riding about 2.5 miles, and hill walking all around.

Brandon View has 5 guest bedrooms, all with an AA 4-star rating, en suite facilities and elegant furnishings and decorations. At breakfast time Helen's menu offers a good choice and a snack menu is also available.

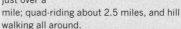

Co Laois

As County Offaly was known as King's County, so Laois (pronounced *leash*) was Queen's County, named after Mary I who "planted" the county with her Catholic supporters in the late 1550s. A new town, Maryborough, was established. It has since been renamed Portlaoise and is now the county town. Those early settlers were mainly smallholders so Co. Laois has none of the great estates like those handed out by Cromwell and Charles II in the southwest counties some 90 years later. But the colonists built some attractive towns and villages, as well as a few notable mansions such as those at Abbeyleix and Emo.

Horse Drawn Caravan, Co Laois

Topographically, Laois has two distinct landscapes: the Slieve Bloom Mountains running along its northwestern border with Co. Offaly, and the green plains that cover the rest of the county. An old traveller's tag asserts that the Laois landscape is, like the local accent, flat and boring: a more sympathetic visitor will appreciate the quiet byways and the gentle, unhurried rhythms of everyday life. Small though it is, the county offers excellent fishing, more than 250 miles of "off road" walking routes and five 18-hole golf courses.

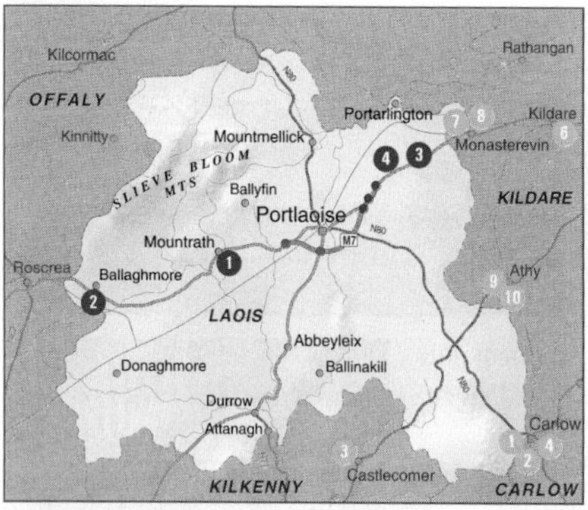

PLACES TO STAY, EAT AND DRINK

Lanigans Lounge Bar, Mountrath	1	Bar with Food	p202
Highway Inn, Borris in Ossory	2	Pub, Food & Accommodation	p202
Delaneys Restaurant, Ballybrittas	3	Restaurant	p203
Emo Court House, Emo	4	House & Gardens	p204

● Denotes entries in other chapters

Bog Cotton, Slieve Bloom Mountains

Portlaoise

When Portlaoise was established in 1556 and named after the reigning Queen as Maryborough, the town was heavily fortified as part of a plan to subdue the local chiefs. These fortifications were comprehensively destroyed by Cromwell's troops and only the outer wall of a tower survives. Depressingly, the most substantial building in Portlaoise today is its top-security gaol which stands in the same street as the county mental hospital. Inevitably, a local wit renamed the street "Nuts'n'Bolts Road". A more cheerful aspect of the town is its abundance of lively pubs – 22 of them at the time of writing.

Around Portlaoise

About 3 miles to the east of Portlaoise, the **Rock of Dunamase** rises from the plain, a geographical feature so distinctive that it even appears on Ptolemy's 1st century map of the known world as "Dunum". Successive generations of warrior-kings made good use of the Rock's strategic position which enjoys uninterrupted views of the low-lying country all around with the **Slieve Bloom Mountains** in the distance. The Rock's lumpy contours are dotted with the weathered ruins of early fortifications, culminating in the remains of the hilltop 12th century castle erected by Dermot MacMurrough, King of Leinster. In 1650 the castle suffered the same fate as so many of Ireland's medieval fortresses – cannonballed into uselessness by Cromwell's artillery.

A mile or so to the east of the Rock of Dunamase, steam buffs will find the **Stradbally Hall Railway** which operates during the summer season. A 19th century steam locomotive, formerly used at the Guinness brewery in Dublin, chuffs along the narrow gauge track and a steam engine rally is held here on the first weekend in August. Another attraction in the village is a **Traction Engine Museum** which also houses a fine collection of vintage cars.

Ballyfin

6 miles W of Portlaoise on the R423

Ballyfin House is regarded by many as the finest sandstone neo-classical house of its period in Ireland. It was designed in the 1700s but when Sir Charles Coote bought it in 1812 he had it redesigned by the architect Richard Morrison. A conservatory and lake were added around 1851 – the former is still popular with locals because of its excellent coarse fishing for pike, rudd and tench. The house is now a secondary school for boys and girls but the grounds are open to the public and provide some scenic walks around the lake and through the surrounding woodlands.

Lanigans Lounge Bar

Shannon Street, Mountrath, Co. Laois
Tel: 0502 32077

Located at the foot of the Slieve Bloom Mountains on the main Dublin-Limerick-Kerry road is **Lanigans Lounge Bar** which dates back to the 1800s and was originally known as Cullens Railway Hotel. It was bought by the Braden family in the 1960s and is now owned and run by John and Mary Lanigan who both have some 30 years experience in the hospitality business and have made this a welcoming lounge bar serving a good selection of excellent food. Jane is an accomplished chef and her menu offers a tempting selection of wholesome and appetising food which is available every day from 12.30pm until 3pm.

The Lanigan are always happy to accept bookings for parties and will serve a full dinner from 6pm to 9pm by appointment. There's a very comfortable lounge bar in dark timber, and a small room to one side where the evening meals are served by candlelight and with an open fire. You'll find that service is both friendly and efficient.

Mountrath

9 miles SW of Portlaoise on the N7

A few miles southeast of the Slieve Bloom Mountains, Mountrath was founded in the 1600s by Charles Coote, a determined entrepreneur whose charcoal-burning ironworks were responsible for devouring many acres of Ireland's natural forests. Mountrath boasts its own 18-hole golf course and there's some good fishing in the area.

Ballaghmore

18 miles SW of Portlaoise off the N7

Ballaghmore sits at the southern tip of the Slieve Bloom Mountains which can be explored by following the **Slieve Bloom Way**, a 31-mile trek that takes you across

Highway Inn

Ballaghmore, Borris in Ossory, Co. Laois
Tel: 087 278 3085

Conveniently located on the main Dublin to Limerick road, the N7, about 5 miles east of Roscrea, the **Highway Inn** is a smart modern hostelry that was completely refurbished when Breda and Michael Carroll arrived here in the summer of 2003. But they retained features such as the wood and slate flooring and have successfully preserve the inn's traditional character. Good home-cooked food based on local produce is served daily from 7.30am until late and the 11 comfortable guest bedrooms are all en suite and equipped with TV and hospitality tray. Credit cards are accepted and there's plenty of parking space.

open moorland, through densely-planted stands of conifers, along the bed of a pre-Ice Age river valley and part of the old High Road to Tara. In Ballaghmore itself, there's a castle which was once an outpost of the Fitzgeralds.

Mountmellick

6 miles N of Portlaoise on the N80

Set within a bend of the River Owenass, Mountmellick was founded in the 17th century by Quakers and flourished as a centre for cotton, linen and woollen manufacturing. Its flourishing industries earned Mountmellick the title "Manchester of Ireland". One of the town's products, "Mountmellick work", became extremely popular in the 1700s. Currently, local people are trying to revive the production of this elegant white-on-white embroidery, decorated with flowers and plants. Samples of Mountmellick work and displays on the town's history can be seen at **Codd's Mill** which serves as the town's heritage centre.

To the west of Mountmellick rise the Slieve Bloom Mountains *"as sweet and delightful as their name"* declared one writer. *"At any season of the year they fill the eye with beauty and the lungs with their fragrant delicious air"*. The 31-mile-long Slieve Bloom Way provides a circular walk around the mountains. The most outstanding views are to be found at the Glendine Gap and the Ridge of Capard.

Portarlington

12 miles NE of Portlaoise on the R4/R420

Handsome Georgian houses with gardens stretching down to the river Owenass and a "French" church where many of the tombstones are engraved with names such as Champ and Le Blanc bear witness to Portarlington's Huguenot forebears. They arrived here in the late 1600s and their

Delaneys Restaurant

Ballintogher, Ballybrittas, Co. Laois
Tel/Fax: 0502 26453

When **Delaney's Restaurant** opened in 1948 it was just a small cottage serving light meals to travellers along the N7, the main Dublin to Cork road. Over the years it has been extended and now comprises two dining rooms seating up to 48 diners. Alice and Tom Delaney took over here in 1998 and, such is the restaurant's popularity, they are planning to expand yet again while retaining the friendly relaxed atmosphere of the current dining rooms with their traditional furnishings and features such as an open fire. The secret of the Delaneys success is the unbeatable combination they offer of quality food at affordable prices. All the ingredients are sourced in Ireland and only the freshest, top quality produce is used.

Food is served from 7am to 9pm (Monday-Friday); 8am to 8pm (Saturday); and 9am to 7pm (Sunday, including Sunday lunch from 12.30pm). Delaney's is a Restaurant with Rooms – 7 comfortably appointed bedrooms, 4 of which have en suite facilities. Ballintogher is a convenient base for exploring this area, the heart of Ireland, with attractions such as Emo Court House & Garden Centre, the Stradbally Steam Museum, Kilkenny Castle, the National Stud and Japanese Garden all within easy reach.

Emo Court House

Emo Village, Co Laois
Tel: 353 502 26572

The attractive village of Emo is dominated by the works of James Gandon (1743-1823), the English-born architect who spent most of his professional life in Ireland. He is probably best known for the dignified Custom House in Dublin, often described as "one of the noblest buildings in Europe". Gandon was also involved in the design of Dublin's Four Courts, the Carlisle (O'Connell) Bridge, and the Bank of Ireland. A lucrative commission from the 1st Earl of Portarlington enticed Gandon from the capital city to this rural corner of County Laois. The Earl desired a stately residence here: Gandon obliged with **Emo Court**, a massively imposing building crowned by a great dome. During the summer season, visitors on guided tours can admire its interior, lavishly appointed with costly Siena marble. All year round, you are free to wander through the extensive landscaped grounds.

In addition to Emo Court, Lord Portarlington's commission to James Gandon specified the building of a church at nearby Coolbanagher and an inn to service the stage coaches bringing guests to his noble home. Gandon delivered, both on time and in budget. Few inns anywhere can claim such a distinguished architect as the one that bears his name.

industrious way of life brought prosperity to this little town. There's an unusual reminder of the town's Huguenot past in the **French Week** held here in July – naturally, the festivities include a snail-eating competition. The **People's Museum** (free) in the Catholic Club has some interesting relics of the Huguenot era and also offers an overview of the town's history stretching back to 4000-year-old axe heads found nearby.

The present town was founded in 1667 by Sir Henry Bennett, Lord Arlington, after whom Arlington, Virginia in the USA is also named. It was one of his descendants who built **Emo Court House** (see panel above), perhaps the finest Georgian mansion in the country, about 5 miles south of the town, at Emo.

Abbeyleix

The town of Abbeyleix grew up around the Cistercian monastery founded here in 1183. The Abbey has long since disappeared but in the **Abbeyleix Heritage House** the curators have garnered abundant materials to present a series of rich displays exploring local and county history. The museum is housed in the former National School Building and the excellent exhibits do full justice to the story of this Heritage Town. One of the displays tells the story of the De Vesci family whose handsome mansion designed by James Wyatt, Abbeyleix House, adds a note of distinction to the town but sadly is closed to the public although its gardens are occasionally open on summer weekends.

It is possible though to visit the **Sexton's House,** a fine example of a mid-1800s cottage which has been restored and fully refurbished to its former style. It's an evocative place with its oil lamps, iron beds and turf fires, and provides an interesting insight into the daily lives of its former inhabitants.

The Abbey may have gone but very much in evidence still is the "improving" work carried out by Abbeyleix's 18th century landlord, Viscount de Vesci. He decided to relocate his uncomfortably close tenants and labourers to a new, elegantly laid-out village set alongside the main coach road, a mile or so away, so that their humble picturesque dwellings no longer marred the view from his own mansion. The final result was one of the finest planned estate towns in the country with spacious tree-lined streets and picturesque period houses.

Another attractive feature of the town is the **Abbey Sense Garden.** Developed in the old walled garden of the Brigidine Convent, the garden was created by people with disabilities for all to enjoy. The attached garden centre includes a selection of plants, concrete garden products, seasonal crafts and garden furniture.

Around Abbeyleix

Ballinakill

4 miles S of Abbeyleix on the R432

Just to the north of the attractive Georgian village of Ballinakill, **Heywood House** (free) has a garden designed by Edwin Lutyens and reputed to have been landscaped by Gertrude Jekyll.

The garden has been restored and is now open to the public. There are some picturesque views of pastoral countryside through the ox-eye windows of Lutyens' sunken terrace and the property consists of formal gardens, woodlands, lakes and architectural features. The house itself was destroyed by fire in 1960 and nothing now stands.

Durrow

6 miles S of Abbeyleix on the N8

Set on the banks of the River Erkina, Durrow is another estate village built by the Duke of Ormond to serve his palatial Palladian mansion, Castle Durrow, built in 1716. The village sits prettily around a green adjoining the estate. The great house is now a convent but visitors can walk up the drive to view it from the outside.

Attanagh

8 miles S of Abbeyleix on the N77

This charming little village right on the border with Co. Kilkenny boasts a unique attraction, the only **Fly Fishing Museum** in the country. It's the creation of Walter Phelan who began collecting fishing memorabilia some 15 years ago and has grown into a comprehensive historical collection on fishing, hunting, poaching and much more. The collection includes reels, rods, game licences, traps, hatching pens, boats, books, pictures and, of course, flies of every kind. If you wish, Walter himself will provide a guided tour.

Donaghmore

14 miles SW of Abbeyleix off the R435

In 1853 the authorities established a parish workhouse some distance outside the village of Donaghmore. It seems far too large a building for such a small area – some 800 paupers were incarcerated here, two of whom on average died each week and were lowered into the mass grave behind the workhouse. The building is now the **Donaghmore Workhouse Museum** and tells the story of the families who lived and died within its walls during and after the Great Famine. Guided or self-guided tours are available and part of the museum is devoted to the role of agriculture in the locality.

Co Leitrim

Even more so than the neighbouring county of Sligo, Leitrim has yet to enter the tourist consciousness. With a total population of less than 26,000 the county is wonderfully uncrowded and unspoilt, sprinkled with lakes offering prime fishing and with rugged mountains sprawling across the northern half. The soil in Co. Leitrim is extraordinarily retentive of water, giving rise to the local joke that land in the county is sold by the gallon rather than by the acre.

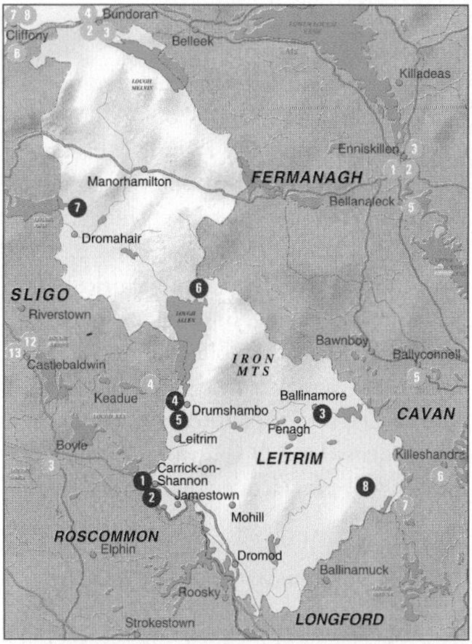

Garadice Lake, Co Leitrim

Only the county town, Carrick-on-Shannon has a well-established visitor attraction with its huge choice of cruises along the Erne Waterway which, including canal links, is navigable for 240 miles, the longest waterway in Europe. Apart from Parke's Castle near the Sligo border and

PLACES TO STAY, EAT AND DRINK

Cryan's Pub, Carrick-on-Shannon	1	Pub with Food	p207
Canal View Country House, Carrick-on-Shannon	2	Guest House	p207
The Commercial & Tourist Hotel, Ballinamore	3	Hotel	p208
Fraoch Ban, Drumshambo	4	B&B	p209
McCready's Restaurant, Drumshambo	5	Restaurant	p209
Mellrose Inn, Dowra	6	Pub, Restaurant & Accommodation	p210
Parke's Castle, Lough Gill	7	Historic Building	p210
Killbrackan Arms, Carrigallen	8	Hotel	p212

● Denotes entries in other chapters

Lough Rynn House near Mohill the county has few buildings of historical importance – this is, after all, a county where the three main interests are fishing, fishing and fishing.

Carrick-on-Shannon

Incorporated as a borough by James I in 1613, Carrick-on-Shannon is a peaceful riverside town set beside a broad stretch of the Shannon and with a population of around 6500. Fishing and river cruising are the major activities as evidenced by the number of fishing tackle shops and the busy marina with its huge fleet of cruisers and pleasure craft.

The town has something of an ecclesiastical oddity in the **Costello Chapel** on Main Street. It is reputed to be the second smallest chapel in the world, just 16 feet long, 12 feet wide and 30 feet high. It was built in 1877 as a mausoleum for Edward Costello and his wife who lie in coffins sunk in the floor either side of the entrance, the lead coffins clearly visible beneath a glass covering. Bizarrely, the chapel stands between two shops in the high street.

Cryan's Pub

Bridge Street, Carrick-on-Shannon,
Co. Leitrim
Tel: 078 20409

A cosy little hostelry at the foot of this bustling town, **Cryan's Pub** has received awards for its food and its traditional Irish music sessions. The pub is run by the brother and sister team of Francis and Liam Cryan – Liam is in charge of the bar and pulls a perfect pint of Guinness; Francis is the chef and produces an appetising range of wholesome, home-cooked Irish cuisine. Food is served every day from 8am to 10pm. Friday night is folk music night, with Saturday and Sunday evenings devoted to traditional music sessions. The pub is open 11am to 11.30pm, Monday to Thursday; 11am to 12.30pm on Friday and Saturday; 11am to 11pm on Sunday.

Canal View Country House

Keshcarrigan, Carrick-on-Shannon, Co. Leitrim
Tel: 071 96 42056 Fax: 071 96 42261
e-mail: canalviewcountryhouse@eircom.net

A spacious and beautifully maintained modern building, **Canal View Country House** stands on a hillside overlooking the Shannon waterway. It's the home of Jeanette and Gerrard Conefrey and since Gerrard is a builder-contractor he ensured that it was built to the highest specifications. There's a large residents lounge with some seriously comfy armchairs or guests can sit outside and watch the riverboats sailing by. Jeanette is a professional cook and each evening between 6pm and 10pm offers superb dinners based on local seafood and meat and accompanied by locally-grown vegetables. Open all year, the house has 6 charmingly furnished guest bedrooms, all en suite and with telephone, TV and hospitality tray.

Across the road from the chapel, the town's original agricultural market area has recently been restored and as the **Market House Centre** now incorporates retail outlets selling local produce, arts and crafts.

St Patrick's Hospital was built as a workhouse in 1841 and witnessed some of the worst horrors of the Great Famine of 1845-48. Hundreds of famine victims, many of them children, were buried in its grounds. A Famine Memorial Garden now occupies the site.

The town hosts an arts festival in June and a traditional music festival, Session on the Shannon, over the last weekend in October.

North of Carrick-on-Shannon

Leitrim

5 miles NE of Carrick-on-Shannon on the R284

Visitors often wonder why the county took its name from this pleasant little village set beside a canal. In medieval times the area was known as West Breffni but in 1585 Elizabeth I decreed that it should become a county. As it happened, the principal family of West Breffni, the O'Rourkes, lived around Leitrim and so that was the name the bureaucrats settled on.

Fenagh

11 miles NE of Carrick-on-Shannon on the R202

Standing on the northern shore of Fenagh Lough, this little village contains the ruins of two Gothic churches, one of them with an unusual east window. They are all that survives of a monastery founded here by St Columba which later became famous as a divinity school under the direction of St Killian. The impressive 17th century **Mausoleum** nearby was erected by Torna Duignan, a former Rector of Fenagh, for his family.

Ballinamore

15 miles NE of Carrick-on-Shannon on the R202/R109

Like most small towns in Co. Leitrim, Ballinamore is primarily a centre for anglers with boats and canal barges for hire and 2-hour river cruises also available. But this former coaching town, with its broad main street, does have a **Heritage and Folk Museum**, housed in the former courthouse of 1830. Some of the museum exhibits are distinctly odd – amongst the items on show is the "authentic detachable shirt collar worn by executed 1916 patriot Seán MacDiamarda". The courthouse building also houses the **Leitrim Genealogical Centre**, an invaluable resource for those

seeking to unearth their family roots in the area.

Just outside the town, on the Shannon-Erne Waterway, **Swan Island Open Farm** is home to more than 50 species of animals and the amenities include a marina, playground, restaurant, picnic area and souvenir shop.

Drumshambo

9 miles N of Carrick-on-Shannon on the R207

Drumshambo is a neat little fishing town set at the southern tip of Lough Allen, one of the three great Shannon lakes – 7 miles long and 3 miles wide. From Drumshambo you can follow a circular route around the lake above which rise some starkly impressive hills and mountains. In the town itself, the **Sliabh an Iarrain Visitor Centre** provides copious information about local traditions in this former coal mining area – the last coal mine hereabouts closed in 1990. One of the most interesting of those traditions was the widespread use of 'sweat houses', best described as a low-tech but more intense Celtic version of a sauna. As well as promoting physical well-being, a steamy (and usually smoky) session in these cramped and uncomfortable ovens was believed to also effect a spiritual and psychological cleansing. Another very different kind of tradition still flourishes in Drumshambo – the celebration of Irish traditional music. In July each year, the

FRAOCH BAN

Downa Road, Drumshanbo, Co. Leitrim
Tel: 07196 41260
e-mail: fraochban@eircom.net

Fraoch Ban – gaelic for 'white heather' – occupies a stunning position enjoying glorious panoramic views across Lough Allen to Corrie Mountain. Built in 1985, this stylish modern house is the home of Mairin Heron, a professional reflexologist who welcomes bed & breakfast guests to this peaceful retreat. There are 4 attractively furnished and decorated guest bedrooms, all with en suite facilities, TV and hospitality tray, and all at

excellent value-for-money rates. Breakfast here is something to look forward to with a wide selection to choose from. Fraoch Ban is open all year; (credit cards not accepted).

MCCREADY'S RESTAURANT

Convent Avenue, Drumshambo, Co.Leitrim
Tel: 071 96 41125
website: www.McCreadysRestaurant.com
e-mail: Brendan@McCreadysRestaurant.com

Overlooking the famous Arigna Mountains and beautiful Lough Allen, **McCready's Restaurant** serves a wide choice of wholesome fare throughout the day, starting with breakfast, through lunches to evening à la carte meals. Business partners Brendan Grenra and Marion McCready are both accomplished chefs and their varied menus include regular favourites such as pan fried pork fillet or half honey roast duck along with less familiar offerings such as Thai Satay

Chicken & Vegetables Stir Fry served on a bed of oriental fried noodles. The elegant 38-cover restaurant has a décor of rich colours – and the service is exceptional.

Melrose Inn

Main Street, Dowra, Co. Leitrim
Tel: 071 9643025

Standing on the main street of this peaceful little village close to Lough Allen, the **Melrose Inn** is as authentic an Irish pub as you could hope to find. The open fire, slate floor and cosy little alcoves all add to the atmosphere and mine hosts, Mel and Rosaleen McLoughlin, are a friendly and welcoming couple who ensure that the craic never flags! In the small lounge/restaurant you'll find a good choice of genuine home-cooked Irish food – beef & spuds, for example, or delicious fresh seafood, all served between 9am and 6pm, every day except Sunday. If you're planning to stay in this tranquil corner of the country, the Melrose has 6 comfortable guest rooms available.

town hosts the **Joe Mooney Summer School** which offers already competent musicians an abundant choice of classes, concerts and set dancing. For the less skilled, these events are enthusiastically supplemented by scheduled and impromptu music sessions in the town's pubs.

Dromahair

8 miles SW of Manorhamilton on the R288

An attractive little village close to the shore of Lough Gill, Dromahair is notable for the evocative ruins of **Creevelea Friary,** the last friary to be founded in Ireland (in

Parke's Castle

Lough Gill, Co Leitrim

Beautifully situated at the eastern end of Lough Gill, **Parke's Castle** stands just a few yards from the lakeside. This appealing 17th century building that rises from the foundations of a much older moated tower house, the stronghold of the Irish chieftain, Brian O'Rourke. O'Rourke came to an unfortunate end, executed at Tyburn for sheltering a survivor of the wrecked Spanish Armada. His estate was acquired in 1609 by a certain Robert Parke who cannibalised the walls of O'Rourke's fortress for his own house. Reflecting the insecurity of the times, Parke surrounded his mansion with bawn walls with picturesque turrets and sloping roofs. The building has been sensitively restored using 17th century building techniques and native Irish oak.

A guided tour of the castle is given every hour and there's also an individual slide show entitled "Stone by Stone", available in four languages. The Castle can be reached by boat from Sligo: other boat trips around the lake and to the enchanting Isle of Innisfree are also available from the castle jetty during the season.

1508) before Henry VIII's suppression of the monasteries some 30 years later. The monks were Franciscans and some fascinating sculptures have survived of St Francis, including one of him preaching from a pulpit to a "congregation" of birds. The Friary occupies a beautiful setting beside the River Bonet.

Beautifully situated at the eastern end of Lough Gill, **Parke's Castle** stands just a few yards from the lakeside (see panel opposite).

Manorhamilton

28 miles N of Carrick-on-Shannon on the N16

The only town of any size in north Leitrim, Manorhamilton stands at the meeting of four mountain valleys, surrounded by striking limestone hills. The scenery is magnificent – steep hillsides, narrow ravines and fertile valleys offer a splendid variety of vistas. Five roads branch off from Manorhamilton through the mountain valleys, each one of them providing a wonderfully scenic route. In the town itself, the main feature of interest is a ruined ivy-clad mansion built in 1638 by Sir Frederick Hamilton who founded the settlement here and gave it his name. A mere 3 years later the local chieftains O'Rourke, O'Connor and Maguire led a rising in which the castle was destroyed. The **Manorhamilton Castle Heritage Centre** tells the story of that rising together with other historical information about this period. The Centre also has a coffee shop, craft area, herb garden and picnic tables.

Just to the south of the town, the well-preserved megalithic tomb at Cashel Bir on the slopes of Benbo is certainly worth a visit.

About 10 miles west of Manorhamilton, in the lovely valley of Glencar Lough, is

Glencar Waterfall

the **Glencar Waterfall**, an impressive sight when it is in full spate. WB Yeats wrote a touching poem set around the waterfall called *The Stolen Child*.

South & East of Carrick-on-Shannon

Jamestown

3 miles SE of Carrick-on-Shannon off the N4

A pleasant Plantation town, Jamestown was founded in 1625 to protect a crossing on the River Shannon. Its founder, Sir Charles Coote, named the new settlement after James I and surrounded it with a wall. The original town gate in the wall still stands on the main street although its arch was removed in the 1970s. Jamestown is a peaceful little place with Georgian houses and wooded river banks where the inexhaustible staple of conversation is fish and fishing.

A mile or so downstream, near Drumsna, a remarkable discovery was made in 1989. Excavations uncovered long stretches of a Stone Age wall, one of the oldest man-made structures in the world. It's been calculated that it would have taken 30,000 labourers some ten years to build the full length of the wall. Drumsna itself is just one street of trim houses leading down to the river but it enjoys a modicum of literary celebrity since it was here in 1848 that Anthony Trollope began writing his novel *The MacDermots of Ballycloran.*

Mohill

9 miles SE of Carrick-on-Shannon on the R201/R202

This busy little fishing centre was the one-time residence of the famous harpist and composer Turlough O'Carolan (1670-1738). At the age of 22 Turlough contracted smallpox and became blind. It was then that he turned to music as a career. Turlough travelled around the houses of the great chieftains where he entertained his noble hosts with his exquisite playing. He was also a heroic drinker and it's said that on his deathbed he asked for whiskey. He was too weak to drink it so he touched the cup with his lips saying "Two old friends should not part without a kiss". A fine statue on the main street commemorates the last of the court bards.

To the south of Mohill, on the lakeshore, stands one of Leitrim's very few stately homes, **Lough Rynn House**, formerly the hereditary seat of the Clements family, Earls of Leitrim. The older part of the house was built in 1833, an exact copy of a house in Ingestry, Staffordshire, and was greatly extended in the flamboyant Scottish Baronial style in 1878. The interior is richly furnished and decorated in the opulent manner of the period.

At that time the house was the centre of a huge 90,000 acre estate and within the grounds there are farm buildings from the 1840s, a picturesque estate office, a charming summerhouse, a dolmen, an arboretum and the ruins of a 17th century castle. Lough Rynn House is currently under extensive renovation but visitors can explore the extensive grounds.

Dromod

12 miles SE of Carrick-on-Shannon on the N4

The **Cavan & Leitrim Narrow Gauge Railway** was opened in 1887 but the sparse population of the area made it a hopelessly uneconomic project almost from the start. Transporting coal kept the enterprise alive for some 70 years but on 31st March 1959,

the last train ran and the track was lifted shortly afterwards. However, the Engine Shed and Water Tower at Dromod have been restored, a new Workshop and Carriage Shed built, and May 1995 saw the introduction of steam hauled passenger trains running along the half a mile of restored track. (The enthusiasts who run the railway hope to extend the line another 5 miles to Mohill where the old station is being restored). The Dromod site is open all year round with diesel trains operating daily and steam trains running from May to October on weekends and by arrangement. There are guided tours of the engine sheds and visitors can also browse in the railway shop.

Cavan & Leitrim Narrow Gauge Railway

Co Limerick

Bordered by the popular tourist counties of Cork, Kerry and Clare, Co. Limerick tends to get overlooked by visitors in search of better known attractions. But this mainly agricultural county has a quiet charm of its own and also some sights as rewarding as anywhere in the country. King John's Castle in Limerick City is one of the best examples of fortified Norman architecture in Ireland; Castle Matrix is a beautifully restored 15th century tower house, and there's an impressive collection of prehistoric monuments in the area around beautiful Lough Gur. The ruins of many Norman castles and monasteries are dotted around the county's green pastures, noted for their lushness – the best dairy cattle come from Limerick and the county is also famous for its horse-breeding. And Adare is certainly a strong contender for the title of "Ireland's Prettiest Village".

Limerick City has been a centre of trade for well over a millennium and although it was once described as having "the grave, grey look of Commerce", in recent years it has revitalised itself, especially around the City Hall area, its Art School has produced some talented clothes designers, and for a city of its size it has a surprisingly vibrant nightlife.

Limerick

The lowest fording point on the Shannon, Limerick was settled by Vikings around AD 922. Irish forces led by Brian Boru ousted them in 1014 but they in turn were conquered by the Anglo-Normans. King John came here in 1210 and built one of the finest castles in his realm - **King John's Castle** (see panel opposite).

Nearby **Castle Lane** celebrates a more recent period – the 18th and 19th centuries, in a streetscape comprising buildings from Limerick's urban architectural heritage. It includes a traditional tavern; an "Officer's Club" which hosts a dinner/theatre entertainment that features a cast of young entertainers displaying the artistry and originality of modern Irish music and dance;

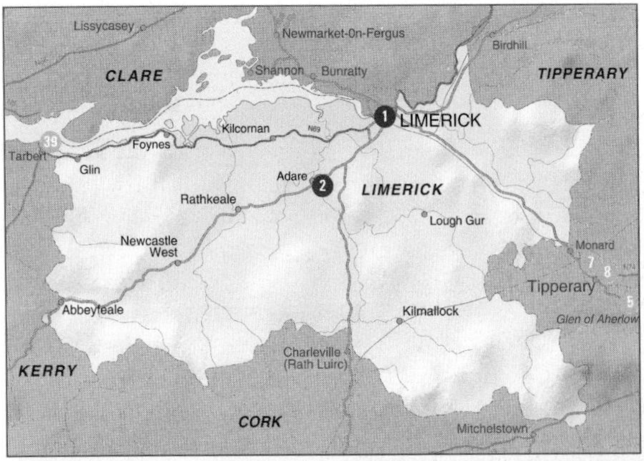

PLACES TO STAY, EAT AND DRINK

King John's Castle, Limerick	1	Historic Building	p215
Adare Heritage Village, Adare	2	Historic Village	p218

Denotes entries in other chapters

King John's Castle

Limerick, Co Limerick

Standing in the heart of Limerick's Medieval Heritage Precinct, **King John's Castle** rises impressively from the waterside, its sturdy round tower guarding the fording place across the river. Badly damaged by Cromwell's troops, the castle was fully restored in 1990, a process which included removing a block of council houses erected in 1935 within the castle walls. The castle now houses an interesting re-creation of what life was like for the medieval garrison. Costumed animators illustrate life as it was in 13th century Limerick and a striking series of six life-sized original wooden sculptures represent characters associated with the history of the castle. King John, as 'Lord of Limerick', minted his own coins here and modern visitors can purchase a replica of the original pieces.

The castle was one of the last strongholds to remain loyal to James II after his defeat at the Battle of the Boyne in 1690. Under the wily command of Patrick Sarsfield, Earl of Lucan, and despite the overwhelmingly superior armaments of King William's soldiers, the Earl resisted the Orange forces for more than a year. He was finally forced to capitulate in October 1691, agreeing to a treaty which promised Catholics the rights they had enjoyed under Charles II. Within months, the English reneged on this part of the treaty, a betrayal that still rankles amongst Limerick people.

and the Limerick Civic Museum. The Civic Museum documents the city's prosperity in Georgian times when it was famous for its production of silverware and lace.

There are even more extensive collections at the **Hunt Museum** in the University campus area. This fine Palladian building of 1765 faces the river and its imposing façade is best viewed from the opposite bank. The Museum's contents were donated by John Hunt, an enterprising antiques dealer of the mid-1900s who had an eye for the main chance but also for fine objects. The collection includes some fine paintings by Renoir, Picasso and Yeats; a superb display of Celtic and medieval art; and an eclectic range of objects from all periods of the past. Amongst many important items are the personal seal of Charles I, the Mary Queen of Scots Cross, a coin revered since the Middle Ages as being one of Judas' 30 pieces of silver, and a magnificent bronze horse

Georgian Houses, Limerick

Cruise Street, Limerick

by Leonardo da Vinci. Guided tours are available or you can just wander around the Museum on your own.

About halfway between the Hunt Museum and King John's Castle, **St Mary's Cathedral** is even older than the castle, dating back to the late 1100s although there were major additions and rebuilding in the 15th century. The cathedral's greatest treasures are its misericords, beautifully carved choir seats of black oak depicting a whole menagerie of real and imaginary animals – boars and griffins, sphinxes and cockatrice amongst them. An interesting feature in the Chapel of the Holy Spirit is the Leper's Squint, a narrow window where people suffering from leprosy could receive communion without infecting the communicants within.

The purpose-built **Limerick Museum** (free), near the cathedral, houses a wide variety of artefacts connected with the city, amongst them a letter written during the 1916 Easter Rising by Padraig Pearse, one of the leaders of the insurrection. Also worth seeing is the Victorian **St John's Catholic Cathedral**, built in the style of Pugin by a London architect, Hardwick, and boasting the tallest spire (280 feet) in the country.

The Irish Chamber Orchestra relocated to Limerick in 1995 and music festivals and performances in the city are now so numerous it's difficult to keep track of them all. In addition to the Summerfest of classical music, the city also hosts the International Marching Band Competition in March, and the "most user-friendly" festival, the Paddy Music Expo, which takes place over the May Bank Holiday and features a full programme of jazz, blues, folk and rock performances as well as talent competitions.

A more recently established celebration is the **Limerick Good Food Festival** in mid-August when international chefs from three continents compete for the Grand Prix Mondial. An open-air barbecue is held in the gardens of City Hall and the city's restaurants vie with each other to produce the most tempting food possible.

Activity of a different kind is reflected in Limerick's claim to be the "Sports Capital of Ireland" – Limerick-born athletes have won no fewer than 6 Olympic gold medals. Rugby, hurling and soccer are undoubtedly the most popular sports but the city also has a modern golf course, a National Hunt horse racing track, and greyhound racing every Monday, Thursday and Saturday evening all year round.

In addition to its world-class athletes, Limerick boasts several other famous sons. Amongst them are the TV personality Terry Wogan, the actor Richard Harris, and Frank McCourt, author of the Pulitzer Prize-winning book *Angela's Ashes*. The **Angela's Ashes Exhibition** can be seen at No.2, Pery Square and includes a life size reconstruction of the McCourt home and images of

Limerick as the McCourts saw it. Evocative pictures contrast the Limerick of those days with the present town and another exhibit follows the making of the film of the book. Interestingly, most of the movie was shot in Dublin and Cork because prosperous modern Limerick possesses no locations that look suitably impoverished. The exhibition is housed in a former coach house at the rear of a meticulously restored Georgian house where an authentic garden of the period has also been faithfully re-created.

Nearby is the People's Park, originally private but donated to the city in 1874. In one corner stands the **City Art Gallery** (free), a gift of Andrew Carnegie and built in 1906 in an uneasy amalgam of Celtic Revival and Arts & Crafts styles. As well as hosting temporary exhibitions, the Gallery has a permanent collection that includes Irish artists from the 18th century to the present, with Jack Yeats well represented.

Around Limerick

Lough Gur

16 miles S of Limerick off the R512

The only lake of any size in Co. Limerick, **Lough Gur** is surrounded by one of Ireland's most important archaeological sites although the most significant artefacts discovered here have been distributed to museums around the world. In the mid-1900s the lake was partly drained, lowering its level by around 9 feet and uncovering such quantities of prehistoric items that whole cartloads were carried away. The most dazzling discovery was an almost perfectly preserved bronze shield dating from around 700 BC, the only blemish to its design of concentric bosses being two nicks caused by the sickle of the reed cutter who unearthed it.

The most impressive of the sites is the vast **Grange Stone Circle**, a perfectly formed circle of 113 stones placed edge-to-edge and pegged into place by smaller stones. In the centre of the circle is a post hole used, it's believed, together with a piece of string, to mark out the faultless circle.

At the **Lough Gur Stone Age Centre** near the lough there are facsimiles of weapons, tools and pottery found in the area, models of stone circles and burial chambers, and an audio-visual presentation recording the story of man's 5000-year-long presence at Lough Gur. During the season the centre offers regular walking tours around the most interesting archaeological features of this historic site.

Kilcornan

11 miles SW of Limerick on the N69

This small village boasts two major tourist attractions and also Co. Limerick's only outdoor Karting track. **Currahchase Forest Park** is one of the finest landscaped grounds in Ireland. For some 300 years the estate was the home of the de Vere family whose most notable scion was the poet and author, Aubrey de Vere (1814-1902). The family's magnificent mansion, Currahchase House was destroyed by fire in 1941 and only the outer shell remains, but the grounds are superb. The 600-acre plantation is maintained by the Irish Forest and Wildlife Service which has provided detailed nature trails, forest walks, picnic areas and an arboretum. **Celtic Park and Gardens** are located on an original Celtic settlement. The Park interprets Ireland's past with exhibits that include a stone circle, a dolmen, a lake dwelling, a stone church and holy well, and a fine example of an early Ringfort.

Foynes

12 miles SW of Limerick on the N69/R521

Between 1939 and 1945, the port of Foynes was an important staging post for air traffic between the United States and Europe. The famous flying boats landed in the bay here, carrying a diverse range of people from celebrities, high-ranking British and American military officers, to refugees. The **Foynes Boat Museum**, housed in the terminal of the original Shannon Airport, recalls this era with a comprehensive range of exhibits, vintage film, graphic illustrations and an audio-visual show.

Foynes and Shannon Airport both claim to have originated Irish Coffee. The Foynes version is that in 1924 the chef at the flying boat terminal, Joe Sheridan, created the warming beverage to comfort some damp and miserable passengers who were stranded there in bad weather. Each year in July Foynes hosts the **International Irish Coffee Festival** when contestants from all around the world vie to make the very best aromatic brew.

Adare

9 miles SW of Limerick on the N20

With its brightly coloured thatched cottages, romantic medieval ruins, ancient stonework and trim gardens, **Adare Village** makes every effort to maintain its claim to be "Ireland's Prettiest Village" (see panel below).

The 2nd Earl of Dunraven who built Adare village, also built a grand mansion for himself and his family. Noble **Adare Manor** is now the Adare Manor Hotel and a delight in every sense. Ranked among Ireland's finest baronial residences when it was completed in 1862, the dream home of the 2nd Earl is a showpiece of Irish architecture, a breathtakingly monumental building which imaginatively combines delicate local craftsmanship with the finest design influences from abroad. There's a Minstrel's Gallery, more than 40 yards long and almost 30 feet high, which was inspired by the Hall of Mirrors at Versailles and has 17th century Flemish choir stalls on both sides. Set beside the gently flowing River Maigue, the Manor remained the home of the Earls of Dunraven until the 1980s. Within the Manor Estate's 840 acres of rolling countryside is the superb 7138 yard championship Adare Golf Course designed by Robert Trent Jones Senior and regarded as amongst the finest created by this world renowned golf architect.

Adare Heritage Village

Adare, Co Limerick

With its brightly coloured thatched cottages, romantic medieval ruins, ancient stonework and trim gardens, Adare makes every effort to maintain its claim to be "Ireland's Prettiest Village". This model estate village snuggles in a wooded setting beside a graceful old bridge over the River Maigue. At its heart is a beautifully preserved 14th century **Augustinian Priory,** part of which is still in use as the Church of Ireland parish church. The story book appearance of the village owes its special qualities to the 2nd Earl of Dunraven who in the 1830s, when landlords in general were replacing thatch with slate, went against the trend and rebuilt Adare with larger thatched houses. Before the Earl's improvements, Adare was notorious for its scruffy, run-down character; today its quaint old cottages are interspersed with upmarket restaurants, art galleries, crafts and antiques shops.

Another attraction in the village is the **Adare Heritage Centre** which includes a Historical Exhibition, tourist information office, craft shop, a Kerry Woollen Mills retail outlet, and a restaurant.

Rathkeale

16 miles SE of Limerick on the N21

The second largest town in Co. Limerick, Rathkeale has a long main street with a fine early-19th century Courthouse and, just outside the town, one of the most striking medieval tower houses in the country, **Castle Matrix**. Built around 1410 for the 7th Earl of Desmond, the castle follows the usual plan for these mini-fortresses – four or five storeys high with the upper floors used as living quarters, the windowless ground floor for storage. The young Walter Raleigh stayed here in 1580 and years later, following his return from a colonising voyage to Virginia, presented his host with some potatoes. The Desmonds claimed that they were the first to grow potatoes in Ireland, a claim hotly contested by the inhabitants of Youghal in Co. Cork.

In the 1980s the castle was bought by Seán O'Driscoll, an Irish-American military expert who used his knowledge of medieval fortifications to restore the building as near as possible to its original state. A tiny chapel was re-created on the top floor and a medieval bedroom on another. The house is furnished with some wonderful Irish pieces, most notably an exquisite 19th century jewel encrusted harp. The house is now the headquarters of the Irish Heraldry Society but can be visited by arrangement. (Tel: 069 64284).

Newcastle West

26 miles SW of Limerick on the N21

This attractive riverside town takes its name from the great castle built in 1184 for the Earl of Desmond. The hall was added in the 1400s and is in a near perfect state of preservation; indeed, part of it is still inhabited. Known as the **Desmond Banqueting Hall** (Duchas), the building is two storeys high and its restored features include an oak musicians' gallery and a limestone hooded fireplace. The hall stands on the main square and is part of a medieval complex that includes a keep, a pele tower, bastion and curtain wall.

Three miles north of Newcastle West is **Ardagh** where in 1868 the famous Ardagh Chalice was discovered in an ancient ring fort. Now in the National Museum in Dublin, the Chalice has been dated to the 8th century AD. It is a beautifully proportioned cup 7 inches high and wrought in gold, silver and bronze with rich settings of enamel, amber, glass and crystal.

Abbeyfeale

38 miles SW of Limerick on the N21

Surrounded by rolling hills and set beside the River Feale, Abbeyfeale claims to be the gateway to Killarney and Tralee. It is also well known as a centre of traditional music, song and dance. There is fishing in the Feale (most of it free) for salmon, sea trout and brown trout. An abbey was founded here in 1188 and what little remains has been incorporated into the present Roman Catholic church.

Glin

33 miles W of Limerick on the N69

This charming village stands on the south shore of the Shannon at a point where the river is 3 miles wide. Once a salmon depot, Glin is now a centre of the dairy industry. Adjoining the village is the lovely demesne of **Glin Castle**, seat of the 29th Knight of Glin whose family, the Fitzgeralds, have lived on this estate almost continuously for 700 years. The present building dates back to the 1780s and stands on the bank of the River Shannon, guarded by three Gothic toy forts. The castle houses an outstanding collection of Irish furniture and paintings, including topographical watercolour prints and political cartoons. The house and grounds are open from mid-March to the end of October

Co Longford

A county of quiet farmlands and brown bogs, with only the occasional low hills, County Longford attracts relatively few tourists but plenty of anglers – there is prime fishing to be enjoyed in its lakes and rivers. But for those who appreciate pastoral calm and a gentle pace of life the county will provide a refreshing change from the busier tourist counties. And it has its fair share of things to see and do. The prehistoric dolmen at Aughnacliffe and the Stone Circles near Granard are both fine specimens of these enigmatic monuments, while the Corlea Trackway at Kenagh is a unique timber "railway" dating from around 3000 BC.

Bog Cutting, Corlea Bog

The county has several major literary associations. Oliver Goldsmith (1730-74), whose play *She Stoops to Conquer* is still frequently revived, was born at Pallas; the novelist Maria Edgeworth (1767-1849) came from the family after whom the village of Edgeworthstown is named; and more recently, the poet and dramatist Patraic Colum (1881-1972) was born in Longford Town, which is where we begin our tour.

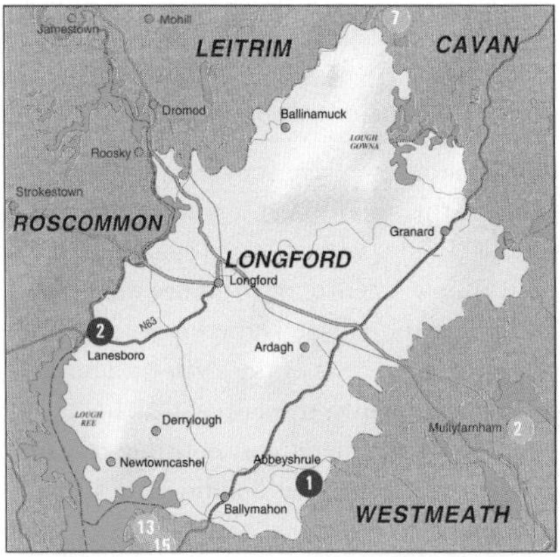

Longford

Set on a slope beside the River Camlin, Longford is dominated by its 19th century grey limestone **Cathedral of St Mel**. St Mel was bishop here around AD 480 and his crozier is one of the treasures in the ecclesiastical museum housed at the rear of the cathedral. Longford has not been lucky

PLACES TO STAY, EAT AND DRINK

The Rustic Inn, Abbeyshrule	1	Pub, Restaurant & Accommodation	p223
Samantha's Restaurant and B&B, Lanesboro	2	Restaurant & Accommodation	p225

● Denotes entries in other chapters

in preserving its past: the ancient fortress (*longphort* in Gaelic) of the O'Farrells and a Dominican priory of 1400 have both disappeared without trace, but some slight remains of a later castle erected by the 1st Earl of Longford in 1627 are incorporated in the old military barracks.

This quiet town really comes alive in July when the week-long **Longford Summer Festival** takes place, with the streets closed to traffic at 6pm and handed over to live pop and rock bands.

Around Longford

About 3 miles northeast of Longford, on the R194 road to Granard, **Carriglas Manor** is a striking Tudor-Gothic style mansion built in 1837 for Chief Justice Thomas Lefroy whose other claim to fame is that he enjoyed a brief romantic liaison with Jane Austen and may well have been the model for Darcy in *Pride and Prejudice*. The Lefroy family is still in residence and it will be one of them who shows you around the house with its elegant Waterford glass, Dutch furniture and family portraits. Visitors can wander around the attractive grounds and there's also a costume museum displaying a hoard of mid-18th century clothes which were discovered in old chests in the manor. The museum is handsomely housed in the former stable block, a striking Classical building designed by James Gandon who was also responsible for two of Dublin's finest buildings, the O'Connell Bridge and the Custom House.

Carriglas Manor Gardens

Ballinamuck

11 miles N of Longford off the R198

This small town in the north of Co. Longford was the arena for the battle that ended the 1798 Rising against the English. The combined Irish and French armies were defeated by a much larger force commanded by General Cornwallis. When the battle was over, 500 bodies lay scattered across the battlefield, - most of them Irish rebels who had refused to surrender. Despite this drastic defeat, the north of the county remained a centre of resistance, so much so that in 1846 an imposing Royal Irish Constabulary barracks was erected in the village. This is now the **1798 Memorial Hall** and incorporates the Ballinamuck Visitor Centre. The exhibits recount the course of the fateful battle and deal with such exploits as the heroic stand of Gunner Magee and the atrocities of the "Walking Gallows".

Granard

15 miles NE of Longford on the N55

A popular angling and riding centre, Granard is a bustling market town with a fondness for festivals. The most celebrated is the **Granard Harp Festival,** held on the second weekend in August, which originated in 1781 and was revived in 1981.

The festivities include parades, concerts, a harp workshop, competitions and ceilis. Then in late October comes the **Granard Pumpkin Festival** which features a wide range of activities from pumpkin baking and pumpkin carving to guess the weight competitions. If you are thinking of entering your own prize pumpkin bear in mind that recent winners have tilted the scales at around 180 lbs. Each spring, the town also hosts an **Easter Eggstravaganza.** To quote from the publicity flyer: "*Eggsciting floats and, for the girls, eggciting blokes, and for the rest of you folks we have eggsciting yolks*". Eggstraordinary.

On a more conventional note, Granard also boasts the largest Norman motte and bailey in Ireland. Built in 1199 and rising some 540 feet above sea level, it is worth walking to the top where a statue of St Patrick gazes out at a view that takes in nine counties, five lakes and a network of rivers. An even more venerable monument than this Norman earthwork is the Stone Circle about 3 miles outside the town. Also known as the **Druid Circle** and the only stone circle in the midlands, this prehistoric construction consists of 24 stones, six of them upright, seven of them placed on their sides and the remainder having fallen.

About 5 miles northwest of Granard, is another prehistoric construction, the **Aughnacliffe Dolmen.** It's a mightily impressive sight. Believed to be around 5000 years old, the dolmen consists of a huge block of stone about 12 feet long, 7 feet wide and 5 feet thick, resting on two supports. The assumption is that these massive neolithic monuments were erected over the grave of a chieftain or other important person and that the stones were originally covered with earth.

Edgeworthstown

8 miles E of Longford on the N4 and N55

The Edgeworth family settled at this crossroads village (known then as Mostrim) in 1583 but it was in the 18th century that the Edgeworths first came to wider notice. Richard Lovell Edgeworth was an author and inventor who is credited with creating the formula for tarmac well before the name of his Scottish contemporary, Macadam, became irrevocably linked with the road-making material. Richard equipped his house with central heating and also devised a water pump that dispensed a coin to anyone who pumped up a certain quantity of water. Richard's brother was the Abbé Henry Essex Edgeworth, confessor to Louis XVI, whom he attended on the scaffold. The Abbé left an eye-witness account of the king's last moments before the guillotine fell and the confessor's robes were drenched in royal blood. Best known of all the Edgeworths, though, was Maria, one of Richard's 22 children. An early campaigner for women's education, Maria made her name at the age of 32 with the novel *Castle Rackrent*. It's an even-handed book, equally understanding of the Anglo-Irish gentry and the impoverished peasantry, and imbued with a truly Irish sense of fun. Sir Walter Scott was an admirer of Maria's work and presented her with an inlaid marble table that is now in St John's Church. In the graveyard outside stands the Edgeworth family vault and, nearby, the grave of Oscar Wilde's sister, Isola, who died while on a visit to Edgeworthstown Rectory.

The Edgeworth family home, The Manor, where literary luminaries such as Scott and William Wordsworth were entertained, is now a nursing home run by the Sisters of Mercy and not open to the public. Another literary connection with Edgeworthstown has no visible memorial. The school on Pound Street where Oliver Goldsmith received his early education is currently just a derelict site. The school that replaced it, on the Athlone road, has been converted into a Visitor and Community Centre.

Ardagh

7 miles SE of Longford off the N4 or R393

Ardagh Village

This pretty village, a National Tidy Towns winner, is surrounded by woods and believed to be the site of a church founded by St Patrick, although today the oldest surviving structure is the ruin of St Mel's Cathedral, dating back to around AD 900. Consecrated by St Patrick himself, St Mel was one of the first Irish bishops. The **Ardagh Heritage Centre**, housed in the former Victorian school, traces the story of this charming village which has a number of pleasant but unremarkable 19th century buildings grouped around the village green.

Abbeyshrule

18 miles SE of Longford off the R393

Just outside Abbeyshrule stand the mournful remains of a 12th century Cistercian abbey but the main reason for seeking out this small village near the

The Rustic Inn

Abbeyshrule Village, Co. Longford
Tel: 044 57424 Fax: 044 57742
e-mail: mcgoey@ireland.com

Charmingly set beside the Royal Canal, **The Rustic Inn** is famous for its good food, drink and entertainment. Mine host Edward McGoey recently took over the running of the inn from his father Ted and is the fourth generation of his family to run this welcoming old hostelry. Although the McGoey family have been here since 1887, the present building dates from 1979 when the premises were completely rebuilt following a major fire. Twenty years later, to mark a major boat rally on the canal a striking wall mural depicting various canal scenes was painted on the inn's rear wall – an extra attraction for customers enjoying their refreshments on the canalside lawn. Right up until the 1940s, the inn's ales were off-loaded at this point from barges.

The Inn takes food seriously, promising – and delivering – exclusive menus and exquisite cuisine, all served in its spacious restaurant which can seat up to 300 guests. The Inn also serves tasty bar food and lunches, and a traditional Sunday lunch which is extremely popular. Music is another major attraction – many of the top Irish artists and musicians of recent years have performed here, amongst them The Dubliners and Sean McGuire. And if you are planning to stay in the area, the Rustic Inn has 4 en suite guest rooms for B&B, and a delightful self-catering property, "Mac's Cottage".

border with Co. Westmeath is its prime fishing. The owner of the Rustic Inn, Ted McGoey, has produced an informative leaflet giving details of the best locations in the many loughs and rivers all around. The local river, the Inny, for example, which runs through the village, "is a top class coarse fishery and..... provides in excess of 60kms of good bank pike fishing". From Ballymahon to Abbeyshrule, the Inny can be a productive wet and dry fly trout fishery and several angling competitions are fished each year on the river.

Small though it is, the village organizes the **Abbeyshrule Annual Fly-In and Airshow** which is held in early August at the General Aviation Airfield just outside the village. The show attracts aircraft from abroad as well as a sizeable UK contingent and the programme includes a lively barbecue and Irish Night at the Rustic Inn.

Ballymahon

14 miles S of Longford on the N55

One of the few places of any size in southern Co. Longford, Ballymahon (population 1,000) is mainly remarkable for its inordinately wide main street. The town stands on the River Inny, renowned for its fine trout. The river is spanned here by a graceful five arched bridge. Ballymahon prides itself on being close to the heart of Goldsmith Country: his mother lived here as a young girl; the author was born at the village of Pallas, 3 miles to the east; and two years later the family moved to Lissoy, 5 miles to the southwest.

Derrylough

15 miles SW of Longford on minor road off the R392

Hidden away in the southwest corner of the county, close to Lough Ree, Derrylough offers sequestered walks alongside the Royal Canal; the ruins of Abbeyderg Augustinian Priory; a charming early-19th dovecote; and a clockhouse memorial tower erected in 1878 which still keeps perfect time. It is worked with its original weights and chains which demand manual winding each week. The mechanism was made by the same company that fitted out London's Big Ben.

Just outside the village is the fascinating **Corlea Interpretative Centre,** a distinctive mustard-coloured building standing in splendid isolation surrounded by windswept bogland on all sides. At this spot, in 1985, a *togher*, an ancient trackway of oak planks, was discovered by men cutting turf. These ancient trackways date back to 3500 BC and were constructed to transport animals and personal belongings across marshy terrain.

The one at Corlea is massive and sturdily built, having endured the pressure of wheeled vehicles over many centuries.

Newtowncashel

11 miles SW of Longford off the R392

Another of Co. Longford's "Tidy Towns", Newtowncashel has a small Cottage Museum, occupying a restored 19th century dwelling, furnished and equipped with typical utensils of the period.

The village is perhaps better known for the famous **Bog Oak Sculptures** produced by the local artist, Michael Casey, using centuries-old oak retrieved from local bogs, allowed to dry out over several years, and then sculpted into intriguing shapes.

Newtoncashel also hosts the Larry Kelly Traditional Music Weekend in early June. Established in 1991, the festival commemorates the legendary fiddle player Larry Kelly and his unique style of fiddle playing. The concerts, sessions and workshops attract traditional music lovers from all over Ireland.

Lanesboro

9 miles SW of Longford on the N63

Sitting at the northern tip of Lough Ree, Lanesboro is a noted centre for coarse fishing and for boat and barge trips around the lough or along the River Shannon. A rather unorthodox attraction, just outside the town, is the power station which offers guided tours.

The station is fuelled by peat, a fossil fuel with which Ireland is still surprisingly well-provided.

SAMANTHA'S RESTAURANT & B&B

Main Street, Lanesboro, Co. Longford
Tel: 043 21558
website: www.samanthasbandb.com

You'll find **Samantha's Restaurant and B&B** in the heart of this picturesque town on the banks of the river Shannon and close to enchanting Lough Ree. Samantha's looks very inviting with its terracotta-coloured walls, colourful window boxes, hanging baskets and potted shrubs and plants. Inside, you can be sure of a warm welcome from owner/manager Samantha Lulham who promises a "professional and friendly home-style service".

The restaurant enjoys a reputation for its consistency in excellent cuisine and specialises in good quality, fresh home-cooked food served in a relaxed and friendly atmosphere. The menu offers something for all tastes – whether it be from the children's menu, the best steaks or vegetarian dishes. An extensive wine list is also available and you'll be served by cheerful and helpful staff.

If you are planning to stay in this attractive part of the county, Samantha's also offers top quality bed & breakfast accommodation. The guest bedrooms have recently undergone major refurbishment but still retain their own individual character and charm. All the bedrooms are fully equipped and decorated to exceptionally high standards. There's a private entrance for B&B guests and converted buildings at the rear provide ample storage space for angling equipment and bicycles.

Co Louth

The smallest of Ireland's 32 counties, Louth covers an area of only 317 square miles, most of it fertile, undulating country with a coastline of sandy beaches interspersed with rocky headlands. But the landscape changes in the north where the mountainous Cooley Peninsula looks across Carlingford Lough to the Mountains of Mourne. Part of the old province of Leinster, County Louth figures prominently in the epic stories of Ireland's misty past. The most famous of these tales tells of Queen Maeve of Connacht who started a war to win a bull she coveted. Maeve had the power to immobilise her enemies with a magical sickness – all save one, the warrior Cúchulainn who single-handedly defeated her troops.

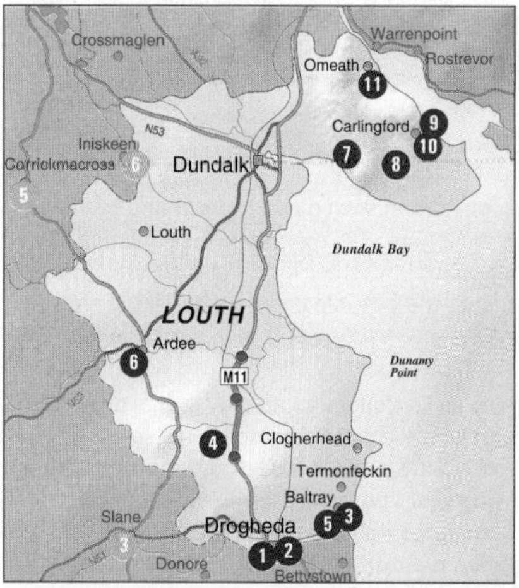

Cooley Mountains, Co Louth

Louth and the neighbouring county of Meath are both rich in prehistoric remains, and the ruins of the great religious

PLACES TO STAY, EAT AND DRINK

Fisherman's Wharf, Drogheda	1	Restaurant & Accommodation	p227
Black Bull Inn, Drogheda	2	Pub with Food	p228
The 19th, Drogheda	3	Pub	p230
Monasterboice, Drogheda	4	Historic Site	p230
Beaulieu House & Gardens, Drogheda	5	House & Gardens	p231
Ferdia Arms, Ardee	6	Pub and Restaurant	p232
Fitzpatrick's Bar & Restaurant, Dundalk	7	Bar & Restaurant	p234
Glenmore Cottage, Carlingford	8	Self Catering	p235
Oystercatcher Lodge & Bistro, Carlingford	9	Bistro & Accommodation	p236
Grove House Carlingford, Carlingford	10	B&B	p236
The Granvue House Hotel, Omeath	11	Hotel	p237

● Denotes entries in other chapters

foundations of Mellifont Abbey and Monasterboice testify to the religious preoccupations of medieval Leinster. There are only two towns of any size in County Louth, both with populations of around 28,000: the port and county town of Dundalk in the north, and Drogheda in the south which is where we begin our tour.

Drogheda

This lively port, hemmed in by hills, began as a settlement around a ford crossing the River Boyne where St Mary's Bridge stands today. When the Vikings arrived in AD 911 they built the first *Droichead Atha*, "bridge across the ford", and so gave the town its name.

Drogheda's most dominant feature is **Millmount**, a huge earthen mound which reputedly contains prehistoric graves although it has never been excavated. The mount is crowned by a Martello Tower which was badly damaged during the 1922 Civil War but has been fully restored and now provides some grand panoramic views of the town. Housed in the nearby 18th century military barracks is the **Millmount Museum** where the exhibits include a wonderful period kitchen complete with a hand-powered vacuum cleaner of 1860, some unique 18th century guild banners, and a Boyne coracle, the circular fishing boat in use from prehistoric times.

Drogheda's tradition of fine workmanship is maintained in the adjacent **Millmount Craft Centre** where the six resident craft workers offer a fascinating range of jewellery, hand painted silks, patchwork & appliqué, fashion knitwear, ceramics and decorative glass.

During the Middle Ages, Drogheda city walls had no fewer than ten gates. Only one survives but it is one of the most perfectly preserved in the country. **St Lawrence's Gate** was built in the late 1200s and it's a

FISHERMAN'S WHARF

Mell, Drogheda, Co. Louth
Tel: 041 983 3800 Fax: 041 984 7425

Two minutes from the centre of Drogheda, in the old townland of Mell, **Fisherman's Wharf** is a converted country house which owner Ann Curry completely re-modelled when she arrived here in 1997. There's a stylish dining room with seating for up to 60 diners where you'll find a good choice of wholesome and appetising food, all of it freshly prepared. The menu includes a succulent home-made steak burger and popular favourites such as Roast Leg of Lamb and Liver and Bacon with Onion Sauce. Amongst the starters are dishes such as deep fried mushrooms in a garlic sauce and home-made soup. Conclude your meal with one of the delicious desserts on offer. Another attraction here is the live entertainment provided each

weekend. Fisherman's Wharf's peaceful location makes this an ideal place to stay.

The 11 guest bedrooms overlook the River Boyne and are attractively furnished and decorated. All of them have en suite facilities and are equipped with colour television and tea/coffee-making facilities. A full Irish breakfast is included in the tariff. Drogheda town is a bustling port with an outstanding museum, the Millmount, an excellent craft centre, a well-preserved medieval gate and two historic churches.

Black Bull Inn

Dublin Road, Drogheda, Co. Louth
Tel: 041 983 7139 Fax: 041 983 6854
website: www.blackbull.ie

A thriving enterprise now, the **Black Bull Inn** has grown from its humble origins when it comprised only the old Crilly Bar and a relatively small lounge. As the owners, John-Paul and Charlie Egan say "Those were the days when the local band "Who's Who" brought the lounge alive on Friday nights while locals jostled and jockeyed for space outside the bar. How times have changed!"

They have indeed. Over the years, the restaurant and dining business has gradually come to the fore and various extensions have helped to transform the Black Bull into one of the finest eating houses in Drogheda – the

"jewel of the Dublin Road". The comprehensive menu offers something for every palate. Amongst the starters you'll find stock pot soup of the day, Prawn Pil-Pil, oak-smoked salmon and warm goat's cheese salad for example.

There's also a choice of appetising open sandwiches – Boyne salmon, crab or steak for example, all freshly prepared and lavishly garnished. Main dishes on offer include seasonal salads, a wide choice of beef burgers made from home-prepared Irish beef, an "Oriental" selection with dishes such as king scallops in coconut and ginger, a wonderful array of poultry, meat and game offerings (roast pheasant in port and redcurrant sauce, perhaps?), fish dishes, steaks and vegetarian options like the tasty pasta provençale. Kids have their own choice of favourites such as fish bites or beef burger with beans and chips. The delicious desserts include profiteroles with butterscotch sauce and meringue nest with fresh fruit. To accompany your meal there's a wide selection of beverages and an extensive wine list with quality wines from both Europe and the New World.

As well as offering outstanding cuisine, the Black Bull is also strong on entertainment. John-Paul and Charlie have opened the lively "Itzabar", designed to attract a youthful clientele. "The recipe has worked well" they say, "enabling a flourishing restaurant business to grow side by side with a modern music bar, a juxtaposition of the old and the new creating a vibrant atmosphere that is simply unique". So, whether your interest is in top quality cuisine or contemporary music (or both) the Black Bull is definitely the place to seek out in Drogheda.

miracle that its two drum towers, four storeys high and supporting a portcullis gate, somehow escaped Cromwell's savage assault on the town in 1649. In that bloody conflict his troops massacred 2,000 of the garrison and citizens. The town's Governor was a primary target for the troops since it was rumoured that his wooden leg was filled with gold. Finding the leg empty, the soldiers used it to beat the Governor to death. Many of Drogheda's citizens sought refuge in **St Peter's Church** and were burnt to death when the soldiers set the 13th century wooden structure on fire. The present church was erected in 1753, an elegant building with a fine porch and steeple designed by the eminent Irish architect Francis Johnston. The graveyard here contains some macabre Golding Cadaver tombstone slabs which depict the horrors of the Black Death and a gruesome, though finely sculpted, memorial of 1520 which dwells on the effects of bodily decomposition.

In Drogheda's main thoroughfare, West Street, there's another St Peter's Church. This imposing Roman Catholic place of worship was erected as a memorial to St Oliver Plunkett, Archbishop of Armagh, who was hung, drawn and quartered in London in 1681 for his alleged participation in the "Popish Plot" fabricated by Titus Oates. The archbishop's body was spirited away by his supporters and his head is now preserved at St Peter's in a special shrine which draws pilgrims from all over Ireland to venerate the relic. Oliver Plunkett was canonized in 1975, the first Irishman to be made a saint for more than 700 years.

On the southern edge of the town, the **Drogheda Heritage Centre** is housed in the former St Mary's Church. One of its exhibits is, rather surprisingly, the death mask of Oliver Cromwell whose troops wreaked such havoc on the town.

Around Drogheda

About 5 miles north-west of Drogheda stand the ruins of **Mellifont Abbey**, established in 1142 as the first Cistercian monastery in Ireland. Construction of the Abbey took fifteen years and its consecration in 1157 was attended by a papal legate, the Irish primate, 17 bishops and the leading lords temporal of Ireland. For almost 400 years the Abbey was one of the most important religious foundations in the country, with 38 other monasteries under its jurisdiction. In 1539, Henry VIII closed them all. The glorious building with its huge pillars supporting a canopy of soaring arches was handed to Sir Edward Moore, ancestor of the Earls of Drogheda, who converted the church into a fortified mansion. His fortifications proved ineffectual against an onslaught by Cromwell's troops in 1649 and by the mid-1800s the shattered building was serving as a pigsty.

Few of the remains rise above shoulder height but a notable exception is the Lavabo, built around 1200. It was originally

Mellifont Abbey

THE 19th

Baltray, Drogheda, Co. Louth
Tel: 041 982 2038 Mobile: 0862 390539

With two 18-hole championship courses nearby it's easy to understand how **The 19**th got its name. Mine host is Eddie Murray, a genial landlord who has been dispensing hospitality for some 15 years. He has decorated The 19th's bar and lounge with a fascinating array of golfing memorabilia to make his golfing patrons feel at home. Open seven days a week, The 19th has a pool table and hosts lively traditional Irish music sessions at the weekend. Wheelchair-friendly, the pub has plenty of parking space, including an area for coaches at the rear.

The 19th doesn't have any guest bedrooms itself but bed & breakfast accommodation can be arranged just 100 yards down the road where golf parties are welcome. Baltray village itself is a quaint little place set near the mouth of the River Boyne and with a 3-mile long beach stretching northwards. On the edge of the village is one of the two championship golf courses; the other is at Termonfeckin, a couple of miles to the north. And 3 miles to the west is Drogheda, a busy port set on both banks of the River Boyne and offering good shopping, an outstanding museum – the Millmount – an excellent craft centre, and historic buildings such as St Peter's Church where the head of St Oliver Plunkett is preserved in a special shrine.

MONASTERBOICE

Drogheda, Co. Louth

About six miles north of Drogheda, **Monasterboice** (*Mainistir Buite*, "Buite's Monastery") is notable for the evocative remains of the monastic settlement founded by St Buite in the 5th century. This small, secluded site contains one of the most perfect 10th century high crosses in Ireland and also one of the tallest surviving Round Towers.

Muireadach's Cross stands 17ft 8in high with every inch of its surface covered with exquisitely carved Biblical scenes ranging from Adam and Eve through to the Crucifixion and a chilling depiction of the Last Judgement. Nearby, the **West Cross** is even taller, 21ft 6in, and although more weathered is equally richly ornamented. Rising high above the crosses is what must have been the tallest **Round Tower** in Ireland before it lost its conical cap. It still stands almost 110ft high and is 51feet across at its base. It used to be possible to enter the tower through the doorway 6ft above ground but the tower has been closed for safety reasons.

octagonal but today only four walls remain standing. The monks would come to the Lavabo before meals to wash their hands in the jets that sprayed from a fountain in the centre. The only other substantial portions of the Abbey still in place are two square towers of the former gatehouse.

About 6 miles north of Drogheda, **Monasterboice** (*Mainistir Buite*, "Buite's Monastery") is notable for the evocative remains of the monastic settlement founded by St Buite in the 5th century (see panel opposite).

Baltray

4 miles NE of Drogheda off the R167

The quaint little village of Baltray boasts a championship golf course and a beach 4 miles long but the most impressive sight here is **Beaulieu House** (see panel below), set on the north bank of the River Boyne. This splendid 17th century mansion built in the Dutch style for Sir Henry Tichbourne is one of the earliest examples in Ireland of an unfortified house. Its interior is almost miraculously preserved with two of the original staircases still in place along with its magnificent two storey high Hall which contains an imposing chimney piece, a large cornice and great arched doorways with elaborate painted pinewood carvings of musical instruments. Among the many fine paintings around the walls are contemporary portraits of William III and Queen Anne, including one by the court painter Jan van Wyck that depicts the king at the Battle of the Boyne. There are also family portraits of the Tichbournes whose direct descendant, Mrs Sidney Waddington, is the present owner of Beaulieu House, the 9th generation of her family to have lived here. Other treasures in the house include a painted ceiling in the drawing room, done in the style of Verrio, the 17th century

Beaulieu House & Garden

Drogheda, Co. Louth
Tel: 041 983 8557 Fax: 041 983 2265

Beaulieu House & Garden, set on the banks of the River Boyne, presents features that are very rare in Ireland. The imposing house was built in 1666 by Sir Henry Tichbourne in a Dutch style that is almost unique in the Republic. It is one of the earliest examples of a non-fortified house of its kind, and its interior is almost miraculously preserved. Two of the original staircases are still in place while the magnificent 2-storey high Hall contains an imposing chimney piece, a large cornice and great arched doorways with elaborate painted pinewood carvings of musical instruments. Amongst the many fine paintings around the walls are contemporary portraits of William III and Queen Anne, including one by the court painter Jan Van Wyck that depicts the King at the Battle of the Boyne. There are family portraits of the Tichbournes whose direct descendant, Mrs Sidney Waddington, is the present owner of Beaulieu House, the 9th generation of her family to have lived here. Other treasures in the house include a painted ceiling in the drawing room, done in the style of Verrio, the 17th century Italian who decorated Windsor Castle and Hampton Court Palace, and a white Carrara marble fireplace showing King Neptune in a shell boat flanked by dolphins.

The Garden at Beaulieu is equally remarkable. It is one of the earliest of Irish walled gardens, dating from around 1732, and Mrs Waddington, who is a keen gardener, has personally tended this delightful spot for half a century. Definitely a sight not to be missed, Beaulieu is open from 1st May to mid-September, Mondays to Fridays.

Italian who decorated Hampton Court Palace and Windsor Castle, and a white Carrara marble fireplace showing King Neptune in a shell boat flanked by dolphins. The house also boasts a lovely walled garden believed to be one of the first to be created in the country, dating from around 1752 – Mrs Waddington, who is a keen gardener, has personally tended this delightful spot for half a century.

Termonfeckin

6 miles NE of Drogheda on the R166

Lying about half a mile inland, Termonfeckin is a peaceful little place which takes its name from St Feckin who founded a monastic settlement here in the 6th century. In the graveyard of the church named after him rises a fine 10th century high cross elaborately ornamented with sculptured figures and interlaced designs. On a hill to the east of the village is

Termonfeckin Castle, a well-preserved small tower house of the 15th and 16th centuries. If you want to see inside, the keys can be obtained from the bungalow across the road. Between the village and the sea is the Seapoint golf course with a parkland and links combination layout designed by local Ryder Cup player Des Smyth.

Clogherhead

8 miles NE of Drogheda on the R166

Clogherhead boasts a fine, safe sandy beach and views across the Irish Sea to the hills of Cumbria in England – and to the controversial Sellafield nuclear plant. The headland known as Clogher Head rises 205 feet from the sea and on its northern shore is the little fishing village of Clogher with a busy small harbour and pier. Carved out of the headland is the Red Cave – so called because of the colour of the rock which is stained by a rusty-looking fungus.

THE FERDIA ARMS

Castle Street, Ardee, Co Louth
Tel: 04168 53675

Frank Lynch is the cheerful host at **The Ferdia Arms**, one of the most popular places to meet and socialise in the historic town of Ardee, which is rapidly developing as a satellite town of Dublin. Dating from 1870, this delightful bar and restaurant retains many original features, including the stone and slate exterior and the Georgian-style windows. Inside, wooden floors, moulded

ceiling panels and sports memorabilia set the scene, and leaded screens create cosy, intimate little nooks.

The Ferdia Arms, which attracts a clientele of local regulars, sports people and tourists, opens at 8 o'clock for breakfast, and the lunchtime and evening menus also feature satisfying country-style home cooking. It's very much at the heart of Ardee's life, with pool and darts the regular pub games and live music (country or pop) on Friday, Saturday and Sunday evenings. It's also a favourite choice for private parties or other special occasions.

The bar takes its name from a famous warrior named Ferdia who was killed at Ardee by his foster-brother Cúchulainn at the Battle of the Táin Bó Cauligne.

Ardee

13 miles NW of Drogheda on the N2

This attractive little market town on the River Dee stands at a strategic crossroads and was often used as a mustering point by the English for their attacks on Ulster. This explains why the town has two castles: the 13th century **Ardee Castle,** whose square keep now houses a museum and gift shop, and **Hatch's Castle** in Market Street which dates from the same period. Ardee stood at the northern boundary of The Pale, the area controlled by the English since the days of Henry II. The territories "beyond the Pale" were regarded as outside the boundaries of a civilized society.

It was at Ardee that the famed Cúchulainn, champion of Ulster, gave battle to his foster brother, Ferdia, the champion of the South. After many days conflict, Cúchulainn slew Ferdia and it was from the fallen hero that Ardee derived its name, *Atha Fhirdhia*.

Collectors of ecclesiastical curiosities should make the short journey from Ardee to the village of Kildernock and its **Jumping Church**. There are two theories as to why most of the end wall of the church here stands 3 feet away from the base on which it was built. The locals' logical explanation is that the wall moved of its own accord in order to exclude the grave of an excommunicated sinner. Meteorologists have come up with the fanciful idea that it was actually a ferocious storm in 1715 that shifted the stonework so neatly.

The graveyard here is also interesting because of the plain, foot-high stone slabs which are some of the earliest tombstones to mark the previously unidentified graves of the poor.

Dundalk

The county town of Louth, Dundalk is a busy manufacturing town, sitting at the head of Dundalk Bay. In Celtic times, as *Dún Dealga*, it was already a fortress (*dún*) guarding the pass through the mountains to the province of Ulster. Vikings, Anglo-Normans and the English followed each other in fighting tooth and nail to command this strategic site. Centuries of unremitting warfare have left few traces of the town's history before things finally settled down, more or less, in the 18th century. The 14th century tower of St Nicholas' Church and the belltower of a Franciscan friary of 1240 are the only significant witnesses to Dundalk's medieval past.

When more prosperous times at last provided Dundalk's Town Fathers with sufficient funds for erecting substantial civic buildings, they possessed no distinctive Irish tradition of public architecture to emulate, so they genuflected to the past. **The Courthouse** for example, completed in 1818, is modelled on the Temple of Theseus in Athens. The Courthouse, still in use, is a lovely, airy building whose classical poise and grace will be a little tarnished for modern-day English visitors by the uncompromising inscription beneath the statue of a Guardian Angel on the plaza outside. The sculpture is dedicated to "*the martyrs in the cause of liberty who fought and died in the struggle against English Tyranny and foreign rule in Ireland*".

Despite those understandable anti-English sentiments of the time, the architects of Dundalk's Roman Catholic **St Patrick's Cathedral** seem to have had no reservations about producing a virtual replica of the exterior of one of England's most distinctive ecclesiastical buildings, King's College Chapel, Cambridge, complete with needle spires, huge mullioned windows and crenellated walls. Financial constraints ruled out any attempt to replicate in St Patrick's interior the 15th

Fitzpatrick's Bar & Restaurant

Jenkinstown, Rockmarshal, Dundalk, Co. Louth
Tel: 00 353 42 9376193

Standing in the heart of the well-known Tain walking trail, **Fitzpatrick's Bar & Restaurant** is a haven for golfers and fishermen alike, and handy for the glorious beaches nearby. It was in 1993 that Danny and Dympna Fitzpatrick established their bar and restaurant in the village of Jenkinstown and since then they have gathered a dazzling array of awards. Fitzpatrick's has been acclaimed Louth Pub of the Year no fewer than 5 times (1998, 2000, 2001,2002,2003); it was the Black and White Irish Pub of the Year in 2001; Lenister Pub of the Year in 2001 and 2002, and All Ireland Pub of the Year 2001.

This outstanding country hostelry is an attractive white-washed building with the Cooley Mountains providing a scenic backdrop. Inside, the walls are smothered with a fascinating array of artefacts and memorabilia – old advertising signs ("I'm jolly well taking Bovril"), vintage kitchen utensils, ancient jugs and mugs, a stag's head and even some signposts. But it's the warmth and hospitality of the owners and staff that really impresses and makes a visit to Fitzpatrick's such a pleasant experience.

If you just want a drink, there's the choice of the atmospheric Shann-Ronan Bar or, if the weather is kind, the adjoining beer garden. If you are looking for a meal, food is served in both the lounge and restaurant and

offers the best freshly-caught Carlingford seafood accompanied by locally grown vegetables. The breads, desserts and petit fours come from the Fitzpatrick's own bakery on the premises.

The menu runs to many pages in which traditional fish and chips sit alongside dishes such as char-grilled marinated salmon prawns provençale; steak & Guinness pie rubs shoulders with beef stroganoff and rib-eye with peppercorn and herb crust; crispy fried duck breast or roast lamb rack on a rosemary and garlic mash. Other pages list vegetarian options, a choice of open sandwiches, full afternoon tea with scones and conserve; fresh raspberry and lemon brulée; a glass of Irish stout, whiskey from the local distillery; or a "Nutty Irishman" liqueur coffee. Food is served from 12.30pm to 10pm, Tuesday to Saturday, from 12.30pm to 3pm on Sunday when a "lunch extravaganza is served that is a local living legend!" Fitzpatrick's has a no-smoking policy; children over 3 years old are welcome; and there's plenty of car parking space. The bar and restaurant are closed on Mondays, Christmas Eve and Christmas Day and also Good Friday.

century glories of its East Anglian model so the lively Gothic contours of the cathedral from outside are considerably more rewarding than the austere interior.

Two other locations are worth a visit. **Louth County Museum**, housed in an impressive 18th century distillery, uses some high tech displays and an audio-visual presentation to tell the story of local industries from coopering to cigarettes, while the top two floors of the building host travelling art exhibitions. A rather unusual attraction, about a mile south of the town on the N1, is the **Carrolls Tobacco Factory**, a striking 1970 building designed by Scott Tallon Walker.

Dundalk makes a good base for exploring the **Cooley Peninsula**, a magically unspoilt area with enchanting views across Carlingford Lough to the Mountains of Mourne. The peninsula was the setting for one of Ireland's best-known myths, the Táin Bó Cúailnge, or the Cattle Raid of Cooley. Although the story is set in the first century AD, the topographical descriptions in the epic tale are so precise that many of the places can still be recognised.

At the western end of the peninsula, near Ravensdale, stands the gigantic **Proleek Dolmen**, accessible via a footpath from the rear of the Ballymascanlon Hotel. The huge capstone that crowns it weighs an incredible 46 tons.

Around Dundalk

Louth Village
9 miles SW of Dundalk on the R171

Why the county should have taken its name from this peaceful little village isn't clear, but it's worth stopping off here just to visit **St Mochta's Church**. According to legend, the original church was built during the course of a single night to provide shelter for its founder, St Mochta, who died in AD 534. The present remains date back to the 1100s and were part of a monastery dedicated to the saint. The high, vaulted roof, reached by way of a shoulder-scraping staircase, is surprisingly graceful for such an early date.

Also in Louth Village is **Knockabbey Castle and Gardens.** The 30 acres of gardens include restored Victorian gardens and parkland, and a medieval water garden which dates back to AD 1050. There is an Interpretative Centre in the 14th century Tower House where visitors can watch a short film on the history and restoration of the castle and gardens.

Carlingford
14 miles NE of Dundalk on the R173

The main settlement on the Cooley Peninsula, the Heritage Town of Carlingford is an attractive seaside resort with some fine

GLENMORE COTTAGE

Glenmore, nr Carlingford, Dundalk, Co. Louth
Tel: 042 937 6199

Glenmore Cottage is a delightful white-washed building dating back to the 1600s and surrounded by wonderfully peaceful open countryside, a perfect rural retreat from which to explore the scenic but little-known Cooley Peninsula. Built in traditional style, the cottage has a comfortable sitting room with an open fire and TV; a kitchen/dining area; **three bedrooms,** a bathroom with shower and a separate shower room. Amenities include a dishwasher and washer/drier. There are some

lovely walks nearby and the popular lakeside resort of Carlingford with its ruined Norman castle, historic buildings and craft shops, is just 5 miles away.

Oystercatcher Lodge & Bistro

Market Square, Carlingford, Co. Louth
Tel: 042 937 3922
website: theoystercatcher.com

Standing right at the heart of the upmarket resort of Carlingford on the shores of Carlingford Lough, the **Oystercatcher Lodge & Bistro** offers top quality cuisine and accommodation. The stylish Bistro, which has won two awards for "Best Dining in Ireland", is particularly noted for its seafood – oysters farmed in Carlingford Lough on beds that have enjoyed an international fame since the mid-1800s, or crab and lobster delivered fresh each day from Dundalk Bay. The chef is Denise McKevitt who together with her husband Brian owns and runs the Oystercatcher. Denise believes that quality ingredients require simple preparation and little adornment and although her speciality is seafood she is also a culinary wizard with meat dishes such as those based on delicious organic Cooley Mountain lamb. From birth these lambs have lived on mountain grasses and herbs which Denise believes gives the meat a very special quality. Brian and Denise spent periods of their lives in the Middle East and America – influences which says Brian "have also infiltrated the menu".

The guest bedrooms at the Oystercatcher are unusually spacious, best described as mini-suites. Elegantly furnished and decorated, they have vaulted ceilings, wooden floors and all modern facilities. Many enjoy wonderful views of Slabh Foye Mountain and all have TV, direct dial telephone, hair dryer, iron and ironing board, and hospitality tray.

Grove House Carlingford

Grove Road, Carlingford, Co. Louth
Tel: 042 937 3494 Fax: 042 938 3851
e-mail: hanrattj@gofree.indigo.ie

Located within walking distance of Carlingford village, **Grove House Carlingford** is an impressive and spacious modern building standing in its own extensive grounds. It was built in 1993 and has been elegantly furnished and decorated by its owner, Wendy Hanratty. The graciously appointed dining room has large windows overlooking the Mourne Mountains and it's here that guests can enjoy a full Irish breakfast with vegetarian options. Breakfast is served from 8.30am to 10pm but an earlier meal can be arranged on request. Grove House has 6 guest bedrooms, all with en suite facilities, TV and hospitality tray.

Children are welcome and large family rooms are available. There are plenty of activities within the immediate area – fishing and hill walking, for example, and the Heritage Town of Carlingford itself is a smart seaside resort with good restaurants, interesting craft shops and notable old buildings. These include the massive ruins of the Anglo-Norman King John's Castle, visited by King John in 1210; a couple of sturdy 15th century dwellings; and The Tholsel, formerly a gate tower in the town's medieval walls.

Carlingford

St Patrick is said to have made his first landfall in Ireland here, the Vikings arrived a few centuries later, but the oldest survival from the past is the impressive bulk of **King John's Castle** down by the water's edge. With walls rising some 70 feet, it is the largest Norman Castle in the country. It was built around 1210 and shortly after its completion King John stayed here, hence the name. Also worth seeking out in Carlingford are the well-preserved Taaffe's Castle and a

beaches and a distinctly medieval feeling in its narrow, terraced streets where at one time there were 32 castellated buildings.

The Granvue House Hotel

Omeath, Co. Louth
Tel: 042 9375 109
e-mail: www.omeath.net/granvuehousehotel.ie

A "grand view" is certainly guaranteed at the **Granvue House Hotel** – in fact, lots of grand views from the mountains and valleys overlooking the village and across beautiful Carlingford Lough. This luxuriously appointed guest house of hotel size proportions is owned and run by Patrice McDonnell and her family and has that genuinely friendly atmosphere you only seem to find in family-run hotels. Guests have the use of an elegant lounge and TV room, exquisitely decorated and lighted, and convenient for the bar, restaurant and rooms. The bar offers a choice of tasty snacks while the superb restaurant serves the best cuisine to be found in these parts with dishes based on fresh local vegetables, fish and meat.

The dining room enjoys a view across the lough that's delightful during the day and magical at night. The guest bedrooms at the Granvue maintain the same meticulous standards evident throughout the hotel – bright, spacious and furnished in warm and cosy colours with luxurious fabrics and discreet lighting. All rooms are en suite and equipped with TV. Amongst the Granvue's specialities are wedding receptions. There's a beautiful spacious ballroom and the hotel's location provides a perfect backdrop for those precious wedding photographs.

fortified house called the Mint. Neither building is open to the public. Close to the Mint and forming an archway over the road, the Tholsel was originally a gate tower in the town walls and later served as Carlingford's gaol.

The hills behind Carlingford provide splendid walking country, with a particularly breathtaking view near the village of Omeath. Another striking feature is Windy Gap, a narrow ravine which, according to the Táin Bó Cúailnge, was carved through the hills by Fergus, Queen Maeve's chief warrior.

Omeath

19 miles NE of Dundalk on the R173

Until fairly recently Omeath was at the centre of the only sizeable Gaeltacht area in this region and it still has a vigorous tradition of singing. With its widely scattered houses – another unusual feature – the village stands at the northern tip of Carlingford Lough and looks across to the towns of Warrenpont and Rostrevor in Co. Down. During the summer months a regular passenger ferry makes the 5-minute journey across the lough to Warrenpoint.

Co Mayo

The County Mayo coastline from Killary Harbour to Killala provides a marvellous sequence of vistas – rugged headlands, roughly-moulded cliffs, sandy beaches and Achill, the largest island off the Irish coast (although it is now linked by road to the mainland). Inland, the landscape is also wonderfully varied with ranges of mountains rising from limestone plains and moorlands studded with countless lakes. It was on one of those mountains, Croagh Patrick, that St Patrick

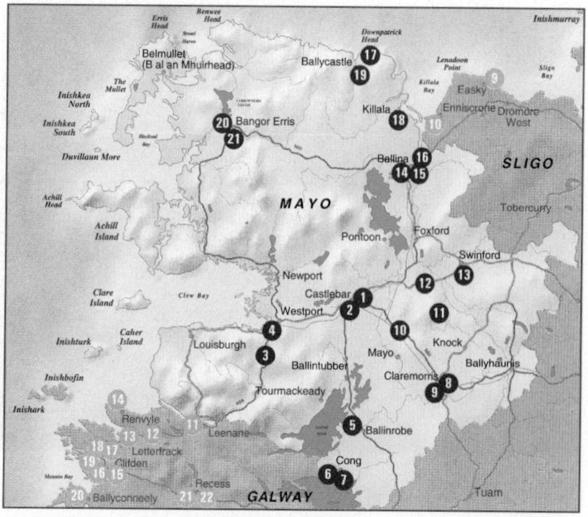

PLACES TO STAY, EAT AND DRINK

Rocky's Bar & Restaurant, Castlebar	1	Bar & Restaurant	p240
The T.F. Royal Hotel & Theatre, Castlebar	2	Hotel	p241
Moher House, Westport	3	B&B	p242
MJ Henehan, Westport	4	Pub, Food & Accommodation	p243
The Valkenburg & Marina's Café, Ballinrobe	5	Pub, Food & Accommodation	p246
Riverside Inn, Cong	6	Pub with Food	p247
Corrib View Villa, Cong	7	B&B and Self Catering	p247
D'Alton Inn hotel, Claremorris	8	Hotel	p248
Mulligan's, Claremorris	9	Pub with Food	p249
The Olde Woods, Balla	10	Pub, Food & Accommodation	p249
Teach O'Hora, Kiltimagh	11	Pub with Food	p250
Village Inn, Castlemorris	12	Pub, Food & Accommodation	p250
Greaney's, Swinford	13	Pub with Food	p251
Chung's at Tullios, Ballina	14	Pub and Chinese Restaurant	p251
Crockets on the Quay, Ballina	15	Pub, Food & Accommodation	p252
The Rocks, Ballina	16	B&B and Self Catering	p252
Downpatrick Head, Ballina	17	Scenic Attraction	p252
Village Inn, Killala	18	Pub with Food	p253
Mary's Cottage Kitchen, Ballycastle	19	Café	p254
Barretts, Bangor Erris	20	Pub, Food & Accommodation	p254
Hillcrest House, Bangor Erris	21	B&B	p255

● Denotes entries in other chapters

Nephin Mountain, Co Mayo

fasted for 40 days and pilgrims on their way to climb the mountain would break their journey at Ballintubber Abbey where Mass has been celebrated daily since its foundation in 1216.

Although Co. Mayo is roughly the same size as Co. Cork, its total population (110,000) is considerably less than that of Cork City alone. Surprisingly, Mayo has never been high on visitor itineraries although that has changed a little since the opening of Knock International Airport, constructed in 1986 to serve the million and a half pilgrims each year who visit the Basilica at Knock where the Virgin Mary appeared in a vision in 1879. But apart from Knock and a few other places such as the delightful Georgian town of Westport, Co. Mayo remains "undiscovered country".

Castlebar

Located in the heart of Mayo's lake country, the county town of Castlebar was founded in the early 1600s by John Bingham, ancestor of the Earls of Lucan. The infamous fugitive Lord Lucan was actually born here. More creditable sons of Castlebar include the inventor of the monorail and the torpedo, Louis Brennan; the former Taoiseach, Charles Haughey; and the world-famous soprano Margaret Burke Sheridan.

The town centre has an attractive tree-lined green and Mall which was once the cricket pitch of the Lucan family. An especially appealing feature of Castlebar is its **Sculpture Trail**, a series of sculptures in various materials – glass, stone, steel, bog pine, scattered around the town.

Originally a market town, Castlebar has kept this tradition and is one of the major shopping centres in the west of Ireland, offering a wide range of interesting shopping areas. The town gets even busier

Rocky's Bar & Restaurant

Tucker Street, Castlebar, Co. Mayo
Tel: 094 24098

It's always a good sign when a restaurant is packed with mostly local people and that's certainly the case at **Rocky's Bar & Restaurant** in Castlebar's town centre. The restaurant's decor is elegantly modern with a striking feature staircase.

Chef Peter Scott has been here since 1999 and has built up a loyal following of customers appreciative of his wholesome and appetising home-cooked menu. A popular element of Peter's menu is the roast beef lunch which is available every day but you'll also find a wide choice of regular dishes as well as daily specials.

Food is served every day from 12,30pm to 6pm; credit cards are accepted.

THE T.F. ROYAL HOTEL & THEATRE

Westport Road, Castlebar, Co. Mayo
Tel/Fax: 094 9023 1111
e-mail: info@tfroyalhotel.com
website: www.tfroyalhotel.com

One of the largest entertainment and hotel complexes in the west of Ireland, the **TF Royal Hotel & Theatre** combines a 3-star luxury boutique hotel and a 300-seat Theatre that stages a wide variety of plays, concerts, ballet and other performances. Recently totally refitted inside and out, the hotel offers mini-suites with spacious executive bedrooms equipped with ISDN line, touch-tone telephone, mini-entertainment centre, and satellite TV and radio. The complex also has a dedicated Business Centre with seminar suites and conference rooms, providing all modern amenities.

during the annual **International Blues Festival,** held over the Whitsun Bank Holiday weekend. A more unusual event is the annual **Celebration of the Senses Festival** in October with inventive performances and displays exploring the five senses of sight, sound, touch, taste and smell. And in early July the **Castlebar International Walking Festival** is a non-competitive event designed to encourage people to rediscover the bogs, rivers, mountains and unspoilt beauty of the area.

If you hear the term "Castlebar Races" don't start thinking horses. It refers to a major clash between the English and Franco-Irish forces in 1798. The Irish troops under General Humbert achieved a crushing victory over the much larger English army commanded by General Lake. The defeated soldiers fled the field at such a pace that the event was tauntingly named the Castlebar Races.

About 5 miles east of Castlebar, the **National Museum of Country Life** (free) celebrates the lives and activities of rural people from the mid-19th to the mid-20th centuries. Their now vanished lifestyles are vividly evoked by exhibits that include the clothes and textiles of those days, furniture and fittings, and the tools used in working the land. A branch of the National Museum of Ireland, the museum's main exhibition gallery is housed in an elegant new building within the grounds of Turlough Park House, a massive Victorian mansion located about 4 miles east of Castlebar.

The Barony of Murrisk

Southwest of Castlebar, the fist-shaped tract of rugged mountains and sparsely-populated plains is known as the Barony of Murrisk from the little town of that name near Westport. The scenery is as splendid as you'll find anywhere in the west of Ireland with two ranges of hills, the Mweelrea Mountains and the Sheefry Hills, providing terrain for serious walkers, and the holy mountain of **Croagh Patrick**, Mayo's most famous landmark. It attracts thousands of pilgrims to the summit where in AD 441 St Patrick fasted for 40 days and nights. In return for this protracted

St Patricks Statue, Croagh Patrick

abstinence the saint received a promise from God that the Irish would never lose their Christian faith. It was from the Precipice of Lugnanarrib nearby that St Patrick sent packing all of Ireland's snakes and toads. At the top of the 2510 feet mountain there is a small modern chapel built with 716 bags of cement carried up the hillside by devout barefoot pilgrims. Each year on the last Sunday of July around 60,000 pilgrims, many of them in bare feet, climb the mountain for a special service. Crowning the hill stands a statue of St Patrick which commands outstanding views extending from the Galway mountains in the south to Achill Island in the north.

Close to St Patrick's statue is the **Famine Monument**, a magnificent piece of sculpture by John Behan depicting a Coffin Ship with skeleton bodies. This poignant memorial was unveiled by President Mary Robinson in 1997 to commemorate the sesquicentennial of the beginning of the Great Famine in 1847.

Westport
11 miles SW of Castlebar on the N5/N59

Set around Clew Bay, Westport is unique among Irish towns in that it was designed, in 1780, to the plan of the well-known Georgian architect James Wyatt. The central Mall with its trees lining both sides of the Carrowbeg River is one of the most gracious thoroughfares in the country; Bridge Street with its cheerful shop and pub fronts is a pleasant place for a stroll, and The Octagon, the town's central square, is the venue for a regular weekly market. The town is noted as a sea fishing centre and holds an annual **Sea Angling Festival** in late June, followed by the **Westport Arts Festival** in October.

MOHER HOUSE
Liscarney, Westport, Co. Mayo
Tel: 098 21360
e-mail: moherbandb@eircom.net
website:
www.homepage.eircom.net/-moherhouse

Moher House is understandably popular with walkers since it lies just off the 140-mile Western Way and is also close to Toachar Padraig, the historic route from Ballintubber Abbey to Croagh Patrick taken by St Patrick himself. The house, which is included in 'The Best B&B in the Country' and 'The Rough Guide', stands in lovely award-winning gardens. It has its own private car park and much else to offer. Owner Marian O'Malley greets arriving visitors with a welcoming afternoon tea and goes out of her way to make this a real "home from home", she will happily drive you to Westport at night if you wish to sample its wonderful Restaurants and Pubs. Marian is an enthusiastic cook with a background in catering so at breakfast time, along with treats such as smoked salmon, Irish yoghurts and cheeses, you'll find her home-made bread and jams.

For the evening meal, there's a choice of home-made soups, steak, lamb cutlets, pork chops, wild salmon or a chicken dish, with the speciality of the house, home-made apple pie, for dessert. To round off the meal, guests are served a complementary Irish coffee. Moher House has peat fires in the lounge and 4 attractively furnished and decorated guest bedrooms, all with en suite facilities, colour TV and hospitality tray. There's plenty to see and do in the area. The house stands beside Moher Lake with its abundant trout and boats for hire; and there's a championship golf course 5 miles away at Westport which was Irelands tidiest town in 2002, and also boasts the fine Georgian mansion, Westport House.

The town's grandest building and Co. Mayo's only stately home open to the public is **Westport House**, standing in fine parkland near Westport Quay. Designed in the 1730s by Richard Castle with later additions by James Wyatt, the mansion is the seat of the Marquesses of Sligo who have successively lived on this spot for more than 400 years. The house is beautifully furnished inside with Irish, Georgian and Victorian antiques, Waterford Crystal, Chinese hand-painted wallpapers and an outstanding collection of paintings, including a *Holy Family* by Rubens. Some of the doors are made of Jamaican mahogany imported from the West Indies by the 1st Marquess who was governor there. (For his time, the Marquess was a comparatively liberal man who freed many of his slaves). The dungeons beneath Westport House are a survival from an earlier building. Children of course love them and they are also well-provided for in the grounds by a rather incongruously inelegant collection of attractions and side-shows. There's also an animal and bird park, flume ride, model railway, 9-hole golf course, boating lake with pedalos, horse-drawn caravan rides and gift shops.

Located in the Tourist Information Centre on James Street, the **Westport Heritage Centre** presents a wealth of historical information about the town. There are some superb photographs from the Lawrence Collection and a fascinating interactive scale model of the town. Other exhibits feature some colourful characters associated with Westport, most notably Granuaile, or Grace O'Malley, the infamous Pirate Queen who ruled the high seas in the 1500s.

Tourmackeady

18 miles SW of Castlebar on minor road off the R330

This Gaelic-speaking village sits on the shore of Lough Mask with the Partry Mountains rising behind it. Scenic Lough Mask, 10 miles long and 4 miles wide, is linked with Lough Corrib to the south by an underground river. On the eastern shore of the lake is Lough Mask House, once the residence of Captain Charles Cunningham Boycott, an English land agent who at a time of great agricultural distress refused to reduce rents on the Mayo estates of Lord Erne. In response, he and his family were totally ostracised and they eventually returned to England having given the language a new term, 'boycotting'.

Louisburgh

14 miles W of Westport on the R335

In 1758 a nephew of the 1st Marquess of Sligo took part in the capture of

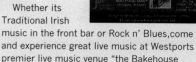

Bertra Strand, Louisberg

Louisburgh, Nova Scotia, from the French. In his honour, the proud uncle re-named this little coastal village after the great victory and replaced its rather shabby buildings with some handsome Georgian houses. The village is still little more than a crossroads but a pleasant base from which to explore the sandy beaches stretching eastwards from the promontory known as Old Head.

This corner of County Mayo has strong associations with a remarkable woman, Grace O'Malley or Gráinne Ni Mháille, whose exploits are still vividly remembered even though she died in the same year as Elizabeth 1, - 1603. Grace's ancestors had been Lords of the Isles for 200 years and Grace fought hard to maintain her regal position against the encroachments of the English. A forceful woman, she unilaterally divorced her second husband by slamming the castle door in his face and then stealing all his other castles. A typical story relates that at the age of 45 Grace was on a sea voyage when she gave birth to her first son, Toby. An hour later, her ship was boarded by Turkish pirates. The battle on the deck was almost lost when Grace appeared wrapped in a blanket and shot the enemy captain with a blunderbuss. Her men rallied, captured the Turkish ship and hanged the crew. Grace O'Malley's colourful life is documented at the **Granuaile Centre** in Louisburgh, open from June to mid-September, which also has a harrowing display on the horrors of the Great Famine.

Reached by passenger ferry from Roonagh Quay, a few miles west of Louisburgh, **Clare Island** was part of Grace O'Malley's domain. The island is dominated by the sheer-sided mass of Knockmore Mountain which rises to more than 1500 feet and although the island is quite small, only 15 miles square and with a population of around 150, there's good walking here, some little-used sandy beaches, and facilities for pony trekking, water-skiing, sail-boarding and fishing. The ruins of Grace's massive castle stand above the tiny harbour and the redoubtable lady herself is reputedly buried in a tomb near the ruined 13th century Cistercian Abbey on the south coast which also has some striking medieval wall paintings.

Northwest of Castlebar

Newport

12 miles NW of Castlebar on the R311

This orderly little 18th century town overlooks **Clew Bay** with its frantically serrated coastline of many-fingered headlands and splattered blobs of islands. Newport is primarily geared to the service of the angling fraternity and rather sadly takes pride in the fact that one of Grace Kelly's ancestors lived for a while at nearby Drimurla. The town is dominated by a huge arched bridge that once carried the railway linking Westport to Achill Island. The railway was built following a public outcry in the 1850s when a boat crowded with migrant workers sailing from Achill to Westport foundered in Clew Bay and everyone on board perished.

Achill Island

The **Westport to Achill Railway** was a delightfully scenic but hopelessly uneconomic venture and in 1936 the company directors had no option but to close it down. Created in response to a terrible tragedy, the railway expired in the wake of another. A few days before its official closure a party of children from Achill who had been harvesting potatoes in Scotland died in a fire at the farmhouse where they were staying. The very last train from Westport to Achill carried the small coffins containing their remains.

Achill Island

30 miles W of Castlebar by the R319

About twenty miles west of Newport, Achill Island is the largest island in the Republic and, since it is now linked to the mainland by a road bridge, one of the easiest to reach. Twenty miles long and 12 miles wide, the island offers a wonderful amalgam of dramatic mountains, the highest sea cliffs (2000 feet) in Europe, sparsely-patronised beaches and, inland, a rich scattering of prehistoric standing stones, stone circles and dolmens. The island also boasts no fewer than five Blue Flag beaches.

A generous influx of government subventions has transformed this once bitterly poverty-stricken area into what is now a comparatively prosperous region. The downside is the large number of characterless modern buildings that have been plonked down seemingly at random and appear totally out of context in such enchanting scenery. Fortunately, their impact on this grand landscape is, so far, still quite negligible. Ignore them and just stand above **Keem Bay** to watch the local fishermen launch into the waves a *currach*, the canvas-covered boat that has served them so well for centuries. You don't need to take a photograph: the image will stay in your mind for years.

South & East of Castlebar

Ballintubber

7 miles S of Castlebar on the N84

Ballintubber Abbey has been called "The Abbey that Refused to Die". Founded in 1216 by Cathal, King of Connaught, near the site of a church built by St Patrick in AD 441, the abbey was suppressed by Henry VIII along with all the other monastic establishments in Britain and Ireland. After its destruction by Cromwell in 1653, the abbey was left roofless but for

250 years the people of Ballintubber continued to attend Mass in wind, rain and snow. The abbey now has the unique status of being the only one in Ireland where Mass has been celebrated every day for more than 780 years. Almost completely restored now, the abbey stands in attractive grounds which are landscaped to portray spiritual themes and the interpretive centre has an informative video which includes scenes of local people performing the annual passion play.

Leading westwards from Ballintubber Abbey, the **Tóchar Phádraig** is the ancient pilgrim path that winds for some 22 miles through the Mayo countryside to the holy hill of Croagh Patrick mentioned above.

Lough Corrib

Ballinrobe

18 miles S of Castlebar on the N84

Located on the Robe River near the eastern shore of Lough Mask, Ballinrobe is a noted angling centre for this lough and the neighbouring lakes of Carra, Conn, Corrib and Cullin. A 4-day wet fly-fishing competition is held here each year, usually in August, but the little town is at its busiest during the race meetings in July which completely fulfil one's expectations of Irish racing – a picturesque course, fine horses and great atmosphere.

Collectors of curiosities will be interested in the huge, stone-stepped pyramid just outside the town. Partly-effaced Roman numerals dates it some time in the 1700s. The pyramid bears the name of George Browne, a member of the family who owned the magnificent Westport House at Westport, but the reason why this strange folly was erected has been lost in the passage of time.

About 2 miles southwest of the town is the great stone fort of **Cahernagollum** and further on stands the **Killower Cairn**, a 22 feet high pillar of stones which is believed to cover a Stone Age passage grave.

Cong

24 miles S of Castlebar on the R346/345

In Gaelic "*cong*" means isthmus, in this case the 3-mile wide nexus of land that separates Lough Corrib from Lough Mask. In fact, the two lakes are linked by a river which flows underground for part of its course. Along the way it has formed great caves in the

Riverside Inn

Cong, Cross, Co. Mayo
Tel: 092 46211 Fax: 094 9546822

Surrounded by stunning scenery and set beside a tiny stream, the **Riverside Inn** stands close to Lough Corrib and the picture-postcard village of Cong. This family pub run by Bridie and Dennis Biggins has a cosy little lounge, open fires, and a spacious public bar with pool table and large screen TV. A major attraction here is the food – good, traditional pub meals, wholesome snacks and all day breakfasts served from 1pm to 5.30pm every day except Sunday. The pub itself is open from 9.30am until late, Monday to Saturday; all major credit cards are accepted, and there's plenty of parking space.

limestone, the most accessible of which is Pigeon Hole.

Cong is a notably picturesque little town and was once a significant religious centre. One of its most impressive sites is the substantial ruin of **Cong Abbey**, founded in 1128 by Turlough O'Connor, King of Ireland. In its heyday the abbey was home to more than 3000 people and its prosperous status is reflected by the exquisite **Cross of Cong**, a 12th century richly ornamented Celtic processional cross enshrining a portion of the True Cross. Made of oak, plated with copper and decorated with exquisite gold filigree Celtic patterns, the cross is now on display at the

Corrib View Villa

Gortacurra, Cross, Cong, Co. Mayo
Tel: 094 9546036/9546199
Fax: 094 9546036
e-mail: corribviewvilla@eircom.net

Enjoying a glorious position looking out over Lough Corrib and the Connemara mountains, **Corrib View Villa** offers a choice of both bed & breakfast and self-catering accommodation. Located less than a mile off the R346 Cong to Galway road, the Villa has been home to Mary Lydon for some 32 years and is an ideal base for touring Connemara and Co. Mayo. Bed and breakfast guests stay in the Villa itself where there are 5 tastefully decorated and furnished guest bedrooms, all with en suite facilities, colour TV and tea/coffee-making equipment. Guests also have the use of a comfortable TV lounge. A full Irish breakfast is included in the tariff and evening meals are available on request.

For those who prefer self-catering, there's a modern self-contained apartment adjacent to the villa, comprehensively equipped and provided with all the amenities necessary for a comfortable holiday. Open all year round, the Corrib View properties stand between two of the world's greatest trout fisheries, Lough Corrib and Lough Mask, but if angling is not your sport of choice, there are plenty of other activities to be enjoyed in the area, including walking, hiking, horse-riding, golf, cruising and boating.

National Museum in Dublin. But there is still much to admire here – fine stone carvings and atmospheric cloisters which give little sign of their partial rebuilding in 1860. The last High King of Ireland, Rory O'Connor, spent the last 15 years of his life at Cong in peaceful meditation following his defeat by the Anglo-Normans. An extraordinary medieval survival here is the monks' fishhouse, a tiny stone building on a platform overhanging the river where they would catch salmon for the refectory table.

Another of Cong's claims to fame is that the village was the shooting location for much of *The Quiet Man*, the immensely popular 1956 film starring John Wayne and Maureen O'Hara. The **Quiet Man Heritage Centre** is an exact replica of "Kate's" White-o-Mornin cottage, complete with thatched roof and whitewashed walls. The interior has been furnished and decorated to re-create a typical Irish cottage of the 1920s. Costumes are available for visitors to wear for a photograph in front of the old fireplace and if you are visiting in June, the Quiet Man Festival includes a midsummer ball at which men are expected to observe the dress code of cap, breeches and waistcoat. There's also an annual John Wayne Lookalike Contest with plans under way for a similar competition to find co-star Maureen O'Hara's double.

The upper floor of the Quiet Man Heritage Centre houses the **Cong Archaeological & Historical Interpretive Centre** which explores the history of the area since prehistoric times.

Mayo Abbey

12 miles SE of Castlebar on minor road off the N60

This tiny village, hidden away in the countryside south of Castlebar, was once the administrative centre of the Diocese of Mayo from which the county takes its name. Mayo Abbey was the seat of the bishop but little

D'ALTON INN HOTEL

Claremorris, Co. Mayo
Tel: 094 71488 / 094 62823
Fax: 094 71408
e-mail: daltoninnhotel@eircom.net

Located at the geographical heart of the glorious west of Ireland, the **D'Alton Inn Hotel** offers excellent cuisine, quality accommodation and top-flight entertainment. The hotel takes its name from the late Cardinal John D'Alton who was born here on 11th October 1882 and went on to become a leading luminary of the Catholic church. Since 1998, the hotel has been owned and run by Sean Gallaher and his twin brother, who over the years have built up its reputation as an ideal venue for special functions – customers can be assured of receiving only the very best of food and service.

The Castle Lounge is a great place for a quiet drink or a late night out, and the newly built state-of-the-art night club with its imaginative décor, hosts some top DJs, boasts two dance floors, and can accommodate up to 500 people. Fine cuisine is another element in the D'Alton Inn's success with a Carvery lunch served daily and an à la carte menu served every evening with dishes based on fresh local seafood, beef and lamb. The accommodation here maintains the same high standards seen throughout the hotel. There are 17 en suite bedrooms each equipped with its own direct dial telephone, Sky digital TV, hairdryer, trouser press and hospitality tray.

Mulligan's

Jane Street, Claremorris, Co. Mayo
Tel: 094 71792

Located on the main street of this thriving little town, **Mulligan's** is the place to go to experience an authentic Irish pub complete with open fire, tiled and wooden floors – and great atmosphere. Geraldine and John Rooney took over here in the autumn of 2002 and have made Mulligan's ***the*** place in town for an excellent Guinness and outstanding food. Geraldine is a gifted cook and her menu offers a wide choice that ranges from snacks to a full à la carte menu based on fresh local produce – generous portions; modest prices. Mulligan's hosts a disco on Saturday evenings and there's a function room for weddings and other celebrations.

The Olde Woods

Main Street, Balla, Co. Mayo
Tel: 09493 65022 Fax: 09493 65243
e-mail: theoldewoods@eircom.net

A well-known local landmark in this village with its broad main street, **The Olde Woods** has been owned and run by the Dempsey family for some 30 years. As well as having an off licence, the pub serves an excellent Guinness and a choice of snacks for those drinking, has a pool table and, during the summer season, hosts live music sessions at weekends. You can also stay here – there are 6 comfortable guest rooms, tastefully furnished and decorated, with en suite facilities, TV and hospitality tray. Evening meals are available for residents by arrangement. The Olde Woods is open daily from 10.30am until late; all major credit cards are accepted.

remains of the once splendid Abbey founded in the 7th century by St Colman. The abbey later became the centre of a famous university where, according to legend, Alfred the Great came to study. One of his sons is reputedly buried here.

Knock

18 miles SE of Castlebar on the N17/R323

More than one and half million pilgrims each year make their way to **Our Lady's Shrine** in the basilica at Knock, the "Lourdes of Ireland". It was here, one rainy evening in 1879, that the Virgin Mary appeared on the gable of the parish church with St Joseph on her right and St John the Evangelist on her left. Angels hovered above the Apparition and the scene was enveloped in a bright light which was seen several miles away. No fewer than 15 people of varying ages witnessed the manifestation. Located in the heart of one of the most desolate and depopulated areas of Ireland, Knock immediately became an important centre of pilgrimage and although no major miracles have been claimed, a huge basilica seating 15,000 was completed in 1976. Architecturally uncompromising, the huge church nevertheless contains some interesting examples of modern art and architecture, and the 32 pillars each contain stone from a different Irish county. Three years after the basilica was consecrated, Pope John Paul II visited the shrine to mark the centenary of the original vision. The opening of Knock International Airport in 1986 brought visitors from all around the world to within a 10-minute drive of the village.

As with most centres of pilgrimage, the village is abundantly provided with shops selling a huge range of religious souvenirs but the **Museum of Folk Life** provides a straightforward account of the visitation and displays artefacts related to it and details of the miracles associated with it.

Ballyhaunis

25 miles SE of Castlebar on the R323/N63

Surrounded by a watery landscape of countless small lakes, this small town near the border with Co. Roscommon has an Augustinian friary that incorporates parts of a church from an earlier foundation. Most of the structure dates from 1641 but there was a major fire only ten years later and the friary was abandoned until restoration began in the early 1900s.

Northeast of Castlebar

Pontoon

11 miles NE of Castlebar on the R310

Pontoon, standing on the neck of land that separates Lough Cullen from Lough Conn, is regarded as one of the most important freshwater angling centres in Ireland, the nearby lakes offering some of the best brown trout and salmon fishing in western Europe. The village is also popular with bird-watchers since the lakes attract a remarkable variety and number of wildfowl.

Foxford

13 miles NE of Castlebar on the N58

Situated on the banks of the River Moy and nestling between the Ox and Nephin

TEACH O'HORA

Main Street, Kiltimagh, Co. Mayo
Tel/Fax: 094 9381138

Teach O'Hora has been owned and run by the O'Hora family since the sixties, the pub is well-established as a popular local hostelry where newcomers will also find a warm welcome. The proprietors are Marty and Marie O'Hora, with Marty concentrating on pulling the finest pint of Guinness in the county, and Marie presiding over the kitchen which produces a wholesome selection of home-cooked dishes that are served daily from 11am until 5pm, except on Sunday. Dating back to the late 1800s, the pub has authentic wooden floors and cosy alcoves with a vintage telephone box providing an unusual feature. Another unusual feature is a life-size cow sitting behind the bar on a bed of straw. A major attraction in Teach O'Hora's is the music every Friday night and a traditional session on Sunday nights, with party nights for all occasions catered for.

VILLAGE INN

Boholo, Castlemorris, Co. Mayo
Tel: 094 84105

The little village of Boholo straddles the crossroads of the N5 and R321 and it's here that you'll find the **Village Inn**. This is a popular venue for anglers as low cost package deals can be arranged for fishing Salmon, Wild Brown Trout and Sea Trout. The world famous River Moy is just 5 minutes drive. Mine hosts at this welcoming hostelry are Bernadette Mountney and Kieran Reid who took over in 2000 and have steadily upgraded the inn's amenities. In the friendly bar customers can enjoy some appetising bar snacks along with a good range of well-maintained ales while enjoying good entertainment. The inn has 5 guest bedrooms which are currently being provided with en suite facilities.

Greaney's

The Square, Swinford, Co. Mayo
Tel: 094 9252558

Occupying a prime site in this small town just off the N5, **Greaney's** was taken over in the autumn of 2003 by Keith and Sandra McFadden who carried out a major programme of refurbishment which has created a very smart and welcoming atmosphere. Both Keith and Sandra are chefs so food is quite an attraction here – all home-cooked using fresh local produce and offering variety and choice at sensible prices. Food is served from 9.30am to 9.30pm every day. The pub itself is open from 9.30am until late – on Friday and Saturday evenings, when there's live music, late means 2am. Credit cards are accepted, and Greaney's has its own car park.

Mountains, Foxford's main visitor attraction is the **Foxford Woollen Mills and Visitor Centre**. Visitors can watch rugs, blankets and tweeds being made, purchase the end products in the Mill Shop and browse around the craft workshops offering original paintings, wood crafts and jewellery.

Ballina

23 miles NE of Castlebar on the N26

Ballina's population of around 8000 makes it the largest town in Co. Mayo. It stands beside the River Moy, one of Mayo's richest salmon and trout rivers. The original settlement here was at Ardnaree on the east side of the river, a site marked by the ruins of Augustinian friary dating from 1427 and now dwarfed by the Victorian **Cathedral of St Muredach** which boasts some particularly beautiful stained glass. During the 18th century Ballina, (pronounced *bally-nah*), developed on the west side of the river and is today a thriving industrial, commercial and tourist centre. It has another claim to fame as the home town of Mary Robinson (née Bourke) who in 1990 became the 7th President of Ireland and the first woman to hold that office.

Near the railway station is perhaps the most remarkable sight in Ballina, the **Dolmen of the Four Maols**, three large rocks capped by a massive boulder and dating back to the Bronze Age. A much later legend asserts that the dolmen marks the graves of a quartet of 6th century foster brothers who killed their eminent tutor,

Chung's at Tullios

Pearse Street, Ballina, Co. Mayo
Tel: 096 70888

A traditional Irish pub and an award-winning Chinese restaurant seems an unlikely combination but it's clearly a successful one to judge from the popularity of **Chung's at Tullios** on Ballina's main street. Owner Kenny Chung hails originally from Hong Kong but his menu offers both top quality Chinese cuisine and traditional European dishes – the best of both worlds! The elegant restaurant with its stylish modern furniture can seat up to 100 and there's also an upstairs function room for special events and celebrations. Credit cards are accepted and the pub has its own car park.

Crockets on the Quay

The Quay, Ballina, Co. Mayo
Tel: 096 75930 Fax: 096 70069
e-mail: info@crocketsonthequay.ie
website: www.crocketsonthequay.ie

Acclaimed as the Black & White Pub of the Year 2002 and Connaught Pub of the Year 2003, **Crockets on the Quay** sets the benchmark standard for what an Irish pub should be. Owned and run by brothers Paul and Alan Murphy and David Smith, Crockets has an elegant restaurant serving outstanding home-cooked food – the lobster, beef dishes and chowder, for example, are truly memorable. Food is available from noon until late every day. The bar and elevated lounge with their dark oak décor are places where you will really want to linger. And if you want to stay longer, Crockets has 8 top quality en-suite guest bedrooms, in the adjoining house.

The Rocks

Behy Baun, Ballina, Co. Mayo
Tel: 096 22140
e-mail: therocks@eircom.net
website: www.therocksguesthouse.info

Just a short walk from the town centre, **The Rocks** offers top class bed & breakfast and self-catering accommodation. This attractive modern house is huge and stands in an extensive garden which is beautifully maintained by your host Margaret Cumiskey who is an enthusiastic gardener. There are 8 guest bedrooms, all en suite, and 2 self-catering units, one sleeping up to 5 guests, the other up to 8. Children are welcome and have their own play area; anglers are provided with a large storeroom, complete with fridge and deep freeze. This outstanding establishment is open all year round and there's plenty of off-street parking.

Downpatrick Head

Ballina, Co. Mayo

Not to be missed is the spectacular view from **Downpatrick Head** where the Atlantic has gouged a huge bay from the mighty cliffs, their summits scoured of all vegetation except grass by the ceaseless ocean winds. The air is full of wheeling birds: terns, gulls, skuas, razorbills and the rather less active puffins. Look out for the puffing holes that spew out tall columns of sea spray when the weather is rough. The most spectacular of these is called Poulnachantinny. It was created, apparently, when St Patrick was fighting with the Devil. The saint landed such a fearsome blow with his crozier that Old Nick was driven clear through the rock and into the sea beneath. In the course of this mighty scrap they also detached part of the headland.

Now known as Doonbristy, this lone stack of rock is crowned by an old ruined fort. On the Head itself, a plaque commemorates those who lost their lives in the aftermath of the 1798 rebellion.

Ceallach, Bishop of Kilmoremoy. They were hanged together by Ceallach's brother across the river at Ardnaree and then buried here.

Ballina is the starting point for the **Tír Sáile**, the North Mayo Sculpture Trail, which follows the coastal route through Ballycastle to Belmullet. Sculptors from Ireland, Britain, Denmark, the US and Japan contributed 15 pieces, each of which was designed with its specific site in mind.

To the north and west of Ballina stretches the unspoilt north coast of Co. Mayo, wonderfully wild and remote. Not to be missed here is the spectacular view from **Downpatrick Head** (see panel opposite) where the Atlantic has gouged a huge bay from the mighty cliffs, their summits scoured of all vegetation except grass by the ceaseless ocean winds.

North & West of Ballina

Killala

9 miles N of Ballina on the R314

Killala enjoys a superb location overlooking Killala Bay and is surrounded by grand scenery. This small seaside resort with its pleasant quayside, 17th century cathedral and an ancient round tower provided the setting for one of the most important events in the rebellion of 1798. On August 22nd of that year, three French warships flying British flags sailed into the Killala Bay. The 1100-strong invasion force took the town by surprise and by nightfall troops were garrisoned in the Bishop's Palace. The British flag on the palace was replaced with a green flag showing a harp and the words *Erin go Bragh* – 'Ireland Forever'. French forces also captured Ballina and Castlebar but their success was short-lived. On September 8th, the Franco-Irish army was crushed by a much larger English contingent under Lord Cornwallis and General Lake at Ballinamuck in Co. Longford. On the R314 north of Killala, a statue of a French soldier and an Irish peasant commemorates a rare moment of Franco-Irish solidarity.

Ballycastle

18 miles N of Ballina on the R314

A small town with a broad main street descending to a fine beach, Ballycastle is best known for **Céide Fields,** the largest known Neolithic farm settlement in the world. It was a local schoolteacher who suspected that the remnants of some kind of settlement lay beneath the blanket bog but it was not until his son became an archaeologist that a dig was organized. As

Mary's Cottage Kitchen

Main Street, Ballycastle, Co. Mayo
Tel: 096 43361
e-mail: marymunnelly@eircom.net

Housed in a charming stone cottage dating back to the early 1800s, **Mary's Cottage Kitchen** is wonderfully atmospheric with its slate floors, open turf fire, exposed beams and pine tables and chairs. Mary Munnelly is an inspired cook whose menu offers an enticing choice of fresh local seafood dishes, daily lunch specials, and a wonderful array of home-baked scones, tarts and cakes. There's a selection of wines to accompany your meal and in good weather you can enjoy your refreshments in the lovely landscaped garden at the rear. The Cottage Kitchen is open daily from 10am to 6pm, April to October; 10am to 6pm, Monday to Friday and 10am to 2pm on Saturdays out of season.

Céide Fields

the team removed the layers of bog a 5000-year-old network of stone-walled fields was revealed. The story is well told at the Visitor Centre which offers an excellent 20-minute audio-visual presentation and there are guided tours around the site. The centre has a restaurant or you can have a picnic outside while enjoying a grand vista of sea and land.

Bangor Erris

26 miles W of Ballina on the N59

A small settlement on the empty road between Ballina and Belmullet,

Barretts

Main Street, Bangor Erris, Co. Mayo
Tel: 097 83451 Fax: 097 83094

Bangor Erris is a popular centre for anglers on nearby Owenduff River and Carrowmore Lough but this busy little village is well worth seeking out to visit **Barretts,** a splendid old family-run pub whose brightly-painted frontage is something of a landmark hereabouts. Mary Barrett's hostelry is full of character and offers excellent ales, a choice of hot snacks – piping hot soup and freshly-cut sandwiches, and comfortable accommodation in 6 comfortable rooms, 3 of which are en suite, the other three have private bathrooms. On Sunday evenings, Barretts hosts live music, either traditional Irish or Country & Western. All major credit cards are accepted.

Hillcrest House

Main Street, Bangor Erris, Co. Mayo
Tel: 097 83494

The Bangor Erris area is famous for its fine fishing and scenic beauty, a powerful combination that brings many anglers and country lovers to Evelyn Cosgrove's charming bed & breakfast establishment, **Hillcrest House** where arriving guests are greeted with a warm welcome and a refreshing afternoon tea. The house has 4 guest bedrooms, 3 of which have en suite facilities, the fourth has a private bathroom at the end of the hall. The guests also have the useful amenity of a Drying Room with showers for fishermen and walkers. A full Irish breakfast is included in the tariff and Evelyn is happy to provide evening meals and packed lunches if required.

Hillcrest House is a participant in the Activity Holidays scheme which provides a comprehensive service for anglers and others – state salmon licence and fishing permits, a full ghillie service with boat and engine if required, full guide service on rivers if required, and up-to-date information on the best fishing locations. The area provides superb angling for wild salmon, sea trout and natural wild brown trout while the Atlantic Ocean yields more than 30 species of sea fish. This is also grand walking country, at the heart of the Western Way and the Bangor Trail; cyclists will enjoy the network of lanes through unspoilt countryside bringing them close to the real Ireland. Golfers too have the benefit of the challenging 18 hole Cain gold links course nearby. Hillcrest House is ITB approved.

Bangor is an angling centre for Carrowmore Lough and the Owenmore River. The name Erris comes from one of the ancient Norman baronies of Ireland.

Belmullet

30 miles W of Ballina on the R313

Belmullet has been described as one of the loneliest towns in Connacht. It stands on a narrow sliver of land linking the mainland to the windswept Mullet Peninsula and, because all the commercial traffic of the peninsula has to pass through the town, its market day is surprisingly bustling. On other days, it has a peaceful, unhurried atmosphere that possesses a charm all of its own. Belmullet is famed for its sea angling and hosts an International Fishing Festival in August; it has some fine beaches and the area is popular with bird-watchers.

Co Meath

Until the mid-1500s, the "Royal County of Meath" – so called because it is home to Tara, seat of the High Kings of Ireland – was combined with Westmeath, making it Ireland's fifth largest, and most powerful, province. Even 5000 years ago this area was clearly an important population centre as the astonishing megalithic cemetery at Loughcrew bears witness. The fertile valley of the River Boyne is also rich in prehistoric tombs with the county as a whole containing by far the richest bounty of such remains in Ireland.

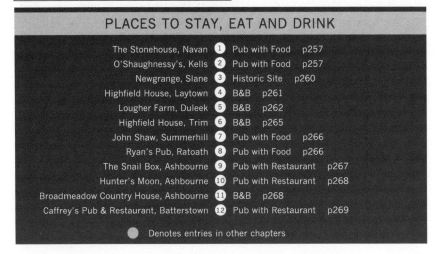

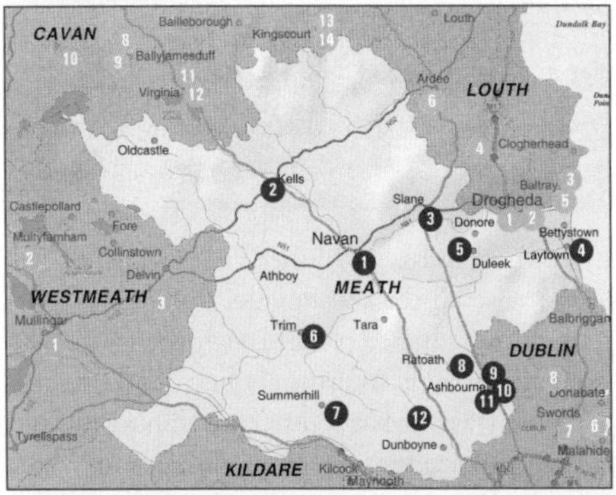

Although the county does have a short coastline, barely 7 miles long, Meath is first and foremost an inland county of rolling green pastures divided into rich plantations and prosperous farmsteads. It was here that one of Ireland's most fateful battles took place, the Battle of the Boyne in 1690, and other memories of the past are vividly evoked by the splendid Norman castle at Trim; the high cross and round tower at Kells; and the holy Hill of Slane.

Navan

Navan, the county town, stands at the meeting of the Boyne and Blackwater Rivers, a strategic location in times past. There is little in the town itself to detain the sightseer but about 1½ miles to the south, on the east bank of the River Boyne, are the impressive ruins of **Athlumney Castle**, a 15th century tower house with a Jacobean manor house added in the early 1600s. It was the home of Sir Lancelot Dowdall, a devout Catholic who after the defeat of James II

PLACES TO STAY, EAT AND DRINK

The Stonehouse, Navan	1	Pub with Food	p257
O'Shaughnessy's, Kells	2	Pub with Food	p257
Newgrange, Slane	3	Historic Site	p260
Highfield House, Laytown	4	B&B	p261
Lougher Farm, Duleek	5	B&B	p262
Highfield House, Trim	6	B&B	p265
John Shaw, Summerhill	7	Pub with Food	p266
Ryan's Pub, Ratoath	8	Pub with Food	p266
The Snail Box, Ashbourne	9	Pub with Restaurant	p267
Hunter's Moon, Ashbourne	10	Pub with Restaurant	p268
Broadmeadow Country House, Ashbourne	11	B&B	p268
Caffrey's Pub & Restaurant, Batterstown	12	Pub with Restaurant	p269

● Denotes entries in other chapters

The Stonehouse

Kennedy Road, Navan, Co. Meath
Tel: 046 9076050 Fax: 046 907 6057
e-mail: stonehousebar@eircom.net

A friendly family-run pub, the **The Stonehouse** was built in 1999 to a very distinctive design – a semi-circular main building flanked by a low tower. This must be one of the most spacious pubs in the country, "so big it could house a football match without annoying the customers" as one patron put it. It occupies both floors of the building and the 200-seater restaurant serves an appetising menu of modern Irish cuisine at value-for-money prices. Food is served from 12.30pm to 8pm (Monday to Wednesday); 12.30pm to 9pm (Thursday to Sunday). Parking is no problem – the town's main car park is just across the road.

at the Battle of the Boyne set fire to his home rather than have it fall into the hands of William's troops. It is said that he watched from the opposite bank of the river as the house blazed throughout the night and then set off for an exile from which he never returned.

Around Navan

Northeast of Navan, about 1½ miles along the Slane road, is **Donaghmore**, the site of an early Christian settlement of which only a well-preserved 10th century Round Tower survives. The single doorway is 12 feet above the ground, its keystone carved with a figure of the crucified Christ. Nearby is the **Donaghmore Workhouse Museum** which devotes itself to telling the story of the families who lived and died within the workhouse walls during and after the Great Famine.

About a mile east of Donaghmore stand the remains of **Dunmoe Castle**, a 15th century building that was destroyed by fire in 1799. The ruins aren't particularly impressive but the glorious view along the River Boyne certainly is.

Kells

10 miles NW of Navan on the N3

This little town on the River Blackwater is best known for the celebrated Book of Kells, the illuminated manuscript produced by the scribes of Iona around AD 800 and

O'Shaughnessy's

Market Street, Kells, Co. Meath
Tel: 046 41110

From the outside **O'Shaughnessy's** looks every inch the authentic Irish pub with its colourful façade and latticed windows. The interior is just as satisfying especially if you are visiting over the weekend when there's live music with a DJ on Friday evening; live music and dancing on Saturday evening; and a sing-along on Sunday afternoon. Owner Gary Conaty took over here in the spring of 2003 and has quickly established O'Shaughnessy's as Kells most lively pub. Good wholesome Irish cuisine is available every lunchtime from 12.30pm to 3.30pm. Credit cards are accepted and the pub has its own car park.

brought to Kells for safe keeping from Viking raids. No trace of Kells monastery, founded by St Columba in AD 550, remains and the original Book is now on display in Trinity College, Dublin, but facsimile copies and CD-ROM versions can be seen in the **Kells Heritage Centre,** housed in a handsome Georgian courthouse of 1801, and in the modern **St Columba's Church.** In the churchyard of St Columba's stand some remarkable early Christian survivals. The **South High Cross** is the largest, most striking, and probably the oldest of the five high crosses in the town, four of which are here in the churchyard. The South High Cross is intricately carved with a wealth of detailed scenes from Biblical stories. The nearby **Round Tower** is one of the best preserved in the country, almost 100 feet high and only lacking its original conical cap. The alignment of the five windows near the top provides a clear view of the five roads entering the town. It's known that the tower was already standing in 1076: in that year Murchadh Mac Flainn, a claimant for the High Kingship, was murdered within its walls.

Just outside the churchyard, **St Colmcille's House** is possibly even older than the Round Tower and is miraculously well-preserved. Its walls are 4 feet thick and those at the sides continue upwards, inclining inwards, to meet in a ridge. Inside, the house measures about 24 feet by 21 feet and its 38 feet height was originally divided into two floors. Modern day visitors enter by a ground floor doorway but the entrance used by the monks can still be seen in the west wall, some 8 feet above the ground.

St Colmcille, (or Columcille), is one of Ireland's most popular saints and has generated some appealing legends. One story recounts that, as punishment for copying a book without authorisation, Colmcille was banished to Iona and forbidden to set foot on Irish soil ever again. The saint contrived an ingenious solution. He strapped sods of Iona turf to his feet and so walked through his beloved Ireland on Scottish soil.

Another cross, the **Market Cross,** stands in front of the Heritage Centre. Originally sited in the market square, the cross was a gift to the town from Jonathan Swift. During the 1798 Rebellion it was used as a gallows to hang local rebels.

The town's rich history is what draws most visitors but Kells also offers several more contemporary attractions. The **Millennium Playground** is ideal for young children and they are also provided with their own toddlers' pool at the **Kells Swimming Pool** which has a 25 metre indoor heated pool and a sauna for the grown-ups. The **Kells Equestrian Centre** has mounts for riders of all ages, while the **Grove Gardens, Tropical Bird Sanctuary & Mini Zoo** is a perfect venue for a family outing. Its 14-acre site includes gardens with an international reputation and is also home to wallabies, raccoons, llamas, rheas, monkeys, camels and many other species of animals and tropical birds.

A little over a mile out of Kells along the Oldcastle road, the R163, a short detour will bring you to the **Castlekeeran Crosses,** all that remains of the *Díseart Chiaráin*, or Hermitage of Ciaran. The four high crosses in this secluded spot are considerably older than those in Kells and their decoration is much simpler. One of them actually stands in the river Blackwater. This unusual siting is explained by an old story which rather improbably claims that St Columba was caught red-handed by St Ciaran as Columba was making off with one of the crosses to his own monastery. In shame, Columba dropped the cross in the river and fled back to Kells.

The Castlekeeran site also has an early Christian grave slab and a fine example of an Ogham stone. Ogham was an early Irish script using just vertical and diagonal strokes in various combinations. It survived until well into the 19th century in some isolated peasant communities where it had the advantage of being completely incomprehensible to outsiders.

Any readers with socialist sympathies might like to make a short detour to the village of **Crossmakeel**, 5 miles west of Kells. This small village was the birthplace in 1852 of Jim Connell, author of the socialist anthem *The Red Flag*. He apparently wrote the whole song during the course of a 20-minute train journey from London's Charing Cross to Lewisham in 1889. After his death, a memorial was erected in Crossmakeel bearing his own epitaph:

Oh, grant me an ownerless corner of earth,
Or pick me a hillock of stones,
Or gather the wind-wafted leaves of trees
To cover my socialist bones.

Oldcastle

12 miles NW of Kells on the R154

This sleepy little town set on the broad plain between the Loughcrew and Cavan hills has some attractive Georgian buildings, a by-product of its 18th century status as the largest yarn market in Ireland. The premier attraction in Oldcastle however is **Loughcrew Historic Gardens** at whose centre is preserved one of Ireland's oldest gardens. Here you'll find a magnificent ancient yew walk; the family church and tower house of St Oliver Plunkett; a walled garden and a watermill. Surrounding this historic area is a wonderful 19th century landscape of parkland, water gardens, specimen trees, follies, rockeries, woodland walks and stunning vistas.

Another attraction lies about 3 miles to the southeast of Oldcastle – the Loughcrew Hills themselves. The loftiest of these, and the highest point in Co. Meath, is **Slieve na Caillighe** (900 feet), "the Mountain of the Sorceress". Scattered across the summits of the three main peaks is a remarkable group of 30 Neolithic chambered cairns. This is one of the major archaeological sites in the country and the area here was comprehensively studied by the archaeologist Martin Brennan in 1980. He formulated a convincing theory that the cairns were aligned to receive the rising sun on significant days such as the spring and autumn equinoxes. Despite their importance, the cairns are little visited, partly no doubt because some fairly extensive walking is involved.

Slane

7 miles NE of Navan on the N2/N52

Slane Village

Standing at the central crossroads of this appealing village are four almost identical Georgian houses. The story goes that they were built by four spinster sisters with a view to keeping an eye on their siblings' behaviour. A different version claims that it was their brother who built the four houses because he was exasperated by their constant squabbling when they were together.

The village was laid out in the 18th century by Viscount

Francis Ledwidge Museum

Conyngham whose plans also included the fine Georgian mill of 1766 that still stands beside the River Boyne. Across the road from the mill is an imposing Gothic gateway, the entrance to the Conyngham family seat, Slane Castle. The castle is now open again after a major fire in 1992 but visitors are vastly outnumbered by the masses who attend the occasional rock concerts held in grounds laid out by 'Capability' Brown. The Rolling Stones, Bob Dylan and Bruce Springsteen have all performed here and U2 recorded *The Joshua Tree* in one of the castle's rooms. The present owner of Slane Castle is Lord Henry Mountcharles, an entrepreneur with many interests in the rock music business. This presumably explains why there's a nightclub held in the castle basement every Saturday evening.

If you drive to Slane from Dublin along the N2 you will find it is an unusually straight road. The road was constructed, so it is said, to enable George IV to waste no time in travelling to Slane and the welcoming arms of his mistress, the Marchioness Conyngham.

To the northwest of the village rises the famed **Hill of Slane** (530 feet). It was here that St Patrick lit the first Paschal fire at Easter AD 433 to proclaim the arrival of Christianity in Ireland. This was in direct defiance of Laoghaire, High King of Tara, who had decreed that the first fire should be lit on the Hill of Tara. Fortunately, Christian forbearance ensured that St Patrick was promptly forgiven. The hilltop views of the Boyne Valley are splendid, and even more impressive if you climb the 60 or

Newgrange

Slane, Co. Meath

Newgrange is a passage grave which predates Stonehenge by a thousand years. The man-made mound is about 300 feet across, rises to 30 feet at its highest point, and is retained by a wall of brilliant white quartzite stones. It's been estimated that some 20,000 tons of stone were dragged here from the Wicklow Mountains, south of Dublin, to build the mound. Access to Newgrange is through the **Brú na Bóinne Visitor Centre** and then by bus to the site. There are guided tours of the inner stone chamber with its intricately decorated stones and the tour concludes with a re-creation of the climactic moment on the morning of the winter solstice, December 21st, when the interior is illuminated by the sun streaming through a narrow "roof-box".

To witness the actual event within the tomb, you need to book years ahead and during the summer season you may also find yourself facing a long wait since the Office of Public Works limits the number of admissions to 600 each day. If you possibly can, visit out of season; if not, visit anyway.

so steps to the top of the Friary Church which was built in 1512 on the site of the church founded here by St Patrick.

After St Patrick, Slane's most famous son is the poet Francis Ledwidge who was born at Slane in 1887. His birthplace, a stone-built labourer's cottage about a mile to the east of the town, is now the **Francis Ledwidge Museum**. On a stone plaque outside the cottage are the lines he wrote for his friend, Thomas MacDonagh, also a poet, who was executed by the British for his involvement in the Easter Rising of 1916: *He shall not hear the bittern cry / In the wild sky, where he is lain / Nor voices of the sweeter birds / Above the wailing of the rain.* Although a nationalist himself, Ledwidge volunteered to fight on the British side in the First World War and died on the battlefield of Flanders on 31 July 1917.

To the east of Slane, within a great loop of the River Boyne is the area known as **Brú na Bóinne**, ("bend of the Boyne"), which contains some of Ireland's most important neolithic remains. The most spectacular of them is **Newgrange**, a passage grave which predates Stonehenge by a thousand years (see panel opposite).

Laytown

20 miles E of Navan on the R150

This little seaside town boasts a splendid sandy beach, six miles long - which is only one mile shorter than the whole of the Meath coastline. Each year, the Laytown Races take place along the strand, the only official strand races remaining in Europe. The town is also home to **Sonairte – The National Ecology Centre**. This is Ireland's premier environmental centre and offers visitors an organic garden; renewable energy interactive park; water, wind and solar exhibits; and educational tours. Facilities include a wholefood organic coffee shop; organic winery; natural gift shop; adventure playground and picnic areas.

Highfield House

Laytown, Co. Meath
Tel: 041 982 7371
e-mail: laytownhighfield@eircom.net

Highfield House enjoys a superb position just 50 yards from a magnificent sandy beach that stretches for six miles – almost the whole of Co. Meath's coastline. This smart modern building, just 30 years old, is the home of Rory and Petra Conway who have been welcoming bed & breakfast guests here since 1999. They have 3 attractively appointed guest bedrooms, all with en suite facilities. A full Irish breakfast which will certainly set you up for the day is served from 8am until 10.30am. A popular amenity here is the spacious balcony with its grand view of the Laytown beach.

You'll find plenty of activities available in the surrounding area – live entertainment, 10-pin bowling, tennis courts, horse riding, an amusement centre and, just over a mile away, a links golf course. Laytown itself is noted for its races which take place along the beach and the only official strand races remaining in Europe. And anyone interested in the environment should certainly pay a visit to Sonairte – the National Ecology Centre, Ireland's leading environmental centre which provides a fascinating insight into issues such as renewable energy, organic gardening and much more.

Bettystown

20 miles E of Navan on the R151

Laytown's twin seaside resort, Bettystown, was the centre of great excitement in 1850 after a beachcomber strolling along the great expanse of sand saw something bright and gleaming. It turned out to be an 8th century brooch, one of the finest examples of the goldsmith's art to have survived from early-Christian Ireland. Remarkably, its intricate Celtic design is reproduced on the back of the brooch, a setting that would only be seen by its owner. Named the **Tara Brooch,** after the capital city of the High Kings of Ireland, it is now on display at the National Museum in Dublin.

Duleek

10 miles E of Navan on the R150

This small village in the valley of the River Nanny takes its name from a church founded here in the 5th century by St Patrick for his disciple St Cianan. For the first time in Ireland the church was built of stone, hence the town's Irish name, *Diamhliag Chianain* – 'the stone church of St Cianan'. Nothing of that church remains – the site is now covered by the ruins of St Mary's, an Augustinian priory founded in 1182. In the village square stands an unusual pillar cross, erected in 1601 by

Genet de Bathe as a memorial to William, one of her husbands. Just outside the village in the hillside cemetery are two 10th century high crosses and, amongst the ruins of a 12th century priory, grave slabs dating back to the 16th and 17th centuries.

Donore

20 miles E of Navan off the N51 or the R152

This little town was chosen by James II as his base before the fateful Battle of the Boyne on 1st July 1690. Just north of here, his 25,000 Irish and French troops were routed by the 38,000 men of William III's army. James fled to permanent exile in France and William's domination of Ireland was assured. The battlefield itself is just off the N51, opposite the turn to Tullyallen. A panoramic plan at the site gives a clear picture of the events that day in which 500 of William's soldiers and 1500 of James' perished.

Donore is the starting point for guided tours of **Newgrange** *(see panel on page 260)*, the most astonishing of the 40-odd neolithic monuments in this area although **Knowth,** 2 miles to the northwest, where excavations are still under way, is likely to be acknowledged as the most complete of the Brú na Bóinne monuments. Twice the size of Newgrange and 500 years older, the site was occupied from around 3000 BC

LOUGHER FARM

Lougher, Duleek, Co. Meath
Tel: 041 982 5346
e-mail: lougherfarm@eircom.net

Only a mile and a half from the fabulous Neolithic monuments at Newgrange, **Lougher Farm** stands in the fertile valley of the River Boyne. It's the home of Patricia and Tom Lenehan who, surrounded by 150 peaceful acres of a working beef farm, have lived here for some 30 years. Their stylish modern farmhouse has 4 well-appointed guest bedrooms, all of them en suite and provided with TV and hospitality tray. Patricia is an

accomplished cook – her breakfasts have acquired a fame of their own! Open all year, Lougher Farm accepts all major credit cards and there's plenty of off-road parking space.

until the 13th century AD. The tunnel to the central chamber is over a hundred feet in length and the chamber itself is richly decorated. The 250 or so decorated stones discovered here constitute around half of all the known Irish passage grave art. While excavations continue, only the exterior can be viewed but the Visitor Centre has some informative displays about Knowth and a third passage grave nearby, Dowth, as well as the other standing stones and cairns within the area.

Hill of Tara

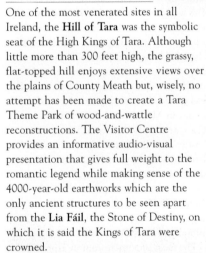

Tara

8 miles S of Navan off the N3

One of the most venerated sites in all Ireland, the **Hill of Tara** was the symbolic seat of the High Kings of Tara. Although little more than 300 feet high, the grassy, flat-topped hill enjoys extensive views over the plains of County Meath but, wisely, no attempt has been made to create a Tara Theme Park of wood-and-wattle reconstructions. The Visitor Centre provides an informative audio-visual presentation that gives full weight to the romantic legend while making sense of the 4000-year-old earthworks which are the only ancient structures to be seen apart from the **Lia Fáil**, the Stone of Destiny, on which it is said the Kings of Tara were crowned.

The origins of the Kingdom of Tara are lost in the mists of time but it reached its peak of power in the 3rd century AD during the reign of the legendary Cormac Mac Art. The kingship was not a hereditary title but one acquired through negotiation or battle. Medieval writers, especially the author of the 12th century *Book of Leinster*, created a highly dubious mythology involving the High Kings, their great banquet hall on the summit of the hill and the five great roads of Ireland that converged on Tara. Only the roads can be authenticated but all the other details are now ingrained in Irish folk lore and these stories invest the historic location with a magic all its own.

The area that gave rise to the idea of a Banquet Hall consists of a long, sunken corridor about 750 feet long and 90 feet wide. Archaeologists believe that in Neolithic times this space was a theatre for priestly and royal processions.

In more recent times, the Hill of Tara was the setting for a mass meeting called by Daniel O'Connell in 1845 as part of his campaign against union with Britain. It was estimated that more than 1 million people gathered here - one in eight of Ireland's population at that time.

Almost half a century later, the Hill saw a smaller scale invasion when a group known as the British Israelites began excavations in the belief that the Ark of the Covenant was buried here. Local people apparently encouraged them in their search by planting Roman coins where they would be easily found. That was all the British Israelites found however, and they soon returned to London. Curiously, another 50 years later, excavations on the site revealed some genuine Roman artefacts.

From the Hill of Tara, winding country lanes lead westward to **Bective Abbey**, a beautiful example of medieval Cistercian architecture in an idyllic riverside setting. Founded in 1146, the Abbey at one time owned one third of Co. Meath and its Abbot held the right to a seat in the British House of Lords, one of only fifteen such peerages granted to the whole of the Pale. The extensive ruins, dating mostly from the 1400s, provide a romantic picture and usually there is plenty of peaceful solitude in which to appreciate them.

Bective Abbey

Athboy

11 miles SW of Navan on the N51

Athboy stands beside the Tremblestown River, its name in Gaelic meaning the "town of the yellow ford". Parts of the town's medieval walls are still intact and the church has an interesting medieval table tomb. A couple of miles outside the town rises the **Hill of Ward**, an Iron Age fort that was once the seat of the High Kings of Ireland. The hill was also the location for the Celtic festival of *Samhain*, held on 1st November to mark the beginning of winter. It was last celebrated in 1168.

Trim

10 miles SW of Navan on the R154

The best approach to this pleasant and historic town set beside the River Boyne is along the R154 from Dublin. This route opens up a striking view of the imposing ruins scattered throughout the town, the most impressive of them being **Trim Castle** which dates back to 1190 and is the largest surviving Anglo-Norman fortress in Britain. The well-preserved ruins sprawl across 2 acres with an outer wall almost 500 yards long and an encircling moat which could be filled from the River Boyne. With its ten D-shaped turrets, sturdy gate towers, barbican and drawbridges, the castle is a noble sight and provided an atmospheric location for scenes in Mel Gibson's film *Braveheart*. The castle is also known as King John's Castle, after the English king who stayed at Trim for a few days in 1210. A later, more reluctant visitor, was Henry, Duke of Lancaster who was imprisoned here by Richard II. The duke later went on to depose Richard and ascend the throne himself as Henry IV.

The most prominent ruin in Trim is the **Yellow Steeple**, all that remains of the 13th century Abbey of St Mary's. It stands on a ridge opposite the castle overlooking the town, a gaunt stone skeleton 125 feet high which in the setting sun takes on the honey colour that gives the tower its name. In front of the Steeple is **Talbot's Castle**, a fortified manor house built in 1415 by the Lord Lieutenant of Ireland, Sir John Talbot.

Highfield House

Mauddin's Road, Trim, Co. Meath
Tel: 046 94 36386 Fax: 046 94 38181
web: highfieldguesthouse.com

Located opposite Trim Castle, just a 2-minute walk from the town centre, **Highfield House** is a handsome stone building dating back to 1810 when it served as a hospital. The house has been very tastefully brought into the 21st century by owners Edward and Geraldine Duignan. Popular with visiting Americans, Highfield House stands in spacious mature gardens and offers far more than most bed & breakfast establishments – laundry and baby-sitting services, for example. The 7 guest bedrooms are all en suite and equipped with TV and hospitality tray. Highfield House is open all year and all major credit cards are accepted. While here take in the lovely town of Trim which is on your route to the West of Ireland and also the Hill of Tara.

It later became a Latin school whose most famous pupil was Arthur Wellesley, 1st Duke of Wellington. He entered Parliament as MP for Trim and it was during his period as Prime Minister, 1828-30, that he reluctantly agreed to the Act of Catholic Emancipation. The duke lived in Dublingate Street, and in nearby Emmet Street there's a statue commemorating his distinguished career.

Nearby stands another of Trim's copious ruins – the remains of the 13th century **Newtown Cathedral**. Destroyed by fire some 500 years ago, it is still worth exploring and trying out the eerie echo in the cloister. Out in the graveyard, look out for the famous **Tomb of the Jealous Man & Woman.** The Elizabethan stone effigies of Sir Lucas Dillon and his wife, Lady Jayne Bathe, are separated by a sword signifying, it is said, Sir Lucas' displeasure at the affair between his wife and brother. Incidentally, if you suffer from warts, soak them in the water trapped in the nooks and crannies of the tomb and they will disappear. The rusty pins lying on the tomb are thank-offerings from sufferers who have been cured.

On the western outskirts of the town, **Butterstream Gardens** has been described as the most imaginative garden in Ireland. Created single-handedly by its owner, beginning in the early 1970s, the skillfully orchestrated plant themes or colour schemes present constantly changing views ranging from the dramatic to the understated. The herbaceous borders, in strictly controlled colour tones, are reckoned by experts to be among the best in Britain. Open daily from 11am to 8pm, May to September, the gardens also have plants for sale.

Butterstream Gardens

John Shaw

Summerhill, Co. Meath
Tel: 046 955 7197 Fax: 046 955 7930

Shaw's was founded in 1902 and has now over 100 years experience in the trade. Nestled within the surrounding hills of the picturesque village of Summerhill, it is renowned for the best food and drink served with experience and hospitality. Located 40 minutes from Dublin City Centre and 6 miles to the N4 going west, it is within easy distance to all top class Golf Clubs and central of all major Racecourses. Shaw's is steeped in history of GAA with a large selection of photographs adorning the walls to bring you through the years.

The open fires are welcoming to visitors and locals alike, and exude warmth and character. So come on in, sit back, relax and enjoy the Irish Must on Thursday nights or kick the heels to DJ/Musicians on Saturday nights. Home cooked lunches prepared daily from local produce are served from 12.30 -2.30pm and evening food is served from 5.00 -8.00pm. John and Clare would be delighted to cater for celebrations such as 18th and 21st birthdays, wedding anniversary's or any other occasions at any time of year. During the summer months catering can be done outside in their comfortable beer garden. A well- stocked Off-Licence also adjoins the premises. Bed & Breakfast is available locally and staff will be happy to advise and assist. Shaw's in Summerhill is not to be missed.

Ryan's Pub

Main Street, Ratoath, Co. Meath
Tel: 01 825620

With its terracotta-coloured exterior **Ryan's Pub** is something of a landmark in the area. It has been owned and run by the Ryan family for some 40 years and has firmly established a reputation for excellent food and well-maintained ales. The building dates from the early 1900s and is meticulously cared for – the exterior is regularly repainted and the spacious car park is cleaned every day. Mine hosts are brothers Michael and Gerry Ryan, perfectionists who make sure that everything is absolutely as it should be.

The outstanding food on offer is all home cooked and includes superb seafood and steak dishes – top restaurant quality at pub prices. Meals are served from noon until 2.30pm, and from 5pm until 9.30pm, Monday to Saturday; from 5pm to 8pm on Sunday. The pub itself is open from 10.30am until late every day except Sunday when the hours are from 12.30pm until 11.30pm. Ratoath itself is a thriving small town within easy driving distance from Dublin and perhaps best known for the nearby Fairyhouse Racecourse where the Irish Grand National takes place on Easter Monday. Also close by are Glebelands and Glebewood Gardens where the beautifully laid-out grounds surround a stately Georgian mansion.

About 10 miles east of Trim, **Dunsany Castle** has been the home of the Plunkett family since the 16th century. The first castle here was built in the 1100s by Hugh de Lacy but the present building is one of the most thriving examples of an Irish castle you are likely to see. It is packed with fine furniture, some unusual Jacobite relics, and a notable art collection which contains a portrait of St Oliver Plunkett, hanged in London in 1682 on trumped-up charges that he was implicated in the "Popish Plot". (The Catholic Plunketts only survived all the vicissitudes of religious persecution because another branch of the family were Protestants and so able to protect their interests to some extent). The grounds at Dunsany Castle are also impressive but they, and the castle, are only open to the public during July and August, and then only from 9am until 1pm, Monday to Saturday, although these opening hours may change.

Summerhill

16 miles SW of Navan on the R158

Summerhill's tree-lined mall was a gift from an improving landlord. It leads to the main avenue of an 18th century mansion once the home of the Earl of Longford but now in ruins. A grove within its grounds contains the remnants of a 16th or 17th stronghold of the Lynch family known as Knock Castle and on the village green are a few medieval fragments including the shaft of a 16th century cross.

Ratoath

10 miles SE of Navan off the N2 or N3

In a country passionate about horse-racing, Ratoath is a very special place – or rather the nearby **Fairyhouse Racecourse** is. On Easter Monday this is the venue for the Irish Grand National, Ireland's premier steeplechasing event. The race covers a gruelling 3 miles and 5 furlongs over a course dotted with hazards such as hedges, ditches and tight turns and has developed from the original steeplechase. The steeplechase was an Irish creation, first seen in Co. Cork in the 18th century when riders raced from one church steeple to another.

Also in Ratoath are **Glebelands & Glebewood Gardens**. The gardens surround a stately Georgian mansion and are set on different levels combining mature trees with an extensive variety of plants and shrubs. Reflective ponds and fountains add to the charm. Set within woodlands, Glebewood Cottage Garden is a younger garden with many interesting features, including a rustic wooden footbridge and several ponds.

Ashbourne

12 miles SE of Navan off the N2

This little town was the only place outside Dublin where local people joined in the

Hunter's Moon

Main Street, Ashbourne, Co. Meath
Tel: 01 835 0104

Conveniently located on the N2 Dublin to Derry road, **Hunter's Moon** was originally built as a coaching inn during the early 1700s. The premises have been greatly extended since those days but the cosy bar still retains a traditional atmosphere. Owner David Farrell bought the pub in 2002 because he had always enjoyed having a pint here. Customers can also enjoy a game of darts or pool, or watch major sporting events on the large screen TV. There's live music on Friday, Saturday and Sunday evenings when the bar stays open until 2.30am.

Every day, throughout the day until 9pm, a good selection of home-made food is available, all based on fresh ingredients and representing excellent value for money. Meals are served in the upstairs restaurant/ lounge. Hunter's Moon also has a large function suite available for weddings, meetings or other functions. All major credit cards are accepted and the pub has its own spacious car park. Ashbourne itself is surrounded by golf courses and yet is only 30 minutes from Dublin City and a few miles southwest is the famous Fairyhouse Racecourse, which on Easter Monday, is the venue for the Irish Grand National, the country's major steeple-chasing event covering a hazardous 3½ mile course.

Easter Rising of 1916. Volunteers led by Thomas Ashe forced the surrender of British forces. A monument in the form of a ship's prow honours the nationalists who died in that insurrection.

Dunboyne

13 miles SE of Navan on the R156/R157

Dunboyne Castle is not a castle at all but an 18th century mansion which replaced an earlier fortress, seat of the Butler family, Lords of Dunboyne. Also near Dunboyne is another 18th century grand house, built in the Palladian style, **Hamwood,** a place that anyone interested in gardens will want to visit**.** Within the grounds of this stately mansion are a walled garden with a restored early 19th

Broadmeadow Country House

Bullstown, Ashbourne, Co. Meath
Tel: 01 8352823 Fax: 01 8352819
e-mail: info@irelandequestrian,com
website: www.irelandequestrian.com

Conveniently located for both Dublin City and Airport, **Broadmeadow Country House** offers the tranquillity of the country side yet is only minutes from the bright lights of Dublin city centre. This delightful house, surrounded by beautiful landscaped gardens, has 8 luxurious en suite bedrooms, 4 star Bord Failte approved, a supper menu is available with wine licence. Facilities include equestrian

centre, tennis courts and numerous Golf courses in the area. Golf packages available on request. (off N2 on the R125) century rock garden; a pine walk planted with cedars, pines, spring bulbs and camellias; and a rose garden fragrant with old-fashioned species. The house was built for Charles Hamilton in 1779: his descendants still live here.

Caffrey's Pub & Golden Miller Restaurant

Batterstown, Co. Meath
Tel: 01825 8479 Fax: 01 825 8491
e-mail: caffs@indigo.ie

Just minutes off the N3 Dublin to Navan road, the delightful **Caffrey's Pub and Golden Miller Restaurant** is well worth making the short diversion. Dating back to 1640, this former coaching inn still has its huge open fireplace but also a spacious modern lounge bar and the elegant Golden Miller Restaurant. Mine host John O'Sullivan arrived here in 1996 and his meticulous standards ensure that everything is absolutely just as it should be. The chef is also a perfectionist, insisting that every single dish gets his seal of approval.

The cuisine here is modern Irish and you can have anything from a bar snack to a full à la carte meal. Food is available throughout the day from 10.30am until 10pm, Monday to Thursday; 10.30am till 10.30pm, Friday and Saturday; and from 12.30pm until 9.30pm on Sunday. All major credit cards are accepted and there's ample parking space. From Caffrey's Pub, lovers of Irish heritage can travel a few miles north to the famed Hill of Tara, the seat of the High Kings of Ireland in medieval times. From the summit of the 300ft high hill, there are extensive views across the central plains of Co. Meath.

Co Monaghan

Drumlins are softly moulded hills created by the melting glaciers of the Ice Age as they retreated northwards. They are found all over northern Europe but nowhere in such profusion as in Co. Monaghan. Viewed from the window of a plane, the landscape has been memorably described as a "basket of eggs". Like the neighbouring county of Cavan, Monaghan is sparsely populated and although well-known to anglers has only recently recognised the need to attract visitors with different interests. Hopefully, the tourism agencies won't try too hard. The real attraction of this neglected area is its authenticity – an unspoiled corner of Ireland completely at ease with itself.

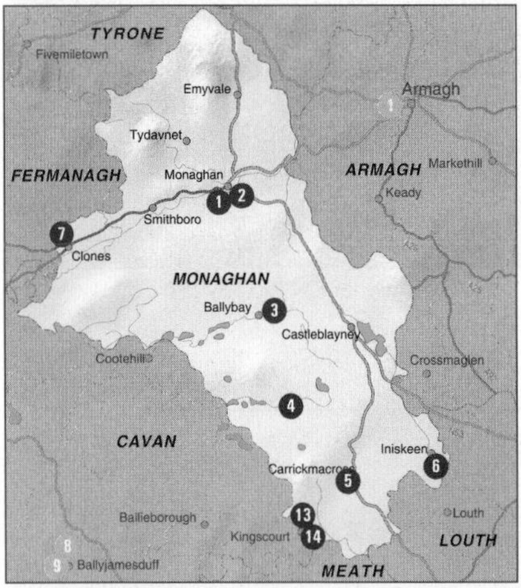

Monaghan

A thriving linen industry in the 18th century endowed Monaghan with a fine legacy of classical and Regency buildings around the town's central square, the Diamond. One of them, the handsome **Market House** of 1792 with some fine carved decorations, is now the tourist office. The most striking sight in the Diamond though is the **Rossmore Memorial,** a huge Victorian drinking fountain with eight grey marble columns and a lofty sandstone canopy. It displaced a 17th century market cross which now stands in another of the town's three squares, Old Cross Square. The third of the town

Rossmore Memorial

PLACES TO STAY, EAT AND DRINK

Louie's, Monaghan	1	Restaurant	p271
Rosefield Farm Guest House, Monaghan	2	Guest House	p271
Maggie Joe's, Ballybay	3	Pub with Food	p272
Lakeview Holiday Apartments, Castleblayney	4	Self Catering	p273
Quigley's, Carrickmacross	5	Pub	p274
Daniel McNello & Co., Inniskeen	6	Pub with Food	p274
Packie Willies, Clones	7	Pub	p275

● Denotes entries in other chapters

Louie's

Glasslough Street
Monaghan, Co. Monaghan
Tel: 047 84255

With its eye-catching red and cream exterior and recently refurbished interior, **Louie's** is a stylish place to eat. Owner Louie O'Leary is also the chef and offers a varied choice that includes an All Day Breakfast; Carvery lunch and à la carte menu. Portions are generous and offer excellent value for money. The air-conditioned restaurant has a wine licence and the modern décor and well-spaced tables all add to the pleasure of dining here. Louie's is open from 9am to 8pm, Monday to Saturday; all major credit cards are accepted and there's good street parking nearby.

Rosefield Farm Guest House

Corbeg, Monaghan, Co. Monaghan
Tel: 047 82181 Mobile: 08683 33201

Situated about 1.5 miles from the town centre, **Rosefield Farmhouse** is much more impressive than it sounds. It's actually a splendid mansion set amidst rolling manicured lawns and is known locally as 'Southfork'. The house is surrounded by a 50-acre working farm with diary stock and poultry, and its bed & breakfast accommodation has been voted No. 2 in all Ireland. Wilfred and Elizabeth Garland are welcoming hosts who make visitors feel instantly at home. The 3 guest bedrooms are huge, all en suite with TV, hospitality tray, trouser press, hair dryer – and lovely views over the garden. Breakfast offers a good choice and packed lunches are available.

squares, **Church Square**, has a delightful Regency Gothic church and a large obelisk commemorating a Colonel Dawson killed in the Crimean War, a period when Monaghan was still a British garrison town. A famous son of Monaghan is also honoured here with a **Statue of Charles Gavan Duffy.** Duffy (1816-1903) was a leading force in the founding of the Young Ireland Movement Irish Tenant League, a co-founder of the influential Nationalist newspaper *The Nation*, and later became Prime Minister of the State of Victoria, Australia.

The award-winning **Monaghan County Museum** (free) on Hill Street has an outstanding collection of prehistoric antiquities, archaeological finds, traditional local crafts, and prints and water-colours from the 18th century to the present day. Housed in the former courthouse of 1829, the museum's most treasured exhibit is the processional **Cross of Clogher**, dating from around 1400 and exquisitely embossed with figures and decoration.

Soaring high above Monaghan is the flamboyant spire of **St Macartan's Catholic Cathedral**, built on a hill just outside the town in the 1860s in the Gothic Revival style popularised by Pugin. An interesting feature here, beneath the impressive hammerbeam roof, is an elaborately scenic memorial to Lieutenant Henry Craven Jesse Lloyd of the Natal Mounted Police *'who fell fighting at Isandula, S. Africa'* in 1879.

Around Monaghan

About 6 miles northeast of Monaghan, near Glaslough, **Castle Leslie** is one of the finest

Italianate houses in Ireland and is lavishly furnished with 16th and 17th century antiques collected by the Leslie family on their Grand Tours. The Leslie family still live in one wing of the castle; the remainder serves as a hotel. Dean Swift stayed here when it was a private house, so did Winston Churchill and Mick Jagger, but the greatest concentration of celebrities at Castle Leslie occurred in June 2000 when it hosted the wedding celebrations of Paul McCartney and Heather Mills.

Castle Leslie

Tydavnet

4 miles NW of Monaghan on the N2

A rather sad tale attaches to the name of this small village. Tydavnet is a corruption of 'Dympna', a 6th century princess who was the daughter of the King of Oriel. He was incensed when she became a Christian so the girl fled to what is now Belgium. Her father pursued her there and killed her. As St Dympna, or Damhait, her relics are still preserved at Gheel.

Emyvale

6 miles N of Monaghan on the N2

A pleasant village set in a picturesque area of woodland and lakes. One of these lakes, Lough Emy, is famous for the number of its wildfowl and swans.

Ballybay

8 miles S of Monaghan on the R162

Ballybay is an attractive little town set on the shore of Lough Major and surrounded by low-lying hills. There are two churches, Catholic and Church of Ireland, each standing on its own hill above the grassy lake. The area around Ballybay with its many lakes and rivers is popular with anglers because of its excellent coarse fishing – especially for bream.

Maggie Joe's

84 Main Street, Ballybay, Co. Monaghan
Tel: 042 974 1225

Eileen and John Meegan spent ages looking for the right pub and, early in 2003, finally found just the thing in Ballybay. Dating back to the late 1700s, **Maggie Joe's** now has a striking gold and black frontage and a small, cosy interior with a stone floor.

It's primarily a wet pub but sandwiches and soups are available all day. John is a Guinness man and takes great pride in pulling a perfect pint.

The other major passion here is music with live sessions of traditional and folk music every Friday, Saturday and Sunday evening.

Lakeview Holiday Apartments

Ballytrain, Shantonagh, Castleblayney.
Co.Monaghan
Tel: 042 974 5060
e-mail: info@lakeview-apartments.com
website: www.lakeview-apartments.com

Hidden away in the undulating countryside of south Monaghan, **Lakeview Holiday Apartments** occupy a beautifully converted stone farmhouse overlooking Ballytrain Lake. The apartments have a 3-star Bord Failte rating and sleep 5-6 guests. Each apartment has a twin room, one double and a sofa bed in the living room. The owners, Brendan and Mary McConnell, have provided just about everything you could want for a comfortable self-catering holiday – even a pub next door which they also own and run. Open all year, the apartments have ample parking space.

Castleblayney

14 miles SE of Monaghan on the N2

Set in the heart of "Drumlin Country", Castleblayney has adopted the title of "The Killarney of the North". The town was established by English colonists and is attractively sited on a narrow strip of land at the head of Lough Muckno, the county's largest stretch of water covering some 900 acres and the venue for the European Coarse Fishing Championships in 1999.

In the 1600s, the lands around Lough Muckno were owned by the Blayney family and it was they who built the original castle. They also developed the town to which they gave their name. The family continued to prosper and by the early 19th century had added the handsome Courthouse, a market house, a Church of Ireland church and, unusually for those times, a Roman Catholic church. They also built a stately three storey Georgian building with five bays.

By the mid-1800s, the Blayneys had fallen on hard times and the house was sold to Henry Thomas Hope, the millionaire owner of the famous Hope Diamond which was reputed to bring bad luck to whoever possessed it. The marriage of Hope's daughter to an English duke doesn't necessarily seem like bad luck but by 1916 the estate was mortgaged and the Hope family departed.

During the 20th century, Hope Castle played many different rôles. From 1900 to 1904 it was the home of the Duke of Connaught, Queen Victoria's third son, who was Commander in Chief of the British forces in Ireland at that time. Later it was used as an Army barracks, a County Hospital, and a guest house run by Franciscan sisters before being purchased by Monaghan County Council.

The house is now the Hope Castle Hotel but part of the grounds has been developed into the delightful **Lough Muckno Leisure Park** set in 900 acres of wooded country, a peaceful place for angling, picnicking and strolling along way-marked forest walks.

Carrickmacross

26 miles SE of Monaghan on the N2

Carrickmacross is an appealing town with a spacious main street and the sparse remains of a castle built by the Earl of Essex to whom Elizabeth I had granted the town. A **Gothic Planters Church** stands at one end of the street, a gracious Georgian courthouse at the other. Traditional shop fronts and stately Georgian houses all add to the charm.

Quigley's

72 Main Street, Carrickmacross,
Co. Monaghan
Tel: 042 966 1403

Located in the heart of Carrickmacross and occupying a late-18th century building, **Quigley's** has all the atmosphere and character you could hope to find in a traditional Irish pub. Joe and Jen Quigley arrived here in the spring of 2003 and are the life and soul of the place. This is a 'wet' pub – no food is served but you'll find an excellent Guinness on draught! On Sunday evenings, live country music provides another attraction. Quigley's is open from 10.30am to 11.30pm, Monday to Wednesday & Sunday; from 10.30am to 12.30am, Thursday to Saturday.

The town's major industry was once the production of fine lace, appliqué work on tulle. The tradition is still alive and well – the work of today's lacemakers can be seen, and bought, at the **Carrickmacross Lace Gallery** in the Market Place.

Carrickmacross's most famous son is the comedian Ardal O'Hanlon, better known as Father Dougal in the Channel 4 series *Father Ted* and as Thermoman in BBC-TV's *My Hero*. Ardal's first novel, *The Talk of the Town*, provides a comic picture of life in a clearly recognizable Carrickmacross.

To the southwest of the town the **Dún a'Rí Forest Park** is an idyllic area, almost 600 acres of woodland looking across to the Mourne Mountains and a ruined Elizabethan fortress. There's a wishing well set into a rocky ledge above the River Cobra, countless places for a peaceful picnic, and a bridge with a story. Apparently, **Sarah's Bridge** is named after a lady who was standing here when a man she had been meeting for 30 years suddenly proposed marriage. She was so startled she fell from the bridge and drowned.

Iniskeen

34 miles SE of Monaghan off the R179 or R178

This small village close to the border with Co. Louth was the birthplace in 1904 of the popular poet, Patrick Kavanagh. There's a small plaque displaying some of his verse and the house where he lived is clearly signposted – but not open to the public.

Daniel McNello & Co.

Inniskeen, Co. Monaghan
Tel: 042 937 8355

Better known to its regulars as Devlin's, **Daniel McNello & Co.** is a fine example of a traditional Irish village pub. Nuala Devlin took over the pub, together with her late husband, some 15 years ago and has recently carried out an extensive refurbishment while retaining the character of the 200-year-old property. An interesting feature of the décor is the gallery of framed tributes from literary luminaries to Inniskeen's most famous son, the poet Patrick Cavanagh. There's no regular food service but sandwiches and snacks are available on request. Open from 10.30am until late every day, the pub also hosts occasional live music sessions.

Kavanagh is buried in the graveyard of St Mary's Church and the church itself is home to the **Patrick Kavanagh Rural and Literary Resource Centre** which has exhibits recording the poet's life and work. An interesting feature here is the specially commissioned series of paintings illustrating scenes from Kavanagh's major work, *The Great Hunger*.

Back in the 6th century, St Deagh founded an abbey at Iniskeen: a round tower and some scant remains are all that have survived.

Smithboro

8 miles SW of Monaghan on the N54

Smithboro lies close to **Rossmore Forest Park,** a popular amenity with beautiful grounds, many pleasant forest walks and plenty of quiet picnic sites. Set among low hills and small lakes, the 692 acre park was originally a private estate.

Clones

11 miles SW of Monaghan on the N54

Pronounced *clo-nez*, Clones is a major agricultural centre and also well known for lace-making. The distinctive variety produced here is crocheted and often features small raised knots known as 'Clones dots'. The town was developed in the early 1600s by English settlers but there are a few

Clones High Cross

survivals from earlier times. In the market place, known as is usual in Monaghan as the Diamond, there's an ancient, deeply carved **High Cross** with scenes from the Old Testament on one side, and New Testament stories depicted on the other. Just a couple of hundred yards from the town centre, a medieval **Round Tower** stands beside the ruins of the Augustinian Abbey founded by St Tiernach in the 6th century.

PACKIE WILLIES

The Diamond, Clones, Co. Monaghan
Tel: 047 51229 e-mail: nquig@hotmail.com

Located in the heart of this friendly market town and dating back to the late 1800s, **Packie Willies** has all the atmosphere and character you associate with an authentic Irish pub. Mine hosts, Nail Quigley and Michael Armstrong, are two young men who have recently taken over here and introduced a striking décor with a 'wood' theme. This is a wet pub – i.e. no food is served – and enjoys the reputation of serving the best pint of stout in Clones. The pub has live music at weekends

and is open daily from noon until late. All major credit cards are accepted.

Co Offaly

The topography of central Ireland is often described as "saucer-shape", and County Offaly represents the lower half of the saucer with the flood-plain of the River Shannon to the north and the heathery Slieve Bloom Mountains providing the rim in the southeast. Most of the county is level plain and bogland – indeed, some of the last remaining tracts of bogland can be visited at Clara and Mongans Bog. But there are also beauty spots such as Victoria Lock near Banagher which one writer compared, perhaps a little over-enthusiastically, with Jamaica. This gentle, unassuming county is also home to one of Ireland's most important early Christian sites, Clonmacnois, and what most experts regard as the country's most perfect 18th century town, Birr, now designated as a Heritage

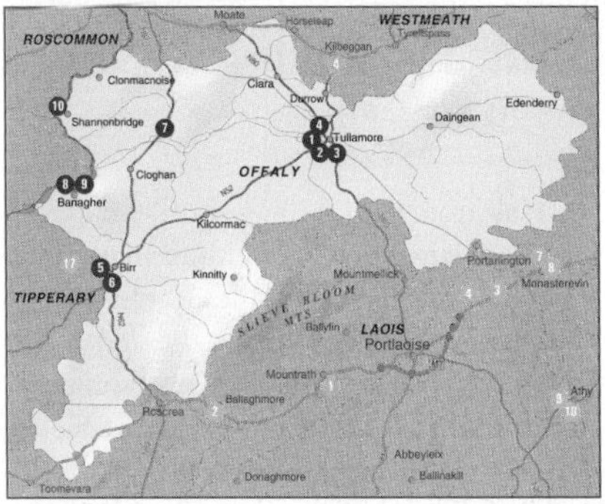

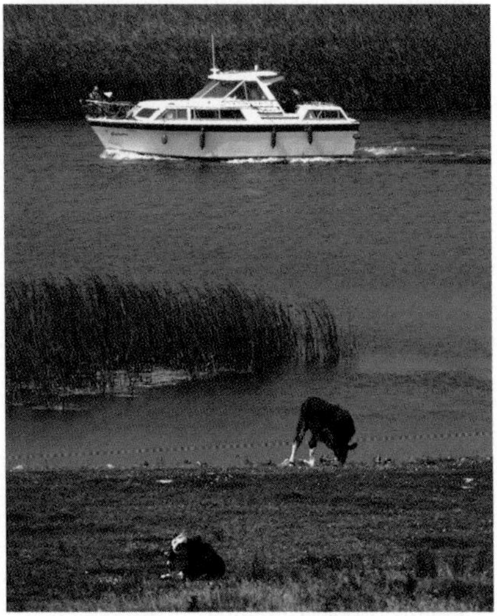

Cruising on the River Shannon

PLACES TO STAY, EAT AND DRINK

Grennan's Country House, Tullamore	1	B&B	p277
Senor Rico Restaurant, Tullamore	2	Restaurant	p278
The Blue Ball, Tullamore	3	Pub with Food	p278
Tullamore Dew Heritage Centre, Tullamore	4	Visitor Attraction	p279
The Maltings Guest House, Birr	5	Guest House	p281
Birr Scientific and Heritage Foundation, Birr	6	Visitor Attraction	p282
Maidin Gheal, Ferbane	7	Restaurant & Bakery	p283
Brosna Lodge Hotel, Banagher-on-Shannon	8	Hotel	p284
The Vine House Bar & Restaurant, Banagher	9	Bar & Restaurant	p284
Laurel Lodge, Shannonbridge	10	B&B and Self Catering	p285

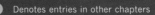

● Denotes entries in other chapters

Town. The Parsons family who created Georgian Birr and later became Earls of Rosse still live at Birr Castle where visitors can see the famous Rosse Telescope.

Tullamore

Offaly's county town, Tullamore owes its extraordinarily wide main street to an early aviation disaster. In 1785, a hot air balloon erupted in flames over the town and the resulting conflagration destroyed no fewer than one hundred houses. The local landowner, Lord Tullamore, although only 21, redeveloped much of the town. It was his family, the Moores, who had come from England as settlers around 1600 and founded the town. Today, Tullamore is the fastest growing town in the Midlands with a population of more than 10,000.

Thirteen years after the great fire, in 1798, the **Grand Canal** reached the town and initiated a half century or so of prosperity. The waterway provided a direct link to Dublin, even though the 45-mile journey took 14 hours. Today, the canal offers modern visitors some pleasant towpath walks. You can also hire a narrowboat here and make your own way along the canal, passing through undulating pastureland and with a better-than-even chance of glimpsing a kingfisher or a lithe otter which can outpace your boat's regulation 4mph by a streamlined speed of 6mph.

It was at Tullamore that the famous Tullamore Dew whiskey and the flavoursome whiskey liqueur Irish Mist were both created. The "Dew" incidentally comes from the initials of the owner of the distillery, Daniel Edmond Williams. The distillery itself has relocated to Clonmel in Co. Tipperary but the **Tullamore Dew Heritage Centre** (see panel on page 279), housed in a canalside warehouse, tells the story of this famous tipple, and of the town where it was born, with the aid of models

Grennan's Country House

Aharney, Tullamore, Co. Offaly
Tel: 0506 55893
e-mail: deirdregrennan@iolfree.ie

Purpose-built in 2001 as a guest house, **Grennan's Country House** stands in unspoilt countryside just outside Tullamore, close to local and regional attractions yet rural enough to provide peace and relaxation. Arriving guests are quickly made to feel at home by owners Deirdre and Pat Grennan who also serve up a complimentary tea tray. Guests have the use of an elegant lounge with an open turf fire and there's a spacious dining room where breakfast is served. A rather special breakfast in fact with a wide choice that includes all the popular favourites as well as kipper, salmon, cake and fruit scones, and a selection of white, brown or soda breads. Packed lunches are available on request.

All the guest bedrooms at Grennan's are en suite and fully equipped with remote control television, hair dryer and tea/coffee-making facilities – cool spring water is also available. The house is fully wheelchair accessible. If you prefer self-catering, there's a 2-bedroom fully furnished luxury apartment on site. Amenities include an en suite bathroom, TV and video. Attractions nearby include the famous Esker Hills golf course which is close enough to walk to, the Kilbeggan Races just 7 miles away, and the major monastic site of Clonmacnois which is only 20 miles distant.

Señor Rico Restaurant

Patrick Street, Tullamore, Co. Offaly
Tel/Fax: 0506 52889 Mobile: 0876 889667
website: www.senorrico.net

Established in 1999, the **Señor Rico Restaurant** is now firmly established as one of the most popular eating out venues in Tullamore – in 2003 it was one of only two local restaurants to receive the prestigious international "Best Restaurant Award". It brings together two of Italy's most popular dining concepts – the Italian family restaurant and a bustling atmosphere. As proprietor Paula Tahraoui puts it "At Señor Rico, everyone's Italian!" Reasonable prices, quality food with a freshness you can see and taste, speedy service and a warm and friendly environment all contribute to the restaurant's success.

The varied menu includes starters such as Melanzane – oven-baked aubergine, courgette and pepper with pesto & melted cheese; pasta dishes such as Taglietelle al Irlandese – green & white pasta with smoked salmon & cream sauce; wonderful meat offerings like the Veal Testarossa – escalope of veal with garlic, chilli and sun-dried tomato; appetising chicken dishes – Chicken Cacciatora, perhaps; and fresh fish like the Monkfish with a roast red pepper and saffron cream sauce. The kitchen is open so you can actually see the chefs preparing your meal. The restaurant is conveniently located directly across from the Garda Station in the centre of Tullamore and is open for lunch from noon until 2.30pm daily; for dinner from 6pm to 11pm, Monday to Saturday, and from 2pm to 10.30pm on Sunday.

The Blue Ball

Blue Ball, Tullamore, Co. Offaly
Tel: 0506 54019
website: www.blueballpub.com

The Blue Ball pub's proud claim is that "We are an hour and a half from anywhere in Ireland!" Not only is it situated right in the centre of Ireland, it is also one of the oldest pubs in the country. The pub dates back to the early 1800s and its unusual name comes from an English trading name for a pub – at a time when people could not read or write a blue ball would be displayed outside the hostelry. This particular pub stands at a crossroads and as other houses were built, the whole settlement became known simply as "Blue Ball". Landlady Carmel Dooley Leonard is a third generation publican born and raised in pub undertaking and auctioneering. Carmel grew up behind the counter of the Midland bar in Kilcormac (about 6 miles down the N52) and today that pub is still run by her mother and brother Colm.

At the moment, the Blue Ball serves light bar food every lunchtime and evening but will happily cater for more intensive fare on order. The pub also caters for all types of parties, specialising in golfing groups since there are golf courses all around. Customers can watch live sporting events such as hurling, football and soccer, and another major attraction is the live traditional Irish music every weekend.

and audio-visual displays. Visitors can also watch bees making honey for the Irish Mist liqueur; try on Victorian costumes; sample a complimentary dram; and take refreshment in the fully licensed café. The centre is open daily, all year round (afternoons only on Sundays).

Around Tullamore

To the southwest of Tullamore, **Charleville Forest Castle** is approached by an avenue beside which stands what is reputed to be the largest oak tree in Europe. The castle is a flamboyant Georgian-Gothic mansion built in 1779 to the designs of Francis Johnston. Johnston was clearly a prime inspiration for the designers who created the sets for the Hammer House of Horror movies of the 1960s - dark recesses, gloomy archways, even a grotto in the grounds, all suggest a sinister medieval provenance but the overall effect is curiously light-hearted. The castle and grounds are open from 11am to 4pm from June to September; weekend afternoons during April and May; and at other times by appointment.

Tullamore Dew Heritage Centre

Bury Quay, Tullamore, Co. Offaly
Tel: 0506 25015 Fax: 0506 25016
e-mail: tullamoredhc@eircom.net
website: www.tullamore-dew.org

Housed in a splendid old Victorian warehouse of 1897 on the banks of the Grand Canal, **Tullamore Dew Heritage Centre** celebrates the history of one of Ireland's favourite beverages. It was back in 1829 that production began of Tullamore's most famous export – Tullamore Dew. The "Dew" part of the name came from the initials of Daniel Edmond Williams, the man who would later own the distillery and promote the virtues, and the sale, of his superb Irish whiskey and the magnificent liqueur, Irish Mist.

These memorable beverages are no longer produced in Tullamore, but the Tullamore Dew Heritage Centre houses a lively and interactive exhibition where the various working stations of the distillery have been re-created. Visitors can wander through the malting, bottling or cooperage areas to name but a few and learn how the whiskey is made.

A wide variety of models, panels and audio visuals record the history of whiskey production in Tullamore and of the town itself. Like so many towns during the Industrial Revolution, Tullamore's prosperity was fuelled by the arrival of the canal. The Grand Canal is an awe-inspiring feat of 18th century engineering and linked Tullamore directly to the rich markets of Dublin and from there to markets abroad.

Exhibits recall key events in the town's history such as the arrival of the barracks in 1716, and the balloon fire of 1785. This caused immense damage but allowed Lord Tullamore, a mere 21 years old at the time, to redevelop much of the town.

The tour of the Centre concludes with a complimentary glass of Tullamore Dew Irish Whiskey or Irish Mist Liqueur thus providing an opportunity to understand why both beverages are so popular amongst the world's connoisseurs.

The Centre's shop displays an array of these famous products and associated merchandise along with famous Co. Offaly crafts – ideal souvenirs of your visit to this part of the country.

Durrow

2 miles N of Tullamore on the N52

A mile or two north of Durrow, just off the N52, is the site of **Durrow Abbey**, yet another of the monasteries founded by St Columba in the 6th century. The famous illuminated Book of Durrow was written here in the following century and is currently housed in Trinity College, Dublin. A medieval church now stands on the site of the Abbey but a 10th century high cross and some fine early tombstones can be seen in the disused cemetery. The church stands next to a grand Georgian mansion, (not open to the public), whose well-maintained grounds provide an elegant backdrop to the tumbledown graveyard.

Daingean

9 miles NE of Tullamore on the R402

Set beside the Grand Canal, this little town was once the seat of the chiefs of Offaly, the O'Conors and was also, briefly, the county town. In the 1500s it was renamed Philipstown in honour of Philip II of Spain, husband of Henry VIII's daughter, "Bloody" Mary. The unhappy marriage only lasted four years (1554-58) but during that time Offaly became known as "King's County" and the title still lingers on.

Edenderry

18 miles NE of Tullamore on the R402

Close to the border with Co. Kildare, this picturesque market town owes its handsome appearance to the Marquess of Devonshire. By marriage he had acquired Blundell's Castle, whose ruins stand on a hill to the south of the town, and as an enlightened landowner did much to improve the little town. A mile or so beyond the castle ruins is the Grand Canal which provides some pleasant towpath walking.

Just over the border, at Carbury, **Ballindoolin House and Gardens** is a popular destination for family outings. Guided tours of the large Georgian house are available while the extensive grounds contain a recently restored two-acre 19th century walled garden, a self-guiding woodland nature trail and tree folklore trail, a children's farmyard and a craft shop.

Kinnitty

16 miles SW of Tullamore on the R440/R421

Kinnitty is a picturesque village set at the foot of the Slieve Bloom Mountains and at the head of a lovely valley running between the hills, Forelacka Glen. Guided walks are a regular activity here during the summer months and a walking festival is held annually in May. For anyone with a love of Irish music, the traditional music sessions held every Friday night in Kinnitty Castle (now a hotel) are not to be missed.

An unusual feature of the village is the extraordinary **Kinnitty Pyramid,** an exact replica of one of the pyramids in Egypt. Built by Richard W. Bernard, its construction took four years and was finally completed in 1830. The pyramid stands in the graveyard behind the Church of Ireland and serves as a tomb for four members of the Bernard family who owned Kinnitty Castle.

Another structure of interest is the High Cross which stands in the grounds of the castle. It came from the monastery founded by St Ciaran in the 6th century at nearby Sierkieran. A curiosity just outside this village is a whitethorn called St Ciaran's Bush which grows in the middle of the road.

A few miles further south is the 15th century **Leap Castle** which is reputed to be the most haunted castle in Ireland. Visitors such as W.B.Yeats and Oliver St John Gogarty all testified to the presence within its rooms of a revoltingly smelly spectre. Even a catastrophic fire in 1922 which left the castle in ruins has not put an end to the ghosts' shenanigans.

Birr

22 miles SW of Tullamore on the N52/N62

Standing at the junction of the Rivers Camcor and Little Brosna, Birr is one of Ireland's finest Georgian towns, beautifully laid out with wide streets and elegant squares and with many dignified houses. The people of Birr have the Parsons family, later the Earls of Rosse, to thank for their handsome town. The lands here were granted to Sir Laurence Parsons in 1620 and became known as Parsonstown. But it was a descendant of his, another Sir Laurence, who began a thoroughgoing "improvement" of the town in the 1740s. **Emmet Square** is the oldest part, completed in 1747 and dominated by the lofty Cumberland Pillar which originally was crowned by a statue of the Duke of Cumberland, the "Butcher of Culloden". Dooly's Hotel, also 1747, is here too, a fine old coaching inn that was accidentally set

Birr Town

THE MALTINGS GUESTHOUSE

Castle Street, Birr, Co. Offaly
Tel: 0509 21345 Fax: 0509 22073
e-mail: themaltingsbirr@eircom.net
website: www.birrnet.com

Occupying a lovely riverside setting beside Birr Castle in the centre of Ireland's finest Georgian town, **The Maltings Guesthouse** is a luxuriously furnished guesthouse and restaurant. Originally built around 1810 to store malt used in the brewing of Guinness, the Maltings was meticulously restored in 1994 and now provides the highest modern standards combined with great charm and character. The stylish licensed restaurant

enjoys soothing river views and there's also a separate bar. Owner Maeve Garry is

always happy to cater for special functions.

The Maltings beautifully furnished and decorated 13 guest bedrooms all have en suite facilities with bath and shower, and are fully equipped with colour TV and direct dial telephone. You can enjoy walking through the nearby Birr Castle Demesne – the largest gardens in the country featuring thousands of trees and plants from all over the world. Golf, fishing and horse-riding can all be arranged and Birr town itself is a pleasure to explore with its elegant Georgian architecture which is at its most striking in Emmet Square and John's Mall.

on fire one night in 1809 by revellers from the Galway Hunt. Since that day, the Hunt has been known as the Galway Blazers.

West of Emmet Square is **John's Mall**, distinguished by some fine Georgian houses with elegant fanlights above the doors. The noble classical building here, with its pillared and porticoed entrance, is John's Hall which now houses the town's Tourist Information Centre. Here you can pick up a leaflet describing a pleasant 50-minute Town Trail which takes in all the major sights.

One of the finest Georgian streets is the majestically tree-lined Oxmantown Mall which leads to the main gates of **Birr Castle**, hereditary home of the Earls of Rosse whose family still lives here. The castle is not normally open to the public

but visitors are welcome to stroll through the 100 acres of pleasure grounds laid out by the 2nd Earl in the 1830s and 1840s. The gardens are the largest in the country and contain many rare specimen trees and shrubs. They also boast the tallest box hedges in the world, about 33 feet high, and no fewer than 50 individual trees were included in the book *Champion Trees of the World*. There are delightful walks around the huge ornamental lake and alongside the rivers that were created specially to enhance the landscape.

Apart from the imposing Gothic exterior of the castle itself, the most fascinating structure here is the colossal **Rosse Telescope** (see panel below) constructed by the 3rd Earl in 1845. With its 72-inch diameter reflector, it was for 75 years the

THE BIRR SCIENTIFIC AND HERITAGE FOUNDATION

Birr Castle, Birr, Co. Offaly
Tel.: 0509 20336 Fax: 0509 21583
e-mail: info@birrcastle.com
website: www.birrcastle.com

Discover the largest telescope in the world for over 70 years; constructed here at **Birr Castle** in the 1840's by the Third Earl of Rosse.The telescope looks and moves just as it did over 150 years ago. Travel through the evolution of astronomy from the 17th century with Gallileo, Newton, Hershell and finally meet the Third Earl of Rosse and his GreatTelescope. Re-live the challenges he had to overcome in order to build the largest telescope in the world, in rural Ireland, in the 1840s. The casting and polishing of the speculum, the building of the observatory and much more... Share in the discoveries of the Third Earl and compare his original drawings of faraway galaxies with photographs taken with contemporary telescopes.

However, at Birr Castle Demesne there is much more than science and technology. The gardens are the largest in the country and feature thousands of

trees and plants propagated from seed that was collected all over the world by three generations of the Parsons family, Earls of Rosse. 50 of these trees are listed in the publication *"Champion Trees of the British Isles.* The Millennium Gardens were created out of the passionate love for gardens of Michael and Anne, the Sixth Earl and Countess of Rosse. Features include a box hedging parterre, in the shape of crossed'Rs' surrounded by the romantic hombearn cloister walk, the Delphinium border, the beautiful PaeoniaAnne Rosse - a hybrid peony developed at Birr and tucked away in an intimate courtyard near the glasshouses, the Pergola with a spectacular Wisteria multijuga which is 90 years old.

largest telescope in the world. The 4th Earl used it to make the first accurate measurement of the temperature of the moon and to catalogue the spiral nebulae.

Also within the castle grounds is the Historic Centre, housed in the former stable block. The exhibits here celebrate the scientific achievements of other members of the Rosse family, amongst them the Lunar Heat Machine invented by the 4th Earl whose younger brother, William, kept up the family reputation by inventing the steam turbine. Not to be outdone, their mother, Mary, Countess of Rosse, displayed considerable talent as one of the earliest women photographers.

the present massive tower house dates from Norman times and has been continuously lived in from the day it was built, more than 800 years ago. It has a magnificent medieval dining room and the castle is furnished with a fascinating collection of antiques, along with weapons and armour going back to Cromwell's time. The castle is open Wednesday to Saturday afternoons, from May through September.

A lane signposted from the castle leads to a local beauty spot, **Victoria Lock,** where the River Shannon runs into two separate channels. One writer found the vegetation here so lush that he compared the scenery to that of Jamaica or Dominica.

Cloghan
16 miles SW of Tullamore on the N62/R357

A few miles northwest of Cloghan, **Cloghan Castle** is the oldest inhabited castle in Ireland. There was a monastery founded here in the 7th century by St Cronan, but

Banagher
22 miles SW of Tullamore on the R439/R356

A major boating centre set beside the Shannon, this appealing little town has one long street descending the hillside to the river and looks across to a Martello tower

MAIDIN GHEAL

Main Street, Ferbane, Co. Offaly
Tel: 090 64 54665

In Gaelic **Maidin Gheal** means "bright morning" and what better way to start the day than by sampling some of the home-baked fare on offer at this delightful bakery and restaurant. You'll find a good selection of home-baked products to take away or, even better, you can settle down in the cosy restaurant with its pine furniture, slate floor and wood-burning stove. The day starts with a wide choice of breakfasts, including a vegetarian one of egg and melted cheese on brown bread served with fried potato, mushrooms and tomato. Lunchtime choices include a variety of appetising chicken dishes along with home-made soup of the day, a salad plate and vegetarian options such as savoury omelettes or a Mushroom Pasta served with

peppers, onions, courgettes and mange tout in a house cream sauce.

All dishes are cooked to order so please allow time for service – if you are in a hurry you can pre-order by telephone. Maidin Gheal also offers a choice of delicious home-made desserts and a tasty selection of sandwiches and toasted sandwiches all freshly made with home-made bread. To accompany your meal there's a choice of beverages that includes Jacob's Creek red and white wine. Maidin Gheal is open from 9am to 6pm, Monday to Saturday, (last orders 5.30pm).

Brosna Lodge Hotel

Banagher-on-Shannon, Co. Offaly
Tel: 00353 (0)509 51350
Fax: 00353 (0)509 51521
e-mail: della@iolfree.ie
website: www.brosnalodge.com

Set close to the banks of the River Shannon, **Brosna Lodge Hotel** is a friendly country house hotel owned and managed by the Horan family. Approved by Bord Failte, the hotel has 14 well-appointed rooms, all en suite with bath and shower, and equipped with multi-channel TV and direct dial telephone. A popular attraction here is Pat's Olde Bar where you can settle down with a pint of creamy Guinness in front of one of the open fires. There is entertainment at weekends. If you're hungry after your travels, ask for the Bar food menu. The menu changes on a daily basis, but you can be sure to find something to suit just your palate. For more substantial fare, sample the appetising food on offer in the well-known Fields Restaurant which is renowned for its quality cuisine, based on fresh local produce, superbly presented and served with a special attention to detail. Awarded Dining Pub of the Year 2003.

After your meal, if you are looking for pure ciúinas (Irish for silence), you'll find it in the mature gardens at the rear of the Lodge. Banagher itself is a tidy, peaceful late-Georgian town where the pace of life seems dictated by the leisurely flow of the river. It consists mainly of one long street running right up to the river where a sweeping bridge links Offaly with Galway.

The Vine House Bar & Restaurant

Westend, Banagher, Co. Offaly
Tel: 059 51463 Mobile: 087 794 7733

Located on the banks of the River Shannon in the attractive tourist town of Banagher, **The Vine House Bar & Restaurant** is extremely popular with both locals and visitors and has been showered with awards. Egon Ronay recommends it for its bar food and atmosphere, it features in the Jameson Pub Guide and it has also been praised by the food writer Gerogina Campbell. There's a spacious courtyard beer garden to the rear, complete with palm trees and ideal for sampling the superb Guinness served here. Lovers of good food will be in gourmet heaven in the cosy restaurant which is full of charm and character.

Amongst the starters, for example, are Galway Bay Oysters served on a bed of seaweed with pigtail lemon, home-made soup, and a Taste of France – ripe Brie pane in the Vine House's own Italian crumb deep fried and served with a fruits of the forest coulis. Main courses include pasta, steak, seafood, meat and poultry dishes with a vegetarian dish of the day always available. Then there are the memorable desserts – Bailey's Cheesecake, Death by Chocolate, passion fruit carrot cake and more. Round off your meal with one of the smooth liqueur coffees on offer.

on the Galway bank. With its handsome Georgian features, Banagher provides an elegant base for exploring both the East Midlands and County Galway. Some of the local shops are well-stocked with wines, spices and exotic vegetables for Continental holidaymakers, while other stores don't seem to have changed since the 1940s. Visitors can hire boats and canoes to explore the Shannon, and there's even a vintage barge offering luxury cruises along the river. The town is peppered with lively pubs featuring traditional music, glorious Guinness and great craic.

An early vacationer at Banagher was Charlotte Brontë who spent part of her honeymoon here in 1854. (Sadly, she was to die the next year in pregnancy). Another literary resident was Anthony Trollope who worked as a Post Office surveyor in the 1840s and wrote his first novel *The Macdermots of Ballycloran* while staying at Banagher.

Not far from Banagher is **Lusmagh Pet Farm,** home to an interesting range of animals and birds that includes rare breeds of farm animals, ostriches, emus, pigs and donkeys. There's also a display of vintage farm machinery and a pre-famine dwelling house. The farm is open, afternoons only, from May to September.

Shannonbridge

22 miles W of Tullamore on the R357/R444

At Shannonbridge a fine, but narrow, 16-arched bridge crosses the River Suck just before it meets the Shannon, and a grey Napoleonic fort guards this strategic junction where three counties meet - Offaly, Roscommon and Galway. The town's main visitor attraction is the "Bog Railway", more properly known as the **Clonmacnoise and West Offaly Railway**. This narrow-gauge railway offers a 5 mile circular tour around the Blackwater Bog and is preceded by a 35 minute video

Laurel Lodge

Garrymore, Shannonbridge, Co. Offaly
Tel: 090 96 74189
website: www.laurelodgefarm@eircom.net

A luxurious and spacious modern farmhouse, **Laurel Lodge** offers visitors a choice of either bed & breakfast, full board or self-catering accommodation in wonderfully peaceful surroundings. Bed & breakfast guests will find 6 comfortable rooms, all en suite and fully equipped with TV and a relaxing residents' lounge also with TV and an open fire. This is prime fishing country so hosts Eamon and Marie McManus have provided a fridge and tackle storage for guests and can also arrange boat hire. There's a pleasant garden, children's playground and a private car park. Anglers will definitely be in their element here. Less than a mile away is the majestic Shannon with its abundant perch, bream, pike, rudd and tench. Only a little further away are the Suck and Brosna rivers and the Grand Canal.

Eamon and Marie understand the angler's ways and are happy to provide an early morning breakfast and supply a packed lunch. Non-anglers will find plenty to keep them busy. There are many fine championship courses in the area; grand walking either alongside the Grand Canal or in the Slieve Bloom mountains and horse-riding. The famous monastic site of Clonmacnoise is just a few miles up the road and no-one visiting this area should miss a journey on the Bog Rail Tour.

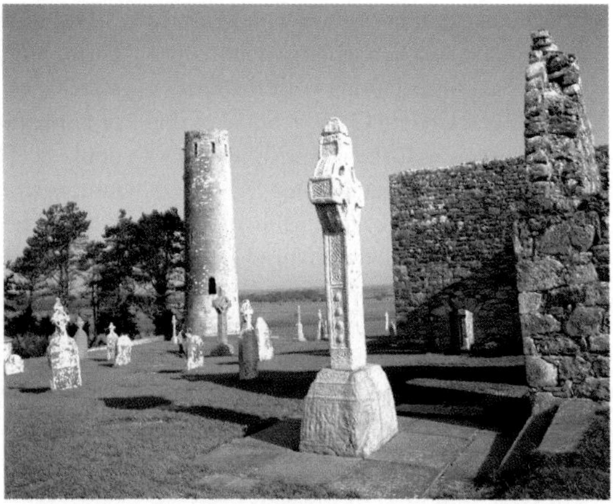

Clonmacnoise Monastic Site

explaining the complex flora and fauna of the area. Visitors are supplied with a *slane*, the special spade for cutting peat, and allowed to cut a few sods of turf in the time-honoured fashion. The railway is operated by the National Peat Board which uses peat from the bog to fuel the massive power station that dominates the landscape. According to the Board, "A few hundred years from now the bog will be an integrated tapestry of fields, woodlands and wetlands", - a prospect that has exasperated conservation bodies trying to save Ireland's fast diminishing areas of natural bogland.

Clonmacnoise

20 miles W of Tullamore on the R444

One of the largest and most impressive monastic sites in Ireland, Clonmacnoise stands in emerald green fields beside the River Shannon. In AD 548, St Ciaran founded a monastery here which was to become the most important religious establishment of its kind in the country, famed as a centre of art and learning throughout Europe. Several of its early treasures have been removed for safe keeping to Dublin, amongst them the superb gold and silver Crozier of Clonmacnoise, and the *Book of the Dun Cow*, one of the earliest and most famous manuscripts in the Irish language.

The extensive site, bounded by an encircling stone wall, contains an astonishingly rich variety of ecclesiastical monuments – the ruins of a 14th century Cathedral, two lofty Round Towers, the finest collection of High Crosses in Ireland, nine churches and numerous carved gravestones. To protect them from the weather, three of the High Crosses, including the magnificent 12 feet high Great Cross, are now housed in the Visitor Centre. The centre also has displays illustrating the history of the site and a video presentation of the life of St Ciaran whose fame still draws pilgrims here for his festival on 12 September.

Clonmacnoise occupied an isolated position, protected on two sides by the river and on the other sides by a boggy plain, passable only by a single *esker*, or raised ridge. Even so, it suffered a series of attacks by Irish, Viking and English raiders, all hoping to plunder not just the riches of the monastery but also the treasures of the Royal City of the High Kings of Connacht who made Clonmacnoise their capital. The last of them, Rory O'Conor, was buried here in 1198.

After surviving so many depredations, the 1000-year-old history of Clonmacnoise was abruptly ended in 1552 when English troops from the garrison at Athlone looted the monastery and left the buildings beyond repair. So much remains, though, that there is a constant stream of tourists visiting the site and for many Irish people Clonmacnoise is perhaps the most evocative of all Ireland's holy places.

Co Roscommon

An inland county, Roscommon nevertheless has an abundance of water. The River Shannon and Lough Ree form its eastern boundary and Loughs Key, Gara and Arrow encircle the county to the north. Smaller bodies of water are scattered across the fertile central plain and the River Suck, beloved of coarse fishermen, forms the boundary with Co. Mayo in the west. The only high ground to be found is on the Sligo and Leitrim border where the Curlew Mountains rise high and wild.

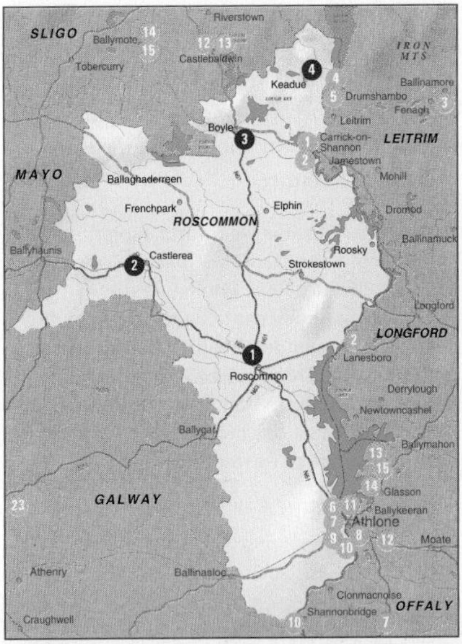

The county boasts some fine buildings, most notably the fine Palladian mansion, Strokestown Park, and the magnificent King House in Boyle. But the pre-eminent attractions of this peaceful county are its uncrowded towns and villages, and its people who seem still to have the time and warmth to make visitors feel truly welcome.

Roscommon

The county town is an appealing little place with attractively restored Georgian and Victorian shops lining the main street, a stately Georgian courthouse, (now a bank), and a grim castellated **Old Gaol** which in the 18th century had the dubious distinction of providing regular employment for Ireland's only hangwoman. "Lady Betty" had been condemned to death herself for the unwitting murder of her own son but when the regular hangman fell ill she volunteered to carry out his duties on condition that her own life be spared. Her position was later made official and she was provided with a salary and accommodation in the gaol. She lived there for some 30 years, dispatching condemned felons from a hinged board fixed outside her third floor window. The Old Gaol now houses a number of shops and restaurants.

The town also boasts two striking medieval ruins. Standing in fields on the

PLACES TO STAY, EAT AND DRINK

The Tatler Inn, Roscommon 1 Pub, Restaurant & Accommodation p288
Tully's Hotel, Castlerea 2 Hotel p290
Chambers Restaurant, Boyle 3 Restaurant p292
Harp & Shamrock, Keadue 4 Pub, Food & Accommodation p293

Denotes entries in other chapters

edge of the town are the ruins of the colossal **Roscommon Castle** (free) a 13th century structure which survived centuries of local feuding before succumbing to Cromwell's troops. The impressive remains include the rounded bastions at the corners and a double-towered entrance gate. In the town itself, **Roscommon Abbey** (free) contains the tomb of its 13th century founder, Félim O'Conor, king of Connaught. The tomb is carved with the figures of eight *galloglasses*, the soldiers who formed the retinue of an Irish chief. The Abbey stands on the site of a much earlier monastery founded by St Coman from whom the town and county take their names.

Roscommon County Museum (free) is a good, old-fashioned museum housed in a former Presbyterian church and its manse. Amongst its treasures are a 9th century inscribed slab from St Coman's monastery; a replica of the 12th century Cross of Cong; and a superb example of a sheela-na-Gig fertility carving.

Around Roscommon

Strokestown

12 miles NE of Roscommon on the R368/N5

A trim little place elegantly laid out in the 18th century, Strokestown has joined the burgeoning ranks of towns hosting festivals of one kind or another. **Strokestown Poetry Festival** was only established in 1999 but already it is attracting well-known poets to its 3-day celebration held in early May. Also drawing visitors to the town is the **County Roscommon Genealogy & Heritage Centre** which stands at one end of the extraordinarily wide main street. The centre is located in the gracious Church of St John, designed in 1819 by the English architect John Nash, and offers a full research service for those with ancestral roots in the county.

Strokestown Park House

But the busiest visitor attraction in Co. Roscommon is undoubtedly **Strokestown Park House** and the associated **Irish Famine Museum** which is housed in the stableyards of the fine Georgian house. Strokestown Park was the seat of the Pakenham Mahon family from the 1660s until 1979 when it was sold to the local garage owner with all its contents intact – everything from antique furniture and furnishings to family archives and toys, even school exercise books from the 1930s. The old schoolroom is still here, with its blackboard, desks and school books, and the main living room, dining room, nursery and library all reflect the family's comfortable rather than ostentatious lifestyle. A unique feature of the house is the gallery in the kitchen from which the lady of the house could keep on an eye on the staff. This lofty distance was maintained even with the weekly list of menus which would be dropped over the railing each Monday morning.

An additional attraction at Strokestown Park is its lovely 4-acre Walled Garden, laid out in the 18th century and now fully restored. The pièce de resistance here is the herbaceous border which has been confirmed by the *Guinness Book of Records* as the longest herbaceous border anywhere in the British Isles.

In stark contrast to the peaceful garden is the harrowing story recounted in the **Irish Famine Museum** which uses a combination of original documents and images in an attempt to explain the circumstances and consequences of the calamitous potato blight of 1845-51 that destroyed the staple, almost the only, food of rural Ireland. Within a matter of days an apparently healthy field of potatoes would be reduced, in the words of one eye-witness, to *"one wide waste of putrefying vegetation"*.

Individuals and charitable organisations in England attempted to relieve the appalling distress but the Whig government of the time refused to commit the really substantial funds necessary – with incredible callousness it decided that this was a problem for private enterprise to resolve. The result was that more than a million Irish died of starvation, another million and a half emigrated to an uncertain future in the United States or Canada. The effects of the famine were aggravated by an epidemic of typhus that caused a further 300,000 deaths: within the space of five years, it's been estimated, Ireland's population of 4 million declined to a little over 2 million.

Roosky

22 miles NE of Roscommon on the N4

The pleasant little village of Roosky sits beside the Shannon at the point where it emerges from Lough Bofin. It's popular with anglers – fishing boats are available and there are also berths for river cruisers.

Castlerea

19 miles NW of Roscommon on the N60

Clonalis House

The third largest town in the county, Castlerea is attractively sited on a wooded stretch of the River Suck. It was the birthplace in 1815 of Sir Walter Wilde, father of the celebrated Oscar.

An even more distinguished family has its seat on the outskirts of the town. **Clonalis House** is the ancestral home of the O'Conor clan which claims to be the oldest family in Europe. As hereditary kings of Connaught, the O'Conors' genealogical tree has been traced back to a certain Feredach the Just in AD 75 although an optimistic chart preserved in the house extends the lineage back to the 15th century BC.

By comparison, Clonalis House (which is still lived in by the O'Conor family) is a relative newcomer – an appealing Victorian mansion in the Italianate style completed in 1878. It contains an interesting miscellany of priceless early-Irish archives, sumptuous

antiques, family portraits documenting the O'Conors' colourful exploits at home and abroad, and a fascinating collection of mementoes. The chapel has a chalice which unscrews into three parts, a useful feature in the days when Catholic worship was proscribed, but perhaps the greatest treasure is the harp once owned by the celebrated blind harpist Turlough O'Carolan (1670-1738), "last of the Irish bards". Clonalis House is open Monday to Saturday from June to mid-September.

A more recent attraction in Castlerea itself is the **Hell's Kitchen Railway Museum & Bar**, the first railway museum of its kind in the Republic. The museum is the fulfillment of a childhood dream for Sean Browne who remembers gazing out of a carriage window at the hundreds of steam engines lined up on the sidings at Mullingar, all of them destined for the scrapyard. In 1994, Sean purchased a 1955 A55 diesel locomotive and this now forms the centrepiece of a remarkable display of railway memorabilia – station boards, signal equipment, bells, lamps and much more. There's also a TV monitor for viewing archival equipment. The array of items has spilled over into the Hell's Kitchen Bar which, like the museum, is open seven days a week, all year.

Frenchpark

7 miles N of Castlerea on the R361

The Rectory at Frenchpark was the birthplace of Douglas Hyde (1860-1949), founder of the Gaelic League and the first President of Ireland. One of his important non-political achievements was the collection of Gaelic stories and folklore from local people. Some of these tales were more than a thousand years old and, with the decline in Gaelic speaking, in serious danger of being lost altogether. Dr Hyde returned to the village in old age and lived at Ratra House (private). He is buried in the graveyard of the simple Planter's Gothic church where his father was rector and which is now the **Douglas Hyde Interpretive Centre**.

Ballaghaderreen

14 miles NW of Castlerea on the N5

Ballaghaderreen sits near the head of the Lung River which empties into Lough Gara northeast of the town. Behind the town rises a range of sandstone hills stretching northeastwards to the shore of Lough Key. Both the Lung and the Breedogue rivers provide good coarse fishing. About 3 miles outside the town stand the **Four Altars** where mass was celebrated in penal times.

Elphin

12 miles NE of Roscommon on the R368

Oliver Goldsmith and Oscar Wilde's father, William, went to school here; the village has been the seat of a bishopric since the days of St Patrick; but the main visitor attraction nowadays is **Elphin Windmill**, the only working mill in the west of Ireland. Unusually, it has a thatched revolving roof and sails that are turned into the wind using earthwheels on a circular track. The mill was built in the early 1700s to grind oats and wheat into meal. It was worked for around a hundred years and then abandoned. In 1992, the derelict tower was acquired by Elphin Area Community Enterprise Ltd and fully restored. Guided tours are given daily throughout the year and if you arrive on a day when there's a stiff breeze blowing you can see the mill in operation.

Boyle

26 miles N of Roscommon on the N61

Generally regarded as the most appealing town in Co. Roscommon, Boyle stands beside the river of the same name with the Curlew Hills rising to the northwest. The most venerable building here is **Boyle**

Chambers Restaurant

The Crescent, Boyle, Co. Roscommon
Tel: 071 966 3614

Located close to the centre of this elegant old town, **Chambers Restaurant** will delight lovers of good food and wine. Peter Doherty's extensive menu offers an enticing selection of modern Irish cuisine with dishes such as King Prawn Kataiffi amongst the starters; Grilled Ostrich au poivre vert, served on rösti potatoes and saffron couscous, as an unusual main course along with poultry, seafood, pasta and vegetarian options. The restaurant itself is elegant and intimate, with widely spaced tables, and is open from 5pm to 10pm, Tuesday to Sunday. At weekends, booking in advance is strongly recommended.

Abbey which despite its town centre location enjoys a tranquil setting beside a rushing stream. The abbey was founded by the Cistercian order in 1161 and suffered the usual succession of attacks by warring Irish tribes. But a surprising amount of the fabric is still intact even though for almost 200 years following the suppression of the monasteries the building housed a military garrison. The 12th century church has some striking Gothic and Romanesque arches and some interesting carvings.

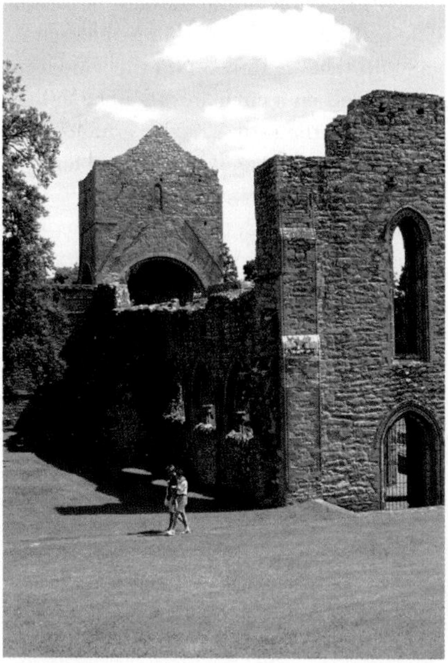

Boyle Abbey

The town also boasts some fine Georgian houses, most notably Frybrook House which has some exquisite 18th century plasterwork and the nearby **King House** built by Sir Henry King around 1730. Half a century later his descendants decided to remove themselves to Rockingham House just outside the town, leaving this stately building beside the River Boyle to become the home of the Connaught Regiment from 1788 and later the Irish Army. In the 1990s, King House was comprehensively restored and re-opened as an intrepretive centre with inventive high-tech special effects and life size models taking visitors through the history of the house and of the people who lived in this part of north Roscommon. Part of King House now serves as the town's tourist information centre.

Located in the grounds of King House, the **Una Bhán Tourism Co-operative Society** is an innovative enterprise which was a well-deserved winner of the National Rural Tourism Award for 1998. The Co-operative is a group of families who have joined together to provide prospective and actual visitors to the area with all-in holiday arrangements, covering accommodation and activities connected with life on the land and local heritage. The Una Bhán complex also includes a Craft Shop stocked with a wide range of hand made traditional crafts, pottery, jewellery, stationery, cards, leather goods, wood creations and much more. Una Bhán incidentally is pronounced *Oona Wawn* and refers to the legend of a beautiful daughter of a local Celtic chieftain. Forbidden by her father to marry the man she loved, Una died of a broken heart and was buried on Trinity Island in nearby Lough Key. Her lover used to swim to the island every night to keep vigil at her grave. He was eventually buried beside her and tradition says that two trees grew up over their graves, entwining together to form a Lover's Knot.

To the east of the town stretches the **Lough Key Forest Park**, formerly part of the vast Rockingham estate and now one of the most extensive (865 acres) and picturesque forest parks in Ireland. Rockingham House itself was burnt to a shell in 1957 but the grounds have been planted with conifers and the attractions on offer include forest walks, boating, fishing and cruising, a bog garden and picnic sites, a caravan park and camping area. Also within the park are the ruins of a McDermott castle and two medieval priories, each standing on its own island in the lake. Guided tours for groups around the park are available by arrangement.

West of Boyle, about 3 miles along the R294, stands the **Drumanone Dolmen**, one of the largest in Ireland with an immense capstone 12 feet long and 9 feet wide. There are more prehistoric remains on nearby Lough Gara where no fewer than 300 *crannógs* have been found. These man-made islands were used by Iron Age farmers as refuges for themselves and their cattle. Astonishingly, some of them remained in use until the early 1600s. The excavations which uncovered these artificial islands also retrieved 31 dug-out wooden boats from the bottom of the lake.

Keadue

34 miles N of Roscommon on the R285

Surrounded by picturesque countryside at the southern end of the Arigna Mountains, is Keadue village which is so beautifully maintained by its residents that it was designated the tidiest town in the whole of Ireland in 1999. It was at Keadue that the last of the Irish bards, Turlough O'Carolan, spent his final years. He died in 1733 and is buried in the ancient cemetery at Kilronan close to the shore of Lough Meelagh. Inside the ruined church is a modern memorial to the blind harpist who is credited with having composed the melody of The Star Spangled Banner. An **O'Carolan Festival** is held over the August Bank Holiday with traditional folk and harp music as the basis of the celebration.

HARP & SHAMROCK

Main Street, Keadue, Co. Roscommon
Tel: 071 964 7288 Fax: 071 964 7951
website: www.harpandshamrock.com

Standing on the main street of this picturesque little village, the **Harp & Shamrock** has all the charm and character you could hope for in an authentic Irish hostelry. An open fire, an eclectic mix of vintage seating and walls covered in memorabilia of the village all add to the appeal. Mine host, Ann Roddy, who has been here since 1989, is a busy lady since she also owns the adjacent village shop and petrol station, but she always has time to make her customers feel at home. Sandwiches are served in the evening as well as meals for guests staying in the comfortable 6 bedrooms, one of which is en suite, the others share 3 bathrooms.

Co Sligo

Just as the spirit of Robbie Burns seems omnipresent in southwest Scotland, so it is with the poet WB Yeats in Co. Sligo. He spent his childhood here, the landscapes and ancient myths of Sligo infuse his best poetry and he is buried at Drumcliffe beneath the huge bulk of Benbulben

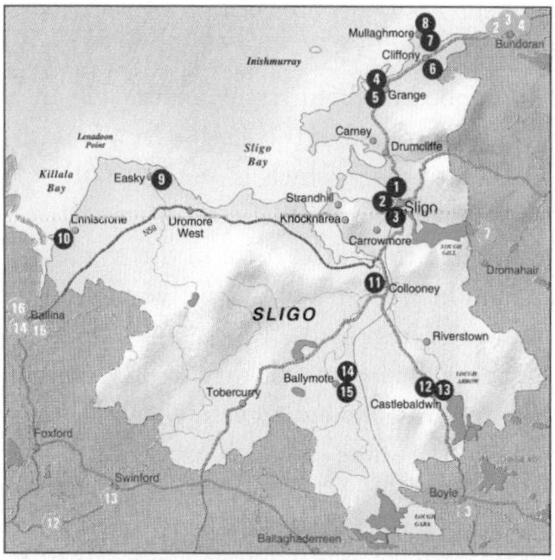

Benbulben

mountain. One of his best-known poems immortalises the lovely lake isle of Innisfree where

"peace comes dropping slow,
Dropping slow from the veil of the morning to
where the cricket sings".

PLACES TO STAY, EAT AND DRINK

Rooftop Restaurant, Sligo	1	Restaurant	p295
Blue Lagoon, Sligo	2	Pub with Food	p295
W.B.Yeats, Sligo	3	Visitor Attraction	p296
John Lang's Bar & Restaurant, Grange	4	Bar & Restaurant	p298
Rowanville Lodge, Grange	5	B&B	p298
The Canavaun Bar, Cliffony	6	Pub with Restaurant	p298
Eithna's Seafood Restaurant, Mullaghmore	7	Restaurant	p299
The Beach Hotel & Leisure Club, Mullaghmore	8	Hotel	p300
The Old Rectory, Easky	9	B&B	p301
The Pilot, Enniscrone	10	Pub with Food	p302
Markree Castle, Collooney	11	Hotel	p303
Cromleach Lodge, Castlebaldwin	12	Hotel	p304
Tower Hill, Castlebaldwin	13	B&B	p305
Higgin's Lounge & Bar, Ballymote	14	Pub with Food	p305
Temple House, Ballymote	15	Hotel	p306

● Denotes entries in other chapters

Co. Sligo is indeed a peaceful place. It came late to the idea of tourism despite possessing magnificent scenery that rivals Killarney and Donegal, a wealth of medieval remains and the largest concentration of megalithic monuments in Ireland. Because visitors are comparatively few the welcome seems even warmer and more heartfelt than in the more frequented areas.

Sligo

Attractively set around the Garavogue River as it flows into Sligo Bay, the county town is the most important in northwest Ireland despite having a population of less than 20,000. The town is well-supplied with traditional inns, music pubs, shops, and its racecourse, on the edge of town, is reckoned to be Ireland's most scenic. There are some pleasant riverside walks and a popular excursion from the town is a boat trip along **Lough Gill** visiting various places en route that have featured in Yeats' poetry, most notably the Isle of Innisfree. The poems are recited at the appropriate sites and the 2½ hour excursion includes a 30-minute stop on the island where there's a craft shop and tea room.

There's also a 24-mile drive around the lake which provides some superb views and rowing boats can be hired from the Blue Lagoon pub at Doorly Park.

In the town itself, there are two cathedrals: the Anglican St John's which dates back to the 14th century and was

Rooftop Restaurant

Wine Street, Sligo, Co. Sligo
Tel: 071 914 4421

Gerry Brady started his **Rooftop Restaurant** in 1998 and has built up a loyal clientele appreciative of the value-for-money fare on offer here. Everything at this self-service-cafeteria style restaurant is freshly prepared and there's a wide choice of dishes with something for everyone, including vegetarians. The menu ranges from all day breakfasts to full lunches, or you can just settle down with a cup of coffee. It's a family-friendly place with a special kids menu available; service is friendly and efficient. The restaurant is open from 9am to 6pm, daily except Sundays and Bank Holidays; and there's a car park close by.

Blue Lagoon

Riverside, Sligo, Co. Sligo
Tel: 071 45407 Fax: 071 44040

Set beside the River Garavogue the **Blue Lagoon** is as traditional an Irish pub as you could hope to find, full of character and charm, and with live music on Saturday and Sunday evenings. Mine host, Peter Henry, has been here for some 40 years now and, amongst other things, is proud of the Blue Lagoon's reputation for serving the finest pint of Guinness in Sligo. Food is available every lunchtime from noon until three – wholesome traditional Irish dishes at value-for-money prices. The real stars here though are Peter and his staff – all friendly, efficient and brilliant at keeping the craic coming!

remodelled in 1730 by Richard Castle, and the Catholic cathedral, a Romanesque-style building completed in 1874.

Sligo Abbey is much older and has endured a more unfortunate history than most such ecclesiastical buildings. Founded in 1252 by Maurice Fitzgerald, Earl of Kildare, the Abbey was destroyed by fire in 1414. It was painstakingly rebuilt but some 220 years later was badly damaged during the sack of Sligo in the rebellion of 1641. The nave, choir and central transept have survived as have some striking 15th century carvings. The grassed inner area, surrounded by arched cloisters, is a peaceful place for meditation or even a picnic.

Sligo Town has many connections with Ireland's greatest poet, an association most dramatically symbolised by the eye-catching modern **Statue of W.B. Yeats** in the town centre which shows him in a serpentine pose with his jacket splayed out like a cobra's hood (see panel below). There's more Yeats material on view at the **Model Arts Centre and Niland Gallery** but here it is the work of Jack Yeats, the poet's brother and the best known Irish painter of the 20th century. His paintings and drawings drew heavily on scenes from Celtic myth and everyday Irish life and the ones on display here have a potent local flavour. Other artists featured include Paul Henry and George Russell, better known as AE. The Centre also hosts three festivals each year: the **Scíobh Literary Festival** in September, an **Early Music Festival** in October and a **Contemporary Music Festival** in November.

About a mile west of the town, **Woodville Farm** will appeal to children with its resident peacocks, pigs, sheep, lambs and hens. There's also a pleasant woodland nature trail.

Immediately north of Sligo town is Rosses Point, a truly beautiful seaside village resort boasting a Blue Flag beach. Out in the bay beyond the point is **Coney Island,** so named because of its multitudinous rabbits. It was the inspiration for naming the pleasure park near New York which was built on ground also infested with rabbits. Out in the channel is the **Metal Man** which marks the deep water channel into Sligo harbour. It was installed there in 1822 and described by Yeats as "the only Rosses Point man who never told a lie".

W.B. Yeats

Sligo, Co. Sligo

Sligo Town has many connections with Ireland's greatest poet, an association most dramatically symbolised by the eye-catching modern **Statue of W.B. Yeats** in the town centre which shows him in a serpentine pose with his jacket splayed out like a cobra's hood.

He is also celebrated in the Yeats Memorial Building, across the river from the Abbey, which houses both the **Sligo County Museum** and the **Yeats Memorial Museum**. They are both small but crammed with interesting items. The County Museum has some fascinating photographs of old Sligo, a display of appealing 19th century sketches and a remarkable 800-year-old firkin of bog butter. The Yeats Museum has many photographs of, and letters by, the poet and the Nobel Prize medal awarded him in 1923 is also on show.

A more academic approach to Yeats is pursued at the headquarters of the Yeats Society, just down the road at Douglas Hyde Bridge, which is the venue for the annual Yeats International Summer School.

North of Sligo

Drumcliffe

4 miles N of Sligo on the N15

Drumcliffe, at the northern end of Rosses Point, is dominated by the mighty ramparts of **Benbulben,** 1730 feet high, its summit as often as not clouded in mist. A monastery was founded here by St Columba in the 6th century and two probable relics from it are the stump of a round tower struck by lightning in 1396 and a 10th century cross. Thirteen feet high, the cross is carved with scenes depicting both Old and New Testament scenes, the only one so decorated in the country.

But the majority of visitors come to visit **Drumcliff Church** and the Visitor Centre in the **Drumcliffe Teahouse** which is dedicated to Ireland's greatest poet. WB Yeats had asked to be buried here, in sight of his beloved Benbulben mountain. In the small churchyard of the plain 19th century church, a simple stone slab marks the **Grave of WB Yeats**. It is inscribed with the epitaph taken from the last poem he wrote:

Cast a cold Eye
On Life, on Death.
Horseman, pass by.

Drumcliff Church

Carney

6 miles N of Sligo on minor road off the N15

Close to the villages of Drumcliffe and Carney is **Lissadell House**, another location closely associated with Yeats who often visited the Gore-Booth family here. The Gore-Booths still live in this fine but austere mansion in the Greek Revival style. The square two storeyed mansion is full of many artefacts gathered by successive generations of the Gore-Booth family displayed in a rather melancholy atmosphere of faded grandeur. Two daughters of the Gore-Booth family were involved in the 1916 rising, one of them, Constance Markiewicz later being condemned to death. Somewhat to her annoyance she was pardoned and went on to become the first British female MP in 1918 and later Minister of Labour in the Dáil's first cabinet. A famous poem by Yeats recalls the two girls at Lissadell:

Light of evening Lissadell
Great windows, open to the south,
Two girls in silk kimonos, both
Beautiful, one a gazelle.

Grange

9 miles N of Sligo on the N15

Lying to the west of Benbulben mountain, the quiet village of Grange was once part of the estate of the 19th century British Prime Minister, Lord Palmerston. To the west of the village the beach is sheltered by the long narrow strip of Streedagh Point. Here, in 1588, three galleons of the Spanish Armada foundered and 1100 bodies were washed ashore. It's said that when the tide is unusually low remains of a ship can

John Lang's Bar & Restaurant

Main Street, Grange, Co. Sligo

Tel/Fax: 071 9163105

The name over the door says **John Lang's** but everyone knows it locally as Burke's, after its owners John and Helen, who have been here some 20 years. John's father had worked here since the 1940's. Built in the mid-1700s, Lang's offers a fascinating blend of old and new – in addition to being a fine old traditional pub it's one of the few remaining genuine Bar/Grocers left in Ireland. Its also an off-licence and undertakers. Good old-fashioned dishes dominate the menu, available daily from 12.30pm to 9pm. The menu is extensive, the portions generous and the prices modest.

Rowanville Lodge

Donegal Road, Grange, Co. Sligo

Tel: 07191 63958

e-mail: Rowanville@hotmail.com

web: www.littleireland.ie/rowanvillelodge.

Enjoying grand views of the Benbulben hills, **Rowanville Lodge** is an impressive modern building with a feature conservatory entrance standing in a spacious garden.

It's the home of Patricia and Matty Hoey who have lived here for some 20 years and make their bed & breakfast guests feel equally at home. There are 3 guest bedrooms (1 triple, 1 double), all en suite and equipped with TV and hospitality tray. An excellent breakfast is included in the tariff; there's ample parking space, and credit cards are accepted. Rowan Villa Lodge is open from March to September.

occasionally be seen. A small park in the village commemorates those who lost their lives.

Cliffony

18 miles N of Sligo on the N15

This trim little village is best known for the

The Canavaun Bar

Donegal Road, Cliffoney, Co. Sligo

Tel: 071 916 6123

The Canavaun Bar has been a family pub since the late 1800s and is now run by Declan Harrison and his mother. Recently redecorated, it's a smart-looking place with a spacious beer garden and a quaint little restaurant offering modern Irish cuisine. Everything on the award-winning menu is freshly prepared and there's a good choice of pizzas which are also available to take away. Food is served from 5.30pm to 10pm daily, except Mondays unless it's a Bank Holiday. The Canavaun hosts live music at weekends and, as we go to press, plans are under way to provide accommodation. Credit cards are accepted and there's ample parking space.

Creevykeel Court Tomb

beach which in 1995 was proclaimed the "best, safest and cleanest in Ireland". From the promontory at Mullaghmore there are some glorious views across Donegal Bay and from the little harbour boats can be hired for the 4-mile trip to **Inishmurray Island**. The last inhabitants of this tiny island, about a mile long and half as wide, gave up the struggle to survive here in 1947 but the deserted island has some interesting antiquities, amongst them one of the country's earliest Christian churches. A great cashel – a wall of uncemented stones – surrounds a group of ruins that includes three beehive cells, three altars and the Well of St Molaise. Even older than the church is the group of rounded stones known as the Cursing Stones. To be effective, you have to turn the stone anti-clockwise as you pronounce your curse. There are about 40 of the stones but an old tradition asserts that nobody has

nearby **Creevykeel Court Tomb** which dates from around 3000 BC and is regarded as one of the finest in Ireland. Upright stones surround a circular court and opposite the entrance are two burial chambers flanked by a wedge-shaped mound of stone.

Mullaghmore

21 miles N of Sligo on the R279

Mullaghmore is an attractive little place with an excellent, safe and sandy Blue Flag

Eithna's Seafood Restaurant

The Harbour, Mullaghmore, Co. Sligo
Tel: 07191 66407
e-mail: eithnaseafood@eircom.net
website: www.eithnaseafood.com

Lovers of seafood can be confident that the fish served at **Eithna's Seafood Restaurant,** located right on the harbour, is really fresh since it will have been caught by local fishermen including your host Phillipe Huel who, together with his wife Eithna, founded this outstanding restaurant in 1990. Eithna supervises the kitchen and, naturally specialises in dishes such as Lobster Thermidor, Donegal Bay prawns, Lissadell mussels and seafood platter. But the menu also offers a choice of meat dishes and a vegetarian Dish of the Day. The home-made desserts are superb and there's a good choice of wines to accompany your meal.

THE BEACH HOTEL & LEISURE CLUB

The Harbour, Mullaghmore, Co. Sligo
Tel: 071 916 6103 Fax: 071 916 6448
website: beachhotelmullaghmore.com

The Beach Hotel & Leisure Club occupies a splendid position overlooking the harbour with grand views of the mountains, beach and Atlantic Ocean. The hotel is well known for its superb cuisine with à la carte, table d'hôte, bar food and fish menus to choose from. To complement your meal, there's an extensive wine list. The hotel has 27 guest rooms, all en suite with direct dial phone, colour TV, hairdryer and hospitality tray. There are also

5 self-catering units. The extensive facilities include a 15 metre heated indoor swimming pool, sauna, steam room, Jacuzzi, hi-tech gym, beauty salon – and an off-licence!

succeeded in counting them twice in succession and coming up with the same number.

West of Sligo

Knocknarea

3 miles W of Sligo off the R292

The walk to the summit of **Knocknarea Mountain** follows a track of strangely moulded limestone with wild flowers growing on either side. At the top rises Medh's Cairn, a huge tower of weather-beaten stones, 33 feet high and 19 feet wide, which is reputed to be the burial place of Maeve, Queen of Connaught. She is believed to have lived around the time of Christ but the cairn is considerably older than that, probably dating from the Bronze Age.

Strandhill

4 miles W of Sligo on the R292

Knocknarea Mountain provides a wonderful backdrop for the popular sea resort of Strandhill where the firm sandy beach stretches for miles and the huge Atlantic breakers attract many bodysurfers, especially over the first weekend in August when the Sligo Open Surfing Championship is held here. Ordinary swimming in the sea

here, however, is not advisable; for a safe swim just walk around the headland to the beach at Cullenamore.

To the southwest of Strandhill there are huge sand dunes and any pebbles you find on the beach may well contain fossil remains. To the east is Sligo's little airport where you can watch small Aer Lingus planes skimming the top of Knocknarea before landing. At the end of the airstrip stands the 10th century **Killaspugbone Church**, reached by way of the beach. It's said that St Patrick tripped on the threshold here and lost a tooth. The tooth was preserved and later enclosed in an exquisite casket, the Fiacal Pádraig, which is now in the National Museum in Dublin although the tooth itself has disappeared.

Co. Sligo has made something of a speciality of seaweed baths. **Celtic Seaweed Baths** has recently revived a Strandhill tradition which prospered throughout the 19th century right up until 1966. Now visitors can once again enjoy a 20-minute soak covered with seaweed as they absorb the minerals and trace elements which, it is claimed, help relieve the symptoms of rheumatism and arthritis, and are useful in the treatment of some circulatory problems. Therapeutic massages and aromatherapy sessions are also available.

Dromore West

20 miles W of Sligo on the N59

Dromore is a picturesque village set on the wooded banks of the river with a terraced waterfall nearby. Pleasant though it is, the area has some sombre memories. **Culkin's Emigration Museum** relives a poignant era when for most people in this part of Ireland emigration was the only hope of a better life. The museum stands on the site of what was once the Shipping and Emigration Agency run by the local draper, Daniel Culkin, to assist local people find a passage to the Americas. Founded in the mid-19th century, the Agency continued to operate right up until the 1930s. The purpose-built modern museum contains some interesting artefacts and features, including the original draper's shop itself.

Easky

24 miles W of Sligo on the R297

The Atlantic rollers crashing onto the beach here have made Easky a favourite spot for surfers – the Surfing Association's Tiki Cold Water Classic is held here over the last weekend in September and the resort has also hosted the national surfing championships. Easky stands at the mouth of the river of the same name which is noted for its abundant salmon and Martello towers at each end of the village are relics of the coastal defences erected during the Napoleonic wars. An earlier defensive building is Rosalee Castle, a former stronghold of the MacDonells, which stands beside the river. About a mile south of Easky, the **Split Rock** is an impressive 10 feet high which ended up here either as

THE OLD RECTORY

Easkey, Co. Sligo
Tel/Fax: 096 49181
e-mail: adlib@eircom.net

Excellent bed & breakfast accommodation in a home-from-home ambiance is to be found at **The Old Rectory**, located just 5 minutes from Easkey's famous surfing beach. This fine old Georgian building, its walls now smothered in Virginia creeper, dates back to 1790. It stands in secluded private walled gardens well-stocked with mature trees and plants, and with a flower garden, formal style vegetable garden and a recently established orchard. There's also some interesting fauna in the form of sheep, hens, donkeys, cats and dogs.

The charming old building is the home of Lorely and Robert Forrester who work as writer/ designer/artists and have filled their house with lots of pictures, books and china. They have 3 guest bedrooms, all doubles with one containing an

additional single bed, and there is a bathroom and shower room for guests' use. A full Irish breakfast is included in the tariff and guests eat together in a friendly *en famille* atmosphere. Easkey village offers pubs, a village shop, an Indian restaurant, Catholic and Protestant churches, a famous salmon river and, of course, the well-known surfing beach. If surfing isn't your thing, there are sandy beaches nearby, salmon and trout fishing, an excellent golf course at Enniscrone, just 6 miles away, good walking in the Ox Mountains and a picturesque coastline to explore.

THE PILOT

Main Street, Enniscrone, Co. Sligo
Tel: 096 36131

Close to the beach and the famous Enniscrone golf club, **The Pilot** is a friendly family pub run by the brother and sister team of Sean and Anne Gilroy. Recently redecorated, it has lots of sailing memorabilia around the walls and a cosy, welcoming atmosphere. As well as a really good pint of Guinness (and other beverages), The Pilot serves excellent home-made food, including fresh fish and outstanding soups, at value-for-money prices. In good weather you can enjoy your refreshments at picnic tables overlooking the main street. Food is served from 1pm to 9pm in summer; 5pm to 9pm in winter.

glacial detritus or because it was thrown some 14 miles from the Ox Mountains by Finn MacCool. According to legend, if anyone passes through the split three times the rock will close on them.

Enniscrone

32 miles W of Sligo on the R297

This popular resort with a sweeping 3-mile-long Blue Flag beach, surfing school and a fine golf course lies close to the Co. Mayo border overlooking Killala Bay and the scenic north Mayo coastline. The town became celebrated for its invigorating hot seaweed baths which can still be experienced at the splendidly Edwardian establishment of **Kilcullen's Bath House.** Patrons immerse themselves in a huge porcelain bath under a blanket of slithery seaweed fronds then rinse off the iodine-rich chocolate-coloured brew with a cold shower. A cup of strong tea in the pleasant tea-room rounds off the experience.

South & East of Sligo

Carrowmore

2 miles S of Sligo off the N4

Only a couple of miles south of Sligo stands one of the most important prehistoric sites in Europe, the **Carrowmore Megalithic Cemetery.** Scattered across the green fields at the foot of **Knocknarea Mountain** are more than 60 dolmens, standing stones and stone circles. The oldest of them were erected around 4000 BC, several hundred years before Stonehenge was built. It's believed that more than half the stones have been removed but Carrowmore is still the second largest megalithic site in Europe after Carnac in Brittany. Incredibly, a plan was mooted in 1983 to turn the site into a rubbish tip. The site is still being excavated each summer by a Swedish archaeological team who in 1999 confirmed that they had

Carrowmore Megalithic Cemetery

found the oldest tomb in Western Europe here, more than 7000 years old. A restored cottage nearby houses an interesting exhibition relating to the site and the excavations.

Collooney

6 miles S of Sligo on the N4

Close to the small town of Collooney, the Owenmore and Unshin rivers combine to force their way through the Collooney Gap between the Ox Mountains and Slieve Daeane. It was near here, during the rebellion of 1798, that a single strategically placed English gun held at bay a combined Franco-Irish force until one of the French officers, the Irish-born Bartholomew Teeling, charged up the hill and shot the gunner dead. The **Teeling Monument** just north of Collooney commemorates this reckless act of bravery. Teeling was later captured by the English and hanged at Dublin.

Collooney's most impressive building is undoubtedly **Markree Castle** (*see panel below*). Now a luxury hotel, the castle overlooks the River Unshin and is approached by a mile-long driveway. It's a stunning sight with its turrets and battlemented towers, two storey oriel windows and arched gatehouse of stone weathered to the colour of pale honey – a complex of glorious buildings surrounded by lush parkland and woods. The oldest parts of the castle date back to 1640 when it was built by the Cooper family. The building was later extended greatly in Victorian times. A magnificent stained-glass window at the top of an impressive oak staircase inside the castle traces the Cooper family tree from the days of King John to the present.

Riverstown

14 miles SE of Sligo on minor road off the N4 or R284

Hidden away in the heart of the south Sligo countryside, the **Sligo Folk Park** at Riverstown is appropriately located for its celebration of the county's rural heritage. One of the highlights is Mrs Buckley's Cottage which is claimed to be the "world's most travelled cottage" since it has been transported to such faraway places as New York. The main Museum and Exhibition Hall contains a fine collection of rural history and agricultural artefacts and the building also hosts regularly changing exhibitions and special events throughout the year. There are also craft workshops, a craft shop, nature trail and a country garden whose home grown vegetables are put to

MARKREE CASTLE

Collooney, Co. Sligo
Tel: 071 67800 e-mail: markree@iol.ie
website: www.markreecastle.ie

The most striking building in Collooney, **Markree Castle** is a unique and spectacular place in which to dine or, even better, spend a few days. The dramatic Victorian Gothic façade conceals a 15th century castle, home of the Cooper family for hundreds of years. Great staircases, carved panelling and vast fireplaces are just some of the impressive features, while the dining room with its ornate mirrors, gilt cherubs and rococo plasterwork will make any occasion seem special. The authentic country house cooking is

complemented by an exceptionally good wine list. Guests can relax in the elegant drawing room with its twin fireplaces and lovely views over the old parterre.

Cromleach Lodge

Castlebaldwin, (via Boyle), Co. Sligo
Tel: 071 916 5155 Fax: 071 916 5455
e-mail: info@cromleach.com
website: www.cromleach.com

Hidden away in the quiet, softly-rolling hills just above Lough Arrow and with the Carrowkeel Cairns in the background, **Cromleach Lodge** is deservedly famed for its wonderful cuisine, splendid accommodation and excellent service. Purpose-built, the Lodge was designed to take full advantage of the wonderful views – every room looks out onto a panoramic scene and the elegant conservatory stretching the length of the building allows guests and diners to sit at leisure and savour the scenery laid out before them.

Just as outstanding is the cuisine on offer here. Moira Tighe, a former Irish Chef of the Year, and her female team of chefs have established a reputation that has travelled far beyond the borders of Co. Sligo. Moira describes their cooking as modern Irish with an emphasis on lightness. They use local organic produce and offer a different menu each evening. Residents can sample the 'Gourmet Tasting Menu' which comprises 6 courses – light portions but intense flavours. For other diners, the 4-course menu offers 5 choices within each course and, as you would expect from a good menu, there are usually fish, meat, poultry, game and vegetarian options. To accompany your meal, you'll find a selection of 100 wines to choose from. The restaurant is open daily from 7pm to 8.30pm (Monday to Saturday); from 6.30pm to 8pm on Sunday. Booking is essential.

The hotel has 3 separate dining areas, allowing guests to feel intimate and secluded. All of these are non-smoking but smoking is permitted in one of the lounges. The Lodge also has a private room which is available for small groups or for family use – children over 7 are welcome in the evening.

The accommodation at Cromleach Lodge maintains the same high standards evident throughout the hotel. There are 10 spacious mini-suite bedrooms each with its own subtle décor carefully chosen by Moira to complement the natural beauty of the landscape. Amenities include TV, mini-bar and hospitality tray. The hotel also has a 'Board Room' which is available for conference or meetings for up to 14 people.

Cromleach Lodge is open from 1 February to 1 November; all major credit cards are accepted but debit cards are not.

Tower Hill

Castlebaldwin, (via Boyle), Co. Sligo
Tel: 071 9666021
e-mail: murielg@gofree.indigo.ie

Conveniently located on the N4 about one mile south of Castlebaldwin, **Tower Hill** stands on the hillside overlooking scenic Lough Arrow. This smart modern farmhouse is the home of Ivan and Muriel Gardiner who run the working mixed farm here and have lived at Tower Hill for more than 30 years. They offer quality bed & breakfast accommodation with four attractive and comfortable rooms available, all of them en suite. There's a residents' lounge with TV and Muriel serves a hearty breakfast. Evening meals and packed lunches are also available if required and there is plenty of parking space.

good use in the Folk Park Coffee Shop & Restaurant.

On the first weekend in August, the village hosts the **James Morrison Traditional Music Festival,** named after the celebrated fiddler who was born in nearby Drumfin in 1893.

Castlebaldwin

18 miles SE of Sligo on the N4

This little town at the foot of the Bricklieve Mountains also lies close to the shore of **Lough Arrow**, a charming spot where the many wooded islands provide a contrast to the bare hills all around. Rowing boats are available to hire. A circular drive around the lake will take you through Ballinafad where there are the ruins of a 16th century castle built to a 13th century design, and also the **National Field Study Centre**. Here visitors can join a guided tour, or take a self-guided tour, over the Sligo Way, the Miners' Way, or the Historical Trail.

From Castlebaldwin village a hillside walk leads to the ancient **Carrowkeel Cemetery,** part of an important Bronze Age settlement which contains 14 cairns, several dolmens and cruciform passage graves, and more than 50 remnants of stone foundations. It's possible to enter one of the roofed tombs where the sun strikes directly into the passage on Midsummer Day, 21st June. Even if prehistoric remains don't excite you, it's worth climbing the hill to enjoy the magnificent panoramic view of Co. Sligo.

Ballymote

14 miles S of Sligo on the R293

This busy little market town is noted as a centre for some of the best coarse fishing in

Higgin's Lounge & Bar

nr Ballymote, Co. Sligo
Tel: 07191 82033

Well hidden away in the countryside, **Higgin's Lounge & Bar** is a popular village pub with a very Irish atmosphere. Tom and Elizabeth Higgins have been here for almost 30 years and have made their pub the centre of village life – there's even a small shop attached. Guinness fans will find that Tom pulls a perfect pint and if you want something to accompany it, some superb sandwiches are available. The lounge is huge – "big enough for a basketball game" – and provides a great setting for the live music sessions held every weekend. The pub is open all day, every day; credit cards are accepted and there's ample parking.

Temple House

Ballymote, Co. Sligo
Tel: 071 9183329 Fax: 071 9183808
e-mail: accom@templehouse.ie
website: www.templehouse.ie

Occupying a beautiful position overlooking Temple House Lake and surrounded by 1000 acres of farm and woodland, **Temple House** is a dignified Georgian mansion offering stylish accommodation in gracious surroundings. The Perceval family have lived here since 1665 and although the house was redesigned and refurnished in 1864 it has retained its ambiance of times past with turf and log fires and some guest rooms with canopied beds.

There are 5 double bedrooms, all centrally heated and with private bathroom, and one single room with shower. The house is delightfully decorated throughout with period furniture and family portraits on the walls. No perfumes please. Closed 30th Nov-1st April.

the country and also boasts a 9-hole golf course and tennis courts. In the 1300s, Richard de Burgo, Earl of Ulster, built a keepless **Castle** of great strength here. His stronghold later passed through many hands, including those of the O'Conors, the MacDermots, the MacDonaghs and, in 1598, the O'Donnells. Red Hugh O'Donnell marched from here to the Battle of Kinsale in 1601. The impressive square structure has round towers at each corner of the 10 feet thick curtain walls, and D-shaped towers in the middle of its east and west walls.

Just outside the town, Temple House is now a hotel but was originally founded by the Knights Templar in the 1300s, expanded in 1560 and comprehensively refurbished in High Victorian style in 1864. One of the most imposing Anglo-Irish mansions ever built, Temple House stands in a lovely 950-acre estate; its restaurant is open to non-residents for dinner.

Also of interest in Ballymote are the remains of the Franciscan friary where the 14th century *Book of Ballymote* was written. Now preserved in the National Irish Academy, the *Book of Ballymote* provided a wealth of historical information and also supplied the key to deciphering the ancient Celtic script known as Ogham. Ogham flourished from the 4th to the 7th centuries AD and is often found carved into the sides of standing stones of that period. Depicted by varying strokes and notches, the Ogham alphabet contained 20 different characters and, unusually, was read from the bottom upwards.

Tobercurry

19 miles SW of Sligo on the N17

Often spelt *Tubbercurry*, this trim market town is well off the tourist trails but fills up with visitors in mid-July when it hosts the **South Sligo Summer School** devoted to traditional Irish music. There are plenty of concerts and pub sessions, set dancing, traditional singing, and classes in various instruments.

Co Tipperary

Tipperary is the most extensive of Ireland's inland counties and also the most prosperous. The county's wealth derives from the undramatic central Golden Vale, a limestone plain that is prime beef and dairy cattle territory, 'planted' with Cromwell's soldiers after his conquest of the country. The Golden Vale is bounded by mountain ranges, the finest of which are the Comeragh and Galtee mountains, and the Glen of Aherlow, but perhaps the most striking landscape feature is the dramatic Rock of Cashel which rises abruptly from the central plain. Its summit is crowned by a wonderful succession of medieval towers, turrets and spires, and the Rock's historic associations with St Patrick and King Brian Boru have made Cashel the most visited site not just in Tipperary but in the whole of Ireland.

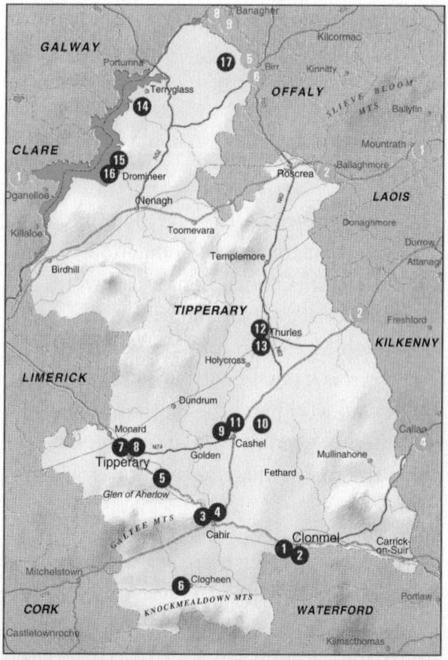

PLACES TO STAY, EAT AND DRINK

Barne Lodge, Clonmel	1	Pub with Food	p308
Benny's Café, Clonmel	2	Café	p308
Killaun, Cahir	3	B&B	p311
The Galtee Inn, Cahir	4	Pub with Restaurant	p311
O'Heney's Bar & Restaurant, Bansha	5	Bar & Restaurant	p312
Ballyboy House, Clogheen	6	B&B	p313
Brown Trout, Tipperary	7	Restaurant	p314
Ballyglass Coutry House Hotel, Tipperary	8	Hotel	p314
Hill House Guest House, Cashel	9	Guest House	p315
Chestnuts, Cashel	10	B&B	p316
Rock of Cashel, Cashel	11	Historic Site	p317
The Castle, Thurles	12	B&B	p317
Horse & Jockey Inn, Thurles	13	Pub, Restaurant & Accommodation	p318
Coolangatta Country House, Nenagh	14	B&B	p320
Whiskey Still, Nenagh	15	Pub with Food	p320
Otway Lodge, Nenagh	16	Guest House	p321
Ardagh House, Killenaule	17	Pub, Food & Accommodation	p322

● Denotes entries in other chapters

The county can also boast some enchanting towns, Clonmel for example; one of the country's largest and best preserved castles at Cahir; and a uniquely beautiful Tudor mansion, Ormond Castle, at Carrick-on-Suir. We begin our survey of the county where most visitors tend to begin: in the southeast.

Clonmel

The county town of Tipperary and its largest settlement with a population of around 13,000 Clonmel enjoys a lovely riverside setting looking across to the Comeragh Mountains of Co. Waterford. The town is a great centre for the greyhound world and the elegant animals can often be seen as they are exercised along the roads, much as racehorses are in Kildare.

A goodly portion of Clonmel's medieval town walls still survive around **St Mary's Church**, a Protestant church with a striking octagonal tower. Although it looks medieval, the West Gate which arches across Main Street was actually rebuilt in 1831 on the site of the earlier gate. The most imposing building in Clonmel is the **Main Guard** in O'Connell Street, said to have been built to a design of Christopher Wren for the main guard of the garrison. Currently being restored, the façade bears two panels dated 1675 showing the coats of arms of the town and of the Palatinate of Ormonde, an administrative district that was dissolved in 1715.

Clonmel's **Town Hall** has a display of civic regalia which includes the mayor's gold chain to which each incumbent adds a new link. A former mayor of Clonmel, an

BARNE LODGE

Cahir Road, Clonmel, Co. Tipperary
Tel: 052 22849 Fax: 052 88281

Once a roadside coaching inn and dating back to the early 1700s, **Barne Lodge** has moved with the times while still retaining a classic traditional atmosphere. Mine hosts Elaine and Del Kirwan arrived here in 2001 and have comprehensively upgraded the Lodge's amenities and are currently planning to add a separate restaurant. Currently, you can enjoy wholesome home cooked food in the bar with dishes based on local lamb, beef and poultry. Food is served throughout the day from

8.30am to 7.30pm; (9pm on Friday, Saturday and Sunday). At weekends, the Lodge hosts popular live music sessions. Credit cards are accepted and there's ample parking.

BENNY'S CAFÉ

O'Connell Mall, Clonmel, Co. Tipperary
Tel: 052 26441

With its wide variety of shops, O'Connell Mall is the place to shop until you drop – the place to drop into then is **Benny's Café**, a friendly and welcoming eatery owned and run by Bernadette Scanlon. Bernadette is also the chef and her menu offers an appetising choice of good old traditional favourites such as Shepherd's Pie and Lasagna, along with other hot snacks and all day breakfasts. The value-

for-money dishes are all home cooked from prime, fresh ingredients and promptly served by bubbly and efficient staff. Food is available every day except Sunday from 8am to 5pm.

Italian named Charles Bianconi (1786-1875), established Ireland's first public transport system when he began running his "Bianconi Cars" (horse-drawn open carts) between Clonmel and Cahir in 1815. They departed from Hearns Hotel on Parnell Street where the original clock that timed the system can still be seen. At one period, Bianconi was running up to 100 of his cars at any one time and his achievement is still celebrated with costumed festivities on his birthday, 6th July.

Transportation of a more recent vintage is on display at the **Museum of Transport**, housed in a former mill in the Market Place. The collection is the personal passion of the owner, Michael Lavin, who over the years has gathered together a fascinating group of exhibits, beginning with the earliest motorised vehicles. Motoring fans will also find a wealth of automobile memorabilia, traffic signs, garage equipment, books and posters.

Clonmel boasts an interesting clutch of literary associations. Laurence Sterne, author of the inimitable *Tristram Shandy*, was born here in 1715; Anthony Trollope worked for a while in the local post office; and George Borrow (1803-81) went to school here.

An unusual, if not unique, attraction at Clonmel is the weekend evening entertainment **Celebrated Tipperary Trials**. These are staged in the former Courthouse where the trials originally took place and each performance depicts a different trial, based on dialogue from the official court transcripts and newspaper reports of the time. The show also includes a presentation of the history of Tipperary in song, dance and story. Tickets are available from the Clonmel tourist office and the admission price includes pre-performance refreshments as well as a sample of the famous local cider.

Around Clonmel

Carrick-on-Suir

12 miles E of Clonmel on the N24

A thriving market town today, Carrick was founded in 1640 by the Duke of Ormonde whose family, the Butlers, had for generations made this area their stronghold. It was an earlier Duke, "Black Tom" Ormonde, who in the 1560s built the superb Elizabethan fortified mansion known as **Ormonde Castle.** "Black Tom" reputedly built the house in expectation of a visit from Elizabeth I, a visit which never came about. The first completely unfortified great house in Ireland, Ormonde Castle is regarded as the finest example of a Tudor manor house in the country, its State Rooms elegantly embellished with decorative plasterwork, including plasterwork portraits. The Long Gallery has a magnificent carved fireplace which adorned Kilkenny Castle for many years before being returned to Ormonde when the house was restored in the 1990s. An old tradition claims that Anne Boleyn was born at the castle but this has never been authenticated. Ormonde Castle

Carrick-on-Suir

is open daily from mid-June to September and the optional guided tours are strongly recommended.

Carrick town itself, although a pleasant enough place, has little else to encourage the visitor to stay although devotees of local history might like to spend an hour or so in the **Heritage Centre** which occupies the former Protestant church. The Centre's prize exhibit is the 17th century church silver presented to the parish by the 3rd Duke of Ormonde.

Cycling enthusiasts will be pleased to note that Carrick's minuscule main square has been renamed after the champion cyclist Sean Kelly who was born in the town.

Just outside Carrick, at Ballynoran, is one of the county's major visitor attractions, **Tipperary Crystal Craft**. Housed in two thatched cottages, the display area and factory lie close to the banks of the Suir River, opposite an ancient tower house. Visitors can watch glass being created by the age-old hand craft method – a skilful use of mouth, hand and timber moulds. In addition to a show room and retail shop where you can view and buy the beautiful crystal items, there are also restaurant facilities and a bureau de change. The site is open daily all year, (no demonstrations on weekdays), and admission is free.

Five miles north of Carrick, the little village of **Ahenny** is worth a short detour to see the two beautiful high crosses in the churchyard. Dating back to the 8th century they are unusual examples of the transitional style between the austere simplicity of the early Christian shaft crosses and the much more elaborately carved crosses seen at Monasterboice and Kells.

Mullinahone

15 miles NE of Clonmel on the R690

North of Carrick the N76 crosses a range of hills, of which Slievenamon (719 feet) is the loftiest, then drops into the valley of the River Anner. Mullinahone sits beside the river, a small village best known for its associations with the writer and patriot Charles Joseph Kickham (1828-1882) whose most celebrated novel, *Knocknagow*, is based on rural life in this corner of Co. Tipperary in Victorian times. A plaque marks the house in Fethard Street where he lived and a Celtic cross stands over his grave beside the Catholic church.

Fethard

10 miles N of Clonmel on the R689/R692

It was back in 1376 that Edward I granted the important little town of Fethard the right to build a town wall. Considerable segments of that wall and one of the gatehouses still stand – the rest of it was demolished by Cromwell in 1650. The town also boasts a 14th century Augustinian abbey, many of whose beautiful arches have survived, as has an interesting collection of gravestones. Another ruin, that of the Templars Castle, can only be reached through the Castle Inn. Fethard also has a charming old church with a square tower and some striking 15th century windows.

Open every Sunday and at other times by arrangement, the **Fethard Folk, Farm and Transport Museum** is housed in the former railway station, near the old town walls. The museum specialises in transport items but also contains thousands of exhibits connected with the people and farming life of the area. There's an extensive and well-equipped playground and collectors' markets and car boot sales are held every Sunday afternoon.

Cahir

10 miles W of Clonmel on the N24

Beautifully set on the River Suir, this appealing little town is dominated by the magnificent 15th century **Cahir Castle**, one of those which Cromwell's troops "knocked about a bit" but which has recently been superbly restored. The castle stands on a rocky islet in the Suir, its great outer walls enclosing three separate 'wards', the inner one protected by a sturdy gate and portcullis. The Irish chieftain Conor O'Brien was the first to erect a fortress here but the present castle was built as a stronghold of the Butler family, Dukes of Ormonde. The massive structure survived largely unscathed from both the assault of the Earl of Essex in 1599 and of Cromwell in 1647. The castle's attractions include an excellent audio-visual show, "Partly Hidden and Partly Revealed", which introduces visitors to all the major sights of south Tipperary.

The town itself has considerable charm, with colourfully painted houses, a broad main square and many traditional shops looking as if they have not changed for decades. Another attractive feature of the town is that Cahir has always been noted for its lack of religious bigotry – at one time Protestants and Catholics used to worship simultaneously in the now-ruined church with only a curtain wall between them.

A fairly recent addition to Cahir's visitor attractions is the **South-East Regional Craft Centre**, housed in a former granary just off the main square. It contains display, sales and exhibition areas designed to serve as a showcase for the finest craftware from the south-east. The centre also provides training studios, demonstration rooms, audio visual rooms and other amenities to encourage the general development of the

KILLAUN

Clonmel Road, Cahir, Co. Tipperary
Tel: 052 41780
e-mail: killaunbandb@eircom.net
website: www.killaun.com

Located on the Clonmel to Waterford road, the N24, about 5 minutes from Cahir, **Killaun** is a delightful detached bungalow surrounded by lovely mature gardens. It's the home of Mrs Jo Doyle who has lived here for some 20 years and provides quality bed & breakfast accommodation, all year round, in three charming guest bedrooms, all en suite and equipped with TV and hospitality tray. Jo has recently spent some 11,000 euros on completely refurbishing the house which is quite immaculate. Golfers, in particular, will find themselves especially welcome at Killaun since Jo is also an enthusiastic golfer.

THE GALTEE INN

The Square, Cahir, Co. Tipperary
Tel: 052 41247 Fax: 052 42638

Dating from the early 1800s and a local landmark for almost 200 years, **The Galtee Inn** is the most popular hostelry in this busy town. It's owned and run by John Malone who has been here for some 32 years and comes from a long line of publicans. He has just finished a complete refurbishment of the pub and it looks very smart with its dark wood tables and chairs. There's a long, narrow bar that leads to an elegant restaurant serving honest-to-goodness authentic home-cooked Irish cuisine – the steaks are especially famous! The appetising food is served every day from noon until 10pm.

craft sector in the region.

The famous Regency architect, John Nash, has two strong connections with Cahir. St Paul's Church was built around 1820 to one of his designs and a very different kind of structure, also designed by him, stands just outside the town on the Clonmel road. (It can also be reach by a 1-mile footpath that starts near the car park of Cahir Castle). The **Swiss Cottage** is an interesting oddity, a delightful thatched "cottage orné" built in the early 1800s for Richard Butler, 1st Earl of Glengall. Recently restored, the interior of this rustic summerhouse contains a graceful spiral staircase and some elegantly decorated rooms. The original hand-painted wallpaper in the Salon, manufactured by the Dufour factory, is one of the first commercially produced Parisian wallpapers. The Cottage is open from March to November; access is by guided tour only.

Also within easy reach of Cahir is **Mitchelstown Cave**, just off the N8 road to Mitchelstown. Visitors are guided through almost half a mile of incredible drip-stone formations – stalagmites, stalactites, huge calcite columns and one of Europe's finest columns, the inspiring Tower of Babel which stands some 30 feet high. There are three massive caverns, one of them measuring 200x160 feet. The cave is open daily throughout the year.

Glen of Aherlow
16 miles W of Clonmel off the N24

In ancient times the lovely Glen of Aherlow, which spreads in a gentle crescent between the Galtee Mountains and the wooded ridge of Slievenamuck, was an important pass between the plains of Counties Tipperary and Limerick. Many battles were fought over this strategic route but today the Glen is a wonderfully scenic and peaceful place. There are some spectacular views, particularly the one about a mile north of Newtown. The scenery can also be enjoyed from the R663 which runs close to the River Aherlow for much of the Glen's 8-mile length.

Clogheen
14 miles SW of Clonmel on the R668

Clogheen is best known as the northern terminus of the **Vee Road** which zig-zags its way through the Knockmealdown Mountains, opening up some spectacular views en route of which the most famous is the panoramic vista from the Vee Gap on Sugarloaf Hill. The road takes its name from the excruciatingly tight hairpin, or V-bend, on the ascent of this hill. About 4 miles west

O'HENEY'S BAR & RESTAURANT

Bansha, Co. Tipperary
Tel: 062 54255

A traditional pub with good food, regular music sessions, guest rooms and self-catering accommodation, **O'Heney's Bar & Restaurant** has it all. Landlord Eamon O'Heney is a larger than life character who has been dispensing hospitality here for more than 16 years. His welcoming hostelry has won awards for both its food and Guinness and the live music sessions every Friday, Saturday, Sunday and Monday evening are understandably very popular. The excellent food served in the Darby & Anchor Restaurant

is all home made – with fresh fish and steaks as the specialities – and is served from 10am to 9pm, Friday to Monday; 10am to 6pm, Tuesday to Thursday.

Ballyboy House

Clogheen, Co. Tipperary
Tel: 052 65297

Nestling beneath the scenic Knockmealdown Mountains, **Ballyboy House** is a handsome Georgian mansion which has been in John and Breeda Moran's family ever since it was built. The gracious interior with its elegant furnishings and décor reflect the house's long history and provide a wonderfully relaxing ambience. Arriving guests are served with complimentary refreshments and a full Irish breakfast with plenty of choice is included in the tariff. Ballyboy House has 5 guest bedrooms, all furnished and decorated to the same high standards and all with en suite facilities.

Guests can enjoy a game of darts or snooker in the games room and there are some lovely scenic walks in the area. There's plenty to see and do in the locality. You can go fly fishing in Ballyboy House's own grounds, there's an 18-hole golf course at nearby Cahir, cycle hire can be arranged and guided mountain walks can be arranged – don't miss the panoramic view at The Vee on Sugarloaf Hill! You can see Farmhouse cheesemaking or explore the incredible caverns within Mitchelstown Cave. Cahir Castle, the curious Swiss Cottage at Cahir and the historic Rock of Cashel are all also within easy driving distance.

The Vee, Clogheen

of Clogheen, the village of Ballyporeen was visited in 1984 by US President Ronald Reagan in search of his Irish roots. In the visitor centre opposite the Ronald Reagan pub there's a photographic display recording the visit and information about the president's great-grandfather who was born in Ballyporeen in 1810.

Tipperary

An important dairy-farming centre, Tipperary is very much a traditional Irish town, its amenities geared up for local people rather than tourists. This honest-to-goodness approach is refreshing, providing as it does an authentic feel of the real Ireland. Despite its agricultural preoccupations, Tipperary suffered badly during the Anglo-Irish and Civil War strife. Various granite statues around the town commemorate heroes of those conflicts and the town's **EXCEL Heritage Centre**

Brown Trout

Abbey Street, Tipperary, Co. Tipperary
Tel: 062 51912

One of Tipperary's most popular restaurants, the **Brown Trout** serves good old-fashioned Irish cuisine – beef, lamb, 'spuds' and fresh vegetable. Chef/patron Sean Buckley is a local man with a great love of Tipperary and an in-depth knowledge of it since he has been cooking here for more than 26 years. The 40-cover restaurant (licensed for wine) has a spacious 'holding area' with comfy sofas and a TV for those awaiting a table. Lunch is served from 12.30pm to 2.30pm. Next door to the restaurant, Sean's B&B has 7 guest bedrooms, with 3 shared bathrooms.

Ballyglass Country House Hotel

Glen of Aherlow Road, Tipperary Town
Tel: 062 52104 Fax: 062 52229
e-mail: info@ballyglasshouse.com
website: www.ballyglasshouse.com

Beside the beautiful Glen of Aberlow, **Ballyglass Country House Hotel** is a handsome Georgian building standing in its own private grounds. This hotel is family run by Bill and Joan Byrne, together with their family. All 10 guest bedrooms are en suite with all facilities. The hotel boasts an excellent restaurant serving tasty dishes based on fresh local produce every evening and on Sundays from noon until 6pm. Adjacent is the Olde Worlde Forge Bar which is an ideal place for a quiet drink in a warm and friendly atmosphere.

displays some poignant memorabilia of the time. There are letters written from prison by Seán Tracey, a violin belonging to Joseph Mary Plunkett, (a poet executed following the 1916 rising), and some moving photographs of the young, fresh-faced officers of the old IRA who were involved in the uprising.

Tipperary is surrounded by scenic countryside, with the Glen of Aherlow and the grand Galtee Mountains lying just a few miles to the south. There is some splendid ridge-walking in the mountains, especially around Lyracappul.

Around Tipperary

Monard

3 miles NW of Tipperary on the N24

The village of Monard lies right on the county boundary, just a few steps away from Co. Limerick. Tipperary Racecourse is little more than a mile distant and the village boasts its very own 18-hole golf course.

Dundrum

8 miles NE of Tipperary on the R661/R505

Gardeners will want to pay a visit to the **Celtic Plantarum Dundrum** (free) on the edge of the village. The 8-acre site offers a dazzling display of some 60,000 plants of more than 2500 varieties and specialises in native Irish plants. Features within the Plantarum have a Celtic theme – a crannóg, dolmen, cairn, fairy fort and so on, and the site includes lakes, a waterfall and water display, and an extensive garden centre.

Dundrum is an attractive village, sitting at the edge of the Galtee Mountains surrounded by wooded hills and farmland. A couple of hundred years ago, 29,000 acres of this land formed the estate of Lord Maude whose agent, or factor, occupied the charming house which now provides the nucleus of Rectory House Hotel.

Golden

8 miles NE of Tipperary on the N74

The little village of Golden sits on the banks of the River Suir from which, at this point, a rocky islet rises and is crowned by the ruined keep of Golden Castle. An even more evocative ruin stands about a mile upstream. Founded around 1190, **Athassel Abbey** was once the largest medieval priory in Ireland and the remains are extensive. The most notable architectural feature of the abbey is its impressive west door. Few visitors seek out this peaceful spot but those who do are rewarded with an almost mystical tranquility.

Cashel

11 miles E of Tipperary on the N74/N8

As PJ Cavanagh puts it **"The Rock of Cashel** jumps out of the Tipperary plains like an Edinburgh Castle in a sea of green".** Cashel is one of Ireland's most historical sites with a magical cluster of medieval buildings crowning the great limestone outcrop that rises spectacularly from the surrounding plain. Legend has it that the Rock was created by the Devil who in one of his understandable rages had bitten a huge chunk of rock from the Slieve Bloom Mountains. He was flying across the plain with the massive rock in his mouth when he caught sight of St Patrick standing ready to found a new church on the site. Outraged, he dropped the rock which fell to earth thus creating this striking feature. It was at Cashel also that St Patrick plucked a

O'Connell held one of his Monster Rallies at Cashel.

The owner of Hill House, Carmel Purcell, has painstakingly and lovingly restored it to its former state of grace. Piece by piece and room by room, she has thrown out all semblances of modernity and replaced them with genuine period Georgian furniture, collected from auctions all over Ireland. "For the first time" she says, "tourists to Tipperary can truly experience what it was like to live in the pampered luxury of Georgian Ireland". Guests can wander into the Great Drawing Room and relax in front of a cosy open fire, examine the volumes in the original Georgian bookcase, and sleep the night away in a spacious 4-poster bed!

HILL HOUSE GUEST HOUSE

Palmershill, Cashel, Co. Tipperary
Tel: 062 61277 Fax: 062 63709
e-mail: info@hillhousecashel.com
website: www.hillhousecashel.com

Few places enjoy such an inspiring view as the one to be seen from **Hill House** – an unobstructed panoramic vista of the Rock of Cashel, one of Ireland's most historic sites, rising from the Tipperary plain. Hill House itself has a fascinating history of its own. Built in 1710, since its earliest days it became the residence of the Ascendancy ruling classes who administered British rule in Ireland. During the 1830s and '40s, it was the home of the Rev. James McDonnell, a great campaigner against the social ills of the

time who in 1846 entertained the 'Liberator' Daniel O'Connell at the house when

Chestnuts

Dualla, Cashel, Co. Tipperary
Tel/Fax: 062 61469
e-mail: bookings@thechestnuts.com
website: www.thechestnuts.com

Extremely comfortable bed & breakfast accommodation in a friendly, homely atmosphere is why guests return to **Chestnuts** in the tranquil hamlet of Dualla. This spacious detached bungalow set within mature gardens is the home of John and Phyllis O'Halloran, formerly farmers but now enjoying their new role as hosts. John is also a DJ on local radio, a country music expert with literally thousands of records in his collection.

Chestnuts is also notable for its excellent food with evening meals available by arrangement. Open all year, Chestnuts has 5 guest bedrooms, all with en suite facilities, and guests also have the use of a comfortable TV lounge.

shamrock and used it to explain the doctrine of the Trinity – God the Father, God the Son and God the Holy Ghost. Since that time the shamrock has been Ireland's unofficial emblem.

A good way to get your bearings in this memorable town is to take the tram tour which departs from the Heritage Centre at the Town Hall. The highlight of the tour is of course the buildings on the Rock itself (see panel opposite).

In the town itself, the **GPA Bolton Library** houses an impressive collection of almost 12,000 antiquarian books and rare manuscripts, the oldest of which date back to the 12th century. The collection includes a microscopic New Testament from the 1860s, two pages from a copy of Caxton's *Chaucer*, and what is claimed to be the smallest book in the world. The Library also has a fine collection of church silver and a display of the altarware used in the original cathedral on the Rock. (The GPA in the Library's name refers to Guinness Peat Aviation which provided the major funding for a complete renovation of the 160-year-old dwelling in which the Library is housed).

In Dominic Street, the **Cashel Folk Village** has a fascinating range of reconstructions of traditional thatched village shops, a forge and other businesses. (Vegetarians would be well-advised to decline a visit to the butcher's shop). There's also a penal Chapel and an extensive display of signs and other commercial memorabilia.

During the summer season, devotees of Irish traditional music can indulge their interest at the **Brú Ború Heritage Centre** which presents a colourful performance of Irish music, song and dance every evening from Tuesday to Saturday inclusive. The

Brú Ború Heritage Centre

Rock of Cashel

Cashel, Co. Tipperary

The oldest structure on the Rock of Cashel is the lofty **Round Tower**, constructed during the 1100s and with an entrance some twelve feet above the ground. **Cormac's Chapel,** built between 1127 and 1134, is the oldest and most beautiful of Ireland's surviving Romanesque churches, its walls ornately carved with beasts and human figures. The chapel takes its name from Cormac, King-Bishop of Munster, who is believed to be buried here in an exquisitely decorated sarcophagus.

The largest structure in this rich complex is the roofless 12th century **Cathedral** which despite its ruined state is still remarkably graceful. In 1647 the cathedral witnessed one of the worst atrocities of Cromwell's war. As his troops, under the command of Lord Iniquin, approached the town, the citizens of

Cashel fled to the sanctuary of the cathedral. Iniquin ordered his soldiers to pile turf around the walls and set it alight. Hundreds were roasted to death.

The nearby **Hall of the Vicars Choral** was built in the 1400s as a grace and favour residence for senior members of the cathedral choir; it now contains a museum displaying St Patrick's Cross, a unique kind of high cross which stands on a broad plinth believed to be the coronation stone of the High Kings of Munster.

complex includes an information centre, genealogy suite, restaurant and a centre for the study and celebration of native Irish traditions. New additions, in the spring of 2001, were an underground theatre and exhibition area tracing the history of Irish music, song and dance.

Thurles

Thurles is a busy market town on the River Suir and is also the cathedral town of the archdiocese of Cashel and Emly, one of the four into which Ireland is divided. The late-Victorian cathedral of 1875, with its lofty 125 feet high campanile modelled on the one in Pisa, Italy, is a landmark for many miles around. Buried in the cathedral is Archbishop Croke who founded the Gaelic Athletic Association in 1884. (The GAA is the governing body of Gaelic football and of what is probably the fastest field sport in the world, hurling). A statue of the Archbishop stands in Liberty Square.

The story of Gaelic games from legendary

The Castle

Two Mile Borris, Thurles, Co. Tipperary
Tel: 0504 44324 Fax: 0504 44352
e-mail: b&b@thecastletmb.com
website: www.thecastletmb.com

Located about 3 miles east of Thurles, on the N75 just off the N8, **The Castle** is an outstanding bed & breakfast establishment with a 5-diamonds rating from the AA. The Duggan family has lived here for more than 250 years – not in the castle itself but in a charming 17th century house with creeper-covered walls. There are 4 very spacious guest rooms, all en suite and provided with TV and

hospitality tray. Joan Duggan is a superb chef and is happy to cook evening meals by arrangement. Guests have the use of a comfortable TV lounge and a well-equipped games room with pool, subbuteo and other amusements.

Horse and Jockey Inn

Horse and Jockey, Thurles, Co. Tipperary
Tel: 0504 44192
e-mail: info@horseandjockey.com.ie
website: www.horseandjockey.com

Where else in the world, one wonders, would you find a village that has taken its name from the local pub? **The Horse and Jockey Inn**, sitting at a busy crossroads in the heart of County Tipperary and serving the stage-coach travellers of the time, was already well-established here in the mid-1700s. A cluster of cottages developed around the inn and over the years this small community became known locally, then officially, by the name of its popular hostelry.

Later that century, in the 1790s, the inn became a regular meeting place for one of the great heroes in the history of Irish independence, Wolfe Tone. He, and the members of his Society of United Irishmen, sought to find a democratic resolution to Ireland's problems with England through Parliamentary reform. Frustrated by the response of English politicians, he became involved in the French-aided rebellion of 1798, was captured, condemned to death but committed suicide before the sentence could be carried out.

The Horse and Jockey's name is significant since several of Ireland's major racecourses and some of its leading training stables are located only a few miles from the inn. It's not unusual for customers to find themselves rubbing shoulders with some of the key players in what is probably the country's most cherished sport – and often in a celebratory atmosphere!

The inn's legendary reputation for unstinted and informal hospitality continues to attract luminaries from not just the sporting world, but also from the Republic's political, commercial and cultural communities. Even while playing host to such well-known local, national and international dignitaries, the Horse and Jockey maintains a homely and friendly Tipperary atmosphere.

A couple of years ago the inn completed an extensive renovation and refurbishment programme and now offers its patrons a spacious lounge and bar, a high quality restaurant and a modern, well-equipped conference centre.

The 33 bedrooms and suites are all provided with state of the art facilities and include specialised accommodation for asthma sufferers and disabled persons.

Happily, the thorough face-lift hasn't changed the heart of the inn. The words of an old poet who sang the praises of the Horse and Jockey Inn many years ago still ring true:

It is there you will find it,
More friendship than is in all Ireland's grounds,
God bless you my Inn, Horse and Jockey,
O where can your likes be found.

times to the present day is vividly presented at **Lár Na Páirce,** housed in an elegant 19th century building on Slievenamon Road. An 18-minute video captures the skill, excitement and colour of the games and the Hall of Fame displays life-size models of the greatest hurlers and footballers, along with the first GAA computer data-base. The centre is open daily, April through October.

Housed in St Mary's Church are two museums dealing with much grimmer subjects. **St Mary's Famine Museum** contains the largest collection of artefacts relating to the Great Famine of 1845-50 held anywhere in Ireland. Exhibits include a book which contains the only existing minutes of a famine food committee; clothing, coinage, newspaper reports and military hardware from the period. **St Mary's War Museum** contains rare memorabilia from conflicts ranging from the Crimean War to Yugoslavia in the 1990s. Tours are available, accompanied by a lecture if requested.

Thurles is also well known for its huge sugar beet factory; its racecourse; its twice-weekly greyhound racing; and the first microbrewery pub/restaurant in Ireland, Dwan, which produces around 6000 litres of beer each week.

Around Thurles

Holy Cross

4 miles SW of Thurles on the R660/R661

The story of **Holy Cross Abbey** is an uplifting saga that spans more than eight centuries and, unusually for Irish medieval churches, has a happy ending. The tale begins in 1168 when Donal O'Brien, King of Munster, founded the Abbey as a worthy shrine for a particle of the True Cross that had been presented to his father by Pope Paschal II. Pilgrims flocked in their thousands to the Abbey to venerate the holy relic. Their donations enabled the Cistercian monks to employ the most accomplished craftsmen to embellish the Abbey with superb features such as the traceried windows and the stone *sedilia*, (seats reserved for the clergy), so delicately sculpted in limestone they resemble the work of a master woodcarver. When Henry VIII officially suppressed the monastery in 1536, the protection of the local magnates, the Earls of Ormonde, allowed the monks at Holy Cross to stay in residence for another century. But Cromwell's ruthless repression of Catholicism finally closed the Abbey. Over the years the fabric deteriorated, the roof collapsed and for 200 years Holy Cross Abbey stood forlornly as one of the *"bare, ruined choirs"* that Shakespeare alluded to. Then, in 1975, funds made available as part of the European Architectural Heritage Year made possible a complete restoration of the Abbey. It is now once again in full use as the parish church for the village.

Templemore

10 miles N of Thurles on the N62

Templemore stands on the plain at the foot of Devil's Bit Mountain (1557 feet). According to legend, the Devil (rather than a glacier) caused the great gap in the mountain by biting out a huge piece. However, disliking the taste, he spat it out and the great chunk flew across the plain, landing to form the mighty Rock of Cashel.

Templemore derives its name from the fact that it developed around a Knights Templar castle and monastery. What little remains of those structures can be seen in the town park where there is also a large lake and swimming pool. The lake contains pike, roach, perch and tench, and there's more good fishing, for brown trout, on the upper reaches of the River Suir near the town.

It is at Templemore that the Irish Gardai (police force) have their training college, housed in a former British Army barracks.

Coolangatta Country House

Kilgarvan Quay, Ballinderry, Nenagh,
Co. Tipperary
Tel: 067 22164
e-mail: coolangatta@eircom.net

In Gaelic '*coolangatta*' means "splendid water view" and **Coolangatta Country House** certainly has one of those, enjoying as it does a lovely position overlooking Lough Derg. This striking modern building completed in 1992 has Scandinavian-style high ceilings with lots of pine and exposed beams. There are 3 spacious bedrooms with private bathrooms, a separate sitting room with TV and tea/coffee-making facilities. Your host, Mary McGeeney serves a splendid breakfast with lots of choices. Mary also arranges traditional music nights and set dancing tuition is available. Coolangatta is open all year round; credit cards are accepted.

Nenagh

The administrative centre of north Tipperary, Nenagh was once an important Anglo-Norman settlement and then a major Franciscan centre until Cromwell's troops destroyed their Friary. The oldest surviving structure in the town is the ruin of **Nenagh Castle**, built in 1217, whose massive circular Keep with walls 20 feet thick still dominates the town. The rest of the castle succumbed partly to the ravages of time, partly to the badly-placed explosives of a farmer trying to rid the castle of its infestation of sparrows' nests.

Located in the Governor's House and Gatehouse of the former county gaol, the **Nenagh District Heritage Centre** has displays that reveal aspects of prison life through the condemned cells, 3D models, and biographical notes of the unfortunates who were executed. Other exhibits include models of the gaol, Lough Derg and two of its lakeside villages, Dromineer and Garrykennedy.

Around Nenagh

Dromineer

7 miles N of Nenagh on the R495

The holiday centre of Dromineer sits on the shore of Lough Derg and has been sensitively developed as a sailing, fishing, cruising and water-skiing resort. A ruined castle stands above the harbour where you

Whiskey Still

Dromineer, Nenagh, Co. Tipperary
Tel: 067 24129
e-mail: whiskeystill@eircom.net
website: www.whiskeystill.com

Dromineer is a small hamlet on the shore of Lough Derg and well worth seeking out in order to pay a visit to the **Whiskey Still**, Declan Collison's outstanding hostelry. Declan has a wealth of experience in the hospitality business and his pub is full of character with lots of interesting collectables distributed around the rooms. Naturally, he stocks a superb selection of fine whiskeys and also offers excellent food with a menu based on fresh fish and other local produce. Outside, there's a smart deck/patio with a grand view of the busy marina and if you visit on a Thursday evening you can enjoy the regular traditional Irish music session.

Otway Lodge

Dromineer, Nenagh, Co. Tipperary
Tel: 067 24133/24273
website: www.flannery@eircom.net

Ann Flannery's **Otway Lodge**, formerly Lord Otway's hunting lodge and before that a military barracks, is now a roomy and comfortable Bed & Breakfast guest house with six en-suite letting bedrooms. The spacious premises, which have been family run for the past 26 years, include a table tennis room and a laundry room is available. A wonderful full Irish breakfast is served to set you up for the day and you can expect the finest hospitality.

Standing in the centre of the village beside Lough Derg, the largest lake on the River Shannon, visitors can enjoy the spectacular views of the water and the surrounding countryside. It's a great base for sporting enthusiasts, with sailing, water skiing and windsurfing on the lake. Boats can be hired and anglers are guaranteed excellent fishing and a choice of local establishments offer a variety of entertainment to round off the day. The owners also have two self catering chalets available for longer stays. Easy parking.

can hire boats or join one of the regular cruises around the 25-mile-long lake which is dotted with wooded islands.

Toomevara

7 miles E of Nenagh on the N7

Backed by the splendour of the Silver Mine Mountains, (where silver and zinc are still being mined), Toomevara has the ruins of a 14th century Augustinian priory church. The village stands at the heart of "Ned of the Hill" country. Ned was an Irish equivalent of Robin Hood and he made life as difficult as he could for the English planter families of the early 1600s. Ned is also credited with writing the lovely song *The Dark Woman of the Glen*.

Birdhill

13 miles SW of Nenagh on the N7

The village of Birdhill lies close to the border with Co. Limerick and just a few miles from the beauty spot known as **Clare Glens**. Here, the River Clare flows through a gorge and splashes down a series of picturesque waterfalls. Swimming is possible in some of the pools and some scenic walks are signposted.

Roscrea

24 miles NE of Nenagh on the N7

A pleasing little town set on a low hill, Roscrea grew up around the monastery founded here in the 7th century by St Cronan. The present ruins date back to the 1100s and, rather bizarrely, are bisected by the main Dublin to Limerick road. On one side of the highway rises a 60 feet high **Round Tower** which typically has a doorway 15 feet up, but untypically has the faint image of a ship on the inner face of a window. The tower was originally 20 feet taller but lost its top section when a cannon backfired in 1798. Across the road

ARDAGH HOUSE

Killenaule, Co. Tipperary
Tel: 052 56224
e-mail: ahouse@iol.ie

Dating back to the mid-1700s, **Ardagh House** is one of the oldest buildings in this busy village a few miles west of Birr. Mine host, Michael McCormick, who has been here since 1995 has recently refurbished his hostelry to the very highest standards. Popular with local people, Ardagh House has a compact bar and a smart lounge/dining area where customers can enjoy wholesome home cooked lunches every weekday. If you are planning to stay in this attractive corner of the county, Ardagh House has 6 attractively decorated guest bedrooms, all with en suite facilities, TV and hospitality tray. Credit cards are accepted.

is the west gable of **St Cronan's Church** and, close by, St Cronan's Cross. It was once highly decorated but nine centuries of exposure to the elements have left it badly weather-beaten. In the centre of the town, the impressive **Gate Tower Castle** was built in the 13th century and now houses a Heritage Centre. Also within the castle's polygonal curtain wall stands **Damer House,** a fine early-18th century town house which was rescued by the Georgian Society whose members also spent years lovingly restoring its magnificent carved pine staircase.

Terryglass

15 miles N of Nenagh on the R493

The picturesque little town of Terryglass occupies a delightful position on the eastern shore of Lough Derg and has been the national winner of the award for Ireland's Tidiest Town.

Terryglass has its origins in the 5th century when St Patrick is said to have visited Tir Dha Glas (the *Land of the Two Streams*) and blessed a large gathering of people saying "This will be the place of my resurrection". A century later, St Columba founded a monastery here which, despite being sacked three times by Viking invaders, continued as a great seat of learning up until 1164 when it was completely destroyed by fire.

Standing forlornly by the lakeside is the ruin of a tower, all that remains of a castle belonging to the Butler family who dominated this part of the country in medieval times.

Co Waterford

More than any other of the southeast counties, Waterford offers a wide variety of landscapes. To the west, unspoiled uplands provide some splendid mountain scenery; in the heart of the county, wooded river valleys wind through fertile farmlands; while the fretted coastline opens up panoramic views of broad bays lined with low cliffs and sandy beaches. Strung along the coast are a handful of fishing villages and holiday resorts of which Tramore is the best known. It is around Tramore that the earliest known inhabitants of the county left their impressive monuments and human remains dating back to 9000 BC.

Waterford City Centre

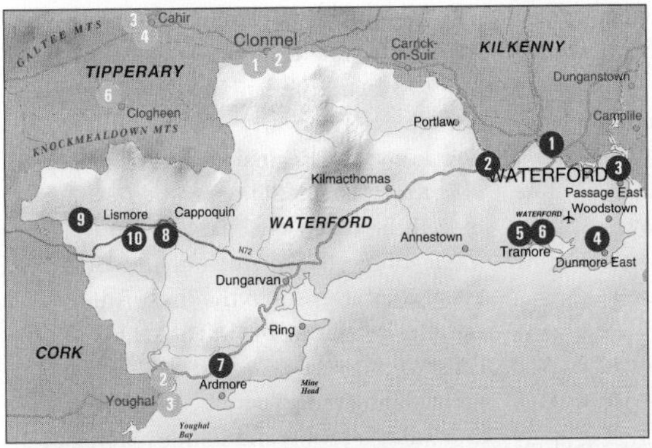

At Ardmore, near the County Cork border, St Declan disembarked in the early 400s, the first Christian missionary to land in Ireland, preceding St Patrick's arrival by several years. Ardmore's splendid 13th century Cathedral, standing on the site of St Declan's monastery, maintains the continuity of

PLACES TO STAY, EAT AND DRINK

Browns Townhouse, Waterford City	1	B&B	p325
The Long Haul Restaurant & Bar, Kilmeaden	2	Bar & Restaurant	p326
Careybridge, Passage East	3	B&B	p327
Strand Inn, Dunmore East	4	Hotel	p328
Glenorney by the Sea, Tramore	5	B&B	p329
Tivoli House, Tramore	6	Accommodation	p330
Newtown Farm Guest House, Ardmore	7	Guest House	p332
The Toby Jug, Cappoquin	8	Hotel	p332
Blackwater Lodge Hotel, Upper Ballyduff	9	Hotel	p333
Pine Tree House, Lismore	10	B&B	p334

● Denotes entries in other chapters

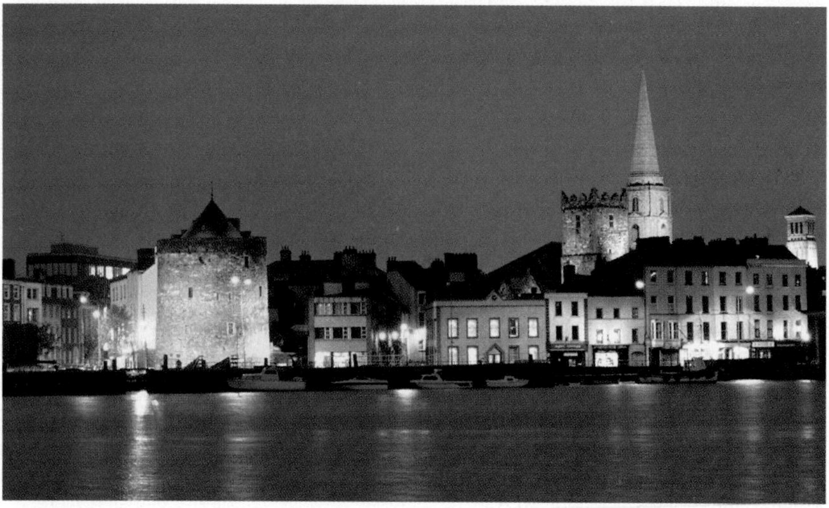

Waterford at Night

Christianity in this area, widely known as Old Parish because it was the first to be established in the country.

Norman survivals in the county include the sturdy Reginald's Tower in Waterford Town while amongst later buildings of note is Curraghmore House at Portlaw, a magnificent Georgian mansion, home of the Marquesses of Waterford for many generations.

Waterford

Centuries ago, Waterford was described in the *Lebor Gabala*, or Book of Invasions, as standing at a "sweet confluence of waters, a trinity of rivers", the three rivers being the Suir, the Nore and the Barrow. This favoured position fostered Waterford's development as the major commercial centre of the southeast and it is still a busy working port.

It was the Vikings who established the first major settlement here in AD 853. They ruled the local Celtic tribe, the Désaí, with an iron rod, forcing them to pay a tribute known as *Airgead Sróine*, or Nose Money. Anyone who defaulted on the payment had his nose chopped off. One of the later Viking leaders, Ranguald, built a tower to guard the harbour. It was rebuilt after the Norman invasion of 1170 and, now known as **Reginald's Tower**, is the oldest surviving building in the town, indeed the oldest civic building in Ireland. Its mighty walls remained impregnable even when it endured the first artillery siege in Ireland in 1495. The massive pepper-pot tower, one of several erected at points along the city walls, has been used as a mint, a prison and military store. Of the walls themselves, extensive stretches are still standing.

Housed in an old granary beside the river, the **Waterford Museum of Treasures** celebrates the town's rich history. There are fascinating artefacts from Viking and medieval times, recovered during excavations in the city centre in the late 1980s and early 1990s: Henry VIII's Cap of Maintenance; and a magnificently illustrated charter from Richard II dating back to 1399.

King Richard is also linked to the city's other major medieval survival, the

Brown's Townhouse

South Parade, Waterford City, Co. Waterford
Tel: 051 870594
e-mail: info@brownstownhouse.com
website: www.brownstownhouse.com

Located on a quiet residential street just a 5-minute walk from the city centre, **Brown's Townhouse** is an elegant late-Victorian property which has been fully modernised by its owners, Leslie and Barbara Brown. All 6 guest bedrooms are en suite and equipped with direct dial telephones, cable television, tea & coffee making facilities. The showers are all oversize and have a pressurised water system with ample hot water. Guests have the use of a spacious lounge with an open fire and at breakfast time you'll find a good choice that includes a full Irish breakfast, Scrambled Eggs with Melted Cheddar, Buttermilk Pancakes with Maple Syrup, fresh home-baked bread and preserves.

Franciscan **French Church**, founded in 1240. It was here that Richard received the submission of the Irish Chiefs in 1395, an act that consolidated Anglo-Norman power in the city for generations. After the suppression of the monasteries, the church served as an almshouse but reverted to being a place of worship when French Huguenot refugees arrived at Waterford in the late 1600s. The church's tower and fine east window are still complete but the building is now roofless.

Two other churches stand close by. The Church of Ireland's **Christ Church Cathedral** is a noble edifice of the 1770s, its handsome Georgian appearance somewhat undermined by one of the tombs preserved from a much older church on the site. The monument to James Rice, Lord Mayor of Waterford, who died in 1482, displays the effigy of a corpse in an advanced state of decomposition. Few details of corporeal decay are omitted, with various creepy crawlies faithfully included in the design. More palatable is the cathedral's 45-minute audio presentation, *Let the Pillars Speak*, which relates Waterford's stirring story from the Norman invasion to the present time.

Christ Church was designed by John Roberts who, unusually, was also the architect for the Catholic **Holy Trinity Cathedral** just a few hundred yards away. The Cathedral was built in 1793 but considerably altered in late-Victorian times which accounts for its ornate, very un-

Old City Walls, Waterford

Georgian appearance.

Another of Roberts' buildings has fortunately been left untouched. **City Hall** in the Mall was built in 1788 as the Merchants' Assembly Hall but has served in its present rôle since 1813. An interesting feature inside is the "Schedule of Mayors" which records more than 600 elders of the city to have held the position since 1284. Also on view is the municipal collection of art which includes work by Jack Yeats, Paul Henry, Séan Keating and others. Tours of the Hall are available by prior arrangement. City Hall is also the venue for The Waterford Show, an evening entertainment of Irish music, story, song and dance presented by performers in Georgian costume. Tickets can be obtained at the Tourist Office on The Quay.

Next door to City Hall, the **Theatre Royal** is a splendid Victorian survival with its tiered horseshoe balconies and flamboyant 19th century décor. It provides an appropriate setting for Waterford's annual opera festival in mid-to-late September.

The **Chamber of Commerce** (1785) in George Street was yet another of John Roberts' buildings and contains what is generally regarded as his *pièce de résistance*, a magnificent cantilevered oval staircase adorned with brilliantly decorative stucco work. Visitors can view the staircase during normal office hours.

A recent addition to Waterford's attractions is the **Municipal Art Gallery** (free) in Greyfriars which celebrates Irish art and includes some fine pieces by Jack Yeats, George Russell, Sarah Purser and Evie Hone.

Wherever you go in Waterford, you'll find the famed Waterford Crystal on display. If you want to see how this exquisite translucent glass is made, there are regular tours of the **Waterford Crystal Glass Factory**, about a mile from the city centre. The theatre at the visitor centre

The Long Haul Restaurant & Bar

Kilmeaden, Co. Waterford
Tel: 051 384234

Co. Waterford's most recommended eating place, **The Long Haul Restaurant and Bar** has been showered with praise by the food critics of *The Times, The Tribune* and *The Independent*. This 400-year-old hostelry is set back from the N25 about 10 miles west of Waterford Town and is sought out by locals and visitors alike. Owner and chef Eugene Lennon has been here since 1997 but his experience in the hospitality business goes back some 20 years. His enticing menus, which change daily, offer an excellent choice of traditional Irish cuisine, meticulously prepared, attractively presented and at very reasonable prices. Before or after your meal, enjoy a drink in the cosy bar with its welcoming open fire.

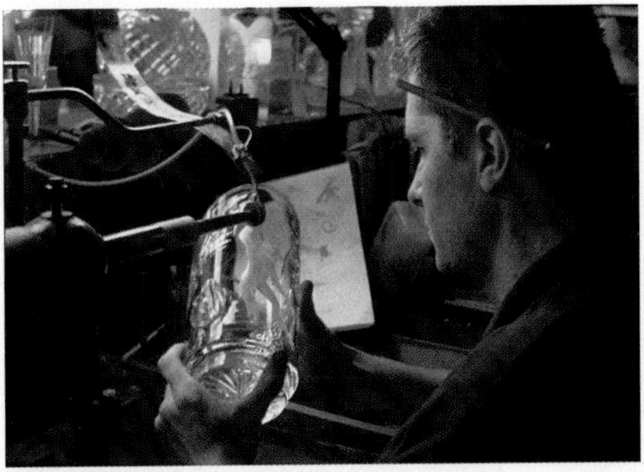

Waterford Crystal Glass Factory

shows a 17-minute audio-visual presentation tracing the ancient craft of glassmaking from Roman times up to the present day.

Around Waterford

Portlaw

10 miles NW of Waterford off the 680

A popular excursion from Waterford is to the village of Portlaw, founded as a model village by a Quaker family, the Malcolmsons. They also established a cotton industry which became noted for its durable tweeds. Adjoining the village is the stately home of the Marquesses of Waterford since 1170, **Curraghmore.** The present building is a grand Georgian mansion set in parkland with gently sloping hills rising behind. The grounds of Curraghmore are considered one of the most beautiful demesnes in the country. They contain an outstanding Arboretum, a bridge built in 1205 for King John to cross the River Clodagh, and a fascinating Shell House, designed and decorated by Catherine, Countess of Tyrone, in 1754. Opening hours of the house and grounds are limited, (details on 051 387102), but group tours are welcome all year round on weekdays by prior appointment.

Passage East

7 miles E of Waterford on the R683

Standing at the neck of Waterford Harbour and framed by rugged hills, Passage East is an attractive little place which was an important port for centuries. Strongbow landed here in 1170 and the following year Henry II landed with 4000 men in 400 ships to drive him out. Passage East's significance as a port has declined over the years but a vehicle ferry still plies the narrow crossing to Ballyhack in Co. Wexford.

Careybridge

Crooke, Passage East, Co. Waterford
Tel: 051 382581 Fax: 051 382029
e-mail: belaire@indigo.io

Enjoying a beautiful location overlooking the Suir estuary, **Careybridge** is an impressive modern house offering luxurious en suite accommodation and a genuinely friendly welcome. Owners John and Rosaleen Walsh take very good care of their guests – especially at breakfast time when the extensive menu includes home-made scones, kippers, eggs Florentine or Benedict, and even Steak & Eggs for a small additional charge. The 3 attractively furnished and decorated guest bedrooms all have en suite facilities and the house is ideally situated for touring the southeast. There are good sandy beaches nearby and Waterford town is just a short drive away.

Woodstown

8 miles SE of Waterford on minor road off the R684

Well-known for its beautiful sandy beach backed by woodland, Woodstown is an ideal place for a gentle stroll or a quiet swim. The nearby Woodstown House Country Estate nestles in 35 acres of wooded parkland just a few minutes from Woodstown Beach. At the heart of the estate stands Woodstown House, an elegant Regency house which was built around 1823 by Lord Carew as a gift for his wife. As a young girl, Lady Carew is said to have danced with the Duke of Wellington at the famous Ball in Brussels given by the Duchess of Richmond on the eve of the Battle of Waterloo. She lived to the great age of 103, dying at Woodstown House in 1901. The house was bought in 1945 by Major C.D. Cholmeley-Harrison who let it during the summer of 1967 to Mrs Jacqueline Kennedy, widow of the American President. The house is now partly devoted to self-catering accommodation.

Dunmore East

11 miles SE of Waterford on the R684

Standing at the mouth of Waterford Harbour, Dunmore East is a picturesque seaside resort with a delightful main street that follows a twisting course from the east cove down to the busy little quay with its

Dunmore East Harbour

crooked harbour wall. The village is framed by red sandstone cliffs overlaid with emerald green turf dotted with golden gorse. Safe bathing beaches boasting the Blue Flag accolade lie at the foot of the cliffs and there are copious facilities for every kind of water sport. Dunmore is a very active fishing port, busy with brightly coloured fishing vessels, and also home to the long-established Waterford Harbour Sailing Club. The town takes its name from the *dun*, or hill fort, of which a few traces remain on nearby Brownstown Head.

STRAND INN

Dunmore East, Co. Waterford
Tel: 051 383174

The **Strand Inn** occupies an ideal location for beach lovers since it stands just 20 yards from the beach and overlooks the quiet bay. The à la carte restaurant, which also enjoys this glorious view, is noted for its excellent sea food dishes. There's also a well-patronised bar which serves food – customers can savour their refreshments inside or on the terrace with its view of the beach. Owned and

run by the Foyle family, this popular hotel has 16 guest bedrooms, all with a 4-star rating, en suite facilities and attractively furnished and decorated.

Tramore

6 miles S of Waterford on the R675

A delightful town where the houses rise one street above another climbing up the hillside. This charming spot remained virtually unknown until the year 1785 when a wealthy Waterford merchant, Bartholomew Rivers, began the development that transformed Tramore from a sleepy fishing village into one of the Emerald Isle's premier resorts. Today, Tramore offers a huge range of holiday amusements in its extensive fun park. **Splashworld** is an all-water experience featuring a bubble pool, river ride, wave machine and water slides, all in chlorine-free, hygienic waters. Outdoors, there's a sandy bathing beach 3 miles long, (Tramore actually means 'big strand'), a fine promenade and good facilities for boating and angling. The Tramore Races are a popular event in the Irish racing calendar, especially the traditional festival meeting

Tramore Beach

Glenorney by the Sea

Newtown, Tramore, Co. Waterford
Tel: 051 281056 Fax: 051 381103
e-mail: glenorney@iol.ie
website: www.glenorney.com

As the name suggests **Glenorney by the Sea** occupies a superb position overlooking the Celtic Sea and within walking distance of the beaches. Guests will receive a warm welcome from owner Marie Murphy who prides herself on providing a real home from home. Glenorney has been recommended by all the top class guides and boasts a 4-Diamond award from the AA plus a Sparkling Diamond award. Guests can relax and enjoy a cup of tea or coffee in the spacious sun lounge overlooking the bay or stroll through the award-winning gardens. All the 6 guest bedrooms, which include 2 family rooms, have en suite facilities and are provided with television, clock radio, direct dial telephone, hair dryer and tea/coffee-making facilities.

At breakfast time you'll find a great choice that includes traditional Irish pancakes and Marie's very special French toast. She takes great care to use only the best of local produce and home baking and preserves. The house has its own secure private parking; Mastercard and Visa are accepted. Tramore provides plenty of activities for holidaymakers. Tramore Golf Club's 18-hole course is just across the road from Glenorney; the wonderful 3-mile long beach is popular with surfers; Splashworld provides a huge variety of water activities, and horse-racing fans are well served by Tramore's own race course.

TIVOLI HOUSE
Tramore, Co. Waterford
Tel: 051 390208

Tivoli House offers quality budget accommodation in a convenient location overlooking Tramore Bay and just a 3-minute walk from the town centre and beach. There's a choice of single, double and family rooms with private bathrooms with showers and, in the adjoining Tivoli Hostel, dormitory rooms; a fully equipped kitchen and dining area; a comfortable TV lounge with fireplace, and an outdoor patio area. Tivoli House was purpose-built as a guest house in 1979 and its owners, Niamh and Avery Coryell, have recently comprehensively refurbished the properties to a very high standard. All major credit cards are accepted.

in August.

Three other features should be mentioned. Despite its spectacular beauty, the Bay has been the graveyard of many a sturdy ship. The greatest calamity of all was the wreck of the *Sea Horse* in 1816 with the loss of 363 lives. The **"Metal Man"** is a huge figure of a sailor which since 1824 has been warning other mariners of the dangers of Tramore Bay. A grey, sombre slab on the **Doneraile Walk** also commemorates that huge loss of life. The Walk itself was laid out in the early 1800s for Lord Doneraile, Tramore's landlord, and offers some splendid panoramic views. Finally, there's the **Knockeen Dolmen** which has been described as the finest specimen of its kind in Ireland but is not easy to find – best to ask for directions locally.

Annestown
12 miles SW of Waterford on the R675

A pleasant little holiday resort with a good sandy beach popular with surfers, Annestown has a 17th century castle (private) but is more famous for being the only village in Ireland without a pub. Apparently, there used to be several inns catering for the nearby barracks but there were so many "donnybrooks", or brawls, that the local landowner closed them all down.

Kilmacthomas
15 miles SW of Waterford on the R676

Located just off the N25 Waterford to Dungarvan road, Kilmacthomas is built on steep slopes either side of the Mahon River and is well known for the durable Irish tweeds manufactured here. To the west rise the **Comeragh Mountains**, a fine range with many peaks above 2000 feet. The highest point, Fascoum (2597 feet) towers above Lough Coumshingaun (pronounced *com-shin-awn*), a mountain tarn enclosed on three sides by 1000 feet high cliffs and very popular with rock-climbers.

Dungarvan
29 miles SW of Waterford on the N25

A busy fishing port and the administrative centre for the county apart from Waterford

Comeragh Mountains

Town, Dungarvan enjoys a picturesque setting, surrounded by low cliffs and gentle hills smothered in pine trees. A pretty arched bridge spans the River Colligan and on the edge of the town are the remains of a castle built by King John in the early 1200s. The centre of the town was redesigned in the early 1800s by the Duke of Devonshire who established the grid pattern of streets around the spacious Grattan Square.

Away from the formal planning of the centre, a maze of narrow alleyways winding between warehouses leads down to the bustling harbour where the attractive old inns naturally specialise in sea food. Collectors of curiosities should make the short trip to the junction of the R672 and N72, northwest of the town. Here stands the **Master McGrath Memorial**, a plain stone monument with an elegant spire erected in 1873. It commemorates not some local worthy but a legendary greyhound that won the Water Cup for coursing three times during the 19th century. The hound is also remembered in popular ballads and in the name of a superior brand of dog food.

The **Dungarvan Museum** (free) in Friary Street traces the development of the town from the Ice Age to Georgian times and includes a maritime display and a historic photographic collection. Those researching their family histories will find plenty of information at the **Abbeyside Reference Archive** which holds a wide variety of photographic material, records, artefacts and memorabilia relating to the history, culture and lifestyle of the area.

Over the Bank Holiday weekend in early May, Dungarvan hosts the **Féile na nDéise**, a festival of traditional music with venues scattered around the town's numerous hostelries.

About 5 miles east of Dungarvan, the beautiful strand at **Clonea** is one of three Blue Flag beaches along the Waterford coast.

Ring (An Rinn)

6 miles SE of Dungarvan

To the southeast of Dungarvan lies the area known as An Rinn, or Ring, an enclave where Gaelic is still the first language for the population of around 1500 and Irish traditions such as set dancing still thrive. During the summer, the language college holds courses in Gaelic. As in many Gaeltacht areas, the village is very scattered with no real centre but there are some excellent bars featuring traditional Irish music and some good walks – along the shore when the tide's out, along the cliff tops at any time. If you are planning to visit over the first weekend in August, book well ahead. This is when the **Ring Oyster Festival** takes place and accommodation is at a premium.

Ardmore

14 miles SW of Dungarvan on the R673

This attractive seaside village boasts a splendid Blue Flag beach, exhilarating views across a wide bay, and the distinction of being one of the earliest Christian settlements in Northern Europe. St Declan brought Christianity to the region around AD 416, almost 30 years before St Patrick's mission began. The area around Ardmore is still known as Old Parish, reflecting its status as the first parish to be established in Ireland. Declan's remains are supposedly buried in St Declan's Oratory and St Declan's Well, to the east of the village, still bubbles up beneath three simple stone crosses. Pilgrims traditionally wash in the cool, fresh water and devotees are especially numerous on the Saint's Day, 24th July.

Ardmore Cathedral, which is mostly 12th century, stands on the site of the monastery founded by Declan. The

Newtown Farm Guest House

Grange, Ardmore, Co. Waterford
Tel: 024 94143 Fax: 024 94654
e-mail: farm@newtownfarm.com
website: www.newtownfarm.com

Just a few minutes from the historic seaside town of Ardmore, **Newtown Farm Guest House** is surrounded by its own farmlands and enjoys wonderful panoramic views of the Atlantic Ocean. As a guest here you can experience a real taste of Ireland – its people, heritage, good food and fishing. Explore Ardmore with its ancient cathedral and round tower, and its superb beach; follow the spectacular cliff walks; visit the heritage town of Lismore and the scenic Mahon Falls, seek out one of the several championship golf courses, or simply retire to the local pub (within walking distance) where you'll find traditional Irish music, pub food and good craic.

At Newtown Farm, owner Theresa O'Connor has created an atmosphere of comfort and attention to detail – Theresa and her staff do all they can to make you feel very much at home. There are seven guest bedrooms, all with great elegance and charm. They all have en suite facilities, a private balcony, television, direct dial telephone and hospitality tray. Guests have the use of the tennis court and horse riding and pony trekking are available on site and nearby. Newtown Farm has a 3-star rating from Bord Failte, and a 4-diamonds grading by the AA. Major credit cards are accepted.

The Toby Jug

Main Street, Cappoquin, Co. Waterford
Tel: 058 52333

Cappoquin is famous for the superb coarse fishing in the Blackwater River and anglers will find the ideal "fishing hotel" in **The Toby Jug**, a friendly, family run business owned by Andrew and Mary Whelan who have been in the hospitality business for more than 21 years. Their hotel is just a 2-minute walk from the river and, by special arrangement with the proprietor of the Lower Blackwater Fishery, hotel guests can reserve fishing on the finest high record beats of the river at very reasonable terms. First class ghillies can be booked, fishing tackle is available on hire, and the hotel has a drying room and rod store for the use of fishing guests.

Good packed lunches are also available or guests can return to eat in the modern dining room which serves tasty, typically Irish meals. To accompany your meal, choose from the many good wines and other beverages available. Guests also have the use of a very comfortable television lounge, cocktail bar and public bar known as the Blackwater Bar. Accommodation comprises 6 spotlessly clean, recently refurbished rooms, all with en suite facilities and individual electric room heaters. A full Irish breakfast is included in the tariff and the hotel is open all year round.

cathedral's exterior is decorated with some remarkably vigorous, if rather weathered, carvings of Biblical scenes such as the Judgement of Solomon, and inside there are several Ogham stones which pre-date St Declan. One of them bears the longest known Ogham inscription in Ireland. Nearby rises an imposing **Round Tower,** reputedly built by the saint in the course of a single night. The graceful tower, 97 feet high, is remarkably well-preserved but cannot be the one so miraculously erected by Declan since it dates from the 11th century.

Cappoquin

10 miles NW of Dungarvan on the N72

From Ardmore the 55-mile long-distance footpath, **St Declan's Way,** links that historic village to the Rock of Cashel in Co. Tipperary. En route, the path passes through Cappoquin at the head of the tidal estuary of the River Blackwater, noted for its excellent coarse fishing. This quiet market town is surrounded by attractive wooded hills and the river valley to the west, skirting the **Knockmealdown Mountains,** is particularly lovely. If you take the **Glenshelane River Walk** it will bring you, after about 3 miles, to Mount Melleray Abbey, a functioning Cistercian foundation where visitors who wish to take time for quiet contemplation are welcome.

Lismore

16 miles W of Dungarvan on the N72

A designated Heritage Town, Lismore lies in the broad plain of the Blackwater Valley and has the distinct feel of a 19th century estate town. The estate in this instance was the property of **Lismore Castle,** the Irish home of successive Dukes of Devonshire since 1753. Earlier owners of the castle included Sir Walter Raleigh. He sold it to

BLACKWATER LODGE HOTEL & SALMON FISHERY

Upper Ballyduff, Co. Waterford
Tel: 058 60235 Fax: 058 60162
e-mail: info@ireland-salmon-fishing.net
website: www.ireland-salmon-fishing.net

Ian and Glenda Powell, the proprietors of the **Blackwater Lodge Hotel & Salmon Fishery** are passionate about salmon fishery and delight in the privilege of being able to cast for these noble creatures on one of the most prolific rivers in western Europe. They know what salmon anglers want and the kind of support services they appreciate. In addition, Glenda is also a qualified fly-fishing instructor – her only regret, she says, "is that as the mother of a young family, I can't get my waders wet as often as I'd like!" When not on the river, Ian and

Glenda make sure their guests are being well looked after. Ian looks after the 'business' end of things, indulging his expertise by selecting the wine list. Glenda ensures that the accommodation, food and facilities are what you would expect from a premier fishing lodge.

All the fish caught by you and your ghillie are yours and once weighed and recorded can be prepared in whatever way your prefer – frozen whole, smoked in the Lodge's own smokery or marinated to the Lodge's own Scandinavian Gravad Lax recipe. Other amenities here include an informal lounge bar with panoramic view of the river, an excellent restaurant where a table d'hôte meal is served in the early evening, and a choice of fully-appointed en suite rooms.

Pine Tree House

Ballyanchor, Lismore, Co. Waterford
Tel: 058 53282
e-mail: pinetreehouse@oceanfree.net
website: www.pinetreehouselismore.com

Pine Tree House enjoys a peaceful location yet is within walking distance of Lismore Castle Gardens, Mount Melleray Abbey and the Towers at Ballysaggart. Approved by Bord Failte, the house has 3 guest bedrooms (1 double; 1 twin and 1 triple-bedded room), all of them attractively furnished and decorated and provided with en suite facilities, television and hospitality tray. Guests receive a warm welcome in the morning in the pleasant dining room where owners Daphne and Shaun Power serve a traditional Irish breakfast for which Pine Tree House has become famous – it will more than set you up for the day! For an evening meal, there are some good restaurants locally or, if you are not going out, you can relax in the company of the family or just find a quiet corner to catch up on some reading.

The house has a charming garden and a large private car park; pets are welcome and there are discounts available for long stay guests. You'll find plenty to see and do without travelling far. Lismore itself is a Heritage town with many historic buildings such as St Carthage's Cathedral and the old Lismore Court House which is now the Heritage Centre. The town has its own 9-hole golf course and is just 30 minutes from the beaches at Dungarvan and Youghal.

Richard Boyle, later 1st Earl of Cork, whose 14th child, Robert, the celebrated chemist and formulator of Boyle's Law, was actually born in the castle. Parts of the grey stone, castellated building overhanging the river date back to the days of King John but the castle was extensively re-modelled by the 6th Duke of Devonshire in the mid-1800s. During this work a dazzling 13th century crozier was discovered hidden in the walls. Dubbed the Lismore Crozier it is now housed in Dublin's National Museum. An earlier refurbishment, in 1814, had also uncovered a treasure hidden in the walls – a bundle of 15th century manuscripts which became known as the Book of Lismore. The texts contain a number of biblical and secular stories. One of the latter tells of three sinners who take a vow of silence. At the end of the first year, one of them finally speaks to question the wisdom of their self-denial. A year later, the second pronounces his agreement. At the end of the third year, the last one says that he is sick and tired of their chattering and decides to return to the outside world.

The noble old castle, towering over the river, is not open to the public but visitors are welcome to explore the attractive gardens, in the afternoons only, from May to September.

Lismore's origins go back to AD 636 when St Carthage founded a monastic complex for both monks and nuns, a foundation which became an important centre of learning despite repeated attacks by Vikings and Normans. The most disastrous visitation however was by the troops of Elizabeth I who almost totally destroyed the medieval cathedral. Its site is now occupied by the Church of Ireland's **St Carthage's Cathedral**, consecrated in 1633 and given a neo-Gothic facelift in the 1820s. The cathedral enjoys a beautiful

Lismore Castle

setting, surrounded by ancient yews and pollarded limes, while the interior contains some interesting tombs and some dazzling stained glass by the English Pre-Raphaelite Burne-Jones.

Housed in the former Court House, **Lismore Heritage Centre** recounts the town's history since its foundation in AD 636 with the help of a multi-media format and an entertaining film presentation. In this award-winning multi-media presentation, "Brother Declan" takes you on an enthralling journey through time, beginning with the arrival of St Carthage in AD 636 and bringing viewers right up to the present.

Another interesting attraction is the **Irish Horse Experience** which is presented by the well-known Ballyrafter Equestrian Centre and available to pre-booked groups of 20 or more. Illustrated by live riding demonstrations, the 30-minute programme covers topics such as the origins, history and legends of the Irish horse; aspects of breeding, and the future of the horse in the 21st century.

Co Westmeath

Set in the heart of this placid county, the Hill of Uisneach was believed to mark the spot where the ancient provinces of Ireland converged, "the navel of Ireland". The hill is something of an exception in this land of woods, rivers and lakes, renowned for its first class angling. Four large lakes lie completely within the county boundaries, it shares beautiful Lough Sheelin in the north with County Cavan, and islet-dotted Lough Ree, over to the west, is noted for its scenic cruises.

The county town, Mullingar, is a busy agricultural centre surrounded by great huntin', shootin' and fishin' country and graced by a fine Palladian mansion, Belvedere House, famous for its gardens and a huge folly known as the Jealous Wall. The only other town of any size is Athlone, a bustling road, rail and waterway centre within easy reach of "Goldsmith Country", the area around Glassan ("The Village of the Roses") which has close associations with the 18th century author of *The Vicar of Wakefield*. And you will surely want to discover the Seven

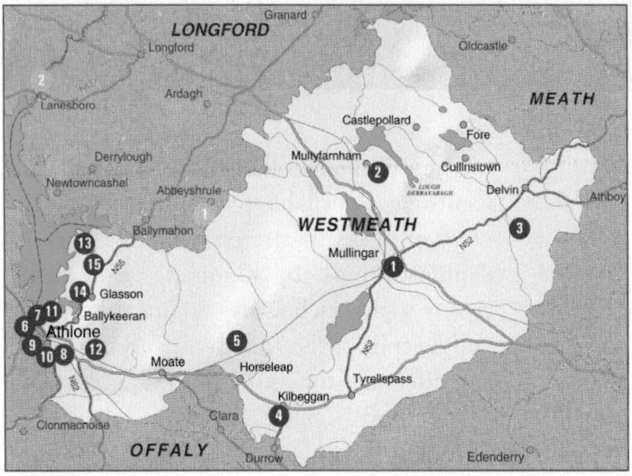

PLACES TO STAY, EAT AND DRINK

Belvedere House, Gardens & Park, Mullingar	1	House & Gardens	p338
An Tintain Restaurant and B&B, Multyfarnham	2	Restaurant & Accommodation	p339
Reynella House, Mullingar	3	B&B	p341
The Game Cock Bar, Kilbeggan	4	Pub	p342
Woodlands Farm, Mullingar	5	B&B	p343
Bonne Bouche, Athlone	6	Restaurant	p344
Riverside Inn, Athlone	7	Pub, Restaurant & Accommodation	p344
Creaghduff Lodge, Athlone	8	Self Catering	p345
Higgin's Pub, Athlone	9	Pub, Food & Accommodation	p345
Lough Ree Lodge, Athlone	10	Accommodation	p346
Cornamagh House, Athlone	11	B&B	p346
Four Seasons, Athlone	12	B&B	p347
Carnakilla Point, Athlone	13	Self Catering	p347
Killinure Chalets, Athlone	14	Self Catering	p348
Inny Bay B&B, Athlone	15	B&B	p348

● Denotes entries in other chapters

Wonders of Fore, hidden away in the Fore Valley, an area of outstanding natural beauty.

Mullingar

Standing on the River Brosna, halfway between Lough Ennell and Lough Owel, Mullingar is almost encircled by the Royal Canal. Standing at the centre of Ireland's cattle-rearing heartland, it's a lively place with some excellent grocery shops, a well-patronised Arts Centre, an equestrian centre, and one of the country's few greyhound racing stadiums. The town's most striking building is the **Cathedral of Christ the King,** a neo-Classical building of white stone whose twin spires soar 140 feet into the sky and, whether intentionally or not, somewhat resemble devotional candles. Inside, there are two interesting mosaics by the Russian artist Boris Anrep, and an ecclesiastical museum which contains many penal wooden crosses and the vestments of St Oliver Plunkett.

Mullingar was formerly a garrison town and the history of those days is recorded in the **Military Museum** at the Columb Barracks. Housed in the old Guard Room, the museum has a display of arms, uniforms and flags from both World Wars, as well as exhibits devoted to the IRA, the War of Independence and the Civil War of the 1920s. Not particularly military but nevertheless fascinating are the long, canoe-like boats which have been found in the boggy floor of the nearby lakes. Originally thought to be Viking craft, they have now been dated as much earlier. Amongst the oddities in the museum is a Military Cycling Handbook which explores this arcane skill with a gravity worthy of the Monty Python team.

Sadly, the most entertaining of Mullingar's museums, The Market House Museum, is currently closed. It was run by volunteers and what it lacked in priceless items it made up for with enthusiasm. Here one can learn all about a genuine local eccentric by the name of Adolphus Cooke. Amongst other peculiar notions, Adolphus was convinced that one of the turkeys strutting about his yard was the reincarnation of his father. He also had the windows of his house made into the shape of spoon-backed chairs, the better to reflect the furniture within. Throughout his life, Adolphus firmly believed that he would be reincarnated as a bee so he arranged to be buried in a tomb resembling a beehive. It stands in the graveyard of Cooksborough church, about 8 miles east of Mullingar. (Incidentally, plans are under way to re-locate the Market House Museum and its artefacts elsewhere in the town).

At the **Mullingar Bronze & Pewter Visitor Centre** (free) visitors can join a factory tour and watch craftsmen at work model making, casting, assembling and finishing their bronze and pewter pieces. There's a gift shop with an extensive range of both bronze and pewter objects at prices to suit all pockets, and a coffee shop serving tea and light refreshments.

Around Mullingar

About 3 miles south of Mullingar, beautifully sited on the shores of Lough Ennell, **Belvedere House & Gardens** (see panel on page 338) is a popular destination for a summer afternoon's outing.

Belvedere House & Gardens is owned and operated by Westmeath County Council which also owns and runs the **Mullingar Arts Centre**. Located in the heart of the town, it reflects a vibrant and thriving community. It boasts an unrivalled programme of concerts, theatre and exhibitions, and also hosts a wide variety of classes and workshops on all aspects of the Arts for both beginners and the experienced. Its exhibition gallery, as well as hosting shows by more familiar names,

Belvedere House, Gardens & Park

Mullingar, Co. Westmeath
Tel: 044 49060 Fax: 044 49002
e-mail: info@belvedere-house.ie
website: www.belvedere-house.ie

Standing in 160 acres of gardens and parkland on the shores of Lough Ennell, **Belvedere House, Gardens and Park** offers visitors one of the finest of Ireland's historic houses together with beautifully restored gardens. The magnificent Palladian house was built around 1740 for Robert Rochfort, later 1st Earl of Belvedere. By all accounts Rochfort was a deeply unpleasant man. After accusing his young wife of adultery with his younger brother Arthur, he kept her prisoner in a nearby house for 31 years. Arthur fled to England. When he returned to Ireland twenty years later, the Earl promptly sued him for adultery. Unable to pay the legal costs, Arthur spent the rest of his life in gaol.

The Earl also quarrelled with another brother, George, who lived at Tudenham House just across from the Earl's mansion. To block out any view of Tudenham House which was built on a far grander scale than Belvedere House, the Earl ordered the building of the Jealous Wall, an impressive Gothic folly said to the most extensive man-made "ruin" in Ireland. It stands three storeys high and extends for 180 feet.

The interior of Belvedere House has recently been completely restored and refurnished using authentic period furnishings. Its most glorious features are the curved balustrade staircase and the dazzling rococo plasterwork ceilings believed to have been created by the French stuccodore Barthelemij Cramillion. The country house historian Marc Girouard wrote of the scrollwork in the drawing-room that *"it flickers and crackles like flames across the edge of the ceilings and stretches out a long tongue into the curved recess of the bow window"*.

The visitor centre at Belvedere House contains exhibits detailing the history of the house and the flora and fauna that flourish in its grounds while in the modern audio-visual theatre the tragic story of the first Earl's wife is told. Outside, there are two restaurants and a shop off the Courtyard; for children, a Discovery and Play Area alongside an Animal Sanctuary.

also provides a platform for up-and-coming artists to display their talent – submissions are always welcome.

A couple of miles south of Belvedere on the N52 a sign points right to **Lilliput.** It's named in honour of Jonathan Swift who was a regular visitor to Westmeath in the early 1700s when he stayed with the Rochfort family at Gaulstown House. It's said that it was when the Dean looked across the expanse of Lough Ennell to the opposite shore and noted the tiny human figures there that he conceived the idea of the Lilliputians featured in *Gulliver's Travels*.

Some 10 miles southwest of Mullingar, at about the geographical centre of the country, is **Uisneach Hill**, the "navel of Ireland". In mythology this was the seat of the High Kings before they moved to Tara. The only evidence for this are thick layers of ashes suggesting that it was the site for fire festivals such as the Beltane, held in the first days of May. *Bealtaine* incidentally is the Irish word for the month of May. Standing atop the hill is an ancient boulder, the **Catstone** ("Stone of Divisions"), 6 metres high and weighing 30 tons. It traditionally marks the geographical centre of the four ancient provinces of Ireland: Leinster, Munster, Connacht and Ulster. If you climb to the summit of the 250 feet hill there are views taking in 20 of the 32 counties that formed the four provinces.

North of Mullingar is the most scenic part of the county, containing the loughs of Derravaragh, Lene and Sheelin, and the enchanting Fore Valley running close to the border with County Meath. The area also boasts one of Ireland's largest and most romantic stately homes, Tullynally Castle, and the ancient ecclesiastical settlement of Fore Abbey. Visitors can also follow the Fore Trail which links the celebrated "Seven Wonders of Fore".

Multyfarnham

8 miles N of Mullingar off the N4

A winner of the "Tidy Towns" award,

Multyfarnham stands on the River Gaine about half a mile from where it flows into Lough Derravaragh. The modern Franciscan **Friary** here was built on the site of one founded around 1260. That friary was suppressed by Henry VIII in 1540 but the monks maintained a presence here, - "a nest of scorpions" as Elizabeth I described them, - until they were scattered by Cromwell's troops in 1651. The old Friary was restored in 1973 and has some striking modern stained glass. The grounds contain life-size stations of the cross, regarded as one of the finest outdoor shrines in Ireland.

Castlepollard

13 miles N of Mullingar on the R354

This neat little town was laid out in the late 17th/early 18th century by the Pollard family with attractive houses set around a

AN TINTÁIN RESTAURANT & GUESTHOUSE

Multyfarnham, Co. Westmeath
Tel: 044 71411 Fax: 044 71434
e-mail: antintain@ireland.com
website: www.antintain.info

Enjoying a picturesque riverside setting in the quaint little village of Multyfarnham, **An Tintáin Restaurant & Guesthouse** offers excellent food and comfortable lodging in wonderfully peaceful surroundings. ('An Tintáin', incidentally, translates as "No home fire like your own home fire"). The building has an old world stone frontage but behind this lies a modern and luxurious, purpose-built 3-star guesthouse and restaurant, furnished and decorated to the highest standards. The 6 comfortable guest bedrooms all have en suite facilities, TV, direct dial

telephone and hairdryer. In the Forge Bar – so named because there's a genuine listed forge on the premises – customers can enjoy a relaxing drink before dining in the fully licensed restaurant with its candlelit tables.

The food served here has featured in Ireland's *Food & Wine* magazine and is inventive and quite outstanding. Amongst the starters, for example, you'll find 'Panirana palachinka s pileshko I zelenchutsi' or you might prefer just saying "Delicious Bulgarian vegetable crepe, stuffed with sweetcorn, peppers, mushrooms and onions". Main dishes are based on quality, carefully sourced ingredients such as Westmeath or Hereford Beef, and Silver Hill Duckling. A vegetarian choice is always listed – other vegetarian dishes are available on request.

large triangular green. Castlepollard is a popular base for anglers drawn here by the abundant roach, pike and trout in nearby Loughs Derravaragh and Lene, and for visitors to **Tullynally Castle**, hereditary home for ten generations of the Anglo-Irish Pakenham family, the Earls of Longford. One of the largest and most stately homes in Ireland, the castle began as a simple tower house in the late 1600s. Then, in the early 1800s, it was remodelled in the Gothic Revival style, - bristling with battlements, towers and turrets. More recently, new ornamental features have been added to the grounds, amongst them a Chinese Garden complete with pagoda and a Tibetan garden of waterfalls and streams . The walled gardens contain a magnificent avenue of 200-year-old Irish yew trees. Guided tours of the house include the Great Hall whose superb acoustics make it an ideal venue for concerts and recitals; the Library started by the 1st Earl's wife in the 1760s and now containing more than 8000 volumes; and a vast Victorian kitchen.

Tullynally Castle

The castle stands in 30 acres of romantic woodland and walled gardens, laid out in the 18th and 19th centuries, which contain many splendid trees, a grotto and two ornamental lakes. The grounds are open to visitors from May to August; the castle itself from mid-June to the end of July every afternoon, and at other times by arrangement.

Fore

16 miles NE of Mullingar off the R195

The **Seven Wonders of Fore** are scattered across the Fore Valley but the local tourist board has produced a useful leaflet detailing the Fore Trail which links them and other places of interest in the valley. The traditional listing of the 7 wonders has "*the anchorite in a stone*" as number six. This refers to the **Anchorite's Cell**, a cubicle 8 feet by 12 feet in the tower of a tiny chapel on the hillside above Fore. The cell was occupied by hermits right up until 1616. The last hermit was a man called Patrick Beglan who had vowed to stay in

Tullynally Castle Gardens

Reynella House

Bracklyn, Mullingar, Co. Westmeath
Tel: 044 64137
e-mail: reynellahouse@eircom.net

Reynella House must be one of the most elegant bed and breakfast establishments in the country. An impressive Georgian mansion built in 1770, it stands in grounds of 155 acres complete with beautifully maintained gardens, a private lake with good coarse fishing, a walled garden, and with some lovely woodland walks.

Since 1992 Reynella House has been the home of Margaret and Patrick Lynch, a friendly and welcoming couple who do everything they can to ensure that their guests have a relaxing stay.

There are 3 guest bedrooms, (2 family rooms; 1 double), one with en suite facilities, the others with private bathrooms. All rooms have TV and hospitality tray.

the cell until he died. Oddly, he broke his neck falling from the tower window. The chapel is kept locked but the key can be obtained from the appropriately named Seven Wonders pub nearby.

At the bottom of the hill is Wonder Number 2: "*the monastery in the bog*", the roofless remains of **St Fechin's Church,** named after St Fechin's Spring nearby from which bubbles up Wonder Number 5: "the water that will not boil". St Fechin founded his monastery here around AD 630 but the present ruins date from the 11th to the 13th centuries. A notable feature of the church is the mighty lintel stone over its west doorway which is carved with a Greek cross within a circle. It weighs over two tons and could only have been put in place by means of a miracle, hence Wonder Number 7: "*the stone raised by St Fechin's prayers*".

The remaining three Wonders are "*the water that flows uphill*", which refers to the river flowing out of Lough Lene where a trick of the light makes it seem as if the water is indeed running upwards; "*the tree that will not burn*", probably a petrified stump but now represented by a tourist board placement of a dead branch, and "*the mill without a race*", the only one of the Wonders that has not been satisfactorily explained.

Other antiquities in and around Fore include the stone gateways that led into the medieval village, and no fewer than 18 crosses, some plain, others carved, of which the best preserved stands in the middle of the village.

Collinstown

14 miles NE of Mullingar on the R395

Collinstown village, once known as the "Maypole", always presents a very pretty appearance, especially during the summer months, with flower-filled gardens and a general air of neatness and order. The village stands close to the southern tip of Lough Lene, a European Blue Flag Lake and a popular venue for swimmers, anglers and scuba divers. The village also has its own pitch and putt course.

Delvin

13 miles NE of Mullingar on the A52/R395

This attractive village set in wooded surroundings boasts a well-preserved 13th century castle in Delvin Castle and another, Clonyn Castle, which stands in ruins in the grounds of the 19th century building that replaced it and took its name. Within the spacious estate of Clonyn Castle is a popular 18-hole golf course. The celebrated writer, Brinsley MacNamara, was born in Ballinvalley near Delvin and some of his works are set in the neighbourhood.

Tyrrellspass

11 miles S of Mullingar on the N52/N6

This delightful Georgian village takes its name from Robert Tyrrell, a late-16th century hero who annihilated a large force of Elizabethan troops with only a small band of men. The winner of many "Irish Tidy Town" awards, the village was formally laid out around the semi-circular green by Jane, Countess of Belvedere, in the 18th century. Amongst the buildings of note here is **Tyrrellspass Castle**. This impressive 15th century tower house retains many of its original features, notably its internal stone spiral staircases. Facilities include a museum, gift shop and licensed restaurant, and medieval banquets are held here regularly during the season. Also worth visiting is **St Sinian's Church** which contains some elaborate tombs to the Belvedere family. One of them commemorates Jane as a countess *"gifted with a masculine understanding"*.

Kilbeggan

14 miles SW of Mullingar on the N6

The main visitor attraction in this neat little town on the River Brosna is **Locke's Distillery**, believed to be the oldest licensed pot still distillery in the world. Established in 1757, pot still Irish malt whiskey was produced here for almost 200 years. In recent years, the local community has been restoring the building and machinery so that the huge old water wheel is now turning again and visitors can follow the process from the grinding of the grain to the casking of the final product. A complimentary glass completes the tour. There's a bar inside the distillery, where you can also sample "the water of life", and a restaurant where you can enjoy a meal in front of an open fire.

About a mile outside the town, **Kilbeggan Race Track** is the only racecourse in Ireland where the races are over jumps under National Hunt Rules – the type of racing the Irish love best. Voted

The Game Cock Bar

Main Street, Kilbeegan, Co. Westmeath
Tel: 0506 321117
Mobile: 086 824 9787

Located close to Kilbeegan's famous racecourse, **The Game Cock Bar** is a fine example of a traditional Irish bar with lots of atmosphere and good craic.

Owner James McNevin, who has been in the hospitality business for more than 20 years, took over here in the summer of 2003 and carried out a comprehensive refurbishment while being careful to maintain the pub's character.

James possesses a wealth of local knowledge so if there's anything you want to know about the area, just ask! A major attraction here is the traditional Irish music sessions that take place every week.

Woodlands Farm

Streamstown, Mullingar, Co. Westmeath
Tel: 044 26414

This charming old country house, its walls smothered with ivy and surrounded by 120 acres of working farm, is located midway between Dublin and Galway, just two and a half miles off the N6 at Horseleap. Your host at **Woodlands Farm,** Mary Maxwell, offers a lovely atmosphere, delicious home cooking and a choice of six guest bedrooms (4 twin/ doubles; 1 family; 1 single), four of which have their own en suite facilities; the other two have private bathrooms. There's a separate guest lounge with comfortable armchairs, television and tea/ coffee-making facilities. Mary is an accomplished cook who serves a wonderful breakfast and is also happy to provide a tasty evening meal.

It's not surprising to find that Woodlands Farm is a Bord Failte Best B&B and also enjoys AA and Frommer approval. Travel Agent vouchers are welcome and there's a 33% reduction for children who will also appreciate the resident pony and donkey! Golf, horse-riding and fishing are all within easy reach, and Woodlands is also conveniently located for visiting the hallowed monastic site of Clonmacnoise where the last High King of Ireland, Rory O'Conor, was buried in 1198.

Locke's Distillery

Race Course of the Year in the past, Kilbeggan hosts a series of meetings throughout the summer months.

Horseleap

14 miles SW of Mullingar on the R391/ N6

This little village stands at a crossroads, close to the geographical centre of Ireland and within inches of the border with Co. Offaly. The unusual name derives from a legend dating back to medieval times. The story goes that the Norman Baron de Lacy was being pursued by a posse of native Gaels, the MacGeoghegans, and only escaped by jumping over the castle drawbridge. Oddly, of the Norman castle in which he found safety, only the drawbridge pillars remain.

Moate

18 miles SW of Mullingar on the N6

This sizeable market town takes its name from the man-made hill known as Mota Grainne Oige which rises beside it. In Celtic times, Grainne Oige (Young Grace) was the wife of the chief of the district, O'Melaghlin.

The major tourist attraction here is the **Dun Na Si Heritage Centre and Park** which offers a microcosm of Irish culture. The Folk Park presents a picture of bygone days with features such as preserved farm machinery, while in the evening and at weekends visitors can enjoy Irish music, song, dance and storytelling at a folklore show. There's also a genealogy research centre for Westmeath and a souvenir shop and restaurant.

Athlone

Straddling the River Shannon just before it flows into Lough Ree, Athlone has been an important strategic location since prehistoric times. Turlough O'Connor built a wattle bridge here and fortified the banks. Brian Boru, High King of Ireland, convened a great assembly at Athlone in AD 1001 and two centuries later the Anglo-Normans replaced an earlier castle with the sturdy fortress known as **King John's Castle.** This remained in use by the military right up until 1969. Although it has been strengthened and extended over the centuries, the castle still retains its classic, uncompromising Norman design. During its long history the castle has seen a great deal of action, most notably in 1690 when supporters of James II withstood a week-

Bonne Bouche

Church Street, Athlone, Co. Westmeath
Tel: 090 72112

Located right in the heart of this historic old town, the **Bonne Bouche** restaurant has been providing good wholesome food for some 23 years. John Mc Loughlin's honest-to-goodness menu includes all the old traditional favourites such as Bacon & Cabbage, Roast Beef and fish dishes along with home-made burgers, quiches, lasagne, sandwiches and light snacks. The 120-seater restaurant is on the first floor above Rick's Bar and is fully licensed. The friendly atmosphere here has made the Bonne Bouche one of Athlone's most popular restaurants, definitely not to be missed. It is open from 10am to 6pm, Monday to Saturday.

Athlone Castle

Riverside Inn

4/5 Castle Street, Athlone, Co. Westmeath
Tel: 090 649 4981 Fax; 090 649 3587

Standing beside the Castle and across the road from the River Shannon, **The Riverside Inn** occupies a fine old building dating back to the late 1700s. Mine host Micheal Ducie, who managed the Hodson Bay Hotel for some 8 years, took over here in the summer of 2002 and has carried out an extensive redecoration and up-grading. Popular with local people, the inn has a huge open-plan lounge with slate and wooden floors and lots of nooks and crannies. This leads to the elegant restaurant which serves excellent home-made food all day. The superior accommodation comprises 15 modern rooms all en suite and including single and family rooms.

long siege here, and again in 1691 when William III's artillery peppered the town and castle with some 12,000 cannonballs.

The circular keep of the castle now houses an interesting museum of folk and local history. Amongst other things, you can learn the approved method of milking a cow, (begin by squirting a few drops on the grass for the fairies), and see the pairs of boots worn by ponies when rolling the lawn, a neat way of protecting the turf from unsightly hoof prints. There are audio-visual presentations on the dramatic Sieges of Athlone in 1690 and 1691, and another on the Story of the Shannon, Ireland's longest river. The museum collection includes two fine examples of **Sheila-na-Gig sculptures**, (prehistoric fertility symbols),

River Shannon, Athlone

Creaghduff Lodge

Creaghduff House, Athlone, Co. Westmeath
Tel: 0902 75891

The two self-catering apartments at **Creaghduff Lodge** provide a genuine experience of rural Ireland. The simple stone building was built some 300 years ago as a boathouse and has recently been restored by owner Allison Couper. Each apartment has its own fitted kitchen, electric cooker and fridge, a dining/sitting area and a bedroom that sleeps 4 with a bathroom en suite. Other amenities include colour TV, washing machine, free linen, and a bait and tackle room with fridge; boats and engines are also available. Children and pets are welcome – a baby-sitting service can be arranged.

Higgins' Pub

2 Pearse Street, Athlone, Co. Westmeath
Tel: 090 6492519

Located on Athlone's west bank, close to the main street, **Higgins' Pub** is as satisfying a traditional Irish inn as you could hope to find. Mine hosts, Tina and Paul Donovan, serve an excellent draught Guinness and also offer a good selection of light meals including home-made soup, sandwiches, baps and filled rolls made to order, salads, BLTs, apple pie and scones, as well as hot meals such as lasagne. Food is served from 10am to 8pm, with breakfast also available from 8.30pm to noon. If you are planning to stay in this historic town, the pub has 4 comfortable guest rooms (2 doubles; 1 triple; 1 family), all en suite with TV and hospitality tray.

Lough Ree Lodge

Dublin Road, Athlone, Co. Westmeath
Tel: 090 64 76738 Fax: 090 64 76477
e-mail: loughreelodge@eircom.net
website: www.athlonehostel.ie

Located just off the N6 and minutes from the town centre, **Lough Ree Lodge** offers outstanding budget accommodation with a choice of single, twin, double or family rooms, as well as small dormitories. There's a fully equipped self-catering kitchen and dining area and a free continental breakfast is served. All 60 rooms are en suite and provided with satellite TV and linen. There are safe lockers, a private TV lounge, pool room, laundry and drying room, and a garden with barbecue area. Owners, Gerry and Geraldine Barry, are adding more self-catering accommodation to be available from September 2004.

Cornamagh House

Cornamagh, Athlone, Co. Westmeath
Tel: 090 64 74171
e-mail: fagg@indigo.ie

Well-signposted from the N55 a mile north of Athlone (turn at Fernhill Garden Centre), **Cornamagh House** is a spacious and attractive building standing in beautifully maintained grounds – owners Mary and Brian Fagg are both avid gardeners. They are also welcoming hosts who have been receiving bed & breakfast guests here for many years, a good proportion of them return visitors. The house has 5 guest bedrooms, all with en suite facilities and all attractively furnished and decorated. The tariff includes a hearty breakfast with plenty of choice.

and a fascinating display devoted to John McCormack, the legendary tenor who was born at Athlone in 1884. The singer's own 78rpm gramophone is among the exhibits, along with a stack of his recordings – visitors can ask for their favourite to be played. A bust of McCormack, who was created a Papal Count in 1928 for his charitable works, occupies a prominent position on the riverside promenade and a plaque marks his house in The Bawn, off Mardyke Street.

If you really want to get into the historical spirit, Viking Tours have a replica longboat and Viking costumes for children to dress up in. In addition to cruises around Lough Ree, the company also offers trips south along the Shannon to the monastic site of Clonmacnoise.

A popular family attraction, located two miles west of Athlone, is **Glendeer Pet Farm**, an award-winning 6-acre open farm which is home to more than 50 species of animals and birds – deer, ostrich, Vietnamese pot-belly pigs, Jacob sheep, Jeresey cows, fancy pheasants and other rare birds and domestic fowl. Throughout December, Glendeer is transformed into Lapland, complete with Santa Claus and his live deer, Dancer and Prancer.

Around Athlone

Ballykeeran

4 miles NE of Athlone on the N55

A popular choice for a day out in this area is to take a boat trip on Lough Ree. The lake is actually an expansion of the River

Four Seasons

Annagh, Ballykeeran, Athlone, Co. Westmeath
Tel: 090 64 74470
e-mail: grennanfourseasons@eircom.net
website: www.athlone.ie/fourseasonsb&b

Built in 1998, **Four Seasons** is a charming modern dwelling offering quality bed & breakfast accommodation. It stands in a quiet country lane just a 10-minute drive from Athlone town centre and close to the N6 Dublin road. Four Seasons is the home of Breda Grennan who has 4 absolutely delightful guest bedrooms, all with en suite facilities and modern amenities. Guests have the use of a lovely lounge with lots of exposed beams and there's a light and airy conservatory-style breakfast room – Breda's full Irish breakfasts are justly famous! Open all year round, Four Seasons has ample parking.

Shannon, about 15 miles long and varying from 1 mile to 6 miles across. Several of the islands have the remains of very early churches, one of them, Inchclearaun, boasting no fewer than six early Christian ruins. Your guide will regale you with stories of Queen Maeve, goddess of war and fertility, who it seems was very active around Lough Ree in mythological times. Also look out for the ruins of 13th century Rindown Castle which stands on a spit of land jutting out into the lake.

Glasson

4 miles NE of Athlone on the N55

Ill fares the land, to hastening ills a prey
Where wealth accumulates and men decay.

Those familiar lines from Oliver Goldsmith's poem *The Deserted Village* were written with Glasson in mind. The poet was lamenting the mid-18th century enclosures which were devastating rural life throughout Britain:

Carnakilla Point

Portlick, Glasson, Athlone, Co. Westmeath
Tel: 0902 85389 Fax: 0902 85953
website: www.shannon-holidays.com

Idyllically set on the shores of Lough Ree and adjoining the splendid Portlick Woodlands, **Carnakilla Point** offers top quality self-catering accommodation in wonderfully peaceful surroundings. The five chalet-style houses (4 with 3 bedrooms; 1 with 2) have been beautifully finished and equipped to the highest standards and are well separated. Proprietor Owen Egan, a master carpenter and conservationist is also an experienced fisherman who knows Lough Ree well. Boats are available for hire, with a gillie if desired, to explore these unrivalled fishing grounds that are well-stocked with pike, trout, bream, perch, roach and rudd. Open all year round; credit cards accepted.

Killinure Chalets

Glasson, Athlone, Co. Westmeath
Tel: 0902 85155
e-mail: manfred@eircom.net
website: www.killinurechalets.com

Beautifully located on the shore of Lough Ree, **Killinure Chalets** offer outstanding self-catering accommodation in peaceful and scenic surroundings. Owners Geraldine and Manfred Walesch have been in the business for some 30 years and are very experienced in catering to their visitors' needs. Each of the 11 attractively designed chalets is comprehensively equipped with just about everything you could possibly want for a relaxed and trouble-free holiday.

A popular amenity here is the well-stocked licensed clubhouse, open to all visitors. Anglers will appreciate the excellent fishing in the lake and boats with outboard motors are available for hire. The Waleschs can provide fishing tackle if required and sea fishing can also be arranged. If your passion is golf, Glasson Golf Course is right next door and Glasson village itself is a trim estate village famous as *The Deserted Village* in one of Oliver Goldsmith's best known poems. It's also known as the "village of the roses" since in the poem Glasson appears as Sweet Auburn which means just that. And just a few miles further is historic Athlone with its sturdy castle and excellent museum which contains an exhibit devoted to the legendary tenor John McCormack who was born here in 1884.

Inny Bay B&B

Annagh, The Pigeons, Athlone, Co. Westmeath
Tel: 090 648 5284 / 090 648 5055
Mobile: 087 637 0237
e-mail: foxed@eircom.net
website www.innybay.com

Part of Lough Ree, Inny Bay is a wonderfully tranquil place and it's here that you'll find the **Inny Bay B&B**, set right on the water's edge and far from passing traffic. It's the home of Deirdre and Paul Foxe who have been welcoming guests at this peaceful spot since 1999. The lake and the Inny River are an angler's paradise with good fishing in the lake and bank fishing available on the river, hire boats are available and fishing trips can be arranged. Quite apart from the breathtaking views, Lough Ree offers a wonderful place to relax and enjoy some tranquility. The Lough has a multitude of small islands, rich in wildlife and Irish History. Guests have the use of a comfortable lounge with an open fire, Sky TV, and tea/coffee making facilities and there's also a pleasant sun room. The 3 guest bedrooms are all en suite and attractively furnished and decorated. A copious Irish breakfast is included in the tariff and evening meals are available by arrangement.

If you enjoy good craic, there's a traditional pub conveniently close while for golfers the 18-hole Glasson Golf Course is just a 10 minute drive away. Another 5 miles brings you to the historic town of Athlone with its mighty fortress known as King John's Castle which now houses an outstanding museum. Ballymahon and Longford are within easy reach in the other direction.

No busy steps the grassgrown
foot-way tread
For all the bloomy flush of life
is fled.

Glasson

In his poem, Glasson appears as "sweet Auburn", the "village of the roses". Today, Glasson is an attractive estate village, built for the many workers on the nearby Waterstown estate.

The local tourist authorities have been zealous in putting up brown and white signs directing visitors to any site connected with Oliver Goldsmith although it has to be said that some of them are less than rewarding. Goldsmith spent his childhood from the age of 2 at the parsonage in **Lissoy,** 3 miles north of Glasson. Only the front and end walls of the building still remain; nothing at all survives of the school he attended here. Forgney Church, where his father served as a curate until 1730, was rebuilt in 1830. At Pallas, his supposed birthplace, the Oliver Goldsmith Society erected in 1974 a larger-than-life statue of the poet, incomprehensibly incarcerated behind bars in a curious kind of grotto.

Co Wexford

The southeast corner of Ireland is the sunniest and driest part of the country and County Wexford is conveniently provided with some excellent beaches lining almost the whole of its east coast. The strands at Curracloe and Rosslare are particularly extensive and even in July and August never overcrowded. Curracloe has an additional interest for film buffs since it was the location for the 'Normandy' beach landings in Stephen Spielberg's film *Saving Private Ryan*. Inland, the gentle countryside of low hills, lush valleys and trim farms is shaped by three great rivers, the Nore, the Barrow and the Slaney. To the northwest, the Blackstairs Mountains form a natural boundary with County Carlow.

Although County Wexford has many prehistoric and medieval monuments, they tend to be on a modest scale with the many 14th century tower houses, for example, merging into the later farmhouses which have grown up around them. The county

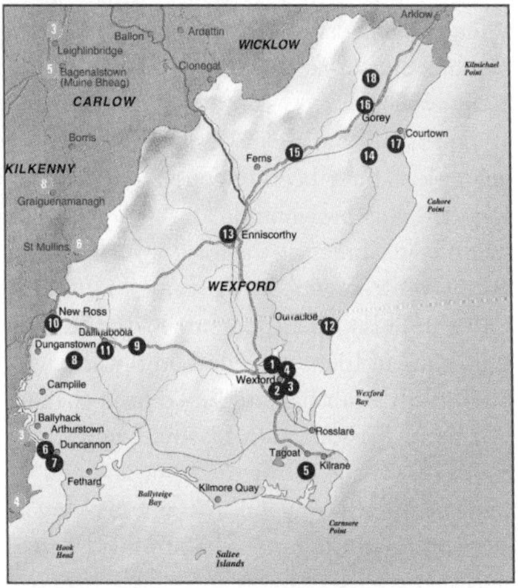

PLACES TO STAY, EAT AND DRINK

Forde's Restaurant, Wexford	1	Restaurant	p351
The West Gate Tavern, Wexford	2	Pub with Food	p352
Harbour Lights, Wexford	3	B&B	p352
Granville House, Wexford	4	B&B	p353
Airdownes Cottages, Broadway	5	Self Catering	p355
Roches Bar & Sqigl Restaurant, New Ross	6	Bar & Restaurant	p356
Duncannon Fort, Duncannon	7	Historic Site	p357
Creacon Lodge Hotel, New Ross	8	Hotel	p358
The Cedar Lodge Hotel, Newbawn	9	Hotel	p360
Thornbury House, New Ross	10	B&B	p361
Horse & Hounds, New Ross	11	Pub, Restaurant & Accommodation	p362
Furlongs Village Bar, Curracloe	12	Pub with Food	p363
Treacey's Hotel, Enniscorthy	13	Hotel	p364
Bootlaces Bar & Lounge, Gorey	14	Pub, Food & Accommodation	p366
Jack's Tavern, Camolin	15	Pub with Food	p366
The Mezz Bar, Gorey	16	Restaurant	p367
Stone Lodge, Gorey	17	B&B	p368
Woodlands Country House, Gorey	18	Guest House	p368

Denotes entries in other chapters

boasts some outstanding gardens, notably at Johnstown Castle near Wexford Town, and the JFK Arboretum at New Ross, established as a memorial to President Kennedy whose forebears lived at nearby Dunganstown.

Wexford Town

The Vikings named the town *Waesfjord* – 'harbour of the mudflats', an appropriate name since it stands beside the muddy estuary of the River Slaney whose silt-laden waters have gradually clogged the once busy deep-water harbour. However, the mudflats, known locally as "slobs", provide a perfect habitat for thousands of wading birds. The **Wexford Wildfowl Reserve** (free) is famous for its wintering wildfowl with species such as Greenland White-fronted Geese, Brent Geese, Bewick's Swans and Widgeon amongst the regular visitors.

Old Wexford has been described as "one of the most atmospheric towns in Ireland" with many of its winding streets so narrow you could shake hands across them. But the only substantial medieval building to have survived is **Westgate.** Built around 1300, it was one of the five gates of the walled city. Now designated the West Gate Heritage Tower it offers a short film retracing the history of the town. Also interesting are the remains of **Selskar Abbey** where Henry II spent the whole 40 days of Lent 1171 in atonement for the murder of Thomas à Becket.

In the centre of Wexford, a small square called the Bull Ring is a reminder of the once popular sport of bull-baiting. The square is now dominated by a statue, the Lone Pikeman, commemorating the rebellion of 1798 when armed only with pikes the townspeople of Wexford fought valiantly against overwhelming odds. A century and a half earlier, Cromwell and his troops had occupied the town, destroyed many of its churches and massacred all but 400 of the town's population of around 2000. The Bull Ring is also noted for the Cape Bar, one of more than 90 bars in the town but the only one which doubles as an undertaker's.

On nearby Crescent Quay stands the statue of a vigorously striding naval officer, Commodore John Barry, a local man who emigrated to Philadelphia and is credited with founding the American Navy during the War of Independence.

Internationally, the town is probably best known for its annual **Wexford Festival Opera**, "Europe's most enjoyable Festival" according to *Reader's Digest*. Held in October, the festival offers the opportunity of seeing lesser-known works by major composers in a wonderfully unstuffy, festive atmosphere. Performances take place in the

FORDE'S RESTAURANT

Crescent Quay, Wexford, Co. Wexford
Tel/Fax: 053 23832 / 22816

Set on the quayside overlooking Wexford Harbour, **Forde's Restaurant** enjoys a glowing reputation for outstanding food and appeared in the list of Ireland's Best 100 Restaurants in both 2003 and 2004. Chef/patron Liam Forde is an accomplished cook with many years of classical training and his menu offers an extensive and enticing choice that ranges from prime fillet steak, through delicious seafood dishes to vegetarian dishes such as cannelloni of wild mushrooms. The 100-cover restaurant is open daily from 6pm to 9.45pm (10.30pm on Saturday); an Early Bird menu is available between 6pm and 7pm, and Sunday lunch is served between noon and 3pm.

Irish National Heritage Park

tiny Theatre Royal, so tickets are hard to come by, but the Festival also offers recitals, concerts, lectures and a lively fringe programme. Wexford's cultural life isn't just confined to the Festival. Throughout the rest of the year the Theatre Royal puts on drama performances and the **Wexford Arts Centre**, housed in an 18th century market house in Cornmarket, has an ever-changing programme of exhibitions, dance and music performances.

One of Wexford's must-see attractions, the **Irish National Heritage Park**. The 35-acre site overlooking the Slaney River depicts human settlements in Ireland from 7000 BC until the arrival of the Normans in the 12th century. Visitors can wander

The West Gate Tavern

Westgate, Wexford, Co. Wexford
Tel: 053 22086

Opposite the West Gate Heritage Centre and close to the Courthouse, the **The West Gate Tavern** is popular with both visitors to the former and those who work at the latter. This traditional hostelry has been owned and run by Michael and Catherine Power since 1988 but its licence dates right back to 1761. It has a compact public bar, full of charm and character, and a spacious lounge where you can enjoy tasty home-cooked food and bar snacks, all prepared from the freshest ingredients possible. There is a variety of live entertainment Monday nights, July-Sept Pub Theatre on Tues and Folk & Blues on Thurs, Ballads & Sinalong on Sundays 6-8pm (winter) or 9-11pm (summer). The Powers also run a bed & breakfast establishment nearby.

Harbour Lights

Kilmore Quay, Wexford, Co. Wexford
Tel: 053 29881

If you are planning to stay in the picturesque little fishing village of Kilmore Quay, you can't do better than **Harbour Lights,** an attractive modern house just 200 yards from the harbour and 500 yards from miles of beach. It's the home of May Bates, a cheerful bubbly lady who has been welcoming bed & breakfast guests here since 1992. Set in extensive, well-maintained gardens, the house has 5 guest bedrooms, all meticulously appointed and provided with en suite facilities, TV and hospitality tray. Guests have the use of a spacious and comfortable residents' lounge and May serves an excellent breakfast with plenty of choice.

Johnstown Castle

through carefully reconstructed full-scale models of ancient homesteads and places of ritual. Burial modes are explained and the county's abundance of archaeological remains interpreted. Guided tours are available and the site includes a Viking shipyard, a nature reserve, a restaurant and a crafts and book shop. The Park is open daily from early April until the end of October.

A couple of miles south of the Park is another major visitor attraction. **Johnstown Castle Gardens** surround Johnstown Castle, a splendid Gothic Revival castellated mansion which is now an Agricultural College. The gardens contain a wealth of colourful shrubs and flowers, ornamental lakes, shady woodland and beautifully maintained walled gardens. The

Granville House

Clonard Road, Wexford, Co. Wexford
Tel: 053 22648
e-mail: emmetcullen@eircom.net
website: www.accommodationireland.net

Conveniently located in a peaceful spot just two minutes from the N25 and only a mile from Wexford town, **Granville House** is an impressive modern building standing in award-winning gardens. It's the home of Emmet and Grainne Cullen who offer luxurious bed and breakfast accommodation in tranquil surroundings. All of the 6 guest bedrooms have en suite facilities with power shower, TV, electric blankets and tea/coffee-making facilities. Guests have the use of a comfortable residents lounge and can also enjoy the superb gardens which contain an extensive range of plants and shrubs that have been carefully tended over the years.

Emmet and Grainne have creatively designed and developed these glorious gardens to include a large aviary to the rear of the house with free-flying doves and other birds, and two water features. At breakfast time guests are offered an extensive choice that includes a full Irish breakfast and fresh fish when available. Granville House, which has a spacious private car park, has been approved by the Irish Tourist Board, Bord Failte, Town and Country Homes and is also recommended by the USA *Best Guide*. It is within easy reach of several beaches, golf courses, fishing, horse-riding, the National Heritage Park and the ferry port of Rosslare.

grounds are open daily all year round and during the winter months entrance is free. Also within the grounds of Johnstown Castle is the **Irish Agricultural Museum** which has extensive displays on all aspects of rural life – farming machinery, domestic objects, carts and carriages, country furniture and reconstructed workshops, and a major exhibit on the Great Famine.

South & West of Wexford

Rosslare Harbour

9 miles SE of Wexford on the R740

Although well known to ferry passengers arriving from Wales or France, most of these arriving visitors speed through Rosslare Harbour en route to better-known attractions. But only a mile or so north from the harbour stretches a 6-mile-long crescent of firm sand and shingle, a popular beach where the bathing is safe at all stages of the tide and local people generally have it to themselves. Similarly, Rosslare town's excellent 18-hole golf course remains for the most part a preserve of Wexford residents.

Rosslare Strand

Tagoat

9 miles SE of Wexford on the N25

About 4 miles south of Rosslare town, in the village of Tagoat, is the **Yola Farmstead Folk Park**, a 5-acre complex of thatched traditional buildings and cottages dating from the late 1700s. Amongst them are a church, forge and working windmill along with a display of bygone farm machinery and rare and endangered species of birds, poultry and animals. Groups can book ahead for one of the traditional Yola banquets with music.

Kilrane

10 miles SE of Wexford on the N25

A couple of miles south of Kilrane, **Lady's Island** as well as being a great location for bird-watching is also a place of pilgrimage. Each year, between 15th August and 8th September, pilgrims make their way across the causeway that links the island to the mainland in order to pay their devotions at the shrine of Our Lady. The most fervent worshippers crawl around the perimeter of the island on their knees; others progress around the shoreline with one foot in the water. Also on the island are the ruins of a 13th century Augustinian priory, a Norman castle and a Round Tower which leans even more alarmingly than the more famous one at Pisa.

Kilmore Quay

14 miles SW of Wexford on the R739

This charming fishing village is set around a busy little

Airdownes Cottages

Broadway, Co. Wexford
Tel: 053 31140

The little village of Broadway lies in the southeast corner of Co. Wexford, only a few miles from Rosslare Harbour and close to several excellent beaches. Here you'll find **Airdownes Cottages**, 2 outstanding self-catering properties developed from attractive stone-built Victorian outbuildings. The two units, converted in 2000, are equipped with all modern conveniences and each can sleep up to 5 guests. These charming cottages are available all year round. Owner Lilian Davis also runs a well-established restaurant close by and an 18-hole pitch and putt course, while only half a mile away is a spacious children's playground complete with bouncy castle.

harbour with whitewashed thatched cottages running alongside the narrow main street. The cottages have walls two to three feet thick, made of clay, straw and stones, and roof frames often made from the strong timbers of ships wrecked by southwesterly storms. Kilmore's modern marina has 55 fully serviced berths and there are regular trips from the quayside during the season to the nearby **Saltee Islands**, two large granite outcrops which support eleven different species of breeding seabirds in late spring and early summer – puffins, kittiwakes, razorbills and gannets amongst them. Boats are also available in Kilmore for fishing trips or cruises along the coast. An event unique to Kilmore is the annual Blessing of the Boats, a service held each year at the end of the summer season.

Kilmore Quay has had its own lifeboat since 1847 and since that date its crew members have saved 111 lives. The history of the lifeboat and the town is recorded in the **Guillemot Maritime Museum**, housed in an old lightship alongside the marina. The 102 feet long ship is complete with all its original furniture, generators and fittings, and contains an extensive collection of maritime pictures, models and many other 'sea antiques'.

If you enjoy seafood, the time to visit Kilmore is in the second week of July when the village hosts the 10-day **Kilmore Quay Annual Seafood Festival** which features events such as a seafood barbecue, a talent competition, outdoor games and activities on the pier, live entertainment and, of course, an abundance of seafood caught by the local fleet and available at prices to suit every budget.

Fethard

22 miles SW of Wexford on the R734

A quiet little resort nowadays, Fethard was once a place of some consequence – important enough for James II to grant it the status of a borough. Little more than a hundred years later though, Fethard's population was so diminished it was stripped of its parliamentary seat. In compensation, the village landlord was granted the then-colossal sum of £15,000.

On the edge of the village stand the remains of **Fethard Castle**, an L-shaped fortified hall house built in the 1400s and incorporating the gate tower of an even older castle. To the southwest of the village, the Hook Head peninsula points a narrow finger of land into the Celtic Sea and forms the western boundary of Waterford Harbour. At the tip of the peninsula, is

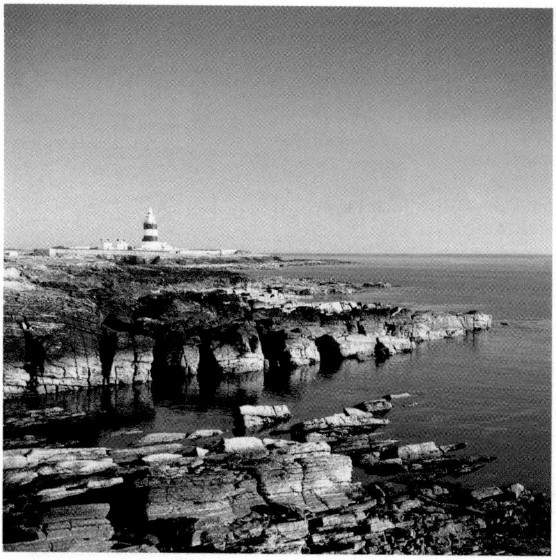

Hook Head Lighthouse

Hook Head Lighthouse which is believed to be the oldest operational lighthouse in Europe and the 4th oldest in the world. Monks were lighting a beacon here in the 5th century but a more substantial structure was erected by the Normans in the late 1100s. The circular keep of this lighthouse is still visible. Guided tours are available and there's also a café and craft shop.

Duncannon

25 miles SW of Wexford on the R733

A pleasant holiday resort boasting a sandy Blue Flag beach, Duncannon stands on a rocky promontory jutting out into Waterford Harbour. It was here that Conan is reputed to have built his *dun*, (hill fort), from which the town takes its name. The

Roches Bar & Sqigl Restaurant

Quay Road, Duncannon, New Ross,
Co. Wexford
Tel: 051 389700 / 389188
Fax: 051 389346
e-mail: sqigl2003@eircom.net

Roches Bar & Sqigl Restaurant is very much a family business. There's Robert Roche, who grew up into the hospitality business with his wife Eileen. Their daughter Cindy who looks after the restaurant and James who is in charge of the bar. Robert's motto is "Classy food in classy surroundings" and that's certainly what you get. In Sqigl Restaurant with its smart modern décor you'll find what the Roches decribe as "cooking that takes inspiration from the classic and infuses it with the modern". There's a choice of either an à la carte or table d'hôte menu, supplemented by an added range of chef's specials every evening.

During the season the restaurant is open daily except Mondays; off season from Wednesday to Sunday. After your meal, step into the adjoining pub with its old world interior, open fire, slate floor and lots of interesting artefacts. There are 3 separate drinking areas and the pub also serves some tasty bar food. In good weather, you can enjoy your refreshments in the beer garden at the rear. Every Saturday night the bar hosts a lively session of traditional music and if you are planning to stay in this scenic part of the county, the Roches have some holiday homes available for rental all year round.

Duncannon Fort

Duncannon, Co. Wexford

Duncannon Fort is a star shaped fortress built on a strategically important promontory in Waterford Harbour. It was built in 1588 in expectation of an attack on the area by the Spanish Armada.

Most notable features of the Fort are the spectacular views over Waterford Estuary, down to Hook Head and across to Passage East, the dry moat and lighthouse, the croppy boy cell where rebels were imprisoned in 1798 and this year the newly opened Maritime Museum, charting the history of the most dangerous coastline in Ireland, the Wexford Coast. Cockleshell Art Centre, Artist's Studio, Café and Craft Shop.

Normans also built a castle here but the site is now occupied by **Duncannon Fort** (see panel above), a star-shaped citadel built in 1588 in expectation of an attack by the Spanish Armada. Visitors can examine the gruesome dungeon in which the "Croppy Boy" of the well-known rebel song was held. Guided tours are available daily during the season (June to September).

Arthurstown

25 miles SW of Wexford on the R733

This small fishing village on the western coast of the Hook Peninsula is a pleasant place to visit. The major visitor attraction, however, lies about 5 miles to the east. **Tintern Abbey** should not be confused with the glorious ruins near Chepstow in South Wales immortalised by Wordsworth in a famous elegiac poem. But there is a strong connection since Wexford's Tintern was named after the Welsh abbey by its founder, William Marshall, Earl of Pembroke. While sailing from Wales to southern Ireland, William's ship was caught in a violent storm. Falling to his knees on the wind-tossed deck, William vowed that he would build an abbey wherever his ship came safely to land. He was true to his word and building began in 1200. The riverside setting is picturesque and the substantial remains, which include the nave, chancel, tower, chapel and cloister of the original building, are imposing and dignified. The Abbey was partly converted into a private residence in 1541 and further adapted over the centuries by the Colclough family who lived here for more than 400 years, right up until the 1960s.

Ballyhack

25 miles SW of Wexford off the R733

Ballyhack is best known locally for its year round vehicle ferry across the harbour to Passage East in County Waterford. But the village is also worth visiting to see **Ballyhack Castle**, a sturdy five storey tower house occupying a steep slope and a commanding position overlooking Waterford estuary. The castle is thought to have been built around 1450 by the Knights Hospitallers of St John, one of the two great

Creacon Lodge Hotel

Creacon Lower, New Ross, Co. Wexford
Tel: 051 421897 Fax: 051 422560
e-mail: info@creaconlodge.com
website: www.creaconlodge.com

Its walls covered with clematis, fuchsia, jasmine, quince and a fig tree, **Creacon Lodge Hotel** looks irresistibly inviting. This luxurious hotel dates back to 1849 and has been carefully restored over the past few years with the emphasis on retaining its country house ambience. The bar and restaurant, for example, were refurbished using 300-year-old pitch pine while the bedrooms, all of which have been individually decorated and are tucked under the roof of

the house, have diamond shaped window panes which offer views of the beautiful gardens. Each of the bedrooms has an en suite bathroom and is provided with colour television and direct dial telephone.

A focal point of the hotel is the spacious drawing room, replete with comfortable armchairs and an ideal place to relax in front of a log fire before and after dinner. There's even a piano for the musically inclined. Another popular amenity is the magnificent rose garden where guests can settle down at picnic tables surrounded by an abundance of roses and other flowers.

Owner Josephine Flood and her staff are particularly proud of their elegant restaurant which offers an interesting selection of dishes using only the finest of local produce that will satisfy the most discerning palate. There's a very comprehensive wine list and a full range of other beverages is available from the bar.

This outstanding hotel is located just outside the town of New Ross which boasts a

history going back to the 6th century when it was one of the country's busiest ports. The first landings by the Normans took place in this area and the landscape is still dotted with reminders of their presence. Many years later, it was from New Ross in 1849 that the great-grandfather of the late American president John F. Kennedy sailed for Boston. The superb JFK Memorial Park is just a 5-minute drive from the hotel and the Kennedy Homestead at Dunganstown, still owned by the Kennedy family, is well worth a visit.

Other attractions within easy reach of the hotel include many fine beaches, numerous quaint villages and, in New Ross itself, the full scale reconstruction of the *SS Dunbrody*, a magnificent three-master which carried many thousands of emigrants across the Atlantic in the 1840s.

Only a two-hour drive from Dublin and about 30 miles from the ferry terminal at Rosslare, Creacon Lodge provides a perfect retreat away from the bustle of city life where guests can relax in the heart of the countryside and enjoy genuine hospitality and fine food.

Ballyhack

military orders founded in the 12th century at the time of the Crusades.

Campile

10 miles SE of New Ross on minor road off the R733

On the outskirts of Campile stand the extensive remains of **Dunbrody Abbey**, one of the finest ecclesiastical ruins in Ireland. The Abbey was founded in 1210 and because it held the right of sanctuary became known as the Monastery of St Mary of Refuge. The site also contains the ruins of Dunbrody Castle which now houses a craft shop selling quality hand-made local crafts. There's a tea room with a small museum mostly concerned with family genealogies, a large doll's house in the form of a scale replica of the castle, a small pitch and putt course and a full size yew tree hedge maze – one of only two in Ireland. The Abbey site is open from April to September.

Dunganstown

4 miles S of New Ross on the R733

This unremarkable little village close to the River Barrow is well established on the tourist route because of **The Kennedy Homestead**, the birthplace of Patrick Kennedy, great-grandfather of President JF Kennedy. Patrick Kennedy left the homestead in 1848 and set sail from New Ross on a wet October day. Now a Cultural Museum and Visitor Centre, the homestead celebrates a family history like no other, one that moves from the steerage quarters on an immigrant vessel to the slums of Boston; from the Court of St James to the White House. The Kennedy family still own and run the farm here and JFK himself visited the house in June 1963. The Homestead is open daily from May to September and at other times by appointment.

A couple of miles to the east, on the slopes of Slieve Coillte, the **John F. Kennedy Memorial Forest** covers an expanse of some 620 acres and boasts a plant collection of international standing with some 4500 types of trees and shrubs from all the temperate regions of the world. Designated a National Park, the site includes a lake, a visitor centre with an audio-visual show and is open daily all year round from 10am.

New Ross

23 miles NW of Wexford on the N25

Set on a steep hill overlooking the River Barrow, New Ross is one of the oldest towns in County Wexford. The centre still has a medieval feel to it, with narrow winding streets which in some places are stepped and so only open to pedestrians. The summer of 2001 saw the opening of a new major attraction – a full scale

The Cedar Lodge Hotel

Carrigbyrne, Newbawn, Co. Wexford
Tel: 051 428386 Fax: 051 428222
e-mail: cedarlodge@eircom.net
website: www.prideofeirehotels.com

Set in the heart of the tranquil Wexford countryside, beneath the slopes of historic Carrigbyrne Forest, **The Cedar Lodge Hotel & Restaurant** is a striking modern building and the perfect place for those seeking to escape the stresses and strains of the everyday world. Owned and run by the Martin family, the hotel has established an impressive reputation for outstanding hospitality, offering fine wines, food and

furnishings complemented by friendly and efficient service. The cuisine is based on the best of local produce and guests can regale themselves on fresh oysters, mussels, lobster, crab, Slaney wild salmon, lamb and much more. The outstanding food is complemented by an excellent wine list that draws on the hotel's extensive cellar of 120 bins dating back to 1955 and is served in the elegant dining room with its roaring log fire beneath a gleaming copper canopy. The menu changes regularly but expect to find appetising dishes such as Dublin Bay Prawn Salad with Mary Rose Sauce amongst the starters, and Filleted Brill with Vermouth or Marinated Guinea Fowl with Coriander as main dishes. After the meal, guests can relax in the beautifully appointed Lounge Bar with its stylish wooden ceiling and elegant furnishings.

Accommodation at The Cedar Lodge maintains the same high standards seen throughout the hotel. All 28 bedrooms are spacious and luxuriously comfortable, enjoy top quality en suite facilities and are all provided with colour TV and direct dial telephone. The hotel is ideally situated for those with a fondness for country pursuits and is also within easy driving distance of many major visitor attractions. Amongst these are the world-famous John F. Kennedy Arboretum with its 4,500 different species of trees and shrubs from all over the world; the Wexford Wildlife Reserve; Waterford Crystal; glorious miles of safe, sandy beaches; the renowned gardens and agricultural museum at Johnstown Castle; the Cistercian abbeys of Tintern and Dunbrody; and many, many more.

Cedar Lodge is conveniently situated just 20 miles from Rosslare Ferry Port, on the N25 road which is the main link between Rosslare and the southwest of Ireland, and is within easy driving distance of several golf courses.

Thornbury House

Irishtown, New Ross, Co. Wexford
Tel: 051 421486

Conveniently located just off the New Ross ring road, **Thornbury House** offers comfortable bed & breakfast accommodation in a friendly and welcoming atmosphere. Bridget and Gerard Martin have been looking after visitors here since 1997 and make every effort to ensure that their stay is as relaxing as possible. There are 9 guest bedrooms, all of a 4-star standard and all with en suite facilities and hospitality tray. A full Irish breakfast is included in the tariff and if you are looking for a tasty evening meal look no further than the Golden Grill restaurant next door which is also owned and run by Bridget and Gerard. You can sit down to a hearty repast of grills or steaks, or simply settle for a takeaway.

Thornbury House has its own private parking and provides an ideal base for exploring this scenic corner of the county. The 18-hole New Ross Golf Club is just a mile away and anglers will find plenty of good fishing within easy reach. New Ross itself, with its winding medieval streets, is an interesting place to explore and you certainly shouldn't miss visiting the famous SS Dunbrody, a full scale reconstruction of the original 3-master which carried many emigrants to the New World in the 1840s.

reconstruction of the original **SS Dunbrody**, a splendid 176 feet long three master which conveyed thousands of emigrants across the Atlantic during the mid-1840s. Visitors to the ship can go below and experience the confined spaces in which passengers endured the 45-day journey. A comprehensive computer data base lists more than two million individual emigrants while audio, visual and interactive displays follow the amazing success stories of some of them, notably the Kennedy family whose forebears lived nearby.

Much more comfortable water travel is available in the regular river cruises which depart from the bridge at New Ross during the summer season. Meals are included in the tariff and the boat is fully licensed.

About 4 miles north of New Ross, the **Berkeley Costume and Toy Museum** displays a wonderful private collection of 18th and 19th century toys, dolls and costumes dating back to the 1720s. Rare dolls, toy carriages and embroidered textiles such as wedding dresses from three generations of one family are amongst the exhibits; a small, pretty garden is included in the visit and on occasions Victorian goat-carriage rides are available for children.

Ballinaboola

20 miles W of Wexford on the N25/R730

This small crossroads village on the N25 is well known to local gardeners since the **Fuschia Nursery** is the only specialist fuchsia grower in Ireland. Plants are propagated from a private collection of more than 1000 varieties, a collection which is constantly updated with imports

Horse & Hounds

Ballinaboola, New Ross, Co. Wexford
Tel: 051 428323 Fax: 051 428471
e-mail: info@horseandhounds.net

The little village of Ballinaboola, about 6 miles southeast of New Ross on the N25, boasts an excellent hostelry in the **Horse & Hounds** inn which has been owned and run by the Murphy family for some 50 years. When the Murphys acquired the business it was just a small country pub but as its reputation for good food, good company and welcoming atmosphere became established the building has been greatly extended. Indeed, as we go to press, work is being completed on a further extension which doubles the amount of accommodation available.

The lively public bar is known as the Fox Hunters Bar in tribute to the local hunt which meets outside during the hunting season to partake of a warming Stirrup Cup. There's also a spacious and comfortable Lounge Bar, an ideal place to relax with a bar meal and a drink.

Food is taken very seriously at the Horse & Hounds. The award-winning restaurant here has, for more than 29 years, prospered under the "watchful eye" of Christy Murphy whose à la carte menu featuring modern Irish cuisine offers an extensive choice of expertly prepared and attractively presented dishes. The menu changes regularly and there are daily specials. Vegetarian options are available and there's also a special mini-menu for children. Food is served all day, starting with breakfast from 7.30am and concluding with evening meals served until 9.30pm.

The wine list here is also rather special, presenting a wide range of European and New World wines at affordable prices. A welcome feature of the list is its small selection of wines by the quarter bottle for those who prefer just a glass or so.

Ballinaboola makes a convenient base for touring southeast Ireland so if you are thinking of staying in the area, the Horse & Hounds is an excellent place to stay. When the current development is finished, 28 guest bedrooms will be available. All of them have en suite facilities, are very comfortable and well-appointed, and some have been specially adapted for wheelchair access. There's ample parking space and credit cards are accepted.

Located roughly halfway between Wexford and Waterford, the inn is close to an 18-hole golf course, the JF Kennedy Park is just 4 miles away, while a little further afield are Enniscorthy Castle and the Blackstairs Mountains.

from around the world. Small cuttings right up to tall fuchsia standards are usually available, along with various other tender perennials, garden plants and shrubs.

North of Wexford

Curracloe

5 miles NE of Wexford on the R742

Curracloe has a superb sandy beach that stretches for miles and boasts a Blue Flag rating. In Steven Spielberg's World War II movie, *Saving Private Ryan*, Curracloe Beach represented Omaha Beach in the opening scenes.

Curracloe Beach

Enniscorthy

14 miles NW of Wexford on the N11/N30

Generally regarded as County Wexford's most pleasing town, Enniscorthy was founded way back in AD 510 by St Senan.

Now a thriving market town, Enniscorthy's most ancient surviving building is the imposing **Enniscorthy Castle** erected in the early 1200s and restored around 1586. The Elizabethan Poet Laureate, Edmund

FURLONGS VILLAGE BAR

Curracloe, Co. Wexford
Tel: 053 37371

The small village of Curracloe, a few miles north of Wexford Town, is well-known for its superb sandy beach, some 6 miles long, and for its excellent pub, **Furlongs Village Bar**. This 200-year-old hostelry, owned and run by Pat and Helen, is famed for its hospitality and relaxed atmosphere where visitors will experience friendly and efficient service in comfortable surroundings. As one visitor put it, "It's a great place to relax and unwind, enjoy a pint of Guinness, and listen to some long stories and tall tales!" The bar, which has recently been completely refurbished, offers darts, pool, bar food available all day and

live music every evening during the summer and at weekends out of season.

Adjacent to the lounge bar is Nellie's Takeaway which serves tasty food all year round. Perhaps the pub's most famous customers were the stars and director of Steven Spielberg's film *Saving Private Ryan*, parts of which were filmed on the beach at Curracloe, standing in for the Normandy beaches. Cast and crew were regular visitors to the bar and it's reported that when Furlongs hosted a pool competition, director Spielberg and star Tom Hanks were both eliminated in the very first round.

Treacy's Hotel

Templeshannon, Enniscorthy, Co. Wexford
Tel: 054 37851
e-mail: info@treacyshotel.com
website: www.treacyshotel.com

One of the best-loved hotels in the southeast, **Treacy's Hotel** offers a unique mix of traditional Irish, authentic European and exotic Oriental styles and tastes all in one breathtaking environment. No expense has been spared to ensure the comfort of guests and the hotel interior has been fitted to the highest standards from top to bottom with attention paid to detail throughout. From the moment you step into the magnificent Reception area guests enjoy the warmest of Irish welcomes from the friendly staff. Dining in the Bagenal Harvey Restaurant is a memorable experience. Beautifully appointed, the restaurant offers a distinguished menu of classic French cuisine, prepared from the finest local produce and complemented by the hotel's own carefully selected wines. In the Chang Thai restaurant, guests can sample exciting Thai specialities prepared by Thai chefs and the stylish themed interior provides a real flavour of the country itself – perfect for both intimate dining and large private parties.

The social centre of the hotel is undoubtedly the popular Temple Bar which has received the prestigious 'James Joyce Pub Award' for being an authentic Irish pub. The bar is beautifully decorated with original paraphernalia from Irish culture over the centuries. Live entertainment is a regular feature here and the mix of guests with local residents makes for a friendly, welcoming atmosphere.

There's yet more entertainment to be found in Benedict's Niteclub whose neo-Gothic décor resembles the mysterious interior of a church – in fact, most of the materials and fittings were actually imported from a closed Benedictine monastery in France!

The hotel has 60 de luxe bedrooms which offer exceptional comfort and are provided with an en suite bathroom, satellite television, direct dial telephone, internet access, hair dryer and hospitality tray. Within the hotel, wheelchair users are well-provided for with an easily accessible custom built toilet and an elevator giving access to room floors.

Treacy's is ideal for the actively inclined. Adjacent to the hotel is the Waterfront Leisure Centre whose amenities include an indoor heated 30-metre-long swimming pool, gymnasium, a sauna with a capacity for 10 people, and Jacuzzi. The gymnasium features trained experts, cardio-vascular and resistance machines. A favourable discount is available to hotel guests for a session in the Centre.

Spenser, owned it for a while shortly after its restoration. The castle now houses the **Wexford County Museum** which has an extensive collection illustrating the storied past of the county in all its varied aspects. The displays include such objects as an ogham stone and a sedan chair, and there are particularly good exhibits commemorating the risings of 1798 and 1916.

The 1798 rebellion is explored in even greater detail at the **National 1798 Centre** which boasts what is probably the best interactive centre in Ireland. The Centre traces the progress of the rebellion, together with events as they happened in Europe, the United States and Australia. The highlight of the show is a dramatic audio visual display, using a curved screen, to simulate the battle of Vinegar Hill which took place just outside the town. A bronze statue in Market Square also recalls the 1798 Rebellion with a fine sculpture of one of its leaders, Father Murphy, and a soldier armed only with a pike.

The town's most impressive church is **St Aidan's Cathedral**, a grand Gothic Revival building of the 1840s designed by Pugin at the time he was also working on London's Houses of Parliament. The Cathedral stands on a commanding site overlooking the River Slaney and provides some grand views along the valley.

In early summer – usually the last week of June or the first week of July – Enniscorthy hosts the week-long **Strawberry Fair** when, as well as enjoying lashings of strawberries, visitors are regaled with music events and street entertainment.

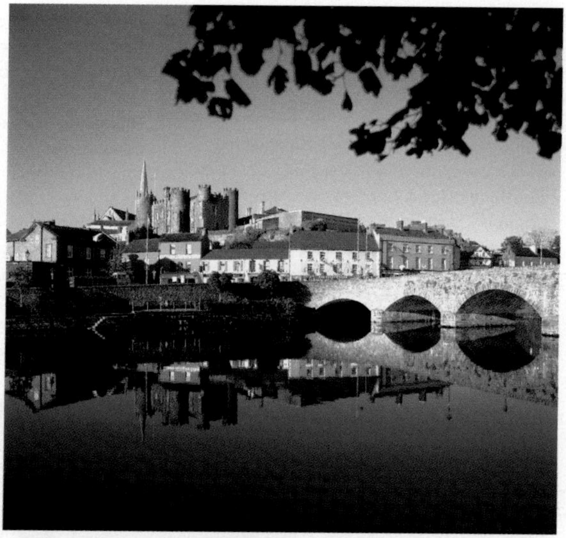

Enniscorthy

Ferns

9 miles NE of Enniscorthy off the N11

Few villages as small as Ferns can boast so rich an historical heritage. An abbey was founded here in the 6th century: its time-worn remains still stand in the graveyard of St Edan's Church. Throughout the Dark Ages, Ferns was the royal capital of Leinster, one of the four great provinces of Ireland in those murky days. It was a King of Leinster, Dermot MacMurrough, holding court in Ferns, who inadvertently paved the way for the Norman invasion of Ireland. Dermot had abducted the wife of another local grandee, Tiernán O'Rourke. Tiernán was understandably aggrieved by losing the love of his life. Hostilities between the two great lords simmered and flared for 14 years. Dermot, temporarily in deep trouble, took the fateful step of seeking help from King Henri of France. The Norman monarch was only too pleased to oblige and took advantage of the invitation to launch a full-scale invasion of Ireland. Later Normans built **Ferns Castle** in the early

Bootlaces Bar & Lounge

Ballycanew, Gorey, Co. Wexford
Tel: 055 27102

Standing right in the heart of the village of Ballycanew, about 4 miles south of Gorey, **Bootlaces Bar & Lounge** occupies what was originally built, in the 18th century, as a private house. It's now a friendly, family-run hostelry owned and run since 1999 by genial hosts Terry and Catherine Holligan. The pub has all the atmosphere you could wish for in traditional Irish fashion and visitors are made to feel very much at home. There's a comfortable lounge and a bar with pool table and open fire. A bar menu with a choice of 2 main courses is served from noon until 3pm, seven days a week.

In summer, customers can enjoy their refreshments in the beer garden where barbecues are held when the weather permits. The pub hosts a regular Quiz Night and at weekends there's music and dancing. Bootlaces has excellent car parking facilities; coaches are welcome. If you are planning to stay in this scenic part of Co. Wexford, the Holligans have 3 self-catering apartments, each with 2 bedrooms, available during the summer months. There are some superb beaches within easy reach and Gorey town golf club is just 5 miles away.

Jack's Tavern

Main Street, Camolin, Co. Wexford
Tel: 054 33174
website: www.jackstavern@aircom.net-diningpubs

Set in the heart of the tranquil Wexford countryside the village of Camolin is well worth seeking out in order to pay a visit to **Jack's Tavern**. Its distinctive bright yellow frontage makes it easy to find and inside you'll find as authentic an Irish pub as you could hope to come across. This friendly hostelry is owned and run by Jack Redmond, a welcoming host whose Guinness is reputed to be as good as any in Wexford! The craic here is good too, one of the reasons why the tavern is popular with locals and visitors alike. Another major attraction is the excellent food on offer.

The tavern's accomplished chef produces a wide range of wholesome and appetising fare with a choice that ranges from tasty bar food to hearty meals. And as befits any self-respecting traditional Irish pub, Jack's Tavern also hosts lively music sessions with local bands playing a wide selection of music that includes traditional Irish music through Country & Western to current pop music. A visit to Jack's Tavern can easily be combined (during the summer months) with a look at nearby Ballymore Historic Features which presents some fascinating insights into the history of this attractive part of the county.

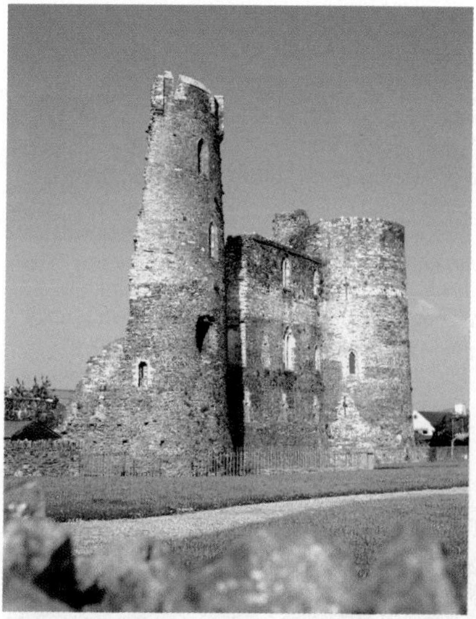

Ferns Castle

1200s – two impressive towers and two curtain walls remain.

Gorey

23 miles N of Wexford on the R471/N11

Gorey, a few miles inland from the coast, is a pleasantly laid out market town and the main shopping centre for the north Wexford coast. This unassuming place became the storm centre of the 1798 insurrection and a granite Celtic memorial cross stands near the spot where the rebels camped on Gorey Hill (418 feet). Many rebels were later held in the Market Hall which was rebuilt in 1809 and now houses the tourist information office. In the Church of Ireland Christ Church, built in 1861, there is some of Harry Clarke's superb stained glass to admire.

Courtown Harbour

22 miles NE of Wexford on the R742

Boasting the lowest rainfall in the south-east and with 2 miles of Blue Flag sandy beach, Courtown is a charming family

The Mezz Bar

22 Main Street, Gorey, Co. Wexford
Tel: 055 21234

Discerning diners can order with confidence at **The Mezz Bar,** secure in the knowledge that chef/manager Vinny Kelly was the Irish winner of the Gordon Ramsey Young Chef of the Year Award, 2002. Vinny's menu offers popular favourites such as steaks and Deep Fried Fillet of Wexford Plaice but also a good choice of less familiar dishes like the Cajun Chicken Caesar Salad or Mexican Style Chicken Fajitas served in a tortilla wrap and topped with tomato and jalepeno sauce. Vegetarians will find tasty alternatives such as the home made Mezz Vegetarian Lasagne or the Mushrooms stuffed with garlic cream cheese, fried in beer batter and served with a salad garni. Other appetising options include venison sausages served with colcannon, red onion relish and Clonakilty pudding or smoked seafood chowder.

Everything is freshly cooked to order and based on fresh, seasonal produce. Desserts, breads and other bakery items are all cooked in-house. For lighter appetites, there's a selection of plain or toasted sandwiches and children have their own menu with mashed potato available as a healthy alternative to chips. Coffee lovers will find an excellent choice that includes a "sumo-sized" espresso and the option of adding a splash of syrup to your favourite coffee – caramel in your latte perhaps, or a dash of roasted hazelnut in your cappuccino.

Stone Lodge

Riverchapel, Courtown, Gorey, Co. Wexford
Tel: 055 25765 Fax: 055 20467
e-mail: stonelodgebb@hotmail.com

Located about half a mile outside the popular resort of Courtown and close to the fine sandy beach, **Stone Lodge** is an impressive dwelling constructed of local stone and with many attractive features such as heavy wood floors and a striking stone fireplace.

The 6 guest bedrooms are all stylishly furnished and decorated, and provided with en-suite facilities, TV and hospitality tray. Your hosts, Claire Mullins and her husband, are a young, friendly couple who make their guests feel very much at home. There's plenty of parking space; credit cards are accepted.

seaside resort with plenty of amusements, an 18-hole golf course and some enticing walks in the surrounding countryside. North of the village is Courtown House which has an ancient 7 feet cross standing in the grounds. Beyond this is another fine beach at Ballymoney, and further north still is Tara Hill, at 830 feet taller than its more famous namesake in County Meath.

Courtown

Woodlands Country House

Killinierin, Gorey, Co. Wexford
Tel: 0402 37125 Fax: 0402 37133
e-mail: woodlands@aol.ie
website: www.woodlandscountryhouse.com

Woodlands Country House is a delightful old building dating back to 1836 and set in 1.5 acres of mature gardens with a courtyard of old stone buildings. This beautiful Georgian residence retains all the characteristics of the period and offers superb accommodation. It's the home of John and Philomena O'Sullivan, a charming couple who bought the house in 1965 and have lovingly restored it over the years. Philomena has a keen eye for antiques and has quite a collection while John is an avid gardener who has created the award-winning gardens with its river and woodland walks.

When you arrive at Woodlands you'll be offered tea and hot scones with home-made preserves and, says Philomena, "most importantly, a friendly chat!" She can also advise you on where to travel and the best sights to see in the area. The house has 6 en suite guest bedrooms, all with treasured period furniture, colour TV, hair dryer and toiletries. Three of the rooms also have balconies overlooking the gardens and local countryside. Here you can relax with a bottle from the extensive wine list or enjoy it in the comfortable guest lounge. Woodlands is renowned for its good food and the breakfast menu offers a wide choice that includes fresh fruit, porridge and a full Irish breakfast.

Co Wicklow

Dubbed the "Garden of Ireland", Wicklow offers visitors a rich mix of attractions. Family holiday-makers flock to the golden sandy beaches at Arklow and Bray; inland, the rolling Wicklow Mountains with their deep heather-clad glens, cascading waterfalls and serene lakes contain some of the finest scenery in

Wicklow Mountains

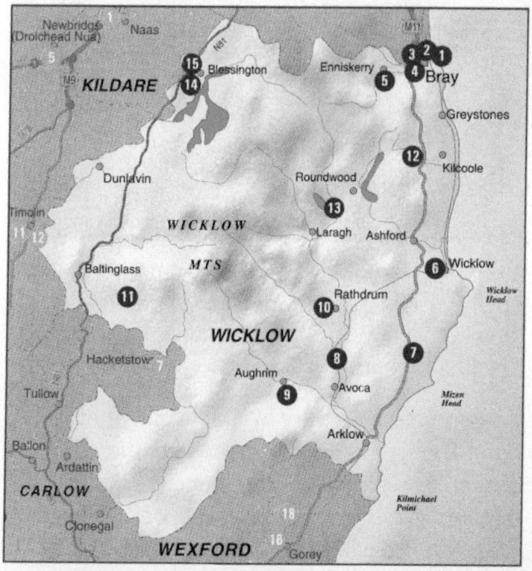

Ireland. Glendalough, in the Wicklow Mountains National Park, is perhaps the most important of all early Christian sites in the country, its origins dating back to the 6th century and its later monastic remains among the most extensive and impressive to have survived.

The county also boasts some magnificent houses and gardens, most notably the glorious Palladian mansion of Russborough House near Arklow, which contains a superb art collection; and the world-famous

PLACES TO STAY, EAT AND DRINK

Vevay Bistro, Bray 1 Bistro p370
Coach Inn, Bray 2 Pub with Food p370
Ulysses, Bray 3 B&B p371
Pine Cottage, Bray 4 B&B p371
Ferndale House, Enniskerry 5 B&B p373
Lissadell House, Wicklow 6 B&B p374
Jack Whites Inn, Brittas Bay 7 Pub with Food p374
The Meetings, Vale of Avoca 8 Pub, Restaurant & Accommodation p376
Lawless's Hotel, Aughrim 9 Hotel p376
Stirabout Lane B&B, Rathdrum 10 B&B p377
Barraderry Country House, Kiltegan 11 B&B p379
Butterfly Hill Farm, Newtownmountkennedy 12 B&B p380
Wicklow Way Lodge, Roundwood 13 B&B p380
Kippure House Estate 14 Self Catering p381
Poulaphouca House, Hollywood 15 B&B p382

● Denotes entries in other chapters

gardens at Powerscourt, laid out in the mid-1800s to a classical pattern. Despite the county's proximity to Dublin, it is surprisingly under-populated and unspoilt – characteristics which have made it a popular location with film and television directors. The county has had starring (if silent) rôles in films such as *Excalibur* and *Braveheart*, and in the hugely successful TV series, *Ballykissangel*.

In this tour of the county we begin by following the coast southwards from Bray before turning inland to explore the Wicklow Mountains National Park.

Bray

Bray developed as a genteel Victorian resort when the railway arrived here in the 1850s and it remains a popular weekend

Vevay Bistro

35 Vevay Road, Bray, Co. Wicklow
Tel/Fax: 01 286 3799
e-mail: vevaybistro@eircom

A qualified and talented chef, James Whelan took over the **Vevay Bistro** early in 2004 and, as we go to press, is completing a comprehensive re-design and refurbishment. James's menu offers a wide variety of dishes with seafood as the speciality of the house. From 8am to 3pm the choice includes a selection of simple lunches while in the evening (from 7pm to 9.45pm) there's a full à la carte menu to choose from with dishes that demonstrate James's masterly culinary skills. The bistro has a full wine licence and if you dine before 7.30pm you can take advantage of the special Early Bird prices.

Coach Inn

Dublin Road, Bray, Co. Wicklow
Tel: 01 286 4674 Mobile: 086 371 5471

As its name suggests, the **Coach Inn** was originally built to service the stage coaches travelling down the east coast routes. Now more than 200 years old this spacious hostelry radiates olde worlde charm and although owners Jim Gill and Thomas Nolan have personally supervised a major reconstruction of the interior they have been careful to retain features such as the natural wood panelling, high-legged stools and slate floors. The result obviously appeals to their customers. Jim says – "We get visitors from all over the globe, from families to old age pensioners!"

Another major attraction here is the outstanding food, available Monday to Saturday from 10.30am until late, and on Sunday from noon until 10.30pm. There's also a Carvery available daily until 5pm. Everything on the menu is home cooked and the lunchtime menu is changed regularly. In the evening, an à la carte menu is served 7 days a week. If you enjoy a pint of Guinness, you'll find that Jim pulls a truly memorable pint!

The Coach Inn accepts credit cards and has its own car park. From the inn it's just a short walk to the centre of Bray with its mile-long beach and manifold resort entertainments.

Bray Seafront

destination for Dubliners so, in addition to its safe, mile-long beach of sand and shingle, the town is well-supplied with all the usual amusements. James Joyce lived in Bray from 1889 to 1891, his residence duly noted in the **Bray Heritage Centre** which also has a good collection of photographs, maps and artefacts illustrating the town's history, and a folklore room. Other attractions include the **National Sea-Life Centre**, home to a wonderful variety of native and tropical fish and, just outside the town, **Killruddery House & Garden**. Many generations of the

Ulysses

The Esplanade, Bray, Co. Wicklow
Tel/Fax: 01 286 3860
e-mail: cojo@indigo.ie

Enjoying a superb position on the seafront and just a short stroll from the town centre, **Ulysses** is a spacious Victorian dwelling dating back to 1860. Owners Colm and Deirdre Jones have made this grand old house into a beautifully furnished and comfortable bed & breakfast establishment. There are 10 guest bedrooms, all en suite and provided with TV and hospitality tray, and most of them enjoying sea views. So does the dining room where Deirdre serves a generous breakfast with plenty of choices. Musicians will feel especially at home here – Colm is an accomplished composer and songwriter and even has his own recording studio at the top of the garden!

Pine Cottage

Windgates, Greystones Road, Bray, Co. Wicklow
Tel: 01 287 2601

Sitting snugly on a plateau carved out of the hillside of Bray Head, **Pine Cottage** is the outstandingly elegant home of Ronnie and Alina Mayberry. Ronnie used to work for Finnish paper manufacturing companies and the architect-designed bungalow contains many beautiful furnishings and decoration of Scandinavian origin. Ronnie and Alina have been welcoming bed & breakfast guests to their lovely home since 2000. The 3 guest bedrooms are all en suite, very spacious and attractively appointed, and visitors have the use of a comfortable lounge which enjoys grand views of Little Sugarloaf Mountain. Golfers are well served with the Bray Golf club just half a mile down the road.

Brabazon family, Earls of Meath, have lived at Killruddery since 1618 and the 17th century French-style garden here is one of the oldest in Ireland still surviving with its original layout. The house itself contains some interesting features – carvings by Grinling Gibbons, Chippendale furniture and a water-powered clock. Just south of the town, **Bray Head** (791 feet) provides an exhilarating coastal walk, overlooked by a huge cross erected to commemorate the Holy Year of 1950.

Around Bray

A couple of miles south of Bray at Kilmacanogue, the large Avoca Handweavers store stands in gardens created by a member of the Jameson whiskey family in the 1870s. The gardens contain the only mature specimen of the Weeping Monterey Cypress in the world. Another 4 miles south, at Kilquade, is the **National Garden Exhibition Centre** which within its 3-acre site displays 16 different themed gardens with names such as the Seaside Garden, the Herb Knot, the Geometric Garden and the Acid Garden. Also on site is a timbered pavilion housing a horticultural shop and a tea room.

Enniskerry

4 miles W of Bray on the R117

The picture-postcard village of Enniskerry, with its splendid backdrop of the Great Sugar Loaf Mountain, was built to serve the 14,000 acre estate of **Powerscourt House** nearby. But the impressive drive, more than half a mile long, only leads to the shell of what was once a magnificent Palladian mansion, designed in 1740 by the German architect Richard Castel for the 1st Viscount Powerscourt. The parlous state of the house seems particularly unfair since it was destroyed by a fire in 1974 just before it was due to be re-opened after a major restoration programme. Only the ballroom, a garden room and a room housing the Visitor Centre are now open to the public but Powerscourt remains one of Wicklow's major visitor attractions because of its glorious gardens. Here, spouting fountains and winged horses, mosaic terraces created with pebbles from Bray beach, tranquil lakes and superb specimen trees create an Arcadian landscape of utter serenity.

Apart from a fragrant **Japanese Garden** added in Edwardian times, the gardens were originally laid out in the mid-1700s and redesigned a hundred years later by Daniel Robertson, an eccentric character who suffered grievously from gout. He directed operations while being trundled around the grounds in a wheelbarrow, swigging the while from a large bottle of sherry. When the sherry was exhausted, so was Daniel and he retired for the rest of the day. This helps to explain why it took more than 100

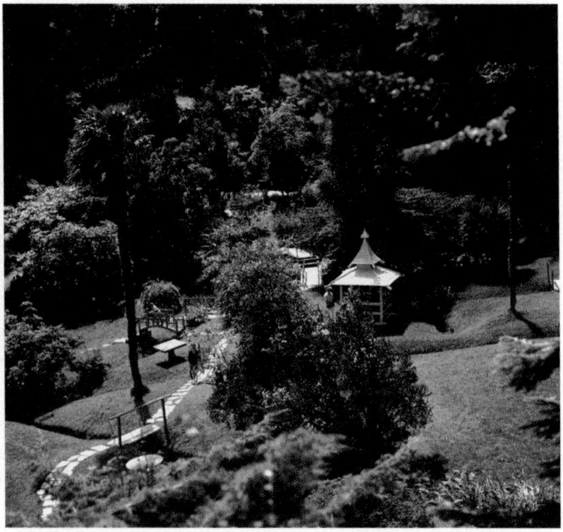

Japanese Gardens, Enniskerry

FERNDALE HOUSE

The Square, Enniskerry, Co. Wicklow
Tel/Fax: 01 286 3518
e-mail: ferndale@eircom.net
website: www.ferndalehouse.com

A handsome early Victorian building, **Ferndale House** was once part of the nearby Powerscourt estate, famous today for its magnificent gardens. Ferndale is the home of Josie and Noel Corcoran who have been welcoming bed & breakfast guests here since 1996 – many of them repeat visitors. Located in the centre of the village, Ferndale is beautifully furnished in period style and its 4 guest bedrooms are all en suite and provided with TV and hospitality tray. Josie makes wonderful breakfasts, offering an extensive choice that includes fresh fruit salad and kippers. Credit cards are accepted and there's ample off street parking.

labourers 12 years to complete the landscaping.

Also within the estate grounds but approached by a different entrance, is the highest waterfall in Ireland. The **Powerscourt Waterfall** plunges some 400 feet over a jagged rock face and the waters then course through a beautiful glen. There are some pleasant riverside walks along this valley which is a popular venue for picnics with tables provided and kiosk refreshments available.

Kilcoole

10 miles S of Bray on the R761

The peaceful little village of Kilcoole will be familiar to viewers of the popular Irish TV series *Glenroe* while golfers will know it better for its two golf courses. One of them, the Druids Glen Golf Course, nestles between the Wicklow Mountains and the Irish Sea. Druids Glen hosted the Murphys Irish Open from 1996 to 1999, was voted European Golf Course of the Year 2000, and was the venue for the Seve Trophy in 2002.

Just outside the village, **Glenroe Open Farm** has often featured in the TV series of the same name and offers a range of attractions that includes a souvenir and home produce shop, coffee shop, picnic areas and farm animals.

Wicklow Town

The Danes named it *Wyking alo*, "Viking meadow" and it became one of their most important settlements. Today, Wicklow's county town is a pleasant sleepy place overlooking a crescent-shaped shingle bay with a ruined Norman castle at its eastern end. Contrasting with the town's brightly-painted houses, the grey stone walls of the former **Wicklow Gaol** (1702) now house a museum dedicated to the 1798 Rebellion with some poignant exhibits detailing the wholesale transportation of rebels and criminals, (some 50,000 were dispatched to Australia), and also the tribulations of the years of the Great Famine. There are regular tours every 10 minutes and the gaol also houses a genealogy centre, a shop and a café.

A good antidote to the gaol's rather sobering displays is a walk around **Wicklow Head** which provides some exhilarating views along the coast and across to the strange profiles of Great and Little Sugarloaf Mountains. On the headland stands **Wicklow Lighthouse**, or lighthouses rather, since there are actually three separate towers.

South of Wicklow Town stretches the 3-mile-long expanse of white sandy beach at **Brittas Bay**, one of the best beaches on

LISSADELL HOUSE

Ashtown Lane, off Marlton Road, Wicklow, Co. Wicklow
Tel: 0404 67458

Located just one mile outside Wicklow Town, **Lissadell House** is a handsome part Georgian-style house set in spacious and beautifully maintained gardens. There are delightful views of the Wicklow hills and countryside and the surrounding area, with its combination of mountains, forests and coastline, is one of the most scenic regions in Ireland. Lissadell House is the home of Patricia Klaue who has been welcoming bed and breakfast guests for some 14 years, many of whom return again and again. There are 4 guest bedrooms, 2 of them with en suite facilities and all attractively furnished and decorated. A full Irish breakfast is included in the tariff and Patricia will provide an evening meal if required.

Facilities for golf, fishing and horse-riding are all nearby, the celebrated Mount Usher Gardens are just a few miles away and the scenic Vale of Avoca lies a little further to the south. Wicklow Town itself is well worth exploring with its ruined castle, brightly painted houses, historic buildings and sandy beach at Brittas Bay. And if you enjoy live Irish music, there are some lively pubs in Wicklow Town where you will be very well entertained!

JACK WHITES INN

Jack White's Cross, Brittas Bay, Co. Wicklow
Tel: 0404 47106 Fax: 0404 47272
e-mail: jackwhites@eircom.net
website: www.jackwhitesinn.com

For many years, **Jack Whites Inn** has been a familiar landmark on the Dublin-Wicklow-Wexford, the N11. For more than 200 years it has stood here, surrounded by beautiful scenic countryside, and the inn's long tradition of hospitality is now continued by Tadhg Kennedy who maintains the hostelry's fine reputation for serving excellent food and drink in its distinctive bars and lounges. This engaging old inn has warm, welcoming fires and cosy snugs ideal for settling down with a deftly pulled pint of Guinness. All year round you'll find outstanding food, served all day and prepared with fresh ingredients and country produce from the surrounding area. Tadhg takes pride in the fact that all his menus and wines are affordably priced.

For special occasions, the inn has an inviting function room where efficient and friendly staff make sure that your event runs smoothly. The inn takes its name from its location at Jack White's Crossroads which in turn is named after a notorious 18th century smuggler who used to land his contraband at what was then the remote beach on Brittas Bay. Today, the 3-mile stretch of beach here, backed by sand dunes, is a popular resort for holidaying Dubliners.

Brittas Bay

Ireland's east coast, with Mizen Head, which features so often in shipping forecasts, at its southern tip.

Around Wicklow

Arklow

14 miles S of Wicklow on the N11

Set around the estuary of the River Avoca, Arklow claims to be one of the ports identified on Ptolemy's famous 2nd century map of Britannia. It was certainly an important port in medieval times and there's still a thriving shipbuilding industry here. Sir Francis Chichester's celebrated transatlantic yacht *Gypsy Moth IV* was built here at John Tyrell's yard, although the boat itself is now moored at Greenwich in London. Arklow's **Maritime Museum** houses a wonderfully motley collection of items with a seafaring connection – a whale's tooth and eardrum, and a model ship made with more than 10,000 matchsticks amongst them. Arklow's own white sand beach has the docks on one side and a gravel extraction plant on the other but about 5 miles south of the town, **Clogga Beach** is quiet and sheltered.

Inland from Arklow lies a peaceful area of leafy glens, mountain streams and gentle rivers. In ancient times gold was mined from Croghan Mountain (2000 feet) and when a sizeable nugget was found there in 1796 a "Gold Rush" ensued during which 2000 ounces were discovered within a few months.

Avoca

12 miles SW of Wicklow on the R752/R754

The late-18th century Romantic poets adored the Vale of Avoca and Avondale. Wordsworth toured these enchanting valleys in the 1790s and was captivated. The Irish poet, Thomas Moore, spent many hours in contemplation on a hill overlooking the **Meeting of the Waters** (where the River Avonbeg flows into the Avoca) and wrote some of his best-known lines:

There is not in this wide world a valley so sweet
As that vale in whose bosom the bright waters meet;
Oh! The last rays of feeling and life must depart
Ere the bloom of that valley shall fade from my heart.

The valleys are particularly glorious in late spring when the wild cherry trees are in blossom but they are delightful throughout the year which means that the main road is nearly always busy. Fortunately, you only have to walk a short distance from the road to find peaceful Arcadian vistas opening up in every direction.

Avoca village was the setting for the popular TV series *Ballykissangel* so "Fitzgerald's Pub" is naturally a great attraction. This charming little hamlet of trim white houses set beside the river is also the home of **Avoca Handweavers** whose appealing range of woollens and knitwear provide popular and practical souvenirs. Their workshops are housed in a group of whitewashed buildings where you'll also find the oldest surviving hand-weaving mill in Ireland, dating from 1723 and still in

The Meetings

Vale of Avoca, Co. Wicklow
Tel: 0402 35226 Fax: 0402 35558
e-mail: info@themeetingsavoca.com
website: www.themeetingsavoca.com

Overlooking the “Meeting of the Waters” where the Avonmore and Avonbeg merge into the Avoca river you will find **The Meetings** which is owned and run by Peter and Marion Moore and their family. Their extensive premises offer a wide range of services in just one stop – add to this beautiful views and scenery and you have the perfect place to stay and rest awhile. The Restaurant offers something for everyone, from a cup of freshly ground coffee and a warm scone to a hearty meal from the day menu, served from 12.30pm to 6pm, and an evening menu running from 6pm to 9pm. The Craft Shop is stocked with a wide selection of knitwear, glassware, pottery, crafts, gifts and souvenirs and also has a Bureau de Change so changing money is never a problem.

The premises has recently been extended to include “Robin’s Nest” which provides excellent en suite pub accommodation overlooking the Meeting of the Waters made famous by the great poet Thomas Moore in 1807. Outside you will find a large beer garden with benches and umbrellas under the shade of an old beech tree where you can relax with a bar snack and a refreshing drink and, on summer evenings and Sunday afternoons, enjoy traditional music.

Lawless’s Hotel & Holiday Village

Aughrim, Co. Wicklow
Tel: 0402 36146 / 36280 Fax: 0402 36384
e-mail: reservations@lawlesshotel.com

Lawless’s Hotel was established way back in 1787 and has retained all the charm and atmosphere of a more leisurely age. The hotel stands right on the river bank and guests can enjoy Brown Trout fishing on more than 30kms of unspoilt mountain river. In the Thirsty Trout Bar and the Snug lounge visitors from around the world mingle with local anglers and farmers in the convivial atmosphere of a genuine Irish pub. An excellent award-winning restaurant and comfortable en suite bedrooms furnished with elegant Victorian or Country Pine décor make this a place that should definitely not be missed.

For those who prefer self-catering, Aughrim Holiday Village stands adjacent to the hotel and is an exclusive development of luxury town houses. Each property can accommodate up to 5 people and each is comprehensively equipped with all modern conveniences. There’s a large sitting room/lounge with open fireplace, television and telephone, while from the fully fitted kitchen French doors lead to a private southwest-facing patio. Immediately beside the village is a 4-acre man-made Angling Park which offers all year round trout fishing with special facilities for the disabled; sea angling is available within a 15-minute drive. Both the Hotel and Holiday Village are located within easy driving distance of up to thirty excellent Golf Courses. Courses can be booked by the Hotel Reception.

operation. Amongst their other achievements the Wynne sisters, who established the business more than 40 years ago, also proudly claim to be the inventors of the car rug. There are daily demonstrations of hand-weaving and the little complex also has a shop and tea room.

Aughrim

16 miles SW of Wicklow on the R753

Aughrim occupies a beautiful position at the meeting point of two rivers, the Ow and the Derry, and several mountain valleys. The most scenic of these is the valley of the River Ow which stretches for about 10 miles to the northwest to Lugnaquilla Mountain (3040 feet). On the western slope of the valley is Ballymanus, the birthplace of Billy Byrne, a doughty leader of the 1798 rebellion.

Rathdrum

9 miles SW of Wicklow on the R752

Northwards from the Meeting of the Waters, the R752 runs through the **Avondale Forest Park** before entering the pleasant little village of Rathdrum. The Park is actually the estate of **Avondale House** which was the home of Charles Stewart Parnell, the great nationalist and advocate of land rights for Irish peasants. The grounds of Avondale House are open daily all year (free) and three rooms in the stately late-18th century mansion, devoted to displays of Parnell memorabilia, are open daily in the season. Parnell is also commemorated in Rathdrum itself by a magnificent bronze statue in the Parnell Memorial Park.

Also worth a visit is the **Kilmacurragh**

Stirabout Lane B&B

36 Main Street, Rathdrum, Co. Wicklow
Tel/Fax: 00353 404 43142
e-mail: stiraboutlane@hotmail.com
website: www.stiraboutlane.com

Located in the heart of the picturesque town of Rathdrum, **Stirabout Lane B&B** offers its guests a *cead mile failte* (a hundred thousand welcomes) – beginning with complimentary refreshments on arrival provided by your hosts, Daphne and Pat. In this home-from-home atmosphere, guests can settle down in the relaxing sitting room with its open turf fire and tea/coffee-making facilities. The spacious, tastefully decorated bedrooms are all en suite and provided with television, hairdryer and clock radio. Ironing facilities are also available.

In good weather, guests can enjoy the mature garden to the rear of the house and there's also convenient off-street parking. At breakfast time, you'll find an appetising choice of tasty home cooking that will set you up well for a day of exploring this attractive area. Rathdrum itself stands high on the western side of the beautiful Avonmore Valley, commanding some magnificent views. It is well-supplied with fine shops, restaurants, pubs and evening entertainment, and may be more familiar than you expected since it has featured in films such as *Michael Collins, Durango, A Love Divided* and even a Spice Girls' video. In addition to abundant facilities for golf and angling, the area also boasts outstanding attractions such as Glendalough (only 10 minutes away), Powerscourt House and Avondale House which is now a museum to the memory of the Irish patriot Charles Stewart Parnell.

Arboretum (free) which is famous for its conifers and calcifuges. They were planted during the 19th century by Thomas Acton together with Davis Moore and his son, Sir Frederick Moore, curators of the National Botanic Gardens in Glasnevin.

About 4 miles west of Rathdrum at Greenan and beautifully set in the Wicklow Mountains, **Greenan Farm Museums and Maze** is a hill farm with a range of museums illustrating rural life in the 19th century. The range includes a period farmhouse museum, a large two storey farm museum and a bottle museum. The mature maze is a real puzzler and the site also offers a farm walk, tearoom and craft shop.

Laragh

9 miles W of Wicklow on the R755

From Rathdrum, the R752 winds through the Avonbeg Valley, also known as the Vale of Clara, to the pleasant village of Laragh, set around a major crossroads and close to one of Ireland's most important spiritual sites, **Glendalough**. Some time in the late 6th century St Kevin, a scion of the royal house of Leinster, came to this secluded valley and for many years lived here as a hermit, sometimes sleeping in the hollow of a tree. Gradually, his sanctity and wisdom attracted many disciples and by the time of his death at a great age, in AD 618, Glendalough was known across Europe as a centre of learning. St Kevin's foundation continued to flourish, despite being sacked twice by Vikings and once again by the English. Each time, the monks patiently restored the buildings until they were finally ousted by Henry VIII.

The oldest surviving building is the **Church of the Rock** which stands on the site of St Kevin's original oratory and has to be reached by boat. The building is about 24 feet by 14 feet on the inside and entered by way of a doorway made of large granite blocks. To the east of the church, in the

Glendalough

cliffside about 30 feet above the lake, is St Kevin's Bed – a tiny hole in the rock which was reputedly used by the saint for meditation and prayer. An ancient legend says that he also used it as a refuge from the unwelcome attentions of a young maiden. When she eventually found his hiding place, St Kevin responded most ungraciously by pushing her into the lake.

The extensive Glendalough site contains a wealth of other ancient buildings – a cathedral built in two phases in the 10th and 12th centuries, a well-preserved Round Tower with a doorway 10 feet above the ground, and numerous crosses, of which the most impressive is the 8th century St Kevin's Cross.

An excellent introduction to all these ecclesiastical treasures is provided at the Visitor Centre where your admission charge includes entrance to an informative exhibition and video show as well as the option of a guided tour if you wish.

Adjoining the Glendalough site is the **Wicklow Mountains National Park Visitor Centre**. The Centre has exhibitions, free lectures during the summer, education courses, and provides comprehensive information about the 49,420 acres of the Park which covers most of upland Wicklow.

Baltinglass

30 miles W of Wicklow on the N81

The little town of Baltinglass lies in a pleasant part of the Slaney valley with Baltinglass Hill (1258 feet) rising abruptly above it. On the summit of the hill are the remains of a large cairn containing a group of Bronze Age burial chambers. It's an easy climb and well worth it for the grand views from the top. To the north of the town stand the ruins of a 12th century Cistercian abbey known as **Vallis Salutis.** The abbey was founded by the King of Leinster, Dermot Macmurrough who is reputedly buried here. Notable among the substantial remains are six elegant Gothic arches on either side of the nave, and sculptures in the south nave.

Ashford

4 miles NW of Wicklow on the N11

This pretty little village on the River Vartry is close to two celebrated beauty spots. To the northwest, **Devil's Glen** is a deep ravine where there are some breathtaking walks high above the rushing river which at one point falls almost 100 feet into the "Devil's Punchbowl". Closer to the village, **Mount Usher Gardens** have grown from a mere potato field in 1860 to become one of Ireland's finest informal gardens today. Four generations of the Walpole family have tended the trees, shrubs and flowers, many

Butterfly Hill Farm

Kilmullen, Newtownmountkennedy,
Co. Wicklow
Tel: 01 281 9218 Fax: 01 281 0145
e-mail: butterflyhillfarm@eircom.net

Tucked away in peaceful countryside but only minutes from the N11, **Butterfly Hill Farm** is a friendly bed & breakfast establishment run by Myrtle Roberts and her husband John who was born on the farm. This charming 200-year-old farmhouse has 4 individually styled and attractive guest bedrooms, 3 of which have en suite facilities, and all of which represent outstanding value for money. Myrtle, who has a passion for handicrafts, is also an excellent cook and serves a wonderful breakfast. Open from February to November, Butterfly Hill is ideally located for visiting the historic attractions of Glendalough and the famous Powerscourt Gardens.

of them rare species, introduced from all around the world and planted in harmony with the natural woodland. The 20-acre gardens are laid out along the banks of the River Vartry with its weirs and waterfalls. Attractive suspension bridges provide vantage points from which to enjoy some spectacular and romantic views. At the courtyard entrance, there are several craft and clothing shops, and a pleasant tea room overlooking the river and gardens.

Roundwood

12 miles NW of Wicklow on the R755

Roundwood enjoys the distinction of being the highest village in Ireland, 780 feet

Wicklow Way Lodge

Oldbridge, Roundwood, Co. Wicklow
Tel/Fax: 01 2818489
e-mail: wicklowwaylodge@eircom.net
website: www.wicklowwaylodge.com

Wicklow Way Lodge is a beautiful residence located in the heart of Ireland's internationally famous Wicklow Way – indeed, the whole area is a walker's paradise. Nestling on the mountainside, the Lodge enjoys some of the most spectacular scenery in Ireland – guests can ramble around the family farm that is set beside the National Park and backs onto Scarr Mountain. The Lodge, which is the home of Marilyn Kinlan, is exquisitely furnished and decorated. The accommodation comprises doubles/twins and one large family room which can take up to 6 people. All rooms have an en suite bathroom, colour television, tea and coffee facilities, and hair dryer. Three of the bedrooms have their own private balcony where guests can relax and enjoy the stunning scenery.

You'll find plenty to see and do in the area. Many outstanding golf courses are close by – Druids Glen (recent host to the Irish Open), Woodenbridge, Roundwood and Powerscourt to name just four, and the ancient monastic city of Glendalough is just a few miles down the road. Other places of interest within easy reach include Powerscourt Gardens and Waterfall, Mount Usher Gardens, and Avondale House & Gardens where the Irish political leader Charles Stewart Parnell was born.

above sea level, and also of having been the home of the great Irish writer James Joyce as a boy. The village lies on the edge of the Wicklow Mountains National Park where red deer and grouse may still be seen and there are opportunities for some wonderful walks.

A unique attraction in Roundwood is **Victors Way** where Victor Langheld has assembled five magnificent works of art from India and set them in what he describes as "an Irish contemplative space". The giant black granite sculptures are a dazzling testament to Indian craftsmanship.

Blessington

20 miles NW of Wicklow on the N81

Tucked away in the northwestern corner of the county, Blessington enjoys a dreamy location alongside the gleaming waters of a lake and with the Wicklow Mountains as a dramatic backdrop. Once a staging post on the coach route from Dublin to Carlow, this attractive village has a wide main street lined by trees and handsome Georgian buildings.

But there's an even more impressive sight nearby, the stately pile of **Russborough House**, a grand Palladian mansion built in the 1740s for Joseph Leeson, 1st Earl of Milltown, a prosperous Dublin brewer. Leeson spared no expense. The house was designed by Ireland's leading architect of the day, Richard Castel; the swirling plasterwork was created by the Francini brothers; and one of the most fashionable painters in Europe at the time, Claude Vernet, was specially commissioned to provide four of the sea-scapes for which he was celebrated.

The palatial building with its two pillared and curving wings looks across to a placid

lake, a commonplace of 18th century landscaping, but this lake is actually a thoroughly modern 20th century reservoir formed by damming the River Liffey and providing Dublin with some 20 million gallons of water a day.

The interior of Russborough House is furnished with a dazzling collection of antiques, tapestries and exquisite porcelain, but the greatest glory of the house is its sumptuous array of paintings – works by Goya, Velazquez, Gainsborough, Rubens and Frans Hals are just some of the masterpieces on display. The paintings come from the collection of Alfred Beit, co-founder with Cecil Rhodes of the De Beer Diamond Company. They arrived at this obscure corner of County Wicklow when Beit's nephew, Sir Alfred Beit, bought Russborough Hall in 1952. Such a treasury of art has attracted some unwelcome attentions. In 1974, Bridget Rose Dugdale stole 16 of the paintings, worth £18 million, to raise funds for the IRA. These were all recovered within a week. There was a second burglary in 1986 and although some of the paintings stolen then were retrieved, security at the Hall is now understandably tight.

Russborough House

Poulaphouca House

Blessington, Hollywood, Co. Wicklow
Tel: 045 864118 Fax: 045 864091
e-mail: poulaphouca@eircom.net
website: www.poulaphoucahouseirl.com

Set within its own 32-acre park, **Poulaphouca House** enjoys an idyllic rural setting on the shores of the Blessington Lakes and close to the scenic Wicklow Mountains. Dating back to 1893, this fine old building has retained its original elegance and olde worlde charm. It's owned and run by the Malone family who have established a reputation for generous Irish hospitality, friendly atmosphere and country style. Outstanding cuisine is another important feature of the hotel's success. The ground floor Victorian-style restaurant, approached by way of the snooker and lounge area, has open fires and large mirrors, friendly approachable staff – and excellent food. The menus change daily but always offer appetising, freshly prepared dishes – traditional Irish Lamb Stew, for example, Aubergine & Courgette Gateau or Poached Darne of Salmon.

The accommodation comprises 6 spacious bedrooms, Victorian in design but equipped with all modern conveniences and enjoying lovely views of the surrounding countryside. With its beautiful surroundings Poulaphouca House is a popular venue for wedding celebrations. By limiting themselves to only one wedding a day, the hotel can give you their full and undivided attention. The hotel also welcomes conferences and other group events. Its facilities include function rooms catering for up to 200, a range of outdoor activities such as clay pigeon shooting – and even its own helicopter pad.

Northern Ireland

To many of its inhabitants, Northern Ireland is still "Ulster", one of the four great provinces of Celtic times, although Counties Cavan and Monaghan which formed a part of Ulster now lie within the Republic. The political entity of Northern Ireland came into being on 22nd June 1921 and, with Cavan and Monaghan excluded, the remaining 6 counties were dominated by Protestants, many of them descendants of Scottish settlers "planted" here in the 1600s.

Giants Causeway, Co Antrim

An almost exclusively Protestant police force, the Royal Ulster Constabulary, and military were established. To compound Protestant control, widespread gerrymandering of constituency boundaries took place, resulting in grotesque anomalies. Two thirds of the population of Derry City, for example, were Catholics but on the City Council Protestants held a two-thirds majority. The smouldering grievances of Catholics resulted in the civil disturbances that began in 1969 and festered throughout the rest of the century.

Slidderyford Dolmen

Happily, the peace process that began with the Easter agreement of 2000 has ushered in a period of stability and visitors are now returning in ever-increasing numbers. There is plenty for them to see and do. Belfast has re-invented itself as a smart and sophisticated centre with wine bars and trendy shops sprinkled amongst its monumental Victorian public buildings such as the City Hall, Grand Opera House and Custom House.

Lower Lough Erne, Co Fermanagh

Co Antrim and Belfast

For most visitors, Antrim is its coast and no tour of Ulster would be complete without a drive along the coastal road. It provides stunning views of the rugged cliffs and passes amazing rock formations, pretty villages, concealed harbours and ancient fortresses. At its north-eastern point Scotland's Mull of Kintyre, just 12 miles away is clearly visible – weather permitting. The road links the nine beautiful valleys known as the Glens of Antrim, skirts the strange rocks of the Giant's Causeway, and finishes (or starts) at the delightful port and resort of Portrush. Inevitably, this cornucopia of attractions leads to heavy traffic during the summer season, and Sundays are notoriously busy most of the year, but there is so much to enjoy that the journey should definitely not be missed. The interior, by comparison, is quiet and peaceful, a patchwork of fertile fields, rolling hills and gently undulating farming country. We begin this survey of the county by following the coastal road from Portrush in the northwest to Larne in the southeast.

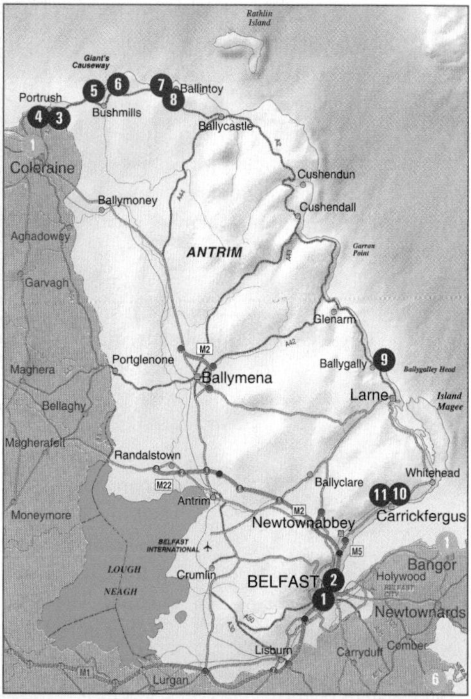

PLACES TO STAY, EAT AND DRINK

Belfast City Hall, Belfast	1	Historic Building	p386
The Lagan Lookout, Belfast	2	Visitor Attraction	p388
Comfort Hotel, Portrush	3	Hotel	p389
Royal Court Hotel, Portrush	4	Hotel	p390
Bayview Hotel, Bushmills	5	Hotel	p392
Giant's Causeway, Bushmills	6	Scenic Attraction	p392
Portcampley, Ballintoy	7	B&B	p393
Fullerton Arms, Ballycastle	8	Pub, Restaurant & Accommodation	p394
Ballygally Holiday Apartments, Ballygally	9	Self Catering	p398
Joymount Arms, Carrickfergus	10	Pub and Bistro	p399
FLAME! The Gasworks Museum, Carrickfergus	11	Museum	p400

● Denotes entries in other chapters

Belfast

One enthusiastic writer has called Belfast the "Hibernian Rio", a description inspired by the city's fine setting, ringed by high hills, sea lough and river valley. One third of Northern Ireland's population, nearly half a million, live in this robust, energetic city with its wealth of self-confident Victorian buildings. But the city's growth has been comparatively recent. Four hundred years ago, the small settlement of Beal Feirst ("the mouth of the sandy ford") had grown little since 1177 when the Anglo-Normans built a castle here. The English returned again in 1604 when James I "planted" Sir Arthur Chichester and the town began to expand around the local linen industry. The arrival of French Huguenots later that century, with their powerful work ethic, boosted development greatly.

But it was during the Industrial Revolution that Belfast really boomed. The growth of industries such as linen, rope-making and shipbuilding doubled the size of the town every ten years. The world's largest dry dock is here and the shipyard's giant cranes tower over the port. Another legacy of this period of prosperity is the staggering number of magnificent Victorian pubs or "gin palaces" scattered around the city.

Today, the city and river front are being transformed once again. Much of the city centre is pedestrianised, with plenty of benches where visitors can sit and listen to street musicians; smart bars and restaurants have sprung up, and there are inexhaustible opportunities for shopaholics. Music, theatre and the arts have experienced a renaissance in the last few years and the whole city demonstrates an optimism seemingly inspired by the ongoing peace process. What hasn't changed is the people – as friendly, welcoming and eager for craic as they have ever been.

Belfast City Centre

At the heart of the city is Donegall Square, a spacious public area dominated by the imposing **City Hall** (free - see panel on page 386) and a huge statue of Queen Victoria who visited Belfast in 1849.

Located on the north side of Donegall Square, the **Linen Hall Library** (free) is the city's oldest library and has been lending books to Belfast's citizens since 1788. It houses a massive collection of early Belfast printed books and a unique accumulation of more than 80,000 publications covering every aspect of Northern Ireland's political life since 1966. Known as the "Political Collection", it includes election posters, political ephemera, scholarly studies, and even prisoners' letters smuggled out of Long Kesh prison. An unusual amenity at the Linen Hall Library is the café in the Reading Room; tours are available..

For connoisseurs of architectural

fantasies, **St Malachy's Church** in Alfred Street is well worth seeking out. Built in 1844, its exterior is an extravagant medley of turrets and battlements, while the sumptuous, wedding-cake interior is notable for its elaborate fan-vaulted ceiling, modelled on the Henry VII Chapel in Westminster Abbey.

About 300 yards to the west of Donegall Square, the lavish **Grand Opera House** of 1895 is another architectural wonder. It boasts an exotic and opulently decorated interior which draws heavily on images from the Orient, with carved elephants supporting the boxes and a glorious painted ceiling. Also in Great Victoria Street is one of the city's gems, the **Crown Liquor Saloon,** an extraordinary gin palace with a glittering, glazed tile exterior and an interior of dizzying High Victorian excess. Gas-lit to this day, it features acres of original wooden panelling, a scrolled ceiling, patterned floor and a long S-shaped bar divided by exuberantly carved screens. A row of wooden snugs, similar to old-style railway compartments, lines one of the walls with carved heraldic beasts at each entry, and the bar staff are dressed appropriately with white aprons and bow ties. This remarkable hostelry is now owned by the National Trust but operates as a normal pub. Just around the corner is another bar that comes a close second to the Crown. **The Britannic** takes its name from the sister ship to the *Titanic* and the bar features plenty of Harland & Wolff shipyard memorabilia along with items from the liner herself.

Great Victoria Street, also known as the Golden Mile, leads the visitor out to the University Quarter. The area around the Georgian University Square has rightly been called a "perfect Victorian suburb", with the stately Tudor-style Queen's University building of 1845 as its focal point. The superb sweep of the Upper Terrace dates from the same time, as does the Lower Crescent which, strangely, is not a crescent at all but straight.

Close by are the **Botanic Gardens** (free) where the magnificent Palm House, built in 1829, is one of the earliest curved glass and

Belfast City Hall

Belfast, Co. Antrim
Tel: 028 902 70456

At the heart of the city is Donegall Square, a spacious public area dominated by the imposing **City Hall** (free) and a huge statue of Queen Victoria who visited Belfast in 1849. Designed by Sir Brumwell Thompson, the Hall was built between 1896 and 1906 in classical renaissance style with a gleaming Portland stone exterior and a sumptuous Italian marble interior. The central dome and corner towers have been unashamedly borrowed from Sir Christopher Wren's St Paul's Cathedral. There are 45-minute guided tours available which take in the palatial entrance hall, robing room, council chamber and views of the magnificent 173 feet high dome whose whispering gallery, oddly, cannot be reached.

The council chamber is, naturally, the grandest room, with hand-carved wainscoting and walls dotted with portraits of British royalty and aristocracy. Outside, at the east side, is a sculptured group commemorating the victims of the *Titanic,* at that time the largest ship in the world, and one of many liners built in the Belfast shipyards.

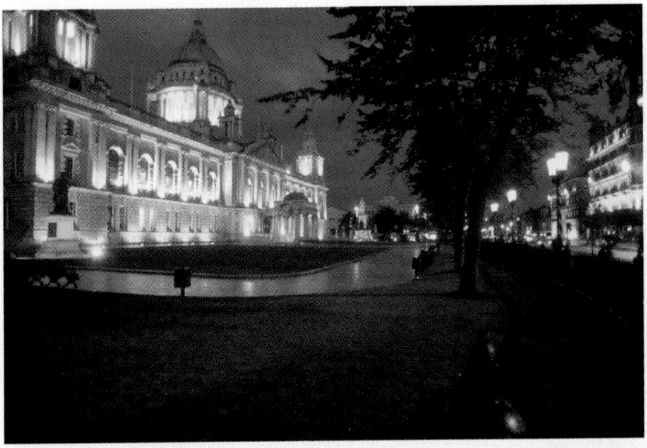

City Hall at Night

iron structures in the world, predating the famous one at Kew Gardens by several years. Within the grounds of the gardens, the **Ulster Museum** (free) houses a colossal collection of exhibits relating to the archaeology, ethnography, art, history and natural sciences of the province. One of the most notable displays is the treasure retrieved from the wreck of the *Girona*, a Spanish Armada galleon which sank off the Giant's Causeway.

Some of Belfast's grandest buildings are banks. The Ulster Bank in Waring Street, for example, has an interior resembling a Venetian palace. Rather more restrained in style is **Clifton House,** an elegant Georgian building of 1744 which is better known as the Poor House since it was originally the Charitable Institute for the Aged and Infirm. Designed by an amateur architect, a paper merchant named Robert Joy, it is crowned by a curious octagonal-based stone spire.

Many of Belfast's finest Victorian buildings were designed by the architect Charles Lanyon. His masterpiece is generally reckoned to be the **Custom House** on Donegall Quay. Although not open to the public, you can admire from the outside this imposing Corinthian-style structure of golden stone, designed in the "Italian manner after Palladio". Lanyon was also responsible for the nearby **Sinclair Seamen's Church** which has become something of a maritime museum. The pulpit is in the form of a ship's prow while other features include navigation lights and the ship's bell from *HMS Hood*. A couple of hundred yards from the church, the towering **Prince Albert Memorial** stands slightly askew because its foundations have sunk into the clay river bank. It's something of a puzzle why such a huge memorial was erected to the Prince since he never visited the city or ever became involved in its affairs, but the lofty clock tower is useful for getting one's bearings as you stroll around the city.

Also in the port area, **Lagan Lookout Visitor Centre** (see panel on page 388) tells the story of the important rôle played by the River Lagan in the development of the city with the help of models, stories and songs. Interactive displays enable visitors to follow the construction of the Lagan Weir and the regeneration of the River Lagan and the surrounding area. The city spent millions of pounds cleaning up the river with the result that for the first time in many years salmon fishing was possible on the day the weir was inaugurated.

Across the river from the Lagan Lookout, **Odyssey** is a colossal leisure complex opened in 2000 and incorporating a 10,000 seat indoor arena, a huge choice of bars, restaurants and shops, a multiplex cinema and the Sheridan IMAX cinema with a screen ten times the size of an ordinary

The Lagan Lookout

1 Dunegal Quay, Belfast BT1 3EA
Tel: 028 9031 1544 Fax: 028 9031 1955

The Lagan Lookout Visitor Centre provides an accessible and informative venue to find out more about Belfast's past and its rise into today's modern city. It provides a unique link that joins the City's industrial past with its evolving future and it tells that story through modern interactive sound and vision.

The location chosen for the Lagan Weir and Lookout is of great historical significance. It is the original site of the ford that crossed the River Lagan. Visit the Lookout and find out about the growth of Belfast over the last 300 years, from its beginnings as a trading port, following its rise through Victorian times and the Industrial Revolution. You can see a display on the world famous, RIMS Titanic built in Belfast and view the fantastic two metre replica of the ill fated ship. Visit "The Big *Fish"* on Donegall Quay and discover a snapshot of Belfast, both past and present.

The Lagan Weir is central to the whole regeneration of the river and the surrounding area. A major engineering achievement, this massive 214 million project provides a new set of lungs for the river. The weir has five gates, which control water levels, ensuring that the mud flats are kept covered. It also acts as a prevention against flooding.

Today the river is undergoing a resurgence to meet changing times. New businesses and new housing developments are rising along its banks and new life is being breathed into its waters. Follow the progress of the changing face of Belfast and capture impressive views of The Odyssey, Belfast's millennium project, or the magnificent Waterfront Hall, situated on Lanyon Place.

The Lookout remains an excellent resource facility for school and college visits, especially those studying Geography, the Environment and History. A resident Education Officer is always on hand to provide specialist knowledge and assistance,

cinema. Also within the complex is **W5,** short for Whowhatwherewhenwhy, a scientific discovery center aimed primarily at children.

On the outskirts of the city, **Cave Hill** (1182 feet) is a notable landmark, known also as Napoleon's Nose because of its profile. If you climb up to the summit, the entire city and its lough are laid out before you in all their glory. The slopes are dotted with Iron Age forts and in ancient times the hill was mined for flint to make tools and weapons. Set on the side of Cave Hill, **Belfast Castle** (free) is a mansion of 1870 built in the style of Queen Victoria's Scottish residence, Balmoral. Its cellars have been transformed into a re-creation of a typical Belfast street in Victorian times, complete with a bar and restaurant. From the main reception room, a splendid Italianate stairway leads down to attractive gardens enjoying fine views of the harbour area. Nearby, **Belfast Zoo** is home to more than 60 endangered species, housed in enclosures which replicate the wild. Set in pleasantly landscaped parkland, the zoo has won many awards for its emphasis on spacious enclosure, its breeding programme, and its mainly small animal collection. Visitors can view penguins and sea lions from underwater and the zoo provides a rare opportunity to see a spectacled bear and a red panda.

About 5 miles to the east of the city and set in 300 acres of gardens, **Stormont** is a splendid neo-classical building of gleaming white stone. It formerly housed the Northern Ireland Parliament and is now the home of the new Assembly. The building is not open to the public but visitors are free to wander through its extensive grounds which also contain Stormont Castle, the official residence of the Secretary of State for Northern Ireland. The Castle is also not open to visitors.

Portrush Harbour

County Antrim

Portrush

5 miles N of Coleraine on the A2/A29

This popular family resort enjoys a splendid position on Ramore Head, a mile-long peninsula jutting out into the Atlantic. Beautiful sandy beaches, (the West and East Strands), run for miles, ending to the east at **White Rocks** – weirdly shaped limestone cliffs which have been weathered into caves and arches. The East Strand is backed by the sand dunes of the famous Royal Portrush Golf Club which provides devotees of the game with one 9-hole and two 18-hole courses. The town is well-provided with all the usual seaside amenities including an all-weather holiday centre, **Waterworld**, which offers flumes, slides, jacuzzis, a sauna, aquarium, restaurant and, oddly, a bowling alley. **Barry's Fairground** has all the traditional amusements and rides; **Fantasy Island** is an indoor adventure playground; and the **Dunluce Centre** has "virtual reality" family attractions including a simulated ghost train. During the season, the Portrush Puffer road train carries passengers on a circular tour of the town and other entertainments include theatre, concerts and firework displays. Towards the end of May, a hilarious **Raft Race** takes place when contestants race each other across the

Royal Court Hotel

Whiterocks, Portrush,
Co. Antrim BT56 8NF
Tel: 028 7082 2236 Fax: 028 7082 3176
e-mail: royalcourthotel@aol.com
website: www.royalcourthotel.co.uk

Overlooking the harbour town of Portrush and its renowned Royal Portrush Golf Club, and enjoying panoramic views of County Donegal and the Scottish Isles, the **Royal Court Hotel** boasts one of the finest locations on Northern Ireland's most famous coastline. It also offers an outstanding range of amenities complemented by meticulous attention to detail along with courteous and efficient service.

Between them, the elegant Restaurant and the Grill Bar cater for every appetite – anything from a snack or table d'hôte lunch, to high tea and à la carte dinner menus. All dishes are prepared using only the finest quality fresh produce and to accompany these culinary treats a selection of fine wines is available.

The accommodation at the Royal Court maintains the same high standards evident throughout the hotel. The 14 guest bedrooms and 4 suites are all luxuriously furnished and decorated and each has an en suite bathroom, large screen colour television, direct dial telephone, tea/coffee-making facilities and a trouser press. The hotel also offers safe-keeping facilities and a bureau de change service.

With its enchanting setting and extensive amenities, the hotel is a popular venue for weddings and other special occasions. With years of experience, the hotel staff pride themselves as wedding specialists, offering 2 superb venues each catering for both the large or smaller wedding and providing the best in scenic views. Professional, caring staff are on hand at all times to make sure that the big day goes off without a hitch, whether it's a small family affair or a grand social occasion.

The Dunluce room overlooks the Skerries and the Atlantic Ocean. Beautiful scenery and more often than not breathtaking sunsets mean that your guests will be able to see some of the best aspects of the beautiful north Antrim coastline. The Dunluce Room can cater for up to 140 wedding guests and up to 200 guests for the evening reception.

The Atlantic Suite, a recently opened function room and conference room can cater for up to 200-500 wedding guests and up to 300 in the evening and boasts magnificent views of Donegal, the Scottish Isles and of course the Atlantic Ocean. Luxurious accommodation is available for you and your guests and the bridal suite has an excellent view, 4 poster bed, large-screen satellite TV, Jacuzzi bath and shower facilities.

harbour on a bizarre assortment of home-made rafts.

One natural feature well worth seeing is the **Cathedral Cave** at the eastern end of the long, sandy beach. The sea and the weather have modelled the soft limestone cliffs into strange shapes and carved out this cave which stretches 180 feet from end to end.

About 3 miles east of Portrush, **Dunluce Castle** is one of the grandest sights in Ireland. This romantic 13th/16th century ruin clings to a crag, almost entirely surrounded by the sea and with a huge cave right underneath. The castle's defenders could enter the cave which slopes up into the castle precincts and repulse any attack from the drawbridge across the deep chasm which is now spanned by a footbridge. In the late 1500s, Dunluce was the stronghold of the MacDonnells, Lords of the Isles, who ruled all the northeastern corner of Ulster from this seemingly impregnable base. But in 1584, the English under Sir John Perrott battered the castle with artillery, forcing "Sorley Boy" MacDonnell and his clansmen to flee. But with the help of a sympathiser in the castle, Sorley Boy ("Yellow Charles" in Irish) was back a few nights later. His men were hauled up the crag in a basket, the English garrison was annihilated and the constable hanged over the wall. Sorley Boy was able to repair the damage to his castle with the rich pickings gathered from the wreck of the Spanish Armada ship, the *Girona*, which sank near the Giant's Causeway in 1588. Sorley Boy later agreed a peace with the English and his son Randal was created Earl of Antrim by James I.

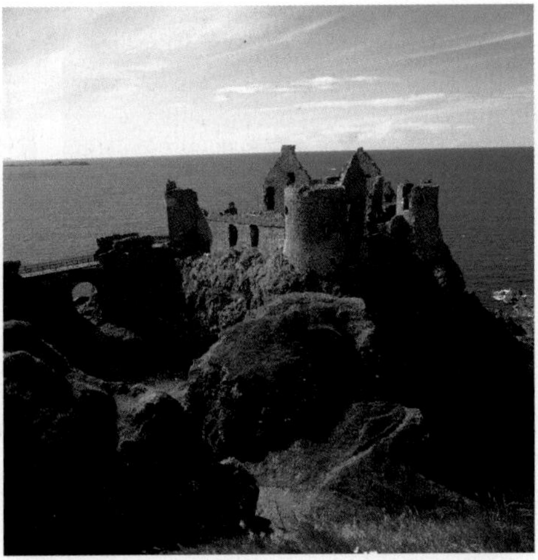

Dunluce Castle

Dunluce Castle suffered another dramatic disaster in 1639 when a great storm swept the castle's original kitchens off the hilltop, along with the cooks and the dinner they were preparing. A few years later, the MacDonnells moved to a less precarious residence at Glenarm in the Glens of Antrim. The extensive ruins of their abandoned castle include two 13th century towers, a Scottish style gatehouse of around 1600, and the remains of a great hall, part of a 17th century house built within the castle walls. Guided tours are available and in calm weather the sea cave can be visited by boat.

Bushmills

12 miles NE of Coleraine on the A2

The quiet little town of Bushmills is known throughout the world for the whiskey that has been legally produced here since 1608, making **Bushmills Distillery** the oldest licit distillery anywhere. Tsar Peter the Great sampled the fiery liquor during his study tour of Europe in 1697 and pronounced himself well pleased. The distillery offers guided tours which last for about an hour and conclude with a tot of the *usquebeagh*, or you can order a hot toddie if you need warming up. Bushmills is barely a quarter of a mile out of town and is clearly signposted.

About 3 miles northeast of Bushmills is

Bayview Hotel

Portballintrae, Bushmills,
Co. Antrim BT57 8RZ
Tel: 028 2073 4100 Fax: 028 2073 4330
e-mail: info@bayviewhotelni.com
website: www.bayviewhotelni.com

Opened in 2001The **Bayview Hotel** is situated in the heart of the picturesque village of Portballintrae, one mile from Bushmills. It is situated overlooking the Atlantic ocean and close to the Giant's Causeway and Old Bushmills Distillery.The 25 luxurious bedrooms available comprise of standard, superior, premier, interlinking and ambulant disabled rooms. This small luxury hotel has its own private car park, Porthole Restaurant and Bar and is the ideal destination for conferencing, golfing, business, travel and leisure. It is a sister hotel to the Comfort Hotel in Portrush.

the spectacular **Giant's Causeway** (free - see panel below), the only World Heritage Site in Ireland and one which has been attracting visitors ever since it was pronounced one of the great natural wonders of the world by the Royal Geographical Society in 1693.

A couple of miles to the east of the Giant's Causeway, the sorry looking remains of **Dunseverick Castle** stand on the cliffs of Benbane Head; only the ruins of a 16th century gatehouse still stand.

Giant's Causeway

Bushmills, Co. Antrim

About three miles northeast of Bushmills is the spectacular **Giant's Causeway**, the only World Heritage Site in Ireland and one which has been attracting visitors ever since it was pronounced one of the great natural wonders of the world by the Royal Geographical Society in 1693.

This extraordinary cluster of black basalt pillars, most of them six-sided although some have as many as ten sides, was formed some 60 million years ago by volcanic activity. As the molten basalt cooled it solidified into some 37,000 columns. Various groups of the stony columns have been given names such as the Organ Pipes, and one, known as Chimney Point has such a strange outline that sailors on the Spanish Armada ship *Girona* mistook it for Dunluce Castle, a mistake which led to the ship's foundering with the loss of more than a thousand lives.

The Causeway takes its name from the legend of the Ulster warrior Finn MacCool who built it so that he could reach his beloved, a giantess on the Island of Staffa where the formation resurfaces off the Scottish coast.

The Causeway is now in the care of the National Trust which has a Visitor Centre here with a coffee shop, craft shop and audio-visual displays. Next door, the **Causeway School** is an interesting re-creation of a 1920s country school, complete with children's toys such as whipping tops and skipping ropes. It's only open during July and August.

Between circa AD 500-800, this was the capital of the kingdom of Dalriada which, based in north Antrim, colonised much of Scotland. Dunseverick was also the terminus of one of the five great roads radiating from Tara, the ancient capital of Ireland.

Ballintoy

15 miles NE of Coleraine on the B15

The dramatic little harbour at Ballintoy with its colourful boats and rock-strewn shore provides a picturesque subject for both amateur and professional painters. The village itself is one of the prettiest along the Antrim coast, its white-painted houses and church creating an almost Mediterranean atmosphere. The village's one-time landlord was Downing Fullerton who endowed the Cambridge college which bears his Christian name and is partly furnished with oak panelling and a staircase taken from Ballintoy Castle which was demolished in 1795.

A popular excursion from Ballintoy is the boat trip around **Sheep Island** (National Trust) just offshore, a great stack with a flat grassy top which is home to an enormous colony of cormorants. The original puffin colony was massacred by rats but the rodents in turn were exterminated and a small number of puffins have recently returned. The boat trips usually continue to the nearby **Carrick-a-rede Island**, famous for its nerve-racking rope bridge. Sixty feet long and suspended 80 feet above the sea, the swaying construction of planks and rope links the island to a commercial salmon fishery. Despite a large sign warning of the danger and the absence of any safety

Fullerton Arms

22-24 Main Street, Ballintoy, Ballycastle,
Co. Antrim BT54 6LX
Tel/Fax: 028 2076 9613
e-mail: info@fullertonarms.co.uk
website: www.fullertonarms.co.uk

Surrounded by some of the most spectacular scenery in northern Europe, the **Fullerton Arms** is a delightful old hostelry with a history going back to the 1700s. At that time, a Dr Fullerton bought Ballintoy village and outlying lands from the Stewart family for the then substantial sum of £20,000. One of his first acts as landlord was to order the closure of an illegal drinking shebeen in the village. Ironically, many years later the same premises were granted a liquor licence and today the building is known as the Fullerton Arms.

Today, this outstanding guest house, bar and restaurant is owned and run by Anne and Lyle Taggart who pride themselves on their high standard of customer service and attention to detail. The lively bar is popular with both locals and visitors. As well as having old world charm and plenty of craic, it also serves one of the best pints of draught Guinness to be found in the north. Special traditional music evenings take place here when you can enjoy the sound of Scottish and Irish reels, jigs and ballads, or admire the footwork of local Irish dancers.

A special pool table area has been set aside for those who enjoy playing bar games, and the bar is also equipped with satellite television for those major sporting events. This is also a good place to eat. A wide selection of food is served, ranging from bar snack meals to evening dining in the fully licensed restaurant. The restaurant is open all year round and can cater for up to 100 guests – large functions, wedding parties, conferences and touring coaches are all welcome. In addition, there is an outdoor function area/beer garden, ideal for those long summer evening events.

The accommodation at the Fullerton Arms enjoys a 3-star rating and comprises 5 doubles, 3 twins, 1 single and 2 family rooms. All the bedrooms are en suite and each is equipped with satellite television, condiments set and tea/coffee-making facilities. Fresh towels are provided daily.

The Fullerton Arms makes an ideal base for exploring the many attractions of north Antrim. A 10-minute walk will bring you to the awe-inspiring Carrick-a-Rede rope bridge that crosses a sea gorge some 80 feet above the water. To the west, the world-famous Giant's Causeway and Old Bushmills Whiskey Distillery are both just 10 minutes away by car; a similar length of journey to the east leads to the seaside town of Ballycastle and the Glens of Antrim.

netting, there's a regular procession of squealing, giggling or frozen-faced tourists crossing the bridge. Carrick-a-rede means "rock in the road" – the "road" being the sea route taken by Atlantic salmon returning to spawn in the rivers.

From Ballintoy harbour, a footpath leads to **Whitepark Bay** (National Trust), a mile-long beach of golden sands backed by grassy dunes. The path continues to the tiny hamlet of Portbraddan whose slate-roofed church, 12 feet by 6½ feet, lays claim to being the smallest church in Ireland.

Carrick-a-rede Island

Ballycastle

16 miles NE of Coleraine on the A2/B67

Ballycastle is a lively little resort town, never more so than in June when it hosts a 3-day festival of Gaelic games, music and dance, the *Fleadh Amhran agus Rince*. In May there's more jollity when the cross-community Northern Lights Festival takes place, but the most time-honoured event occurs on the last Monday and Tuesday of August. **Ould Lammas Fair** has been held here ever since the MacDonnells were granted a charter in 1606, making it Ireland's oldest popular fair. It used to last for a whole week but is now a 2-day event featuring sheep and pony sales along with several hundred street stalls shoehorned into the Diamond (Market Square) and along Fairhill Street. An old, but still popular song, asks *Did you treat your Mary Ann / To dulse and yellow man / At the Ould Lammas Fair in Ballycastle-O?* "Dulse" is an edible seaweed; "yellow man" a bright yellow toffee so rock-hard it requires a hammer to break it into fragments.

Whitepark Bay

Ballycastle was extensively developed during the mid-1700s by its landowner, Colonel Hugh Boyd, and many attractive houses of that period have survived. The handsome Classical parish church with its octagonal spire was also built at that time. Its square tower is marked by a huge clock face, completely out of proportion to the tower, while inside there's a dazzling star-spangled blue ceiling and some grandiose monuments to the Boyd family.

Another monument, in the form of a picnic site on the sea front, commemorates a crucial moment in the history of telecommunications. It was from here, in 1898, that the 24-year-old Guglielmo Marconi made the world's first successful cross-water wireless transmission to Rathlin Island, about 5 miles distant.

The boomerang-shaped **Rathlin Island** is a popular destination for boat trips from Ballycastle – a 45-minute journey. Girded by high white cliffs for most of its coastline, the island is nowhere more than a mile wide. The cliffs are home to tens of thousands of seabirds whose incessant murmurings sound like the inside of a beehive. They vastly outnumber the 100 or so human residents on the island.

The cliffs are perforated by many caves, the most famous of which is Bruce's Cave where Robert the Bruce took refuge after his defeat at Perth by the English in 1306. According to legend, it was here that he observed a spider repeatedly trying to reach the roof of the cave and formulated the apophthegm *"If at first you don't succeed, try, try and try again"*. Bruce did try again, returning to Scotland and defeating the English at the Battle of Bannockburn. In calm weather, Bruce's Cave can be visited by boat.

Restrictions on visitor's cars make Rathlin a peaceful place nowadays but the island has witnessed some horrific events. In AD 795 its inhabitants were the first victims in Ireland of Viking raiders; in 1575 English forces led by the Earl of Essex slaughtered every one of the women, children and old people whom the MacDonnells had sent here believing it to be a place of safety. In 1642 the MacDonnells on Rathlin Island were again under attack, this time from their Scottish enemies, the Campbells. From a hill in the middle of the island, now called *Cnoc na Screedlin*, "the hill of screaming", the distraught MacDonnell womenfolk looked on helplessly as the Campbells butchered their husbands and sons. For an insight into Rathlin Island's chequered history, its culture and ecology, a visit to the **Boathouse Centre**, just around the bay from the harbour, is recommended.

Continuing eastwards from Ballycastle along the A2 for a couple of miles brings you to Ballyvoy and the ruins of **Bonamargy Friary** founded by the MacQuillan family around 1500. It is notable for the tombs of "Sorley Boy" MacDonnell of Dunluce Castle fame, his son Randal, 1st Earl of Antrim, and his grandson the 2nd Earl who died in 1682. The 2nd Earl's tomb provides evidence that even at this late date Irish was still a living language in this area. As well as English and Latin epitaphs there are two Irish inscriptions. One translates as "Every seventh year a calamity befalls the Irish"; the second, "Now that the Earl has departed, it will occur every year". A slab in the main aisle marks the grave of Julia MacQuillan who insisted on being buried here so that even in death she would be humbled by the feet of passing worshippers.

From Ballyvoy a minor road leads to **Fair Head**, also known as Benmore. From its 600 feet-high summit there are wonderful views over to Rathlin Island and the Scottish islands of Islay and the Paps of Jura, and the Mull of Kintyre, only 13 miles away but seeming much closer. Wild goats live among the rocks below the cliffs. On the top of the headland, Lough na Cranagh is a small lake with a beautiful *crannóg* – a man-made island built in the early Christian period.

Cushendun

27 miles N of Larne on the B92

A short detour off the A2 on the B92 leads to the striking little village of Cushendun, once a fashionable watering place and distinguished by its very un-Irish architecture. Most of the buildings were designed by Clough Williams-Ellis, better known for his fantasy village of Portmeirion in Wales. He was commissioned by Ronald McNeill, 1st (and last) Lord Cushendun, and his Cornish wife Maud to create a setting with a Cornish theme. So the houses, built between 1912 and 1925, are of rugged white-washed stone with roofs of slate. Williams-Ellis also designed Lord Cushendun's large neo-Georgian house, fronted by an odd five arch arcade, which is now a home for the elderly. The tiny village, (population about 70), is owned by the National Trust which fussily preserves its pristine appearance.

The Poet Laureate John Masefield knew Cushenden well since he married a daughter of the Crummelin family. The Crummelins lived at Cave House (now a Catholic retreat), a substantial mansion which is set in an amphitheatre of cliffs and can only be reached by passing through a 60-feet-long tunnel in the red sandstone cliff.

To the west of the village, in Craigagh Wood, is a rock where clandestine Masses were said during the 18th century. The stone is carved with a crucifixion scene and is said to have been brought here from Iona. Nearby, the **Gloonan Stone** is indented with two hollows made, according to legend, by St Patrick when he knelt to pray here. *Glúna* is the Irish word for knees.

Cushendun lies at the head of Glendun, the wildest of the Antrim Glens and there's a marvellously scenic walk from the village up to waterfalls.

Cushendall

24 miles N of Larne on the A2

This delightful village with trim, colour-washed houses set along a spectacular shore lies at the point where three of the nine Glens of Antrim converge, hence its claim to be the "Capital of the Glens". In mid-August the Heart of the Glens Festival takes place here with an abundance of traditional music, sporting events and a huge street céili, but at any time throughout the year the local pubs offer a good choice of dancing and traditional music. The village's most striking building is **Turnly's Tower** which dominates the main crossroads. It was built in 1809 by a nabob of the East India Company, Francis Turnly, as "a place of confinement for idlers and rioters". After serving as the town's lock-up for more than a century, it became a private dwelling and was inhabited until a few years ago.

From the village, an exhilarating cliff-top walk leads to the ruins of **Layde Old Church** which dates back to the 13th century and was the chief burial place of the MacDonnells whose gravestones still fill the churchyard. South of the village, **Ossian's Grave** is even older. This prehistoric court grave is named after the legendary poet Ossian whose supposedly ancient works were in fact the creation of an 18th century literary fraudster.

A mile or so south of Cushendall, the A43 strikes off into Glenariff, a broad and fertile valley flanked by steep mountain sides, a landscape described by William Thackeray as "Switzerland in miniature". About 5 miles along this road is **Glenariff Forest Park** which has several way-marked paths, including a Waterfall Trail leading to a series of spectacular waterfalls bearing evocative names such as *Ess na Larach*, (the Mare's Fall) and *Ess na Crub*, (the Fall of the Hooves). Some of them can be viewed from a timber walkway first erected more than a hundred years ago.

Glenarm

12 miles N of Larne on the A2

This appealing little village is one of the oldest of the glen settlements, dating back to the 13th century. Its narrow main street, lined with colour-washed cottages, broadens out as it approaches the impressive gateway of Glenarm Castle. The castle, the home of the Earl of Antrim, is only open to the public for a few days in summer but if you walk through the gateway into Glenarm Forest there's a good view of this curious building which has been likened by many to the Tower of London.

Ballygally

5 miles N of Larne on the A2

Continuing southwards from Glenarm, the A2 passes through Ballygally where the very

BALLYGALLY HOLIDAY APARTMENTS

210 Coast Road, Ballygally,
Co. Antrim BT40 2QQ
Tel: 02828 583061 Fax: 02828 583100
e-mail: info@ballygally.net
website: www.antrimcoastandglens.co.uk

Set on the beautiful Antrim coast, the village of Ballygally is an ideal centre for exploring the Glens of Antrim and the world-famous Giant's Causeway. Enjoying a superb location in the village, overlooking Ballygally beach and with magnificent views over the Irish Sea to Scotland, the **Ballygally Holiday Apartments** provide luxury accommodation in a wonderful setting. The seven award-winning apartments are furnished to a very high standard and each has an elegantly furnished lounge with picture windows.

They each have a fully equipped kitchen with a range of modern appliances including laundry facilities, dishwasher and microwave. One, two and three-bedroom apartments are available, all centrally heated, with a luxury bath/shower room, and each is equipped with television, video, modem telephone, trouser press and hairdryer. Weekly linen and a daily towel service are provided. On arrival,

guests will find a complimentary breakfast starter pack ready for them and a resident manager is always on hand to assist in any way. Other amenities include an outside picnic area, a fax facility and private car parking. Activities available in the area include golf, fishing, boating, swimming in the sea or at Larne Leisure Centre, a children's playground, and a wonderful variety of walks.

Scottish-looking 17th century plantation castle is now a hotel, its dungeons converted into a welcoming bar (despite the attentions of a resident ghost). At nearby **Carnfunnock Country Park** the attractions include a walled garden, a "time garden" with an interesting collection of sundials, a maze in the shape of Northern Ireland, a 9-hole golf course, craft shop, miniature railway and many beautiful walks.

Larne

18 miles N of Belfast on the A8

The 60-mile scenic stretch of the Antrim coast comes to an end at the busy industrial port of Larne which is the terminal for ferries to Stranraer and Cairnryan – the shortest sea crossings between Ireland and Scotland. On clear days, the Scottish coast is plainly visible from the promenade and from the Curran, a long gravel spit curving southwards from the town. The Curran is an archaeologist's dream. Many thousands of neolithic flint flakes, arrowheads and tools have been discovered here, providing evidence that this was one of the first parts of Ireland to be inhabited. At the southern tip of the Curran stand the ruins of **Olderfleet Castle**, originally a Viking foundation but rebuilt in stone during the 13th century. Its present setting is deeply unromantic, surrounded almost entirely by an industrial park. Perhaps the town's most striking building is the 95 feet high **Round Tower** that overlooks the harbour. Modelled on the lines of an ancient Irish round tower, it was erected in 1888 as a memorial to James Chaine, a County

Antrim MP who was the driving force behind the establishment of shipping routes from Larne to Scotland and the Americas. Before his death, James carefully stipulated the manner of his burial. He was to be interred "in an upright position in a private enclosure overlooking the entrance to the lough, so that even in death he could still watch the passing ships". And so he was.

Carrickfergus

10 miles S of Larne on the A2

Carrick, a rock; *Fergus*, King of Dalriada: - the name of this seaside town derives from the misfortune of King Fergus who was shipwrecked nearby during one of his frequent voyages between his Irish and Scottish possessions. The sea front area is dominated by the massive bulk of **Carrickfergus Castle**, its lofty four storey tower perched on a rocky promontory above the busy port. Built around 1180 by the Anglo-Norman John de Courcy, the castle was in continual military use until 1928 and is extremely well-preserved. King John slept here in 1210; the French occupied it for a short while in 1760. During a siege in 1315 by Edward Bruce the Irish defenders were on the brink of surrendering because they had no food. Happily, they managed to capture eight of the Scotsmen whose bodies furnished sufficient sustenance for the Irish to continue their defiance for a few more days.

The castle now houses the **Cavalry Regimental Museum** which displays an impressive array of weapons and armour. Costumed guides, life-size model figures and a video presentation provide a fascinating insight into the castle's various triumphs and disasters. Visitors can buy a joint ticket which also gives entry to the **Knight Ride** trip, Ireland's only themed mono-rail ride, which transports passengers through 1000 years of the town's colourful history, complete with all the appropriate sounds

JOYMOUNT ARMS

16-18 Joymount, Carrickfergus,
Co. Antrim BT38 7DN
Tel: 02893 351850 Fax: 02893 359303
e-mail: joymountarms@aol.com

For good food, reasonable prices and a cosy atmosphere make your way to the **Joymount Arms** in Carrickfergus. Long established in the area, it was brought under new ownership in 2002 and the owners have recently renovated an adjoining house to incorporate "ownies", its new bistro. The bistro's extensive menu offers everything from traditional steaks and calf liver to Belgian mussels and Jamaican red snapper. You can dine and relax under the old beams as friendly and efficient staff attend to your needs.

Upstairs, a function room holds up to 90 people and cater for parties, weddings and private dinner functions. Here diners can overlook the stunning view of the sea as they enjoy the sumptuous food prepared by top class chef Johnny Richie, formerly of Bureau in Whiteabbey and TATU in Belfast.

The relaxed and friendly atmosphere and professional staff form a big part of the Joymount Arms success. With open fires and traditional surroundings regular live music, sports coverage, quizzes and the best pint of guiness in the area. The Joymount Arms is a must for good food and drink and a great craic.

and smells.

Carrickfergus boasts some literary connections. The Restoration playwright William Congreve grew up in the castle where his father was a soldier; Jonathan Swift's first clerical appointment was at Kilroot, just outside the town, where he wrote *The Tale of a Tub* between 1694 and 1696; and the poet Louis MacNeice (1907-63) spent a despondent childhood here which he recalled in his far from complimentary poem, *Carrickfergus* (1937).

MacNeice's father was the minister at the **Church of St Nicholas,** originally built by John de Courcy in 1205 but extensively altered in 1614. Of interest here are the leper's squint; a crooked aisle or *skew* that symbolises Christ's inclined head on the cross; and, in the baptistery, a stained glass window depicting St Nicholas in his role as Santa Claus, complete with sledge and reindeer.

American visitors, especially, will find the **Andrew Jackson Centre** of interest. The parents of the 7th President of the United States set sail from Carrickfergus in 1765 and the reconstructed traditional thatched farmhouse here contains exhibits on President Jackson's life and career, his Ulster relations and rural Ulster life. Located within the gardens of the Andrew Jackson Centre, the **US Ranger Centre** tells the story of this elite combat unit whose first unit was formed at Carrickfergus in June 1942. The exhibition material has been donated by Ranger veterans and includes uniforms, vintage radio equipment, documents and photographs.

As a change from castles, visitor centres and museums a visit to The **Gasworks Museum of Ireland** (see panel below) is recommended. Built in 1855 to produce gas for the town's street lamps, this is the only Victorian coal-fired gasworks in Ireland.

In and around Antrim Town

Antrim Town is set a little way back from the shores of Lough Neagh, the largest stretch of inland water in the British Isles, 17 miles long and 11 miles wide. The lough is famous for its eels which spawn in the Sargasso Sea, take 3 years to swim across the Atlantic and then wriggle their way up the River Bann during the spring. Some 20

FLAME! The Gasworks Museum of Ireland

44 Irish Quarter West, Carrickfergus,
Co Antrim BT38 8AT
Tel: 028 9336 9575

Carrickfergus boasts Ireland's sole surviving coal gasworks and is one of only three left within the British Isles.

It was opened in 1855 and supplied the town with gas for over 100 years. It stopped making gas in 1967 and finally closed in 1987. It is now fully restored and open to the public.

See how gas was made from coal in Europe's largest serving set of horizontal set of retorts. Meet the manager and his wife and listen in on the workers. In addition you'll also get a great view of the town from the top of the gasholder!

million of them make the transatlantic crossing each year but nowadays as many as possible are caught at Coleraine and transported to Lough Neagh by tankers. Once released into the lough's waters, it takes another 12 years for the eels to fully mature. They are then harvested and treated at the main fishery at Toomebridge, where the River Bann enters the lough. Visitors are welcome at this friendly co-operative managed by local fishermen and farmers.

Antrim

16 miles NW of Belfast off the M2

Antrim is a prosperous town whose population has rocketed over the last 20 years, with new housing and shopping developments swamping its ancient core of which little now remains. One remarkable survivor, though, is the 9th century **Round Tower**, (just north of the town centre), which is in almost perfect condition. Of Antrim Castle, built in 1662 for Viscount Massereene and Ferrard, only a mutilated tower still stands following a disastrous fire in 1922. But the lovely **Antrim Castle Gardens** surrounding the castle are well worth a visit. They have been carefully restored to the original patterns created by the distinguished French landscape gardener, André Le Nôtre (1613-70), designer of the excruciatingly formal gardens at Versailles. The original design for Antrim Castle Gardens was also pure geometry: a rigid pattern of circular parterres, radial paths and ruler-straight avenues. Fortunately, nature always wins. Overarching trees now soften the harsh lines of Le Nôtre's grid-like view of what a garden should be. Antrim Castle's former carriage house and stable block has also been renovated and is now home to the **Clotworthy Art Centre**, a theatre and art gallery which hosts exhibitions of the work of both local and international artists.

On the Randalstown Road, **Shanes Castle** is the family seat of the O'Neills of Clandeboy. The demesne is regarded as one of the most beautiful and well-maintained in Ireland with a rich variety of fauna, flora, insect and bird life, along with a herd of feral deer. The Castle itself has been in ruins since a fire in 1816 but the peaceful setting, the striking remains and the unique Camellia House make it well worth a visit.

Antrim also boasts an 18-hole golf course on the lake shore, excellent trout fishing, a large indoor sports complex with two swimming pools, and there are pleasure boat cruises on Lough Neagh departing from the Six Mile Water marina.

Crumlin

12 miles S of Antrim on the A52

Crumlin lies a few miles south of Belfast International Airport so it's an appropriate location for the **Ulster Aviation Heritage Centre** which occupies a former US air base. Amongst the aircraft on display are a Wildcat, Sea Hawk, Buccaneer and the amphibian Sea Hawker. The Centre also possesses a unique collection of photographs, documents and artefacts exhibited in the old wartime buildings, and a reference library. The centre is open on Saturdays from 1pm to 6pm, or by arrangement.

Lisburn

8 miles SW of Belfast off the M1

In 2002, Lisburn was created a city, one of only five towns in Britain to be honoured in this way as part of Queen Elizabeth's Golden Jubilee celebrations. Located on the River Lagan in the southern tip of County Antrim, Lisburn was once an important linen town, flourishing under the leadership of the Huguenot Louis Crommelin in the late 17th century. The history of that industry is vividly presented at the **Irish Linen Centre & Museum**, housed in the 18th century Assembly Rooms in the Market Square. Visitors can try their hand at scutching or spinning or watch the only hand loom linen weavers at work in Ireland today in the purpose-built workshop, purchase samples in the craft shop or enjoy refreshments at the café in the modern annex where there are art displays and lunchtime recitals. Virtually all of Lisburn's older buildings were destroyed by a catastrophic fire in 1707 which, along with most of the town, also laid waste to its 17th century castle. The Cathedral was so badly damaged it had to be rebuilt. Only the size of a parish church, the Cathedral contains some interesting tablets and monuments, and the tiny graveyard is the last resting place of Louis Crommelin who brought such prosperity to the town.

A recent addition to Lisburn's attractions is the **Island Arts Centre,** located on an island in the River Lagan, which has a varied programme of concerts, exhibitions and other artistic events.

Devotees of real ale will want to pay a visit to the **Hilden Brewery**, about a mile outside Lisburn in the village of Hilden. Established in 1981, it's one of only two real ale breweries in Ireland and occupies the courtyard of a 19th century mansion that once belonged to the Barbours, one of Lisburn's greatest linen manufacturing families. Visitors can watch (and smell) the aromatic process, browse through the historical exhibition and refresh themselves in the Tap Room Restaurant.

At **Brookhall Historical Farm** the attractions include farm animals, some of them rare breeds, agricultural items from bygone days, some lovely gardens, a fishing lake, an historic 12th century church and also a farm tea house.

Just to the south of Lisburn is a much less enticing location – the Long Kesh prison, notorious for its H-block cells, hunger strikes and "dirty protests" by prisoners, and the murder in 1998 of the LVF leader Billy Wright by the INLA that generated a wave of retaliatory killings across the north. The prison can be clearly seen from the M1 motorway.

Ballymena

10 miles N of Antrim on the A26

Located at the heart of a prosperous farming region, Ballymena was mostly settled during the 17th century by incomers from southwest Scotland and the lowland accent and intonation is still very evident here. A thriving linen industry formed the basis of the town's steady development, greatly aided by the arrival of Huguenot weavers in the 1680s. There's a lively major market every Saturday but for the rest of the week the blackstone basalt buildings and austere-looking churches make Ballymena seem a rather dour place.

A striking exception is the **ECOS Environmental Centre,** a bold modern building where the interactive exhibits are devoted to highlighting environmental issues: bio-diversity, sustainability and alternative energy production. The Centre stands within a 150-acre park which has some attractive walking and cycling trails.

You only have to travel a few miles east of Ballymena to arrive at one of Ireland's most evocative Christian sites, **Slemish Mountain**. It was on the slopes of this extinct volcano that St Patrick herded swine. As a child, he had been captured on the coast of Britain by pirates and brought here where he worked as a slave for 6 years for the local chieftain, Miluic, before making his escape. Slemish is a place of pilgrimage on St Patrick's Day, 17th March, when many thousands of the devout make the steep climb to the summit. If you join them, even if you are not a believer, it's difficult not to succumb to the feeling that there is a truly mystical presence here.

Portglenone

10 miles W of Ballymena on the A42

For many years, right up to the mid-1700s, the bridge at Portglenone was the only crossing of the 35-mile-long River Bann apart from Coleraine near the estuary. Originally, it was a drawbridge which would be lifted at night to protect the village from the "tories", or outlaws, infesting the forests on the opposite bank. Canadian visitors may well be interested in the plaque at 48 Main Street, facing the attractive market square. It was in this shop that Timothy Eaton learnt the drapery business during the years 1847-52, working 16 hours a day and sleeping under the counter. He emigrated to Toronto where he made a fortune in the retail trade.

Ballymoney

8 miles SE of Coleraine on the A26

Set in the valley of the River Bann, the market town of Ballymoney developed from a huddle of houses around two medieval castles. Nothing remains of the castles and most of what you see today was built in the 19th century, including the 1866 red and yellow brick Town Hall. There is however a terrace of small Georgian houses on Cockpit Brae which takes its name from the sport beloved of local carters who drove stage coaches between here and Belfast. To the north, close to the River Bush, is Gary Bog, one of the largest remaining bogs in Ireland, but Ballymoney's prime attraction is the popular **Leslie Hill Open Farm**. The farm has been owned by the Leslie family for 10 generations and the layout of the 500-acre estate has altered little over the last 230 years. The present owners, James Leslie and his wife, have restored the old farm buildings which now contain displays of vintage horse-drawn implements and tools, vehicles ranging from carts to carriages, and wage books, account books and other documents showing how farming, and life in general, has changed over four centuries.

The Leslies have also restored and improved the walks through the woodlands and around the lakes, and re-made the large walled garden where you can pick your own fruit in season. Younger children will no doubt be more interested in the variety of animals that have their home here, amongst them some rare breeds and a herd of docile red deer. Also within the farm are an adventure playground, picnic area beside a duck pond, a tea room and craft shop.

Co Armagh

Although it is the smallest county in Ulster, Armagh has some surprisingly varied scenery. The south is drumlin country; there is wild open moorland in the central area; and to the east, mountains and rocky glens. Around Loughgall in the north the apple orchards are an enchanting sight in May when the trees are in full blossom. A distinctive feature of the Armagh landscape is its network of dry-stone walls dividing the farmland into tiny fields – a legacy of the Gaelic tradition of dividing land equally between all members of the family.

The ancient city of Armagh was in prehistoric times the seat of the kings of Ulster who were crowned at nearby *Emain Macha*, (Navan Fort). Few medieval buildings have survived but there are many good Georgian houses both in Armagh itself and at the National Trust properties of The Argory and Ardress House. While travelling through the county keep an eye open for a game of road bowls in progress. Also known as 'Bullet' this sport is unique to Armagh and Co. Cork and gives a clear indication of the comparative lack of road traffic here.

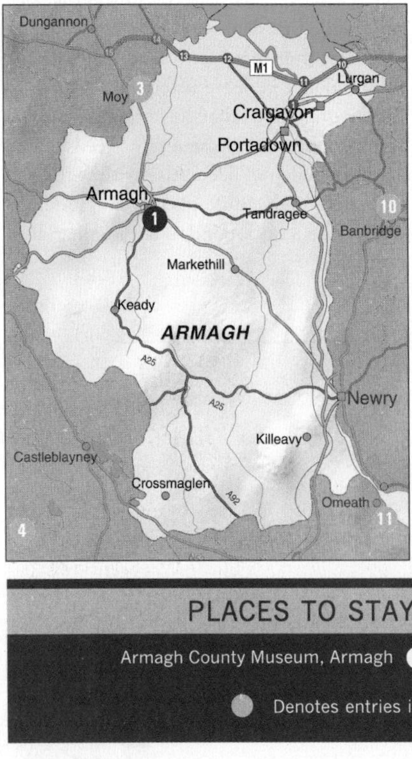

Armagh

The ecclesiastical capital of Ireland for more than 1500 years, Armagh is a delightful place to wander around. According to tradition, St Patrick himself chose Armagh as the centre of his mission in Ireland. The first church was built in AD 445 and the same site has been in use for 1500 years.

The city's prosperity in the 18th century is reflected in its numerous listed Georgian buildings, especially in the Mall – a large expanse of urban parkland, formerly a racecourse, which was one of many gifts to the city from Archbishop Robinson who held the post for 30 years until 1795. On the east side of the Mall, the **Armagh County Museum** (free - see panel opposite) occupies one of the most distinctive buildings in Armagh, similar in appearance to a small Greek temple. It was originally built as a school. The exhibits range from prehistoric artefacts, through military costumes, wedding dresses, and natural history specimens to a display recounting

PLACES TO STAY, EAT AND DRINK

Armagh County Museum, Armagh (1) Museum p405

Denotes entries in other chapters

Armagh County Museum

The Mall East, Armagh BT61 9BE
Tel: 028 37 523070

Located near the centre of St Patrick's cathedral city, a visit to **Armagh County Museum** is an ideal way to experience a flavour of the orchard county. The unique character of the Museum's architecture makes it one of the most distinctive buildings in Armagh where the collections reflect the lives of those people who have lived, work or are associated with the county.

Discover a rich and varied legacy revealed in objects ranging from prehistoric artefacts to household items from a bygone age. There are military costumes, wedding dresses, ceramics, natural history specimens and railway memorabilia. Admission free. Opening hours; Mon-Fri 10am-5pm; Sat 10am-1pm & 2pm-5pm.

the story of Ireland's worst railway accident when two passenger trains collided outside Armagh in 1889. Eighty-nine people lost their lives; many of them are buried in the churchyard of St Mark's nearby.

The city has two cathedrals, both of them dedicated to St Patrick who founded the first church here in AD 445. **St Patrick's (Roman Catholic) Cathedral** with its soaring twin towers stands impressively atop one of Armagh's seven hills. The foundation stone was laid in 1840 but the disaster of the Great Famine delayed construction and the cathedral was not completed until 1873. The seat of the Cardinal-Archbishop of Armagh, the cathedral has a sumptuous interior with walls completely covered by colourful mosaics, in hues that range from sky-blue to terracotta pinks and oranges, much gilding and fine stained glass. Amongst the mosaics are medallions representing many of the saints of Ireland. Armagh's other cathedral, the Church of Ireland one, was originally built in AD 445 but has been destroyed and rebuilt no fewer than 17 times. The present building in the Gothic style was completed in 1834. It contains some fine monuments, strange and interesting carvings, and in the Cathedral Library of 1711, just down the hill, there's a copy of *Gulliver's Travels*, annotated by Dean Swift himself.

At the **St Patrick's Trian Visitor Complex** there are three quite separate exhibitions. One of them, housed in a Presbyterian Meeting House of 1722, explores the 'Land of Lilliput' with a narration delivered by a 20 feet giant and other models, and also details Jonathan

Armagh Cathedral

Swift's associations with Armagh where he lived for a while. The second exhibition, 'The Armagh Story', offers a multi-media account of the city's development from prehistoric times up to the present day. The third, 'Patrick's Testament', takes a closer look at Ireland's patron saint through material contained in the ancient manuscript, *The Book of Armagh*. The complex also incorporates a former bank, now the tourist information centre, and the bank manager's house of 1800 which has become the Pilgrim's Table Restaurant.

Further insights into Armagh's Georgian past can be gained at the **Palace Stables Heritage Centre & Demesne**. The Palace was another of Archbishop Robinson's 'improving' additions to the city, a somewhat austere Georgian mansion which is now the headquarters of the Armagh District Council. Tours are available by prior arrangement. The Heritage Centre occupies the former stables and courtyard of the palace and includes a 'Day in the Life' exhibition featuring costumed actors portraying life around the stables as it might have appeared on a typical day, 23rd July 1776. The courtyard also has a craft shop and restaurant.

The Demesne, or parkland, surrounding the Palace and stables is beautifully landscaped with laid out walks, orienteering and horse trails, adventure play area, and a Garden of the Senses. The ruins of **Armagh Friary,** the longest friary church in Ireland (163 feet) stand near the entrance to the Centre. The extensive grounds also feature a lovely temple-like Chapel with some exquisite wood carvings, an Ice House, a Victorian conservatory, and a Servants' Tunnel which was used to bring food from the detached kitchens – Archbishop Robinson had a sensitive nose and detested the lingering smells from cooking.

Two other visitor attractions in the city are the **Observatory**, built in 1791 as another of the Archbishop's benefactions, and the comparatively recent **Planetarium** of 1968 where digital video technology allows audiences in the Star Theatre to fly through space and a state-of-the-art stereo system provides the appropriate sound effects. Visitors can handle rocks more than 3 billion years old and a 4 billion-year-old meteorite.

A couple of miles west of Armagh is **Navan Fort** (free), a colossal earthworks which is all that remains of the great palace built by Queen Macha in 300 BC. It was here that Deirdre of the Sorrows met her lover, Noísí, and where the warrior kings of Ulster and of the Irish equivalent of the Knights of the Round Table, the Knights of the Red Branch, met and feasted. The feats of these genuine historical figures, and particularly their greatest champion Cuchullain, have passed into legend and are recounted in the songs and stories of the Ulster Cycle. The entire complex of Navan Fort was destroyed in AD 330 by the three Cullas brothers so there is little to see apart from the earthen mounds.

Around Armagh

Portadown

11 miles NE of Armagh on the N3

Formerly a prosperous linen manufacturing town, Portadown is set around the River Bann but it was the arrival of the Newry to Lough Neagh canal in the 1730s that provided the basis for its growth. An exhibition detailing the history of the canal and its importance to the town is presented at **Moneypenny's Lock** (free) where there's a restored lock-keeper's house, stables and a bothy. The lock can be reached by a peaceful walk along the canal towpath from the car park in Castle Street.

A few miles to the west of Portadown are two fine houses, both of them National Trust properties. **Ardress House** is a 17th century manor house, much altered in the following century so that its appearance is now that of a Georgian mansion. Inside, there's some outstanding plasterwork and a good collection of paintings while outside there's a sizeable working farmyard, children's playground and wooded grounds. Not far away is **The Argory,** a striking neo-classical building overlooking the River Blackwater which has changed little since it was built in the 1820s. Many of the original contents are still in place and there's a charming early-Victorian sundial garden. A curiosity here is the rare acetylene gas plant of 1906 in the laundry yard which still provides light for the interior.

Markethill

6 miles SE of Armagh on the A28

A mile or so to the north of Markethill is **Gosford Forest Park**. Several of the nature walks around the estate were first devised by Jonathan Swift when he visited the Earl of Gosford here between 1728 and 1730. The house he stayed in burnt down in 1805 and was replaced by a stunning mock-Norman castle with a large square keep flanked by a sturdy round tower. Within the grounds stand some fine old walnut trees, a walled garden and, in the arboretum, Dean Swift's Chair, a half-moon seat where the author of *Gulliver's Travels* would sit in fine weather, writing and composing his poems.

Killeavy

3 miles SW of Newry off the B113

Tucked away in the southeastern corner of the county, close to the border with Co. Down, Killeavy village is remarkable for its "conjoined churches" – two churches from different eras sharing a common gable wall. The church to the west is one of the most important pre-Romanesque churches in the country; the other dates back to the 13th century. The twin churches stand on the site of a 5th century nunnery founded here by St Bline. A granite slab in the church marks her grave and a little way up the hillside is a holy well dedicated to her which pilgrims visit on her feast day, the Sunday nearest 6th July.

Co Down

With farmlands that are among the most fertile in Ireland, more than 200 miles of attractive coastline, the magical Mountains of Mourne creating a mystical bulwark to the south, and a wealth of interesting historical buildings, Down is indeed a favoured county. The sheltered waters of Strangford Lough are popular with sailing enthusiasts, and for sea anglers there is prime sea-fishing off Ardglass and

Mountains of Mourne

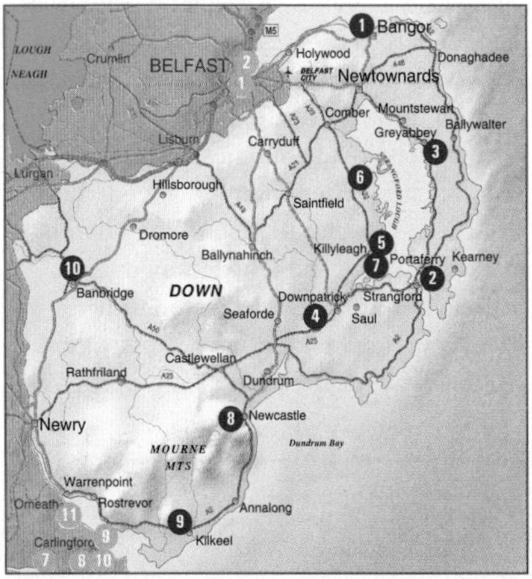

Portavogie. The county is also rich in prehistoric monuments, with numerous cairns, standing stones and dolmens dating back to 3000 BC scattered around Strangford Lough and the Lecale district. As if that weren't enough, the county also claims to have the driest and sunniest climate in Ireland.

The area has strong connections with St Patrick who made his final landing on the shore of Strangford Lough in AD 442 and is believed to be buried at Downpatrick – at least according to the people of Co. Down but their claim is hotly disputed by Armagh.

PLACES TO STAY, EAT AND DRINK

Tara Guest House, Bangor	1	Guest House	p409
Exploris Aquarium, Portaferry	2	Visitor Attraction	p413
Mervue B&B, Newtownards	3	B&B	p413
The Mill at Ballydugan, Downpatrick	4	Café, Restaurant & Accommodation	p415
The Hill Cottage, Downpatrick	5	Self Catering	p416
The Barn at Ballymacashen, Killinchy	6	Self Catering	p417
Dufferin Coaching Inn, Killyleagh	7	Pub, Restaurant & Accommodation	p417
Mountains of Mourne, Newcastle	8	Scenic Attraction	p419
Cranmore B&B, Kilkeel	9	B&B	p420
Downshire Arms Hotel, Banbridge	10	Hotel	p421

● Denotes entries in other chapters

Bangor

Bangor Harbour

Bangor's attractive Victorian and Edwardian architecture reflects its popularity as a seaside resort during those eras. The town still attracts many day visitors from Belfast and is well provided with all the usual amusements as well as offering some splendid Victorian parks. One of these, **Ward Park,** has two large ponds supporting a range of wildfowl and a resident flock of barnacle geese. Bangor also boasts a weekly open air market, plenty of pubs and eating places, and some good beaches, the best of which is Ballyholme Bay.

Of Bangor's once important and influential abbey, founded by St Comgall in AD 586, nothing remains. Today, the oldest building in the town is the fine **Old Custom House and Tower** of 1687 which stands on the seafront and now houses the tourist information office.

Bangor Castle, now the Town Hall, is actually a Victorian mansion built in 1852. Its former outbuildings house the **North Down Heritage Centre** (free) which has some striking displays highlighting the

archaeology, early-Christian history and natural history of the area. These are enhanced by audio-visual presentations and sound effects tapes. Prize exhibits here include the Ballycroghan Swords, dating from 500 BC and a 9th century handbell found near Bangor. Uniquely for a local museum, there's also a Jordan Room which displays a remarkable collection of Far Eastern wares amassed by a locally-born diplomat, Sir John Jordan. The centre has a rather superior restaurant which is used at times for evening events such as musical recitals and other arts performances.

A popular destination for family outings from Bangor is the **Pickie Fun Park** on The Promenade. A modest entrance fee provides access to swan-shaped pedal boats, paddling pools, a mini-railway, go-karts and a playground.

Around Bangor

Holywood

6 miles W of Bangor on the A2

This small residential town beside Belfast Lough has some fine sandy beaches and a lovely coastal walk that runs eastwards for 15 miles to Helen's Bay. The major visitor attraction here is the **Ulster Folk & Transport Museum** which ranks among the best museums in the country. The open air part of the complex represents town and country life in Ulster around 1910, complete with a farm using the methods and equipment of a bygone age. The 30-odd buildings are all authentic, painstakingly removed from their original sites throughout Ulster and re-erected here. The indoor galleries demonstrate how food preparation, clothing, farming and other everyday occupations and lifestyles have changed over the years. The road and railway transport exhibits include 'Old Maeve', the largest locomotive ever built in Ireland; a unique collection of vintage motor vehicles and bicycles, including one of the notorious De Lorean sports cars; whilst another building houses the Titanic Exhibition, a tribute to Belfast's shipbuilding heyday. The museum is open all year round but opening times vary.

On the outskirts of the town, **Redburn Country Park** offers woodland walks and some grand views of Belfast City, Belfast Lough and the Antrim hills. In spring, the woodland floor is carpeted with a spectacular azure haze created by thousands and thousands of bluebells in full bloom.

Donaghadee

6 miles E of Bangor on the A2/B21

This pleasant seaside town was for many years the arrival port for ferries from Portpatrick in Scotland, the shortest sea-crossing possible. A remarkable succession of well-known visitors stepped ashore here: Peter the Great; James Boswell; John Keats; Daniel Defoe; Franz Liszt (plus piano); and an elderly William Wordsworth. Many of these celebrities stayed at Grace Neill's Inn on the High Street. The advent of larger steam-powered boats requiring a deeper harbour caused the ferry service to be transferred to Larne in 1849 and Donaghadee settled into a gracious decline.

Behind the town rises a large prehistoric mound known as **The Rath.** It is now a public park and crowned by a castle-like building, The Moat, which was built to house explosives used in the construction of the harbour. From this point, it's possible to see the hills of Galloway in southern Scotland. Also in view is an elegant lighthouse designed by Sir John Rennie, famed for his Eddystone Lighthouse. The lighthouse has a rather bizarre literary connection since its walls were once painted by the boisterous Irish writer, Brendan Behan, when he was (briefly) employed by the Commission for Irish Lights.

From the little harbour there are regular ferries during the season to the **Copeland Islands,** a couple of miles offshore. Uninhabited since the 1940s, the islands provide some pleasant picnic spots and good fishing. One of the smaller islands, Cross Island, is now an RSPB bird sanctuary and the Society arrange cruises to visit its noted bird observatory.

About a mile outside Donaghadee, the five acres of **Breezemount Farm** are home to a number of top quality Angora goats whose coats are sheared in January and August and then processed at various centres to produce beautiful mohair socks, scarves, stoles and general knitwear. At present there is no charge for visitors as most people purchase some of the goods available but please phone beforehand to arrange your visit.

Newtownards

5 miles S of Bangor on the A20

A busy manufacturing town, Newtownards stands near the northern tip of Strangford Lough and although the town was founded in 1244 the only ancient remains are those of a ruined Dominican priory – some striking pillars and semi-circular arches are all that have survived. Today, the most impressive building in Newtownards is the former Market House of 1765. It now serves as both town hall and arts centre and faces onto the spacious square which is crammed with market stalls every Saturday.

A mile or so southwest of the town rises the prominent landmark of **Scrabo Tower** (free), built in 1857 as a memorial to the 3rd Marquis of Londonderry for his relief efforts during the Great Famine. If you are prepared to tackle the 122 steps to the top there are some splendid views across Strangford Lough and across the Irish Sea to Scotland. The tower stands within the **Scrabo Country Park** (free) which has some splendid woodland walks and also contains the old quarries where the celebrated Scrabo stone was extracted.

A couple of miles north of Newtownards, the **Somme Heritage Centre** recalls the part played by the Irish and Ulster Divisions in the most horrific and futile battle of World War I. The battle of the Somme lasted for five months, from July to November 1916. When the Germans finally retreated, the British forces had won a few miles of shell-pocked mud at the cost of 600,000 lives. At the Centre here, staff in battledress recount the terrible story and the re-created frontline trenches underline the horror.

Just across from the Centre, **The Ark** is Ireland's first rare breeds farm and is home to more than 80 rare species of cattle, pigs, sheep, goats, ponies, ducks, poultry and llamas in 40 acres of countryside. Other attractions include picnic sites, play areas and a tea room.

Comber

9 miles S of Bangor on the A22

Set beside the River Enver, noted for its sea trout, Comber is a pleasant little town with some good antiques shops. To the south of the town, **Castle Espie Wildfowl and Wetland Centre** has a resident population of ducks, geese and swans, and some 7000 visiting birds over the course of a year. The centre is run by the Wildfowl and Wetlands Trust which provides hides and you can also view the birds from the coffee shop and art gallery.

In Comber itself, the 80-seater **Tudor Cinema** was built by Noel Spence, an addict of B movies. He has re-created perfectly the ambience of mid-20th century filmgoing with red velvet seating, footlights and staff in gold braid. Noel programmes his favourite movies, classics like *Attack of the Fifty Foot Woman* for example; there's no entrance fee but donations are welcome.

The Ards Peninsula

Running east and south from Newtonards, the Ards Peninsula is a long, thin hook of land that almost encloses Strangford Lough, with only a narrow channel near Portaferry allowing access from the Irish Sea. The east coast has long stretches of sandy beaches and on the Strangford side there's an endless variety of views from sensitively sited car parks and lay-bys. The area's attractions include one of the only two working windmills in Ireland. It's located near the seaside village of Millisle, at Ballycopeland, and visitors can enjoy a guided tour of the late-18th century windmill and follow the milling process from corn into flour.

Ballywalter

14 miles SE of Bangor on the A2

A thriving port in the 1600s, Ballywalter still has a busy harbour area which gives the village character and vitality. Just south of the harbour is the Long Strand, a wide stretch of beach offering safe bathing and facilities for all kinds of water sports. Car fanatics will be interested in the **Ballywalter Mini Collection**, a private collection of 30 varieties of this popular car which includes an ex-works Paddy Hopkirk rally car. The display can be visited by arrangement only, (tel: 028 4458098).

A few miles south of Ballywalter, near the village of Ballyhalbert, Burr Point is the most easterly place in Ireland, and another couple of miles further south, **Portavogie** is one of Northern Ireland's most important fishing ports. Few visitors leave without purchasing some of its famous giant prawns and herrings.

Kearney

3 miles E of Portaferry off the A2

This small coastal village on the low rocky coastline at the tip of the peninsula owes its spick and span appearance to the fact that it is owned by the National Trust. The Trust has restored some of the whitewashed cottages here to the authentic vernacular style of a traditional fishing village. There are some splendid views across to Scotland, the Isle of Man and the Mountains of Mourne, and a lovely coastal walk leads to Knockinelder, a beautiful sandy beach to the south. Seals are regularly seen basking on the rocks between Kearney and Knockinelder.

Portaferry

19 miles SE of Belfast on the A2

Portaferry has a magnificent setting looking out across the narrow strait connecting Strangford Lough with the sea. The powerful current which rushes through the Narrows carries 400 million gallons of water with every tide – no wonder the Vikings named the lough "Strong Fjord". A regular 5-minute-long car ferry service across the Narrows links the town to the village of Strangford and the county town of Downpatrick.

Portaferry is a busy boating centre, never more so than during the town's annual **Gala Week and Regatta** in July when the music pubs are open almost 24 hours a day and the traditional Galway boats called hookers sail here to share in the festivities. For an insight into Portaferry's maritime history and the general environment of Strangford Lough, a visit to the **Portaferry Visitor Centre** (free), housed in a former stable, is recommended. The centre also has an informative video introducing the tower houses of Co. Down.

Portaferry is home to **Exploris** (see panel opposite), the only aquarium in Northern Ireland, which provides a showcase for thousands of species native to the area, amongst them stingrays which you are invited to touch and sharks which you are not. Thousands of species are on view and

Exploris Aquarium

The Rope Walk, Castle Street, Portaferry,
Co Down, Northern Ireland BT22 1NZ
Tel: 028 4272 8062 Fax: 028 4272 8396
e-mail: info@explorls.org.uk
website: www.exploris.org.uk

Exploris is Northern Irelands only public aquarium and Seal Sanctuary. Exploris presents the wonders of the Irish Sea, in the conservation village of Portaferry, on the shores of Strangford Lough, one of the most important marine sites in Europe. The Touch Tanks at Exploris give you the opportunity to touch and hold a variety of living marine animals. Stroke a friendly ray. Feel the suction power of a starfish. The Touch Tanks are run by experienced guides at regular intervals throughout each day. Exploris rehabilitates Northern Ireland's sick, injured or orphaned seals in the N.I.E Seal Sanctuary.

You are taken through the seal's journey back to health and eventual release. There are special viewing points for visitors to see the seals. The nature of rehabilitation means there are times when there are no seals in the sanctuary. If you are interested in viewing the seals, please call ahead for more information.

in 1999 a new seal sanctuary was added to the attractions.

Greyabbey

12 miles SE of Newtonards on the A20

From Portaferry the A20 runs northwards, hugging the shoreline of Strangford Lough and providing a succession of grand views. Only a handful of small villages stand on this side of the lake, the most interesting of which is Greyabbey which is noted for its clutch of antique shops and art galleries. The village takes its name from Grey Abbey (free) whose extensive ruins nestle in beautiful parkland on the edge of the village. Founded in 1193 by Affreca, daughter of the King of Man, it was the first truly Gothic structure in Ireland, with graceful pointed lancet windows and an impressive west door on which the carved decoration can still be made out. The monks here were Cistercian, an Order with

Mervue B&B

28 Portaferry Road, Greyabbey, Newtownards,
Co. Down BT22 2RX
Tel: 028427 88619 Mobile: 077 9196 4862
e-mail: herondf@yahoo.co.uk

Beautifully located with lovely views across Strangford Lough, **Mervue B&B** provides an ideal base for exploring the Ards Peninsula and surrounding area. This attractively furnished and decorated property with its well-tended gardens full of colour is the home of Ann Heron, a friendly lady who makes her guests feel very welcome. There are 3 comfortable guest bedrooms, all tastefully decorated and provided with en suite facilities, and Ann's generous breakfast offers plenty of choices – including home-made bread and preserves. There are good restaurants and pubs and Greyabbey itself is noted for its antique shops, art galleries and the extensive ruins of its medieval Abbey.

Mount Stewart Gardens

a great knowledge of plants, both wild and cultivated, and they made use of this in their practice of medicine. At Grey Abbey they had their own 'physick' garden and this has been carefully re-created. Based on medieval paintings and texts, the garden contains more than 50 different medicinal plants and herbs. The surroundings are as soothing and tranquil as they would have been when Affreca chose this setting more than 800 years ago.

Mount Stewart

10 miles SE of Newtownards on the A20

The mild micro-climate of Strangford Lough favoured the creation of **Mount Stewart Gardens** (National Trust), the inspired work of Edith, 7th Marchioness of Londonderry (1879-1959), a leading political hostess of her day. She laid out the gardens in the 1920s with colourful parterres, ornamental lakes, noble trees and many rare and tender plants. Her gardeners crafted some striking topiary that includes a harp, an appropriately coloured Red Hand of Ulster, and various animals which allude to the marchioness' pet names for her politician friends. Within the grounds there's a lovely Temple of the Winds modelled on the Tower of Andronicus Cyrrhestes in Athens and commanding a splendid view of the lough.

Mount Stewart House (National Trust) is also open to the public. It was the birthplace in 1769 of Lord Castlereagh who, as Chief Secretary for Ireland, secured the passage of the Act of Union in 1800. The Act terminated Ireland's nominal self-government, transferring all executive decisions to Westminster. In return, Prime Minister Pitt promised Irish Catholics the freedom to practise their hitherto proscribed religion, a pledge he was unable, because of political opposition, to honour. That unfulfilled promise added yet more poison to the long-festering resentment between England and Ireland.

Those dark political consequences do nothing to diminish the charm of Mount Stewart House itself. The mansion is richly furnished and contains some interesting political memorabilia, as well as a collection of fine paintings the most notable of which is the huge canvas by George Stubbs depicting the celebrated racehorse, Hambletonian.

In and around Downpatrick

Downpatrick

23 miles SE of Belfast on the A7

Downpatrick and the surrounding area is rich in associations with St Patrick. He sailed up the Slaney River in AD 432, landing near Downpatrick where he is believed to have founded its first church. The present **Downpatrick Cathedral** is comparatively recent, completed in 1826 but incorporating some parts of a 12th century cathedral on the same site. Some 18th century box pews have also survived,

THE MILL AT BALLYDUGAN

Drumcullen Road, Ballydugan, Downpatrick, Co. Down BT30 8HZ
Tel: 028 4461 3654 Fax: 028 4483 9754
e-mail: ballyduganmill@aol.com
website: www.ballyduganmill.com

When it was built in 1792 **The Mill at Ballydugan** incorporated the very latest state-of-the-art technology, its eight vast floors producing flour, bran and starch and providing an economic boost for the rural economy. But less than 70 years later the Mill lay desolate and abandoned. It wasn't until a century and a quarter later that Noel Killen, a local contractor renowned for his love of traditional Irish buildings, bought the old mill and after many years of hard work restored the grand old giant to its former state of grace. Now a listed building, the Mill offers a wide range of amenities.

On the ground floor, The Wheelhouse Café serves a good choice of wholesome and appetising refreshments while on the floor above, in The Lecale Restaurant, you'll find an enticing menu featuring top quality Irish cuisine. The second and third floors are devoted to quality accommodation – 11 en suite bedrooms offering classic comfort. The fourth floor now provides unique and adaptable function facilities catering for banquets, intimate wedding receptions and conferences. Not content with all this, Neil has also established a permanent exhibition detailing the history of the mill, the process of reconstruction and the mill's place in the economy of South Down.

each marked with a brass plaque bearing the name of its owner.

No-one knows for sure where St Patrick was buried – both Downpatrick and Armagh lay claim to being the saint's final resting place. Pilgrims to Downpatrick were so certain that he, along with St Columba and St Brigid, were buried near the cathedral they scrabbled a deep hole in the churchyard in the hope of finding their remains. In 1900, the church authorities covered the hole with a huge granite boulder inscribed with a cross and the single name PATRIC. The saint is also commemorated by a huge 35 feet high granite statue on the summit of Slieve Patrick across the valley.

Downpatrick itself is a charming collection of late Georgian and early Victorian buildings set on two low hills. Its 18th century gaol now houses the **Down County Museum** (free) and the **St Patrick Heritage Centre**. The former has some interesting exhibits of Stone Age artefacts and local history; the latter tells the story of St Patrick using extracts from his autobiography, *Confessions*, and also runs a video featuring other locations around the town associated with him.

Anyone with the slightest interest in steam locomotives will be delighted with the **Downpatrick Railway Museum** in Market Street. There are working engines here; a photographic display and a model railway in the former station house. The Museum can arrange steam train rides along a restored section of the Belfast-Newcastle main line to the grave of Magnus Barefoot, a Viking king, and also offers footplate driving courses.

Saul

2 miles NE of Downpatrick off the A25

The small village of Saul overlooks Strangford Lough and holds a special place in Irish history for it was here that St

Patrick is said to have made his first landing in Ireland in AD 432. He converted the local lord, a man called Dichu, who presented the saint with a barn, a *sabhal*, hence the name of the village. A much later church now occupies the site with an impressive round tower standing nearby.

Strangford

7 miles NE of Downpatrick on the A25

Thousands of travellers pass through this tiny village, either boarding or leaving the regular vehicle ferry that links it to the Ards Peninsula. It's worth stopping off though to visit **Castle Ward** (National Trust) – an 18th century mansion which is famed for being divided into two architectural styles. One façade is classical, the other Gothick. This split personality is due to the differences between its original owners, Bernard and Anne Ward, later Lord and Lady Bangor. The interior is equally schizophrenic – half the rooms are classical in style (his preference), whilst the others, such as the Saloon and the Boudoir with its fan-vaulted ceiling, are Gothick (her favoured style).

The house is stunningly situated, surrounded by farmland, landscaped gardens and lakes, one of which, Temple Water, is overlooked by a graceful pedimented temple. An underground passage links the house to the stableyard where there's a Victorian pastimes centre where children can dress in clothes from the period and play with popular Victorian toys; a late-19th century laundry; a well-stocked gift shop and a restaurant. Also within the grounds are a defensive tower built in 1610, a sawmill and a recently restored water-powered corn mill which has regular working demonstrations. For three weeks during June, Castle Ward becomes the Irish Glyndebourne, with opera performances and elaborate picnics in the grounds.

Killyleagh

5 miles N of Downpatrick on the A22

Located at the southwest corner of Strangford Lough, Killyleagh is a plantation town and port laid out in a gridiron pattern. Its impressive hilltop **Castle** has 13th century origins but these can hardly be detected now as it was rebuilt in 1666 and again in 1850 when the exuberant Disney-style turrets and cones were added. But its soaring towers, stalwart battlements, bawn wall and picturesque gatehouse provide an excellent photo-opportunity. Groups can visit the castle by prior arrangement.

Outside the castle gates, in Frederick Street, a plaque records the achievements

The Barn at Ballymacashen

88c Saintfield Road, Ballymacashen, Killinchy,
Co. Down BT23 6RW
Tel: 028 9754 2399 Fax: 028 9754 2469
e-mail: thebarn@ballymacashen.freeserve.co.uk
website: www.ballymacashen.freeserve.co.uk

Self-catering accommodation in a converted farm building of character is on offer at **The Barn at Ballymacashen,** a charming old property set in rolling countryside. The open plan living area is on the upper floor, comprising kitchen, dining and living room with an open fire and bed settee. The kitchen is fully equipped with cooker, fridge, dishwasher and washer/dryer. On the ground floor are 2 bedrooms (1double; 1 twin) and a bathroom with bath, shower and WC. Belfast and Lisburn are both only 12 miles away and the surrounding area has many golf courses.

of Killyleagh's most famous son, Sir Hans Sloane, who was born here in 1660. He became physician to George II and on his death at the grand old age of 93 bequeathed his fabulous library and collections to the nation. They formed the basis of the British Museum which stands on the site of his London home, Montagu House.

Saintfield

10 miles NW of Downpatrick on the A7

Enjoying regular success in the annual "In Bloom" competitions, Saintfield is a pretty little town with many Georgian buildings – the consequence of having to rebuild after the town was almost completely destroyed

Dufferin Coaching Inn

31 High Street, Killyleagh,
Co. Down BT30 9QF
Tel: 028 4482 8229 Fax: 028 4482 8755
e-mail: dufferin@dial.pipex.com
website: www.dufferincoachinginn.co.uk

The Dufferin Coaching Inn stands majestically on the main street of this historic town on the shore of Strangford Lough. This is a traditional country pub, owned and run by Kitty and Morris Crawford, lying in the shadow of the 16th century Killyleagh Castle. Renowned throughout Ulster for its excellent food, drink and friendly atmosphere, The Dufferin Arms is a wonderful place where visitors can relax by the open fire and wile away the evening. Recommended by Taste of Ulster, the food here in the Cellar Restaurant is absolutely delicious, the very best of country kitchen style cuisine.

The Dufferin Arms is however much more than just a pub with a restaurant. A choice of accommodation is also offered by the Arms. There are 6 luxury en suite bedrooms, some with 4-poster beds, and overnight guests have the use of a comfortable residents' lounge and a library.

An additional and unusual attraction is the Siglu, a clear-walled igloo-like structure originally designed as a schnapps and gluhwein bar for skiers and now providing an ideal venue for parties, barbecues and corporate events in Delamont Country Park.

in the Battle of Saintfield in 1798. Today, much of the town centre has been designated a Conservation Area and this is where many of the antique dealers for which the town is famous have their premises. Located to the south of Saintfield, **Rowallane Gardens** have been described as one of the National Trust's finest ornaments. The 50-acre site was once just rough ground punctuated by granite outcrops but is now a series of lovely gardens. Created by Hugh Armytage Moore in the 1920s the gardens are noted for their spectacular displays of rhododendrons, azaleas, rare trees, shrubs and plants.

Ballynahinch

25 miles S of Belfast on the A24/A49

Set among many low, rounded drumlins Ballynahinch is a thriving market town which was laid out in the first half of the 17th century by the Rawdon family who also built a fine mansion for themselves, Montalto House. In the following century another family, the Kers, became the landlords of Ballynahinch and it was they who created the town's pleasant terraces and the large shops with their fine façades.

Two miles south of Ballynahinch, on the south slopes of Cratlieve Mountain, rises the striking man-made formation known as the **Legananny Dolmen**. Silhouetted against the skyline and surrounded by a desolate landscape, it has a brooding, mystical presence. The tapering capstone of the dolmen is supported by two 6 feet portal stones at the front and a smaller stone at the rear. Found almost exclusively in Britain, Ireland and France, dolmens were constructed as burial chambers for royal and noble persons and in their original state were almost certainly covered by a mound of earth. There are many good examples across Ireland but the proportions and elegant structure of Legananny Dolmen have made it the best known, often featuring on tourism brochures and guide book covers.

Seaforde

6 miles SW of Downpatrick on the A24

This tiny village is nevertheless home to a popular visitor attraction, **Seaforde Gardens & Tropical Butterfly House** which has a large flight area with hundreds of free-flying exotic butterflies. There are also reptiles and insects (behind glass!). The surrounding grounds also offer a maze and play area, nursery garden, shop and tea room. An appealing feature is the Moghul Tower from the top of which visitors can survey the attractive gardens.

Dundrum

9 miles SW of Downpatrick on the A2

Once a thriving fishing port, Dundrum is now mainly of interest because of **Dundrum Castle**, one of the finest Norman castles in Northern Ireland. Built around 1177 as part of John de Courcy's coastal defences, it stands on a steep hill above the town. The circular tower keep is a rare feature in Irish castles and although the fortress was 'slighted' (rendered militarily useless) by Cromwell's troops in 1652, for once they skimped the job and the extensive remains include a fortified gateway, drum towers and a central donjon with a fine spiral stairway winding its way up inside the wall.

Murlough National Nature Reserve, a mile south of the town, preserves a sand dune system with heath and woodland surrounded by estuary and sea, rich in botany and wildlife. Guided walks are available or you can follow the way-marked nature trail with an information guide.

About 4 miles to the west of Dundrum, **Castlewellan Forest Park** in the foothills of the Mountains of Mourne is renowned for its arboretum and superb gardens. The arboretum was established in 1740 and its sheltered, south-facing position has encouraged the growth of some magnificent exotic species of trees. There's a 3-mile trail around the lake, marked with sculptures created from the park's natural materials and at the visitor centre the Queen Anne-style courtyard houses a charming tea room.

Newcastle

23 miles E of Newry on the A2

One of Northern Ireland's premier seaside resorts, Newcastle is beautifully situated at the western end of the extensive sandy beach that fringes Dundrum Bay with the huge bulk of Slieve Donard providing a scenic backdrop. The town is also a noted golfing resort boasting two 18-hole courses, one of them the world-famous Royal County Down Club. For family visitors, the **Tropicana Pleasure Beach** provides a whole range of entertainments including a heated outdoor fun pool, giant slides and an adventure playground. For poor weather days, the **Saintfield's Museum of Childhood** has a fine collection of vintage toys and dolls while Route 66 is Ireland's only museum featuring American automobiles and memorabilia of the 1930s, with jukeboxes and films of cars adding to the nostalgic appeal.

Newcastle

On the outskirts of the town stretches the **Tullymore Forest Park** in the foothills of the Mountains of Mourne. There are some lovely walks here, passing between banks of rhododendrons, over quaint bridges spanning deep ravines and rushing rivers, and past some unusual Gothic follies. In the arboretum there's a magnificent Cork Oak and the visitor centre contains wildlife and forestry exhibits, a lecture theatre and tea room.

Newcastle is the main tourist centre for the Mountains of Mourne which extend 15 miles southwestwards from the town (see panel below).

Mountains of Mourne

Newcastle, Co. Down

Newcastle is the main tourist centre for the Mountains of Mourne which extend 15 miles southwestwards from the town. Amongst them is the highest mountain in Northern Ireland, Slieve Donard, which rises from the sea to a height of 2796 feet. Altogether, there are some 48 peaks although the word seems inappropriate for what are mostly rounded summits clad in purple heather in late summer. Just one road leads through these granite mountains so they can only be fully appreciated on foot.

Fortunately, a network of ancient tracks criss-cross the moorlands and upland pastures - leaflets detailing the most popular walks can be obtained from the Newcastle tourist information centre on the main Promenade. For serious climbers, the Northern Ireland Mountain Centre in Newcastle runs climbing courses but these must be booked at least two weeks in advance.

Annalong

7 miles S of Newcastle on the A2

Annalong is a picturesque little fishing resort where the stone houses cluster around a deep, double-walled harbour. Many of the houses are built of Mourne granite extracted from the mountains which provide an awesome backdrop to the village. On the edge of the village, **Annalong Mill** is an early 19th century corn mill which is still working and open to visitors.

Kilkeel

12 miles S of Newcastle on the N2

Unless you've completely lost your sense of smell, you will quickly realise that Kilkeel's main business is fish. Trawlers crowd the harbour which is surrounded by canneries and the main excitements here are the fish auctions that take place on the quayside. In the summer Kilkeel hosts a Harbour Festival and the **Nautilus Centre** has an exhibition on the fishing industry, a fish shop, gift shop, café and conference centre.

In the churchyard here is buried Kilkeel's most infamous son. William Hare was born at Kilkeel sometime around 1800 and as a young man moved to Edinburgh where he owned a lodging house. When one of his lodgers died owing him rent, Hare and his accomplice William Burke sold the body to a medical school for £7.10s. Subsequently, they murdered a further 15 people before being caught. Hare turned king's evidence and was released; Burke was hanged. Hare returned under a different name to his home town where he was soon reduced to being an inmate of the workhouse. His identity was only revealed when a former medical student in Edinburgh, a Dr Reid, visited the workhouse and recognised him. Hare is buried in Kilkeel's riverside graveyard in the area once reserved for workhouse paupers.

Cranmore B&B

163 Newcastle Road, Kilkeel,
Co. Down BT34 4NN
Tel: 028417 62021 Fax: 028417 69956
e-mail: cranmore@fsmail.net
e-mail: yvonne@cranmorehouse.com
website: www.cranmorehouse.com

Cranmore B&B is a smart modern house set back from the Newcastle to Kilkeel road and enjoying views across the Irish Sea. It's the home of Yvonne Fitzpatrick, a friendly and welcoming lady who does everything she can to make her guests feel at home. They have the use of a comfortable lounge where Yvonne has nurtured some very healthy-looking pot plants! There are 3 guest bedrooms, each with its own en suite facilities and attractively furnished and decorated. Breakfast is something to look forward to at Cranmore – a wide choice that includes Yvonne's own home-made bread. Special dietary requirements can be catered for.

You'll find plenty to see and do in the area. There's an 18-hole golf course just a couple of miles down the road and walkers and cyclers can explore the scenic Mourne Mountains a few miles to the north. Kilkeel is a busy fishing port and hosts a Harbour Festival in the summer, while the Nautilus Centre is devoted to the history of fishing in the area. Other attractions in the vicinity include the working mill at Annalong, Saintfield's Museum of Childhood at Newcastle, and the Tullymore Forest Park.

West Down

Newry

30 miles SW of Downpatrick on the A1/A25

As part of Queen Elizabeth's Golden Jubilee celebrations in 2002, Newry was one of the two towns in Northern Ireland to be awarded the status of a city. The most important commercial centre in the area, Newry occupies an anomalous position, straddling the border between Down and Armagh. As if to symbolise this unusual situation, Newry's Town Hall stands on a bridge over the Clanrye river, its offices divided equally between the two counties. Located inside the Hall, the **Newry Museum** (free) has a good local history display and an intriguing collection of other exhibits amongst which is Nelson's table from *HMS Victory*.

When Newry's canal opened in 1741 it was the first in the British Isles and the new waterway established Newry's position as the pre-eminent trading centre for the region, a status it has never lost. The economic boom wasn't translated, as in other prosperous Georgian towns, into stylish squares and terraces, and the most distinctive building in the town is the Catholic Cathedral, an uncompromising granite structure with a more attractive Byzantine-style interior and some outstanding stained glass.

Banbridge

10 miles N of Newry on the A1/A26

Once an important linen town, Banbridge has little to detain tourists nowadays but the town enjoys fame of a kind because of its unusual main street. The street climbs a steep hill which in the days of stage coach travel presented a major travel hazard. When the coach operators threatened to bypass Banbridge the town fathers had a deep underpass cut in the central part of the road and a bridge constructed across it.

Dromore

14 miles SW of Belfast on the A1

The small town of Dromore stands beside the River Lagan and was for centuries the ecclesiastical capital of the diocese of Dromore. The cathedral here was built in the 1660s by Bishop Jeremy Taylor who, unusually, is buried inside the altar. Embodied in the south wall is a stone inscribed with a cross and known as St Colman's Pillow. It's believed to be a relic of the monastic foundation created here by St Colman around AD 600. It was one of the saint's successors who erected a High Cross in the Market Square. By the late

1880s this was in a ruinous state so its fragments were incorporated in a restoration of the cross which now stands beside the bridge over the Lagan.

Another survival is the set of stocks in the market square which are still occasionally used for imprisoning local brides and grooms before a wedding. A good time to visit is on the last Saturday in September when a lively horse fair takes place.

Hillsborough

4 miles NE of Dromore off the A1

With its fine Georgian architecture, Gothic planter's church, tea rooms and well-stocked antique shops, Hillsborough has been described as one of the most English-looking villages in Ulster. There's a lovely circular walk around the lake which takes about an hour to complete and begins near an impressive ruined fort built in 1650 by Colonel Arthur Hill after whom the village is named.

Nearby **Hillsborough Forest Park** covers an area of almost 500 acres which provides ample space for a variety of different walks. The whole of the lake area is a forest wildlife sanctuary and home to a wide variety of birds and animals.

The Hill family seat, **Hillsborough Castle** was built around 1797 and between 1925 to 1973 was the residence of the Governor of Northern Ireland. It then functioned as a stately-home-away-from-home for visiting VIPs and is now the official residence of the British Secretary of State for Northern Ireland. Within the grounds are some magnificent gardens, a Quaker burial ground, a Greek temple, and Lady Alice's circular temple, built in 1880. Tours of the castle and gardens are available by arrangement.

In early September Hillsborough village hosts the **World Oyster Eating Championships** in which contestants from as far afield as Japan, Canada, Russia and New Zealand attempt to swallow as many of the molluscs as they can in 3 minutes. The current record is 97 – more than one oyster every 2 seconds.

Co Fermanagh

More than a third of Co. Fermanagh lies under water – either lakes or rivers. It's an enchanted landscape, bounded in the northwest by Lower Lough Erne and in the southeast by Upper Lough Erne, two beautiful lakes linked by the winding River Erne. Tiny wooded islets dot the loughs, many of them with early-Christian ruins and evidence of even older, pagan cultures. Naturally, this is prime fishing country, the quality of the coarse fishing almost legendary.

This was also plantation country and there are many planter castles scattered around the trim little towns and villages. Fermanagh boasts two outstanding stately homes, Florence Court and Castle Coole, both near Enniskillen. Other places of major interest include the Marble Arch Caves and the famous Belleek Pottery, renowned for its extraordinarily elaborate and delicate wares.

Sheel-na-gig Statues, White Island

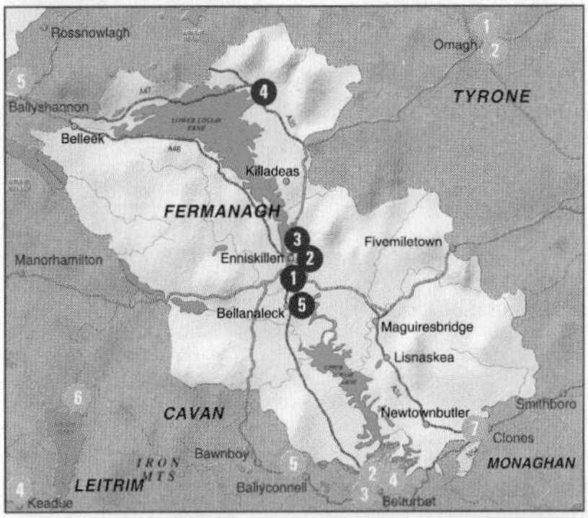

Enniskillen

Surrounded by water, the county town of Enniskillen is beautifully located on an island between the Upper and Lower Loughs Erne. Its skyline is dominated by **Enniskillen Castle**, occupying a picturesque site beside the water. Much modified over the years, the castle's 15th century Keep now houses both a Heritage Centre devoted to Fermanagh life and customs, and the Regimental Museum of the Royal Inniskilling Fusiliers and Dragoons. The

PLACES TO STAY, EAT AND DRINK

Oscar's, Enniskillen		Restaurant	p424
Willowbank House, Enniskillen		B&B	p424
Horseshoe & Saddler's Restaurant, Enniskillen	3	Pub with Restaurant	p425
Lough Erne Hotel, Kesh	4	Hotel	p426
Florence Court, Bellanaleck	5	House & Gardens	p427

Denotes entries in other chapters

town's close connections with these famous regiments have in the past made Enniskillen a target for terrorist attacks, most horrifically on Remembrance Day in 1987 when an IRA bomb killed eleven people and injured another 61. Happily, more peaceful times have returned to the town which had always been noted for the good relations between its Catholic and Protestant communities.

The centre of the town is a tangle of medieval lanes and a winding main street which skips through six different names along its length. Naturally, there are plenty of bait and tackle shops, and the gift shops are well-stocked with the delicate cream-coloured pottery made at Belleek. As an unusual souvenir of the area you might want to buy one of the locally-produced brooches made from fishing flies. More gift

possibilities are on offer in the town's former **Buttermarket,** erected in 1835, which is now a crafts-and-arts centre where you can watch craftspeople at work producing quality pottery, knitwear and leather items. There's also a craft shop displaying quality crafts from all over Ireland, a coffee shop, and the attractive paved courtyard is used in summer for street theatre, buskers and craft fairs.

One of the stateliest buildings in Enniskillen is the Portora Royal School on the edge of the town. Founded by Charles I in 1626, the present building dates from 1777 and its distinguished alumni include Oscar Wilde and Samuel Beckett.

Enniskillen boasts a beautifully maintained open space, **Forthill Park,** set on a steep hill above the town. Crowning the summit is the Cole Monument, built in

OSCAR'S

Belmore Street, Enniskillen,
Co. Fermanagh BT74
Tel/Fax: 028 6632 7037

The award-winning **Oscar's** restaurant is named in honour of Oscar Wilde who had many connections with Enniskillen. So in the downstairs dining area, designed as a kind of library, you'll find various portraits of the author and even a re-creation of Oscar's cell in Reading Gaol. Owner Dermot McGee is a qualified chef and his enticing menu offers a good choice of classic modern Irish cuisine, including fresh seafood, along with European and Asian dishes. Dinner is served throughout the year, lunches also during the season, but at any time booking ahead is strongly advised. Oscar's is fully licensed; credit cards are accepted.

WILLOWBANK HOUSE

60 Bellevue Road, Enniskillen,
Co. Fermanagh BT74 4JH
Tel/Fax: 028 6632 8582
e-mail: joan@willowbankhouse.com
website: www.willowbankhouse.com

Enjoying glorious panoramic views over Lough Erne but only 3.5 miles from Enniskillen, **Willowbank House** offers top quality bed & breakfast accommodation in wonderfully peaceful surroundings. Your hosts, Joan and Tom Foster, have been welcoming guests here since 2001 and their AA 4-Diamond rated accommodation comprises 5 ground floor guest bedrooms, all with en suite facilities, colour TV and hospitality tray. There's a comfortable lounge overlooking the lake, as does the garden/patio area. Joan is an accomplished cook and serves an outstanding breakfast and the room rates offer good value for money. Credit cards accepted.

Lower Lough Erne

1857 to commemorate Sir Galbraith Lowry-Cole who was one of Wellington's Generals. There are superb views from the top of the monument but you will have to negotiate 108 steps before you can enjoy them.

Enniskillen's position at the southern tip of Lower Lough Erne makes it an ideal starting point for boat trips around this fascinating lake. Several of the islands can be visited – Boa Island and Devenish Island both have interesting Celtic or early-Christian relics, and **White Island** is noted for its eerie statues. There are eight of them, ranged against the wall of a 12th century church, and like many of the sculptures discovered in Fermanagh they have a distinctly pagan air about them. **Devenish Island** is famous for its perfect 12th century Round Tower (95 feet high), ruined Augustinian priory and an intricately carved 15th century high cross in the graveyard.

A mile or so south-east of Enniskillen stands a masterpiece of Palladian architecture, **Castle Coole** (National Trust). Built in Portland stone to a design by James Wyatt, the house was completed in 1798 and is generally regarded as the most perfect house of its era in Ireland. It was erected at enormous expense for the Earl of Belmore who spent equally lavish sums on its magnificent furnishings. The guided tour of the house conducts visitors through a luxuriously ornate State Bedroom, a much more functional Servant's Tunnel, and includes an inspection of the Earl's luxurious private coach which is still garaged in its original 18th century coach house.

Landscaped parkland leads down to the River Erne and nearby is the Ardhowen Theatre, occupying a lovely lakeside position. Established in 1986, the theatre offers a lively programme of plays, operas, variety shows, and dance and jazz performances. Travelling to the theatre by

THE HORSESHOE & SADDLER'S RESTAURANT

66 Belmore Street, Enniskillen,
Co. Fermanagh BT74
Tel: 028 6632 6223 Fax: 028 6632 5076

For more than half a century the Coalter family have been dispensing excellent food and drink at **The Horseshoe & Saddler's Restaurant**. A coaching inn dating back to 1830, The Horseshoe now offers an outstanding and extensive menu with dishes based on the freshest of locally produced ingredients with all the meat products coming from its own butcher's shop next door. To complement your meal, the wine list brings together many of the best wines

from around the world at reasonable prices. At weekends there's live music and for special occasions the inn has a spacious Function Room that can cater for up to 250 guests.

THE LOUGH ERNE HOTEL

Main Street, Kesh, Co. Fermanagh BT93 1TF
Tel: 028686 31275
e-mail: info@loughernehotel.com
website: www.loughernehotel.com

Comfortable rooms in a peaceful setting, outstanding food, lively bars, great craic and friendly, attentive staff all combine to make **The Lough Erne Hotel** an ideal location for a relaxing break. You can enjoy superb food in the Bridgewater Restaurant, overlooking the river, where the menu includes dishes such as fresh Fermanagh trout with almonds, thick juicy fillet steaks or, for really hearty appetites, the huge Lough Erne Hotel Mixed Grill. Food is also served in the lounge and bar throughout the day but wherever you choose to eat your meal will have been prepared from the freshest and finest ingredients.

The hotel offers a choice of accommodation. You can stay in one of the hotel's 12 exceptionally comfortable and cosy rooms, all of them en suite and well-equipped and including one with an elegant 4-poster bed. If you prefer self-catering, the hotel also has a choice of 5 cottages or 4 studio apartments set beside the sparkling waters of the river Glendurragh. The cottages have 2 twin-bedded rooms; the apartments are designed for one or two guests. With its lovely setting and superior amenities, the hotel is also a popular venue for weddings and other functions, and can cater for up to 200 guests.

boat from Enniskillen makes a visit even more memorable.

A really satisfying day trip from Enniskillen is to follow the sign-posted drive around the entire expanse of Lower Lough Erne. Driving north from Enniskillen along the A32, the road passes the ferry point for Devenish Island. Fork left on the B32 to pass the town's small airport before reaching the little town of Killadeas.

Around Enniskillen

Killadeas

6 miles N of Enniskillen on the B82

Killadeas is an angling, boating, sailing and cruising centre and, naturally, enjoys a marvellous view of Lough Erne. In the graveyard of the little church here stands the **Bishop's Stone**, one of the most striking examples of an early Christian carved stone. On one side there's an obviously pagan image of a troubled-looking face; on the other, a bishop with bell and crosier. The graveyard also contains other curiously carved stones which are believed to date from the 7th or 8th centuries, amongst them a rounded pillar which was possibly a pagan phallic image.

Continuing northwards from Killadeas, the route passes **Castle Archdale Forest Park** (free) from whose marina there's a ferry to White Island and then along the north shore of the lake to Belleek.

Belleek

25 miles NW of Enniskillen on the A47

Belleek stands right on the border with Co. Donegal. An ancient joke for anglers is that it's possible here to hook a salmon in the Republic and land it in Northern Ireland. The town is famous for its distinctive pottery – beautifully crafted lustreware which is produced primarily for its decorative rather than its utilitarian qualities. At the **Belleek Visitors Centre** (free) a video presentation explains the production process and is followed by a 20-minute guided tour of the pottery which was established in 1857 and is the oldest and most famous in Ireland. The Pottery Shop has the complete product range on show and for sale and the Centre also includes an award-winning restaurant where, naturally, your refreshments are served on the finest Belleek tableware.

Skilled craftsmanship of another kind is on view at **Fermanagh Crystal** (free) where you can watch fine pieces being created and even commission a work of your own. Also in Belleek, located on the banks of the River Erne, **Explore Erne** provides the opportunity of exploring the length and breadth of the Lough Erne without getting your feet wet. A huge video wall displays an informative video explaining how the 50 miles of lough were formed; how Lough Erne has influenced the lives of local people; and how the lakes have contributed to travel, recreation and industry in Fermanagh.

From Belleek, the A46 hugs the southern shore of the lake for most of the 25 mile journey back to Enniskillen. Along the way, it passes the **Lough Navar Forest**, where there's a 7-mile circular drive through the forest that includes a breathtaking panorama over the lake from the Magho Viewpoint (1000 feet).

Two short detours will bring you to the remains of two castles, both of which were destroyed by fire. About 10 miles before Enniskillen, **Tully Castle** was built by Sir John Hume around 1613 and burned by his enemies, the Maguires, in 1641.

The castle has a formal garden and visitor centre. Five miles further on, signposted from the main road, a country lane leads to **Castle Monea** (free), an imposing plantation castle built by Michael Hamilton around 1618. It is remarkably well preserved considering that it has suffered no fewer than three separate fires. It was put to the torch during the Great

Florence Court

Bellanaleck, Co. Fermanagh BT92 1DB
Tel: 028 6634 8249

About five miles southwest of Bellanaleck, **Florence Court** is regarded as one of the most important houses in Ulster. Beautifully situated beneath the steep mountain of Benaughlin, the house was built for John Cole, father of the 1st Earl of Enniskillen, and completed in 1775. It was named after Florence, his wife. One of the chief glories of Florence Court is the exceptional embellished rococo plasterwork, seen at its best above the stairs and in the dining room. The house contains fine Irish furniture, including an 18th century rococo armchair in the library, an Irish writing cabinet which dates from 1730 and an unusual 18th century bed.

The house is surrounded by a large area of parkland, garden and woodland, including a recently restored walled garden where the pink and white roses are especially attractive in early summer. Florence Court's most notable tree, the Irish yew, grows in a much wilder part of the estate. From its seedlings have grown every other Irish yew anywhere in the world. This 260-year-old original was one of two found in the Fermanagh hills in the 1740s. Also within the grounds are a recently restored water-powered sawmill, an ice house, a replica of a Victorian summer house, a shop and tea room.

Rebellion of 1641, again during the Jacobite uprising of 1689, and finally abandoned after another, accidental, fire in 1750.

Bellanaleck

3 miles S of Enniskillen on the A509

Bellanaleck is a pleasing little town with a marina where you can hire cruisers and rowing boats to explore this little-known wetland area. But if you plan on walking around Bellanaleck, wellington boots are recommended! The town is well-known for Gault's Crafts which specialises in beautiful hand-knit Aran sweaters created by local knitters, but also has a wide range of other items – blackthorn sticks and shillelaghs (made on the premises); hand-woven tweed, rugs, scarves and hats; Belleek and Donegal china; and much more.

A visit to **Florence Court** (see panel on page 427) can be combined with an exploration of the **Marble Arch Caves**, three miles to the west. This is one of Europe's finest showcaves, a fascinating underworld of stalactites and stalagmites glistening in winding passages and huge caverns. The 75-minute guided tour begins by boat and then continues on foot past limestone formations, rivers and waterfalls. An especially interesting feature is the "Moses Walk", so-called because the dammed walkway crosses a lake, with more than three feet of water on either side. During the high season the guided tours can be fully booked and after heavy rain the caves may close for safety reasons so it's advisable to telephone before setting out (tel: 028 6634 8855).

Maguiresbridge

8 miles SE of Enniskillen on the A4/A34

The maze of waters around Maguiresbridge present quite a challenge for the explorer so if you plan to explore this wonderfully tranquil area a detailed map is a necessity. Old folk traditions still linger here – you may well come across someone possessing the secret of unorthodox cures for animal and human ailments.

Newtownbutler

18 miles SE of Enniskillen on the A34

Covering almost two thousand acres of woodland, farmland and loughs which support a wide variety of rare plants and abundant wildlife, the **Crom Estate** (National Trust) is one of Ireland's most important nature conservation areas. Trails around the estate take in the ruins of Crom Old Castle built on the shore of the lough in 1610 by Michael Balfour, Laird of Mountwhinney. The castle survived two sieges during the troubles of 1689 but was destroyed by an accidental fire in 1764. The yew trees within the ruins are reputed to be the oldest in Ireland. Other buildings of interest within the estate are The Old Farmyard, built as a model farmyard in the 1830s and now the Visitor Centre, a Victorian schoolhouse, summer house, and a splendidly over-the-top Boathouse with decorated bargeboards and battlements. Boats can be hired to explore the islands that form part of the estate or for fishing expeditions. There are good facilities for visitors with disabilities and the Visitor Centre has a tea-room and shop.

Co Londonderry

County Londonderry, or Derry as it is commonly known locally, is a beautiful and compact area with a rich and varied scenery. To the south, the Sperrin Mountains sprawl across into County Tyrone with their highest point, Sawel (2240 feet), right on the county border. To the north lies the Atlantic coast, lined with magnificent beaches of surf-washed sand and popular resorts such as Portstewart and Castlerock. Inland lies an inviting landscape of scenic hills, glens and river valleys. These well-wooded acres are the result of the "plantations" of the early 1600s when English Protestant colonists were granted huge tracts of land by James I. The story of that crucial episode in Ulster's history from which so much good and bad has flowed is told in the Plantation of Ulster Visitor Centre at Draperstown. Much of the interest in the area centres on the ancient and historic city of Derry which stands on a commanding site overlooking a broad curve of the River Foyle and this is where we begin our survey of the county.

Mussenden Temple

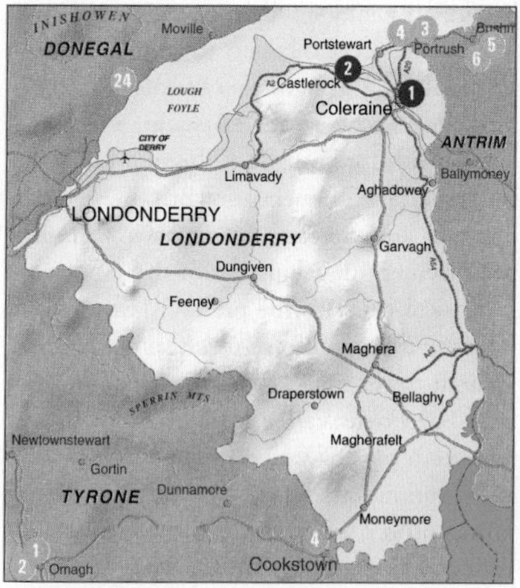

Derry

In the year AD 546 a virulent plague devastated the people of Donegal. Amongst those who fled across the River Foyle into what is now Londonderry was a charismatic monk named Colmcille, better known today as St Columba. On a mound surrounded by oak trees, "*doire*", he established a monastery whose wealth and importance steadily grew over the years, reaching its

PLACES TO STAY, EAT AND DRINK

Strawberry Fayre Tea Rooms, Coleraine	1	Tea Rooms & Bakery	p432
Musseunden Temple, Castlerock	2	Historic Building	p433

● Denotes entries in other chapters

peak in the 12th and 13th centuries.

Throughout the late Middle Ages the town declined. Elizabeth I tried to establish English rule in Ulster by means of a brutal military campaign which destroyed most of Derry's medieval buildings. It was her successor, James I, who in 1609 granted Derry to the Irish Society of London "for the promotion of religion, order and industry". Along with other English and Scottish Protestant settlers, this energetic body rebuilt the city, laying it out according to the best contemporary principles of town planning, and creating a street plan which has survived almost intact to the present day.

They surrounded their new town with walls 25 feet high and 28 feet thick – an impregnable defence that has never been breached. Derry was the last walled city built in Ireland and the only city on the island whose ancient walls survive complete. There are walkways along the one mile circuit of the walls which offer some grand views of the city and the River Foyle.

The settlers also built **St Columb's Cathedral** (1633), the first post-Reformation cathedral to be built in Britain. A fine example of the style known as Planters' Gothic, the cathedral is one of the most important 17th century buildings in the country. Nearby is the Bishop's Palace where one bishop's wife, Cecil Frances Alexander, penned the well-known hymns *There is a Green Hill Far Away* and *All Things Bright and Beautiful*.

The peaceful period of reconstruction and progress of the early 1600s was soon shattered. Derry was besieged during the rebellion of 1641, again during the Cromwellian wars and, most significantly for Ulster's subsequent history, in 1689. On this occasion it was the deposed James II who attacked the city. As his troops approached, 13 apprentice boys rushed to the city gates and secured them. During the 135-day siege that followed, the people of Derry were reduced to eating rats, dogs and the starch used for laundering linen. Almost one quarter of the inhabitants perished, a death toll which is commemorated in the skeleton emblazoned on the city's coat-of-arms. Despite their plight, Derry's citizens defiantly proclaimed their policy of "No Surrender", and to this day repeat that slogan during the controversial "Apprentice Boys Marches" through the town that take place each year on 12 August, the day on which troops supporting William of Orange (William III) finally captured the town.

Following William's victory, the 18th and 19th centuries provided an era of comparative prosperity but the late 1900s saw the eruption of sectarian divisions in the Troubles. But following a major programme of investment and redevlopment in the 1990s, Derry is once again a vibrant, buzzing city and a delight to visit.

Now the second largest town in Ulster, Derry offers a wide range of visitor attractions. The **Tower Museum,** which has won awards for both Best Museum in Ireland and in the whole of Britain, contains a comprehensive display outlining the turbulent development of the city from geological times to the present day. The building is a modern re-creation of an ancient tower house that once stood on the site. The **Foyle Valley Railway Centre** features a narrow gauge (3 feet) railway with working models and a 1934 diesel railcar on a 2-mile track along the river valley; and the **Harbour Museum** (free) includes a replica of the 30-feet long curragh in which St Columba sailed to Iona and an authentic 15th century longboat recovered from the bed of the Upper Bann river. Also worth a visit is the **Derry Craft Village** (free) in Shipquay Street, a re-created traditional stone village where you'll find a range of traditional craft shops and the stylish Boston Tea Party tea room.

In addition to St Columb's Cathedral, Derry's other buildings of interest include the **Courthouse** of 1813, which is a notable example of Greek Revival architecture; the neo-Gothic Victorian **Guildhall** (free) containing some excellent stained-glass windows depicting the history of Derry and, in a very different vein, the **Free Derry Mural** in the Bogside, a much photographed and repainted emblem of Catholic resistance.

A mile or so outside Derry, the **Earhart Centre & Wildlife Sanctuary** (voluntary donation invited) commemorates Amelia Earhart, the first woman to fly the Atlantic solo in 1932. A sculpture marks the spot in the field where the intrepid American aviator landed after her 13¼ hour flight.

Around Londonderry

Limavady

15 miles NE of Londonderry on the A2

Founded in the early 1600s by an enterprising Welshman, Thomas Phillips, Limavady enjoys a lovely situation in the Roe Valley, surrounded by mountain scenery to the north and southeast. This bustling market town has expanded greatly over recent years but some attractive features of the past have survived. An elegant six arch bridge of 1700 spans the River Roe and the Main Street leading to it has some decorous Georgian buildings. One of them, No. 51, was the home of Jane Ross who in 1851 heard a passing itinerant fiddler playing a magically wistful tune. She noted it down and the old folk melody has endured as the *Londonderry Air*, ("Danny Boy"). Jane Ross and her three younger sisters, all unmarried, are buried across the road at the 18th century parish church which is notable for its collection of several hundred tapestry kneelers, each one different.

A few years before Jane Ross recorded Ireland's most famous tune for posterity, W.M. Thackeray had stopped for ale at an inn in Main Street and was swiftly beguiled by the barmaid's bright eyes. His popular poem *Sweet Peg of Limavady* was the result.

The town's most famous son, (in New Zealand at least), was William Massey, Prime Minister of that country from 1912 to 1925. A plaque in Irish Green Street records his birth there in 1856.

A couple of miles south of the town, the **Roe Valley Country Park** is a scenic gem, 3 miles of wooded gorges and floodplain meadows. Ireland's first hydro-electric power station, opened in 1896, is located within the park with much of the original equipment still intact. There's also a small weaving centre and a visitor centre.

Feeny

15 miles SE of Londonderry on minor road off the A6

The Feeny area, meaning "wooded place", lies in the foothills and valleys of the North Sperrins range, surrounded by some splendid scenery and many sites of archaeological and historical interest. Standing stones, stone circles, a chambered grave, raths (circular earthen defences) and a prehistoric sweathouse are just some of the ancient remains scattered around the area. **Banagher Glen National Nature Reserve** (free), about 2 miles southwest of Feeny, contains ancient oak woodland of national importance and is one of the last remaining semi-natural woodlands in Northern Ireland. To the northeast are the quietly impressive ruins of **Banagher Old Church**, founded around 1100 by a local saint named Muiredach O'Heney. The saint is buried in a well-preserved mortuary in the churchyard. His tomb stands on a sandhill and if you grasp a handful of the sand from beneath his grave into your possession you will be granted the power to bring luck to yourselves and others. Poet Seamus Heaney tried it and look what happened to him.

Dungiven

15 miles SE of Londonderry on the A6

This small market town set beside the River Roe is notable for the ruins of the 12th century **Dungiven Priory,** set on a bluff above the river just south of the town. The shattered remains of the once rich and powerful monastery contain the finest medieval tomb in Ireland. Cooey Na Gall O'Cahan, Chief of the O'Cahan clan, died in 1385. His stone effigy lies under an elaborately traceried canopy; beneath it, in niches sculpted into the sarcophagus, stand six warriors in kilts representing the Scots mercenaries from whom Cooey earned his nickname *Na Gall*, "of the foreigners". It's almost 300 years since the Priory was last in use but it remains something of a shrine for those seeking a cure for illness or disability. An ancient tree within its precincts flutters with votive offerings – handkerchiefs, dresses, even socks.

Coleraine

The county's second largest town after Derry, Coleraine developed around the banks of the River Bann and this area remains the most attractive part of the town. The river splashes noisily over a picturesque weir, whitewashed lock-keepers' cottages maintain watch over the locks upstream at The Cutts, and downstream there's a large and thriving boating marina. Apart from a handsome Town Hall, most of Coleraine's buildings are severely functional

STRAWBERRY FAYRE TEA ROOMS & BAKERY

1 Blagh Road, Coleraine,
Co. Londonderry BT52 2PG
Tel: 02870 320437

Had Finn Macool been around today he might well have joined the visitors stopping by at **Strawberry Fayre Tea Rooms and Bakery** on his way to the Giant's Causeway from Coleraine. The tea rooms provide a perfect excuse for a run out in the car explains Nevin Hamilton, owner of this family-run tea room and bakery business housed in a renovated school house. Popular with day trippers, tourists and local people, its success comes

not only from its location but also because of the quality and mouth-watering array of food on offer. The lunch menu changes daily with dishes featuring Northern Ireland produce – beef, chicken, pork or salmon – all freshly prepared as you wait.

The fruit and vegetable garden is at the heart of the accompanying salads and fruit desserts. Seated comfortably in the softly coloured restaurant (which is non-smoking) your eye is taken by the wonderful array of sweets on the long serving table and the rows of newly baked cakes, scones, wheatens etc, all available to purchase.

The bakery and tearoom products are made without artificial additives, using only natural ingredients to produce good food prepared by qualified staff. The tea room has ample car parking in the playground with easy access for disabled customers.

but, with the campus of the University of Ulster located here, the town is always lively in term time.

About a mile south of the town, **Mountsandel** claims to be the earliest known inhabited place in Ireland. There's not a great deal to see at this 200 feet high oval mound overlooking the river but the post holes and hearths of wooden dwellings are estimated to be 9000 years old.

Around Coleraine

Castlerock

5 miles NW of Coleraine off the A2

This pretty seaside resort is noted for its fine sandy beach that runs for about a mile westwards from the mouth of the River Bann. An open air heated swimming pool by the beach, a championship 18-hole golf course and good sea and river fishing all add to the appeal. About a mile south of the village, **Hezlett House** (National Trust) is a single storey, 17th century thatched rectory with an unusual cruck-truss roof construction. This was a pioneering method of building which involved balancing curved timbers (crucks) in pairs to form a series of arches and building the house around this frame. Smothered in Virginia creeper, the house is now furnished in late Victorian style and has a small display of vintage farm implements.

About 2 miles east of Castlerock, **Mussenden Temple** (National Trust)is one of the most photographed sights in Ireland (see panel below).

Portstewart

4 miles N of Coleraine on the A2

Two miles of magnificent strand sheltered by rocky headlands, (now protected by the National Trust), attracted Victorian holidaymakers to Portstewart; a century later wind-surfers flock here to ride the great breakers which crash down on the long sandy beach which is firm enough to drive a car along. There's a breezy cliff-side walk that passes trim Victorian villas and an imposing Gothic mansion, now a Dominican nunnery and college.

Portstewart has always had a rather more genteel atmosphere than its twin resort, Portrush, just across the border in County Antrim. Portstewart's Victorian town fathers, for example, insisted that the

Mussenden Temple

Castlerock, Co. Londonderry

About two miles east of Castlerock, **Mussenden Temple** (National Trust), perched on eroding cliffs above the 6-mile-long Magilligan Strand, is one of the most photographed sights in Ireland. Modelled on the temples of Vesta at Rome and Tivoli, the elegant domed structure was built in 1783 as a "summer library" by the eccentric Frederick Augustus Hervey, Anglican Bishop of Derry and 4th Earl of Bristol. An unorthodox cleric, he once organised a curates' race along the sands at Downhill, the winners being rewarded with benefices in his diocese. He was also unconventional for his time in his tolerance of Catholics, permitting a weekly Mass in the Temple since there was no local Catholic church.

A great traveller and art collector, the Earl-Bishop's progress around the Continent can still be detected by the number of hostelries that re-named themselves the "Hotel Bristol" following a visit by the free-spending English milord. The Temple was originally just a landscape adornment for the Bishop's **Downhill Palace**, a grandiose mansion last occupied by US troops during World War II and now in ruins.

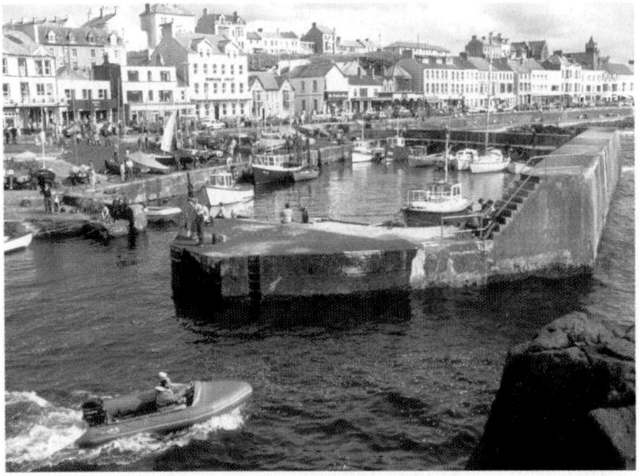

Portstewart Harbour

railway station should be located a good mile from the town centre to discourage the influx of the less desirable class of tourist. It's a much more welcoming place nowadays, offering a choice of two 18-hole golf courses, two 9-hole courses, good bathing, tennis, boating and sea fishing.

Aghadowey

7 miles S of Coleraine on the B66

This small riverside village lies close to the County Antrim border, conveniently located for exploring both the Causeway Coast and the Sperrin Mountains. It's a wonderfully peaceful place for holidaymakers with plenty of activities and attractions within easy reach and some welcoming places with excellent amenities to stay at.

Garvagh

10 miles S of Coleraine on the A29

The small town of Garvagh is attractively situated in the foothills of the Carntogher Mountains and beside the River Bann, another river famous for its salmon. Garvagh has an unusually wide main street because until the early 1800s the houses here all had their gardens at the front.

From 1620 onwards, the Canning family played an important part in the development of Garvagh. One of their descendants, George Canning, became Prime Minister of Great Britain for a few months before his untimely death in August 1827.

Another celebrated son of Garvagh is Denis O'Hempsey, the famous harpist who was born here in 1695. Denis was only 3 years old when he almost died from a virulent attack of smallpox. He eventually recovered, but the vicious infection left him blind. The loss of sight seems to have stimulated his sensitivity to sound. Denis found solace in music – above all in the music of the traditional Irish harp. He became an accomplished performer and made a comfortable living playing to middle-class drawing room audiences across the country. He even visited Scotland where he played before Bonnie Prince Charles at Holyrood in 1745. Denis was 97 years old when he attended the great Harp Meeting in Belfast in 1792. After his dazzling performance, the other harpists refused to play, protesting that their modest talents were unworthy to be heard in the wake of such a genius. Denis died in 1807, aged 112. His harp, a gift to him from the residents of Garvagh in 1713, is now on display in the Guinness Museum, Dublin.

Just outside the town, **Arkhill Farm** has many animals for children to see, smell, hear, touch and feed. Visiting groups have full use of a specially equipped education room and the outhouses are used for 'hands-on' activities. The farm shop sells arts and crafts, organic fruit and vegetables. There is access for the disabled and the farm is open all year round.

Maghera

22 miles S of Coleraine on the A29

Pleasantly located at the eastern end of the Sperrin Mountains, the little town of Maghera was once an important ecclesiastical centre, the seat of a bishop. **Maghera Old Church** stands on the site of a 6th century monastery founded by St Lurach. Its fine 12th century west door is decorated with animal and floral designs crowned by a massive lintel carved with a crucifixion scene. The tower, dating back to the 1600s, conveniently provided the priest with a first floor apartment over the shop. Westwards from the town, a scenic route traverses the Glenshane Pass through the Sperrins to Londonderry.

Magherafelt

28 miles S of Coleraine on the A31

Magherafelt is one of several plantation towns in the area, its spacious and orderly layout created by the Salters' Company of London to whom James I had granted the land. The town provides a convenient angling centre for the Moyola River and there are pleasant drives along the shore of nearby Lough Neagh. In March each year, Magherafelt hosts a lively Arts Festival.

A popular excursion from Magherafelt is a visit to **Springhill** (National Trust), about 5 miles south. This 17th century whitewashed manor house contains family furniture, paintings, ornaments and curios. An important costume collection is housed in part of the extensive outbuildings which include a fortified barn also dating from the 17th century and two barns in the Dutch style. There are secluded walled gardens and woodland walks.

Bellaghy

26 miles S of Coleraine on the A54

Bellaghy is yet another of Londonderry's plantation towns, created in 1622 by the Vintners' Company. Its plantation castle, **Bellaghy Bawn,** still stands and is one of the best surviving examples of this form of defensive architecture. Although most of its fortifications were destroyed in 1641, the imposing circular tower remains. It has been imaginatively restored and now contains interpretive displays spanning the 7000 year old history of settlements in the area.

There is also a major exhibition celebrating Bellaghy's most famous son, Seamus Heaney, one of the greatest of contemporary poets and winner of the Nobel Prize for Literature in 1995. Seamus himself provides the narration for a fascinating video, *A Sense of Place*, in which he explains how the local scenery and characters inspired much of his poetry. The Bawn's library contains a comprehensive collection of his works, including first drafts and rare editions, and there's also a small café here.

Draperstown

6 miles S of Coleraine on the B41

Draperstown is another of County Derry's plantation villages created, as the name indicates, by the London Company of Drapers. So it's an appropriate location for the **Plantation of Ulster Visitors Centre** where audio-visual technology and computer-enhanced images tell the story of James I's attempt to "Anglicize" Ulster by granting huge estates to English and Scottish settlers. The Centre also has displays on Hugh O'Neill and the fateful "Flight of the Earls" in 1607 when Ulster's lords abandoned their homeland.

Co Tyrone

Lying in the heart of Ulster, Tyrone is one of the most beautiful of the inland counties, with the Sperrin Mountains in the north and well-wooded tracts in the southeast which gave rise to the frequently quoted tag, "Tyrone among the bushes, where the Finn and Mourne run". This is primarily a farming county and the whitewashed stone farmhouses with their brightly coloured doors are a distinctive feature of the landscape. The least populated of the Six Counties, Tyrone has a peaceful charm all of its own.

The county has a good number of prehistoric remains of which the Beaghmore Stone Circle in the Sperrins is the most remarkable. Very few of the handsome Georgian houses built by the planters are open to the public but Tyrone boasts one of Ireland's major visitor attractions at the Ulster American Folk Park which celebrates the strong links between the peoples of Ulster and North America.

Omagh

Tyrone's county capital is a prosperous, busy place but with a limited number of attractions for the visitor. Two exceptions are the fine classical **Courthouse** and the **Catholic Cathedral of the Sacred Heart** with its irregular twin spires, a building which has been described as "the poor man's Chartres Cathedral". Completed in 1893, the cathedral soars above the town and is flanked by the Courthouse built some 30 years earlier.

The Courthouse was believed to be the target of the terrorists who in 1998 exploded a bomb in the main street, an atrocity which left 29 people dead and 200 injured. A **Memorial Garden** marks the place where they lost their lives.

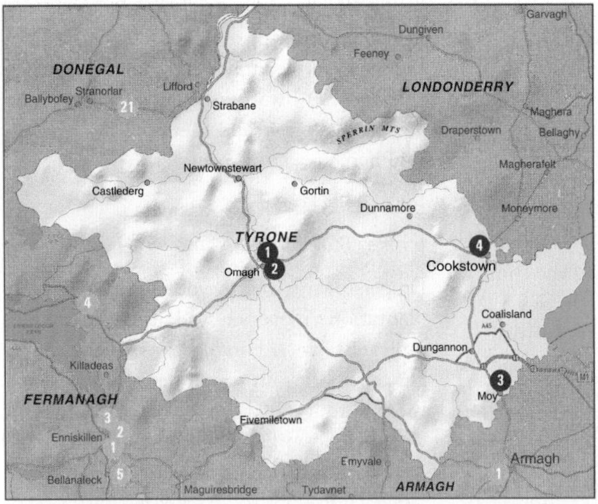

PLACES TO STAY, EAT AND DRINK

- Silver Birch Hotel, Omagh ① Hotel p437
- Ulster-American Folk Park, Omagh ② Visitor Attraction p439
- The Ryandale Inn, Moy ③ Hotel p440
- The Belfast House, Cookstown ④ Bar and Accommodation p442

● Denotes entries in other chapters

THE SILVERBIRCH HOTEL

5 Gortin Road, Omagh, Co. Tyrone BT79 7DH
Tel: 02882 242520
e-mail: info@silverbirchhotel.com
website: www.silverbirchhotel.com

The spacious reception and foyer area at **The Silverbirch Hotel** gives a foretaste of the lavish and modern surroundings, and relaxed and informal atmosphere of this friendly family-run hotel. It stands in beautifully landscaped mature gardens, a picturesque setting which has made the hotel a popular venue for weddings. Another major attraction here is the quality of the food. You can treat yourself to a choice from the comprehensive selection of dishes based on fresh local produce that's on offer in the Buttery Bar and Lounge or, for a more formal or quiet experience, settle down in the elegant à la carte dining room.

For grander occasions, the hotel's banqueting facilities can cater for up to 300 guests. Wedding receptions are the

Silverbirch Hotel's speciality but it has a number of rooms available to suit whatever size of business or social event – and each room has its own bar facilities. The accommodation here maintains the same high standards evident throughout the hotel. There are 46 bedrooms, all luxuriously furnished, en suite and provided with multi-channel TV, direct dial telephone, hair dryer, trouser press and hospitality tray. The hotel is conveniently located close to a number of visitor attractions, golf courses and shops.

Omagh is the home town of the celebrated playwright Brian Friel, (*Translations* and *Philadelphia, Here I Come*), and also of the song-writer Jimmy Kennedy whose greatest hits were *Red Sails in the Sunset* and *The Teddy Bears' Picnic*.

A popular souvenir to take home from Omagh is one of the statuettes or plaques made of peat cut from the Black Bog which stretches to the east of the town.

Within easy reach of the town are some excellent Forest Parks. To the north is **Gortin Glen** which has a 5-mile forest drive with some well-sited lay-bys to enjoy the splendid views, and way-marked trails. To the northwest is **Baron's Court Forest Park** where Bessy Bell Hill provides a spectacular overview of the Sperrins, Lough Erne and Co. Donegal. To the south, **Seskimore** is noted for its collection of ornamental birds and domestic fowl.

Omagh's most popular visitor attraction is the **Ulster-American Folk Park** (see panel on page 439) on the A5 three miles north of Omagh.

Around Omagh

Gortin

8 miles N of Omagh on the B48

The small village of Gortin lies close to the foot of the Sperrin Mountains, surrounded by woodland and with the Gortin Glen Forest Park a couple of miles to the east. According to legend, St Patrick himself built the local church which is still in use to this day.

About 3 miles south of Gortin is one of County Tyrone's major visitor attractions, the **Ulster History Park**. There are full-scale reconstructions of Irish buildings from 7000 BC up to the 17th century, videos and displays, and best of all a guided tour around the site during which visitors can enter a foul-smelling deerskin-covered teepee, learn how to make a flint, and

explore a ring fort and medieval castle.

Gortin village itself lies on the Ulster Way, not the main 34 mile route which follows an arduous course through the mountains, but a gentler 10 mile stretch which runs through woods and farmland and ends at another visitor attraction, the Ulster American Folk Park.

Newtonstewart

8 miles N of Omagh on the N5

Attractively laid out in the 1600s as a plantation town, Newtonstewart stands at the confluence of the rivers Strule and the Glenelly where they meet to form the River Mourne. This strategic spot was once guarded by two medieval castles of which very little remains.

Co. Tyrone is well supplied with a diverse range of museums and the **Gateway Centre & Museum** is one of the most fascinating. Much of the collection was a gift from local historian Billy Dunbar and includes a multifarious display of items such as a threepenny bit engraved with the Lord's Prayer, a Bordalous (a mini-chamberpot named after a French priest dreaded for his interminable sermons), man traps, vintage packaging, stereoscopes and war memorabilia. Other exhibits include antique toys, a device for lifting hedgehogs, and photographic and agricultural equipment dating from the 19th century.

Castlederg

14 miles NW of Omagh on the B50/B72

Castlederg is a pleasant place to wander around. It sits on one bank of the River Derg, on the other stand the ruins of **Castlederg Castle** which has one of the shortest histories of any Irish castle. It was built in 1619 and destroyed during the Rebellion of 1641. In the **Castleberg Visitor Centre**, there's an interesting display honouring the American frontiersman and adventurer, Davy Crockett, whose family emigrated from the Castlederg area. The exhibit includes a model of the Alamo fort where Davy made his last stand in 1836.

Strabane

20 miles N of Omagh on the A5

This large market town stands beside the River Mourne looking across to its twin town, Lifford in Co. Donegal. To the east stretch the Sperrin Mountains, wonderfully empty of humans but rich in wildlife.

The best introduction to this area of solitude and peace, a walker's paradise, is to visit the **Sperrin Heritage Centre** at Cranagh, a few miles east of Strabane. There are hi-tech exhibitions and an audio-visual presentation on the area's natural history and, since there's "gold in them thar hills", visitors can try their luck at panning for it. You can discover the only place where the cloudberry grows and learn about the origins of the St Brigid Cross. Made of rushes in the rough shape of a swastika, you will see them hanging above the doors around here to ward off evil. The Centre also has a craft shop and an excellent tea room, the only one for miles around.

In Strabane, American visitors in particular will be interested in **Gray's Printing Shop** in Main Street, now owned by the National Trust. It was here that John Dunlap, the printer of the American Declaration of Independence and also of America's first daily newspaper, the *Pennsylvania Packet*, learned his trade in the mid-1700s.

There's another strong American connection to be found at Dergalt, a couple of miles east of Strabane. **Wilson House** is a small, traditional farmer's house which was the 19th century home of the father of Woodrow Wilson, 28th President of the United States. And 2½ miles from Woodend Cottage, Cowancor is the ancestral home of the 11th President, James Knox Polk.

Ulster-American Folk Park

Castletown, Omagh, Co. Tyrone BT78 5QY
Tel: 028 8224 3292

Omagh's most popular visitor attraction is the **Ulster-American Folk Park** on the A5 three miles north of Omagh. This outstanding museum tells the story of the great waves of emigration from Ulster during the 18th and 19th centuries and how they fared across the Atlantic. In the Old World area of the Park stand some fascinating restored buildings - thatched craftsmen's cottages, a forge, schoolhouse and Presbyterian meeting house. Peat fires still burn in the cottages

and there are regular demonstrations of old skills such as candle-making, fish-salting and horse-shoeing. There's also an indoor exhibit re-creating an Ulster main street as it would have appeared around 1900.

The New World section displays log houses, a Pennsylvania farmstead, a covered wagon and a full scale replica of an emigrant ship. Disney and others have given theme parks a bad name but the exhibits at the Ulster-American Folk Park have a satisfying stamp of authenticity. The Park was endowed by a generous grant from the Mellon banking family who founded Pittsburgh, Pennsylvania. Their ancestor, Thomas Mellon, was born at the village of Camphill near Omagh and emigrated to America in 1818. His family homestead at Camphill is one of the more substantial of the cottages re-located here. The Park is open all year round and has a gift shop, café and a major reference and research library containing a wealth of material such as emigrants' letters, ships' passenger lists and newspaper articles of the time.

Fivemiletown

14 miles S of Omagh on the A4/B122

The village's name came from a popular misconception that it was 5 miles equidistant from the surrounding villages of Clabby, Clogher and Colebrooke, which in fact it isn't. Sir William Stewart built a plantation castle here during the reign of James I. Its remains can be seen on the north side of the main street. Fivemiletown stands right on the border with Co. Fermanagh with the mass of Slieve Beagh (1221 feet) rising to the south.

A nearby attraction is the **Coach and Carriage Museum** at Blessingbourne. Among the numerous coaches on display is an 1825 London-to-Oxford stage coach; an even older private coach of 1790; and a country doctor's buggy dating from 1910.

The Ryandale Inn

16-19 The Square, Moy, Co. Tyrone
Tel: 028 0778 4629 Fax: 028 8778 9911
e-mail: info@theryandale.com
website: www.theryandale.com

The Ryandale Inn stands in the heart of the attractive village of Moy, about midway between Dungannon and Armagh, and offers luxurious en suite accommodation and an excellent fully licensed restaurant. This family run business is owned by Vincent and Marian Daly, a friendly and welcoming couple who make sure that their guests are extremely well looked after.

The hotel has two bar areas and a spacious restaurant which is noted throughout the county for its superb cuisine.

It can seat up to 60 diners – ideal for that special occasion – and food is served throughout the day from 9am to 9.30pm.

The accommodation comprises 14 charming bedrooms, each with its own unique character and tasteful furnishing. All of them are en suite and equipped to the highest standard with every facility the discerning traveller could ask for.

Music lovers are well served here with live performances 3 nights a week and dancing every Saturday evening. There's also a nite-club which is situated away from the main building.

The Ryandale is well-established as one of the most popular venues in the area for wedding celebrations. It stands on a one acre site with a large garden which provides a beautiful backdrop for photographs. Another attraction is the interesting range of menus designed to suit all tastes and budgets. The function suite can accommodate up to 400 guests and the hotel offers advice on the planning of every aspect of your reception from arranging floral displays and table plans to your evening entertainment. Friendly and efficient service is another bonus – when you choose the Ryandale you can relax in the knowledge that everything will be perfect with nothing left to chance.

Moy itself is an attractive estate village set beside the River Blackwater and its residents are proud of having won the "Best Kept Village Award" in 1992. It boasts eight pubs, two restaurants, an attractive library with the Hobson Room and its own Health Centre. Within a few miles are the tourist attractions of the Argory and Ardress House, both of which are open to the public, and the Blackwater River Park which offers bream fishing, canoeing, and sub-aqua enthusiasts.

The museum also exhibits an interesting collection of antique horse-drawn farm machinery.

Fivemiletown is a good place to join the **Clogher Valley Scenic Route,** a 25 mile circular drive that wanders along country lanes, through woodlands and over hills, taking in *en route* Slieve Beagh and Fardross Forest where there's a spectacular viewpoint across the Clogher Valley. Just beyond Fardross Forest you'll see an extraordinary hilltop tower. This is **Brackenridge's Folly**, named after George Brackenridge who built it as his mausoleum so that "the squirearchy who had looked down on him during his lifetime were compelled to look up to him after his death".

East Tyrone

Moy

5 miles SE of Dungannon on the A29

Tucked away in the southeast corner of Co. Tyrone, Moy was built in the 18th century by Lord Charlemont. Its street design, for reasons known only to his Lordship, is based on the town plan of Marengo in Lombardy, Italy. The village, with its wide tree-lined square, is attractively set beside the River Blackwater which forms the boundary here with Co. Armagh.

About 4 miles northeast of Moy, **The Argory** is a National Trust property set in wooded countryside and overlooking the Blackwater river. The elegant house dates from 1820 and additional attractions include a sundial garden and tea room. Entrance is by guided tour only.

Dungannon

28 miles SE of Omagh on the A29/A45

From their hilltop fortress at Dungannon the O'Neills ruled Ulster for more than five centuries but all traces of their medieval castle have disappeared beneath the present O'Neill's Castle which is actually a late-Georgian mansion. The town now has the typical appearance of a planter town, with a planned main street, a Royal School founded by James I, and some attractive Georgian terraces. Another building of interest is the police station in the town centre which looks like a castle with projecting apertures for missile throwing. The extraordinary official explanation for this unusual structure is that the building was originally intended as a fort designed to guard the Khyber Pass in Afghanistan but a flustered government clerk mixed up the plans. Presumably, somewhere in southern Afghanistan, there is now a homely Irish police station protecting the wild mountain pass.

Just outside the town, **Tyrone Crystal** at Killybrackey has tours all year round allowing visitors to view the delicate processes of hand-blowing and hand-cutting involved in creating this world-famous product. There's also a factory shop and café.

American visitors especially will be interested in seeking out the little village of Ballygawley, (about 13 miles southwest of Dungannon), or rather the smallholding a couple of miles to the east which is now known as the **Grant Ancestral Homestead.** It was once farmed by the maternal ancestors of Ulysses S. Grant (1822-85), hero of the American Civil War and 18th President of the USA. Grant's great-grandfather, John Simpson, was born here in 1738 and his tiny two roomed thatched cottage has been restored and furnished in typical 19th century style. The surrounding working farm has a display of 19th century agricultural implements and is stocked with traditional breeds. The site also includes a wildlife pond and butterfly garden. The homestead is open from April to September, Monday to Saturday.

Cookstown

8 miles N of Dungannon on the A29

Cookstown was originally built in the early 1620s as a planned plantation town by one Alan Cook, a Scotsman. Less than 20 years later, during the 1641 uprising, the town

THE BELFAST HOUSE

3 Orritor Street, Cookstown, Co. Tyrone
Tel: 0288 676 9759

Located right in the centre of the town, **The Belfast House** is an impressive building displaying an unusual and interesting style of architecture. For more than half a century this welcoming hostelry has been owned and run by the Conway family and is popular with both locals and tourists alike.

The bar has all the charm and character you could hope to find – as well as a pool table and live music at weekends. The Belfast House also offers quality bed & breakfast accommodation with 6 guest bedrooms available, all stylishly furnished and with en suite facilities and hospitality tray.

was captured by Irish rebels and burnt to the ground. The ruins stood abandoned for almost a century before Cook's grandson laid out a new town with a main street stretching for almost a mile and a half – the longest main street in Ireland it is claimed.

To the west of the town, the **Drum Manor Forest Park** contains a demonstration shrub garden, a walled butterfly garden and an arboretum. There are nature trails passing lakes and a heronry, a forest trail for the disabled, a perfumed garden for the blind and a café. Nearby is the **Wellbrook Beetling Mill** (National Trust). At this water-powered 18th century linen hammer mill the process of "beetling" took place – the stage in linen manufacture when the cloth is hammered to produce a sheen. Another National Trust property, to the northeast of the town at Moneymore, is **Springhill House**, a charming 17th century manor house complete with family belongings and with a costume museum.

Dunnamore

8 miles W of Cookstown off the A505

This area is notable for its many prehistoric monuments of which the most impressive are the extraordinary **Beaghmore Stone Circles**, a couple of miles to the north of Dunnamore. Discovered by peat-cutters in the 1930s, there are seven circles in all, six of them in pairs. The odd one out is scattered with more than 800 upright stones, known as the Dragon's Teeth, and the site also includes ten rows of stones and a dozen burial mounds, some with cremated human remains still inside. The stones are not particularly lofty, (the tallest ones are less than 4 feet high), but the organisation involved in constructing the circles and their uncanny alignment to the movements of the sun, moon and stars testify to the sophistication of the Bronze Age people who occupied this lonely site from 2000 to 1200 BC.

TOURIST INFORMATION CENTRES

ACHILL
The Sound, Achill Island, Co. Mayo
Tel: 098 45384

ADARE
Adare Heritage Centre, Adare, Co. Limerick
Tel: 061 396255 Fax: 061 396610
Open: All Year

ANTRIM
16, High Street, Antrim, Co. Antrim BT41 4AN
Tel: 028 9442 8331 Fax: 028 9448 7844
e-mail: abs@antrim.gov.uk
Open: All Year

ARAN ISLANDS
Kilronan, Inishmore, Co. Galway
Tel: 099 61263
Open: All Year

ARDMORE
Sea Front Car Park, Ardmore, Co. Waterford
Tel: 024 94444

ARKLOW
Coach House, Upper Maiin Street,
Arklow, Co. Wicklow
Tel: 0402 32484

ARMAGH
St Patrick's Trian Visitor Complex, 40 English Street, Armagh, Co. Armagh BT61 7BA
Tel: 028 3752 1800 Fax: 028 3752 8329
Open: All Year

ATHLONE
Athlone Castle, Market Square,
Athlone, Co. Westmeath
Tel: 0902 94630

BALLINA
Cathedral Road, Ballina, Co. Mayo
Tel: 096 70848
Open: All Year

BALLINASLOE
Keller's Travel Agency, Main Street,
Ballinasloe, Co. Galway
Tel: 090 964 2131

BALLYCASTLE
7 Mary Street, Ballycastle, Co. Antrim
Tel: 028 2076 2024 Fax: 028 2076 2515
Open: All Year

BANBRIDGE
200 Newry Road, Banbridge, Co. Down
Tel: 028 4062 3322 Fax: 028 4062 3114
Open: All Year

BANGOR
34 Quay Street, Bangor, Co. Down
Tel: 028 9127 0069 Fax: 028 9127 4466
website: www.northdown.gov.uk
Open: All Year

BANTRY
Old Courthouse, Bantry, Co. Cork
Tel: 027 50229

BELFAST
Belfast Welcome Centre, 47 Donegall Place,
Belfast
Tel: 028 9024 6609 Fax: 028 9024 0960
e-mail: infor@nitb.com
website: www.goto-belfast.com
Open: All Year

BIRR
Market Square, Birr, Co. Offaly
Tel: 0509 20110

BLARNEY
Blarney Woollen Mills, Blarney, Co. Cork
Tel: 021 438 1624
Open: All Year

BOYLE
Market Street, Boyle, Co. Roscommon
Tel: 079 62145

BUNCRANA
Railway Road, Buncrana, Co. Donegal
Tel: 074 936 2600

BUNDORAN
Main Street, Bundoran, Co. Donegal
Tel: 071 984 1350

CAHERCIVEEN
Old Library, Main Street, Caherciveen, Co. Kerry
Tel: 066 947 2531

CAHIR
Castle Street Car Park, Cahir, Co. Tipperary
Tel: 052 41453

CARLOW
Tullow Street, Carlow, Co. Carlow
Tel: 0503 31554
Open: All Year

CARRICKFERGUS
Heritage Plaza, Carrickfergus, Co. Antrim
Tel: 028 9336 6455 Fax: 028 9335 0350

CARRICK-ON-SHANNON
The Old Barrel Store, Carrick-on-Shannon, Co. Leitrim
Tel: 071 962 0170
website: www.leitrimtourism.com

CARRICK-ON-SUIR
Heritage Centre, Main Street, Carrick-on-Suir, Co. Leitrim
Tel: 051 640200
Open: All Year

CASHEL
Cashel Heritage Centre, Cashel, Co. Tipperary
Tel: 062 61333

CASTLEBAR
Old Linen Hall, Linenhall Street, Castlebar, Co. Mayo
Tel: 094 902 1207

CAVAN
1 Farnham Street, Cavan, Co. Cavan
Tel: 049 433 1942
website: www.cavantourism.com

CLIFDEN
Market Street, Clifden, Co. Galway
Tel: 095 21163

CLIFFS OF MOHER
Liscannor, Co. Clare
Tel: 065 708 1171

CLONAKILTY
25, Ashe Street, Clonakilty, Co. Cork
Tel: 023 33226

CLONMACNOISE
via Shannon Bridge, Clonmacnoise, Co. Offaly
Tel: 0905 74134

CLONMEL
8 Sarsfield Street, Clonmel, Co. Tipperary
Tel: 052 26500
Open: All Year

COLERAINE
Railway Road, Coleraine, Co. Derry BT52 1PE
Tel: 028 7034 4723 Fax: 028 7035 1756
e-mail: coleraine@nitic.net
website: www.colerainebc.gov.uk
Open: All Year

CONG
Abbey Street, Cong, Co. Mayo
Tel: 092 46542

COOKSTOWN
The Burnavon, Burns Road, Cookstown, Co. Tyrone
Tel: 028 8676 6727

CORK
Aras Fáilte, Grand Parade, Cork, Co. Cork
Tel: 021 427 3251 Fax: 021 427 3504
e-mail: user@cktourism.ie
Open: All Year

DINGLE
Strand Street, Dingle, Co. Kerry
Tel: 066 915 1188

DONEGAL
The Quay, Donegal, Co. Donegal
Tel: 074 972 1148 Fax: 074 972 2762
website: www.donegal.ie

DONGLOE
Car Park off Main Street, Dongloe, Co. Donegal
Tel: 075 21297

DROGHEDA
Bus Eireann Station, West Street, Drogheda, Co. Louth
Tel: 041 983 7070
website: www.drogheda-tourism.com
Open: All Year

DOWNPATRICK
St Patrick Visitor Centre, 53a Market Street, Downpatrick, Co. Down BT30 6LZ
Tel: 028 4461 2233 Fax: 028 4461 2350
website: www.stpatrickcentre.com
Open: All Year

DUBLIN
14, O'Connell Street Upper, Dublin
Tel: 01 747733
College Green. Tel: 01 711488
website: www.visitdublin.com
Baggot Street Bridge. Tel: 01 765871
Open: All Year

DUNDALK
Jocelyn Street, Dundalk, Co. Louth
Tel: 042 933 5484 Fax: 042 399 8070
Open: All Year

DUNGARVAN
Courthouse Building, Dungarvan, Co. Waterford
Tel: 058 41741 Fax: 058 45020
Open: All Year

ENNIS
Arthur's Row, Town Centre, Ennis, Co. Clare
Tel: 065 682 8366 Fax: 065 682 8350
e-mail: info@shannon-dev.ie
website: www.shannon-dev.ie
Open: All Year

ENNISCORTHY
Town Centre, Enniscorthy, Co. Wexford
Tel: 054 34699

ENNISKILLEN
Wellington Road, Enniskillen,
Co. Fermanagh BT74 7EF
Tel: 028 6632 3110 Fax: 028 6632 5511
e-mail: tic@fermanagh.gov.uk
website: www.fermanagh-online.com
Open: All Year

GALWAY CITY
Aras Fáilte, Forster Street, Galway, Co. Galway
Tel: 091 537700 Fax: 091 537733
e-mail: info@irelandwest.ie
Open: All Year

GIANT'S CAUSEWAY
Bushmills, Co. Antrim
Tel: 028 2073 1855
Open: All Year

GLENGARRIFF
Main Street, Glengarriff, Co. Cork
Tel: 027 63084

GOREY
Market House, Main Street, Gorey, Co. Wexford
Tel: 055 21248
Open: All Year

HILLSBOROUGH
Council Offices, Hillsborough, Co. Down
Tel: 028 9268 9717 Fax: 028 9268 9016
Open: All Year

KENMARE
Kenmare Heritage Centre, Main Street,
Kenmare, Co. Kerry
Tel: 064 41233

KILDARE TOWN
Main Square, Kildare, Co. Kildare
Tel: 045 521240

KILKEE
The Square, Kilkee, Co. Clare
Tel: 065 905 6112

KILKEEL
28 Newcastle Street, Kilkeel, Co. Down
Tel/Fax: 028 4176 2525
Open: All Year

KILKENNY
Shee Alms House, Rose Inn Street,
Kilkenny, Co. Kilkenny
Tel: 056 51500 Fax: 056 63955
e-mail: info@southeasttourism.ie

KILLALOE
Lock House, The Bridge, Killaloe, Co. Clare
Tel: 061 376866

KILLARNEY
Beech Road, Killarney, Co. Kerry
Tel: 064 31633 Fax: 064 34506
Open: All Year

KILLYMADDY
Ballygawley Road, Killymaddy,
Co. Tyrone BT70 1TF
Tel: 028 8776 7259 Fax: 028 8776 7911
Open: All Year

KILRUSH
Town Hall, Kilrush, Co. Clare
Tel: 065 905 1577

KINSALE
Pier Road, Kinsale, Co. Cork
Tel: 021 477 2234 Fax: 021 477 4438

KNOCK
Knock Airport, Knock, Co. Mayo
Tel: 094 938 8193
Open: All Year

KNOCK VILLAGE
Knock, Co. Mayo
Tel: 094 938 8193

LARNE
Narrow Gauge Road, Larne, Co. Antrim
Tel/Fax: 028 2826 0088
Open: All Year

LETTERKENNY
Neil T. Blaney Road, Letterkenny, Co. Donegal
Tel: 074 912 1160 Fax: 074 912 5180
Open: All Year

LIMAVADY
7 Connell Street, Limavady, Co. Antrim
Tel: 028 7776 0307
Open: All Year

LIMERICK
Arthurs Quay, Limerick, Co. Limerick
Tel: 061 317522 Fax: 061 317939
Opon: All Year

LISBURN
Irish Linen Centre, Lisburn, Co. Antrim
Tel: 028 9266 0038 Fax: 028 9260 7889
Open: All Year

LISMORE
Heritage Centre, Lismore, Co. Waterford
Tel: 058 54975
website: www.lismoreheritage.com
Open: All Year

LISTOWEL
Saint John's Church, Listowel, Co. Kerry
Tel: 068 22590 Fax: 068 23485

LONDONDERRY
44 Foyle Street, Londonderry, Co. Derry
Tel: 028 7126 7284 Fax: 028 7137 7992
website: www.derryvisitor.com
Open: All Year

LONGFORD
Market Square, Longford, Co. Longford
Tel: 043 46566

MIDLETON
Jameson Heritage Centre, Midleton, Co. Cork
Tel: 021 461 3702

MONAGHAN
Market House, Pearse Street,
Monaghan, Co. Monaghan
Tel: 047 81122
website: www.monaghantourism.com

MULLINGAR
Dublin Road, Mullingar, Co. Westmeath
Tel: 044 48650 Fax: 044 40413
e-mail: info@ecoast-midlandstourism.ie
website: www.ecoast-midlands.travel.ie
Open: All Year

NAVAN
Ludlow Street, Navan, Co. Meath
Tel: 046 907 7273 Fax: 046 907 6025
website: www.meathtourism.ie

NENAGH
Connolly Street, Nenagh, Co. Tipperary
Tel: 067 31610 Fax: 067 33418

NEWCASTLE
10-14 Central Promenade, Newcastle,
Co. Down BT33 0AA
Tel: 028 4372 2222 Fax: 028 4372 2400
e-mail: newcastle@nitic.net
website: www.newcastle.tic.org
Open: All Year

NEWGRANGE
Newgrange Visitor Centre, Newgrange, Co. Meath
Tel: 041 988 0305
Open: All Year

NEWPORT
Main Street, Newport, Co. Mayo
Tel: 098 41895

NEW ROSS
The Quay, New Ross, Co. Wexford
Tel: 051 421857

NEWTOWNARDS
31 Regent Street, Newtownards,
Co. Down BT23 4AD
Tel: 028 9182 6846 Fax: 028 9182 6681
Open: All Year

OMAGH
1 Market Street, Omagh, Co. Tyrone BT78 1EE
Tel: 028 8224 7831
(after hours: 028 8224 0774)
Fax: 028 8224 0774
Open: All Year

OUGHTERARD
Main Street, Oughterard, Co. Galway
Tel: 091 552808 Fax: 091 552811
e-mail: oughterardoffice@eircom.net
Open: All Year

PORTAFERRY
The Stables, Castle Street, Portaferry,
Co. Down BT22 1NZ
Tel: 028 4272 9882 Fax: 028 4272 9822

PORTLAOISE
James Fintan Lalor Avenue, Portlaoise, Co. Laois
Tel: 0502 21178

PORTRUSH
Dunluce Centre, Sandhill Drive,
Portrush, Co. Antrim BT56 8BF
Tel: 028 7082 3333 Fax: 028 7082 2256
e-mail: portrush@nitic.net

PORTSTEWART
The Library, Town Hall, The Crescent,
Portstewart, Co. Derry BT55 7AB
Tel: 028 7083 2286

ROSCOMMON
Harrison Hall, Market Square,
Roscommon, Co. Roscommon
Tel: 0903 26342

ROSSLARE
Rosslare Harbour, Rosslare, Co. Wexford
Tel: 053 33232 Fax: 053 33421

SALTHILL
The Promenade, Salthill, Co. Galway
Tel: 091 520500

SHANNON AIRPORT
Shannon Airport, Co. Clare
Tel: 061 471664 Fax: 061 471661
Open: All Year

SKIBBEREEN
North Street, Skibbereen, Co. Cork
Tel: 028 21766 Fax: 028 21353
Open: All Year

SLIGO
Aras Reddan, Temple Street, Sligo, Co. Sligo
Tel: 071 916 1201 Fax: 071 916 0360
e-mail: irelandnorthwest@eircom.net
website: www.ireland-northwest.travel.ie
Open: All Year

STRABANE
Abercorn Square, Strabane, Co. Tyrone
Tel: 028 7188 3735 Fax: 028 7138 2264

THOOR BALLYLEE
Yeats Tower, Gort, Thoor Ballylee, Co. Galway
Tel: 091 631436

TIPPERARY
James Street, Tipperary, Co. Tipperary
Tel: 062 33466

TRALEE
Ashe Memorial Hall, Tralee, Co. Kerry
Tel: 066 712 1288 Fax: 066 712 1700
Open: All Year

TRAMORE
Railway Square, Tramore, Co. Waterford
Tel: 051 381572

TRIM
Mill Street, Trim, Co. Meath
Tel: 046 37111
Open: All Year

TUAM
Mill Museum, Tuam, Co. Galway
Tel: 093 25486

TULLAMORE
Tullamore Dew, Heritage Centre, Bury Quay, Tullamore, Co. Offaly
Tel: 0506 25015
Open: All Year

WATERFORD
Waterford Treasures, The Granary, The Quay, Waterford, Co. Waterford
Tel: 051 875823 Fax: 051 877388
e-mail: info@southeasttourism
Open: All Year

WESTPORT
James Street, Westport, Co. Mayo
Tel: 098 25711 Fax: 098 26709
Open: All Year

WEXFORD
Crescent Quay, Wexford, Co. Wexford
Tel: 053 23111 Fax: 053 41743
Open: All Year

WICKLOW
Rialto Centre, Fitzwilliam Square, Wicklow, Co. Wicklow
Tel: 0404 69117 Fax: 0404 69118
Open: All Year

YOUGHAL
Market Square, Youghal, Co. Cork
Tel: 024 20170

LIST OF ADVERTISERS

Other

A

B

D

E

INDEX OF TOWNS, VILLAGES AND PLACES OF INTEREST

A

B

C

D

H

I

J

K

L

M

P

Q

R

S

T

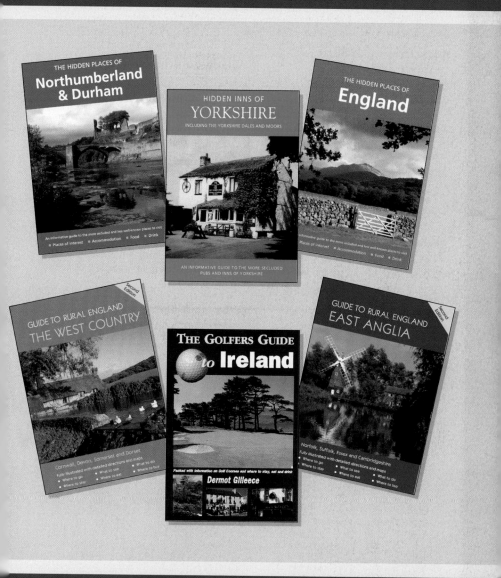

HIDDEN PLACES ORDER FORM

To order any of our publications just fill in the payment details below and complete the order form. For orders of less than 4 copies please add £1 per book for postage and packing. Orders over 4 copies are P & P free.

Please Complete Either:

I enclose a cheque for £ ______ made payable to Travel Publishing Ltd

Or:

Card No: ______ Expiry Date: ______

Signature: ______

Name: ______

Address: ______

Tel no: ______

Please either send, telephone, fax or e-mail your order to:

Travel Publishing Ltd, 7a Apollo House, Calleva Park, Aldermaston, Berkshire RG7 8TN

Tel: 0118 981 7777 Fax: 0118 982 0077 e-mail: karen@travelpublishing.co.uk

	Price	*Quantity*
Hidden Places Regional Titles		
Cambs & Lincolnshire	£7.99	....
Chilterns	£7.99	....
Cornwall	£10.99	....
Derbyshire	£8.99	....
Devon	£8.99	....
Dorset, Hants & Isle of Wight	£8.99	....
East Anglia	£8.99	....
Gloucs, Wiltshire & Somerset	£8.99	....
Heart of England	£7.99	....
Hereford, Worcs & Shropshire	£7.99	....
Highlands & Islands	£7.99	....
Kent	£8.99	....
Lake District & Cumbria	£8.99	....
Lancashire & Cheshire	£8.99	....
Lincolnshire & Notts	£8.99	....
Northumberland & Durham	£8.99	....
Sussex	£8.99	....
Yorkshire	£8.99	....
Hidden Places National Titles		
England	£10.99	....
Ireland	£10.99	....
Scotland	£10.99	....
Wales	£10.99	....

	Price	*Quantity*
Hidden Inns Titles		
East Anglia	£7.99	....
Heart of England	£7.99	....
Lancashire & Cheshire	£7.99	....
North of England	£7.99	....
South	£7.99	....
South East	£7.99	....
South and Central Scotland	£7.99	....
Wales	£7.99	....
Welsh Borders	£7.99	....
West Country	£7.99	....
Yorkshire	£7.99	....
Country Living Rural Guides		
East Anglia	£10.99	....
Heart of England	£10.99	....
Ireland	£10.99	....
North East of England	£10.99	....
North West of England	£10.99	....
Scotland	£10.99	....
South of England	£10.99	....
South East of England	£10.99	....
Wales	£10.99	....
West Country	£10.99	....

Total Quantity ______

Post & Packing ______

Total Value ______

READER REACTION FORM

The *Travel Publishing* research team would like to receive readers' comments on any visitor attractions or places reviewed in the book and also recommendations for suitab le entries to be included in the next edition. This will help ensure that the *Country Living series of Rural Guides* continues to provide its readers with useful information on the more interesting, unusual or unique features of each attraction or place ensuring that their visit to the local area is an enjoyable and stimulating experience. To provide your comments or recommendations would you please complete the forms below and overleaf as indicated and send to:

The Research Department, Travel Publishing Ltd,
7a Apollo House, Calleva Park, Aldermaston, Reading, RG7 8TN.

Your Name:

Your Address:

Your Telephone Number:

Please tick as appropriate:

Comments ☐ Recommendation ☐

Name of Establishment:

Address:

Telephone Number:

Name of Contact:

Reader Reaction Form

READER REACTION FORM

Comment or Reason for Recommendation: